THE RIGHT TO VOTE

THE RIGHT TO VOTE

The Contested History of Democracy in the United States

ALEXANDER KEYSSAR

BASIC
BOOKS

A Member of the Perseus Books Group

Published by Basic Books
A Member of the Perseus Books Group

Designed by Rachel Hegarty

Library of Congress Cataloging-in-Publication Data
Keyssar, Alexander.
   The right to vote : the contested history of democracy in the United States /
Alexander Keyssar
      p.   cm.
   Includes index.
   ISBN 0-465-02968-X
   1. Suffrage—United States—History.   2. Voting—United States—History.   I. Title.
JK1846.K48 2000
324.6'2'0973—dc21   00-034299

00 01 02 03/10 9 8 7 6 5 4 3 2 1

For Natalie

CONTENTS

PART III

PREFACE

I have come to believe that books have fortuitous or unforeseen beginnings, and this one is no exception.

A half dozen years ago, I began to draft a different book, a highly quantitative study of working-class participation in electoral politics in the United States. My outline for that book—developed after several years of research—called for a stage-setting chapter about the legal and political history of the right to vote. I envisioned that chapter as a simple preamble to a detailed investigation of the ways in which working people did and did not participate in elections.

But when I sat down to write the chapter, I ran into trouble. The story line, tracing the evolution of the right to vote in the United States, began to zig and zag at unpredictable moments. Easy generalizations wilted when I tried to mold them into forceful arguments or undergird them with documentary evidence. Moreover, the evidence I had on hand, drawn from standard sources, looked increasingly skimpy and incomplete. I went back to the library for a few months and then tried again. Without success. The more I wrote, the further I seemed to be from the finish line. The chapter kept getting longer, as did my list of unanswered questions.

Eventually I realized that the chapter with which I was wrestling was a book in itself. The subject, the right to vote, was of almost self-evident importance to American history and contemporary politics; remarkably little had been written about it; and I could not really make sense of electoral participation until I had a deeper understanding of the laws that shaped and structured that participation. I also realized that I wanted to write about the history of suffrage: the richness of the issues, their intricacy and importance, had captured my attention and imagination. Americans had debated, and fought over, limitations on the right to vote from the revolution to the late twentieth century, and those debates and contests told much about the meaning of democracy in American political life and culture. My stacks of computer printouts went back into the filing cabinet, and I went back, yet again, to the library.

The book that has emerged from this detour is longer, and perhaps more ambitious, than I originally intended. My sojourn with the sources convinced me that the many different strands to this story—including women's suffrage, the voting rights of African Americans and immigrants, residency and property requirements, literacy tests, felon and pauper exclusions—were closely intertwined with one another and could only be understood as part of a single fabric; similarly, the ups and downs in the narrative, the shifting and uneven mix of gains and losses, could only be comprehended as part of a lengthy chronicle. Consequently, I have tried to write a comprehensive, multifaceted history of the right to vote in the United States, from the nation's birth to the present, a history that encompasses not only national laws and policies but also developments in the fifty states.

Writing such a book, trying to explore such an enormous terrain, has many intellectual rewards for an author. Yet it is also a humbling experience. Although surprised initially by the absence or scarcity of systematic scholarly studies, I have been dependent nonetheless on the labors of scores of scholars who have carefully mined particular veins, who have examined specific themes, individual states, and colorful historical actors. This book would not have been possible had I not been able to build on their efforts. No one, moreover, is more aware than I of the work that remains to be done, of the many patches of terrain that have never been carefully scrutinized. As my own labors draw to a close, one of my strongest hopes is that this book will open the doors to further inquiry, that it will spark other studies of the history of suffrage, as well as the broader history of democracy, in the United States and elsewhere.

A word about a self-imposed limit to this inquiry: this is a book about the legal and political history of suffrage; it is not a study of political practice or participation. Inescapably, questions will arise about the relationship between the legal structures and the practice of politics, about the precise— and quantitative—impact of voting laws on political behavior. Those questions, for the most part, will not be fully answered in this volume; but I do hope to address them, as completely as I can, when I return to writing the history of electoral participation that gave birth to this book in the first place.[28]

—⦅⦆—

This book has been a long time in the making, and it still would be were it not for the generous assistance that I received from many institutions and individuals. Having the opportunity to express my thanks is one of the (long-imagined) pleasures of sending a manuscript off to press. The Dean's Office of the School of Humanities and Social Science at the Massachusetts Institute of Technology provided a grant that launched the research, and it continued with the help of a research fund provided by Duke University. A fellowship from the John Simon Guggenheim Memorial Foundation gave me time to think about the materials that I was collecting. A year spent in what a friend has called "academic nirvana," the Center for Advanced Study in the Behavioral Sciences, offered me stimulating intellectual company as well as the opportunity to write without interruption—except for the thoughtful hours that I happily spent staring out the window at San Francisco Bay.

The research for this book could be gathered only by casting a wide net, and over the years that net was held by a small army of student (and ex-student) research assistants. Indeed, so many have toiled in this project that I have sometimes believed that my research was responsible for the decline in the national unemployment rate. Among those who served particularly long stints were Greg Bylinsky, Ewan Campbell, Cypria Dionese, Conrad Hall, Stephen Hartzell, Roger Michel, Katie Ratte, Chris Seufert, Teddy Varno, and James Worthington. I thank them all, as well as the many others whose indentures were of shorter duration. Two people deserve special mention. Courtney Bailey has worked on and off this project for years; her thoughtful attentiveness and long hours helped me to gain control of unwieldy legal materials and made it possible for me to finish the endnotes. Laura Thoms rightfully deserves credit as co-author of the appendix. Tables always look neat and simple in print, but these tables began as clumsy boxes of photocopied documents, some of which traveled with Laura wherever she went. Translating these documents into their current tidy form took more than two years of careful sifting and cross-checking; without Laura's indefatigable efforts, the tables might still be in boxes.

Many colleagues helped me to find new sources, clarify my thinking, and sharpen my prose. Too numerous to mention are the scholars, archivists, and librarians who over the years have fielded my phone calls and e-mails about particular (often arcane) details: they know who they are, and I thank them. Closer to home, Sydney Nathans and Peter Wood generously responded to my queries about times and places that they know better than I. Larry Goodwyn, Bill Reddy, and David Montgomery posed challenging questions that I have since tried to answer. Feedback from seminar presentations at the Newberry Library, the Charles Warren Center at Harvard University, the Center for Advanced Study, the Ecole des Hautes Etudes in Paris, the University of California at Santa Cruz, and Yale University stimulated my thinking about various pieces of the project. Valuable comments on portions of the manuscript were offered by Nancy Cott, John Demos, Robert D. Goldstein, Linda Kerber, Marc Kruman, Jonathan Prude, and James C. Scott. Benjamin I. Page read the entire manuscript, improving the product while encouraging the producer. My thanks to all of them.

The logistical process of getting the book to press was made vastly easier by the cheerful efforts of Deborah Carver-Thien and Andrea Long. My agent, Jill Kneerim, gave me sound advice and warm support at moments when both were needed. Tim Bartlett has been a model editor, committed to the project, deft and thoughtful in suggesting revisions, patient about waiting for me to produce them. Michael Wilde has been a remarkable copyeditor; Richard Miller has superintended the production process with care, consideration, and good humor. Basic Books merits special thanks for its willingness to publish the appendix tables as a contribution to scholarship.

This book is dedicated to my daughter, Natalie. For years, she has fallen asleep (and now, as a teenager, awakened) to the sound of tapping at my computer across the hall. An ardent democrat in her own right, she has particularly strong convictions about the role of universal suffrage within the family. I can't honestly say that Natalie helped in the production of this book (indeed recently she commented that it was amazing that I finished it "with one of me around"), but I hope she knows what a pleasure it always is when she interrupts me.

Introduction

*A*MERICANS DON'T VOTE MUCH ANYMORE. In recent decades, only half of all potential voters have actually shown up at the polls for presidential elections; in state and local contests, turnout has been even lower, often dropping to 20 or 25 percent. Barring the unforeseen, these patterns appear certain to continue in the early years of the new millennium.[1]

Such low levels of popular participation suggest that our democracy, two centuries after the nation's founding, has become dispirited, if not lethargic, and that the act of voting is not greatly prized. Yet Americans do place a high value on democratic institutions, and white Americans, at least, have long thought of themselves as citizens of a democratic nation—indeed, not just any democratic nation, but *the* democratic nation. According to our national self-image—an image etched in popular culture and buttressed by scholarly inquiry—the United States has been the pioneer of republican and then democratic reforms for two hundred years, the standard bearer of democratic values on the stage of world history. As the influential political theorist and founder of the *New Republic*, Herbert Croly, put it in 1909, the United States is the "Land of Democracy," a nation "committed to the realization of the democratic ideal." Similarly, in a famous address to Congress in 1965, President Lyndon B. Johnson maintained that Americans had "fought and died for two centuries" to defend the principle of "government by consent of the governed" and the conviction that "all men are created equal." From the late eighteenth century through the cold war, Americans have regarded their own political institutions as models of popular government and self rule.[2]

Implicit in this democratic self-image is the belief that the right to vote is, and long has been, widely distributed among Americans, that the United States has something very close to universal suffrage. (The phrase has been historically elastic; here it means simply that all adult citizens have the right to vote.) As every schoolchild learns, thousands of soldiers fell at Gettysburg so that government "of the people, by the people, and for the people" would not perish from the earth—and presumably a government of and by the people was one that the *people* selected. Indeed, in popular usage, the term *democracy* implies that everyone, or nearly everyone, has the right to participate in elections; the image of a democratic United States is that of a nation with universal suffrage. And rightly so: although a nation certainly could have universal suffrage without being a democracy, a polity cannot be truly democratic without universal suffrage.

In recent years, in fact, there has been a reasonably good fit between the image and reality of voting rights in the United States. As Congressional Quarterly's *Guide to U.S. Elections* concluded in 1985, with a trace of patriotic hyperbole, "by the two hundredth anniversary of the nation, the only remaining restrictions [on the franchise] prevented voting by the insane, convicted felons, and otherwise eligible voters who were unable to meet short residence requirements."[3] To be sure, many scholars and activists remain deeply concerned about our "turnout problem," about the ways in which the electoral system may discourage voting, and about the extraordinary growth in the number of persons disfranchised because they have committed felonies. Yet the vast majority of American adults do possess the right to vote, and formally at least, the United States has universal suffrage.[4]

This was not always the case, however—not by a long shot. Until the 1960s most African Americans could not vote in the South. Women were barred from voting in a majority of jurisdictions until 1920. For many years, Asian immigrants were disfranchised because they could not become citizens, and Native Americans lacked the right to vote far more often than they possessed it. In the early nineteenth century, moreover, states generally granted the franchise only to property owners, and well into the twentieth century paupers often were prohibited from voting. The list could, does, and (in later chapters) will go on: for much of American history, the right to vote has been far from universal.

Why was this the case? Why were so many Americans, in different places and at different times, denied the right to vote? How could Americans have thought of themselves as democratic while they possessed such a restricted franchise? Most fundamentally, perhaps, how, why, and when did the laws governing suffrage change? These questions are central in political history, critical to an understanding of the evolution of democracy; they also are central to our conceptions of what it means to be an American.

Yet these questions rarely have been asked—or answered. The history of the right to vote in the United States has received far less scrutiny than the subject would seem to warrant. There exist, to be sure, important monographic studies of the voting rights of African Americans, focusing particularly on the post–Civil War period (when African Americans were enfranchised and then disfranchised) and on the 1950s and 1960s (when they were reenfranchised).[5] There is also a rich literature—beginning with the writings of key participants—chronicling the movement for women's suffrage.[6] In addition, historians have produced several synthetic accounts of the ways in which the franchise was reconfigured between 1800 and 1850.[7]

Yet thus far, no modern, comprehensive history of the right to vote has been written. The last attempt to survey the evolution of the franchise in the United States was made fifty years ago; the most recent scholarly effort, written by historian Kirk Porter, was published in 1918.[8] There has been, in effect, no attempt to explore in any systematic way the sweep of this story over a long period, the links between different strands of the history (e.g., suffrage for women and the voting rights of immigrants), or the overall sources and rhythms of change in the breadth of the franchise. Which is remarkable in a nation that so publicly prizes its democratic history.

This scholarly silence appears to have several different sources. Foremost among them is what one might call a progressive or triumphalist presumption: a deeply embedded, yet virtually unspoken, notion that the history of suffrage is the history of gradual, inevitable reform and progress. (In England, as historian Herbert Butterfield has famously noted, such presumptions have yielded a "Whig" interpretation of history.)[9] The inventor of this idea—or at least its most well-known early celebrant—was Alexis de Tocqueville. Writing in 1835 in *Democracy in America*, de Tocqueville observed (or rather predicted) that

> Once a people begins to interfere with the voting qualification, one can be sure that sooner or later it will abolish it altogether. That is one of the most invariable rules of social behavior. The further the limit of voting rights is extended, the stronger is the need felt to spread them still wider; for after each new concession the forces of democracy are strengthened, and its demands

increase with its augmented power. The ambition of those left below the qualifying limit increases in proportion to the number of those above it. Finally the exception becomes the rule; concessions follow one another without interruption, and there is no halting place until universal suffrage has been attained.[10]

De Tocqueville's "rule of social behavior" certainly rings a bit mechanistic to modern ears, but the broad outlines of his forecast have seemed to many analysts to match the American experience. The standard narrative, consequently, goes as follows: at the nation's founding, the franchise was sharply restricted, but thereafter one group of citizens after another acquired the right to vote. Most propertyless white men were enfranchised during the first half of the nineteenth century; then came African Americans; then women; then African Americans again; and finally, even eighteen-year-olds. The precise causes and dynamics of change may have been less straightforward than de Tocqueville believed, but viewed from afar, the major events in American suffrage history appeared to fit the de Tocquevillian model of change that was straightforward, unidirectional, and inevitable.[11] "The history of the American suffrage has been one of steady and irresistible expansion," noted Harvard historian and political scientist William B. Munro in 1928. "One limitation after another has been swept away by constitutional amendments and laws—religious tests, property qualifications, race discriminations, and finally exclusion on grounds of sex."[12]

Interestingly—but not surprisingly—this progressive presumption has had greater currency during some periods than others. Roughly a century ago, when some of the first histories of suffrage were written (and when the breadth of the franchise was a very live issue), de Tocqueville's notion was far from preeminent. An impressive study of suffrage in Michigan in the nineteenth century, for example, concluded that change was not at all unidirectional: "The tendencies which were so markedly toward liberality and extension in the earlier half of the century," wrote Mary Jo Adams, "have been scarcely less clearly in the direction of conservatism in the later half."[13] The same conclusion was reached in 1897 by James Schouler, in the first article about American voters ever published in the *American Historical Review*. More or less simultaneously, writer and professor of constitutional history Francis N. Thorpe characterized the evolution of voting rights as contingent rather than inevitable; there had been, he wrote, a "struggle for the franchise, now lasting a century."[14] Two decades later, Kirk Porter's history of suffrage, reflecting the emphasis on conflict so characteristic of his era's historians, depicted a "vigorous" century-long "fight" over the right to vote, driven by "materialistic considerations."[15]

By the middle of the twentieth century, however, this sense of conflict and contingency had receded; perhaps because women finally had gained the franchise and because cold war liberalism provided a congenial ideological climate, the idea of an inexorable march toward universal suffrage became preeminent. "One of the easiest victories of the democratic cause," proclaimed political scientist E. E. Schattschneider in 1960, "has been the struggle for the extension of the suffrage. . . . The struggle for the ballot was almost bloodless, almost completely peaceful and astonishingly easy." It is testimony both to the paucity of historical research and to the ideological power of triumphalism that Schattschneider, a learned and insightful critic of American politics, could pen such sentences despite the violent struggles over suffrage in the post–Civil War South—and while most blacks remained voteless. Similarly, in 1978, an eminent and concerned trio of political scientists could identify "the history of the franchise" simply as "the history of the removal of barriers based on economic condition or sex or skill and often the lowering of the age threshold. . . . The result is a system with wide political rights equally available to all citizens." This triumphalist spirit also informed the only scholarly synthesis written during this period, Chilton Williamson's study of colonial and antebellum reform, tellingly subtitled *From Property to Democracy*.[16]

More important, the progressive presumption appears to have dampened interest in the subject, to have deflected the spotlight of inquiry away from the history of the right to vote, even at a time when the struggle for voting rights was generating conflict and violence in the South. "Invariable rules of social behavior" and "irresistible expansions"—by whatever name—are phenomena that tend to be taken as historical givens rather than as problems inviting research. The expansion of democratic political rights in the United States was not deemed to require explanation; it was the nation's natural destiny. Accordingly, many mid-twentieth-century historians—particularly those of the consensus persuasion—were likely to agree with Munro that the history of suffrage was "a long and not a very interesting story."[17] This opinion was shared by the revisionist social historians of a slightly later generation (including the author), at least in part because we were inclined to view electoral politics as mere superstructure and thus irrelevant or of scant interest.[18] Within the scholarly community, the evolution of the right to vote attracted attention primarily among students of comparative politics, who were interested less in historical inquiry or specific national histories than in theory building.[19]

This book is an attempt to break the odd silence about the history of suffrage, to take a new look, with fresh eyes, at a venerable, if neglected, subject. It offers a chronicle of the history of the right to vote in the United States from the late eighteenth century to the present, an account of the evolution of the laws—municipal, state, and federal—that have defined and circumscribed the American electorate. It is a narrative detailing the ways in which women, African Americans, industrial workers, immigrants, and many other groups (or categories of individuals) acquired, and sometimes lost, the right to vote.

This book also is an attempt to puzzle over the story, to avoid taking familiar things for granted, to interrogate the past with wonder. It is well known, for instance, that only property owners could vote at the end of the eighteenth century, but why exactly was this the case? Why in fact did it take so long for women to gain the right to vote? Or, for that matter, why did the right to vote expand at all? Why did those who were already enfranchised, such as property-owning white males, cut anybody else in on the deal? It is by no means self-evident, as one looks at modern history, that individuals who possess political power will (or can be expected to) share that power with others, millions of others. Why did it happen, and why did the right to vote expand at certain times and certain places, while contracting in others?

To pose such questions is to inquire both into the origins of democracy and into the obstacles or threats to the existence of democratic polities. The two inquiries necessarily accompany and implicate one another: as global politics in the twentieth century have made clear, democracies do not thrive under all conditions, and democratic yearnings do not necessarily produce durable democratic institutions. The United States is not and has not been an exception in this regard. Our history is complex, at times contradictory, befitting a nation that began as a republic that tolerated slavery.[20] The evolution of democracy rarely followed a straight path, and it always has been accompanied by profound antidemocratic countercurrents. The history of suffrage in the United States is a history of both expansion and contraction, of inclusion and exclusion, of shifts in direction and momentum at different places and at different times.

In addition to charting such shifts and reversals, this book offers a framework for understanding and explaining them—a framework that may well provoke controversy and perhaps inspire further research. Stated briefly, the argument is as follows: The expansion of suffrage in the United States was generated by a number of key forces and factors, some of which have long been celebrated by scholars, journalists, politicians, and teachers. These include the dynamics of frontier settlement (as Frederick Jackson Turner pointed out a century ago), the rise of competitive political parties, the growth of cities and industry, the flourishing of democratic ideals and beliefs, and effective efforts at mobilization on the part of the disfranchised themselves.[21]

Yet alongside these factors was another, less celebrated force: war. Nearly all of the major expansions of the franchise that have occurred in American history took place either during or in the wake of wars. The historical record indicates that this was not a coincidence: the demands of both war itself and preparedness for war created powerful pressures to enlarge the right to vote. Armies had to be recruited, often from the so-called lower orders of society, and it was rhetorically as well as practically difficult to compel men to bear arms while denying them the franchise; similarly, conducting a war meant mobilizing popular support, which gave political leverage to any social groups excluded from the polity. While it may seem less exceptional and romantic than the frontier, without doubt war played a greater role in the evolution of American democracy.[22]

The history of suffrage in the United States was also shaped by forces that opposed or resisted a broader franchise, forces that at times succeeded in contracting the right to vote and often served to retard its expansion. Once again, most of these forces or factors have long been recognized: racist and sexist beliefs and attitudes, ethnic antagonism, partisan interests, and political theories and ideological convictions that linked the health of the state to a narrow franchise.

One important factor, however, has received little or no attention: class tension. The concept of class, of course, has long carried heavy ideological freight and at times has been the great unspoken word in America's officially classless society. Yet class conflict and class differences have played a vital role in many chapters of American history, and the right to vote is no exception. A wide-angle look at the full span of suffrage history—considering all restrictions on voting rights throughout the nation—strongly suggests that class tensions and apprehensions constituted the single most important obstacle to universal suffrage in the United States from the late eighteenth century to the 1960s. Contrary to a great deal of received wisdom about the history of American politics and labor, the formation and growth of an industrial working class, coupled with the creation of a free black agricultural working class in the South, generated a widespread, potent, and sometimes successful opposition to a broad-based franchise in much of the nation. In 1898, in the city of New Bedford, Massachusetts—to cite one of many little-known examples—this opposition was sufficiently strong that striking textile workers were threatened with disfranchisement because their employers claimed that the strikers had accepted public relief and consequently were "paupers" who could not legally vote.[23] This incident, as well as others like it, does not appear in standard histories of suffrage.

A caveat: to emphasize the significance of class is not to diminish the salience of race, gender, or ethnicity, all of which have been central to the history of voting rights; nor is it to substitute a monocausal interpretation for more complex or nuanced interpretations of the past. Race, class, gender, and ethnicity (a category that can house religion as well) have always been overlapping, dynamic, intertwined dimensions of identity and experience. Race and ethnicity are common determinants of class position, while class often has structured the significance of gender, racial, and ethnic boundaries and divisions. Historically, the formation of an industrial working class in the United States has been shaped by the presence of racially or ethnically distinctive supplies of labor, as well as by the gendered segregation of jobs and the reconfiguration of women's work. Class, race, gender, ethnicity, and religion all have played a part in the history of the right to vote in the United States, and their interaction lies at the heart of this narrative. But the particular role of class in this history is both fundamental and relatively unexamined.

It is class—and its link to immigration—that shapes the periodization of the story. There were, in fact, four distinctive periods, or "long swings," in the history of the right to vote in the United States. The first was a pre- and early industrial era during which the right to vote expanded: this period lasted from the signing of the Constitution until roughly 1850, when the transformation of the class structure wrought by the Industrial Revolution was well under way. The second period, stretching from the 1850s until roughly World War I, was characterized both by a narrowing of voting rights and by a mushrooming upper- and middle-class antagonism to universal suffrage. The third era, lasting until the 1960s, was contoured differently in the South than in the North, but throughout the nation was marked by relatively little change in the formal breadth of the franchise; in the North this period also was distinguished by state-sponsored efforts to mitigate the significance and power of an unavoidably growing electorate. The fourth and last period, inaugurated by the success of the civil rights movement in the South, witnessed the abolition of almost all remaining restrictions on the right to vote. During each of these periods, the right to vote was contested; at times, the breadth of suffrage was a major political issue; at stake always was the integration (or lack of integration) of the poor and working people into the polity.

To describe the history of the right to vote in these terms—as a protracted yet dynamic conflict between class tensions and the exigencies of war, with a trajectory far from unilinear—is to suggest that the experience of the United States has been less unique or exceptional than has oftentimes been claimed.[24] Wars, class tensions, ethnic antagonisms, and shifting gender roles have been staples of western experience over the last two centuries, and it is hardly surprising that conflicts over the franchise that constitute such a well-known feature of European history had counterparts on this side of the Atlantic. Social class shaped the evolution of voting rights not only in Britain and Japan but in New York and Texas. Wars influenced the breadth of the suffrage in the United States, as well as in Norway, France, and Germany. Gender was a critical issue everywhere. Race and ethnicity separated the enfranchised from the disfranchised not only in the United States but—as the recent history of Europe makes clear—wherever there has been migration or empire.[25]

Indeed, almost all of the forces and factors that shaped the history of the right to vote in the United States were present in other nations. The American story, contrary to popular legend, was not a unique amalgam of the frontier, the democratic spirit, and egalitarian principles; it was not an exceptional example of democratic destiny and idealism.

Yet the history of suffrage in the United States is certainly distinctive in many ways, several of which merit bold headlines. The United States was indeed the first country in the western world to significantly broaden its electorate by permanently lowering explicit economic barriers to political participation. De Tocqueville was not hallucinating when he described (and seemed overwhelmed by) a vibrant, powerful democratic spirit in the early nineteenth century. The United States also was exceptional, however, in experiencing a prolonged period during which the laws governing the right to vote became more, rather than less, restrictive. Finally, despite its pioneering role in promoting democratic values, the United States was one of the last countries in the developed world to attain universal suffrage. Linking and accounting for these headlines is one of the tasks of the tale that follows.

Telling this tale, exploring the complex evolution of the right to vote, should shed light on both the strength and fragility of democratic institutions in the United States. In so doing, it leads inescapably to the reframing of portraits of key episodes in American political history—including the dramatic successes of the Know-Nothings in the 1850s, the debates surrounding the Fifteenth Amendment during Reconstruction, the rise of urban political machines, the programmatic efforts of "good government" reformers, the institutionalized dominance of a two-party system after 1896, the political thrust of the New Deal, and the civil rights movement of the 1950s and 1960s. In addition, examining this slice of our past might help us to understand that most distinctive and paradoxical feature of contemporary American politics: the low, class-correlated turnout of voters. America's formally democratic institutions are ones in which most Americans do not participate. The nation's public culture celebrates the insignificance of class boundaries, yet the wealthy and well educated are far more likely to go to the polls than are the poor and those lacking education.[26] These are paradoxes that history has created—and can also illumine.

PART I

The Road to Partial Democracy

The same reasoning which will induce you to admit all men who have no property, to vote, with those who have, . . . will prove that you ought to admit women and children; for, generally speaking, women and children have as good judgments, and as independent minds, as those men who are wholly destitute of property; these last being to all intents and purposes as much dependent upon others, who will please to feed, clothe, and employ them, as women are upon their husbands, or children on their parents. . . . Depend upon it, Sir, it is dangerous to open so fruitful a source of controversy and altercation as would be opened by attempting to alter the qualifications of voters; there will be no end of it. New claims will arise; women will demand the vote; lads from twelve to twenty-one will think their rights not enough attended to; and every man who has not a farthing, will demand an equal voice with any other, in all acts of state. It tends to confound and destroy all distinctions, and prostrate all ranks to one common level.

—JOHN ADAMS, 1776

It seems to me sir, that we should not abandon the principle that all men are to have some participancy in the affairs of government, particularly when they may be called upon to contribute to

the support of that government. These people. . . are subject to
pay taxes, they are liable to be called on to perform road labor and
various other duties; and, sir, they . . . when the tocsin of war has
sounded, rally to the field of battle. Shall we say that such men
shall not exercise the elective franchise?

—MR. DAVIS OF MASSAC, ILLINOIS,
AT THE ILLINOIS CONSTITUTIONAL CONVENTION, 1847[1]

*A*T ITS BIRTH, THE UNITED STATES WAS NOT a democratic nation—far
from it. The very word *democracy* had pejorative overtones, summoning up
images of disorder, government by the unfit, even mob rule. In practice, moreover, relatively few of the new nation's inhabitants were able to participate in
elections: among the excluded were most African Americans, Native Americans, women, men who had not attained their majority, and adult white males
who did not own land. Only a small fraction of the population cast ballots in
the elections that elevated George Washington and John Adams to the august office of the presidency.

To be sure, the nation's political culture and political institutions did become more democratic between the American Revolution and the middle
of the nineteenth century. This was the "age of democratic revolutions," the
epoch that witnessed the flourishing of "Jacksonian democracy." The ideal
of democracy became widespread during these years, the word itself more
positive, even celebratory. Owing in part to these shifting ideals and beliefs—and also because of economic and military needs, changes in the social structure, and the emergence of competitive political parties—the
franchise was broadened throughout the United States. By 1850, voting was
a far more commonplace activity than it had been in 1800.

Yet the gains were limited. Longstanding historical labels ought not obscure the restricted scope of what was achieved. The American polity may
have been set on an unmistakably democratic course during the first half of
the nineteenth century, but the United States in 1850 stood a long way from
"universal suffrage." Significantly, this phrase had begun to appear in public discourse, but the institution lagged far behind. Indeed, some Americans
who had been enfranchised in 1800 were barred from the polls by midcentury. Change was neither linear nor uncontested: the sources of democratization were complex, and the right to vote was itself a prominent political
issue throughout the period.

ONE

In the Beginning

Today a man owns a jackass worth fifty dollars and he is entitled
to vote; but before the next election the jackass dies. The man in
the mean time has become more experienced, his knowledge of
the principles of government, and his acquaintance with
mankind, are more extensive, and he is therefore better qualified
to make a proper selection of rulers—but the jackass is dead and
the man cannot vote. Now gentlemen, pray inform me, in whom
is the right of suffrage? In the man or in the jackass?

—BENJAMIN FRANKLIN, *The Casket, or
Flowers of Literature, Wit and Sentiment* (1828)

AS THE MEN WHO WOULD LATER BE CALLED "the framers" of the United
States Constitution trickled into Philadelphia during the late spring of
1787 (most of them arrived late), they had weighty issues on their minds:
whether the Articles of Confederation should be revised or replaced with an
altogether new plan of government; how the federal government could be
made stronger without undermining the power of the states; resolving the
already brewing conflict over the apportionment of representatives between
large and small states; and contending with the freighted and divisive matter of slavery. Although the Revolutionary War had been won and independence achieved, a great deal still appeared to be hanging in the balance:
as James Madison portentously noted, "it was more than probable" that the
plan they came up with would "in its operation . . . decide forever the fate
of Republican Government."[1]

With George Washington presiding and the energetic, carefully prepared Madison shaping many of the terms of debate, the fifty-five delegates to the convention wrestled, in closed sessions, with these and many other issues throughout the hot and humid summer. That they would succeed in devising a constitution acceptable to the twelve states that had sent them (not to mention Rhode Island, which had declined the invitation to attend) was far from certain; several impasses were reached in the first two months of deliberation, and by the end of July, many of the delegates were frustrated, impatient, and tired. Eighty-one-year-old Benjamin Franklin, described by one of his fellow delegates as "the greatest philosopher of the present age," trudged wearily back and forth to the sessions, occasionally having to be carried in a sedan chair.[2]

By mid-September, a constitution had been drafted and signed, and delegates began returning home to promote its ratification. The Articles of Confederation were to be scrapped; the increased—but restrained—powers of the federal government had been specified; the issues of state representation and slavery had been compromised; and a great many details outlining the operation of a new republican government had been etched in parchment. What British leader William E. Gladstone a century later would call "the most wonderful work ever struck off at a given time by the brain of man" was complete. The western world's most durable and perhaps most celebrated written blueprint for representative government was soon to become the fundamental law of North America's new nation.

Remarkably, this new constitution, born in celebration of "republican government," did not grant anyone the right to vote. The convention's debates about suffrage, held during the doldrums of late July and early August, were brief, and the final document made little mention of the breadth of the franchise. Only section 2 of article 1 addressed the issue directly: it declared that in elections to the House of Representatives "the Electors in each State shall have the Qualifications requisite for Electors of the most numerous Branch of the State Legislature." More obliquely, section 1 of article 2 indicated that the legislature of each state had the right to determine the "manner" in which presidential electors would be selected, while article 4 entrusted the federal government with a vague mandate to "guarantee to every State in this Union a Republican Form of Government." Otherwise, the Constitution was mute—from which much would follow.

The Received Legacy

For more than a decade before the founding fathers arrived in Philadelphia, individual states had been writing their own suffrage laws. These laws almost everywhere were shaped by colonial precedents and traditional English patterns of thought. The lynchpin of both colonial and British suffrage regulations was the restriction of voting to adult men who owned property. On the eve of the American Revolution, in seven colonies men had to own land of specified acreage or monetary value in order to participate in elections; elsewhere, the ownership of personal property of a designated value (or in South Carolina, the payment of taxes) could substitute for real estate.[3]

Both in England and in the colonies, property requirements had long been justified on two grounds. The first was that men who possessed property (especially "real property," i.e., land and buildings) had a unique "stake in society"—meaning that they were committed members of (or shareholders in) the community and that they had a personal interest in the policies of the state, especially taxation. The second was that property owners alone possessed sufficient independence to warrant their having a voice in governance. As Henry Ireton had argued in England in the seventeenth century, "if there be anything at all that is the foundation of liberty, it is this, that those who shall choose the law-makers shall be men freed from dependence upon others." And the best way to be "freed" from such dependence, or so it was believed, was through the ownership of property, especially real estate. Conversely, the ballot was not to be entrusted to those who were economically dependent, because they could too easily be controlled or manipulated by others. Such control may have seemed particularly plausible in the six colonies in which voting was viva voce—although advocates of secret paper ballots pointed out that disfranchisement was not the only solution to that problem. Indeed, implicit in the argument for independence was another notion, often unspoken but especially resonant in the colonies, where economic opportunities were believed to abound: that anyone who failed to acquire property was of questionable competence and unworthy of full membership in the polity.[4]

These concerns also prompted other restrictions on voting. Many colonies instituted residency requirements to exclude transients who presumably lacked the requisite stake in the colony's affairs;[5] for similar reasons, some made citizenship, of England or the province, a prerequisite for voting.[6] To guarantee that those who were dependent could not vote, several colonies formally barred all servants from the polls, while others expressly excluded paupers. Women too were prohibited from voting, because they were thought to be dependent on adult men and because their "delicacy" rendered them unfit for the worldly experiences necessary for engagement in politics.[7] In addition, there were limitations on the franchise that had more to do with social membership in the community than with a person's independence or stake in society. Freedmen of African or Amerindian descent were denied the ballot in much of the South.[8] In seventeenth-century Massachusetts, only members of the Congregational church could vote; in the eighteenth century, Catholics were disfranchised in five states and Jews in four.[9]

As these details suggest, aside from property qualifications, there were no firm principles governing colonial voting rights, and suffrage laws accordingly were quite varied. Not only Catholics and Jews, but also Native Americans, free blacks, and nonnaturalized aliens could vote in some places and not in others.[10] Women were barred expressly in several colonies, including Virginia, but statutes elsewhere made no reference to gender, and in at least a few Massachusetts towns and New York counties propertied widows did legally vote.[11] Absentee landowners were enfranchised in Virginia in 1736, which often meant that they could vote in more than one place. In practice, moreover, the enforcement or application of suffrage laws was uneven and dependent on local circumstances.[12]

Of equal importance, the qualifications to vote in local elections—especially in the cities and larger towns—often differed from those needed to vote for colonial or provincial officers. These differences had two sources. The first was political or institutional. Royal charters for incorporated cities frequently spelled out precise suffrage rules, and those rules commonly granted political citizenship to men who had commercial affairs—rather than a residence—within the city limits. The breadth of the franchise in New York City, Perth Amboy, New Jersey, and Norfolk, Virginia, for example, was determined not by colonial general assemblies but by royal declaration and by the appointed officers who controlled the municipal corporations. The second reason for this municipal–colonial difference was economic: city and town dwellers possessed different types of property than did farmers, and consequently they sought to define property requirements in terms other than acreage or land. Although differently configured, city and town suffrage qualifications were not uniformly more strict or more lenient than were the qualifications for voting in the countryside.[13]

Did the right to vote expand or contract during the colonial era? Were the colonies becoming more or less democratic, in their suffrage rules? The evidence is mixed. Some broadening of the franchise certainly occurred: religious restrictions, for non–church members and Protestant dissenters, tended to be relaxed in the late seventeenth and eighteenth centuries; municipal corporations began to grant the franchise to freeholders as well as men of commerce; and both Massachusetts and Virginia enacted laws that reduced the property requirements for voting.[14] Yet the colonial era also witnessed some statutory contraction of the suffrage. The initial laws restricting the franchise to property owners generally were passed only decades after the colonies were settled, and in several colonies, including Pennsylvania, Rhode Island, and Virginia (which had a notably nonlinear franchise history), property requirements became more stringent over time.[15] Moreover, the legal exclusion of Catholics, as well as African Americans, mulattoes, and Native Americans, took place primarily in the eighteenth century.[16] Whether these laws altered rather than codified existing practices is unclear; but the statutes seem to have been more restrictive by the middle of the eighteenth century than they had been in the seventeenth.[17]

What also is unclear is just how many people could and did vote. This issue is a source of controversy among historians, some of whom conclude that colonial America was a land of middle-class democracy in which 80 or 90 percent of all adult white males were enfranchised, while others depict a far more oligarchic and exclusive political order.[18] In fact, enfranchisement varied greatly by location. There certainly were communities, particularly newly settled communities where land was inexpensive, in which 70 or 80 percent of all white men were enfranchised.[19] Yet there were also locales— including coastal towns (e.g., Ipswich, Massachusetts), farming counties (Westchester, New York, and Chester, Pennsylvania), cities (e.g., Philadelphia and Boston), and even some frontier settlements (Kent, Connecticut)—where the percentages were far lower, closer to 40 or 50 percent.[20] Levels of enfranchisement seem to have been higher in New England and in the South (especially Virginia and the Carolinas) than they were in the mid-Atlantic colonies (especially New York, Pennsylvania, and Maryland); not surprisingly, they also tended to be higher in newer settlements than in more developed areas. On the whole, the franchise was far more widespread than it was in England, yet as the revolution approached, the rate of property ownership was falling, and the proportion of adult white males who were eligible to vote was probably less than 60 percent.[21]

The Revolution and the Vote

> The ultimate end of all freedom is the enjoyment of a right of
> free suffrage.
>
> —"A WATCHMAN," *Maryland Gazette*, 1776

The "shot heard round the world" signaled the beginning of a new era in the history of the franchise. By challenging Britain's right to rule the colonies, the American Revolution sparked a far-reaching public debate about the nature and sources of legitimate governmental authority. The issue of suffrage was always near the center of that debate: if the legitimacy of a government depended on the consent of the governed (one of the key rhetorical claims of the revolution), then limitations on suffrage were intrinsically problematic, since voting was the primary instrument through which a populace could express or withhold consent.[22]

Did the colonial franchise restrictions, then, have to be abolished? The question loomed large, and in many of the former colonies, the revolutionary period—stretching from the mid-1770s to the ratification of the Constitution—witnessed heated public exchanges and sharp political conflict over the franchise; in some locales, men voted—or were prevented from voting—through the use or threat of force. Challenges to the traditional class restraints on suffrage were critical ingredients in the democratic, rather than anti-imperial, thrust of the revolution.[23]

The conflict over the franchise that erupted during the revolution involved—as such conflicts always would—both interests and ideas. The planters, merchants, and prosperous farmers who wielded power and influence in late-eighteenth-century affairs had an unmistakable interest in keeping the franchise narrow: a restricted suffrage would make it easier for them to retain their economic and social advantages. Conversely, tenant farmers, journeymen, and laborers (not to mention African Americans and women) had something to gain from the diffusion of political rights. Landowners would maximize their political power if the franchise were tied to freehold ownership, while city dwellers, shopkeepers, and artisans had a direct interest in replacing freehold requirements with taxpaying or personal property qualifications.

Yet the debates were not simply a self-interested shouting match between the haves and the have nots or between men who owned different types of property. For one thing, the haves were hardly unanimous in their views; nor presumably were the have nots, who left fewer written records. Further-more, ideas—whether or not independent of interests—mattered to the haves and have nots alike. Participants in debates about the franchise surely were influenced by their own material interests, but they also were trying to grasp or invent ideas that meshed with social reality and harmonized with deeply held values. This was always true in American history, and never more so than during the revolution—an era of political experimentation and war in which ideas about politics possessed exceptional valence. Received notions were being looked at with fresh eyes, held up against the backdrop of changed circumstances; new ideas had to be tested against models of history and human nature. The founding fathers—and mothers, sons, and daughters—were trying to envision a new polity as well as a new state, and they felt some urgency about getting it right.

Throughout the ex-colonies, political leaders put forward several different arguments—some traditional, at least one new—to justify the retention of restrictions, particularly property restrictions, on the franchise. Implicit in these arguments was the claim that voting was not a right but a privilege, one that the state could legitimately grant or curtail in its own interest. Indeed, in early English usage, the word *franchise* referred to a privilege, immunity, or freedom that a state could grant, while the term *suffrage* alluded to intercessory prayers. Even Pennsylvanian James Wilson, a signer of both the Declaration of Independence and the Constitution, and one of the more democratic of the founding fathers, described suffrage as a "darling privilege of free men" that could and should be "extended as far as considerations of safety and order will permit."[24]

One such consideration was the stake in society notion inherited from the colonial period. Only men with property, preferably real property, were deemed to be sufficiently attached to the community and sufficiently affected by its laws to have earned the privilege of voting.[25] Sometimes this argument was given a negative cast, with proponents insisting that the propertyless, if enfranchised, would constitute a menace to the maintenance of a well-ordered community.[26] Defenders of property qualifications also maintained (as the British had to the colonists) that representation could be virtual rather than actual, and that consequently there was no need to enfranchise the poor. The interests of the propertyless, like those of women and children, could be represented effectively by wise, fair-minded, wealthy white men.[27]

Those who opposed any expansion of suffrage also relied heavily on the belief that in order to vote a person had to be independent. This venerable

idea, a staple of republican thought in the eighteenth century, was given influential expression in the late 1760s by Sir William Blackstone in his *Commentaries on the Laws of England.*

> The *true* reason of requiring any qualification, with regard to property, in vot-
> ers, is to exclude such persons as are in so mean a situation that they are es-
> teemed to have no will of their own. If these persons had votes, they would
> be tempted to dispose of them under some undue influence or other. This
> would give a great, an artful, or a wealthy man, a larger share in elections than
> is consistent with general liberty. If it were probable that every man would
> give his vote freely and without influence of any kind, then, upon the true
> theory and genuine principles of liberty, every member of the community,
> however poor, should have a vote in electing those delegates, to whose charge
> is committed the disposal of his property, his liberty, and his life. But, since
> that can hardly be expected in persons of indigent fortunes, or such as are
> under the immediate dominion of others, all popular states have been obliged
> to establish certain qualifications; whereby some, who are suspected to have
> no will of their own, are excluded from voting, in order to set other individ-
> uals, whose wills may be supposed independent, more thoroughly upon a
> level with each other.[28]

Blackstone's reference to persons who were "in so mean a situation" that
they had "no will of their own" (a phrasing that Blackstone appears to have
lifted, without attribution, from Montesquieu) was repeated endlessly during
the revolutionary era.[29] In debates everywhere, from Massachusetts to New
Jersey to Maryland to South Carolina, lawyers, merchants, and farmers defended property qualifications by quoting or paraphrasing Blackstone and by
invoking the spectre of a demagogue coming to power through the manipu-
lation of dependent men and women.[30] Even Thomas Jefferson, perhaps the
most democratic leader of the revolution, accepted Blackstone's equation of
property with independence and the right to vote—although Jefferson sought
to solve that distasteful equation by advocating the distribution of free land to
the propertyless.[31] Thomas Paine also believed, in the 1770s, that voters
should be personally independent, but by 1795 the experience of two revolutions had changed his mind and led him to advocate universal suffrage.[32]
    Remarkably, the argument that the poor should not vote because they had
"no will of their own" coexisted with an altogether contradictory argument,
often expressed by the same people: the poor, or the propertyless, should not

vote because they would threaten the interests of property—that is, they would have too much will of their own. If men without property could vote, reflected the judicious conservative, John Adams, "an immediate revolution would ensue."[33] Indeed, the almost obsessive incantation of Blackstone's phrase may well have been a refraction, a semiconscious mask, of class apprehensions, a sign that the well-to-do feared not that the poor would have no will of their own but precisely the opposite. Sober and scholarly as the argument for independence may have sounded, there was little in American political experience to suggest that the poor would be misled by an "artful" or "wealthy" politician to the ruin of the republic; it was far more likely, as a rebellion of hard-pressed western Massachusetts farmers demonstrated in 1786, that men who were financially strapped would band together to defend their own interests. Operatively, then, the primary thrust of Blackstone's words was to defend the material interests of the propertied. By invoking his arguments, Blackstone's North American followers were performing an impressive feat of ideological alchemy: providing an ostensibly egalitarian defense of an overtly anti-egalitarian policy.

The issue of inequality also lay at the heart of the most innovative, and distinctively American, justification for property restrictions: a pessimistic view of the nation's future class structure. Even at the new nation's birth, even as the glorious future of the republic was being proclaimed up and down the seaboard, some of the revolution's leaders were cautioning that economic expansion and the growth of "manufactures" would bring greater inequality and new political dangers. This theme, which would be echoed in political debates for a century, was voiced by Madison at the federal constitutional convention:

> in future times a great majority of the people will not only be without landed but any other sort of property. These will either combine under the influence of their common situation; in which case, the rights of property and the public liberty will not be secure in their hands: or which is more probable, they will become the tools of opulence and ambition, in which case there will be equal danger on another side.

By referring to "future times," Madison was tacitly acknowledging the limited applicability of Blackstone's thinking to the late-eighteenth-century American world in which freeholders were numerous. Yet presciently anticipating that the rise of "manufactures" would transform the nation's social structure, Madison advocated a property requirement that would serve the nation in a nineteenth-century future in which the propertyless—possessing either too much or too little will of their own—would be numerically predominant and politically powerful. Property qualifications, in effect, would function as a bulwark against the landless proletariat of an industrial future.[34]

Arrayed against these conservative views was a set of equally cogent, if somewhat experimental, arguments in favor of extending the franchise, particularly to men who did not own property. The most broadly framed of these arguments was simple: voting was a "natural right" that the state could not suspend, except in the most extreme circumstances. The idea that voting was a right, even a natural right, had become increasingly widespread in the eighteenth century (its ancestry dated to antiquity) and was embraced by many small farmers and artisans, as well as by the most radical leaders of the revolution, such as Franklin, Thomas Young of Pennsylvania, and Ethan Allen of Vermont.[35] The rural town of Richmond, Massachusetts, for example, declared its opposition to a proposed state constitution in 1780 because "excluding persons from a share in representation for want of pecuniary qualifications is an infringement on the natural rights of the subject." Similarly, the town of Greenwich objected that the "people" were "deprived of their natural rights" because it was the "right of the people to elect their own delegates."[36] The notion that voting was a right also was mobilized on behalf of African Americans: "the depriving of any men or set of men for the sole cause of colour from giving there [*sic*] votes for a representative," proclaimed the town of Spencer, Massachusetts, was "an infringement upon the rights of mankind."[37]

The idea that voting was a natural right or even a right at all was rhetorically powerful: it meshed well with the Lockean political theory popular in eighteenth-century America, it had a clear antimonarchical thrust, and it had the virtue of simplicity. The language of rights was resonant and fresh in late eighteenth-century America, and the notion that voting was a right that inhered in individuals rather than property was welcome as well as liberating. Franklin's pointed query about the right to vote belonging to the jackass rather than the man became so widely known that references to "Franklin's jackass" appeared in constitutional convention debates fifty years later.

Yet there was a problem with this vision of suffrage as a right, a problem both political and rhetorical. During the revolutionary period and in later decades, as its proponents quickly discovered, there was no way to argue that voting was a right or a natural right without opening Pandora's box. If voting was a natural right, then everyone should possess it. Did this mean that not just every man (including poor men) should vote, but women as well? What about African Americans—and recently arrived aliens? Or children? If there was a "right" to suffrage, wasn't it wrong or immoral to deprive any group or individual of that right? How could one justify denying anyone his or her natural—or socially acknowledged—rights?

This was precisely the point John Adams made in his letter (quoted earlier) to James Sullivan in 1776, a point he was to reiterate for years.[38] Once it was acknowledged that people had a *right* to vote, it would be difficult to deny the suffrage to anyone: there would "be no end of it," as Adams observed. Adams and other conservatives, moreover, were well aware that most of those who invoked natural rights on behalf of the propertyless did not want there to be "no end of it": they did not believe, for example, that women or African Americans or minors should vote.[39] Their conception of natural rights was not universal, and their embrace of rights claims therefore could easily be exposed as instrumental and inconsistent. This dynamic—the embrace of rights arguments by advocates of an expanded suffrage met by a conservative counterargument emphasizing the unacceptable contents of the Pandora's box—was to be repeated for almost two centuries.[40]

In part because they feared the universalist implications of natural rights claims, most proponents of a broader franchise offered more limited and specific arguments for changing the voting laws. One such argument was that property qualifications ought to be replaced by taxpaying requirements, because all taxpayers (not just property owners) were contributing to the government and affected by its policies. Such a change would enlarge the electorate; it also would shift the primary basis of an individual's claim to membership in the polity from his independence (as established by the ownership of property) to his stake in, and vulnerability to, state policies (as someone required to pay taxes). Taxpaying requirements, as historian Marc Kruman has argued, were not simply watered-down versions of property qualifications; they derived from a different premise: that all those who paid taxes had the right to defend themselves against potentially unfair government policies. The logic of "no taxation without representation" had a domestic as well as anticolonial application.[41]

Linked to this argument was another, drawn directly from republican theory and prevailing conceptions of the social contract: "that law to bind all must be assented to by all."[42] For society to function smoothly, for the social contract to operate, people had to be given the opportunity—directly or through chosen representatives—to consent to or oppose laws. Denying people the franchise made that impossible and was consequently an invitation to disorder, anarchy, and tax evasion. "No man can be bound by a law that he has not given his consent to, either by his person, or legal representative," declared a western Massachusetts citizens committee in 1779.[43] "We view it both unfair and unjust to tax men without their consent," concluded a town meeting in New Salem in 1780.[44]

The significance of popular consent also helped to undermine the idea of virtual representation. The purpose of representation, in republican theory, was to provide the governed with a feasible mechanism through which they could express or withhold their consent to laws or policies promulgated by a government. To say that men could be fairly represented by those whom they had played no part in choosing rang just as false as the royal claim that the colonists were adequately, if virtually, represented by British members of Parliament. As historian Gordon Wood has pointed out, the increasingly pluralist and particularistic conception of representation that emerged during the revolution subverted arguments for a limited franchise.[45]

The final cluster of arguments for expanding the franchise was rather different: these favored extending the right to vote to everyone who was serving, or had served, in the army or the militia. The grounds for such an expansion were partly moral: it was not fair to ask propertyless men to risk their lives in defense of independence and then refuse them the right to vote. "Shall these poor polls who have gone for us into the greatest perils and undergone infinite fatigues in the present war . . . shall they now be treated by us like villains?" queried the citizens of Northampton, Massachusetts, in 1780.[46] It was an "injustice" to disfranchise men who "have fought and bled in their country's cause," concluded residents of nearby Lenox.[47]

Embedded in this view was also a clear, if not always articulated, conception of the links between the rights and obligations of citizenship: a man who served in the militia or the army was entitled to all the rights of a citizen, including the right to vote. As one Pennsylvania editorialist wrote, the franchise should belong to "every man who pays his shot and bears his lot." Similarly, a Philadelphia pamphleteer (probably Thomas Young) insisted that "every man in the country who manifests a disposition to venture his all for the defense of its liberty, should have a voice in its council." The power of such arguments went well beyond implicit theories of citizenship: as would be true throughout American history, the notion that soldiers should be enfranchised was an emotionally resonant one to all men who had fought or even those who knew what military service was like. "Perils," "infinite fatigues," and "bled" were concrete words, evoking the intensity and horror of wartime experiences that amply earned a man the right to choose his leaders and participate in politics.[48]

These principled reasons for enfranchising men who bore arms were to be heard repeatedly in the course of American history. So too was a more pragmatic and political argument: recruiting and retaining an army would be difficult if soldiers or potential soldiers were prohibited from voting. Franklin voiced this view at the constitutional convention, in opposition to a call for a national freehold qualification. "It is of great consequence," the oldest delegate declared, "that we should not depress the virtue and public spirit of our common people; of which they displayed a great deal during the war, and which contributed principally to the favorable issue of it." He contrasted the willingness with which captured British seamen "entered the American service" with the patriotism of imprisoned American sailors, who had refused to "redeem themselves" from British prisons by fighting for the enemy. Franklin attributed the Americans' superior valor to their morale, to their knowledge that they were the "equal" of their "fellow citizens," and warned that the patriotism of the "common people" could be undermined by property qualifications on the franchise. Franklin's point was a resonant one in a new and vulnerable nation that had been compelled to offer significant economic and legal incentives to the poor in order to raise a revolutionary army. Wars were not fought by property owners alone (they often did not fight at all), and it was in the national interest to enfranchise everyone who might be called upon in an hour of need.[49]

Given these widely disparate and sharply conflicting views of suffrage, it is hardly surprising that the breadth of the franchise—and particularly the desirability of property requirements—became a major focus of controversy during the revolutionary era. Arguments for and against a more democratic suffrage were voiced in newspapers, broadsides, provincial assemblies, town meetings, gatherings of militiamen, and constitutional conventions, as well as taverns, inns, city streets, and private homes. The very act of declaring independence from Britain compelled the residents of each colony to form a new government, and the process of forming new governments inescapably brought the issue of suffrage to the fore.[50] Who should be involved in creating a new government for an ex-colony? For a new government to be legitimate, who had to consent to its design and structure? And how broad should suffrage be in a republic? The answers to these questions varied from one state to the next. (For a summary of the suffrage laws adopted, see table A.1.)

The most influential and, perhaps, dramatic expansion of the franchise occurred in Pennsylvania during the first months of the revolution. The key actors in the drama were members of the highly politicized Philadelphia militias who seized the early initiative in Pennsylvania's rejection of British rule. As early as March 1776, the Committee of Privates, speaking for rank-and-file militiamen drawn from the city's "lower" and "middling sorts," announced its readiness to discard colonial suffrage requirements: it asked the provincial assembly to enfranchise the "brave and spirited Germans and others" who had "cheerfully" joined the militia associations, yet were "not entitled to the privileges of freemen electors." Later in the spring, the committee also demanded that militiamen be permitted to elect their own officers and that all taxpaying militia associators be allowed to vote for delegates who would draw up a new state constitution.[51]

Backed by prominent reformers such as Franklin, Young, and Paine, and allied with western farmers who had long been underrepresented in the colony's government, the militiamen succeeded in electing a constitutional convention dominated not by the traditional elites but by artisans, lesser merchants, and farmers. That convention, in the fall of 1776, produced the most democratic constitution in the thirteen original states: it abolished property requirements and enfranchised all taxpaying adult males as well as the nontaxpaying sons of freeholders. Since Pennsylvania had a poll tax—meaning a "head" tax or a tax on all household heads—this effectively enfranchised the great majority of adult males. Despite fierce opposition from the Quaker upper classes that had controlled the colonial government, the constitution relocated the boundaries of the population regarded as having "a sufficient common interest with and attachment to the community." Those new, more ample boundaries remained in place despite the state's conservative swing in the 1780s.[52]

In Maryland, militia associators also spearheaded the attack on the colonial franchise with even greater militance, but less ultimate success. The precipitant of militia action was a provincial decision in 1776 to limit voting for delegates to a constitutional convention to men who met the colonial property qualifications. In half a dozen counties, militiamen rebelled, insisting that all taxpaying associators be permitted to vote. In Arundel County, armed men who could not meet the franchise requirement actually marched on the polls, demanded the right to vote, and threatened to "pull the house down from under" the election judges. When they were refused and the polls closed, they declared that they would lay down their arms. In other counties, militiamen and local citizens appointed their own election judges, who in turn allowed all associators to vote. The state's governing authorities, however, displayed little tolerance for these rebellions, ordering new elections with strict enforcement of the property qualifications. The constitutional convention itself, perhaps chastened by the tumult, significantly lowered, but did not abolish, the property requirement; and the state's Declaration of Rights reiterated the principle that the right of suffrage ought to be possessed by "every man having property in . . . the community."[53]

The political dynamics of revolution generated a broader franchise in a half dozen other states as well. In New Jersey, a decentralized movement for reform, backed by artisans, city dwellers, and small landowners, succeeded in abolishing the freehold requirement for voting; a new provision, however, was instituted granting suffrage only to persons worth fifty pounds in proclamation money.[54] In Georgia, despite significant opposition, the freehold qualification was abandoned in 1777 and replaced by a more flexible requirement that any twenty-one-year-old white male could vote who possessed "ten pounds value," was "liable to pay tax in" the state, or belonged "to any mechanic trade."[55] New Hampshire, after six years of difficulty agreeing on the text of a constitution, decided in 1782 to substitute a taxpaying qualification for the provincial freehold requirement.[56]

In New York and North Carolina, the right to vote was enlarged, with conflict resolved through bicameral compromise. In the Empire State, despite the activism of New York City's already enfranchised artisans, the conservative Whigs who dominated state politics preserved property requirements for voting for all offices. Yet the requirement was reduced (to a twenty-pound freehold or a forty-shilling tenancy) for elections to the state assembly, while remaining far more substantial for senatorial elections. New York also took the step (mirrored less formally elsewhere) of constitutionally abolishing oral voting.[57] In North Carolina, similarly, demands for manhood suffrage were rebuffed, but some liberalization of the law did take place: a taxpaying qualification was introduced for the lower house of the legislature, while the state retained a fifty-acre freehold requirement in elections for the state senate.[58]

In only one state, Vermont, was a man's ability to vote completely detached from his financial circumstances. The residents of what would become the Green Mountain State adopted a constitution in 1777 that was closely modeled on that of Pennsylvania. The farmers of Vermont went a step further, however, eliminating not only property requirements but tax-paying qualifications as well. That they took such an unprecedented step was a reflection both of the region's relatively egalitarian social structure and the rather unruly political—and military—process that led to the writing of a constitution. For Vermonters, the revolution was a rebellion, led by Ethan Allen and his band of Green Mountain Boys, against both Britain and the state of New York, to which the region technically belonged. Since Vermont was unique in not having a government when independence was declared, delegates to its constitutional convention were selected not by an existing state assembly but by popular elections held in the region's townships. This democratically selected convention produced the first state constitution to abolish slavery and to institute anything close to universal manhood suffrage. In campaigning for statehood, Allen (who had become the head of the state's militia) and his colleagues pointed repeatedly to the difference between Vermont's broad suffrage and the freehold requirements still prevailing in New York. When Vermont finally entered the union in 1791, any adult male who took the Freeman's Oath could vote.[59]

Vermont was a revealing but exceptional case. Even the partial liberalization of voting requirements was by no means universal: in five states, there was little or no change at all. Rhode Island and Delaware retained their colonial laws, with relatively little public turmoil; Connecticut did the same, despite pressure for reform from militiamen, among others. In South Carolina, demands for change produced only a nominal revision of the property requirements; and in Virginia—where the subject produced great debates and considerable eloquence from notables such as George Mason and Thomas Jefferson—the constitution adopted in 1776 ended up reiterating voting laws that had been put in place forty years earlier.[60]

Massachusetts, moreover, actually stiffened its requirements for voting.[61] Throughout the revolutionary period, the Bay State was wracked by regional and ideological conflict: the relatively conservative established leadership of its eastern counties squared off repeatedly against more radical and democratic factions centered in the west. In 1778, a convention drafted a compromise constitution that would have permitted all taxpaying, white freemen to vote for the lower house of the state legislature, while retaining a property requirement for senate and gubernatorial elections. Yet this constitution was overwhelmingly rejected by the state's citizens, in part—but only in part—because it was insufficiently democratic. Numerous towns objected to its racially discriminatory suffrage provision: it "deprives a part of the human race of their natural rights, merely on account of their color," explained the citizens of Westminster. Others refused to accept the persistence of any property qualifications on voting, which made "honest poverty a crime."[62]

A year later, a new constitution was drafted, largely by John Adams: it dropped the racial exclusions but reinstituted property requirements that were more stringent than those of the colonial era. Members of the constitutional convention (chosen by an electorate that included all freemen) justified this conservative tilt in a published address that was remarkably overt in its class bias and contempt for the propertyless:

> Your Delegates considered that Persons who are Twenty-one Years of age, and have no Property, are either those who live upon a part of a Paternal estate, expecting the Fee thereof, who are but just entering into business, or those whose Idleness of Life and profligacy of manners will forever bar them from acquiring and possessing Property. And we will submit it to the former class, whether they would not think it safer for them to have their right of Voting for a Representative suspended for [a] small space of Time, than forever hereafter to have their Privileges liable to the control of Men who will pay less regard to the Rights of Property because they have nothing to lose.[63]

Forty-two towns, most of them in the west, objected strenuously to the proposed suffrage qualifications. "Taxation and representation are reciprocal and inseparably connected," declared the town meeting of Stoughton. Belchertown's citizens insisted that denying the franchise to adults was to deprive them of "that liberty and freedom which we are at this day contending for." The eastern town of Mansfield responded to the convention's stated rationale by noting that "many sensible, honest, and naturally industrious men, by numberless misfortunes," never acquire property "of the value of sixty pounds." Despite these objections, and thanks to a remarkably stacked and undemocratic method of counting the "votes" of the commonwealth's communities, the new constitution was declared ratified in 1780. Its suffrage provision reflected the convention's view that those who lacked property were unworthy of full citizenship—or in the words of one prominent eastern merchant, "the people at large, in any numbers together, are nearly as unfit to choose legislators . . . as they are in general to fill the offices themselves."[64]

The revolutionary period, in sum, witnessed a broad range of reactions to economic restrictions on the franchise. Although often overshadowed by

other issues (such as taxation or the structure of future legislatures), the
breadth of the franchise mattered greatly to citizens of the thirteen original
ex-colonies and the new state of Vermont. In every state, there was pressure
for suffrage reform, as well as conservative opposition to a less class-biased,
more economically inclusive franchise. The outcomes of these conflicts followed no clear regional pattern; they seem instead to have been shaped
largely by the strength of local elites and by the particular political processes
that unfolded in each state. The overall result was a mixed bag of substantial changes, cosmetic alterations, and preservation of the status quo.[65]

On noneconomic fronts, however, proponents of suffrage reform fared
better. The disfranchisement of Roman Catholics and Jews was brought to
an end—although in South Carolina it remained necessary to "acknowledge
the being of a God."[66] Free African Americans were tacitly enfranchised in
North Carolina, Massachusetts, New York, Pennsylvania, Maryland, and
Vermont.[67] (They remained voteless in Georgia, South Carolina, and Virginia.) In New Jersey, the revolutionary-era constitution permitted women
to vote (a development to be discussed at length in subsequent chapters).

Alongside these substantive matters, several important legal and jurisdic-
tional issues also were shaped, or structured, during the revolutionary period.
The first was that suffrage was defined as a constitutional issue: all of the
early state constitutions (except that of Delaware) treated the right to vote as
a matter of fundamental—and thus constitutional—law, rather than statute
law. Implicit in this treatment was the notion that suffrage requirements
ought to be durable and difficult to change; legislatures and governors alone
were not entrusted with the power to tamper with the right to vote. In theory
at least, the franchise could be broadened or narrowed only through constitutional revision or amendment.[68]

In addition, the revolution witnessed the perpetuation and, in some instances, the reinforcement of the distinction between state and municipal
voting rights. In cities that possessed charters from the colonial period, the
right to vote in municipal elections continued to be determined by city officials and charter rules; in almost all of the twenty-five cities incorporated
during the revolutionary era, municipal voting rights were specified in new
charters. Despite the constitutional character of state voting requirements,
legislatures—which could grant new charters—were granted the power to
define the electorate for nonconstitutional (including local) offices.[69]

The most common manner in which municipal voting rights differed
from the state suffrage was in the configuration of property restrictions: in-

creasingly, urban residents who did not own real property could vote if they met either a personal property or a taxpaying requirement. The principles of state law were, in effect, adapted to urban conditions. In some locales, however, the differences were more substantial. Nine of the cities chartered during the revolution granted the franchise to nearly all adult males; and Massachusetts, in the 1780s, passed a series of laws that gave the right to vote in town meetings to all men who could meet a minimal taxpaying requirement.[70]

On the whole, municipal voting rights tended to broaden more rapidly than did the right to vote in state elections, probably because of pressure from propertyless urban citizens.[71] There were important exceptions to this trend, however, notably among cities with prerevolutionary charters. In Norfolk, Virginia, for example, a closed corporation of merchants continued to govern the city without the electoral participation of most inhabitants; only in the late 1780s did the state government, responding to petitions from the populace, grant municipal suffrage to those who could already vote for state legislators. In so doing, the commonwealth was tacitly setting a precedent, ruling that municipal charters were not inviolable. In Philadelphia and New York, similarly, local elites sought to preserve, or impose, a restrictive municipal suffrage in order to retain political control of their cities: in both urban centers sharp conflict over the suffrage—and over the state's right to intervene in the affairs of municipal corporations—persisted into the postrevolutionary era.[72]

The States and the Nation

It was at the end of the revolutionary period that the role of the federal government in determining suffrage requirements was written into constitutional law. Under the Articles of Confederation, the states had retained complete control over the franchise. But the Constitution of the United States forged a link between state suffrage rules and the right to vote in national elections: those who participated in elections for the "most numerous Branch of the state legislature" were automatically entitled to vote for members of the House of Representatives. These were the only national offices for which the Constitution demanded a popular electoral process of any kind.

This rather peculiar and indirect national mandate was a compromise, an outgrowth both of an ideologically divided constitutional convention and the practical politics of constitutional ratification. The issue of suffrage came to the floor of the convention in late July 1787, when the delegates were fatigued from months of debate and speechmaking; after a brief discussion, the issue was consigned to a committee of detail, with instructions for the committee to consider designing property and citizenship requirements for voting in na-tional elections. The committee of detail worked for more than a week, while other delegates took a break: Washington and several of his colleagues went fishing. In its deliberations, the committee weighed the possibility of a fed-eral property requirement, as well as several proposals that would have given the federal government the power to impose its own suffrage laws at some fu-ture time. The issue was "well considered by the committee," claimed James Wilson, who noted further that it was "difficult to form any uniform rule of qualifications for all the states." In the end, the committee's recommendation was to tie suffrage for the House of Representatives to state franchise re-quirements in elections to the lower house of each state legislature.[73]

The committee's proposal prompted a short but sharp debate in the con-vention early in August. That debate revolved around concerns that the franchise would be too broad. Pennsylvania merchant Gouverneur Morris, sounding an array of familiar conservative notes, led the attack, insisting that a national freehold requirement was necessary to prevent the growth of aristocracy.

> The aristocracy will grow out of the House of Representatives. Give the votes to people who have no property, and they will sell them to the rich. . . . We should not confine our attention to the present moment. The time is not distant when this country will abound with mechanics and manufacturers, who will receive their bread from their employers. Will such men be the secure and faithful guardians of liberty? Will they be the impregnable barrier against aristocracy?[74]

His views were seconded by Madison, who argued that the corruption of Parliament in England had occurred because the "qualification of suffrage" was too low in the "cities and boroughs." Madison also maintained that "the freeholders of the country would be the safest depositories of republican lib-erty," although he acknowledged that it might be impolitic to impose a free-hold requirement on those "states where the right was now exercised by every description of people."[75]

The views of Morris and Madison were challenged both by conservative advocates of higher property qualifications and by proponents of a more popular suffrage. George Mason of Virginia maintained that "every man having evidence of attachment to, and permanent common interest with, the society, ought to share in all its rights and privileges." Nathaniel Gorham, a Boston merchant, correctly pointed out the flaws in Madison's understanding of British politics and observed that he had never "seen any inconvenience from allowing such as were not freeholders to vote . . . the elections in Philadelphia, New York, and Boston, where the merchants and mechanics vote, are at least as good as those made by freeholders only." Franklin vehemently maintained that "depositing the right of suffrage in the freeholders exclusively" would "injure the lower class of freemen. . . . The common people of England," he maintained, "lost a great portion of attachment to their country" because of their disfranchisement. Franklin also advanced his argument that a freehold suffrage requirement would undermine the loyalty of sailors and soldiers; not coincidentally, perhaps, a few hours before Franklin spoke, the city of Philadelphia had welcomed home 800 militiamen who had been serving on the northwestern frontier.[76]

Although Morris's proposal for a national freehold requirement was beaten back, it was notable that no argument was put forward on the convention floor in favor of a uniformly broad national suffrage. Perhaps owing to the absence of some of the revolution's most democratic leaders (including Jefferson, Paine, Samuel Adams, and Patrick Henry), there was no formal debate about the possibility of a national standard more inclusive than the laws already prevailing in the states. Indeed, the records of the federal convention and state constitutional conventions suggest that most members of the new nation's political leadership did not favor a more democratic franchise: Madison's views were more typical of the founding fathers than were those of Jefferson or Franklin. The well-to-do Elbridge Gerry of Massachusetts (whose name would be immortalized in the word *gerrymander*), speaking at the end of the convention, described "Democracy" as "the worst . . . of all political evils."[77] This conservative consensus also was expressed in the Northwest Ordinance of 1787 (an act reaffirmed by the first Congress in 1789), which instituted a freehold requirement in the territories northwest of the Ohio River. In the largest piece of terrain directly controlled by the federal government, citizens and aliens alike had to own fifty acres of land in order to vote.[78]

The decision made by the constitutional convention, however, stemmed at least as much from practical politics as from ideology. The convention accepted the committee of detail's formulation, with slight revisions, largely because of its desire to avoid jeopardizing the ratification of the new constitution. Any national suffrage requirement was likely to generate opposition in one state or another, and a narrow national suffrage, such as a free-hold qualification, seemed capable of derailing the Constitution altogether. As Oliver Ellsworth of Connecticut observed, "the right of suffrage was a tender point, and strongly guarded by most of the state constitutions. The people will not readily subscribe to the national Constitution, if it should subject them to be disfranchised." Madison reiterated the point in the *Federalist Papers*: "One uniform rule would probably have been as dissatis-factory to some of the States as it would have been difficult to the conven-tion."[79] By making the franchise in national elections dependent on state suffrage laws, the authors of the Constitution compromised their substan-tive disagreements to solve a potentially explosive political problem.

The solution they devised, however, had a legacy—a long and sometimes problematic legacy. The Constitution adopted in 1787 left the federal gov-ernment without any clear power or mechanism, other than through con-stitutional amendment, to institute a national conception of voting rights, to express a national vision of democracy. Although the Constitution was promulgated in the name of "We, the people of the United States," the in-dividual states retained the power to define just who "the people" were. Stated somewhat differently, citizenship in the new nation—controlled by the federal government—was divorced from the right to vote, a fact that was to have significant repercussions for almost two centuries.[80]

—◁▥◁∫▷▥▷—

The American Revolution, in sum, produced modest, but only modest, gains, in the formal democratization of politics. In more than a third of the states, colonial restrictions on suffrage (or close approximations thereof) re-mained in force; elsewhere the suffrage was broadened, in some places sig-nificantly, in others not. Overall, the proportion of adult men who could vote in 1787 was surely higher than it had been in 1767, yet the shift was hardly dramatic, in part because changes in the laws were partially offset by socioeconomic shifts that increased the number of propertyless men. By 1790, according to most estimates, roughly 60 to 70 percent of adult white men (and very few others) could vote.[81]

Yet the contribution of the revolution went beyond the legal changes etched in the state constitutions. The experience of the revolution—the po-litical and military trauma of breaking with a sovereign power, fighting a war, and creating a new state—served to crack the ideological framework that had upheld and justified a limited suffrage. The concept of virtual representation was undermined; the notion that a legitimate government required the "consent" of the governed became a staple of political thought; and a new, contagious language of rights and equality was widely heard. For many participants, values and principles at the heart of the revolution were difficult to reconcile with the practice of denying voting rights to men simply because they were poor or African American. At the same time, the experience of fighting a long and drawn-out war, with a popular rather than professional army, illuminated the importance of the "common people" to the fate of the new nation. By the end of the revolution, the policy of keeping those common people from the polls had become significantly harder to defend than it had been in 1770.[82]

TWO

Democracy Ascendant

The course of things in this country is for the extension, and not the restriction of popular rights.

—NATHAN SANFORD, NEW YORK
STATE CONSTITUTIONAL CONVENTION, 1821

*T*HINGS CHANGED RAPIDLY IN THE NEW NATION. The population of the United States was less than four million in 1790; by 1820 it was nearly ten million, and by 1850, more than twenty million. Cities grew, seaboard counties became more densely inhabited, and millions of settlers spilled into the western reaches of Massachusetts, New York, Pennsylvania, Virginia, and the Carolinas. Vast new territories were added by purchase or conquest, and wars were fought against Britain and Mexico. Commerce expanded, thousands of workers carved canals through the earth, steam-powered ships made their way up and down the Mississippi, and the South grew dependent on the cash crop of cotton. In the Northeast, particularly after the War of 1812, manufacturing industries, led by textiles, became increasingly prominent features of the economic and physical landscape.

This fast-moving assembly of changes created pressures for the states to significantly revise the blueprints for governance that they had drawn during the era of the revolution. To many citizens of early-nineteenth-century America, the first state constitutions, written during the tumult of the revolution, appeared either flawed or obsolete—or both. Between 1790 and the 1850s, every state (there were thirty-one by 1855) held at least one constitutional convention, and more than a few held several. The issues addressed by these conventions were many, but almost invariably a key concern was the distribution of political power among the increasingly diverse residents of each state. Indeed, disputes over political power, rights, and influence—including the breadth of the franchise and the apportionment of state legislative seats—were often what prompted states to call constitutional conventions in the first place.

That these conventions could gather at all, that the people of the states could select delegates to reshape their governing institutions, was itself a highly valued legacy of the political leadership of the revolutionary generation. In 1820, members of the Massachusetts constitutional convention paid tribute to that legacy by standing in silence and removing their hats as eighty-five-year-old John Adams, a delegate from Quincy, slowly entered the State House to take his seat. They even elected Adams—the principal author of the document they were about to revise—president of the convention, but he declined the honor. Nine years later in Virginia, in an eerily similar scene, seventy-eight-year-old James Madison, weakened by a recent illness, nominated his even more frail but slightly younger colleague, James Monroe, to be president of that state's convention. Monroe accepted the position, but had to be helped to the speaker's chair by Madison and the somewhat more spry seventy-four-year-old Chief Justice of the United States, John Marshall.[1]

Once these conventions settled down to work, however, the founding fathers played minor roles. While Adams sat in the State House, his fellow delegates opened the Pandora's box of suffrage reform that he had been so eloquently describing since 1776. Madison could do little to prevent Virginia's warring factions from producing a constitution so unsatisfactory that it would have to be replaced within twenty years. For better or worse, the torch had been passed to a new generation of political leaders equipped with different ideas and compelled to confront significantly altered historical conditions.

The Course of Things

> To attempt to govern men without seeking their consent is usurpation and tyranny, whether in Ohio or in Austria. . . . I was looking the other day . . . into Noah Webster's Dictionary for the meaning of democracy, and I found as I expected that he defines a democrat to be "one who favors universal suffrage."
>
> —NORTON TOWNSHEND,
> OHIO CONSTITUTIONAL CONVENTION, 1850

Nearly everywhere, the laws governing the right to vote in the United States were greatly elaborated and significantly transformed between 1790 and the 1850s. In addition to the fundamental changes wrought by constitutional conventions, state legislatures frequently supplemented (and sometimes altered) constitutional provisions with statute law; and courts intervened to interpret both the constitutions and the statutes.[2]

One cluster of legal changes involved the physical act of voting. At the nation's founding, the concrete procedures for voting varied widely from state to state and even from town to town. In some locales, particularly in the South, voting was still an oral and public act: men assembled before election judges, waited for their names to be called, and then announced which candidates they supported; in one variant of this process, common in Virginia, men inscribed their names in a poll book underneath the name of the candidate they preferred. Elsewhere, state constitutions or statutes required that voting be conducted by written ballot, to protect voters against intimidation. By the mid-nineteenth century, nearly all states insisted that votes be cast through written ballots, placed in a box or handed to an official. As the number of offices to be filled through elections grew, printed ballots gradually replaced handwritten ones, and political parties themselves began to prepare printed ballots, both to assist and monitor their voters. Abuses of this system were (sometimes) checked by the passage of laws requiring all ballots to be of uniform size and color or by insisting that ballots be placed in envelopes before being deposited. Not surprisingly, the laws governing such procedures were often the subject of partisan wrangling.[3]

Other legal developments were essentially administrative, reflecting a need to translate broad precepts into detailed rules governing the conduct of elections. Most states, for example, had to define what it meant to be a resident or inhabitant. They had to decide how and when lists of eligible voters would be assembled, what documents had to be presented as proof of citizenship, and how challenges to a voter's eligibility should be handled. Some state legislatures also had to specify the ways in which a personal property requirement could be met: Did a promissory note count as personal property? Similarly, race had to be given an operative definition. Just how white did you have to be in order to vote? One half, three quarters? An increasingly voluminous body of law offered answers to such questions.[4]

Far more significant were the substantive changes in voting requirements that marked the era, particularly those that lowered economic barriers to voting. Between the end of the American Revolution and the beginning of the Civil War, the economic and class lines that had so clearly circumscribed the electorate in the eighteenth century became blurred, even indistinct. The sources of this important shift were complex; but first, a brief chronicle of the events.

The property qualifications for suffrage that had begun to erode during the revolution were gradually dismantled after 1790. (See tables A.2 and A.3.) Delaware eliminated its property requirement in 1792, and Maryland followed a decade later. Massachusetts, despite the eloquent opposition of Adams and Daniel Webster, abolished its freehold or estate qualification in 1821; New York acted in the same year. Virginia was the last state to insist on a real property requirement in all elections, clinging to a modified (and extraordinarily complex) freehold law until 1850. And North Carolina finally eliminated its property qualification for senatorial elections in the mid-1850s.[5] Alongside these developments was another, of equal importance: none of the new states admitted to the union after 1790 adopted mandatory property requirements in their original constitutions.[6] By the end of the 1850s, only two property requirements remained in force anywhere in the United States, one applying to foreign-born residents of Rhode Island and the other to African Americans in New York.

Yet the demise of property requirements was not identical to the eradication of economic qualifications. Several states had taxpaying requirements even in 1790; a number of others instituted such requirements when they abolished property qualifications, and several of the new western states, including Ohio and Louisiana, also insisted that voters be taxpayers. Although taxpaying requirements were conceptually distinct from property qualifications (paying a tax demonstrated one's membership in a community but not one's Blackstonian independence), they nonetheless preserved the link between a person's financial status and his right to vote. Moreover, depending on the size and nature of the tax, these requirements could keep substantial numbers of voters from the polls; ironically, the barrier was lowest in those states that had a regressive (but usually insubstantial) poll tax on all household heads.

The democratic momentum that overwhelmed property requirements, however, also undermined taxpaying qualifications. Between 1830 and 1855, six states relinquished their insistence that voters pay taxes, leaving only six others with taxpaying clauses, several of which were quite minimal. By 1855, thus, there were few formal or explicit economic barriers to voting. (See tables A.2 and A.3.)

This broadening of state voting requirements was paralleled by changes both in federal policy and in municipal voting laws. In 1808, Congress modified the property qualifications in the Northwest Ordinance; three years later it acted more decisively, enfranchising all free white males who had paid taxes and resided in the territory.[7] Subsequent acts of territorial organization for other regions generally permitted either taxpayer or white male suffrage.[8] Similarly, congressional enabling acts (authorizing territories to become states and to hold constitutional conventions) became increasingly liberal in their suffrage provisions. Representatives to the constitutional conventions of Ohio (1802) and Indiana (1816) were chosen by adult male citizen taxpayers who met a one-year residence requirement; Illinois in 1818 did not even insist on a taxpaying qualification; and several decades later, all free white male inhabitants of Michigan (1835) and Wisconsin (1846) were able to participate in the founding elections.[9] The franchise in the District of Columbia followed a similar path: a taxpaying requirement, adopted in 1802 when the city was first incorporated, was dropped in 1855.[10]

The patterns of change in municipal voting laws were more variegated. Differences between state and city (or town) voting requirements persisted into the nineteenth century, sometimes as a legacy of colonial practices, but more often because individual locales wanted to control the entry portals into their political communities. In some cities and towns, municipal suffrage laws were more liberal than those in force for state elections, as had been true in the late eighteenth century. In Massachusetts, for example, male citizens who were "liable to be taxed" remained able to vote for town officers despite the property qualification that applied to state elections until 1820.[11] New Jersey's laws were similar, while numerous towns and counties in Mississippi, including Greenville, Holmesville, and Shieldsborough, simply ignored the state taxpaying requirement and granted the suffrage to all "citizens of the town."[12]

More often, the eligibility gap was reversed: in contrast to the eighteenth-century pattern, cities and towns that had their own franchise requirements during the first half of the nineteenth century tended to have relatively strict eligibility rules. This was true not only in cities such as New York, where property qualifications were a holdover from colonial charters, but also in new municipalities such as Chicago, which, in its first charter (1837), enfranchised taxpayers only—even though Illinois did not have a taxpaying requirement.[13] Comparably strict suffrage requirements could be found in all the towns of Maine and Tennessee, in Milwaukee, Louisville, St. Louis,

Memphis, Richmond, and Petersburg, Virginia; some municipalities (in Alabama and Indiana, among other places) even adopted freehold requirements.[14] The relative stringency of these municipal laws was generally justified by the increasingly widespread notion that the distinctive responsibility of local government was financial administration—from which it seemed to follow that only those who contributed to the municipality's finances ought to elect its officials. As novelist James Fenimore Cooper put it in 1838, "towns and villages regulating property chiefly, there is a peculiar propriety in excluding those from the suffrage who have no immediate local interests in them."[15]

Still, the most significant trend affecting municipal elections was the convergence of state and local eligibility requirements. Almost everywhere, between 1790 and the 1850s, state suffrage laws and municipal suffrage laws became identical. Behind this convergence were two important, and related, shifts in law. The first was the early nineteenth-century deterioration and then collapse of the notion that municipal charters were inviolable. The second was the ascent of a broad concept of state supremacy, the idea that municipalities legally ought to be regarded as administrative creatures of the state, rather than as separate sovereignties of any type. This second notion became known in the late nineteenth century as Dillon's rule (thanks to the exhaustive and pioneering scholarship of jurist John Dillon), but it was already well established in American law before the Civil War.[16] One of its implications was that state legislatures could set the franchise in municipal elections and compel cities and towns to adopt the same suffrage provisions as the state.[17]

Which is exactly what state legislatures did, sometimes for partisan reasons, sometimes for the sake of principle—and usually because they were asked to intervene by the disfranchised residents of cities. Pennsylvania's legislature altered the franchise in Philadelphia in 1796; New York State overrode New York City's charter in 1804; the state legislature in Missouri broadened the St. Louis franchise in the 1840s; and Virginia finally brought Richmond into line in the 1850s.[18] Although the idea persisted that municipalities had to perform special tasks that might warrant special suffrage requirements (Michigan adopted separate rules for school elections as early as 1837) there was a presumption, by the 1850s, that state suffrage regulations would and did apply to all elections.[19]

In some states, the right to vote also was broadened along axes that were not economic or financial. Almost everywhere states tinkered with their resi-

dency rules, which had become increasingly salient once property qualifications had been eliminated. In several states, including Delaware, Pennsylvania, South Carolina, Indiana, and Michigan, residency requirements were
shortened, opening the polls to large numbers of migrants who previously had
been barred.[20] In Ohio, widespread migration led to a shift in the entire con-
ceptual underpinning of residency rules, increasing the weight given to an individual's right to vote while limiting the power of communities to decide
who their official residents were.[21]

Far more dramatic, and perhaps surprising, was the extension of the franchise to aliens—although the history of alien (i.e., noncitizen) voting was
anything but unidirectional. At the end of the eighteenth century, the line
separating citizens from aliens was not clearly or consistently drawn, either
in law or in practice.[22] Some state constitutions specified that voters had to
be citizens, while others conferred the franchise on "inhabitants"; the federal government, hoping to encourage settlement, expressly permitted aliens
to vote in the Northwest Territories.[23] Thus in many locales, foreign-born
men who had not been naturalized by the federal government but who did
meet property, taxpaying, and residence requirements were able to participate in elections.[24]

The status of aliens was in flux, however. The federal government
changed the procedures and qualifications for naturalization every few
years, settling on a durable formula only in 1802, when Congress declared
that any foreign-born white male who met a five-year residency requirement could become a citizen three years after formally announcing his intention to do so.[25] In addition, the distinction between citizens and
inhabitants became the subject of litigation in Ohio, Illinois, and other jurisdictions.[26]

Between 1800 and 1830, moreover, numerous states opted to clarify ambiguous wording in their constitutions to protect themselves against a perceived or potential influx of (undesirable) foreign-born voters. While revising
their constitutions, New York, Massachusetts, Connecticut, Vermont, Maryland, and Virginia all replaced "inhabitant" with "citizen"; New Jersey performed the same alchemy by statute.[27] (New Jersey seemed uniquely cavalier
about altering suffrage qualifications by statute rather than constitutional
amendment.) Not surprisingly, the western states followed suit: almost all of
the new states joining the union between 1800 and 1840 conferred the right
to vote exclusively on citizens.[28] (The one exception was Illinois, which permitted aliens to vote for several decades after the state was organized in

1818.) By the Jacksonian era, aliens were barred from the polls nearly everywhere. (See table A.4.)

Then the pendulum swung back, particularly in the Midwest. Although
Illinois by a narrow vote decided to limit the franchise to citizens in 1848,
other states in the upper Midwest moved in the opposite direction. Wisconsin was the pioneer, adopting in 1848 what became known as "alien intent" or
"declarant non-citizen" suffrage: building on the two-step structure of the
naturalization laws, the franchise was extended to aliens who had lived in the
United States for two years and who had filed "first papers" declaring their intention to become citizens.[29] Not coincidentally, the population of Wisconsin in 1850 was 35 percent foreign born, the highest of any state.[30] Michigan
and Indiana soon passed similar laws, as did the federal government for the
territories of Oregon and Minnesota.[31] In the late 1850s, Kansas, Minnesota,
and Oregon all adopted alien suffrage, and after the Civil War a dozen more
states in the South and the West did likewise (again joined by various territories administered by the federal government). Outside of the Northeast, declarant, noncitizen suffrage therefore became commonplace, permitting
hundreds of thousands of previously excluded voters to go to the polls.[32] Although the constitutionality of alien suffrage was heatedly debated in the
mid-nineteenth century (opponents often claimed that states were usurping
federal power by conferring the franchise on those who were not naturalized),
state courts consistently upheld such provisions.[33] In 1840, for example, the
Illinois Supreme Court affirmed that the state's constitution granted "the
right of suffrage to those who, having by habitation and residence, identified
their interests and feelings with the citizenry . . . although they may be neither native nor adopted citizens."[34]

Sources of Expansion

> It ought to be remembered, Sir, that manufacturers are rapidly
> increasing; and their employers may bring them in regiments to
> the polls.
>
> Sir, if they come in regiments to the polls to vote; they go in
> regiments to fight the enemies of their beloved country.
>
> —LEGISLATIVE DEBATE, CONNECTICUT, 1818

Why was the franchise broadened—and broadened so dramatically? Why
were property requirements jettisoned almost everywhere and taxpaying

requirements abandoned in most states? Why were men who were not even citizens permitted to vote? Why, in sum, was the suffrage enlarged nearly everywhere in the United States, North and South, along the coast and inland?

Not surprisingly, no single factor can explain this upsurge of democracy—not even a factor as capacious as Frederick Jackson Turner's frontier. Although insightful, Turner's famous vision of the frontier as a democratizing force cannot account for the relatively early democratization of much of the eastern seaboard.[35] The much-celebrated broadening of the suffrage during the first half of the nineteenth century indeed was spawned not by one change but several, by the convergence of different factors, present in varying combinations in individual states. Among them were three important socioeconomic and institutional developments: widespread and significant changes in the social structure and social composition of the nation's population; the appearance or expansion of conditions under which the material interests of the enfranchised could be served by broadening the franchise; and the formation of broadly based political parties that competed systematically for votes.

Most fundamentally, perhaps, all of the states that had property requirements in 1790 witnessed an increase in the number and proportion of adult males who were unable to meet those requirements. Up and down the eastern seaboard, from Boston to New York to Baltimore to Richmond to Wilmington, North Carolina, the urban population grew rapidly, swelling the ranks of those who owned no real property and sometimes no property at all. Artisans, "mechanics," laborers, even small merchants and shopkeepers—an increasingly large and prominent slice of the population of nearly all cities and large towns was disqualified for economic reasons.[36] In some states, there was also an increase in the proportion of *farmers* who could not meet property requirements—because they were tenants, their holdings were too small, or because of shifts in leaseholding patterns. In both northern Louisiana and western North Carolina, for example, the rapid growth of newly settled counties and parishes, dominated by small farms on just-cleared land, spelled a sharp increase in the population of ineligibles.[37] A similar pattern resulted from the shift, in Virginia, from leases for life (which were counted as freeholds) to shorter-term leases (which did not).[38] In the North, farm tenancy was on the rise, and in some locales, including upstate New York, farmers who purchased land through installment mortgages did not become eligible to vote until they had made their last payment and secured legal title to their lands.[39] Meanwhile, in the West, the slow, cumbersome, and erratic process of gaining title to lands was preventing many settlers from voting.[40] Swelling the ranks of the voteless in the North were hundreds of thousands of immigrants excluded by increasingly widespread citizenship requirements.

These changes in the social structure created significant and growing clusters of men who were full participants in economic and social life but who lacked political rights. Not surprisingly, at times these ineligible citizens themselves exerted significant pressure to enlarge the franchise, particularly when they were concentrated in cities, neighborhoods, or distinct rural districts. Between 1790 and 1835, from the Southeast to Michigan, voteless men petitioned legislatures and constitutional conventions to broaden suffrage requirements. Maryland's early decision to drop property qualifications was hastened by years of agitation by the propertyless residents (including many "mechanics") of politically dominant Baltimore; in the 1840s, men who could not meet North Carolina's senatorial freehold requirement held mass meetings to demand the right to vote in all elections, while German and Irish aliens petitioned for their own enfranchisement in Milwaukee.[41] In Virginia, the War of 1812—which, according to historian J. R. Pole, "gave the greatest single stimulus to the movement for suffrage extension"—created conditions that accelerated such protests and gave them a patriotic cast. When gathered together to be mustered into the militia, men signed petitions affirming and protesting their disfranchisement. In a Shenandoah muster of 1,000 men, 700 claimed they could not vote; in Loudoun, the figure was 1,000 out of 1,200.[42]

Perhaps the most eloquent expression of protest emanating from the voteless themselves was the "Memorial of the Non-Freeholders of the City of Richmond," presented on October 13, 1829, to the Virginia Constitutional Convention. Chief Justice John Marshall, who was far from sympathetic with the nonfreeholders, delivered the memorial to the convention, without comment. More angry than pleading in tone, the memorial charged that Virginia's freehold requirement was an unjust usurpation of power that violated the commonwealth's celebrated Declaration of Rights.

> [It] creates an odious distinction between members of the same community; robs of all share, in the enactment of the laws, a large portion of the citizens, bound by them, and whose blood and treasure are pledged to maintain them, and vests in a favoured class, not in consideration of their public services, but of their private possessions, the highest of all privileges.

The nonfreeholders, "comprising a very large part, probably a majority of male citizens of mature age," ridiculed the notion that the possession of land established that a man was "wiser or better." "Virtue" and "intelligence" were "not among the products of the soil." The memorial also pointed out that landless men were not considered too "ignorant" or "depraved" to serve in the militia.

> In the hour of danger, they have drawn no invidious distinctions between the sons of Virginia. The muster rolls have undergone no scrutiny, no comparison with the land books, with a view to expunge those who have been struck from the ranks of freemen. If the landless citizens have been ignominiously driven from the polls, in time of peace, they have at least been generously summoned, in war, to the battle-field.

The nonfreeholders conceded that the right of suffrage was a "social right" rather than a "natural right," and that "it must of necessity be regulated by society. For obvious reasons, by almost universal consent, women and children, aliens and slaves, are excluded." Yet those exclusions were "no argument for excluding others" along indefensible economic lines. "We have been taught by our fathers, that all power is vested in, and derived from, the people, not the freeholders," the memorial claimed, echoing the Declaration of Rights. "They alone deserve to be called free, or have a guarantee for their rights, who participate in the formation of their political institutions."[43]

Powerful as their words may have been, the nonfreeholders of Richmond had little success: the Virginia convention of 1829–30, despite the presence of an extraordinary group of political notables, produced a muddled and confusing suffrage law that effectively retained a freehold requirement. "No one can understand it," concluded one contemporary.[44] (For the incomprehensible text, see table A.2.) This disappointing yet illustrative outcome reflected a stalemate in the deeply contentious political life of the commonwealth. For nearly three decades, residents of the rapidly growing western counties had been clamoring for a new constitution: foremost among the changes they (and their scattered eastern allies) sought were the abolition of the freehold requirement for voting and a redistribution of seats in the lower house of the legislature, based on each county's white population alone. Virginia's most revered founding father, Thomas Jefferson, had joined this cry for reform. In 1816, he wrote a letter to one of the leaders of the reform movement endorsing suffrage for all free white males. In 1824, shortly before his death, he criticized the state's government as violating "the principle of equal political rights."[45]

Yet the eastern slaveowners who dominated the commonwealth's government had fiercely resisted such changes; the "odious landed aristocracy" (as they were called by reformers) was deeply reluctant to even hold a constitutional convention, fearing both the immediate loss of political power and setting in motion a democratizing dynamic that might eventually undermine slavery itself. When a convention finally was forced on them by a popular referendum, Virginia's conservatives fought tooth and nail against every major proposal for change. Thanks to a delegate selection system that favored the eastern counties, they prevailed.[46]

Virginia's convention of 1829–30 was a vivid demonstration of the ways in which the issue of suffrage was interlaced with other questions of political power and representation. The convention also demonstrated the difficulties faced by men who lacked the franchise as they sought political power. The nonfreeholders of Richmond, as well as their numerous nonvoting allies in the west, could not generate constitutional reform simply by signing petitions and holding meetings. As was true throughout the nation, the disfranchised were unable to precipitate change by themselves. When the right to vote was enlarged, it happened because some men who were already enfranchised actively supported the cause of suffrage expansion.

Why did voting members of the community sometimes elect to share their political power with others? In numerous cases, it was because they saw themselves as having a direct interest in enlarging the electorate. One such interest was military preparedness and the defense of the republic. In the wake of the Revolutionary War and again after the War of 1812, many middle-class citizens concluded that extending the franchise to the "lower orders" would enhance their own security and help to preserve their way of life, by assuring that such men would continue to serve in the army and the militias. The nation's experience during the War of 1812 underscored this concern: the federal government had great difficulty recruiting and retaining soldiers and eventually had to call on militia forces to bolster the army.[47]

In nearly every subsequent debate over the suffrage, from New York to Illinois to Massachusetts to Alabama, the issue of soldiers was invoked— not simply as a question of fairness (how unjust to withhold the ballot from "the poor and hardy soldier who spills his blood in defence of his country") but also as a matter of security.[48] In Connecticut, worried leaders expressed the view that the state's militias had not performed well during the war because the men who served were unenthusiastic about protecting a government they played no role in choosing; in 1820, Massachusetts convention delegate Reverend Joseph Richardson feared that the "ardor" of the disfranchised "would be chilled . . . when called upon to defend their country." Between 1817 and 1820, three states—Connecticut, New York, and Mississippi—exempted militia members from property or taxpaying requirements. Thirty years later, North Carolina gubernatorial candidate David S. Reid declared that he "would like to see the brave men who periled their lives in the War against Mexico, received at the ballot-box upon terms of equality."[49]

In the South, the issue had an added twist: enfranchising all white Southerners was a means of making sure that poor whites would serve in militia patrols guarding against slave rebellions. However much diehard reactionaries such as John Randolph of Virginia might have feared that broader suffrage would unravel the fabric of slave society, there were other political leaders who believed that it would contribute to white solidarity. A delegate to Virginia's convention pointedly noted that "all slave-holding states are fast approaching a crisis truly alarming, a time when freemen will be needed—when every man must be at his post." Was it not then "wise . . . to call together at least every free white human being and unite them in the same common interest and Government?"[50]

Economic self-interest also played a role in the expansion of the franchise, particularly in the Midwest. As territories began to organize themselves into states, inhabitants of sparsely populated regions embraced white manhood suffrage, in part because they believed that a broad franchise would encourage settlement and in so doing raise land values, stimulate economic development, and generate tax revenues. After 1840, similar concerns helped to propel the alien suffrage laws, as new states of the old Northwest competed with one another for settlers. Granting full political rights to immigrants appeared to be economically advantageous as well as democratic; that this was so was testimony to the desirability—or at least perceived desirability—of the franchise.

Nowhere was this case made more strenuously (though unsuccessfully) than in Illinois, where the 1847 constitutional convention unfolded against the backdrop of a mountain of public debt. "Is it our policy, as a state burdened with debt and sparsely settled, to restrict the right of suffrage, and thus prevent immigration to our soil?" queried one convention delegate. "Should we not . . . hold out to the world the greatest inducement for men to come amongst us, to till our prairies, to work in our mines, and to develop the vast and inexhaustible resources of our state?" demanded a delegate from Joe Davies County. "We cannot obtain this class of population without holding out to them inducements equal to those of other states; and as we are burthened with a debt, we should have those inducements greater than elsewhere."[51]

Perhaps the most common way in which the fortunes of the already enfranchised were concretely linked to the cause of suffrage reform was through political parties and electoral competition. Early in the nineteenth century, the Federalist and Republican parties competed actively for votes in many states; in others (such as New York in the 1820s), contests between organized political factions were commonplace. By the 1830s, competition between Whigs and Democrats dominated political life, reflecting the creation of a strong and vibrant national party system: not only were elections systematically contested, but both party loyalty and party identification became prominent elements of public life. In this competitive political culture, the issue of suffrage reform inescapably attached itself to partisan rivalries.

To some degree, particularly during the first quarter of the nineteenth century, the involvement of political parties in debates over suffrage was a straightforward reflection of ideological differences, an outgrowth of beliefs and values. The Federalists, rooted among the northeastern elites and confident in their own leadership, tended to oppose any broadening of the franchise; the more egalitarian Jeffersonian Republicans viewed expansion more favorably. Decades later, the ideological gap between the Whig and Democratic parties was even more pronounced. The Democrats, heirs to the Jeffersonians, embraced an individualist, competitive vision of society, in which the pursuit of self-interest was altogether legitimate and in which all (white) citizens were entitled to political rights—in part to defend themselves against the encroachments of government. The Whigs, on the other hand, clung to a more organic and hierarchical social vision, believing both in a more active state and that it was best for public affairs to be conducted by society's "natural" leaders. They consequently were inclined to resist efforts to enlarge the polity.[52]

Yet the significance of political parties in the evolution of suffrage went beyond matters of ideology: the elementary dynamics of electoral competition created a stimulus for reform. Put simply, in a competitive electoral environment, parties were always alert to the potential advantage (or disadvantage) of enfranchising new voters and potential supporters. The outcomes of electoral campaigns could easily depend on the size and shape of the electorate; it was natural therefore for parties, at least in some circumstances, to try to broaden the franchise because they wanted to win elections, whatever their views about democratization.

These dynamics probably did not play a significant role in the evolution of suffrage between 1790 and the mid-1820s. Although parties and factions did exist, the political arena was not acutely competitive, particularly once the Federalists started disintegrating in the face of the War of 1812. More important, popular participation in electoral politics was limited: turnout levels were low and many offices were filled either by appointment or by legislative, rather than popular, vote. In some states, there was not even any popular balloting for the presidency. The institutions of politics changed dramatically by the late 1820s and the 1830s, however, with the spread of popular elections, the formation of the Democratic Party as the nation's (and the western world's) first mass-based political organization, and the subsequent emergence of the second party system. Electoral politics became a form of public theater, parties themselves began to print written ballots (deemed acceptable by the courts), the mobilization of voters became a critical activity for both the Democrats and the Whigs, and electoral turnout rose dramatically, from 27 percent in 1824 to 56 percent in 1828 to 78 percent in 1840. It was in this more modern political universe that the partisan pursuit of new voters became clearly visible. The Democratic embrace of alien suffrage, for example, was unmistakably motivated in part by the party's desire to enroll and win the support of immigrant voters.[53]

The nature of partisan competition, moreover, was such that if any party or faction—out of conviction or political self-interest—actively promoted a broader franchise, its adversaries experienced pressure to capitulate.[54] This dynamic was manifested most distinctly in circumstances where different suffrage restrictions applied to different offices. In both New York and North Carolina, for example, voters had to meet a stiff property requirement to participate in senatorial elections, while many more people were eligible to vote for state representatives. As a result, once any political organization began to support abolition of the senatorial property qualification, it became politically risky for others to endorse the status quo—because their parties (or factions, in the case of New York) could be punished at the polls by men who were already voting in some elections.[55] A similar scenario could unfold if there were a sizable gap between municipal and state voting regulations, as occurred in St. Louis in the 1850s.[56]

Such was the scenario played out dramatically in North Carolina in the late 1840s and early 1850s. State politics had been dominated by the Whigs until David S. Reid, a long-shot Democratic candidate for governor, embraced the cause of suffrage reform, somewhat to the surprise of his fellow Democrats. In the election of 1848, Reid did much better than expected (there was no property requirement in gubernatorial elections) and aided by a wave of support from the landless was elected governor in 1850, promising a constitutional amendment to eliminate the property qualification for senatorial voting. Once elected (and reelected), Reid pursued that goal, declaring that the "elective franchise is the dearest right of an American citizen" and complaining that 50,000 free white men were disfranchised by the state's constitution. Sobered by political reality, the Whigs abandoned their opposition to suffrage reform: by the early 1850s, they saw the wisdom of tacitly approving a measure that they had denounced in 1848 as "a system of communism unjust and Jacobinical."[57]

A more common scenario unfolded when two parties were fairly evenly matched, and a broadening of the franchise appeared likely to be of particular benefit to one. In Connecticut, for example, the Republicans stood to gain far more than the Federalists from the abolition of property requirements; in Pennsylvania in 1837, the Democrats expected to benefit from a halving of the residency requirement; and throughout the Midwest, the Democratic Party seemed likely to attract far more alien voters than the Whigs.[58] In each of these instances, and many others, support for democratization stemmed in part from partisan self-interest.[59] Once suffrage reform appeared possible, however, what might be called an endgame dynamic often came into play: the parties that formerly resisted reform would drop their opposition, regardless of their convictions, because they did not want to risk antagonizing a new bloc of voters. In the 1840s and 1850s, for example, in both Ohio and New Jersey, the Whigs ended up capitulating to Democratic demands because they feared the political damage that might result from appearing hostile to men who might well gain the franchise anyway.[60]

These partisan dynamics also point to the ways in which suffrage sometimes was expanded as a political compromise or tactical concession. The Massachusetts convention of 1820–21, for example, was dominated by a well-organized faction of conservatives who generally opposed democratization of the state government: as was true in New York (and later in Virginia), the constitutional convention had been forced on them. The Bay

State's conservatives, however, were willing to tolerate expansion of the franchise as long as seats in the powerful state senate continued to be allocated on the basis of property rather than population.[61] Similarly, in North Carolina, the final acquiescence of the most conservative Whigs to "free suffrage" for senatorial elections was prompted by their desire to maintain a favorable legislative apportionment system and to fend off a constitutional convention that might adopt further reforms.[62] Partisan compromises and tactical maneuvering also marked the New York convention of 1821 and Virginia's final "reform" convention of 1850.[63] Conceding suffrage reform could be a means of taking the steam out of democratic movements while retaining or reconstructing institutional structures that would keep dominant factions and elites in power.

Ideas and Arguments

Alongside the shifts in the social structure and in political institutions—and surely linked to them—was another factor that played a critical role in the expansion of suffrage: a change in prevailing political ideas and values. Stated simply, more and more Americans came to believe that the people (or at least the male people—"every full-grown featherless biped who wears a hat instead of a bonnet") were and ought to be sovereign and that the sovereign "people" included many individuals who did not own property. Restrictions on the franchise that appeared normal or conventional in 1780 came to look archaic in subsequent decades. Franklin's oft-cited view that the right to vote should belong to the man and not the ass began to look commonsensical rather than radical. The shift in political temper was evident in the decisions of states admitted to the union after 1800 not to impose any pecuniary qualifications on suffrage. It also surfaced throughout the nation in newspapers, in the occasional treatise, in public debate: at William and Mary College, in both 1808 and 1812, the graduating students who gave commencement addresses seized the occasion to proclaim their support for universal suffrage. "The mass of the people," declared one newspaper in 1840, "are honest and capable of self-government." Not everyone embraced such ideas, but the tide of political thought was flowing in the direction of democracy.[64]

This ideological tilt, grounded in social changes that had swept the nation, was readily apparent at numerous constitutional conventions that debated and acted on proposals to enlarge the franchise. These debates generally were heated, and many of the views expressed echoed those heard at the end of the eighteenth century. But the ideological spectrum had shifted, its centerpoint sliding to the left—which was reflected not only in the substance but in the emphases, tones, and language of the debates.

Delegates who advocated the elimination of property requirements (the central obstacle to a broader suffrage) from the outset were more aggressive and more confident in their arguments than their predecessors during the revolutionary period. These delegates paid their rhetorical respects to the founding fathers, but pointed out that the "framers" had unfortunately "retained a small relic of ancient prejudices" that it had come time to be "rid of." As retired Senator Nathan Sanford of New York noted in 1821, the ideas that had shaped the first constitutions came from "British precedents," from the British notion of "three estates" that ought to be represented in Parliament. "But here there is but one estate—the people." David Buel, a young lawyer from Rensselaer County, pointed out that social conditions had changed: "without the least derogation from the wisdom . . . of the framers," it had to be understood that their embrace of property qualifications came in response to "circumstances which then influenced them, but which no longer ought to have weight."[65]

Reform delegates frontally attacked the notion that those who owned property were somehow better qualified to vote than those who did not. "Regard for country," argued J. T. Austin of Boston in 1820, "did not depend upon property, but upon institutions, laws, habits, and associations." William Griffith of New Jersey, writing under the name of Eumenes, declared that it was simply an irrational prejudice, unsupported by any evidence, to claim that the ownership of "fifty pounds clear estate" made someone "more a man or citizen," or "wiser than his neighbor who has but ten pounds," or "more honest." The eloquent nonfreeholders of Richmond went a step further in 1829: "to ascribe to a landed possession, moral or intellectual endowments, would truly be regarded as ludicrous, were it not for the gravity with which the proposition is maintained, and still more for the grave consequences that flow from it." Linked to such views was a complete and sometimes contemptuous dismissal of the Blackstonian notion that only real property ownership gave a man sufficient independence to be a trustworthy voter. One Virginia delegate, after a detailed, logical dissection of the claim that broadening the franchise would permit the rich to manipulate the poor, concluded that the "freehold test" had no merit "unless there be something in the ownership of land, that by enchantment or magic converts frail erring man, into an infallible and impeccable being."[66]

Some advocates of reform insisted, as their predecessors had in the late eighteenth century, that voting was a natural or universal right. New Yorker James Cheetham, writing in 1800, invoked the Declaration of Independence ("all men are created equal") to support the notion that "the right of suffrage cannot belong to one man without belonging to another; it cannot belong to a part without belonging to the whole."[67] In the late 1840s and 1850s, the most radical advocates of democracy even mustered natural rights arguments to support the enfranchisement of African Americans, women, aliens, and paupers. On the whole, however, natural rights or universal rights arguments were notably scarce in convention debates, at least in part because reformers were well aware that such arguments would immediately provoke the conservative Pandora's box counterattack. Josiah Quincy, a staunch defender of property requirements, leapt on a Massachusetts reformer's claim that "every man whose life and liberty is made liable to the laws, ought therefore to have a voice, in the choice of his legislators." Is not this argument, argued Quincy, "equally applicable to women and to minors? . . . The denial of this right to them shows that the principle is not just."[68]

To avoid such counterattacks, many who favored a broader suffrage retreated to the argument that voting was a qualified "right" that only some possessed. *Niles' Register*, the voice of manufacturing interests in Connecticut, maintained that voting was "the natural right of every citizen, who is bound by the law to render personal services to the state, or aid its revenue by money." Similarly, a delegate to the Ohio convention in the early 1850s insisted that voting was "a matter of right" for "a man who is the subject of government, and shares in its burthens." In 1846, in New York, a delegate urged that blacks be granted "the common rights of freemen."[69]

As such language suggests, most proponents of an expanded suffrage, while rejecting the conservative view that the franchise was a privilege that the state could limit however it wished, took the position that voting was a right, but a right that had to be earned: by paying taxes, serving in the militia, or even laboring on the public roads. As Nathan Sanford put it, "those who bear the burthens of the state should choose those that rule it."[70] That simple proposition meshed well with the rhetoric of the revolution, and the principle lent force to demands that all taxpayers vote and that it was an injustice to withhold the franchise from those who fought for the nation and served in its militias. (The military service argument also was mobilized to support the enfranchisement of aliens and African Americans.)[71] There was, to be sure, one glaring inconsistency in the proposed application of this principle: the exclusion of women who paid taxes and shared the burdens of the state; but this was an inconsistency that most found easy to overlook.

The centrality of the notion of an earned right made clear that the goal of most suffrage reformers was not a universal right to vote but rather the enfranchisement of what New Yorker Samuel Young described as "the intermediate class." Future president Martin Van Buren was more precise, as he maneuvered the New York convention toward rejection of both the status quo and demands, from a radical faction, for universal suffrage. Van Buren's stated goal was "clothing with the right of suffrage" a "class of men, composed of mechanics, professional men, and small landholders" that constituted the "bone, pith, and muscle of the population of the state." Such men, of course, comprised a core constituency of the Democratic Party that Van Buren was so instrumental in building.[72]

Underlying these arguments for expanding suffrage to include "mechanics, professional men . . . small landholders" and others like them was a curiously static vision of the future. Although conservatives (as will be discussed) repeatedly raised the specter of the growth of manufacturing and the appearance of a large, urban proletariat, reformers—in the Northeast between 1800 and 1830 and substantially later in the Midwest—dismissed that specter as a scare tactic. David Buel, for example, acknowledged that if he believed that manufacturing would become predominant and that enormous disparities in wealth loomed in the nation's future, then he would "hesitate in extending the right of suffrage"; but, to the contrary, he was convinced that "the farmers in this country will always out number all other portions of our population." Moreover, the "supposition that, at some future day, when the poor shall become numerous . . . they may rise, in the majesty of their strength, and usurp the property of the landholders, is so unlikely to be realized that we may dismiss all fear arising from that source." His views were seconded by convention delegates throughout the nation, including the redoubtable Daniel Webster.[73]

The movement for franchise expansion thus was grounded in the conviction that the relatively agrarian and egalitarian United States of the early nineteenth century would permanently endure. Only rarely did a reformer, such as J. T. Austin of Boston, argue that suffrage should be broadened even if we did become "a great manufacturing people." "God forbid," declared Austin, but if it should happen, he shrewdly observed that it would be "better to let . . . the laborers in manufactories" vote. "By refusing this right to them, you array them against the laws; but give them the rights of citizens . . . and you disarm them."[74]

The argument against property requirements gained momentum and became easier to make with each passing decade, in part because reformers
could cite a growing number of states where no property qualifications were
in force and no calamities had ensued. David Buel made this point as early
as 1820. A decade later, a delegate to the Virginia convention claimed that
there were no property qualifications in "twenty-two out of twenty-four sister republics," none of which had ended up in "tumults, confusion, civil dis-
cord, and finally despotism."[75] In the South, the momentum for reform was
reinforced by intensifying anxiety about slave revolts and the increasing fusion of prosuffrage arguments with the defense of slavery. As Senator
Charles Morgan put it at the Virginia convention of 1829–30, "we ought to
spread wide the foundation of our government, that all white men have a
direct interest in its protection."[76]

In response to this array of arguments, conservative defenders of property
qualifications, who were present and vocal at all the conventions, offered the
same ideas put forward in the eighteenth century but with different emphases and in different proportions. Conservatives insisted that voting was
not a matter of right but "wholly a question of expediency," and as noted
earlier, they were quick to point out the inconsistencies in any rights arguments put forward by reformers. They also maintained, in the words of
Samuel Jones, author of a lengthy treatise published in 1842, that "on the
question, who shall be admitted to the exercise of the right of suffrage, the
public safety ought to govern." The most sharp-edged conservatives, such as
Warren Dutton of Massachusetts, claimed that "in this country, where the
means of subsistence were so abundant and the demand for labor great," any
man who failed to acquire property was "indolent or vicious."[77]

Notably, however, the conservatives rarely reiterated the classical Blackstonian argument that property ownership alone could provide the "independence" required of voters. Although the idea did occasionally surface,
and Josiah Quincy attempted a brief—and quickly ridiculed—evocation of
Blackstone by arguing that property qualifications actually aided the poor
rather than the rich, the eighteenth-century linkage of independence to
property or freehold ownership was largely absent from public debate. If the
fallible and sometimes weary eyes of one reader of convention transcripts
can be trusted, the once-totemic phrase that the franchise should not be
granted to "such persons as are in so mean a situation that they have no will
of their own" was never uttered in the constitutional conventions. This pow-

erful image of the late eighteenth century simply did not mesh with the social realities or values of the 1820s and 1830s.[78]

Indeed, as Gordon Wood has pointed out, nineteenth-century conservatives—faced with the charge of being aristocrats at heart—ceased to claim that the ownership of landed property was intrinsically linked to a man's character, that real property was a source of gentility, independence, and impartiality. Instead, they retreated to a defense of agriculture as a preeminent economic interest and to a celebration of the virtues of those who cultivated the soil. Among farmers, declared New York Federalist (and later Whig) James Kent, "we always expect to find moderation, frugality, order, honesty, and a due sense of independence, liberty, and justice. . . . Their habits, sympathies, and employments necessarily inspire them with a correct spirit of freedom and justice." In Virginia, it was argued that freeholders deserved special political rights because they paid most of the state's taxes and provided the funds to pay for wars. Such arguments, of course, were less redolent of aristocracy, but they undercut the notion that the *owners* of land possessed special qualities that entitled them to wield a disproportionate amount of political power.[79]

In fact, the conservative case for the maintenance of property requirements, particularly in the Northeast, rested less on the alleged virtues of freeholders than on the fear that the growth of industry would create a large, propertyless, and dangerous urban proletariat. This was a partial reincarnation of the Blackstonian argument, complete with its internal contradictions, yet in a more anxious, fearful, and industrial form. "Manufacturers are rapidly increasing; and their employers may bring them in regiments to the polls," declared a Connecticut legislator. In Massachusetts, Josiah Quincy developed the argument in detail:

> Everything indicates that the destinies of the country will eventuate in the establishment of a great manufacturing interest in the Commonwealth. There is nothing in the condition of our country to prevent manufacturers from being absolutely dependent upon their employers, here as they are everywhere else. The whole body of every manufacturing establishment, therefore, are dead votes, counted by the head, by their employer. Let the gentlemen from the country consider, how it may affect their rights, liberties, and properties, if in every county of the Commonwealth there should arise, as in time there probably will, one, two, or three manufacturing establish-

ments, each sending as the case may be, from one to eight hundred votes to
the polls depending on the will of one employer, one great capitalist. In such
a case would they deem such a provision as this of no consequence? At present it is of little importance. Prospectively of very great.[80]

Quincy was, in effect, maintaining that industrial workers would "have no
will of their own." At the same time, the equally conservative Chancellor
Kent voiced the opposite—and more common—fear: that those who
worked in manufacturing would have too much will of their own and would
threaten the interests of property. A freehold requirement for the New York
Senate, Kent argued, was necessary to protect

> against the caprice of the motley assemblage of paupers, emigrants, journeymen manufacturers, and those undefinable classes of inhabitants which a
> state and city like ours is calculated to invite. This is not a fancied alarm. Universal suffrage jeopardizes property, and puts it into the power of the poor
> and the profligate to control the affluent.

Kent went on to maintain that

> there is a constant tendency in human society, and the history of every age
> proves it; there is a tendency in the poor to covet and to share the plunder of
> the rich; in the debtor to relax or avoid the obligation of contracts; in the majority to tyrannize over the minority, and trample down their rights; in the indolent and the profligate to cast the whole burthens of society upon the
> industrious and the virtuous.

Although New York was still dominated by cultivators of the soil, it was, according to Kent, well on the road toward inequalities of a type that would
spawn bitter class conflict.

> The disproportion between the men of property and of no property is daily
> increasing; and it will be fallacious to expect that our people will continue the
> same small farmers as our ancestors were. . . . As our wealth increases, so also
> will our poor. . . . What has been the progress of the city of New York? In
> 1773, it contained only 21,000 inhabitants; in 1821, 123,000 souls. It is evidently destined to become the London of America. . . . And can gentlemen
> seriously and honestly say, that no danger is to be apprehended from those

combustible materials which such a city must ever enclose? . . . The poor man's interest is always in opposition to his duty; and it is too much to expect of human nature, that interest will not be consulted.[81]

Clearly, Kent and his many allies were not simply worried that the propertyless lacked good and independent judgment; they were overtly hostile to manufacturing workers and the urban poor. Not only would the "motley assemblage" be covetous and threatening, it also would be, in the words of another New York delegate, a repository of "ignorance, vice, and corruption." This imagined future compelled Kent to refuse to "bow before the right of universal suffrage. This democratic principle cannot be contemplated without terror."[82]

Similar visions of a dangerous and degraded urban population were evoked, in the Midwest, by opponents of alien suffrage. One Illinois delegate in 1847 declared that "the majority of foreigners who came here" were "ignorant, and . . . none but such, and criminals and paupers, came here at all." Another, claiming that Massachusetts was already spending huge sums to support "her foreign pauper population," feared that the urban masses of the Northeast would soon come to Illinois "and cast their votes in competition with our own citizens, even while sucking from us the life blood of our bosoms." Everywhere conservatives voiced the apprehension that eliminating property qualifications would inescapably send the nation careening down the slippery slope that led to universal suffrage. "Once break loose from the freehold qualification," wrote a Virginian in 1825, "and it will soon be found that every argument against that qualification goes the whole length of justifying and requiring universal suffrage, and in a few years we shall have this worst of evils entailed upon us." Moreover, as Kent ominously warned, "universal suffrage, once granted, is granted forever, and never can be recalled. . . . However mischievous the precedent may be in its consequences, or however fatal in its effects, universal suffrage never can be recalled or checked, but by the strength of the bayonet."[83]

Ironically, perhaps, the conservatives' portrait of the nation's future proved far more accurate than the benign, static vision offered by Republican and Democratic reformers. Yet the prospect of a society dominated by manufacturing and cities teeming with hundreds of thousands of poor, rootless workers did not seem credible to most Americans in 1820 or even 1840. In the absence of that specter, the conservative case for preserving or (as in Pennsylvania in the 1830s) reinstituting property qualifications was unpersuasive as well as incongruent with widely accepted political values. Granting exclusive political rights to landowners and others who possessed considerable property did in fact smack of aristocracy and indeed was inconsistent with the quasi-egalitarian rhetoric of the revolution and the early republic.

In contrast, an aura of commonsensical fairness enveloped the reformers' basic notion that anyone who shared the burdens imposed by government should have a voice in choosing that government. In the rapidly growing, energetic, and increasingly urban society of Jacksonian America, large numbers of propertyless men were known by their neighbors, relatives, and friends to be altogether capable and worthy of exercising the franchise. "If a man can *think* without property, he can *vote* without property," observed one delegate to the Louisiana convention of 1845.[84] However blinkered their vision of the future, advocates of a broader suffrage were presenting arguments that were more consonant with the predispositions and experience of a majority population. Samuel Jones seriously misgauged the temper of the times when he wrote in 1842 that the "principle of natural law and of our own government, that all men are created equal" ought to have no bearing on the breadth of the suffrage and that "universal suffrage . . . would be a gross violation of it." To most Americans, that much-quoted principle could not easily be separated from the right to vote, and the principle created a strong, if not always articulated, presumption in favor of granting the franchise to adult, white men.[85]

Such a presumption contributed not only to the eradication of property qualifications but also to the stunningly swift abolition of taxpaying requirements in all but a handful of states. By 1855, half of the states that ever had taxpaying requirements—including those that had substituted them for property ownership—had gotten rid of them. To be sure, Massachusetts and Pennsylvania, as well as a handful of other states, voted to retain tax provisions, on the grounds that *only* those who shared the burdens of the state ought to have a voice in governance. Elsewhere, however, this last major, explicit link between a person's financial circumstances and the suffrage—a link so favored by many democratic reformers of the 1810s and 1820s—was dissolved with little fanfare. By the beginning of the Civil War, tax provisions had been eliminated even in most municipal elections.[86]

Shifts in ideology were only partly responsible. Taxpaying provisions also were opposed, by many Whigs as well as Democrats, because they were difficult to enforce and led to substantial fraud. Moreover, broadly stated tax

FIGURE 2.1   Property and Taxpaying Requirements for Suffrage: 1790–1855

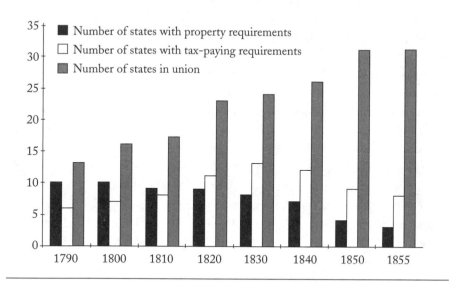

requirements could prove difficult to translate into coherent, concrete policies. In New York, for example, the state legislature struggled with problems that arose between lessors and lessees in the 1820s: If a lessee paid tax on a property, was the owner then disfranchised? Or, if the lessor paid the tax, presumably from the rent paid by the lessee, did the lessee lose his right to vote? In 1825, Governor DeWitt Clinton pointed to such problems as a reason to do away with the taxpaying provision altogether; he also pointed out that the prospective elimination of a general state tax could end up disfranchising masses of citizens. In 1826, sweeping aside the arguments for taxpayer suffrage that had been voiced so persuasively by Nathan Sanford, Martin Van Buren, and David Buel only six years earlier, New York amended its constitution to remove the taxpaying qualification.[87]

With the ascendancy of the second party system, taxpaying restrictions also were undermined by the dynamics of partisan politics: parties and factions vied to wear the increasingly popular mantle of democracy while simultaneously accusing one another of circumventing the law for their own advantage. Most commonly, campaigns to terminate taxpaying provisions were launched by Democrats, but the Whigs usually jumped on the bandwagon quickly, both to shore up their democratic credentials and because they believed that Democrats were corruptly evading the law anyway. In Southern states such as Louisiana and Virginia, eliminating taxpaying requirements was viewed, once again, as mortar solidifying the edifice of white supremacy.[88]

By the middle of the nineteenth century, thus, the nation had taken significant steps in the direction of universal white male suffrage. Spurred by the development of the economy, shifts in the social structure, the dynamics of party politics, the diffusion of democratic ideals, the experiences of war, and the need to maintain militias, the states, the federal government, and municipalities all had dismantled the most fundamental obstacles to the participation of men in elections. The impact of these reforms on the size of the electorate varied from state to state and is difficult to gauge with precision, but it surely was substantial. A careful study of New York before 1820 indicates that two thirds of adult males were unable to meet the freehold requirement to vote for the senate, and one third were unable to meet the much lower property requirement for voting for the legislature; the reforms therefore tripled the electorate for senatorial elections and increased it by 50 percent for the assembly. Similarly, in North Carolina, abolition of the freehold requirement doubled the electorate for senatorial elections, while the Virginia reforms of 1851, applying to all elections, increased the size of the polity by as much as 60 percent.[89]

The consequences were not everywhere so dramatic (in New Jersey and Massachusetts, for example, the growth of the electorate was more modest), but in every state where property and taxpaying qualifications were abolished, thousands and sometimes tens of thousands of men were enfranchised. The expansion of the suffrage in fact played a key role in the enormous upsurge of political participation in the 1830s and 1840s, when turnout in some locales reached 80 percent of all adult male citizens. De Tocqueville's declaration that "the people reign over the American political world as God rules over the universe" was more than a little hyperbolic; but his celebratory enthusiasm was far more closely matched by the reality of the United States in 1850 than it would have been in 1800.[90]

THREE

Backsliding and Sideslipping

According to our general understanding of the right of universal suffrage, I have no objection ... but if it be the intention of the mover of the resolution to extend the right of suffrage to females and negroes, I am against it. "All free white male citizens over the age of twenty-one years,"—I understand this language to be the measure of universal suffrage.

—Mr. Kelso, Indiana
Constitutional Debates, 1850

*H*ISTORY RARELY MOVES IN SIMPLE, STRAIGHT LINES, and the history of suffrage is no exception. Significant as the broadening of the franchise was in the first half of the nineteenth century, it does not tell the whole antebellum story. While the major thrust of legal change was toward increasing the number of voters, laws also were passed that tightened voting requirements. Some of these were administrative in origin, giving specificity to vaguely worded constitutional mandates. Others were designed to fill specific quadrants of the large space opened up by the abolition of property and taxpaying requirements. Still others were a response to the profound economic, social, and political changes transforming the nation: as the United States began to wrestle with the impact of industrialism, sectional conflict, immigration, and westward expansion, the first clouds of an antidemocratic reaction were forming on the horizon.

Women, African Americans, and Native Americans

One of the earliest acts of suffrage restriction—or retraction—was the disfranchisement of women in New Jersey in 1807. Both the state's constitution of 1776 and an election law passed in 1790 granted the right to vote to all "inhabitants" who otherwise were qualified: this was interpreted locally to mean that property-owning women could vote. New Jersey's policy was exceptional—although throughout the new nation there were individuals who followed the logic of "stake in society" arguments across the customary border of gender and concluded that women (such as widows) should be enfranchised if they possessed property and were not legally dependent on men. Why the state of New Jersey embraced this minority view is unclear, but the enfranchisement of women was definitely not inadvertent and appears to have been grounded at least in part in factional politics. As different political groups struggled to gain ascendancy during and just after the revolution, they tried to enlarge their potential constituencies, one of which was female.

Yet what partisan politics could give, it also could take away. By the early nineteenth century, the balance of political power had shifted, charges of voting fraud were rampant, and the Federalists, as well as two competing groups of Republicans, concluded that it was no longer to their advantage to have all "inhabitants"—including women, aliens, and African Americans—in the electorate. After the impulse to clean up politics had been bolstered by a flagrantly corrupt election to select the site for a new courthouse in Essex County, New Jersey's legislature took it upon itself to declare that "no person shall vote in any state or county election for officers in the government of the United States or of this state, unless such person be a free, white male citizen." Those who supported this retrenchment made little or no mention of the incapacity or incompetence of women; they were simply fighting corruption, correcting a "defect" in the constitution, and clearing up "doubts" about the composition of the electorate. Once that constitutional defect had been corrected, women everywhere in the nation were barred from the polls.[1]

African Americans were the target of a far more widespread movement, in the North as well as in the few pockets of the South where free blacks had sometimes voted. As tables A.4 and A.5 make clear, the number of states that formally excluded free African Americans was relatively small at the nation's founding, but it rose steadily from 1790 to 1850. States that had permitted blacks to vote during the first years of independence, including New Jersey, Maryland, and Connecticut, limited the franchise to whites before 1820. New York excluded the vast majority of blacks (by instituting a racially specific set of property and residence requirements) in the same constitution in which it removed property qualifications for whites. In 1835, North Carolina added the word *white* to its constitutional requirements, and Pennsylvania, which had such a liberal constitution during the revolutionary era, did the same in 1838, two years after its supreme court had ruled that blacks could not vote because they were not "freemen." Of equal importance, every state that entered the union after 1819 prohibited blacks from voting. In the late 1840s and early 1850s, moreover, many states (including New York, Ohio, Indiana, and Wisconsin) reaffirmed their racial exclusions, either in constitutional conventions or through popular referenda. By 1855, only five states (Massachusetts, Vermont, New Hampshire, Maine, and Rhode Island) did not discriminate against African Americans, and these states contained only 4 percent of the nation's free black population. Notably, the federal government also prohibited blacks from voting in the territories it controlled; in 1857, the Supreme Court ruled that blacks, free or slave, could not be citizens of the United States.[2]

The sources of this exclusionary impulse shifted somewhat over time. Early in the period, there was an almost matter-of-fact quality to decisions to bar African Americans, who were widely believed to be inferior and lacking in potential republican virtues. Since slaves obviously were ineligible to vote and most free blacks could not meet property and taxpaying requirements, formally expressed racial barriers would affect relatively few people, especially in the North. Yet with each passing decade the free black population grew, the abolition of property requirements made it possible for poor, uneducated blacks to vote, and inhabitants of Northern states grew increasingly apprehensive about the prospect of attracting black migrants from the South.

More important, perhaps, was an efflorescence of racism: while abolitionist sentiment was growing, so too were sharply antagonistic, fearful, and hostile attitudes toward blacks. This hardening of attitudes was discernible in the language with which the issue was discussed. At the New York convention in 1821, for example, a delegate opposed to black suffrage rather temperately had described blacks as "a peculiar people, incapable, in my judgment, of exercising that privilege with any sort of discretion, prudence, or independence." Twenty-five years later, one of his successors at the "peo-

FIGURE 3.1   Race Exclusions for Suffrage: 1790–1855

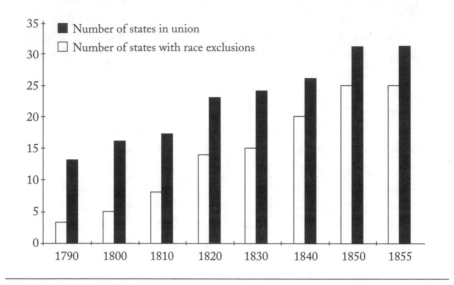

ple's convention" of 1846 belligerently declared that "nature revolted at the proposal" for black enfranchisement.[3]

In some states, the issue became enmeshed in party politics. In New York, for example, Republican factions were hostile to black voting between 1810 and 1820, in part because they feared (correctly) that blacks would constitute a Federalist voting bloc, especially in New York City; politically active blacks, throughout the North, tended to support the Federalists because of their opposition to slavery. Similarly, in later decades, Democratic opposition to African-American suffrage was reinforced by the (equally correct) conviction that most blacks would vote for Whigs—who were more antagonistic to slavery and who, despite their conservatism on class issues, could imagine a place for African-American voters in an organic social order. The membership of both major parties, however, tended to be divided on the issue, and outside of the border states (as well as the South, of course), the electoral stakes were small. In the North in 1850, blacks constituted more than 2 percent of the population in only one state, New Jersey, and many areas that witnessed heated debates on the subject (e.g., Ohio and Indiana) had populations that were less than 1 percent black.[4]

Indeed, northern antagonism to black voting was grounded far less in party politics than in hostile, or at best condescending, white attitudes toward blacks. Numerous delegates to the conventions, often equipped with anti–black suffrage petitions from their constituents, reiterated the notion that suffrage was not a natural right but "a kind of franchise bestowed or withheld as the public good demanded," and they were adamant that blacks were altogether lacking in qualities that could serve the public good. "No pure negro has wishes and wants like other people," declared one Indiana delegate in 1850. "The distinction between these races has been made by the God of Nature," insisted another. "The black race has been marked and condemned to servility, by the decree of Omnipotence; and should feeble man claim to erase from them the leprosy which God has placed upon them?" "Every negro was a thief, and every negro woman far worse," noted a Wisconsin spokesman. Even in freedom, blacks could not be "elevated" enough to make them the equals of whites, and any policy that promoted the "amalgamation" of the races would only lead to the "degradation of the white man." These stridently racist views were galvanized by the fear of black migration: in New York, Pennsylvania, Wisconsin, and elsewhere, convention delegates claimed that enfranchising blacks would only encourage freedmen and runaway slaves to flock to their states. A delegate from Wisconsin insisted that an extension of the suffrage "would cause our state to be overrun with runaway slaves from the South." Blacks at the time constituted two tenths of 1 percent of the state's population.[5]

Northern blacks, of course, resisted efforts to strip away their political rights. In Philadelphia, a gathering of African Americans issued an angry public statement called the *Appeal of Forty Thousand Citizens, Threatened with Disfranchisement, to the People of Pennsylvania.* "We ask a voice in the disposition of those public resources which we ourselves have helped to earn; we claim a right to be heard, according to our numbers, in regard to all those great public measures which involve our lives and fortunes," the statement declared. Similarly, New York's African-American population protested against the state's discriminatory property qualification, and in Providence, blacks—thanks to an extraordinarily complex political situation—succeeded in getting their political rights restored.[6]

Some whites also were forceful advocates of black suffrage, from the early nineteenth century through the 1850s. In 1821, in New York, a delegate countered the claim that blacks were a "peculiar people" by maintaining that they were instead "a peculiarly unfortunate people" that white society should endeavor to help. At all of the major state conventions, there were delegates who argued that if blacks were men, then they deserved to possess the rights of men. In 1846, a New York delegate "called upon the convention to decide whether the colored people were men or not. If they were men, he claimed for them the enjoyment of the common rights of men; otherwise, make them slaves to you and your children and trample them in the dust forever."[7] That same year, a Wisconsin delegate developed this moral argument more amply and eloquently, grounding the case in both religious and political principles:

> the sentiment that "all men are born free and equal" is a just and right principle . . . the negro has rights as sacred and as dear as any other race; and . . . these rights can only be secured by placing in his hands the instrument of defense—the ballot—which is provided by our institutions as the safeguard of political rights. We live as has been often repeated in this hall, in an age of progressive democracy, an age whose characteristic is a spirit that breaks over the barriers and superstitions of the past and looks through the disguises of rank and nation to a common nature coming from an impartial God. In its political effects it discards the prerogative of a few to govern and looks to the rights of all . . . this spirit is opening a grand law of humanity more comprehensive than all others, that looks farther than the skin to say who shall have rights and who shall be maintained in the free enjoyment of what the God of nature has given them. . . . Because a man is born with a dark skin, he is forever to be disfranchised! This is a terrible, damnable doctrine, and as false as it is terrible. It is a doctrine that will not stand the scrutiny of the spirit of the age; neither will its apologists stand with clean hands at a tribunal where there is no respect of persons.[8]

Such language was echoed in one state after another, in petitions from white and black citizens, and by convention delegates themselves; the argument was buttressed by the claim that granting blacks the vote would help to elevate their condition, while disfranchisement would attach a "stigma" that would throw "an obstacle in the way of their improvement." Attorney Charles Chauncy maintained in Pennsylvania in 1838 that it was "our duty to do everything that lies in our power, to elevate and to improve the condition of the colored race . . . instead of cutting them off." Other advocates pointed out that the very term *white* was ambiguous in its meaning: "Does it mean only Anglo-Saxons?" queried an Ohio delegate. "Does it embrace all Caucasians? This interpretation would include many who are darker than some it would exclude." Still others played the military card, quoting General Andrew Jackson's praise of black soldiers who took up arms during the War of 1812, and insisting that those who fought for their country, and might fight again, should not be denied the franchise.[9]

Such arguments, compelling as they may sound to twentieth-century ears, carried little weight, either in constitutional conventions or among the population at large. Black suffrage was an emotionally charged issue that could not be reached through rational argument or fine distinctions. In few conventions were votes on the issue even close; at the Indiana convention of 1850, one delegate even offered the barbed jest of an amendment "that all persons voting for negro suffrage shall themselves be disfranchised." Political leaders frequently voiced the fear that any constitution including black suffrage could not be ratified by the electorate, and they were probably right. With the exception of Rhode Island, all of the popular referenda held on the issue resulted in overwhelming mandates for an exclusively white suffrage. Much of the populace believed that blacks were inferior, and outside of the slave states, feared their presence. Permitting African Americans to vote seemed all too likely to open the doors to migration and "amalgamation," and thus to diminish the significance of whiteness and citizenship.[10]

The political rights of the nation's other racial minority, Native Americans, were a less inflammatory issue. To be sure, fears were expressed in Texas that "hordes" of Mexican Indians "will come moving in . . . and vanquish you at the ballot box though you are invincible in arms"; and at California's founding convention, one delegate voiced the conviction—surely widely shared—that it was "absolutely necessary" to include a constitutional provision that "will prevent the wild tribes from voting." In addition, many constitutional conventions held brief debates about whether Indians were or were not "white." The Michigan convention, for example, came to the remarkable conclusion that Indians ought to be considered white because the word *white* simply meant "not black": "the word white was used in contradiction to the black alone, and though the Indian was copper-colored, he was not to be classed among the latter." The prevailing view in much of the nation, however, was that Native Americans, whether officially white or not, ought not be excluded from the franchise on *racial* grounds: as long as they were "civilized" and taxpaying, they should be entitled to vote. As was true of many policies toward Native Americans in the nineteenth century,

Indians were regarded as possessing the raw (but uncivilized) potential for full (white) personhood.[11] (See table A.4.)

Nonetheless, the ability of Native Americans to participate in politics was narrowed between 1790 and the 1850s. In some states, they were barred because they were finally judged not to be legally white, and only whites were eligible to vote. More distinctively, Native Americans were kept from the polls through a series of court decisions and legal declarations that circumscribed their ability to become citizens. The citizenship status of Native Americans was ambiguous in early American law (the constitution specified that Indians "not taxed" were not to be counted in the census for the purposes of legislative apportionment), but beginning with Chief Justice Marshall's landmark decisions of the 1830s, their legal status began to be clarified—in a negative direction. Indian tribes were "domestic, dependent nations," according to Marshall, and thus individual Indians, living with their tribes, were aliens, even if born in the United States. Twenty years later, the Dred Scott decision affirmed this interpretation, while suggesting a path toward citizenship: Indians (unlike blacks) could, if they left their tribes and settled among whites, "be entitled to all the rights and privileges which would belong to an immigrant from any other foreign people." At roughly the same time, however, the attorney general ruled that Indians could not become citizens through the conventional process of naturalization because the naturalization laws applied only to whites and to foreigners—and Indians were not actually foreigners, because "they are in our allegiance." The upshot of this juridical Catch-22 was that Indians could become citizens only by treaty or by special acts of Congress, even if they did settle among whites and pay taxes.[12]

Congress did in fact attempt to naturalize some tribes in their entirety, usually in return for a tribal agreement to accept a limited allotment of land; but congressional actions affected only a small number of Native Americans. Meanwhile, several states formally moved to disfranchise all Indians, or Indians "not taxed," or members of specific tribes, while others expressly limited suffrage to citizens or to "civilized" Indians who were "not a member of any tribe." (Georgia even gave full citizenship rights to individually named Cherokee Indians who surrendered any legal claims to their lands.) Although these latter provisions were commonly construed as extensions of the franchise, their applicability was limited. On the whole, Native Americans were understood to be potential voters, but few in fact ever were able to vote during the antebellum era.[13]

Paupers, Felons, and Migrants

In addition to restrictions focused on people's identities, laws also were passed that targeted their behavior. In drawing—and redrawing—the boundaries of the polity, each state contended not only with issues of race and gender but also with adult, white men who occupied the social margins of the community. Despite the abolition of property requirements, most Americans did not believe that all adult white males were entitled to full membership in the political community.

One restriction preserved a link between economic status and enfranchisement: paupers were denied the right to vote in twelve states between 1792 and the late nineteenth century. (See table A.6.) Although the precise definition of *pauper* was debated in constitutional conventions and in the courts, these laws clearly were aimed at men who received public relief from their communities or from the state: those who lived in almshouses or were given "outdoor relief" (generally in the form of food, fuel, or small amounts of cash) while residing at home. These pauper exclusions were not archaic carryovers of colonial precedents; they were generally new constitutional provisions, often adopted at the same conventions that abolished property or taxpaying requirements.[14]

The exclusion of paupers constituted a direct rejection of claims that suffrage was a right that ought to be universal among white males: it drew a new border around the polity, making clear that individuals had to maintain a minimal level of economic self-sufficiency in order to possess political rights. The rationale for these measures was Blackstonian: a man who accepted public support surrendered his independence and therefore lost the capacity to function as a citizen. Paupers, according to one Delaware delegate, were not "freemen in the whole extent." "The theory of our constitution," declared Josiah Quincy, "is that extreme poverty—that is pauperism—is inconsistent with independence." "When a man is so bowed down with misfortune, as to become an inmate of a poor house . . . he voluntarily surrenders his rights," claimed a member of the New Jersey committee that drafted its law in 1844. Advocates of these laws frequently invoked a vivid, if implausible, image of the trustees or masters of poorhouses marching paupers to the polls and instructing them how to vote.[15]

The prospect of disfranchising a community's poorest residents caused some discomfort, and even outrage, among citizens of both parties. In the New Jersey convention of 1844, Democratic delegate David Naar, a judge

and sephardic Jew whose family had recently emigrated from the West In-
dies, fiercely opposed the notion that "paupers have made a voluntary surrender of their liberties." "Does any one of his own will and choice become
a pauper? No one, sir, except from the necessity of the case!" He also pointed
out that "the working men . . . are sometimes bowed down by misfortune,
and shall they be deprived of the right of voting? Which of us can say that
some day or other he may not become a pauper?" A former overseer of the
poor supported Naar, saying that "he had seen citizens of the first families
in our State borne to the poor house from misfortune: and now shall we set
a mark upon them and rank them with criminals?" In several states, such as
Wisconsin, the idea of disfranchising the unfortunate was too distasteful,
leading to the rejection of proposals for pauper exclusions; but elsewhere,
and with the support of some Federalists, Republicans, Democrats, and
Whigs, paupers were defined out of the polity.[16]

As legal historian Robert Steinfeld has perceptively pointed out, the pauper exclusion laws expressed a shift in the prevailing concept of independence, a shift precipitated by the abolition of property requirements.
Independence had come to be perceived less in economic than in legal
terms: paupers were legally dependent on those who ran poorhouses and
administered relief, and often were required to perform labor in return for
aid. While they were paupers (the laws were generally interpreted by courts
to apply only to men receiving aid at the time of elections), they lacked
"self-ownership," which limited their capacity to act or vote independently.
Implicitly, the pauper exclusion laws were drawing a distinction between
wage earners, whom many viewed as sufficiently independent to be enfranchised, and men who had surrendered legal control of their own time and
labor. Yet, as Naar suggested, there was also a class edge to these laws—
since they constituted a warning to the working poor that misfortune, or
failure to be sufficiently industrious, would deprive them of their political
rights. That warning, as Naar surely was aware, was all the more resonant—
and seemed all the more unfair—after the jarringly sharp economic down-
turn of 1837.[17]

The right to vote also was withheld from another group of men who violated prevailing social norms, those who had committed crimes, particularly felonies or so-called infamous crimes. (These were crimes that made a
person ineligible to serve as a witness in a legal proceeding.) Disfranchisement for such crimes had a long history in English, European, and even
Roman law, and it was hardly surprising that the principle of attaching civil

disabilities to the commission of crimes appeared in American law as well. The rationale for such sanctions was straightforward: disfranchisement, whether permanent or for an extended period, served as retribution for committing a crime and as a deterrent to future criminal behavior.[18]

States began to incorporate such provisions in their constitutions in the late eighteenth century. Eleven states disfranchised those convicted of infamous crimes (and sometimes specified crimes such as perjury, bribery, or betting on elections) between 1776 and 1821; by the eve of the Civil War, more than two dozen states disfranchised men who had committed serious crimes. (See table A.7.) In some instances, these exclusions were specified in state constitutions; in others, the constitutions authorized legislatures to pass laws barring certain offenders from the polls. In almost all cases, the disfranchisement implicitly was permanent, although the New York Constitution of 1846 stipulated that men who were pardoned for their crimes would be reinstated in the voting rolls, a principle likely applied elsewhere as well. Rarely did such constitutional or legislative acts occasion much debate, but it is notable, from a late-twentieth-century perspective (felons are now disfranchised almost everywhere), that such provisions were neither universal nor uniform.[19]

In several states, the franchise also was restricted by lengthening state or local residency requirements. (As noted in the previous chapter, the reverse was true in some locales.) The need for residency rules was widely agreed upon: particularly in the absence of property or taxpaying qualifications, it seemed sensible to restrict the franchise to those who were familiar with local conditions and likely to have a stake in the outcome of elections. How long the necessary period of residence ought to be was less obvious. The average requirement tended to be one year in the state and three or six months in an individual township or county, but there were strenuous advocates of both longer and shorter periods.[20]

Those who favored lengthy residency requirements were generally seeking to prevent "vagrants and strangers," "sojourners," or transients of any type from voting. "There is little propriety," observed James Fenimore Cooper, "in admitting the floating part of the population to a participation" in government. Most of these floating men were manual workers, deemed to be ignorant of local conditions and a source of electoral fraud. In 1820, "hundreds of men . . . from New Hampshire" were reported to be flocking into Massachusetts each spring to vote in elections; in Wisconsin, convention delegates advocated a lengthy period of residence to exclude a "numerous class" of migrant miners from Illinois; in Ohio, the "transient, homeless hands of canal boats" were said to be determining the outcome of elections in towns that bordered the canals. Elsewhere in the Midwest, apprehensions focused on railroad workers (whose votes allegedly could be controlled by railroad corporations) and on farmhands who could be shipped from county to county for political purposes. These concerns became more acute as economic development heightened the visibility of migrants. Nonetheless, anxiety about the transient population generally was overridden by those who believed that lengthy residency requirements would unjustly disfranchise "wandering mechanics," men whom "poverty obliged to remove from one township to another," or even farmers who commonly leased their land for a year or eighteen months and then moved on. Some Midwesterners also argued that shorter periods of residence would encourage much-needed settlement.[21]

Not surprisingly, there was a partisan dimension to these debates. Federalists and then Whigs tended to favor longer periods of residence, because they were wary of the unsettled and the poor and suspected that most transients would vote for the Republicans or Democrats. The Democrats shared this analysis, advocating shorter residency requirements in the hope of enfranchising more of their own supporters. This partisan split became more pronounced in the 1840s as the issue was infused with conflicting and sometimes antagonistic popular attitudes toward the mobile foreign-born.[22]

Most of these debates resulted in a standoff, but some states did end up lengthening their residency requirements. New York, in 1821, did so for those who could not meet the taxpaying requirements for legislative voting. Maryland adopted a six months' local requirement in 1850, aimed almost entirely at the immigrant population of Baltimore; and Virginia, that same year, increased the state residency requirement from one year to two. In addition, Florida adopted an unusually long residency requirement of two years in 1838. In 1845, a coalition of Whigs and Democrats from the southern parishes of Louisiana, fearing the potential power of immigrants flooding into New Orleans, succeeded in doubling the state residency requirement from one year to two, while demanding a full year's residence in the parish. Residency also would be voided by an absence of ninety days or longer. Meanwhile, in Ohio, a complex, even bewildering, series of laws was passed, as Whigs and Democrats fought over residence rules for more than two decades. The upshot was the maintenance of a one-year state requirement and a shorter local-residence requirement, coupled with the appointment of election judges who had the power to reject any voter's claim to be a legal resident. This was followed by the passage of a Whig-sponsored law that instituted a new system of voter registration applicable only to selected communities and towns and to "canal counties" where rates of transience were high.[23]

Registration and Immigration

Ohio was not the only state where concern about transients—and particularly foreign-born transients—sparked interest in the creation of formal systems of voter registration. Massachusetts had adopted a registration system in 1801, South Carolina instituted a limited registration requirement for the city of Columbia in 1819, and New York considered the possibility in 1821 (and did require that voters present "proper proofs" of their eligibility). Most states, however, did not keep official lists of voters or require voters to register in advance of elections.[24]

Beginning in the 1830s, the idea of registration became more popular, particularly among Whigs, who believed that ineligible transients and foreigners were casting their votes for the Democratic Party. At the same time, a landmark Massachusetts court case, *Capen v. Foster*, ruled that registry laws were not unconstitutional impositions of new voting qualifications but reasonable measures to regulate the conduct of elections. In 1836, Pennsylvania passed its first registration law, which required the assessors in Philadelphia (and only Philadelphia) to prepare lists of qualified voters: no person not on the list was permitted to vote. Although the proclaimed goal of the law was to reduce fraud, opponents insisted that its real intent was to reduce the participation of the poor—who were frequently not home when assessors came by and who did not have "big brass" nameplates on their doors. At the constitutional convention of 1837, Democratic delegates from Philadelphia responded by introducing a constitutional amendment mandating a uniform, statewide registry system; the proposal was resoundingly defeated by rural delegates.[25]

In New York, the 1830s witnessed the beginning of a prolonged partisan struggle over voter registration. Early proposals for a registry were unmistakably designed to hinder the voting of Irish Catholic immigrants and thereby reduce Democratic electoral strength. In 1840, Whigs succeeded in passing a registry law that applied only to New York City, which contained the largest concentration of Irish voters. That law was repealed two years later, but throughout the 1840s and 1850s an emerging coalition of Republicans and Know-Nothings continued to press for a formal system of registration. (Regarding the Know-Nothings, see chapter 4.) In Connecticut, similarly, the Whigs passed a registry law in 1839. Since it did not require the registrars to be drawn from both parties, Democrats denounced the act as a "disfranchising law" and replaced it, in 1842, with a law that shifted the burden of registration from the voter to town officials. Proposals for registries also were floated in other states. Yet nearly everywhere outside of the Northeast, registration systems were rebuffed as partisan measures that would weaken the Democratic Party while infringing the rights of immigrants and the poor.[26]

Apprehensions about immigrant voting in the 1840s, particularly in the Northeast, also gave birth to new and untried ideas for limiting the franchise. In New York, New Jersey, Indiana, Maryland, and Missouri, constitutional conventions considered proposals to institute literacy tests, or even English language literacy tests, for prospective voters. "The least we can require," noted a New Jersey delegate in 1844, "is this very simple manifestation of intelligence." Such a law, he claimed, would encourage parents to educate their children. "Let fathers understand—let mothers understand, that before their sons wear the livery of American freemen they must be able to read." Samuel Jones stated the issue more severely: "persons wholly destitute of education do not possess sufficient intelligence to enable them to exercise the right of suffrage beneficially to the public." Although the image of an educated electorate clearly had its attractions, these proposals were rapidly rebutted: there were many fine, upstanding citizens who happened to be illiterate or barely literate (even Andrew Jackson, it was claimed, had difficulty spelling his own name) but were perfectly capable of responsibly exercising the franchise. Without a system of universal education, moreover, a literacy requirement would be, as one delegate put it, "a blow at the poor."[27]

Advocates of restriction also put forward another proposal explicitly aimed at immigrants: they sought to prevent naturalized citizens from voting until they had held citizenship for one, five, ten, or even twenty-one years. The expressed goal of this proposal was to prevent the partisan, mass naturalization of immigrants that allegedly occurred on the eve of elections; the proposal also would give immigrants time to become fully acquainted with American norms and values (and diminish the Democratic vote). In the 1840s and early 1850s, laws of this type were proposed in New York,

New Jersey, Missouri, Maryland, Indiana, and Kentucky. Yet not until the Know-Nothing successes of the later 1850s (see chapter 4) were any literacy or "waiting period" restrictions actually imposed—although New York, in 1846, did institute a system through which registrars could interrogate naturalized citizens and demand written proof of their eligibility. Notably, the concern about immigrant voters in the Northeast was mounting at precisely the same time that many Midwestern states were extending the franchise to nondeclarant aliens.[28]

———

By the early 1850s, therefore, several groups or categories of men (and one group of women) had lost the political rights they possessed a half century earlier. Although the franchise on the whole had been broadened, new barriers were erected, targeting specific—and smaller—populations. These barriers were expressions of the nation's reluctance to embrace universal suffrage, of the limits to the democratic impulses that characterized the era. After the 1820s, such barriers—as well as proposals for additional restraints on the franchise—were also a response to socioeconomic change, as the economy became more industrial, large numbers of immigrants arrived at the nation's shores, and the impending crisis over slavery threatened to release significant numbers of African Americans not only from bondage but from the South. Despite the democratic ethos of the era, the transformation of American society was setting in motion a crosscurrent of apprehensions about a broadly democratic polity, apprehensions that would prove to be harbingers of things to come.[29]

Democracy, the Working Class, and American Exceptionalism

Americans have long taken pride in what they see as the exceptional qualities of political development in the United States, qualities that distinguish American history from that of other, particularly European, nations. Prominent among these exceptional features are the longstanding tradition of political democracy and the relatively small role played by class in American social life and politics. For much of the twentieth century, scholars and writers have linked these two ingredients, locating their convergence in the uniquely early and quite uncontested enfranchisement of the American working class in the years before the Civil War. According to the standard, widely accepted narrative, American workers—unlike their counterparts

nearly everywhere in Europe—gained universal suffrage (or at least universal white male suffrage) early in the process of industrialization and thus
never were obliged to organize collectively to fight for the franchise. As a
result, workers were able to address their grievances through the electoral
process, they were not compelled to form labor parties, and they developed
partisan attachments to mainstream political organizations. All of which—
or so it has been argued—had profound implications for the subsequent
evolution of American politics and American labor, including the absence
of a strong socialist movement in the United States.[30]

The traditional account does have some validity. Many American workers indeed were enfranchised decades before their counterparts in Europe
(although just how many remains unclear). Moreover, as leading labor historian David Montgomery has recently pointed out, the acquisition of the
franchise by thousands of artisans, craftsmen, and mechanics in antebellum
America led to important legal changes that served the interests of working people.[31]

Nonetheless, the traditional account, grounded in a triumphalist, or
Whig, history of suffrage, misses a critical dimension of the story. Put simply, to the extent that the working class was indeed enfranchised during the
antebellum era (and one should not ignore that women, free blacks, and recent immigrants constituted a large portion of the working class), such enfranchisement was largely an unintended consequence of the changes in
suffrage laws. The constitutional conventions that removed property and
even taxpaying requirements did not deliberately intend to enfranchise the
hundreds of thousands of factory operatives, day laborers, and unskilled
workers who became such a prominent and disturbing feature of the economic landscape by the mid-1850s. Certainly not immigrant, and especially
Irish Catholic, operatives, laborers, and unskilled workers.

Although conservatives such as James Kent and Josiah Quincy had
warned that lowering the barriers to voting would end up giving substantial
political power to such undesirables, the proponents of suffrage reform dis-
counted that possibility. New Yorker David Buel, it will be remembered, declared that if he shared Kent's vision of the future, he would not have
advocated the elimination of property qualifications. Buel, however, was
convinced that New York would remain an overwhelmingly agricultural
state and that there was nothing to be feared from the relatively small urban
population of New York City. Similarly, Martin Van Buren, another staunch
supporter of a broader franchise, made clear that he opposed "universal suf-

frage" and that the constitutional revisions of 1820 were intended only to enfranchise the respectable middling strata of society.[32]

Indeed, the broadening of the franchise in antebellum America transpired before the industrial revolution had proceeded very far and before its social consequences were clearly or widely visible. The data presented in tables A.2 and A.8 lend some factual and statistical muscle to the point. As these tables indicate, there were relatively few manufacturing workers in the northern states when property qualifications were abolished or new constitutions without property restrictions were adopted. (Since the South remained overwhelmingly agricultural, these states are omitted from table A.8.) In New York in 1820, for example, persons engaged in agriculture outnumbered those in manufacturing and commerce combined by a ratio of almost 4 to 1; in Illinois, the ratio was 10 to 1; even in Massachusetts, the ratio was 3 to 2. Everywhere in America, the number of people engaged in agriculture greatly outnumbered those working in manufacturing alone when property and taxpaying requirements were abolished. The enormous surge in manufacturing began after 1820 and in some places, after 1840. That surge led to a dramatic shift in the ratios of farmers to workers: by 1850, persons who earned their living in agriculture were actually outnumbered in five states. But this new, and permanent, tilt in the relative importance of industry occurred twenty years or more after the suffrage laws had been changed.

What this points to, of course, is that the American polity did not make a deliberate and conscious decision to enfranchise the working class that the industrial revolution was in the process of creating. Massachusetts, New York, Pennsylvania, and other states did choose to entrust the ballot to farmers who leased rather than owned land, to small shopkeepers who owned little or no property, and to artisans, mechanics, and craftsmen who constituted the visible—and not very large—working class of the early nineteenth century. These men were all deemed to possess the republican virtues of manliness, self-sufficiency, and independence of judgment that were thought to be required of voters. Stable and respectable employment, as well as property ownership, made a man worthy of full political citizenship. Yet few of the delegates to constitutional conventions—and probably few of the people who elected them—believed that suffrage ought to be so universal as to embrace a large, urban proletariat of a type that existed in England and that, it was hoped, would never become part of the American world. Such a proletariat did eventually appear on this side of the Atlantic, but only after the suffrage laws, nearly everywhere, had been reformed. The broadening of suffrage in the United States took place in the absence of a large or very developed industrial working class.[33]

This comparative perspective can be extended to the South. In Europe (and elsewhere), resistance to universal suffrage was grounded not only in opposition to the enfranchisement of industrial workers but in an equally powerful opposition to the extension of political rights to the peasantry—to the millions of men, many of them illiterate, who lived in poverty, toiling on farms large and small. The American peasantry, however, was peculiar: it was enslaved. As Benjamin Watkins Leigh observed at Virginia's constitutional convention of 1829, "slaves, in the eastern part of this state, fill the place of the peasantry of Europe." "In every civilized country under the sun," Leigh argued, "some there must be who labor for their daily bread" and who were consequently unfit to "enter into political affairs." In Virginia and throughout the South, those who labored for their daily bread were African-American slaves—and because they were slaves, they never became part of the calculus, or politics, of suffrage reform. When the political leaders of Virginia or North Carolina or Alabama decided to abolish property or taxpaying qualifications, they did not remotely imagine that their actions would enfranchise the millions of black men who toiled on the cotton plantations and tobacco farms of the region.[34]

In both the South and the North, thus, economic barriers to enfranchisement were dropped in social and institutional settings that permitted political leaders to believe that the consequences of their actions would be limited, far more limited than they would have been in Europe. The relatively early broadening of the franchise in the United States was not simply, or even primarily, the consequence of a distinctive American commitment to democracy, of the insignificance of class, or of a belief in extending political rights to subaltern classes. Rather, the early extension of voting rights occurred—or was at least made possible—because the rights and power of those subaltern classes, despised and feared in the United States much as they were in Europe, were not at issue when suffrage reforms were adopted. The American equivalent of the peasantry was not going to be enfranchised in any case, and the social landscape included few industrial workers. What was exceptional about the United States was an unusual configuration of historical circumstances that allowed suffrage laws to be liberalized before men who labored from dawn to dusk in the factories and the fields became numerically significant political actors.

A Case in Point: The War in Rhode Island

The exception that proves this rule—at least for the North—was Rhode Island, where a property requirement remained in place until long after a sizable industrial working class had emerged. Rhode Island did not draw up a new constitution during the revolutionary era and continued to be governed by a colonial charter that granted the franchise to "freemen"; as defined by the General Assembly, this term included only those who owned real estate valued at $134 or rented property for at least $7. In the eighteenth century, nearly three quarters of all adult males were able to meet such requirements. The rapid growth of Providence and of manufacturing centers (particularly textile mills) in the state's Blackstone valley, however, changed that proportion dramatically: by the 1830s, substantially less than half of the adult white males in the state could vote, and many of those who lacked the franchise were immigrant workers. Compounding the maldistribution of political power was a system of legislative apportionment weighted heavily in favor of the rural counties in the southern half of the state.[35]

Several different political factions, as well as the disfranchised themselves, attempted to promote suffrage reform during the first quarter of the nineteenth century, but they were rebuffed by a coalition of conservatives and landowners who controlled the legislature and enjoyed, among other benefits, minimal and infrequent taxes on landed property. Opposition to the colonial charter picked up steam, however, in the early 1830s; it was sparked initially by a group of radical workingmen of whom carpenter and activist Seth Luther became the most celebrated spokesman. Luther, who had served a stint in debtors' prison in the early 1820s, was a gifted orator and one of New England's foremost critics of the inequalities created by industrialization. In his *Address on the Right of Free Suffrage*, he claimed that there were "twelve thousand vassals" in Rhode Island

> who submit to be taxed without their own consent, who are compelled to perform military duty, to defend the country from foreign invasion and domestic commotion; to protect property frequently not their own; in fact, who are obliged by the will of a minority, to bear all the burthens of a nominally free government, and yet have no voice in the choice of the rulers, and the administration of that government.

Luther denounced the class prejudice that kept workingmen from voting, insisted that the laws of Rhode Island violated the federal Constitution's

guarantee of a republican form of government, and suggested that the Declaration of Independence be rewritten to indicate that "all men are created
equal, except in Rhode Island."[36]

Despite Luther's fiery rhetoric, and in part because workingmen became
pessimistic about the possibility of enfranchisement, the movement for suffrage reform (and reapportionment) was taken over by a group of middle-
class reformers, many of whom were Whigs. They were led by Thomas
Dorr, a successful Providence attorney from a well-to-do Rhode Island family. Dorr, who had attended Exeter and entered Harvard at the ripe age of
fourteen, was known as a man of integrity and principle who unequivocally
embraced causes he believed were righteous. The reformers launched a
Constitutionalist Party that sought to write a new state constitution and
correct numerous defects in the state's government. After two years of agitation, they succeeded in convincing the General Assembly to hold a constitutional convention—which proceeded to reject, by overwhelming
margins, demands for taxpayer suffrage, reapportionment, and the aban-
donment of the colonial charter. Clearly at stake was nothing less than control of the state's government: the combination of a broad franchise and
reapportionment would produce a dramatic shift in power, which landowners were fiercely committed to resisting.[37]

The conflict came to a boiling point in 1841, when mechanics and workingmen, believing that they could never redress any of their economic grievances until they possessed political rights, formed a new, militant suffrage
organization. Their demands for change were backed not only by the reformers of the mid-1830s but also by the Democratic Party, which viewed an expansion of the franchise as the key to its own electoral fortunes. Dorr by this
time had abandoned the Whigs and become the head of Rhode Island's
Democratic Party. This broad coalition of reform advocates openly derided
the state's existing constitution as an anachronism. "If the sovereignty don't
reside in the people, where in the hell does it reside?" queried one member of
the new Rhode Island Suffrage Association.[38]

Convinced that further appeals to the state's government were futile, the
Suffrage Association convened a People's Convention in October 1841.
There they drafted a new constitution that granted the franchise to all adult
white men who met a residency requirement of one year; it also reappor-
tioned the legislature to increase the representation of Providence and the
industrial towns of the north. The most contentious issue to surface at the
convention was black suffrage: after a lengthy debate, shaped in part by the

fear of including a potentially unpopular element in what was already a radical document, the People's Convention voted to restrict suffrage to whites, a decision that led both blacks and abolitionists to oppose the new suffrage movement.[39]

Supporters of the People's Convention organized a statewide referendum on the new constitution: to their delight, when the votes were counted in January 1842, 14,000 people, a clear majority of all adult male Rhode Islanders, had voted to ratify their constitution. To Dorr and his followers, this expression of popular will meant that their constitution was now the legitimate, fundamental law of the state; they were further heartened when an alternative constitution, proposed by the Landholders' Convention (representing the charter government), was defeated in a referendum. Tension mounted during the spring of 1842, as supporters and opponents of suffrage expansion denounced one another in street confrontations, in pamphlet wars, speaking tours, and rhetorical appeals to the federal government. Tensions were exacerbated further when the reformers proceeded to hold elections under the new constitution: although turnout was disappointing, a new legislature was elected and Dorr voted in as governor.[40]

Meanwhile, the conservatives, now organized as the Law and Order Party, succeeded in persuading the General Assembly to pass a series of laws aimed at "certain designing persons . . . endeavoring to carry through a plan for the subversion of our government." These laws (called the Algerine laws by suffragists, in reference to the well-known contemporary tyrant, the Dey of Algiers) imposed harsh penalties on those who were candidates in unauthorized elections and on those who presided at meetings held under the People's Constitution. Any person who attempted to assume office under the People's Constitution would be guilty of treason and subject to life imprisonment.[41]

The Algerine laws successfully splintered the Suffrage Association— since many backers of reform were reluctant to risk jail terms for the cause. A growing fear of civil or even military conflict, moreover, led many moderate supporters of suffrage reform to distance themselves from Dorr and his more radical, generally working-class, allies. Nonetheless, in early May, the People's government marched into Providence surrounded by thousands of supporters, including armed militia companies, to inaugurate Dorr as governor and open a session of the new legislature. That legislature promptly swore in state officials, passed a wide array of new laws, and repealed the Algerine restrictions on political activity. The new legislature also instructed Dorr to inform the United States Congress and the President of the United States that Rhode Island had a new government.[42]

For several weeks thereafter, things remained at a standstill, with two different groups claiming to be the legitimate government of the state. The nation's attention was riveted on the unprecedented conflict, with reactions closely following partisan lines. Democrats, including Andrew Jackson and Martin Van Buren, embraced the Dorrites, endorsing the right of "the people" to "alter and amend their system of government when a majority wills it." Whigs, in contrast, denounced the reformers as pernicious advocates of rebellion and anarchy.[43]

The stalemate was broken on the night of May 18, when Dorr and a small group of armed followers attempted to exercise their sovereign power by assembling in front of the state arsenal and demanding that it be turned over to them. When their demands were refused, they attacked the arsenal, but both of their cannons misfired, and the Dorrites were then beaten back. Dorr himself promptly left the state, his followers scattered, and some, including Seth Luther, were sent to prison. Over the course of the next few months, radical suffrage advocates attempted a few other military escapades (resulting in several deaths), with similarly disheartening and tragicomic results. The charter government remained in control of the state, backed by federal troops sent by Whig President John Tyler; political support for Dorr was undercut by dismay at his adventurism; and the Dorr War ended with more whimper than bang. In 1843, Dorr, after spending more than a year in quasi-exile (largely in states controlled by Democrats who refused to pursue him), returned to Rhode Island, where he was promptly arrested, convicted of treason, and sentenced to life in prison, at hard labor. Twenty months later, his health ruined by imprisonment, he was quietly released from jail, in part at the behest of his former adversaries.[44]

Despite their victory, the Law and Order Party and the charter government were at least mildly chastened by the events of 1841–42, and they drew up a new constitution with a somewhat broader suffrage. All native-born adult males were permitted to vote if they met a minimal taxpaying requirement; consistent with Whig principles (and perhaps out of gratitude for their nonsupport of Dorr), the conservatives also enfranchised taxpaying blacks. The far more numerous immigrant working-class groups that had supported the rebellion, however, were not treated as generously. Foreign-born naturalized citizens were obliged to meet the existing property qualification, as well as a lengthy residence requirement. In addition, only property owners were permitted to vote for the city council of Providence or on any matters affecting taxation and financial policy in all cities and towns. The electorate in effect remained circumscribed by class and ethnic boundaries, and the state settled into an era of political apathy in which relatively few people bothered to vote.[45]

The final legal chapter of the rebellion was written in the Supreme Court's decision in the landmark case of *Luther v. Borden* in 1848. The case had arisen in 1842, when Martin Luther, a Suffragist, sued Luther Borden for illegal breaking and entering: Borden was a Rhode Island military official who had been sent by the charter government to arrest Luther. The Suffragists claimed that the government that had dispatched Borden had been nullified by the ratification of the People's Constitution and thus that Borden lacked any legal authority to enter Luther's home and arrest him. The claim that the People's Constitution had become the legitimate blueprint of Rhode Island's government was justified by appealing to article 4 of the U.S. Constitution, which guaranteed to each state "a republican form of government." What was at stake in the lawsuit was the capacity, under federal law, of a popular majority of any state to create or re-create its own governing institutions. The Supreme Court dodged the issue, offering little sympathy to the Suffragists and no judicial support for the theory that a majority of the people could erect their own government in place of one ruled by a minority. The Court affirmed a lower court ruling that Borden had not trespassed, and asserted that the definition of "a republican form of government" was a political issue to be decided by the "Political Department" and not by the judiciary.[46] The Court in effect declined to interpret the Constitution as requiring state governments to be democratic.

The bizarre culminating events of the Dorr War ought not obscure the significance of a political conflict that enveloped the state for more than a decade and gripped the nation for months. In Rhode Island, by the 1830s and 1840s, the abolition of pecuniary qualifications for voting clearly would have meant enfranchising a working-class majority, including thousands of factory operatives, many of whom were Irish Catholics. Faced with that prospect, the state's ruling minority resisted reform with a ferocity not seen elsewhere. Chancellor Kent's pessimistic vision of the future was a reality in Rhode Island by 1840, and inhabiting that reality—as opposed to David Buel's benign world in which farmers and other property owners would always predominate—the middle and upper classes were willing to go to extraordinary lengths to prevent any significant expansion of the right to vote.

What happened in Rhode Island highlights the critical fact that the reforms of the antebellum era were not designed or intended to enfranchise a large, industrial, and partially foreign-born working class. There is, moreover, little reason to think that other industrializing states would have avoided similar conflict and tumult—culminating in similarly restrictive suffrage laws—had they delayed franchise reform for another generation or more.

PART II

Narrowing the Portals

The right of suffrage, being the creature of the organic law, may be modified or withdrawn by the sovereign authority which conferred it, without inflicting any punishment on those who are disqualified.

—*Anderson v. Baker* (OCTOBER 1865)

*A*FTER 1850, CONFLICT OVER THE RIGHT TO VOTE heightened dramatically. For the next seventy years, the issue was often on center stage, and always backstage, in American political life. Heated public debates surrounded the post–Civil War enfranchisement of African Americans, as well as their disfranchisement a generation later. Advocates of women's suffrage fought battle after battle in the states and in Washington. Workers, immigrants, transients, Native Americans, paupers, and the illiterate often found themselves contending with rules that would, or did, bar them from the polls.[1]

The diverse forces and dynamics that had promoted an expansion of the franchise before the 1850s remained active. The demands of war and the pressure to enfranchise soldiers and ex-soldiers prompted various efforts to broaden the right to vote; political parties jockeyed even more incessantly to shape the electorate to their advantage; thinly populated states sought to stimulate settlement through generous suffrage regulations; deeply held democratic convictions inspired thousands, if not millions, of individuals to support and fight for universal suffrage; and the disfranchised themselves pressed vigorously for inclusion in the polity.

Yet there was a shift in temper after midcentury, marked by a heightened resolve on the part of those seeking to contract the right to vote or limit its further expansion. This shift was grounded in the deepening changes occurring in the nation's economic and social structure, changes that (among other things) greatly enlarged the industrial and agricultural working class. Importantly, this sprawling, regionally diverse working class—dependent and assertive in many of the ways that Blackstone and Chancellor Kent had imagined—consisted increasingly of men and women who were racially, ethnically, and culturally unlike old-stock white Americans. In the South, the abolition of slavery gave birth to a class of black freedmen living in a state of interdependence and hostility with their former masters; because the Radical Republicans were convinced that freedom would be illusory without political rights, these freedmen were enfranchised during Reconstruction. In the North and the West, millions of foreigners from Ireland, Asia, southern and eastern Europe—men and women who were non–English speaking, Catholic, and Jewish—arrived to work in the rapidly growing factories and mines, to build railroads, roads, and cities; they too were, or might become, voters. North and South, thus, the potential electorate in 1880 or 1900 looked very different than it had in 1840.

Moreover, these working people and poor people—skilled tradesmen, factory operatives, miners, agricultural laborers, sharecroppers—acquired some political and electoral strength, particularly at local levels. During and after Reconstruction, southern blacks were elected to office, put forward programs to promote their own education and economic welfare, and played a decisive role in many electoral contests. In the North, prolabor third parties became prominent in numerous cities and towns, while political machines with large, foreign-born constituencies flexed their muscles in most urban centers. Labor organizations also formed periodic alliances with the major political parties, especially the Democrats, to promote prolabor legislative agendas.[2]

These changes, occurring with great speed, unfolding in scores of different ways in individual states and municipalities, spawned a significant reaction against democracy and universal suffrage in certain strata of American society. Southern white leaders came to believe, with good reason, that they could not control their region if the black population remained enfranchised.

Northern elites, as well as many middle-class, old-stock Americans, also feared that they would lose control of politics and state power to men who did not share their interests and values. "We have received," noted an unsigned article in the *Atlantic Monthly* in 1879,

> an almost unlimited immigration of adult foreigners, largely illiterate, of the lowest class and of other races. We have added at one stroke four millions and more of ignorant negroes to our voting population. . . . The result of such tremendous changes is that our system moves with increasing difficulty, and its faults become more conspicuous and more threatening.

As a consequence, a

> feeling of distrust and fear in regard to the holders of sovereign power . . . is manifesting itself more and more among the most intelligent classes of the community. No careful observer can have failed to notice the change of sentiment in this respect. . . . Thirty or forty years ago it was considered the rankest heresy to doubt that a government based on universal suffrage was the wisest and best that could be devised. . . . Such is not now the case. Expressions of doubt and distrust in regard to universal suffrage are heard constantly in conversation, and in all parts of the country.

Such views were indeed echoed "in all parts of the country." The buoyant optimism about popular participation, so visible in the 1830s and 1840s, gave way to apprehension and fear by the late 1870s and 1880s. The high tide of faith in democracy in the United States was reached at midcentury; thereafter it ebbed. In the words of the *Atlantic Monthly*, "the democratic principle . . . reached its culmination about 1850."[3]

The result was a long period, stretching into the second decade of the twentieth century, marked less by the exuberant forward march of democracy than by often mean-spirited battles and skirmishes over suffrage: while various social groups and political factions supporting them fought to broaden the franchise, others struggled, sometimes frantically and often with success, to block the road to the polls. These years did not, as they are commonly portrayed, witness an ongoing enlargement of democracy, marred only by the well-known and exceptional disfranchisement of southern blacks between 1890 and 1910; quite the contrary. The exceptional event, the aberration from prevailing patterns, was the temporary enfranchisement of African Americans under the extremely unusual conditions of

Reconstruction. The dominant trend of the era was toward a narrowing of the franchise: in many states, the years between 1855 and World War I constituted something of a slow Thermidor, a piecemeal rolling back of gains achieved in earlier decades.

Several distinct yet related stories unfolded during this period. One was the highly contentious effort to enfranchise—and then to disfranchise— blacks in the South in the decades that followed emancipation. Second was the battle for political rights that enveloped working-class men, many of them immigrants, in the North and the West. Third was the halting movement toward suffrage for women, a story with its own distinctive dynamics and—at the very end of this period—a happier conclusion. All of these stories included episodes of both enfranchisement and disfranchisement; all involved the intersection of class tensions with racial, ethnic, religious, gender, and cultural differences. Overall, the period witnessed a checkered tale of motion forward, backward, and sideways, of local peculiarities and surprises, of a rapidly changing, increasingly heterogenous society contending awkwardly with its own professed political values.

FOUR

Know-Nothings, Radicals, and Redeemers

*I*N JANUARY 1865, AS THE CIVIL WAR was drawing to a close, Andrew Tait and fifty-eight other African-American residents of Tennessee addressed a lengthy petition to a convention of pro-Union whites meeting in Nashville to discuss changes in the government of the state. They "most respectfully" asked for "a patient hearing of your honorable body in regard to matters deeply affecting the future condition of our unfortunate and long suffering race." Those "matters" were simply stated. The petitioners asked the convention "to complete the work begun by the nation at large, and abolish the last vestige of slavery," to "cut up by the roots the system of slavery, which is not only a wrong to us, but the source of all the evil which . . . afflicts the State." The petitioners requested a transformation of the judicial system, so that blacks could testify in court and be freed from the "malignant persecution" they suffered at the hands of angry Confederate rebels.[1]

Finally, they asked for citizenship and the right to vote. Acknowledging "that the negro suffrage proposition may shock popular prejudice at first sight," the petitioners observed that this was not "a conclusive argument against its wisdom." After all, popular opinion had maintained blacks could not be good soldiers, an assertion that had been amply disproven. Indeed, the heroic military service of blacks during the Civil War was a good reason to enfranchise them. "Nearly 200,000 of our brethren are to-day performing military duty in the ranks of the Union army," they pointed out. "Thousands of them have already died. . . . If we are called on to do military duty against the rebel enemies in the field, why should we be denied the privilege of voting . . . ? The latter is as necessary to save the Government as the former." Reaching to broader principles, the petitioners also noted that "this is a democracy—a government of the people." If men were "good law-abiding citizens . . . why deny them the right to have a voice in the election of its rulers?" In addition, "the most rich, intelligent, enlightened and prosperous" states, such as Massachusetts, had long permitted blacks to vote and had "never had reason to repent the day when she gave them" the franchise.[2]

Not surprisingly, the petition offered a plea as well as arguments: "How boundless would be the love of the colored citizen . . . how enthusiastic and how lasting would be his gratitude," Tait and his fellow residents wrote, "if his white brethren were to take him by the hand and say, 'You have been ever loyal to our government; henceforward be voters.'" Several weeks later, the Union convention voted in favor of a state constitutional amendment to abolish slavery—but it declined to act on the question of suffrage.[3]

Immigrants and Know-Nothings

The first targets of the nation's shifting political mood in the 1850s were working-class immigrants, especially those from Ireland. Although foreshadowed by the public debates of the 1840s, a full-blown nativist movement surfaced only during the following decade, precipitated by an extraordinary surge in immigration after 1845. Between that year and 1854, nearly 3 million foreigners arrived, equal to roughly 15 percent of the population in 1845; in 1854 alone, the flow reached a record high of 427,833, a figure that would not be surpassed until the 1870s. Most of these immigrants came from Ireland or Germany, with the Irish, in particular, remaining in the cities of the Northeast: by the mid-1850s, more than one fifth of all residents of Boston and New York were Irish-born.[4]

The immigrants who came to the United States during this period (and most other periods) were of two types. Some—to deploy categories developed by historian Dirk Hoerder—were "settlers" who typically intended to farm and buy land: usually farmers or artisans in their country of origin, they often brought enough capital with them to purchase a small amount of land or start a business. The second group consisted of "workers" who lacked capital or easily marketable skills and took jobs in manufacturing, transportation, and construction. The distinction between these two streams of immigrants was a significant one throughout American history, in part because natives tended to respond more positively to the more middle-class settlers than to workers.[5]

Indeed, in the 1850s, foreign-born settlers were not only welcomed to the United States but often encouraged to participate in politics. As noted in chapter 2, laws permitting declarant noncitizens to vote after a limited residence period were passed in Wisconsin, Minnesota, Michigan, Indiana, Oregon, Kansas, and Washington territory between 1848 and 1859. All of these states were predominantly agricultural, thinly populated, and hoping to encourage settlement: their immigrant populations, actual and prospective, consisted primarily of farmers. One delegate to the Indiana Constitutional Convention of 1850 supported the enfranchisement of noncitizens with the observation that most immigrants to the state were "upright, honorable, and industrious" Germans: "wherever they settle, though it were a desert . . . they soon make it blossom like a rose." Although there were always dissenters, state constitutional conventions commonly adopted alien suffrage laws by large and decisive majorities.[6]

Workers, however, were a different story. They were generally poor; they crowded into densely populated, often squalid urban neighborhoods; they were commonly depicted as rowdy rather than "upright, honorable, and industrious"; and most were Irish Catholic. Although their labor was welcome and there was substantial sympathy for the desperate poverty that had impelled them to emigrate, their religion, ethnicity, and class converged to cast doubt on their desirability as members of the polity. The upsurge of anti-immigrant sentiment in the 1850s, although often stated in more general terms, was rooted in antipathy to the unmistakably working-class Irish. Notably, the one state that abolished declarant suffrage during this period was Illinois, where a substantial Irish population already had appeared in Chicago.[7]

Those who objected to immigrant participation in politics cited several reasons. Some natives regarded recently arrived immigrants, even citizens, as insufficiently tutored in American values and the workings of American democracy; others feared that Catholics were controlled by the Pope and would seek to undermine Protestant society. Charges that immigrants corrupted elections by voting illegally and selling their votes were commonplace, as were stories of politically motivated mass naturalizations in the days before elections. (Bulk naturalizations shortly before elections certainly did occur, although it is not clear that they were illegal; the more general charges of corruption, according to recent historical research, were greatly exaggerated.) Whig and then Republican objections were strengthened by the tendency of many immigrants to drink alcohol and vote Democratic,

while abolitionists came to regard immigrants as a proslavery voting bloc
that would help to keep the planter aristocracy in power in the South.[8]

As noted earlier, such sentiments were translated into a variety of proposals in the 1840s, most of which were not passed by constitutional conventions or state legislatures.[9] Political nativism moved to the foreground of
the political stage, however, when the Know-Nothings burst onto the scene
in 1853–54. Originally a secret organization called the Order of the Star
Spangled Banner, the Know-Nothings went public in 1853, organized a
new political party, the American Party, and for a few years captured the
spotlight of American politics. The Know-Nothings dominated political
life in the Northeast, parts of the Midwest, and even southern states with
sizable immigrant populations, such as Louisiana and Maryland. Their so-
briquet arose from the order's instructions to members to refuse to tell non-
members anything about the order.[10]

By 1854, the Know-Nothings had a million members, as well as lodges
in all northern states. Their platforms and programs, which varied from
state to state, contained a strange and shifting mix of ingredients. On the
one hand, the Know-Nothings expressed disdain for the existing party system, opposed the extension of slavery, and endorsed a host of genuinely progressive reforms, including strengthened lien laws for mechanics, property
rights for married women, and an expansion of nonsectarian public schools.
At the same time, they gave voice to unvarnished ethnic and religious bigotry, denouncing and caricaturing immigrants in general, and Catholics in
particular. To join the Order of the Star Spangled Banner, one had to be a
native-born, white male adult, with no personal or familial connection to
Catholicism.[11]

Although the Know-Nothings' nativism was partially grounded in disapproval of the social behavior of immigrants (e.g., their alleged intemperance
and proclivity to crime), its core was political: they feared that immigrants,
especially Catholics, wielded too much electoral power and would use it to
subvert American values and institutions. To combat this threat, they proposed that federal laws be changed to require a twenty-one-year (rather
than five-year) waiting period prior to naturalization—or even permanent
denial of citizenship to the foreign-born. The Know-Nothings also advocated significant changes in state voting laws, including registration systems, literacy tests, and in the absence of a change in naturalization laws, a
twenty-one- or fourteen-year postnaturalization residence period before a
foreign-born male could vote. Recognizing that the nation benefited from
the labor of immigrants, the Know-Nothings never endorsed a suspension

of immigration. What they sought instead was to restrict the political rights of immigrants until they had been "nationalized" through prolonged immersion in the American way of life.[12]

The Know-Nothings stunned the nation's political elite by scoring huge electoral successes between 1854 and 1856. They won gubernatorial elections in nine states and controlled legislative branches in at least a half dozen; their vote was particularly strong in states and cities with sizable immigrant populations, including Massachusetts, Maine, Connecticut, New Jersey, New York, Michigan, and parts of Ohio, as well as cities such as Baltimore, New Orleans, and Pittsburgh. Supported by a fairly broad cross section of society, including many merchants, manufacturers, professionals, and native-born workers who saw immigrants as competitors for jobs, the Know-Nothings were victorious enough to kill off the faltering Whig party and briefly emerge as the primary alternative to the immigrant-friendly Democrats.[13]

In the wake of these successes, state legislatures and constitutional conventions in much of the North seriously considered imposing restrictions on immigrants who sought to vote. Know-Nothings, backed by some Whigs and later Republicans, sponsored legislation to repeal alien suffrage provisions, institute registration systems and literacy tests (from which taxpayers in certain cases would be exempted), require lengthy residence periods for the foreign-born, and prevent immigrants from voting for years after they were naturalized. Such laws were necessary, declared one Know-Nothing editor, because "Romanism" was "a Political as well as Religious system," and the "Irish rabble" in particular were herded to the polls by their priests. Most of these efforts, which had a partisan as well as nativist thrust, failed. In some states, the Democrats were strong enough to defeat restrictive legislation; in others, Whigs and Republicans helped to block the Native American program because they found it ideologically objectionable and feared losing the electoral support of German immigrants. Notably, states such as New Jersey and Indiana, with large German as well as Irish populations, rebuffed the nativist program. The Know-Nothings also were unable to alter federal naturalization laws.[14]

Yet the nativist movement did have some striking successes. In New York, in 1859, a coalition of Know-Nothings and Republicans passed a registry law designed to "purify" the ballot box; this purification was deemed necessarily only in New York City and New York County. A handful of states, including four in New England, accepted a Know-Nothing proposal to prohibit state judges from naturalizing immigrants: federal judges were preferred, because they were believed to be less inclined to tolerate politically driven mass naturalizations. Oregon, in 1857, dealt with its threatening immigrants, who were Chinese rather than Irish, by limiting the franchise to whites. The impulse even had success in those (generally urban) pockets of the South that had attracted immigrants: in 1860, for example, secessionist Georgia disfranchised propertyless whites, largely in response to the rapid growth of an Irish working-class population in Augusta and Savannah.[15]

Most important, the Know-Nothings and their allies succeeded in changing the substance of suffrage law in two industrial states with large Irish working-class populations, Massachusetts and Connecticut. Their success was most pronounced in Massachusetts, where the Know-Nothings elected a governor and won control of the legislature in 1854, retaining considerable power throughout the decade. Most Know-Nothing support came from the eastern half of the state, which was rapidly industrializing and home to hundreds of thousands of Irish immigrants. In 1857, Massachusetts passed a law requiring prospective voters to demonstrate their ability to read the Constitution and to write their own names: such laws, according to the Know-Nothings, would keep the "ignorant, imbruted Irish" from the polls. (Connecticut had passed similar legislation in 1855.) This law had a class as well as anti-immigrant edge, but its class effects were softened by a grandfather clause that exempted all citizens over sixty or who previously had voted. The Know-Nothing legislature also approved a postnaturalization waiting period of fourteen years, which failed to become law only because the complex mechanics of constitutional change required that any amendment be approved by a two-thirds majority in two successive legislatures. Two years later, however, the newly ascendant Republicans joined with the Know-Nothings to pass a compromise amendment, ratified by a large popular majority, imposing a two-year waiting period before naturalized citizens could vote. Massachusetts and Maine also passed laws requiring immigrants to present their naturalization papers to local officials three months before elections.[16]

After the mid-1850s, the Know-Nothings quickly disappeared from view, as nativism was eclipsed by sectional politics and the Republican Party gained the support of many former Know-Nothing backers. Although the Republicans succeeded in part by embracing some of the nativist agenda, they quickly turned their attention to other issues and were increasingly sensitive to the political risks they ran, particularly in the Midwest, by associating themselves too closely with anti-immigrant politics. As Edward L. Pierce, a Republican from Chicago, wrote in a letter published in Boston,

at the very moment that the character of foreign immigrants is vastly improving, when we are receiving those from Germany and Switzerland, who come
with understanding in their heads, instincts of freedom in their hearts and
money in their pockets, we should be . . . cautious lest . . . we do not also shut
out a great good and . . . convert our natural friends into unnatural enemies.

Abraham Lincoln, in response to a letter from German Americans about
the Massachusetts two-year amendment, declared that

I am against its adoption in Illinois, or in any other place, where I have a right
to oppose it. Understanding the spirit of our institutions to aim at the eleva-
tion of men, I am opposed to whatever tends to degrade them. I have some
little notoriety for commiserating with the oppressed condition of the negro;
and I should be strangely inconsistent if I could favor any project for curtail-
ing the existing rights of white men, even though born in different lands, and
speaking different languages from myself.

During the Civil War, Radical Republicans, prompted both by egalitarian
principles and electoral pragmatism, led a successful campaign to repeal the
two-year amendment in Massachusetts. Literacy tests remained in force,
however, both in the Bay State and in Connecticut, an enduring reminder
of the nation's first major skirmish in what would become a prolonged
struggle to restrict the political rights of foreign-born men who were flooding into the cities and workplaces of an increasingly industrial society.[17]

Race, War, and Reconstruction

The Civil War refocused the national debate about suffrage. Most obviously, four years of armed conflict, as well as the challenge of reconstructing
the nation after the war, brought the question of black voting rights to the
foreground of national politics. As important, the process of wrestling with
the issue of black enfranchisement raised critical questions, largely ignored
since the writing of the Constitution, about the role of the federal government in determining the breadth of the franchise. Although political leaders eventually drew back, they veered remarkably close to a profound
transformation of the principles shaping the size and composition of the
nation's electorate.

At the outset of the war, only five states, all in New England, permitted
blacks to vote on the same basis as whites; a sixth, New York, enfranchised

African Americans who met a property requirement. Not surprisingly, the Civil War unleashed new pressures to abolish racial discrimination. The abolition of slavery turned four million men and women into free citizens who had a new claim on political rights; African Americans were loyal supporters of the Union cause and the Republican Party; they also had fought and died to preserve the Union, in considerable numbers. Indeed, by 1865, the traditional argument that men who bore arms ought to wield the ballot was applicable to more than 180,000 blacks. As General William Tecumseh Sherman himself noted, "when the fight is over, the hand that drops the musket cannot be denied the ballot."[18]

Freedmen themselves, as well as northern blacks, asked for—and sometimes demanded—the right to vote: hardly had the war ended when freedmen throughout the South began to write petitions, hold meetings, and parade through the streets to press for an end to racial barriers to voting. In Wilmington, North Carolina, freedmen organized an Equal Rights League, demanding that blacks be granted "all the social and political rights" that whites possessed. In 1865, the highly politicized black community of New Orleans put together a widely participated-in mock election to demonstrate the strength of their resolve; in Maryland, blacks held conventions and marches to further their demands. Former soldiers, ministers, free blacks, and artisans all played prominent roles in this political activity, joined by thousands of others who insisted that suffrage was their right and their due. To African Americans, enfranchisement not only constituted a means of self-protection but was a critical symbol and expression of their standing in American society.[19]

Many northern whites agreed. Between 1864 and 1868, the more militant and egalitarian Radical wing of the Republican Party included an increasing number of men who embraced "impartial" or "universal" suffrage; intellectuals and ministers, as well as politicians, offered forceful and eloquent pleas for the egalitarian cause. As early as 1865, for example, New York's influential Protestant minister Henry Ward Beecher offered a multipronged argument for universal suffrage. "The broad and radical democratic doctrine of the natural rights of men," Beecher declared, "shall be applied to all men, without regard to race, or color, or condition." Suffrage "is not a privilege or a prerogative, but a right. Every man has a right to have a voice in the laws, the magistracies, and the policies that take care of him. That is an inherent right; it is not a privilege conferred." Beecher added a Christian layer to the argument by asserting that natural rights were God given, that "the negro" should vote "because he came from God, and goes to God again." Yet Beecher, like other advocates of black suffrage, went beyond the issue of rights. Even if one rejected the claim that suffrage was a right, he maintained, blacks had "earned" the franchise through their "heroic military service" and their "unswerving fidelity to the Union." Beecher also offered a cautionary argument that only rarely had been heard in antebellum debates about enfranchising the lower classes. Responding to those who insisted that it would be dangerous to enfranchise "ignorant" blacks, he maintained,

> it is far more dangerous to have a large under-class of ignorant and disfranchised men who are neither stimulated, educated, nor ennobled by the exercise of the vote . . . to have an ignorant class voting is dangerous, whether white or black; but to have an ignorant class and not have them voting, is a great deal more dangerous . . . the remedy for the unquestionable dangers of having ignorant voters lies in educating them by all the means in our power, and not in excluding them from their rights. . . . Nothing so much prepares men for intelligent suffrage as the exercise of the right of suffrage.[20]

Most white Americans, however, did not share such views. In the South, the prospect of black enfranchisement not only violated two centuries of structured and deeply rooted racism but also threatened the postwar white goal of regaining political, social, and economic control over the black population. More surprising was the ongoing hostility to African-American suffrage in the North: the racist beliefs common in the 1840s remained widespread after the Civil War, and fear of black migration to the North was intensified by emancipation. As a result, the cause of impartial suffrage suffered a damaging string of electoral defeats: between 1863 and 1870, proposals to enfranchise blacks were defeated in more than fifteen northern states and territories. Most of these decisions came in public referenda, and the vote rarely was close. Indeed, prior to the passage of the Fifteenth Amendment, only Iowa and Minnesota, in 1868, adopted impartial suffrage, and the Minnesota vote was facilitated by wording that masked the subject of the referendum. Although most northern Republicans supported black suffrage, Democrats adamantly were opposed, and they generally were joined by enough Republicans to guarantee popular or legislative defeat of any reforms. Notably, this partisan alignment contrasted sharply with the lineup on immigrant voting in the 1850s.[21]

Despite the breadth and intensity of opposition, however, the political dynamics of Reconstruction led to a pathbreaking series of steps by the federal government to override state control of the franchise and grant political rights to African-American men. At the center of these dynamics were conflicts that unfolded between Republicans in Congress and President Andrew Johnson and his (generally) Democratic supporters after the end of the Civil War. Johnson's approach to the task of Reconstruction, begun in 1865, was to offer lenient terms to southern states so that they could be restored quickly to the Union. Despite some early vengeful rhetoric, Johnson's program demanded few reforms and virtually guaranteed that political and economic power in the South would remain in the hands of whites, including those who had supported the rebellion. Alarmed at this prospect and at the resistance of many southern leaders to policies emanating from Washington, the Republican-controlled Congress began to formulate its own program in 1866. Although relatively few Republicans at that juncture advocated black enfranchisement, they did seek to guarantee the civil rights of blacks and promote greater racial equality in southern society.[22]

To further that end, the moderate majority of Republicans in Congress negotiated the passage of the Fourteenth Amendment in June 1866. A compromise measure, the amendment was designed to punish Confederate political leaders (by preventing them from holding office), to affirm the South's responsibility for a share of the national debt, and to protect southern blacks without arousing the racial fears of northern whites. Although denounced by some (but not all) Radical Republicans as too tepid, the amendment nonetheless altered the constitutional landscape. By declaring that "all persons born or naturalized in the United States" were "citizens of the United States and of the State wherein they reside," the amendment at long last offered a national definition of citizenship and confirmed that blacks were indeed citizens. The amendment also prohibited states from passing laws that would "abridge the privileges or immunities" of citizens or deny them "the equal protection of the laws."[23]

In its direct references to suffrage, the Fourteenth Amendment was a double-edged sword. Since most congressional Republicans—whatever their personal beliefs—were convinced that northern whites would not support the outright enfranchisement of blacks, the amendment took an oblique approach: any state that denied the right to vote to a portion of its male citizens would have its representation in Congress (and thus the electoral college) reduced in proportion to the percentage of citizens excluded. The clause would serve to penalize any southern state that prevented blacks from voting without imposing comparable sanctions on similar practices in the North, where blacks constituted a tiny percentage of the population. Although this section of the amendment amounted to a clear constitutional frown at racial discrimination, and Congress hoped that it would protect black voting rights in the South, the amendment, as critics pointed out, tacitly recognized the right of individual states to erect racial barriers. Wendell Phillips sharply attacked the amendment for this very reason, calling it a "fatal and total surrender." Of equal importance to many, the use of the word *male* constituted a de facto recognition of the legitimacy of excluding women from electoral politics.[24]

However tepid or double-edged the Fourteenth Amendment may have been, it was fiercely opposed by President Johnson, white Southerners, and northern Democrats who argued that it would create "mongrel" governments and was an intolerable intrusion of the federal government into an arena constitutionally reserved to the states. Both Johnson and the Democrats campaigned vigorously against ratification. Meanwhile, the state governments that Johnson had sponsored in the South legally codified various forms of racial discrimination while doing little to stop campaigns of violence against blacks and white Republicans who tried to vote or run for office. In New Orleans, one of the most flagrant incidents of violence left thirty-four blacks and four whites dead, with scores of others wounded, when they attempted to hold a convention favoring black suffrage. Deeply disturbed by such developments and emboldened by substantial electoral victories in the fall of 1866, congressional Republicans approached the issue more aggressively in the winter of 1866–67. To more and more Republicans, many of whom were changing their views in the cauldron of circumstance, black enfranchisement began to appear essential to protect the freedmen, provide the Republican Party with an electoral base in the South, and make it possible for loyal governments to be elected in the once-rebellious states.[25]

Congress first signaled its shift in perspective by passing a law ending racial qualifications for voting in the District of Columbia. Republicans, such as Charles Sumner of Massachusetts and Frederick Frelinghuysen of New Jersey, justified such action with potentially far-reaching arguments that echoed those of Reverend Beecher: the franchise was a right that belonged to all citizens, and black sacrifices on the battlefield had to be recognized and rewarded with enfranchisement. President Johnson vetoed the legislation, maintaining that it was wrong to enfranchise "a new class, wholly unprepared" for democracy "by previous habits and opportunities." Congress overrode the veto and weeks later passed a bill prohibiting racial bars in any existing or future federal territories. Going a step further, Congress then proceeded to insist that Nebraska and Colorado adopt impartial suffrage as a prerequisite for admission to statehood. Even some Republicans (as well as the president)

balked at this, insisting that Congress lacked the power to set voting requirements for new states. Radical Republicans, however, defended the unprecedented step by arguing both that new states were the creations of the federal
government and that imposing suffrage rules was sanctioned by article 4 of
the Constitution, which authorized the United States to "guarantee to every
state in this union a republican form of government." Sumner acknowledged
that the founding fathers had tolerated discrimination and that racial bars to
voting "may be 'republican' according to the imperfect notions of an earlier
period," but he insisted that in post–Civil War America impartial suffrage was
a necessary ingredient of republican government.[26]

   This surge of activity, fed by continued southern intransigence, culminated in the passage of the Reconstruction Act of March 1867. The act, the
legal centerpiece of Radical Reconstruction, denied recognition to the existing state governments of the South and authorized continued military
rule of the region under the control of Congress. In order to terminate such
rule and be fully readmitted to the Union, each southern state was required
to ratify the Fourteenth Amendment and to approve, by manhood suffrage,
a state constitution that permitted blacks to vote on the same terms as
whites. President Johnson vetoed the bill, but his veto was quickly overridden. To rejoin the political nation, the states of the Confederacy were now
compelled to permit blacks to vote.[27]

   Under the protective umbrella of the Reconstruction Act, politics in the
South were transformed. In 1867 and 1868, African Americans, working
with white Unionists and Republicans—most of whom came from poor or
modest circumstances—elected new state governments, wrote progressive
constitutions that included manhood suffrage provisions, and ratified the
Fourteenth Amendment; black enthusiasm for political participation was
so great that freedmen often put down their tools and ceased working
when elections or conventions were being held. (The progressive nature of
these constitutions is evident in the details of the suffrage laws—on issues
ranging from taxpaying qualifications to residency—contained in tables
A.10 to A.15.) By June 1868, seven states, with manhood suffrage, had
been readmitted to the Union, and the process was well under way elsewhere. All this was achieved despite fierce opposition from upper-class
whites, who feared that a biracial alliance of blacks and nonelite whites
would superintend the erection of a new and inhospitable economic and
political order. The intensity of white hostility was manifested in a petition
that conservatives in Alabama sent to Congress, denouncing the enfranchisement of "negroes,"

in the main, ignorant generally, wholly unacquainted with the principles of free Governments, improvident, disinclined to work, credulous yet suspicious, dishonest, untruthful, incapable of self-restraint, and easily impelled . . . into folly and crime . . . how can it be otherwise than that they will bring, to the great injury of themselves as well as of us and our children, blight, crime, ruin and barbarism on this fair land? . . . do not, we implore you, abdicate your own rule over us, by transferring us to the blighting, brutalizing and unnatural dominion of an alien and inferior race.

Nor was southern opposition purely rhetorical: antiblack and anti-Republican violence flared up throughout the region, often spearheaded by the rapidly growing Ku Klux Klan.[28]

Republican achievements in the South, however, were accompanied by a succession of electoral defeats in the North. Not only were impartial suffrage referenda defeated in a handful of states, but the Republicans suffered sharp losses in the elections of 1867. The Democrats gained ground from the Atlantic to the Pacific, winning in New York and California and electing mayors in three of the largest cities in Ohio. Interpreted by both parties as the consequence of Republican support for black suffrage, this electoral swing led the Republicans to seek more moderate ground—in part out of fear that they could lose the 1868 presidential election and thereby bring a premature end to Reconstruction. Accordingly, the party nominated the uncontroversial General Ulysses Grant for the presidency and adopted a platform that supported black suffrage for the South while advocating state control of electoral rules in the North. Despite this tilt toward moderation, the Republicans did not fare well in the 1868 elections: although Grant was victorious, the winning margin was surprisingly slim, and the Democrats continued to gain ground in Republican strongholds.[29]

The Strange Odyssey of the Fifteenth Amendment

Within days of the 1868 election, the Republicans shifted course, as Radicals, in and out of Congress, announced that they would press forward with a constitutional amendment to enfranchise African Americans. The elections had created a quandary for supporters of impartial suffrage. On the one hand, the decline in support for the Republican Party, as well as the referenda outcomes in 1867 and 1868, underscored the strength and breadth of opposition to black enfranchisement. On the other hand, Republicans sensed that control of the national government might be slipping from their grasp, that white Southerners were intensifying their opposition to black equality, and that something had to be done soon to guarantee black political rights, particularly in the event that the Democrats returned to power in the South or nationally.

Election results also indicated that black voters might be important to the fortunes of the Republican Party in northern as well as southern states. As Senator Charles Sumner declared to his fellow Republicans,

> You need votes in Connecticut, do you not? There are three thousand fellow-citizens in that state ready at the call of Congress to take their place at the ballot box. You need them also in Pennsylvania, do you not? There are at least fifteen thousand in that great state waiting for your summons . . . be assured they will all vote for those who stand by them in the assertion of Equal Rights.

In addition to such pragmatic considerations, many Republicans were uncomfortable with the glaring inconsistencies in the party's posture toward black suffrage in the North and in the South. A constitutional amendment, then, had several perceived virtues: it would end the party's hypocrisy, benefit its candidates, and firmly cement the political rights and power of blacks in the South. Moreover, as a federal amendment, rather than an act of Congress, it could avoid constitutional adjudication in the courts and would be easier to enact than a long series of state constitutional referenda: once it left Congress, an amendment would be subject to ratification only by state legislatures, most of which were in the hands of Republicans.[30]

What ensued was a prolonged debate in January and February 1869, about the contents and passage of a suffrage amendment. The debate, unfolding in a Republican-controlled Congress, was dramatic and extraordinary: members of Congress were well aware that the subject was momentous and that it marked the first time since the constitutional convention in Philadelphia that the national government of the United States had grappled directly and extensively with the issue of voting rights. Both chambers of Congress echoed with eloquent speeches, deeply felt idealism, and carefully nuanced historical and theoretical arguments—as well as intense political maneuvering and sharp rivalry between the two houses. The debate began with a strategic focus on the rights of African Americans, particularly in the South, but it soon broadened into a far-reaching consideration of the meaning of democracy and the power of the national government. For several months, the outcome was very much in doubt.

The first version of the amendment to be placed on the table was authored by Representative George S. Boutwell, an influential Massachusetts Republican who had long been a defender of black rights. The amendment stated simply that "the right of any citizen of the United States to vote shall not be denied or abridged by the United States or any State by reason of race, color, or previous condition of slavery of any citizens or class of citizens of the United States." Criticism of Boutwell's draft came from two directions. Democrats and a few conservative Republicans opposed such an amendment because they did not believe blacks were qualified to vote and because they regarded the amendment as an infringement of states' rights; they cited the Federalist papers and the debates in Philadelphia as proof that the wisdom of the founding fathers was being fatally ignored. At the same time, some Radicals wanted a more sweeping and comprehensive amendment, such as the one proposed by Ohio Republican Samuel Shellabarger. Shellabarger's amendment prohibited the states from denying or abridging the voting rights of any adult male of "sound mind," except those who had engaged in rebellion against the United States or committed other "infamous" crimes. Although Shellabarger's version, like Boutwell's, was phrased negatively—it did not actively confer suffrage but rather prevented states from denying suffrage—it implicitly would have ended not only racial discrimination but also property, tax, nativity, and literacy requirements. In so doing, this version of the amendment would have taken a giant step toward a nationally mandated and nationally uniform suffrage. Shellabarger's amendment was rejected decisively by the House; Boutwell's then was passed by a large and partisan majority.[31]

In the Senate, a draft very similar to Boutwell's was introduced by moderate Republican Senator William M. Stewart of Nevada. Although Democrats opposed the amendment, they had only twelve votes in the Senate, and early in the deliberations it was clear that debate would center on the choice between a narrow amendment such as Stewart's or broader language that would ban various kinds of discrimination in voting and office holding. A proposal embodying the second approach was put forward by Massachusetts Senator Henry Wilson, a shoemaker by trade, a longtime foe of slavery, and later vice president of the United States. Wilson's amendment prohibited discrimination "among the citizens of the United States in the exercise of the elective franchise or in the right to hold office in any State on account of race, color, nativity, property, education or creed." This version avoided some of the criticism leveled at Shellabarger's by tacitly permitting suffrage qualifications based on age and residence.[32]

Wilson and his allies, many from the Midwest, mounted a powerful array of arguments in favor of a broadly phrased amendment. They voiced a prescient fear (as had Shellabarger) that an amendment such as Stewart's or Boutwell's would end up being circumvented by southern states that could disfranchise blacks through literacy, tax, or property requirements. In addition, Wilson maintained shrewdly that his proposal might have the best chance of being ratified by the states, because it effectively would enfranchise everyone (including many immigrant supporters of the Democrats) and not appear to be granting special privileges to African Americans. At the heart of the argument, however, were beliefs and principles, some long held, some shaped by the tumultuous events of the previous decade. Wilson himself had been a Know-Nothing and an opportunistic nativist whose views had changed in the course of the war and the early years of Reconstruction. Wilson insisted that he supported an amendment, despite the unpopularity of black suffrage, because "it is right, absolutely right"— and there is little reason under the circumstances to doubt his sincerity. Wilson also pointed out that broadening the amendment to erase all discrimination (other than by age, residence, and gender) was a logical outgrowth of the reasoning that sanctioned the enfranchisement of blacks. A broad amendment would institutionalize the very principles the nation claimed to embody:

> Let us give to all citizens equal rights, and then protect everybody in the United States in the exercise of those rights. When we attain that position we shall have carried out logically the ideas that lie at the foundation of our institutions; we shall be in harmony with our professions; we shall have acted like a truly republican and Christian people. Until we do that we are in a false position, an illogical position—a position that cannot be defended; a position that I believe is dishonorable to the nation with the lights we have before us.

Senator John Sherman of Ohio, acknowledging that his own views had shifted over time, echoed Wilson's words, recognizing the uniqueness of the historical moment while looking to the future of the nation and the Republican Party.

> I believe that since we are compelled by our position to adopt an amendment to the Constitution of the United States, since public opinion requires it, since the necessity for protecting four millions of freed people in the southern States compels us to treat with this question, we ought to deal with it

with all the lights of our modern civilization, with all the lights of our modern constitutions, and plant our work upon the solid basis of impartial, and you may say, universal suffrage.

It seems to me, as the Republican party are about to lay the foundation for a political creed, that the broadest and safest and best foundation for it is universal suffrage.[33]

Other supporters pointed to more specific benefits that would result from ending nearly all barriers to voting. Simon Cameron of Pennsylvania, with the Know-Nothing agitation clearly in mind, favored Wilson's amendment "because it invites into our country everybody; the negro, the Irishman, the German, the Frenchman, the Scotchman, the Englishman, and the Chinaman. I will welcome every man, whatever may be the country from which he comes, who by his industry can add to our national wealth." Senator Oliver P. Morton of Indiana also viewed a broad amendment "as a safeguard against any future Know-Nothing excitements." In addition, Morton explicitly invoked the language of natural rights to attack property and literacy qualifications for voting.

I think there is no more principle, there is no more justice in requiring a man to have a certain amount of property before he shall be allowed to exercise this right that is indispensable to the protection of his life, liberty, and happiness than there is in requiring him to have a white skin. If the right of suffrage is a natural right, if it belongs to all men because they have a right to have a voice in the Government that controls their action . . . how can you make it depend upon property?

He continued:

The same may be said in regard to educational tests. I believe all educational tests in this country are humbugs. . . . When you come to consider the question of voting as a natural right, what right have you to take it from a man because he cannot read and write? . . . He has his rights to defend and preserve just like other men, and the right of suffrage is just as important to him as it is to anybody else.

Morton also argued that an amendment dealing exclusively with race would imply that the federal government sanctioned other restrictions on voting. Such an amendment would say to the states:

"While you shall not disfranchise a man on account of color, you may disfranchise him because he has not got property." Are we willing to place ourselves as a Senate, and are my Republican friends willing to place themselves
a party, before the country on that ground?

   In regard to nativity . . . we say to the States, "You cannot exclude men because of their color, but you are still left at liberty to exclude them because of
their nativity." Are we prepared to say that? I am aware that the question of
colored suffrage has brought the subject before Congress; but, now that it is
here, we are bound . . . to consider and to guard against all the abuses that
may arise upon that subject.[34]

Morton and his fellow advocates of the Wilson amendment were, in effect, turning the tables on those critics of suffrage expansion, going back to
John Adams, who had long claimed that "rights" arguments in behalf of
any particular suffrage extension opened up a Pandora's box—because the
same arguments could justify anyone's enfranchisement. Morton and Wilson acknowledged that enfranchising blacks on the grounds that voting
was a right or natural right carried the implication that all adult male citizens should be enfranchised. Unlike most of their predecessors, however,
they embraced rather than dodged that implication: to be consistent and to
set the matter to rest, once and for all, the franchise indeed should be further extended rather than limited. To be sure, most Republicans—even
most Radical Republicans—remained reluctant to let women out of the
Pandora's box, but these advocates of a broad constitutional amendment
nonetheless were staking out new ground in public debate for the cause of
universal suffrage.

   The Wilson amendment did not go unchallenged. Vehement criticism of
the proposal came from several different quarters. Many Senate Democrats
remained hostile to black suffrage (and thus to any amendment) on substantive grounds. James Doolittle of Wisconsin maintained that African
Americans were "incompetent to vote" and that Congress should not try to
"enforce this unnatural equality." James Bayard of Delaware voiced at great
length the fear that conferring "political power on an inferior race" would
lead both to racial conflict and the destructive commingling of "the negro
and the Caucasian." Blacks, according to Bayard, were "more animal" and
"indolent" than whites, and any "crossing" of the two races would lead to a
degeneration of the "moral nature" and life expectancy of their offspring.
That the Wilson amendment sanctioned black office holding, as well as suffrage, only intensified the opposition.[35]

Some moderate Republicans also objected to the office-holding provisions, while others opposed the Wilson amendment precisely because it would eliminate a range of barriers to the franchise. Senators from the West were apprehensive that it would enfranchise the Chinese. Several northeastern Republicans wanted states to retain the power to circumscribe the voting rights of immigrants. Roscoe Conkling of New York, a powerful figure in the Senate, maintained that municipalities and states ought to be able to impose property requirements in elections dealing with taxes and financial matters. As two bellwethers of Republican opinion, the *New York Times* and the *Nation*, pointed out, many Republicans in fact favored literacy or educational tests and saw no reason to jettison them with a constitutional amendment. For all of these reasons, key Republicans, such as Stewart, insisted that the Wilson amendment would have no chance of being ratified and that protecting the rights of blacks in the South depended on congressional passage of a narrowly constructed amendment.[36]

The most frequently voiced reason for opposing the Wilson amendment was not that it would empower an "inferior" people but rather that it would produce a "radical and revolutionary" transformation of the relationship between the federal government and the states. As Senator James Dixon of Connecticut pointed out, at issue was not simply who voted but "who shall create . . . the voter." The Wilson amendment would vest that power in the federal government and in so doing alter the Constitution while undermining the autonomy and authority of the states. Wilson and other Radicals replied that the "republican guarantee" clause of article 4 already gave the federal government the power to regulate the franchise. Nonetheless, the *New York Times*, which endorsed the House version of the amendment, claimed that Wilson's proposal "travels over new ground, dictates terms for which the country is not prepared, and goes far toward extinguishing the vital forces of State authority." Democrats, of course, were broadly committed to preserving the power of the states, but even moderate Republicans, in the Senate and the House, worried that the Wilson amendment would upset the balance of state and federal authority enshrined in the Constitution. To be sure, such arguments offered critics of the amendment a convenient, apparently principled means of opposing franchise extension without sounding undemocratic or racist, but they also reflected a (probably unrealistic) desire to shore up federalism in an era when the exigencies of war and the economic program of the Republican Party were shifting power toward Washington.[37]

Congressional debate about the breadth of the Fifteenth Amendment unfolded in the course of a byzantine legislative process. After several weeks of discussion, the Senate first rejected the Wilson amendment and then, shortly later, approved a slightly revised version. The Senate's resolution was rejected overwhelmingly by the House, which asked for a conference committee to resolve the differences between the House and Senate versions. The Senate declined a conference and instead passed a narrower variant of the amendment, similar to Stewart's original draft. In response, the House, led by Representative John Bingham of Ohio, darted in the opposite direction: it approved language very close to that of the Wilson amendment, leaving out only the ban on education or literacy tests. The reasons for the House's change of direction are unclear, but its new proposal was supported by some Democrats who may have been hoping to kill the amendment altogether by making it unacceptably broad. Faced with a second round of conflict between the two chambers, the congressional leadership then appointed a conference committee that included Boutwell, Conkling, and Stewart among its members.[38]

The conference committee startled everyone, particularly Wilson and his supporters, by agreeing on a draft very close to Boutwell's and Stewart's original propositions: a narrow amendment that made no mention of office-holding or suffrage issues other than race. The committee was roundly denounced for having exceeded its authority and betrayed the Republican cause: instead of shaving the differences between the two chambers (the customary charge of conference committees), it had come forth with language far narrower in scope than each had already approved. One member of the conference committee, Senator George Edmunds of Vermont, shared this outrage and refused to sign the committee's report.

Yet time was becoming short. Congress would remain in session for only a few days longer, and procedural rules demanded that conference reports be voted up or down, without substantive amendments. There was too little time to thrash out a new text, and there were risks in holding the matter over until the next congress. Faced, thus, with a choice between a narrowly phrased amendment and the possibility of no amendment at all, advocates of broad-gauged democratization surrendered. Wilson declared that he would vote reluctantly for the "lame and halting" conference report because "at this late hour" it was "the best I can get." Morton, still fuming at the conference committee, announced he would take "half a loaf when I cannot get a whole one; but nevertheless I want to say that it is pretty hard to accept the half loaf when a whole one or almost a whole one has been offered." With several disheartened senators, including Edmunds and Sumner, declining to vote at all, on February 26, 1869, Congress passed the Fifteenth Amendment. It read simply:

The right of citizens of the United States to vote shall not be denied or abridged by the United States or by any State on account of race, color, or previous condition of servitude—

The Congress shall have power to enforce this article by appropriate legislation.[39]

That the Wilson amendment (or some variant thereof) came so close to passage is a remarkable fact, testifying to the ways in which the Civil War and Reconstruction invigorated and extended (in some quarters, at least) the democratic convictions that had flourished at midcentury. The extraordinary circumstances surrounding the war propelled many Americans to support black suffrage, and as happened periodically in American history, contending with the issue of race provoked new thinking about democratic rights in general. By the late 1860s, large segments of the nation's citizenry and political leadership were prepared to embrace universal male suffrage, and some men were even ready to endorse women's suffrage (see chapter 6). Such views, held primarily by Republicans, certainly were consistent with the party's "free labor" ideology and its vision of a nation populated by autonomous, independent citizens. Nonetheless, the embrace of universal male suffrage was notable, given the Republican Party's all-too-recent association with nativism and the Know-Nothings, as well as its links to a Whig Party that often had opposed extensions of the franchise. As had been true during the era of the American Revolution, people were changing their minds, and ideologies were being retailored. It was fitting that Henry Wilson, a self-educated shoemaker, first elected to the Senate by a Know-Nothing legislature and known more as a practical politician than an ideologue, became the late 1860s standard bearer of universal suffrage.

Why Congress failed to pass a broader version of the Fifteenth Amendment is a question that might well take a book to answer satisfactorily. Yet even without a detailed study of the maneuvering, politicking, and happenstance that must have been present behind the scenes, certain things seem clear. One is that the narrow version of the Fifteenth Amendment probably represented the center point of American politics, the consensus view even within the Republican Party. Most Republicans—and most Americans—did not travel the same ideological road as Henry Wilson and Oliver Morton. They accepted black suffrage but were not prepared to let loose the other inhabitants of the Pandora's box. As the *New York Times* noted approvingly, the changes in suffrage law "have sprung not from any conviction of injustice or unfairness . . . but from the new emergencies created in the progress and by the results of the civil war." Indeed, the debates in Congress revealed the limits, the jagged edges, of democratic thought and political practice among Republicans as well as Democrats. The primary hindrances to further democratization were concerns about ethnicity and class (as well as sex) that had been so prominent in the 1850s and that still shaped the thinking of many political leaders. What opponents of a broad amendment rejected in the end was the abolition of discrimination based on nativity, religion, property, and education. They wanted to retain the power to limit the political participation of the Irish and Chinese, Native Americans, and the increasingly visible clusters of illiterate and semiliterate workers massing in the nation's cities. As Henry Adams astutely observed, the Fifteenth Amendment was "more remarkable for what it does not than for what it does contain."[40]

Ethnic and class issues remained prominent during the ratification process. On the West Coast, especially in California, opposition to the Fifteenth Amendment was fueled by the anti-Chinese furor that would sour the region's politics for decades: whites, including many working-class whites, feared that the amendment would enfranchise the Chinese, encourage further Chinese immigration, and lower the wages and living standards of white workers. (That the Chinese could not become citizens in the late 1860s did little to extinguish such fears.) Consequently, state legislatures in the western states (excepting Nevada) refused to ratify the amendment—despite the tiny African-American presence in the region.[41]

An even more baroque drama was played out in Rhode Island. The state's Republican middle class was divided over the amendment owing to a widely bruited-about claim that the Irish could be considered a race and that the Commonwealth's property qualification for the foreign-born therefore would be construed as racial discrimination. The Democrats also were split, with one faction ready to override the national party's opposition to the amendment in the hope that it might indeed enfranchise propertyless immigrant workers. In the end, Rhode Island did ratify the amendment, but only in 1870, long after other New England states had acted and only when it appeared that the state's vote might be critical to passage. What made this political conflict particularly curious—and revealing of the complex linkages between class and race—was the fact that blacks had been enfranchised in Rhode Island since the 1840s.[42]

For these reasons, among others, ratification did not appear to be a sure thing. Although the moment was as propitious as it ever would be (Republicans controlled most state legislatures and President Grant actively sup-

ported the measure), opposition to the amendment was widespread and intense; it was passed easily only in New England, where blacks already voted,
and in the South, where the federal government had already intervened to
compel black enfranchisement. (Ratification of the amendment was made a
condition for readmission to the Union for four southern states.) Elsewhere,
battles over ratification were closely fought and heavily partisan. Democrats
argued that the amendment violated states' rights, debased democracy by enfranchising an "illiterate and inferior" people, and promised to spawn an un-
holy (and contradictory) mixture of intermarriage and race war. Republican
legislators replied that black men had earned the franchise through their
heroism as soldiers and that the amendment was needed to finally put the
issue of black rights to rest; given the narrow boundaries of the amendment,
they often avoided claiming suffrage as a universal right. What neither party
mentioned much was that partisan interests were at stake, particularly in the
border, midwestern, and mid-Atlantic states, where the black population
could boost the fortunes of the Republicans. In the end, most of these close
contests were won by the Republicans, and the Fifteenth Amendment became part of the Constitution in February 1870.[43]

African Americans jubilantly celebrated the amendment's ratification.
Thousands of black voters, including military veterans with their wives and
children, marched in triumphant parades throughout the country. Frederick
Douglass, speaking in Albany in late April, declared that the amendment
"means that we are placed upon an equal footing with all other men ... that
liberty is to be the right of all." Longtime abolitionists such as William
Lloyd Garrison and Wendell Phillips were no less enthusiastic: the amendment, according to Phillips, was "the grandest and most Christian act ever
contemplated or accomplished by any Nation." Among less engaged and activist citizens, feelings were more muted, evoking the satisfied but fatigued
sentiment that the *New York Times* had voiced in March 1869. "The adoption of this amendment will put an end to further agitation of the subject,"
editorialized the *Times*, "and thus leave the Government of the country free
to deal with its material interests and with ... more pressing questions." As
Congressman and later President James Garfield noted, now that they were
enfranchised, "the fortunes" of African Americans were "in their own
hands."[44]

The Fifteenth Amendment was certainly a landmark in the history of the
right to vote. Spurred by pressure from blacks, deeply felt ideological convictions, partisan competition, and extraordinary conditions created by an in-
ternecine war, the federal government enfranchised more than a million men

who only a decade earlier had been slaves. Moving with a speed reflecting rapidly shifting circumstances, Congress and state legislatures had created laws that would have been unthinkable in 1860 or even 1865. In the Fourteenth and Fifteenth Amendments, the words *right to vote* were penned into the nation's Constitution for the first time, announcing a new, active role for the federal government in defining democracy. Yet momentous as these achievements may have been, the limitations of the Fifteenth Amendment were, as Henry Adams pointed out, as significant as its contents: the celebrations of the black community would soon prove to be premature, and the unresolved tension between federal and state authorities would vibrate for another century. Contrary to the optimistic conclusion of the *New York Times*, the nation had not finished with the issue of black suffrage.

The Lesser Effects of War

The Civil War also had an impact on other suffrage-related matters. One unusual, but not surprising, consequence was the appearance of a new qualification: loyalty. Both the federal Reconstruction Act and the constitutions adopted by Reconstruction governments in a half dozen southern states disfranchised prominent Confederates because of their role in the rebellion. Although more draconian provisions were considered—in 1868 one angry Virginia conservative complained that the draft constitution ought to read "no white man shall vote"—these punitive measures ended up affecting only a few thousand men, usually temporarily.[45]

Other consequences of the war cut in the opposite direction, toward expansion of the franchise. For the first time, states were obliged to contend head-on with the issue of absentee voting: reluctant to deny the franchise to men who were bearing arms to defend the Union, nineteen states enacted laws enabling soldiers in the field to vote. In so doing, they established a precedent for loosening the links between residence and participation in elections. The experience of war also led to the enfranchisement of some military veterans who failed to meet existing qualifications: Massachusetts, for example, voted to exempt ex-soldiers from the pauper exclusion in its constitution.[46]

Similarly, declarant aliens, many of whom were serving or had served in the army, were enfranchised in ten states or federal territories in the 1860s. The war, however, attached new strings to noncitizen voting. After a series of contested legal actions in the states, Congress specified in 1863 that aliens who had declared their intention to become citizens were subject to the military draft. A short while later, President Lincoln signed a proclamation offering declarant aliens the choice of becoming eligible for the draft or renouncing their intention to become citizens and leaving the country within sixty-five days. An exception was made for declarants who had already voted: they were not given the option of renunciation and were immediately vulnerable to the draft. The path connecting military service to voting had begun to carry traffic in both directions.[47]

The South Redeemed

> I cannot do justice to my own feelings without . . . commenting upon . . . that great fifteenth amendment . . . the hearts of the Virginia people have never approved it, and true Virginians can never approve it. We do not believe that the colored man is the equal of the white man, and that is what the fifteenth amendment means.
>
> I wish to put myself on record here as being opposed to what is known as manhood suffrage. I believe that the greatest mistake that any people ever made was made when the Convention of 1850 adopted manhood suffrage. I believe that the right to vote, as it is generally conceived by some ignorant politicians, is not a right but a privilege.
>
> —R. L. GORDON, CONSTITUTIONAL
> CONVENTION OF VIRGINIA, 1901–2

Even before Reconstruction came to a quasi-formal end in 1877, black voting rights were under attack. Elections were hotly contested, and white Southerners, seeking to "redeem" the region from Republican rule, engaged in both legal and extralegal efforts to limit the political influence of freedmen. In the early 1870s, both in the South and in the border states, districts were gerrymandered (i.e., reshaped for partisan reasons), precincts reorganized, and polling places closed to hinder black political participation. Georgia, Tennessee, and Virginia reinstituted financial requirements for voting, while local officials often made it difficult for freedmen to pay their taxes so that they could vote.[48]

Far more dramatic was a wave of what historian Eric Foner has called "counterrevolutionary terror" that swept the South between 1868 and 1871. Acting as the military, or paramilitary, arm of the Democratic Party, organizations such as the Ku Klux Klan mounted violent campaigns against blacks who sought to vote or hold office, as well as their white Republican allies. In 1870 alone, hundreds of freedmen were killed, and many more badly hurt, by politicized vigilante violence. Although the Klan was never highly centralized and actions generally were initiated by local chapters, its presence was felt throughout the region. Whites of all classes (but not all whites) supported the Klan, its leadership often drawn from the more "respectable" elements of society; support was so widespread that Republican state governments, as well as local officials, commonly found it impossible to contain the violence or convict offenders in court.[49]

The national government did not stand by idly. In May 1870, stretching the limits of its constitutional powers, Congress passed an Enforcement Act that made interference with voting a federal offense, punishable in federal courts—which presumably were more reliable than state courts. This first enforcement act was followed by others, including the Ku Klux Klan Act, which, among its provisions, authorized the president to deploy the army to protect the electoral process. These acts, pioneering efforts to enforce the Fourteenth and Fifteenth Amendments with federal machinery, gave enough support to sympathetic state and local officials to produce crackdowns on the Klan and similar organizations. As a result, violence declined in 1872. A few years later, however, the incidence of violence rose sharply again, and this time the federal government responded less forcefully. By the mid-1870s, many northern Republicans, including President Grant, had lost their enthusiasm for policing the South; preoccupied with an economic depression and labor conflict in the North, they wearily drifted toward a "let alone policy." In September 1875, one Republican newspaper referred to the Fourteenth and Fifteenth Amendments as "dead letters."[50]

The Redeemers who were gaining power throughout the South in the 1870s had goals that were at once political, social, and economic. Most immediately they sought to drive the Republicans from power and elect Democrats, an objective hard to attain in a fully enfranchised South. Limiting black voting therefore was a means to a precise end; but it was more than that. Keeping freedmen from the polls was also a means of rebuffing broader claims to equality, a way of returning blacks to "their place," of making clear that, whatever the Fourteenth Amendment said, blacks did not enjoy full citizenship.

There were important class dimensions to this political and racial agenda. Freedmen not only were men of a different race, they also constituted the primary labor supply of the agricultural South. Emancipation and Reconstruction threatened white control over needed black labor, and white landowners and merchants sought both to halt the erosion of labor discipline and to utilize the state to enforce their dominance. It was no accident that the Klan targeted economically successful blacks or that it tried to keep freedmen from owning land. When Redeemer governments came to power, they commonly passed draconian vagrancy laws (subjecting anyone without a job to possible arrest) as well as legislation prohibiting workers from quitting their jobs before their contracts expired. The Redeemers also enacted laws that harshly punished petty theft, gave landlords complete control of crops grown by tenants, and reduced the proportion of tax revenues that went to education and social improvements. The resistance to black voting was rooted in class conflict as well as racial antagonism.[51]

The pace of Redemption was quickened by the presidential election of 1876 and the subsequent removal of the last federal troops from the South. At roughly the same time, the Supreme Court (in *U.S. v. Cruikshank* and *U.S. v. Reese*) challenged key provisions of the enforcement acts, largely on the grounds that the acts were too vaguely worded and too loosely tied to race to be enforceable under the Fifteenth Amendment. In 1878, moreover, Democrats won control of both houses of Congress for the first time in twenty years. The upshot of these events—which reflected the North's growing fatigue with the issue of black rights—was to entrust the administration of voting laws in the South to state and local governments. Between 1878 and 1890, the average number of federal prosecutions launched annually under the enforcement acts fell below 100; in 1873 alone there had been more than 1,000.[52]

In the Deep South, the Republican Party crumbled under the onslaught of Redemption, but elsewhere the party hung on, and large, if declining, numbers of blacks continued to exercise the franchise. Periodically they were able to form alliances with poor and upcountry whites and even with some newly emerging industrial interests sympathetic to the probusiness policies of the Republicans. Opposition to the conservative, planter-dominated Redeemer Democrats, therefore, did not disappear: elections were contested by Republicans, by factions within the Democratic Party, and eventually by the Farmers' Alliance and the Populists. Consequently, the Redeemers, who controlled most state legislatures, continued to try to shrink the black (and opposition white) electorate through gerrymandering, registration systems, complicated ballot configurations, and the secret ballot (which served as a de facto literacy test). When necessary, they also resorted to violence and fraudulent vote counts. In 1883, a black man in Georgia testified to a Senate committee that "we are in a majority here, but you may vote till your eyes drop out or your tongue drops out, and you can't count your colored man in out of them boxes; there's a hole gets in the bottom of the boxes some way and lets out our votes."[53]

This period of limbo and contestation, of participation coexisting with efforts at exclusion, started coming to an end in 1890. One key ingredient in the shift was Congress's failure to pass the Federal Elections Bill, commonly known as the Lodge Force Bill. The bill had its origins both in Republican outrage about the conduct of elections in the South and in national partisan politics. National elections were extremely close and fiercely contested in the late 1870s and 1880s; congressional majorities were unstable; and in 1884 Grover Cleveland became the first Democratic president since before the Civil War. In the eyes of many Republicans, the Democrats' success, their ability to wield national power, was illegitimate, dependent on wholesale violations of the Fifteenth Amendment in the South. In its 1888 platform, the Republicans charged—and many Republicans believed— "that the present Administration and the Democratic majority owe their existence to the suppression of the ballot by a criminal nullification of the Constitution and laws of the United States." After that year's elections, the Republicans had a chance to do something about it: they had won the presidency and control of both houses of Congress.[54]

With the support of President Benjamin Harrison, congressional Republicans, led by two Massachusetts leaders, George Frisbie Hoar in the Senate and Henry Cabot Lodge in the House, drafted legislation to expand and strengthen the enforcement acts of the 1870s. Although the Supreme Court in the mid-1880s had shifted course and upheld several provisions of these acts, Republicans were convinced that stronger medicine was needed—both to end suppression of the black vote in the South and eliminate the growing problem of fraud in congressional elections throughout the nation. The bill that they drafted, the Federal Elections Bill, was ostensibly nonpartisan and nonsectional in its goals: it authorized federal circuit courts, on petition of a small number of citizens from any district, to appoint federal supervisors of congressional elections. These supervisors were entrusted with a raft of responsibilities, including attending elections, inspecting registration lists, verifying information given by doubtful voters, administering oaths to challenged voters, preventing illegal immigrants from voting, and certifying the count. As important, the bill gave federal officials and courts the power to overturn election results that had been declared and certified by state officials. Although the seventy-five-page bill made little mention of force (the label "force bill" was applied by opponents), the House (but not the Senate) version did authorize the president to utilize the army, if necessary, to guarantee the legal conduct of elections.[55]

Most Republicans supported the Federal Elections Bill for a mixture of partisan and principled reasons. The Republicans certainly stood to gain from fair elections in the South and from less corrupt elections in some Democratically run northern cities; they also were likely to control the federal machinery that they were attempting to create. Yet there was more to the force bill than a partisan grab for advantage. Men such as Hoar, who had voted for the enforcement acts of the 1870s, were the partial heirs of the Radical Republicans, appalled by what was occurring in the South, enraged that the hard-won victories of war and Reconstruction were being undermined by fraud and violence. Hoar believed equal rights to be a core value of the Republican Party and that "in all these race difficulties and troubles, the fault has been with the Anglo-Saxon." Lodge, younger and more ambitious, aspired to Charles Sumner's Senate seat and had long imbibed abolitionist and radical sentiments. The freedmen, he maintained in a carefully argued speech echoing the debates over the Fifteenth Amendment, "took their muskets in their hands and went to the front by regiments. They died in the trenches and on the battle-field by hundreds for the Government which up to that time had only fastened their chains more securely. . . . Such loyalty and fidelity . . . demand some better reward . . . than the negro has ever received." Lodge continued,

> The Government which made the black man a citizen is bound to protect him in his rights as a citizen of the United States, and it is a cowardly Government if it does not do it! No people can afford to write anything into their Constitution and not sustain it. A failure to do what is right brings its own punishment to nations as to men.[56]

The Democrats, of course, fiercely opposed the bill, denouncing it as "a scheme to rob the people of the States of the dearest right of American citizenship." They argued that it was partisan, hypocritical, unnecessary, unacceptably expensive, and potentially dictatorial; they also claimed it to be an unconstitutional assertion of federal dominance over the states. (The Republicans defended the bill's constitutionality by citing both the Fourteenth Amendment and Supreme Court cases of the 1880s.) In the House, where the bill actually came to a vote, no Democrats supported it.[57]

What sank the Federal Elections Bill, however, was not Democratic hostility but rather parliamentary maneuvering, happenstance, and division among the Republicans. Within the Republican Party, debates about ideology and political strategy had been brewing since Reconstruction. On one side stood those, like Hoar, who believed that the party's identity should remain closely tied to equal rights and that its best chance for national political dominance was to dissolve the solidly Democratic South by insisting on black suffrage, on a "free ballot and a fair count." Dissenters to this view, such as Pennsylvania's powerful Senator Matthew S. Quay, preferred to emphasize the party's procapitalist, pro-economic development, protariff views; they were convinced that such an approach would attract a new white constituency in the South while shoring up Republican support elsewhere. Although adherents of the latter view were not necessarily opposed to the elections bill, they did not see it as essential or high-priority legislation.

As a result, the bill became stalled in the Senate after being narrowly passed by the House (thanks to Speaker Thomas Reed's forceful maintenance of party discipline). Quay and his Pennsylvania colleague, J. Donald Cameron, maneuvered to postpone consideration of the elections bill until the short session of Congress, because they wanted the Senate to act first on the McKinley tariff. Then, during the short session, the silver Republicans from the West, led by Senator Stewart of Nevada, joined with the Democrats to again delay discussion, to permit Congress to consider a measure dealing with the coinage of silver. Stewart, who had been one of the principal authors of the final draft of the Fifteenth Amendment, opposed the Lodge Force Bill because he claimed that it was unenforceable and that only time and education could mend the racial divide in the South. When the elections bill finally came to the floor, it was met by a Democratic filibuster—which ended, early in 1891, when the Senate, to the surprise of many, voted to halt debate to take up an apportionment act. This decisive procedural vote, effectively killing the elections bill, passed the Senate by a vote of thirty-five to thirty-four, with nineteen abstentions.[58]

The Senate vote brought congressional efforts to enforce the Fifteenth Amendment to a halt. Once again, by a small margin, the federal government backed away from a significant expansion of its role in shaping electoral law and guaranteeing democratic rights; once again, this occurred not only because the nation and the Congress were divided, but also because of back-door political dealing and accidents of timing. Congress's decision in January 1891 was not as consequential as were its actions on the Fifteenth Amendment, but it nonetheless signaled to the South that the federal government was not prepared to act energetically to guarantee the voting rights of blacks. Several years later, when Democrats again gained control of both

Congress and the presidency, they amplified that signal by repealing the enforcement acts of the 1870s. Whatever the Fourteenth and Fifteenth Amendments said on paper, the right to vote was back in the hands of the states. Not until the 1960s, when the Lodge Force Bill was reincarnated as Lyndon Johnson's Voting Rights Act, did Congress again seriously consider federal intervention in southern politics.[59]

The year 1890 also marked the beginning of systematic efforts by southern states to disfranchise black voters legally. Faced with recurrent electoral challenges, the annoying expense of buying votes, and controversy surrounding epidemics of fraud and violence, Democrats chose to solidify their hold on the South by modifying the voting laws in ways that would exclude African Americans without overtly violating the Fifteenth Amendment. Experiments with these legal strategies had occurred in the 1870s and 1880s, but it was between 1890 and 1905 that they became the primary weapon in enforcing and institutionalizing Redeemer rule. In deploying this weapon, white Democrats turned back the clock on the broadly progressive franchise provisions that had been etched into most Reconstruction-era state constitutions. (See tables A.10 to A.15.)[60]

Mississippi led the way in 1890. Unnerved by the federal government's consideration of a Federal Elections Bill, Senator James Z. George, who had played a key role in the state's violent redemption from Republican rule, led a campaign to hold a constitutional convention that would transform Mississippi's suffrage laws. The impulse for restriction came largely from the state's elites and black-belt counties, and initially was opposed by Democrats and Populists in predominantly white locales. After granting concessions to the white counties on apportionment and other issues, George and his allies secured passage of provisions that would remove blacks from Mississippi political life while technically adhering to the Fifteenth Amendment. These provisions included a sharp increase in the residency requirement ("the negro is . . . a nomadic tribe," opined the state's attorney general), the institution of a two-dollar poll tax, and the imposition of a literacy test that required potential voters to demonstrate that they could understand and interpret the Constitution.[61]

In short order, other states followed suit, adopting—in varying combinations—poll taxes, cumulative poll taxes (demanding that past as well as current taxes be paid), literacy tests, secret ballot laws, lengthy residence requirements, elaborate registration systems, confusing multiple voting-box arrangements, and eventually, Democratic primaries restricted to white voters. Criminal exclusion laws also were altered to disfranchise men convicted of minor offenses, such as vagrancy and bigamy. These restrictions sometimes were written into state constitutions; elsewhere they simply were passed as statutes by state legislatures. (See tables A.10, A.11, A.13, A.14, A.15.) The overarching aim of such restrictions, usually undisguised, was to keep poor and illiterate blacks—and in Texas, Mexican Americans—from the polls. "The great underlying principle of this Convention movement . . . was the elimination of the negro from the politics of this State," emphasized a delegate to Virginia's constitutional convention of 1901–2. Literacy tests served that goal well, since 50 percent of all black men (as well as 15 percent of all whites) were illiterate; and even small tax requirements were a deterrent to the poor. Notably, it was during this period that the meaning of *poll tax* shifted: where it once had referred to a head tax that every man had to pay and that sometimes could be used to satisfy a taxpaying requirement for voting, it came to be understood as a tax that one had to pay in order to vote.[62]

Many of the disfranchising laws were designed expressly to be administered in a discriminatory fashion, permitting whites to vote while barring blacks. Small errors in registration procedures or marking ballots might or might not be ignored at the whim of election officials; taxes might be paid easily or only with difficulty; tax receipts might or might not be issued. Discrimination also was built into literacy tests, with their "understanding" clauses: officials administering the test could, and did, judge whether a prospective voter's "understanding" was adequate. "Discrimination! Why, that is precisely what we propose," intoned future Senator Carter Glass at Virginia's constitutional convention of 1901–2. "That, exactly, is what this Convention was elected for—to discriminate to the very extremity of permissible action under the limitations of the Federal Constitution, with a view to the elimination of every negro voter who can be gotten rid of, legally, without materially impairing the numerical strength of the white electorate." Discrimination, as well as circumvention of the Fifteenth Amendment, was also the aim of the well-known grandfather clauses that exempted men from literacy, tax, residency, or property requirements if they had performed military service or if their ancestors had voted in the 1860s. The first southern grandfather clause was adopted in South Carolina in 1890; with exquisite regional irony, it was modeled on the anti-immigrant Massachusetts law of 1857.[63]

Such laws were not passed without controversy. Contrary to twentieth-century images of a monolithic solid South, there was substantial white opposition to new restrictions on the franchise: many upcountry whites, small farmers, Populists, and Republicans viewed such laws as a means of suppressing dissent, a self-interested and partisan grab for power by dominant, elite, often black-belt Democrats. Legislation thus was not always enacted when first proposed, and there were at times prolonged and bitter debates about the dangers of "reform." Egalitarian voices were raised, insisting that it was "wrong" or "unlawful" to deprive "even one of the humblest of our citizens of his right to vote . . . no matter how humble, or poor, or ignorant, or black, he may be." Critics also maintained that "it is safer, easier, and more practicable to govern ignorant people as fellow-citizens than as subjects." More commonly, apprehensions were voiced about the laws' potential to disfranchise whites. A delegate from a predominantly white county in Texas asked whether a proposed poll tax had a "covert design" since "it afflicts the poor man and the poor man alone." Proponents of suffrage restriction, however, drowned such objections in rhetoric stressing the urgency of black disfranchisement while assuring whites that their political rights would not be subverted. "I told the people of my county before they sent me here," declared R. L. Gordon at Virginia's constitutional convention in 1901, "that I intended . . . to disfranchise every negro that I could disfranchise under the Constitution of the United States, and as few white people as possible."[64]

Despite such claims, many advocates of so-called electoral reform were quite comfortable with the prospect of shunting poor whites aside along with African Americans. One little-noticed irony induced by the Fifteenth Amendment was that it led southern Democrats to resurrect class, rather than racial, obstacles to voting, a resurrection that was altogether compatible with the conservative views and interests of many of the landed, patrician whites who were the prime movers of disfranchisement. "I believe in the virtue of a property qualification," proclaimed Gordon of Virginia, who, as noted earlier, openly decried his state's embrace of manhood suffrage in 1850. Gordon's views apparently were shared by politicians in Alabama, who altered the preamble to the state's constitution in 1901, relabeling suffrage a "privilege" rather than a "right." As tables A.11 and A.13 reveal, Alabama's progressive constitution of 1875 had expressly banned both property and education requirements for suffrage; the new constitution imposed an amalgam of the two. Similarly, a New Orleans newspaper attacked manhood suffrage as "unwise, unreasonable, and illogical," and Louisiana's disfranchising laws targeted not only blacks but a political machine supported by working-class whites, many of them Italian. One Alabama disfranchiser publicly avowed his desire to eliminate "ignorant, incompetent, and vicious" white men from the electorate, while a Virginia delegate re-

vived the notion of virtual representation in an attempt to mitigate the significance of legislation that would keep many whites from the polls. Such
statements, moreover, were not mere window-dressing designed to mask
the racial intent of the new laws; as historian J. Morgan Kousser has pointed
out, it was far riskier for politicians to publicly sanction white disfranchisement than to demand black exclusion.[65]

Indeed, the late-nineteenth-century effort to transform the South's electorate was grounded solidly in class concerns as well as racial antagonism.
Not only was the disfranchisement of poor whites palatable to many of their
better-off brethren, but the exclusion of black voters also had significant
class dimensions. Ridding the electorate of blacks was a means of rendering
most of the agricultural laborers of the rural South politically powerless, of
restoring the "peasantry" to its pre–Civil War political condition. Taking
this step would permit post-slavery agriculture to be organized and economic development to be promoted while landowners and businessmen
wielded unchallenged control of the state.

To be sure, the upper classes were not alone in advocating black disfranchisement: the movement was actively supported by many poor and lower-
middle-class whites, just as the Know-Nothing effort to disfranchise
immigrants was backed by some native-born workers. Yet the presence of a
racial and political schism within the lower classes did not blunt (though it
did complicate and disguise) disfranchisement's class edge. In the black-
belt, cotton-growing counties that remained at the core of the South's economy, a large majority of the laboring population was vulnerable to the new
laws; in the region as a whole, the threat of a troublesome electoral alliance
between blacks and poor whites could be eliminated. As historians have
long noted, the political order of the new South was structured by class as
well as racial dominance. In the words of an Alabama trade unionist, "the
lawmakers . . . made the people believe that [the disfranchising law] was
placed there to disfranchise the negro, but it was placed there to disfranchise
the workingman."[66]

The laws, of course, worked. In Mississippi after 1890, less than 9,000 out
of 147,000 voting-age blacks were registered to vote; in Louisiana, where
more than 130,000 blacks had been registered to vote in 1896, the figure
dropped to an astonishing 1,342 by 1904. Throughout the region the black
electorate was decimated, and many poor whites (as well as Mexican Americans) went with them. Just how many persons were barred from the polls
is impossible to determine, but what is known is that both registration and
turnout (calculated as the percentage of votes cast divided by the number of

men of voting age) dropped precipitously after the electoral laws were re-configured. By 1910, in Georgia, only 4 percent of all black males were registered to vote. In Mississippi, electoral turnout had exceeded 70 percent in the 1870s and approached 50 percent in the decade after the Redeemers came to power: by the early twentieth century, it had plummeted to 15 percent and remained at that level for decades. In the South as a whole, post-Reconstruction turnout levels of 60 to 85 percent fell to 50 percent for whites and single digits for blacks. The enlargement of the suffrage that was one of the signal achievements of Reconstruction had been reversed, and the rollback had restored the southern electorate to—at best—pre–Civil War proportions. Just as Henry Wilson and his allies had predicted, the South successfully took advantage of the narrowness of the Fifteenth Amendment to circumvent and undermine its intent.[67]

What this meant for the history of the twentieth-century South is well known: the African-American population remained largely disfranchised until the 1960s, electoral participation remained low, and one-party rule by conservative Democrats became the norm. Viewed through a wider lens, these developments also signified that in a major region of the United States the nineteenth-century trend toward democratization had been not only checked, but reversed: the increasingly egalitarian institutions and convictions forged before the Civil War were undermined, while class barriers to electoral participation were strengthened or resurrected. The legal reforms of the late nineteenth and early twentieth centuries created not just a single-party region but a class-segmented as well as racially exclusive polity. Large segments of the rural, agricultural working class—America's peasantry—were again voteless, and industrialization, which became increasingly important to the region after 1880, took place in a profoundly undemocratic society.

All of which, it must be noted, took place without great protest from the North. Although Republican politicians and newspapers routinely criticized the disfranchising laws, the Federal Elections Bill of 1890 was never revived, and scattered efforts to enforce the Fourteenth Amendment—by reducing the congressional representation of southern states—garnered little support. As important, the Supreme Court upheld the legality of all of the major techniques of disfranchisement. In 1898, for example, it ruled that Mississippi's literacy test did not violate the Fifteenth Amendment because the law creating the test was not, on its face, designed to discriminate against blacks. This constitutional standard, applied widely in the Gilded Age and during the Progressive era, flew in the face of both the consequences of the disfranchising laws and the explicitly discriminatory intentions proclaimed by their authors. Making enforcement of the Fifteenth Amendment even more difficult, the Court also ruled that the federal government had the power to charge states, but not individual actors, with violations of the amendment's principles: an individual who interfered with an African American's attempt to vote was beyond the reach of federal law.[68]

The only exceptions to the Court's extraordinary willingness to ignore the realities of southern political life arose in 1915, when it ruled that grandfather clauses in Oklahoma and Maryland were so blatantly discriminatory that they violated the Fifteenth Amendment. By 1915, however, the South's new electoral structures were solidly in place, and grandfather clauses, in any case, were only minor building blocks of the system. The North in effect tolerated disfranchisement in the South—in part from weariness, in part due to the partisan interests of the Democratic Party, and in part because Northerners too had been losing faith in democracy.[69]

FIVE

The Redemption
of the North

The great bulk of the American people have ever since the country was settled been property-owners, taxpayers, and people of considerable intelligence and business experience, and the reason that the establishment of universal suffrage by the abolition of the property qualification came about so easily was that it made no practical change in the seat of the sovereignty. It left power just where it had always been. The additions it made to constituencies, in the shape of ignorant and penniless voters, were so trifling that they attracted no attention and produced no change in the character either of legislation or administration. It is only now in our own day, and only in the great cities, that the possibility of the severance of political power from intelligence and property has been brought home to people as a practical question, and the results of the rule of mere numerical majority been made visible. If this severance had existed when the Government was founded, the republican form would assuredly never have been adopted; or, had it been adopted, it could never have been maintained, and the country would long since have gone the way of the South American republics. No such men as formed the bulk of the earlier settlers would ever have attempted the formulation of a political system in which the power was to be lodged in the hands of the proletariat; and the men who formed and overthrew all restrictions on the electoral franchise in the first half of this century only did so, democratic as they were, because they saw plainly that the change would rob neither property nor intelligence of its supremacy.

—ANONYMOUS, *The Nation*, 26 APRIL 1877

*L*ATE-NINETEENTH-CENTURY POLITICS was a rough-and-tumble sport, acutely partisan, engaging the energies and attention of millions of people. National elections were closely contested; control of Congress changed hands frequently; presidents were elected by razor-thin margins and sometimes with less than a majority of the popular vote. In the West as well as the North, politics was a mass activity, shaped by increasingly professional party organizations: public demonstrations and parades were common; electoral turnout was high; urban political machines, both Republican and (more often) Democratic, traded services for the votes and loyalty of hundreds of thousands of city dwellers. Although party identifications were strong, third parties frequently cropped up and remarkably often gained substantial influence in state and local governments. The Greenback Labor Party, the Knights of Labor, the Grange, the Farmers' Alliances, the People's Party, the Socialist Party—all wielded local or even statewide power at some point between the end of the Civil War and the turn of the century.

The issues animating political life were big ones, sparked by the rapid spread of industrialization, fanned by class and interest-group conflict. The tariff and the money supply (which affected prices and the availability of credit) were issues in every national election. Railroad rates and regulation often dominated state political contests. City dwellers fought over the development and financing of increasingly necessary water, sewer, and transport systems. Embedded in all such issues were conflicts over corporate power and uncertainty about the proper role of the state: farmers and shippers pressed the states and Washington to protect them against the predations of railroads that controlled access to markets; workers sought legislation to shorten the hours of labor; small businesses cried out against monopolies; and urban consumers demanded regulation of utility companies. To be sure, not everything was high seriousness and political economy: the sale of liquor, for example, was a life-and-death issue in many elections. Yet on the whole, politics revolved around the myriad consequences of the increasingly evident triumph of industrial capitalism.

After 1900—or after the critical election of 1896, which yielded a new and long-lasting partisan alignment—the tone of political life shifted, although the dominant issues remained the same. The fate of the South was settled (removing one key contentious issue from the political arena), the Republican Party securely dominated much of the Northeast and Midwest, and third-party rebellions became infrequent. Electoral turnout fell, North and South, while the major political parties suffered a decline in enthusiasm and loyalty. The apocalyptic language of late-nineteenth-century politics—a language of crisis and perceived conflict—gave way to a more metallic and optimistic language of problem solving and expertise. Progressive reformers sought to tame, without frontally challenging, corporate power, utilize the state to contain economic conflict, and bureaucratize instruments of governance. Progressives also continued efforts to cleanse politics of corruption, diminish the influence of parties, and make public administration more efficient. Thanks in part to these reformers' efforts and those of their late-nineteenth-century predecessors, most key features of the modern American state had been erected by 1920, on the foundation of an equally modern national, industrial economy.

Losing Faith

The Civil War and the crisis surrounding black voting rights provided only a temporary check against the current of antidemocratic sentiments that first roiled the political waters in the 1850s. By the middle of the 1870s, a scant few years after passage of the Fifteenth Amendment, leading intellectuals and politicians voiced deep reservations about universal or manhood suffrage—which is how they described the breadth of the franchise in the wake of the Civil War. Although many had been abolitionists and had supported the republican drive for black enfranchisement, these critics publicly lamented the expansion of the franchise that had occurred before mid-century and opposed universal suffrage in terms far more sweeping and systematic than the Know-Nothings had done. Their criticisms of a broad suffrage were not mere revivals of early-nineteenth-century conservatism. Grounded in the realities of industrial, capitalist society, they constituted a more modern critique of democracy, capable of influencing and justifying voting laws well into the twentieth century.

The most influential critics of universal manhood suffrage were clustered in the cities of the Northeast, particularly Boston and New York. From Protestant, often elite, backgrounds, generally Republican but only loosely tied to the party, they constituted a somewhat self-conscious intelligentsia, publishing their views in widely read journals such as the *Atlantic Monthly*, *The Nation*, and the *North American Review*. Among their ranks were historian Francis Parkman, editor E. L. Godkin, descendant of two presidents Charles Francis Adams, Jr., and somewhat later, prominent Ivy League academics. Yet the pendulum swing away from unrestricted suffrage was never confined to this small group of reformist intellectuals or the class to which they belonged; across the nation, political figures voiced similar concerns. So too did newspapers: the *Washington Post* in 1899, for example, urged that "poor white" Southerners, and white "sansculottes" everywhere be disfranchised. Such sentiments even took root among the more settled and established segments of the working class. As was often true, restrictions on suffrage for those at the bottom of the social ladder received backing from men who were only one rung up.[1]

One source of this conservative reaction was the dismal course of events in the South: not only was Redemption gaining ground, but reports were widely circulated (though largely inaccurate) that Reconstruction governments elected with black votes were incompetent and corrupt. The key precipitants of this ideological swing, however, resided in the North, in the dramatic—even shocking—transformations in economic and social life that inescapably reverberated into politics. Between 1865 and 1900, the United States became the leading manufacturing nation in the world, and its industrial output eclipsed that of agriculture. While the country's population rose from roughly 35 million to nearly 75 million, nonfarm employment tripled: at the turn of the century, more than 10 million people worked in manufacturing, mining, construction, and transportation.[2]

When Americans who had come of age in the 1840s and 1850s gazed outward after the Civil War, what they saw was unfamiliar and disturbing: new industries, large and impersonal workplaces, private corporations wielding enormous economic and political power, and economic panics that created new problems such as mass unemployment. They saw abandoned farms, railroads crisscrossing vast stretches of country, and—distressingly—cities of unprecedented size and complexity. In 1870, only New York and Philadelphia had populations greater than 500,000; by 1910, there were eight, three of which contained more than a million people. Moreover, these cities increasingly were governed by political organizations, or machines, as critics called them, that the traditional elites could not control or even understand.

What Americans also witnessed—and apparently feared—was the extremely rapid growth of an immigrant working class. Interrupted by the Civil War, the flow of immigrants that had begun in the 1840s resumed quickly after Appomattox: the nation's expanding industries needed labor, and that labor was supplied by men and women from Europe and to a far lesser extent Asia and Mexico. Between 1865 and World War I, nearly 25 million immigrants journeyed to the United States, accounting for a large proportion of the nation's World War I population of roughly 100 million. The vast majority of these immigrants were propertyless workers rather than settlers. The Irish and Germans continued to arrive, joined by growing numbers of southern and eastern Europeans: men and women who did not speak English, whose cultures were alien, and most of whom were Catholic or Jewish. By 1910, most urban residents were immigrants or the children of immigrants, and the nation's huge working class was predominantly foreign-born, native-born of foreign parents, or black.[3]

In the eyes of many old stock Americans, this mass of immigrant workers was an unwelcome addition to the electorate. Poor, uneducated, ignorant of American traditions, the foreign-born men peopling the nation's industries seemed to lack the judgment, knowledge, and commitment to American values necessary for salutary participation in elections. It was not their foreignness alone or their class position by itself that rendered them suspect; rather it was the combination of the two, the melding of class and cultural attributes and interests, the fusion of poverty, dependence, ignorance, difference, and militance. One sign of immigrants' unsuitability as voters was their apparent inclination toward radicalism. These were the voters who backed "demagogue" Ben Butler's quasi-populist, anti-establishment campaigns in Massachusetts in the 1870s, as well as Knights of Labor and socialist candidates in later decades; these were the men who allegedly tossed bombs at Haymarket in 1886, who struck and rioted against the railroads in 1877, at Pullman in 1894, and Lawrence in 1912. It was likely not a coincidence that several prominent attacks on universal suffrage were published immediately after the strikes of 1877 and Butler's 1878 campaign.

Equally compelling evidence of their unfitness was the support that poor, foreign-born voters gave to political machines, to so-called boss rule. The clientelist politics of the machines, grounded in ethnic loyalty and the exchange of favors for votes, appeared to be a plague, incubated in immigrant neighborhoods and infecting the entire body politic. By the late 1860s, this political plague had brought the notoriously corrupt Tweed ring to power in New York, and in subsequent decades, only slightly less notorious machines were flourishing in cities such as Boston, Philadelphia, Cleveland, and San Francisco.

Critics of manhood suffrage thus anchored their views in the claim that the democratic principles so widely celebrated in earlier decades had been rendered obsolete or even hazardous by changes that had occurred in the composition of the electorate. The unnamed author of the 1877 article published in *The Nation* (quoted at the opening of this chapter) offered the (probably accurate) historical argument that "the republican form would assuredly never have been adopted" and "restrictions on the electoral fran-

chise" would never have been removed before 1850 had previous generations faced the prospect of putting power "in the hands of the proletariat."
America's most celebrated historian, Francis Parkman, made the point more
vividly in "The Failure of Universal Suffrage," a widely read article published in 1878:

> A New England village of the olden time—that is to say, of some forty years
> ago—would have been safely and well governed by the votes of every man in
> it; but, now that the village has grown into a populous city, with its factories
> and workshops, its acres of tenement-houses, and thousands and ten thou-
> sands of restless workmen, foreigners for the most part, to whom liberty
> means license and politics means plunder, to whom the public good is noth-
> ing and their own most trivial interests everything, who love the country for
> what they can get out of it, and whose ears are open to the promptings of
> every rascally agitator, the case is completely changed, and universal suffrage
> becomes a questionable blessing.

Perhaps consciously, Parkman's retrospective analysis clearly echoed Chancellor Kent's famous prediction in 1821 that a broad franchise would en-
danger the nation once manufacturing had taken hold.[4]

Indeed, opponents of universal suffrage consistently couched their opinions in language redolent with class, ethnic, and racial hostility; in telling
contrast to the 1850s, anti-Catholic language was rare and muted.[5] "Universal Suffrage can only mean in plain English," wrote John Quincy
Adams's grandson, Charles Francis Adams, Jr., "the government of ignorance and vice:—it means a European, and especially Celtic, proletariat on
the Atlantic coast; an African proletariat on the shores of the Gulf, and a
Chinese proletariat on the Pacific." In 1883, eminent geologist Alexander
Winchell denounced the "evils which germinate in the American system of
universal suffrage." The United States must "diminish the power of the
worst classes . . . to deny the existence of classes among us is to dispute with
the multiplication table." Writing from New York in 1890, Edward Godkin, editor of the influential and widely read *Nation*, lamented that "it was
unfortunate that the change in the constitution of this state in 1846, establishing universal suffrage, occurred simultaneously with the beginning of
the great tide of emigration which followed the Irish famine. Its result was
that the city was soon flooded with a large body of ignorant voters." Early
in the twentieth century, writer and former diplomat William L. Scruggs
concluded that "in its last analysis, universal suffrage is but another name

for a licensed mobocracy; and a licensed mobocracy is nothing less than 'organized anarchy,' pure and simple." A decade later, another critic decried the fact that "the improvident, the ignorant, the vicious, the stupid, the lazy, the drunken, the dirty—the whole mass of scum and dregs of society" had the same electoral power as "the mature, the useful, the industrious, the intelligent." In Texas, Mexican immigrants were described as a "political menace," as "foreigners who claim American citizenship but who are as ignorant of things American as the mule."[6]

Aside from their ignorance and vices, what was objectionable about these voters was that they purportedly were prone to voting illegally, irresponsibly, and against the interests of their betters. Charges of corruption and naturalization fraud were repeated endlessly: electoral outcomes were twisted by "naturalization mills" that, with the aid of "professional perjurers and political manipulators," transformed thousands of immigrants into citizens in the weeks before elections. (Just how substantial—or insubstantial—such charges may have been is discussed in detail later in this chapter.) Moreover, even if their votes were legal, they were inappropriately cast, bartered for jobs or favors from a boss. "The suffrage is nothing to [the immigrant]," observed reformer and labor economist John R. Commons, "but a means of livelihood." Several critics, including Winchell, offered an updated Blackstonian specter in which a working-class, rather than aristocratic, demagogue took advantage of the poor: universal suffrage, he maintained, "establishes the way to demagogism. The ignorant, uncultured, or dissipated voter most willingly yields to the persuasions of one of his own class."[7]

Others stated unabashedly that the voting poor constituted a threat to property. "There is probably no sweeter experience in the world than that of a penniless laborer . . . when he learns that by casting his vote in the right way he can strip the rich merchant or shipowner of a portion of his gains," wrote one critic. Universal suffrage "gives power to the communistic attack on property," concluded Parkman. "Communism and social chaos are the only possible finality of such a tendency," echoed Winchell. Framing the matter more broadly—and probably more accurately—Parkman concluded that the "masses" had values antithetical to the American tradition: "Liberty was the watchword of our fathers, and so it is of ourselves. But, in their hearts, the masses of the nation cherish desires not only different from it, but inconsistent with it. They want equality more than they want liberty."[8]

Faced with the "evils" stemming from a broad suffrage, these critics utterly repudiated the notion, so prevalent in the mid–nineteenth century, that voting was a right or even a natural or inalienable right. As early as

1865, Godkin maintained that the franchise was "not a right, but a trust committed to each individual more for the benefit of the rest of the nation than for his own." That same year, a Maryland court ruled that suffrage was not "among the rights of property or person"; it was instead "a matter of mere state policy." Parkman was even more hostile, deriding the "theory of inalienable rights" as "an outrage to justice and common sense," reflecting a "superstition . . . respecting the ballot."

> The means are confounded with the end. Good government is the end, and the ballot is worthless except so far as it helps to reach this end. Any reasonable man would willingly renounce his privilege of dropping a piece of paper into a box, provided that good government were assured to him and his descendants.[9]

Thirty years later, such opinions remained current: an editorial in *The Outlook* (a Christian "family newspaper"), for example, juxtaposed the theory of suffrage as a right with the notion that it was a matter of efficacy, a "means to an end." "One view is that suffrage is a natural right: that it is the prerogative of the freeman: that every man of sound nature, mentally and morally, and of full age, has a right to an equal share with his fellow men in the government of the State of which he is a member." In contrast, the "other view," which *The Outlook* endorsed,

> is that suffrage is simply a means for exercising the functions of government . . . that no one has a right to share in this government unless he is competent to know what are the rights of his fellow-citizens and to take whatever action may be necessary for their protection; that suffrage is merely means to an end and that end a just government, and that whatever conditions of suffrage at any particular time and in any particular community will secure the best government are the conditions which the community should adopt and maintain.

The implication of this reasoning was unmistakable: if suffrage was simply a "means to an end," and if broad suffrage produced poor governments, then it was perfectly legitimate to narrow the portals to the voting booth. Ironically, perhaps, rejecting the notion that suffrage was a right was made easier by the contemporaneous agitation for women's suffrage: reversing the "slippery slope" argument, critics argued that since women did not vote, suffrage obviously was not a right.[10]

Not everyone bought this restrictionist logic, even among the elite. Many supporters of black suffrage in the South continued to insist that voting was

a right, as did advocates of women's suffrage; moreover, some liberal Northerners publicly took issue with democracy's critics. One particularly pointed
rebuttal came from John Martin Luther Babcock, who in 1879 published
"The Right of the Ballot: A Reply to Francis Parkman and Others Who
Have Asserted 'The Failure of Universal Suffrage.'" Babcock, a minister and
erstwhile poet from Groton, Massachusetts, was alarmed by the burst of attacks on "universal suffrage, or what in this country is called such," particularly since the attacks emanated from "an element that claims to be the 'best'
in our society." Babcock's "reply" to Parkman and others was multipronged.
He argued that "the idea of human rights" was "the safeguard alike of society
and of man. . . . One may be willing, for the sake of discrediting the ballot, to
repudiate the idea of natural rights; but he must also be willing to repudiate
the most inspiring lessons of our history." Zeroing in on the class dimensions
of Parkman's views, Babcock pointed out that the ballot was a necessary bulwark against exploitation, that the "poor multitudes may be oppressed with
safety" if they lack "political power." A broad franchise, moreover, was in the
interest of all classes because it would "unite the different elements of society
in harmonious fellowship" and because without it the polity would contain
"the seeds of violent dissolution." Babcock acknowledged the imperfections
and corruption of contemporary political life but insisted that such flaws were
not peculiar to a democratic "system of government." The "republic," he
claimed, would be "perfected . . . by establishing justice and equity among
men," not by the "overthrow" of "natural rights."[11]

Babcock's arguments were echoed and supplemented by numerous other
writers and political figures. Most insisted that suffrage was indeed a right,
that society "should give the ballot to every man simply because he is a
man." Only slightly less common was the argument (drawing in part on the
writings of John Stuart Mill) that possession of the franchise was educational, that it would serve to stimulate and uplift the poor and the ignorant,
creating a wiser and sounder polity in the not-too-distant long run. Some
defenders of democracy dismissed the fear that "working men will unite in
support of measures intended for their benefit as a class, without regard to
the welfare of other classes": the working class, they insisted, simply was too
diverse and divided to form an electoral bloc. Others, including former abolitionist and Republican Congressman George W. Julian, maintained that
the "evils which now blacken our politics" ought to be blamed not on universal suffrage but on "corporations," "capitalists," and "a mercenary and
corrupt leadership." The notion that men with property were the best cus-
todians of the republic in fact seemed to fly in the face of the track record

of the era's robber barons: "wealthy men control our railroad corporations," a contributor to *The Nation* pointed out. "What has been the degree of honor and regard for the public good with which these institutions have been managed?"[12]

The intellectual counterattack against critics of universal suffrage made clear that northern liberals, "literary men," those who in later decades would be called opinion makers, were deeply divided over the issue. There were passionate advocates of a broad franchise just as there were passionate critics, and there is no way to tell how many men, literary and otherwise, fell into each camp. What was noteworthy about this public debate—which foreshadowed and then mirrored debates in statehouses across the country—was not the relative strength of the two camps but rather that the debate took place at all. Within a few years of passage of the Fifteenth Amendment, a significant segment of the intellectual community was announcing its distrust of democracy and rejecting the claim that suffrage was a right. The discourse had changed, and the breadth of the franchise—particularly extension of the franchise to the poor, uneducated, and foreign-born—was once again a live issue.

In contrast to the debates of the 1830s and 1840s, advocates of a broad suffrage were back on the defensive: the terms of public discussion were being set by men who believed that universal suffrage had failed, that it was neither viable nor desirable in the socially heterogeneous, industrial world of the late nineteenth century. As scores of contemporary commentators noticed, the tides of political thought had shifted again, and that shift endured well into the twentieth century. In 1918, two Yale historians concluded a two-volume comparative history of voting with the comment that "if the state gives the vote to the ignorant, they will fall into anarchy to-day and into despotism to-morrow." A decade later, William B. Munro, professor of history and political science at Harvard, declared that "eliminating the least intelligent stratum" of the electorate was essential to the nation's well-being.[13]

Despite their shared diagnosis, the intellectuals and reformers who were losing faith in universal suffrage were not of one mind about the prescription. Some, such as Godkin, believed that nothing could be done to shrink the electorate. "Probably no system of government was ever so easy to attack and ridicule," he wrote in 1894, "but no government has ever come upon the world from which there seemed so little prospect of escape. It has, in spite of its imperfections and oddities, something of the majesty of doom." Beneath Godkin's sonorous rhetoric was a shrewd perception of political realities: introducing new barriers to suffrage was far more difficult than simply retaining those already in place. Men who possessed the franchise, and their representatives, could combat—and politically punish—those who sought to disfranchise them. Consequently, Godkin regarded it as "a mere waste of time to declaim against" universal suffrage: the challenge to "educated men" was to develop ways of having good government despite universal suffrage.[14]

Proposals for achieving such a goal began to find their way onto the public agenda in the 1870s and remained there for decades. Among them were less frequent elections, at-large rather than district voting, increased public accountability for office holders, and state control over key arenas of municipal administration. Another proposal that garnered considerable attention was to remove public offices from the electoral sphere and make them appointive. As the *Atlantic Monthly* observed in 1879, "the right of voting cannot be taken away, but the subjects of voting can be much reduced." It was "absurd" to involve the electorate in "the selection of judges and sheriffs, and district attorneys, of state treasurers and attorney-generals, of school commissioners and civil engineers." Democracy in effect could be salvaged by circumscribing its domain.[15]

Other critics were more optimistic about the possibilities of changing the size and shape of the electorate. Some advocated reinstituting property and tax qualifications or imposing literacy tests on prospective voters. More subtle approaches also were proposed, including longer residence periods, stricter naturalization laws, waiting periods before new citizens could vote, complex ballot laws, and elaborate systems of voter registration. Wherever such ideas originated, their endorsement by well-known liberal spokesmen helped to speed their circulation through the political cultures of the North and West, where they quickly acquired a life and importance that reached far beyond the world of northeastern intellectuals.[16]

Purifying the Electorate

The laws governing elections in most states were revised often between the Civil War and World War I. Many states, new and old, held constitutional conventions that defined or redefined the shape of the electorate as well as the outlines of the electoral process. State legislatures drew up increasingly detailed statutes that spelled out electoral procedures of all types, including the timing of elections, the location of polling places, the hours that polls would be open, the configuration of ballots, and the counting of votes. As

had been true before the Civil War, many of these laws were straightfor-
wardly administrative, creating needed electoral machinery and translating
broad constitutional precepts into concrete, enforceable rules.[17]

Other laws were more controversial, inspired by partisan interests, enacted to influence the outcome of elections. Prominent among them were
laws that affected the weight, or value, of votes cast. The apportionment of
state legislative as well as congressional seats was a key issue, generating recurrent conflicts, particularly between urban and rural areas. Linked to apportionment was the location of district boundaries in states and within
cities: gerrymandering was a routine form of political combat, practiced by
both major parties against one another and against any upstart political organizations. Similarly, technical rules governing the presence of parties and
candidates on the ballot also were subjects of contention—since they could
encourage, or discourage, third parties and fusion slates. Minute legal details could and did shape the choices offered to voters and the weight of individual votes.[18]

Nonetheless, the most critical laws remained those that determined the
size and contours of the electorate. These were of two types. First and most
important were those that set out the fundamental qualifications that a man
(or woman) had to meet in order to become an eligible voter. The second,
of increasing significance, established the procedures that a potential voter
had to follow in order to participate in elections. Both types remained under
state control, since the Constitution and federal courts continued to say little about suffrage, except with regard to race. In every state, changes in both
substantive and procedural laws were proposed and debated, often giving
rise to reforms and commonly generating political and ideological conflict.

The legal changes considered by constitutional conventions and legislatures cut in both directions. Some were aimed at enlarging the franchise—
either substantively (e.g., by eliminating tax requirements) or procedurally
(e.g., by keeping the polls open longer hours, to make it easier for working
people to vote). In the early twentieth century, several states, alarmed at the
decline of turnout in the middle and upper classes, even considered making
voting compulsory—thereby making exercise of the franchise an obligation
as well as a right.

More typical of the era, however, were efforts to tighten voting requirements. Justified as measures to eliminate corruption or produce a more
competent electorate, such efforts included the introduction of literacy
tests, lengthening residency periods, abolishing provisions that permitted
noncitizen aliens to vote, restricting municipal elections to property owners

or taxpayers, and the creation of complex, cumbersome registration procedures. Stripping voters of the franchise was a politically delicate operation
that generally had to be performed obliquely and without arousing the ire
of large and concentrated groups of voters.[19]

The political dynamics of reform defy easy characterization: any full understanding would require dozens of in-depth studies of individual states
and cities. Still, certain overarching patterns are visible. Efforts to restrict
the franchise commonly emanated from the middle and upper classes, from
business and rural interests, as well as professionals; resistance to these efforts, as well as sentiment in favor of looser voting requirements, tended to
be concentrated in the urban working class. Republicans were far more
likely than Democrats, or third-party advocates, to favor restrictive reforms.
Partisan competition played a larger role, and ideology a smaller one, than
had been true during the first two thirds of the nineteenth century. Issues
of military recruitment and mobilization were not much of a factor until
World War I.[20]

Yet there were exceptions to nearly all of these trends. The partisan lineup
was not consistent, either geographically or over time; the middle and upper
classes were never homogeneous in their views or interests; segments of an
ethnically divided and fluid working class periodically championed the
cause of restriction; and political machines, long regarded as powerful en-
gines of electoral expansion, sometimes judged that it was in their interest
to freeze the size of the electorate. The politics of suffrage were shaped by
vectors of class, ethnicity, and party, but these vectors were never identical
nor even consistently parallel to one another. The battle lines were bent further by the omnipresent shadow of demands for the enfranchisement of
women and by the indirection of proposals that would only partially disfranchise (or enfranchise) members of particular groups. This was more
guerilla than trench warfare.

Money and the Vote

> If the law of Massachusetts had been purposely framed with the
> object of keeping workingmen away from the polls it could
> hardly have accomplished that object more effectually than it
> does. It probably was drawn up with just that sinister purpose in
> view. In order to register it is necessary for the workingman to
> lose a day or at least half a day in presenting himself personally
> to substantiate his right to vote—no small sacrifice in the case of

the hardly driven and badly paid workers in the cotton mills and other poorly remunerated industries. Then, again, the payment of the poll tax of $2 is a prerequisite to voting . . .

The registration and poll-tax law of Massachusetts is essentially unjust and un-American. It virtually debases the right of suffrage to a part of the tax collecting machinery, and instead of making it really, as it is in theory, the birthright of every American citizen renders it a privilege to be secured by a money-payment.

—*Journal of United Labor*
(Knights of Labor), 1889

Contrary to received wisdom, economic requirements for voting were not a dead issue after 1850. In addition to being resurrected in the South, such requirements persisted in some northern states and were revived or debated anew in others. (See tables A.10 and A.11.) Although difficult to justify because they violated popular ideological norms, economic qualifications continued to offer opponents of universal suffrage a direct and potentially efficient means of winnowing out undesirable voters.

The unpopularity of economic qualifications was manifested in three states (Massachusetts, Rhode Island, and Delaware), which abolished longstanding property or tax requirements at the end of the nineteenth century. In Massachusetts, the abolition was accomplished by the Democrats, with substantial labor and Irish Catholic support. For decades, the tax requirement had served as an obstacle to poor people's voting and as a drain on the treasuries of both political parties, who often paid the taxes of their constituents. By the late 1880s, the Democratic Party—with more working-class supporters and thus greater financial exposure—reportedly was spending $50,000 at each election to pay the poll taxes of its supporters. Taking advantage of a brief moment of statewide electoral strength, the Democrats pushed through a constitutional amendment repealing the tax requirement in 1891. While campaigning for repeal in the face of vociferous conservative opposition, Governor William Russell claimed that the "tax deprives a man of his vote because of his poverty only" and warned that continued deprivation would only prompt the poor to adopt violent means of seeking change. According to Boston's mayor, the abolition of the poll tax led to an immediate 21 percent increase in the number of persons on the city's voting lists.[21]

In adjacent Rhode Island, the Democratic Party also led a campaign against economic qualifications but with less satisfactory results. (Rhode Island was the last state to require property ownership to vote.) Passed in the

1840s, its electoral laws permitted foreign-born citizens to vote in state elections only if they owned real property; the laws further barred all those without property from voting in city elections in Providence. Combined with an apportionment system heavily biased in favor of rural voters, these laws—which disfranchised roughly one fifth of the state's males and nearly 80 percent of potential municipal voters in Providence—very effectively kept a Republican elite in power.

By the 1880s, however, the Republicans were faltering, in part because of the growing electoral strength of the native-born children of Irish immigrants and because of corruption so flagrant that it repelled some of their traditional constituents. Supported by a coalition of middle-class reformers, advocates of women's suffrage, and labor, the Democrats successfully pressured Republicans into holding a referendum on the franchise in 1888. The electorate then approved the Bourn amendment, which eliminated the statewide property qualification for immigrants. The victory, however, was incomplete: the Bourn amendment extended the property requirement for municipal elections to all cities as well as to town meetings dealing with financial matters. At the same time, it imposed an annual registration requirement on propertyless voters. Consequently, suffrage reform remained an issue in Rhode Island well into the twentieth century, with the Democrats annually introducing legislation to repeal the municipal property requirements. These efforts bore fruit only in 1928, when men and women who did not own property finally were permitted to vote in city elections.[22]

In Pennsylvania, attempts to repeal a taxpaying requirement were even less successful. The issue came to the fore at the constitutional convention of 1872 73: the convention's committee on suffrage recommended that the tax qualification be dropped, a recommendation supported by Democrats and reform Republicans, including the committee's chair, H. Nelson McAllister. McAllister, presenting the committee report, argued that "the right of suffrage" was perhaps not an "absolute personal right" but was a "natural social right," belonging "to a man because he is a man," not "because he is a taxpayer." McAllister found repugnant the prospect "of excluding from the right of suffrage any man on the face of the earth because he is poor." Yet McAllister and his allies ran up against the powerful Republican political machine that ruled the state for decades and was well known for paying the taxes of its supporters. William Darlington, a machine Republican, objected strenuously to this "fundamental change" in the state's laws, a change that would allow "those to vote . . . who have no manner of stake in the government." His colleague, Charles Bowman, declared that he would "never vote" for a proposition "by which vagabonds and stragglers shall have a right to step up to the election polls and cast a vote which will count just as much as the man whose property is taxed thousands of dollars." Thanks more to their political muscle than the power of their arguments, the defenders of a taxpaying requirement carried the day, and the qualification was carried over into the new constitution. Fifteen years later, opponents sponsored a constitutional amendment to repeal the requirement, but the electorate, mobilized by the still-powerful machine (now headed by Matthew Quay, who played a key role in defeating the Lodge Force Bill), overwhelmingly rejected the amendment. Until the 1930s, the only success achieved by reformers was the passage in 1897 of a weakly enforced law that required citizens to pay their taxes themselves.[23]

Meanwhile, a handful of states that did not have property or taxpaying requirements considered imposing them, causing disputes in constitutional conventions in Indiana, Ohio, Colorado, Missouri, and Texas. (The last occurred in 1875, long before the great sweep of southern disfranchisement.) In the 1870s, the electorate of Maine narrowly rejected the adoption of the state's first taxpaying requirement, and the California constitutional convention of 1878–79, which expressly banned property requirements, declined to inscribe in its constitution a similar ban on poll tax restrictions.[24]

In many locales, there were serious debates regarding the implementation of more politically palatable economic qualifications: selective ones that would apply in some elections but not others. The most celebrated contest occurred in New York in the late 1870s, when a commission appointed by the Democratic governor, Samuel Tilden, recommended the creation of a board of finance to control taxation and expenditures in each of the state's cities. In the largest cities, this board was to be elected by men who owned and had paid two years of taxes on property valued at $500 or more; potential voters also could become eligible by establishing that they had paid an annual rent for two years of at least $250. In lesser cities, the same principles would apply, but the valuations were lower. Aimed at New York City's Democratic machine and at working-class voters throughout the state, this proposal was endorsed by the business community, the state's social and financial elite, prominent politicians, major newspapers and magazines, and leading liberal reformers such as Godkin. Characterized by supporters as a means of lowering taxes and making clear to voters "that municipal affairs are business affairs, to be managed on business principles," the measure would have deprived a sizable majority of the state's urban population from participating in decisions affecting municipal taxes or expenditures. The

Republicans introduced the measure to the legislature as a constitutional amendment, where it was approved in 1877. New York, however, required that proposed amendments be passed by two successive legislatures before being submitted to a popular vote, and the following year—unhappily for advocates of municipal property requirements—Democrats gained a legislative majority and blocked passage of the amendment.[25]

Although defeated in New York, selective or municipal economic qualifications were imposed in cities and towns scattered throughout the country. The legislature in Maryland had the authority to impose taxpaying requirements in all municipal elections, and it did so for numerous towns and cities, including Annapolis. Municipal tax qualifications also appeared in Kentucky, Vermont, Texas, and eventually some communities in New York—as well as Rhode Island. Michigan in 1908 decided that only owners of taxable property could vote on any referendum question "which involves the direct expenditure of public money or the issue of bonds." Arizona, Oklahoma, and Utah passed similar legislation, and New York in 1910 restricted school board voting to either the parents of school-age children or property owners in the school district. Kansas, early in the twentieth century, adopted a technique that would be emulated for decades: it created new governmental entities—drainage boards, in this case—that possessed highly specific yet crucial powers, and for which only taxpayers could vote. (For a listing of various tax and property qualifications, see tables A.10 and A.11.)[26]

The legality of selective economic prerequisites for voting was affirmed consistently by the courts. In 1902, for example, the New York Court of Appeals upheld a state law that permitted the village of Fulton to restrict voting on financial propositions to those owning property in the village. Distinguishing between the right to vote in general state elections and the right to vote on municipal financial matters, the court ruled that the legislature had the right and duty "to protect the taxpayers of every city and village in the state." "And what better or more effective method of preventing . . . abuses and protecting . . . taxpayers could be devised," queried the court, "than to restrict the right of voting upon propositions for borrowing money or for contracting debts, to the persons who are liable to be taxed for the payment of such debts?" Similarly, the supreme court of Kansas found a way to rule that the taxpaying requirement for drainage board elections was constitutional, despite the fact that the Kansas Constitution—like many others written at midcentury—expressly banned property and tax qualifications for voting. The court concluded that the precedent established by the enfranchisement of women in school board elections made clear that the provisions of the state constitution applied only to those offices and elections explicitly mentioned in the constitution itself. The U.S. Supreme Court made clear that it too did not see anything unconstitutional about taxpaying or property requirements in *Myers v. Anderson* in 1915. Although the Court overturned the Maryland law that limited suffrage in Annapolis to taxpayers, it did so only because of a grandfather clause that permitted nontaxpayers to vote if they were the descendants of men who had been legal voters in 1868. The Court thus found the law to be racially discriminatory in violation of the Fifteenth Amendment; at the same time, however, it noted that economic discrimination in the form of a property requirement was presumed to be "free from constitutional objection."[27]

This same reasoning permitted numerous states to continue excluding paupers from the franchise. As table A.6 indicates, a dozen states, all in the Northeast and the South, barred from the franchise any man who received public aid. In addition, four states excluded inmates of poorhouses or charitable institutions, and many more throughout the country prohibited such inmates from gaining a legal residence in the town or city where the institution was located. Paupers therefore could not vote unless they were able to travel to their community of origin, an unlikely prospect. With the exception of Arkansas, no state repealed its pauper exclusion law, while many of the statutes aimed at inmates were passed after the Civil War.[28]

The reach of the laws, however, was narrowed. Whatever ambiguity might once have existed regarding the definition of *pauper*, it was well understood in the late nineteenth century that the term applied only to men who received public support. Legislatures and courts also took steps to clarify the temporal dimensions of the exclusions, usually (but not always) specifying that a man was barred from the polls only if he was a pauper at the time that an election was held: prior pauperism was not grounds for disfranchisement. In Massachusetts, the House of Representatives asked the Supreme Judicial Court in 1878 to give an advisory opinion regarding "whether a person who is admitted to have been, and to have ceased to be, a pauper, must have ceased to be such for any definite period of time before he can exercise the right of suffrage." The court concluded that no such period of "probation" was required. "The disqualification of pauperism or guardianship, like that of alienage or nonage, is not required to have ceased to exist for any definite period of time, in order to entitle a man . . . to exercise the right of suffrage." New Hampshire was less generous: anyone receiving aid within ninety days of an election was disqualified.[29]

Despite the temporal limitations, pauper exclusions prevented thousands of men in Massachusetts (and perhaps hundreds of thousands nationwide) from voting. As important, the disciplinary edge to the laws remained sharp: the reason that the Massachusetts House of Representatives sought an opinion from the Supreme Judicial Court was that it hoped to apply the pauper exclusion law to all men who had received relief at any time during the year preceding an election. To do so, it considered requiring local overseers of the poor to report the names of such men to election officials. The legislature's concern stemmed from the dramatic increase in the number of persons seeking public relief during the prolonged depression of the 1870s. Despite abundant evidence that those people were jobless "through no fault of their own," many respectable citizens were convinced that men who sought relief were "slackers," "loafers," and "tramps" who needed to be disciplined: not coincidentally, the same legislature that sought to extend the pauper exclusion law passed "anti-tramp" legislation making it a crime for a jobless man to travel from town to town in search of work. As Charles T. Russell, a critic of these laws, noted, those who advocated the redefinition of *pauper* to include "a person who has within a year received public assistance" believed that paupers were not unfortunate but unworthy, that "once a pauper always a pauper."[30]

That the pauper disqualification could serve as a means of social discipline also was revealed in the course of a strike in New Bedford, Massachusetts, in 1898. When striking textile workers sought public relief to help tide them over months without income, they were told by city officials that receiving such relief would disqualify them from voting in the next election. The announcement sparked an uproar in New Bedford, particularly when one striker, despite illness in his family, withdrew his application for aid so that he would not be disfranchised. After the mayor had been informed of his plight, legal guidance was sought from the city solicitor, who then dug up the Supreme Judicial Court's 1878 opinion and announced that relief recipients could vote if they had ceased receiving aid by election day. The solicitor's report was front-page news in the overwhelmingly working-class city, and advocates of disfranchisement backed off. Nonetheless, the message was clear: poverty could cost workingmen their political rights. Turning to the state for aid had a price and would transform a needy worker into something less than a full citizen. The national magazine of the machinists' union reported on the case in detail, observing that "if the capitalistic class succeeded in robbing every man of his vote who was forced to apply for relief, it wouldn't be long before a great percentage of our citizens would be voteless. There is nothing they fear so much as a vote."[31]

Immigrants Unwelcomed

> In my judgment, whenever the United States finds itself at war with a foreign country, and realizes the need of soldiers, the need of strong bodies, brawny arms and brave hearts, they will be liberal enough in extending the right of suffrage and the facilities to become citizens to our foreign born fellow men. But in times of profound peace, when war's dread alarms are not sounding through the land, they relapse back into the old channel, and require them to serve an apprenticeship before they shall become voters or citizens of the United States.
>
> —Mr. Burns, Ohio
> Constitutional Convention, 1874

Overtly class-based economic restrictions were accompanied by legal changes expressly designed to reduce the number of "undesirable" immigrants who could vote. Beginning in the 1890s, the nation witnessed the growth of a significant movement to restrict immigration altogether, one source of which was widespread middle-class anxiety about the impact of the foreign-born on politics, particularly urban politics. The effort to keep immigrants from the polls, however, was somewhat distinct from the movement for outright restriction, and it bore fruit long before Congress passed the pathbreaking restriction and quota acts of 1921 and 1924.[32]

One critical step in this campaign was the revocation of state laws that permitted noncitizen declarants (those who had lived in the United States for two years and formally filed declarations of their intent to become citizens) to vote. As described in chapter 2, such laws became common in the Midwest in the mid-nineteenth century, and they also were enacted in parts of the South and West after the Civil War. Yet even before the last of these laws were passed, in the 1880s and 1890s, the pendulum of public opinion had begun to swing in the opposite direction. (See table A.12.) As the ratio of immigrant workers to settlers soared and the need to encourage settlement diminished, granting the franchise to noncitizens seemed increasingly undesirable and risky.

At the Ohio Constitutional Convention of 1873–74, for example, a committee recommendation in favor of enfranchising declarant aliens produced days of stormy debate. Ohio was one of the few midwestern states that had not authorized noncitizen voting, and proponents of the new law, many of them Democrats and some foreign-born, offered a variety of arguments for bringing the state in line with its neighbors. Enfranchising aliens who had filed "first papers" would encourage migration, attach immigrants to American institutions, and justly reward loyal aliens who had fought in the Civil War or might serve in the military in the future. Denying noncitizens the vote stigmatized the foreign-born and implied that they were inferior to recently enfranchised blacks. Opponents of alien suffrage countered with Parkmanesque images of ignorant, foreign-born paupers ill-equipped to participate in democratic politics. They also contended that suffrage ought to derive from citizenship, that it was unconstitutional for the state to usurp the federal government's authority to create citizens, and that it was "dangerous to confer suffrage upon those who owe their allegiance to foreign powers." Reflecting the heat of a simultaneous debate about women's suffrage, some opponents further maintained that it would be unseemly, if not unjust, to enfranchise alien males while women remained voteless.

Embedded in these opposition arguments were strident emotions, a xenophobia that interlaced left-over Know-Nothingism with newly intensified anxieties about racial equality. Lewis D. Campbell, a delegate from the small town of Butler, insisted that the racial equality provisions of the Fourteenth and Fifteenth Amendments heightened the menace of immigration. If alien suffrage were permitted,

> it will be granted not only to the unnaturalized foreigner who comes here from European countries, but also to the unnaturalized African who might be brought over . . . by Dr. Livingstone; and should he capture in the jungles of that benighted land . . . a specimen of the connecting link between man and the animal, as described by the theory of Darwin, and bring him to Ohio, that link could not only claim to become a citizen of the United States, but without naturalization . . . claim to be a sovereign, a voter and an officeholder. . . . The Chinese, the Japanese, and even the Ashantees, who are now at war with England . . . could become voters.

Campbell also feared that wealthy "foreign capitalists," such as "the Rothschilds," could control American elections by "colonizing" aliens into key electoral districts. Just how widespread the fear of blacks, Jews, and the missing link may have been is impossible to determine, but Campbell, a Republican-turned-Democratic Congressman and vice-president of the constitutional convention, was hardly the only delegate to voice xenophobic concerns. After a week of debate, the proposal to enfranchise aliens in Ohio was defeated.[33]

The debate in Ohio was unusually prolonged and colorful, but there was nothing unusual about either its content or the outcome of the vote: most states rejected alien suffrage proposals in the late nineteenth century, and beginning with Idaho territory in 1874, states that had permitted noncitizens to vote began to repeal their declarant alien provisions. This rollback picked up steam in the wake of the depression of the 1890s and the assassination of President McKinley by an immigrant in 1901; it accelerated again during and after World War I, when concerns about the loyalty of the foreign-born contributed to a rare instance of wartime contraction of the franchise. The last state to permit noncitizens to vote was Arkansas, which abolished the practice in 1926.[34] (See table A.12.)

While alien suffrage was being phased out, numerous states placed new obstacles in the path of immigrant voters: most commonly these were supported by some Republicans, opposed by Democrats, and justified on the grounds that they would reduce fraud. One such obstacle was to require naturalized citizens to present their naturalization papers to election officials before registering or voting. Although not unreasonable on its face, this requirement, as lawmakers knew, was a significant procedural hurdle for many immigrants, who might easily have lost their papers or been unaware of the requirement. "A sad feature" of New Jersey's requirement, observed the *New York Herald* in 1888, "was that many persons will be deprived of their vote, as their papers are either worn out, lost, or mislaid." Particularly when coupled with provisions that permitted anyone present at the polls to challenge the credentials of immigrant voters, these laws placed substantial discretionary power in the hands of local officials.[35]

Another method, mildly echoing Know-Nothing demands, was to prohibit naturalized citizens from voting unless they had been naturalized well before any specific election. Couched as an antidote to mass election-eve naturalizations, these laws placed a unique burden on foreign-born citizens and prevented aliens from deciding to become citizens because they had become interested in the outcome of a particular election. (Since few aliens became citizens as soon as the five-year minimum residency period had expired, such decisions were likely not unusual.) Indeed, in 1887, the Supreme Judicial Court of Massachusetts overturned the commonwealth's statutory one-month waiting period on the grounds that it was not a "reasonable" regulation of electoral procedures but was instead "calculated injuriously to restrain and impede in the exercise of their rights the class to whom it applies." This logic, however, was not embraced in other courts: five states did impose waiting periods on the foreign-born. In New York and California, immigrants had to wait a full ninety days after naturalization before they could vote. (See table A.12.)[36]

The concerns that prompted such efforts to keep immigrants from the polls also contributed to the tightening of federal immigration and naturalization laws between 1880 and the 1920s. Keeping undesirable immigrants out of the country or keeping them from being naturalized was viewed as one of the best "safeguards of the suffrage" by many who were apprehensive about immigrant voters. Immigration and naturalization laws in fact had changed very little between 1802 and the 1880s, although Congress in 1870 passed a law specifying that "aliens of African nationality and persons of African descent," as well as whites, were eligible to be naturalized. (Exactly what *white* meant was debated in the nation's courts for decades.) Beginning in 1882, however, Congress began to narrow the channels through which the flow of European immigrants passed. In that year, it enacted a law that barred convicts, "lunatics," "idiots," and people likely to become public charges from entering the United States. A head tax of 50 cents was imposed on each immigrant, and steamship companies were required to screen their passengers and provide return passage for any who were refused admission. In subsequent years, the list of undesirables was extended to include contract laborers, polygamists, those suffering from dangerous contagious diseases, epileptics, professional beggars, and anarchists.[37]

Between 1906 and 1910, Congress also codified the naturalization laws, prohibiting many "undesirable" foreign-born residents from becoming citizens, setting a time limit on the validity of declarations of intent, and requiring candidates for naturalization to write their own names and present ample proof (including witnesses) of their eligibility and continuous residence in the United States for five years. These laws were unabashedly aimed at making it more difficult for men and women to become citizens, and by all accounts they succeeded, reducing the proportion of immigrants who could vote. Some judges, moreover, applied a political litmus test to potential citizens, refusing to naturalize men "with the slightest sympathy for the principles of Socialism" or trade unionism. In 1912, a federal judge in Seattle even revoked the citizenship of a naturalized citizen who espoused socialism.[38]

The most controversial reform of the naturalization laws was the imposition of a literacy or education test on candidates for citizenship. This idea was first introduced in Congress by Henry Cabot Lodge in 1895: although passed with bipartisan support, it was vetoed by President Grover Cleveland early in 1897. For the next two decades, it was reintroduced almost annually, garnering the support of a unique, if not bizarre, coalition of northern professionals, many Republicans, southern Democrats, anti-Catholics, anti-Semites, and the American Federation of Labor. Although unstated, the bill's target was clearly the "new" immigrant population, eastern and southern Europeans who had high rates of illiteracy (more than 20 percent in 1914) and who generally were regarded as less desirable than their English, German, Scandinavian, and even Irish predecessors. There also was an unmistakable class thrust to the proposal: as one supporter tellingly argued,

> the theory of the educational test is that it furnishes an indirect method of excluding those who are undesirable, not merely because of their illiteracy but for other reasons . . . there is a fairly constant relation between illiteracy, the amount of money brought by the immigrant, his standard of living, his tendency to crime and pauperism, [and] his disposition to congregate in the slums of cities.

After the turn of the century, literacy requirements for naturalization twice more were passed by Congress and vetoed, first by William Howard Taft and then by Woodrow Wilson. During World War I, however, concerns about the loyalty of the foreign-born, coupled with a new emphasis on the "Americanization" of immigrants, gave a boost to the measure, and in 1917 Congress mustered enough votes to override Wilson's second veto.[39]

Intense as apprehensions about poor European immigrants may have been, they paled in comparison to American attitudes toward the Chinese and other east Asians: by the final quarter of the nineteenth century, most Americans—and especially those on the West Coast—wanted not only to keep the Chinese from voting but to halt Chinese immigration and even deport those who were already here. The center of anti-Chinese agitation was California, which housed a sizable population of Chinese migrants (but less than 100,000), many of whom had been recruited to help build the nation's railroads. Feared because of their willingness to work for low wages and despised for racial and cultural reasons, the Chinese had never been a significant political presence because they had almost always been treated as nonwhite and therefore ineligible for citizenship. Nonetheless, the Chinese became the target of fierce racism during the depression of the 1870s, one consequence of which was the passage of a series of federal laws, beginning in 1882, that strictly limited and then halted Chinese immigration. (Later variants of the law also banned the Japanese.) Such restriction, according to a congressional committee, was necessary in order to "discourage the large influx of any class of population to whom the ballot cannot be safely confided." It was widely agreed that the Chinese, "an indigestible mass . . . distinct in language, pagan in religion, inferior in mental and moral qualities," constituted such a class.[40]

But these federal laws were not sufficient to satisfy western xenophobes. In California in the late 1870s, anti-Chinese agitators, led by small businessman and Irish immigrant Denis Kearney, took command of the fledgling Marxian Workingmen's Party and used it as a vehicle to capture control of the San Francisco city government and gain significant influence in state politics. The program of Kearney's party, reminiscent of the Know-Nothings, contained an amalgam of progressive, anti–big business (and antirailroad) proposals, rhetoric denouncing the mainstream political parties, and a slew of measures designed to remove the Chinese from the state's economic and political life. One proposal even called for disfranchising anyone who hired a Chinese worker.[41]

Although working class and lower middle class in origin, Kearney's movement quickly succeeded in garnering broad support for the anti-Chinese elements of its program. As a result, the California Constitutional Convention of 1878–79, heavily populated by Workingmen's delegates, passed almost without objection a series of anti-Chinese articles. One delegate claimed that without such laws, California would become "the mercenary Mecca of the scum of Asia—a loathsome Chinese province." Although many of these measures were thrown out by the courts, the suffrage provision of the 1879 constitution remained in force until 1926. It specified that "no native of China" (the wording was aimed at circumventing the Fifteenth Amendment's ban on racial barriers) "shall ever exercise the privileges of an elector in this State." The convention's formal address to the people of California declared that this article was "intended to guard against a possible change in the naturalization laws so as to admit Chinese to citizenship." Similar provisions appeared in the constitutions of Oregon and Idaho.[42]

Educated Voters

> A knowledge of the language of our laws and the faculty of informing oneself without aid of their provisions, would in itself constitute a test, if rigorously enforced, incompatible with the existence of a proletariat.
>
> —CHARLES FRANCIS ADAMS, JR.
> "PROTECTION OF THE BALLOT" (1869)

> The great danger of the proposed reform (?) is that it strikes at
> the root of free government by substituting a qualification of ac-
> quirement for the qualification of nature, i.e., Manhood, the only
> qualification that can safely be set upon the republican franchise.
> . . . If a republic can be got to admit that the right to vote is de-
> pendent upon the ability to read and write it may just as consis-
> tently decide that that right is a privilege dependent upon the
> ability to pay a certain amount of taxes.
>
> —*Coast Seamen's Journal*, 1896

Perhaps the most popular method of constricting the electorate was the literacy or education test. Massachusetts and Connecticut had adopted such
tests in the 1850s, and support for them became widespread beginning in
the 1870s, as the memories and taint of Know-Nothingism faded. Requiring voters to be literate, particularly in English, had a number of apparent
virtues: it would reduce the "ignorance" of the electorate and weed out sizable numbers of poor immigrant voters (outside of the South, the native-
born population was almost entirely literate); moreover, it would do so in a
way that was ideologically more palatable than taxpaying restrictions or
waiting periods for the foreign-born. Literacy tests did not overtly discriminate against particular classes or ethnic groups, and literacy itself was a re-
mediable shortcoming. While the federal government was debating an
education test for citizenship, the states began to entertain the possibility of
imposing their own tests on potential voters.

An indirect and limited means of promoting a literate electorate was the
adoption of the secret or Australian ballot (which first appeared in Australia
in 1856 and then was implemented in England in 1872). For much of the
nineteenth century, voters had obtained their ballots from political parties:
since the ballots generally contained only the names of an individual party's
candidates, literacy was not required. All that a man had to do was drop a ballot in a box. Since ballots tended to be of different sizes, shapes, and colors, a
man's vote was hardly a secret—to election officials, party bosses, employers,
or anyone else watching the polls. (In theory, a voter could write his own ballot, or "scratch" names from a party ballot, but it was difficult to keep such actions confidential.) The Australian ballot was an effort to remedy this
situation and presumably the corruption and intimidation that flowed from it:
it was a standard ballot, usually printed by the city or state, containing the
names of all candidates for office; the voter, often in private, placed a mark by
the names of the candidates or parties for whom he wished to vote.[43]

The first American experiment with the Australian ballot, in Louisville in 1888, was rapidly followed by its adoption almost everywhere in the United States. Despite (or perhaps underscored by) the opposition of machine politicians, the democratic virtues of secret voting were widely apparent. The Australian ballot was, however, an obstacle to participation by many illiterate foreign-born voters in the North, as well as uneducated black voters in the South. In some states, this problem was remedied by expressly permitting illiterate voters to be assisted or by attaching party emblems to the names of candidates; in others, it was compounded by complex ballot configurations that easily could stymie the illiterate. (An Ohio court in 1909 issued a nonbinding dictum questioning whether the state's ballot laws constituted an unconstitutional, back-door education test.) In more than a few states, including New York, rules governing the physical appearance and comprehensibility of the ballot were a partisan battlefield for years. (See table A.13.)[44]

Both before and after adoption of the Australian ballot, many states considered adding more direct and robust literacy tests to the qualifications required of voters. The argument for doing so was three-pronged. Its core, of course, was that illiterate men lacked the intelligence or knowledge necessary to be wise or even adequate voters. A voter who cannot read, insisted E. L. Godkin, "may be said to labor, for all political purposes, under mental incapacity." A delegate to Michigan's constitutional convention of 1907 maintained similarly that "it is of the highest importance that any man who is called upon to perform the function of voting should be not only intelligent but also be able to find out for himself what the real questions before the public are." A second justification, aimed particularly at new immigrants, was that English-language literacy was essential for the foreign-born to become properly acquainted with American values and institutions. The third was that tying voting to literacy would encourage assimilation and education, which would benefit American society as well as immigrants themselves.[45]

Reasonable as these arguments sounded, they often sparked vehement opposition, much of which was grounded in the (accurate) perception that literacy requirements discriminated against foreign-born citizens and were designed to reduce their electoral strength. In New York, where education tests were proposed at constitutional conventions in 1846, 1867–68, 1894, and 1915, a delegate derided them in 1915 as "another attempt upon the part of the rural communities of this State to restrict the voting capacity of the city of New York where the greatest number of foreigners have their homes." In many states, opponents attacked the proposals as shameful revivals of Know-Nothingism, insulting to immigrants, and violating American traditions: "if literacy were a valid test of voting . . . nearly fifty percent of our early settlers . . . the men who are idolized to-day as the pioneers of civilization . . . would not be entitled to vote." Virtue and intelligence were not confined to the literate, and it was fundamentally unfair to deny people the rights, while imposing the obligations, of citizenship. "You will disfranchise many a man who understands what he is voting on just as well as we do," declared a Michigan delegate. "If a man is ignorant, he needs the ballot for his protection all the more," insisted a New York Democrat in 1868. "If you disfranchise a man because he cannot read and write," argued a member of Missouri's convention in 1875, "then, in my judgment you ought not to call upon him to repair the public highways, you ought not ask him to pay taxes . . . you ought not to call upon him when the enemy invades your country." One of his colleagues even satirized the proposed literacy test and the benefits that it would purportedly bring to his state:

> We might go a step further, and I have no doubt my friends will join me in this. It is desirable that a man should not only know how to read and write but that he should be educated in the higher branches. We might graduate this thing, and say that in 1876 he shall read and write, that in 1878, at the next biennial election he should understand Geography and that in 1880 he shall understand Arithmetic, and we might thus proceed gradually from Arithmetic to English Grammar, and from English Grammar to History, Moral and Mental Philosophy . . . we should have a generation by the time the 19th century closes the most intelligent, the most prosperous, the most happy here in the State of Missouri upon the face of the habitable globe.[46]

The opposition was sufficiently strong that most states outside of the South declined to impose literacy tests. Not surprisingly, northern Democrats, who counted the urban poor among their constituents, generally voted against education requirements. So too did politically organized ethnic groups, regardless of their party affiliation—which helps to explain why no English-language literacy tests were imposed in the Midwest: the German and Scandinavian communities of the Midwest, though often allied with the Republicans, vehemently opposed education requirements. Missouri rejected a literacy test in 1875, as did Michigan in 1907, and Illinois on several occasions, up to and including 1920. In New Mexico, a sizable Spanish-speaking electorate went so far as to write into the state's first constitution that "the right of any citizen . . . to vote . . . shall never be restricted, abridged, or impaired on account of inability to speak, read, or write the English and Spanish languages." In New York, the Democrats, backed by the Irish and later the Italian and Jewish communities, successfully resisted a test until after World War I.[47]

Nonetheless, by the mid-1920s, thirteen states in the North and West were disfranchising illiterate citizens who met all other eligibility requirements. (See table A.13.) In all of these states, the Republican Party was strong; several had large immigrant populations that played important roles in party competition; a handful of others were predominantly rural states with small but visible clusters of poor foreign-born voters; several also had significant Native American populations. In Massachusetts and Connecticut, Republicans were able to beat back recurrent Democratic efforts to repeal the laws that had been passed in the 1850s. Massachusetts, in 1889, demanded that anyone who had not voted for four years had to take a new literacy test; by a ten-to-one majority, voters in Connecticut in 1895 endorsed an amendment specifying that literacy had to be "in the English language." Wyoming, where only 2 percent of the population was foreign-born, instituted a literacy requirement in 1889 both to disfranchise miners and guard against a future influx of immigrants.[48]

Five years later, California enacted a constitutional amendment that disfranchised any "person who shall not be able to read the Constitution in the English language and write his name." The amendment (a precursor of which had been defeated in 1879) originated more in grass-roots pressure than in organized partisan conflict. The idea first was broached in the assembly by a Republican veteran of the anti-Chinese agitation: bipartisan opposition to it crumbled in the face of a petition campaign and then an advisory referendum signaling that nearly 80 percent of the electorate supported an education requirement. Aimed diffusely at the Chinese, Mexican Americans, "the ignorant foreign vote," and "hosts of immigrants pouring in from foreign countries," the amendment—which contained a grandfather clause exempting current voters—then was passed by the legislature with little opposition.[49]

Remarkably, New York, which had the largest immigrant population in the nation, also passed a constitutional amendment instituting a literacy requirement in 1921: prospective voters were obliged either to pass a stringent English-language reading and writing test administered by the Board of Regents or present evidence that they had at least an eighth-grade education in an approved school. Although similar proposals had been defeated in earlier decades, the Republican-dominated legislature, backed by reform organizations such as the Citizens' Union, succeeded in pushing the amendment through in the aftermath of the war and the antiradical, anti-immigrant Red Scare of 1919. The amendment, which had the potential of disfranchising, among others, hundreds of thousands of Yiddish-speaking Jews, was backed overwhelmingly by upstate voters and even received a majority in New York City. Support for a literacy test also may have been strengthened by the recent enfranchisement of women, which was believed likely to "produce 189,000 more illiterate voters."[50]

The potential impact of these literacy laws—all of which were sanctioned by the courts—was enormous. According to the census (which relied on self-reporting), there were nearly 5 million illiterate men and women in the nation in 1920, roughly 8 percent of the voting-age population. Other sources suggest that in fact the figure was much higher. Twenty-five percent of men who took an army literacy test during World War I, for example, were judged to be illiterate and another 5 percent semiliterate. To be sure, education tests were not always rigorously administered, and several states "grandfathered" men and women who could already vote. Still, literacy requirements, North and South, could be a potent weapon. In New York (the only locale for which data exist), roughly 15 percent of all those who took the English-language literacy test between 1923 and 1929 (55,000 persons out of 472,000) failed; and it seems safe to assume (as did contemporaries) that many more potential voters did not take the test because they thought they had little chance of passing. Thus a reasonable estimate is that a minimum of several hundred thousand voters—and likely more than a million—were barred by these tests, outside of the South. In 1900, one reformer, echoing others, lamented that a literacy test "does not go far enough: it places the hod-carrier who knows his alphabet on a level with the President of Harvard College." Yet there were surely some hod carriers who did not know their alphabet well enough to attain that exalted parity.[51]

Migrants and Residents

> No one knows better than the learned counsel on the other side and the lawyers of this committee the difficulty in modern times of proving a person's residence, no matter what his position in life may be. It has required the Supreme Court to tell Nat Thayer and William F. Weld and John H. Wright where they lived. And the more migratory the population, the poorer the person, the less worldly effects with which he is endowed, the more difficult becomes the question at any particular day or hour where he is

residing. He is not a householder, he owns not even a trunk, his worldly goods are on his back or in his pocket, and where he lives it is difficult, of course difficult, to say, whether it be in a palace on the Back Bay or in a pigstye in Ward 17.

—Argument of Arthur T. Johnson
in a contested election case,
Massachusetts, 1891

Arthur T. Johnson was right: the difficulty of defining or establishing residence indeed was becoming more complex "in modern times," and "the poorer the person," the greater the complexity. As an historian of Boston would discover almost a century later, that city's population was extremely mobile in the 1880s, and rates of mobility rose as one descended the occupational hierarchy. In the city as a whole, only 64 percent of all residents in 1880 were still living there a decade later; for blue-collar workers, the proportion was substantially lower. Indeed, the number of persons who lived in Boston at some point in the 1880s was three times as large as the number who ever lived there at the same time. Boston was not unusual—nor were the 1880s.[52]

Given the peripatetic lives of Americans in general and workers in particular, it is hardly surprising that residency qualifications for voting often were in dispute. In contrast to other dimensions of electoral law, however, these disputes more often were juridical than political. Court cases abounded as citizens challenged their exclusion from the polls (or the inclusion of others) because of their failure to meet residency requirements. At the heart of such conflicts was the difficulty of defining *residence*, particularly in light of the increasingly accepted legal notion that sheer physical presence in a community for a specified length of time was not sufficient for a person to be considered a resident. As the Supreme Court of Colorado put it in 1896,

We think the residence . . . contemplated [by the constitution] is synonymous with "home" or "domicile," and means an actual settlement within the state, and its adoption as a fixed and permanent habitation; and requires not only a personal presence for the requisite time, but a concurrence therewith of an intention to make the place of inhabitancy the true home.

Physical presence thus had to be accompanied by the intention of remaining in a community for what the courts came to describe as "an indefinite period." Although the concept was reasonable, intention could be difficult to ascertain or prove. Consequently, courts found themselves evolving criteria to gauge the intentions of both individuals and groups (such as ministers and railway workers, who were often on the move), as they tried to apply broadly stated laws to extremely varied situations. On the whole, the insistence on intention tended to make legal residence harder to establish, especially for men whose occupations demanded mobility, but the rules were frequently interpreted with considerable sensitivity to individual circumstances.[53]

Although the rules developed by state courts differed from one another, on one major issue there was uniformity: no jurisdiction questioned the legitimacy of statutes or constitutional amendments establishing residence qualifications—even lengthy residence qualifications—for voting. In 1904, moreover, the U.S. Supreme Court, in *Pope v. Williams*, affirmed the constitutionality of residency qualifications and state efforts to enforce them. Ruling on a Maryland law that required persons moving into the state to make a declaration of intention to become state residents one year before they could cast their ballots, the Court ruled that the "statute does not violate any Federal right of the plaintiff." The Maryland law "is neither an unlawful discrimination . . . nor does it deny to him the equal protection of the laws, nor is it repugnant to any fundamental or inalienable rights of citizens."[54]

While the courts debated the definition of residence, it was left to constitutional conventions, and sometimes legislatures, to determine the appropriate length of residency requirements. In much of the nation, there was a broad consensus that a year's residence in the state was necessary and sufficient for a man to responsibly exercise the franchise, although in many midwestern states the consensus period was six months. More controversial were local, county, and district requirements. Those who favored relatively long periods of residence (usually three to six months) commonly argued that voters needed time to "become very largely interested in the local politics of a county or precinct" and to become "identified with the interests of the community." Almost always, such arguments contained ingredients of class apprehension. "The citizens of any precinct have the right of protection against a floating population," noted an Illinois delegate in 1870. "Our state," observed one of his colleagues, "is now a great railroad state. There are a great number of operatives in the service of these various railroads, who might be transferred to a particular locality . . . and the permanent residents would have their interests voted down by these casual and temporary residents." In some instances, the class fears were directed upward: "great interests" or "designing politicians" could take advantage of short residency periods to "colonize" men into a particular district in order to win an election.[55]

Opponents of long residency requirements responded in kind: a member of Pennsylvania's constitutional convention in 1872–73 objected that a proposed precinct residence rule would disfranchise thousands of working men who were compelled to move from place to place so that they could live near their places of employment: "You absolutely deprive them of the right to vote, just because they are so poor and so unfortunate that they are forced to change their places of dwelling within two months of election day." "Laboring men and mechanics, as a general thing," insisted a California politician, "cannot live in one place as long as ninety days." In New York in the 1870s, residents of some rural counties, as well as the New York State Teachers Association, also petitioned for shorter county residence requirements.[56]

In the end, as table A.14 reveals, residency rules did not change much outside of the South. California and Colorado increased their required periods of residency, many states tinkered with precinct and county requirements, and Minnesota in 1893 passed an extraordinary law preventing migrant lumbermen and construction workers from gaining residence. As a rule, however, the issue generated only muted partisan warfare, and the prevailing patterns in 1920 were very similar to those in place in 1870. Notably, no state in the North or West, except Rhode Island briefly, adopted the punitive, two-year requirements that were becoming common in the South.

These years also witnessed the codification of residency rules for three increasingly large groups of men whose situations were anomalous: residents of almshouses and other custodial institutions, soldiers and sailors, and students. As noted earlier, many states enacted laws that prevented inhabitants of public (and even private) custodial institutions from becoming legal residents of the communities where those institutions were located. The same rule was applied to military personnel, although most states (to avoid the appearance of disfranchising soldiers) also specified that soldiers and sailors who were away from home did not lose their residence in their original communities. (See table A.14.)

The most difficult case proved to be students at colleges, seminaries, and other institutions of higher learning. In many states, there was substantial sentiment in favor of prohibiting students from gaining residence in the communities where they attended college: claiming that students were not truly members of the community, political leaders cited anecdotes of students being paraded to the polls to vote en masse, of unscrupulous politicians enlisting students to cast their ballots, and of students (who did not pay taxes) voting to impose tax increases on permanent residents. There was, however, a notable degree of resistance to such laws, grounded perhaps in a reluctance to keep respectable, middle-class, native-born men from voting. "I cannot see the propriety of . . . discriminating against intelligent young men attending college," insisted a Pennsylvanian in 1873. Many states did end up specifying that students could not gain legal residence by attending educational institutions, although the courts—and occasionally the legislatures as well—made exceptions for those who did not have other domiciles and could establish their intention to remain in the community where they were studying.[57]

The notion that legal residence was tied as much to intention as physical presence inexorably led states to consider mechanisms for absentee voting—for men and women who were temporarily away from home but intended to return. Although there were venerable precedents for men casting their ballots without being physically present at polling places (in seventeenth-century Massachusetts, for example, men whose homes were vulnerable to Indian attack were permitted to vote without leaving their abodes), absentee voting was rare before 1860: only Oregon, in 1857, made it possible for men who were temporarily away from home to vote. Yet, as noted in chapter 4, the Civil War—and the desire to permit soldiers to vote during the war—severed the link between voting and physical presence in a community. After the war, more and more states made it possible for absent soldiers to vote, particularly if they were stationed within their home state. The laws sometimes specified that they could vote anywhere in the state for statewide offices and anywhere in the district in congressional elections; casting ballots by mail was not the norm. World War I added a new urgency to the issue, since nearly three million men were inducted into the army. Accordingly, by 1918, nearly all states had made provisions for men serving in the military to cast their ballots, at least in time of war.[58]

Soldiers opened the gates to a broader dispensation. The logic of allowing nonresident military personnel to vote seemed to apply almost equally well to others whose jobs forced them to be away from home on election day. The city of Somerville's delegate to the Massachusetts Constitutional Convention of 1917–18 made the point at some length:

> there is a very clear-cut analogy . . . between the votes of the soldiers and
> sailors on the one hand and such citizens as trainmen and traveling salesmen
> on the other . . . we are saying here . . . that the absent soldiers and sailors
> should not be deprived of their enfranchisement at an election . . . because the
> State or the Nation has extended its own hand and removed these men, for
> the time, out of their place in the body politic . . . we also have an industrial

situation, or rather, an industrial system, and by that system, through no fault of their own, men are removed from their places in the body politic and deprived of their rightful votes. The system of industry which is doing that, which removes these men, is also in the interest of the public good. The sacrifices of the soldiers and sailors are more spectacular, and they are more impressive, but for the common good, these men removed from the voting booth by the system of industry, are toiling and sacrificing. Therefore, it seems to me that the analogy is a perfect one.

Whether or not the analogy was perfect, it was widely accepted: by the end of World War I, more than twenty states had provided for absentee voting on the part of anyone who could demonstrate a work-related reason (and in a few cases, any reason) for being absent on election day. Concerns about fraud generally were alleviated by tight procedural rules and requirements that absentee ballots be identical to conventional ones.[59]

The provision of absentee ballots, however, did not address the largest issue raised by residency requirements: their disfranchisement of everyone who changed residences shortly before an election or who relocated from one state to another in the year before an election. If one accepts the findings of scholars of geographic mobility, the impact of durational residency qualifications had to be substantial, particularly among blue-collar workers, many of whom moved from place to place incessantly. Precisely how substantial is beyond the scope of this study, but a conservative estimate would be that 5–10 percent of the nation's adult population failed to meet the residency requirements at each election; for manual workers, the figure was surely higher—high enough to have potentially changed the outcomes of innumerable elections.[60]

Keeping Track of Voters

The edifice of voting law acquired one additional pillar between the Civil War and World War I: pre–election day registration. Before the 1870s in most states, there were no official preprepared lists of eligible voters, and men who sought to vote were not obliged to take any steps to establish their eligibility prior to election day. They simply showed up at the polls with whatever documentary proofs (or witnesses) that might be necessary. To be sure, Massachusetts was registering voters as early as 1801, and a few other states implemented registration systems before 1850, but registration was uncommon before the Civil War. Moreover, as noted in chapter 3, most antebellum proposals for registration systems were rejected as unnecessary and partisan.

Between the 1870s and World War I, however, the majority of states adopted formal registration procedures, particularly for their larger cities. The rationale for requiring voters to register and have their eligibility certified in advance of elections was straightforward: it would help to eliminate fraud and also bring an end to disruptive election-day conflicts at the polls. Especially in urban areas, where corruption was believed to be concentrated and voters were less likely to be known personally to election officials, advance registration would give the state time to develop lists of eligible voters, check papers, interrogate witnesses, and verify the qualifications of those who wished to vote. Although machine politicians objected to registration systems because they were discriminatory (especially if instituted only in cities) and many small-town officials thought they were expensive and unlikely to work, proponents were generally able to override these objections with some ease.[61]

Yet the devil was in the details. However straightforward the principle of registration may have been, the precise specifications of registration laws were a different and more contested matter. How far in advance of elections did a man or woman have to register? When would registration offices be open? Did one register in the county, the district, the precinct? What documents had to be presented and issued? How often did one have to register? All such questions had to be decided, and since the answers inescapably had implications for the composition of the electorate, they were a frequent source of contention.

Three examples reveal the contours of the terrain. In New Jersey, a state with a long and colorful history of electoral disputes, Republicans instituted registration requirements in 1866 and 1867. All prospective voters had to register in person on the Thursday before each general election: anyone could challenge the claims of a potential registrant, and no one was permitted to vote if his name was not on the register. In 1868, the Democrats gained control of the state government and repealed the registration laws, stating that they penalized poor men who could not afford to take time off from their jobs to register. In 1870, the Republicans returned to power and reintroduced registration, this time making it applicable only to the seven cities with populations greater than 20,000. Six years later, the law was extended to all cities with more than 10,000 persons and to adjacent communities; at the same time, in a concession to party organizations, the registration procedure was liberalized, permitting any legal voter (such as a party worker) to enroll others by affidavit. During these years, and for decades thereafter, the two parties also feuded over the hours that polls would be open: when the Republicans were able to, they passed laws closing the polls at sunset on the grounds that illegal voting was most likely to occur after dark; the Democrats protested that "sunset laws" kept workers from voting, and when in power, they extended the hours into the evening.[62]

These partisan battles continued to rage (Republicans imposed more stringent registration procedures on Newark and Jersey City in 1888), although for a time the touchstone of conflict became ballot reform rather than registration. During the Progressive era, however, registration became the centerpiece of efforts, spearheaded by middle-class reformers, to limit corruption and reduce the electoral strength of immigrants, blacks, and political machines. In 1911, a package of two bills, the Geran Act and the Corrupt Practices Act, was introduced into the state legislature by a coalition of independents, Republicans, and a few Democrats. After heated debate, during which urban Democrats succeeded in removing some of the legislation's most onerous features, the bills were passed, creating a registration system that applied to every city with a population greater than 5,000 persons. Personal registration was now required, and it had to be renewed whenever a voter moved or failed to vote in an election. Prospective voters were given only four days in which they could register, and at registration a man was obliged not only to identify himself and his occupation but to give the names of his parents, spouse, and landlord, as well as a satisfactory description of the dwelling in which he lived. To no one's surprise, these reforms sharply depressed turnout, particularly among blacks and immigrants.[63]

In Illinois, a durable registration system was hammered into place in the 1880s. It was crafted by the business and social elites of Chicago, who were dismayed by their loss of political control of the city to allegedly corrupt Democratic politicians. Their primary vehicle of reform was the Union League Club, founded in 1879 to promote a third term for Ulysses Grant and to push for reforms that would "preserve the purity of the ballot box." In the early 1880s, the club began to promote registration reform to replace a weak system that had been in effect since 1865. At the same time, it engaged in a kind of political vigilantism, hiring investigators to check polling places and offering a $300 reward to those who helped in the apprehension and conviction of anyone who voted illegally in Chicago in 1883. Despite the club's efforts, the only "fraudulent" voters apprehended eventually were acquitted in court. Yet in 1885, a registration law drafted by the club's members and backed by the city's commercial establishment was passed by the state legislature.[64]

The act provided for the creation of a board of election commissioners, to be appointed by the county courts, in any city or town that chose to adopt registration. (Chicago did so before the 1886 elections.) These commissioners—each of whom was obliged to post a $10,000 bond—were responsible for dividing their communities into precincts containing a maximum of 450 voters. They were to appoint election judges and clerks, who actually administered the process of registration as well as elections in each precinct. To register, a prospective voter had to appear in person before the election judges, on the Tuesday of either the third or fourth week prior to an election. If an applicant's qualifications were challenged (by a judge or any other voter), he was required to file an affidavit of eligibility, which then would be verified by the judges. Following the two days of registration, the clerks, assisted by the police, conducted a house-to-house canvass of the precinct to verify the names of all adult male residents and compile a "suspected list" of improperly registered voters. Anyone whose name appeared on the so-called suspected list would be removed from the election rosters unless he appeared before the judges again, on the Tuesday two weeks prior to any general election, and made a convincing and verifiable case for his eligibility. A new general registration, repeating all of these procedures, was to occur every four years. This "act regulating the holding of elections" was amended, during the following decade, to require that one of the two registration days be a Saturday, that a general registration be held every two years rather than four, and that every proprietor of a lodging or boarding house give the election judges the names and "period of continuous residence" of all tenants.[65]

Three details of the Illinois law revealed its restrictionist thrust. The first was the small size of the precincts: although justified as a means of insuring that election judges would be familiar with their constituents, the creation of tiny precincts meant that anyone who moved even a few blocks was likely to have to register again and meet a new thirty-day residency requirement. The second telling feature was more obvious: there were only two days on which a person could register, a small window by anyone's reckoning. Finally, the burden of proof, for a person who was challenged or whose name showed up on the remarkably labeled suspected list, was placed on the prospective voter himself. A man whose credentials were questioned had to take the time and effort to speedily establish his own eligibility. The Urban

League Club congratulated itself that "the foundations for honest elections were now firmly laid."[66]

In California, the registration laws evolved in stages. In the 1850s and early 1860s, men could establish their eligibility through their own declarations; widely voiced concerns about fraud, particularly in San Francisco, led not to statutes but to organized armies of poll watchers who kept an eye on elections. This informal vigilance (a term frequently invoked by the city's elite) was supplanted in 1866 by the California Registry Act. The act was sponsored by a predominantly Republican faction of the Unionist Party: although Democrats denounced the bill as a "fraud and a swindle" and "an act of hostility to the Democratic party," broadly based worries about corruption guaranteed its passage through the legislature.[67]

The Registry Act instructed county clerks throughout the state to prepare Great Registers that would include the names of all legal voters. To enroll, a prospective voter had to appear in person before the county clerk and present evidence of his eligibility, if he was not known personally to the clerk. To the dismay of the Democrats, naturalized citizens were obliged to present their original, court-sealed naturalization papers. In the absence of such papers, an immigrant's eligibility could be established only through the testimony of two "householders and legal voters" and by residence in the state for a full year, double the normal requirement. The Registry Act, moreover, imposed a remarkable deadline on prospective voters: registration had to be completed three months before a general election.[68]

Despite their fears, the Democrats did extremely well in the 1867 elections and became supporters of voter registration—in part because they worried about future Republican chicanery. Five years later, the legislature revised the Registry Act, tightening it in some respects, liberalizing it in others. A special procedure was created to permit registration after the three-month deadline, and the evidentiary burden placed on naturalized citizens was lightened. Yet voters who moved from one county to another were presented with a new obstacle: before registering, they had to present written proof that their prior registration had been canceled.[69]

A more significant tightening of the law, targeted only at San Francisco, took place in 1878. The "Act to regulate the registration of voters, and to secure the purity of elections in the city and county of San Francisco" was sponsored by Republicans and designed, at least in part, to rebuff the insurgent and anti-establishment Workingmen's Party. The act removed control of the city's elections from the elected board of supervisors and vested it instead in a board of commissioners consisting of the mayor and four appointed county officials; it also created a registrar of voters, appointed by the governor, who was empowered to purge the registers of names suspected to be fraudulent. The 1878 act required each voter to reregister in person before every general election, and most important, it terminated city and countywide registration, demanding that voters register within their own electoral precinct. The precincts were to be created by the commissioners and could not include more than 300 voters. In San Francisco, as in Chicago, any man who moved out of a very small neighborhood was obliged to reregister.[70]

During the Progressive era, California's registration laws were revised further, making it somewhat easier for many men to vote. Naturalized citizens who lacked papers no longer were required to present affidavits from registered voters; paperwork was standardized; the number of places where a person could register was increased; registration was permitted until forty days before an election; and voters who moved could cancel their previous registration while registering in their new place of residence. A few new requirements, however, were added. Biannual registration became compulsory everywhere, not just in San Francisco, and all landlords and lodging-house keepers were required to provide registry officers with lists of their tenants. If a registered voter's name did not show up on these lists, he was sent a citation through the mail demanding that he appear before the election commissions to verify his eligibility within five days. If he failed to appear "at the time appointed, his name shall be stricken from the register of voters."[71]

The examples of New Jersey, Illinois, and California suggest the significance of the fine print in the extremely lengthy and detailed registration statutes adopted by most states from the time of the Civil War through the aftermath of World War I. Nearly everywhere, such laws emerged from a convergence of partisan interest with sincere concern about electoral fraud; the extent to which they prevented honest men from voting varied over time and from state to state. The length of the registration period, its proximity to the date of an election, the size of registration districts, the frequency of reregistration, the necessity of documentary evidence of eligibility, the location of the burden of proof—all of these and others were critical details, subject to dispute, change, and partisan jockeying. Moreover, a close examination of the laws of nearly two dozen states reveals little in the way of national trends. To cite one example, some states, including New York and Ohio, began to insist on annual personal registration in large cities, while others simultaneously were moving toward systems of permanent registration. Much depended on local conditions and local episodes.

New York City in 1908 took a swipe at Jewish voters, many of whom were Socialists, by holding registration on the Jewish sabbath and on the holy holiday of Yom Kippur.[72]

The political dynamics revealed in New Jersey, Illinois, and California frequently were replicated elsewhere. Republicans and reform-minded middle-class independents tended to be the prime movers behind registration itself and behind provisions likely to have a disproportionate impact on poor, foreign-born, uneducated, or mobile voters. Similarly, legislators from rural and semirural districts tended to favor stringent registration requirements that would apply only to city dwellers. (Rural political leaders generally argued that it would be a hardship for their constituents to travel twice each fall, first to register and then to vote.) Resistance to strict registration systems generally came from urban Democrats, from machine politicians who correctly regarded the new laws as attempts to reduce their electoral strength. Yet the targets of registration laws were not always corrupt machines. In 1895, the Republicans who dominated Michigan's legislature passed a reregistration law expressly designed to disfranchise foreign-born voters who supported Detroit's indisputably honest reform mayor, Hazen Pingree. "It will take off the books just about enough Pingree votes to prevent his ever becoming mayor again," declared the bill's sponsor. Pennsylvania's Republicans—who for decades resisted registration laws that would have harmed their own political machine—took similar action against a crusading reformer in Pittsburgh in 1906.[73]

Indeed, in most cities, the machines learned to live with and take advantage of the systems of registration that were imposed on them. They rapidly mastered techniques for insuring that their own voters were registered, and when in power, they often embraced the registration laws as a means of keeping other men and women from voting. As political scientist Steven Erie has pointed out, once securely ensconced, the Irish political machines that dominated city politics in numerous cities often displayed little interest in mobilizing new voters, particularly southern and eastern European immigrants. (In some states, such as Massachusetts, friction with the Irish led numerous new immigrants to support Yankee Republicans.) By mobilizing their own constituencies and supporting cumbersome registration laws that made it difficult for others to vote, Irish political machines could keep a ceiling on their expenses, while reducing threats to their own power—a stance that may well have contributed to the decline in political conflict over registration during the Progressive era. Political machines flourished during this period, with and without strong registration systems.[74]

Meanwhile, state courts sanctioned the creation of registration systems, as long as they did not overtly narrow the constitutional qualifications for voting. Even when state constitutions did not authorize or instruct legislatures to pass registration laws (more than twenty did so by 1920), the courts generally were sympathetic. "A wise system of registration," concluded an Ohio court in 1885, was an efficacious means "to prevent fraud, insure integrity at the polls, and enable the honest and qualified elector to exert his just influence." The courts did occasionally overturn statutes that seemed too restrictive, such as an Ohio law that opened the registration rolls for only seven days each year and made no provision for voters who happened to be absent during that period. Yet on the whole they endorsed registration as a reasonable component of electoral administration. Courts also upheld the legitimacy of registration laws that applied only to particular classes of cities, despite objections that such laws violated the equal protection clause of the Fourteenth Amendment. As a rule—outside of the South, at least— the courts applied the same principles to primary elections as to general elections.[75]

The impact of these laws was highly variable and depended not only on the details of the laws themselves but also on the ability and determination of political parties to get their own voters registered. Quantifying such an impact is beyond the scope of this study, but it can be said with certainty that registration laws reduced fraudulent voting and that they kept large numbers (probably millions) of eligible voters from the polls. In cities such as Philadelphia, Chicago, and Boston, only 60 to 70 percent of eligible voters were registered between 1910 and 1920; in wards inhabited by the poor, the figures were significantly lower. In San Francisco between 1875 and 1905, an average of only 54 percent of adult males were registered. Electoral turnout dropped steadily during precisely the period when registration systems were being elaborated, and scholars have estimated that one third or more of that drop, nationally, can be attributed to the implementation of registration schemes.[76]

In some places the impact was far more dramatic and instantly visible. In New Jersey, for example, the passage of new registration laws in the early twentieth century was immediately followed by such a sharp plunge in turnout, particularly in the cities, that a New Brunswick newspaper concluded that "the critics who declared that the Geran Act would result in the disfranchisement of thousands were justified." Similarly, in Pittsburgh in 1907, the newly created registration commission crowed, in the private minute books of its meetings, that "the figures speak for themselves as to the good results obtained under the operation of the Personal Registration Act." The number of men registered to vote had dropped from 95,580 to 45,819.[77]

Postscript: Fraud, Class, and Motives

Proponents of ballot reform and elaborate registration procedures—as well as other measures, such as early poll closings—invariably defended such steps as necessary to prevent fraud and corruption. Legislative debates were sprinkled heavily with tales of ballot-box stuffing, miscounts, hordes of immigrants lined up to vote as the machine instructed, men trooping from precinct to precinct to vote early and often. The goal of reform, according to its advocates, was not to shrink the electorate or to prevent certain social groups from voting, but to guarantee honest elections. Unsurprisingly, historians—guided by a written record largely composed by the literate, victorious reformers— often have echoed this perspective: late-nineteenth-century and Progressive- era political reformers have commonly been portrayed as honest middle- and upper-class citizens who were trying to clean up politics, to end the corruption practiced by ethnically based political machines and their unscrupulous business allies.[78]

That such portraits are too monochromatic—and misleading—is suggested by the utterances of the reformers themselves: their antagonism toward poor, working-class, and foreign-born voters was thinly disguised at best, and many of them unabashedly welcomed the prospect of weeding such voters out of the electorate. Still, the question of fraud remains: Was corruption so rampant that the reformers' motives can be taken at face value, that their intentions can be viewed as democratic, whatever the consequences? Should registration laws and ballot reform be understood primarily as weapons in the battle against election fraud, or as techniques for diminishing the breadth of democracy?

The available evidence—inescapably fragmentary and uneven—does not offer definitive answers to such questions. On the one hand, fraud and corruption clearly did exist: complaints came not only from upper-crust reformers but from labor organizations and Populists; moreover, the memoirs of politicians contain numerous acknowledgments of improper and illegal practices. On the other hand, recent studies have found that claims of widespread corruption were grounded almost entirely in sweeping, highly emotional allegations backed by anecdotes and little systematic investigation or evidence. Paul Kleppner, among others, has concluded that what is most striking is not how many but how few documented cases of electoral fraud can be found.

Most elections appear to have been honestly conducted: ballot-box stuffing, bribery, and intimidation were the exception, not the rule.[79]

The evidence also suggests that urban, machine politicians and their ethnic constituents were not alone in skirting or ignoring the borders of legality. Boss Tweed of New York, living in splendor from the abundant kickbacks he received through his largely Irish "organization," was surely the most well-known corrupt politician of the late 1860s and 1870s. But perhaps the most celebrated instance of electoral irregularity in the 1890s occurred in rural Adams County, Ohio, where 90 percent of the electorate, entirely from "old and excellent American stock," was being paid to vote. In addition, coercive pressure to vote (and to vote the right way) came not only from political machines, democratic and republican, but also from employers and corporations.[80]

To cite one little-known but graphic example: in 1914, general elections were held in Huerfano County, Colorado, which at the time was embroiled in a prolonged strike of coal miners against Colorado Fuel and Iron and several other coal companies. The bitter strike already had produced the infamous Ludlow massacre of striking families living in a tent city; it also prompted the federal government to send troops to maintain order. The elections resulted in a victory for the Republican slate of candidates, headed by the powerful sheriff, J. B. Farr. A lawsuit brought by the Democrats, however, revealed a remarkable set of irregularities. The Republicans, working with Colorado Fuel and Iron, had drawn precinct boundaries so that seven precincts in the county were located entirely on company-owned land. On registration days and election day, company guards refused to permit anyone to enter these precincts who was thought to be a union member, an agitator, or a labor sympathizer. Foreign-born scabs who lived in the mining camps then were marched to the polls by company officials: since many were illiterate, they were given printed cards containing the letter *R* and illegally assisted by election judges. These voters were instructed to move the cards along the ballot and place their mark beside any name that had a party designation of *R*. Nearly 90 percent of the vote went to the Republicans in these "closed" precincts, enough to overcome a Democratic majority elsewhere in the county. The violations of the law were so flagrant that the Colorado Supreme Court eventually voided the election, overturning the decision of local (Republican) judges who claimed to have seen no evidence that fraudulent votes had been cast.[81]

What transpired in Huerfano County was not the type of fraud that agitated the relatively well-off and largely Republican men who pushed for strict registration systems and other "honest ballot" reforms. These reformers, who were so sensitive to the dubious practices of urban political machines, rarely mentioned abuses by employers, and their support for registration procedures applicable only to cities ignored the possibility of rural corruption. Many of the reformers, moreover, ended up joining the Democrats in turning a blind eye to the flagrant disfranchisement of blacks and poor whites in the South. The measures they proposed to "purify the ballot box" were aimed largely at particular ballot boxes and particular voters.

This is not to say that reformers' claims about fraud were mere window dressing, cynical efforts to mask partisan motives or antidemocratic intentions; such cynicism surely was present among some advocates of registration laws and ballot reform, but there was more to it than that. As Kleppner and others have pointed out, corruption was a word with many meanings, and reformers deployed the term to refer to practices that seemed (to them) inappropriate as well as illegal. Paying people to get out the vote seemed corrupt, as did paying poll taxes so that constituents could vote—even if there were no direct partisan strings attached to the payments. Reformers also believed that votes were corrupt when they were prompted by narrow self-interest—as, for example, when a man voted the way his ward boss asked him to, in return for the favor of a job or a free coal delivery.[82]

In addition, it seems altogether likely that many proponents of electoral regulation were genuinely offended by the state of political practices: they believed that fraud was epidemic, particularly in the cities. Yet that belief was itself linked to and shaped by class and ethnic tensions. Respectable middle-class and upper-class citizens found it easy to believe that fraud was rampant among the Irish or among new immigrant workers precisely because they viewed such men as untrustworthy, ignorant, incapable of appropriate democratic behavior, and not a little threatening. Stories about corruption and illegal voting seemed credible—and could be magnified into apprehensive visions of systematic dishonesty—because inhabitants of the slums (like blacks in the South) appeared unworthy or uncivilized and because much-despised machine politicians were somehow winning elections.

An analogy in our time might be the widespread notion that many recipients of welfare, usually black and Hispanic, were "cheating the system" in the 1980s and 1990s. Despite the lack of systematic evidence, Ronald Reagan's oft-repeated anecdote about a woman who drove a Cadillac to pick up her welfare check seemed persuasive and resonant to Americans who were predisposed to see poor people of color as lazy and dishonest. The late-nineteenth-century reaction to Francis Parkman's portrait of the electorate was similar: political leaders felt justified in modifying electoral laws based on anecdotes and broadly stated impressions. In both cases, widespread convictions were spawned by germs of fact, cultured in a medium of class and ethnic (or racial) prejudice and apprehension.

Two Special Cases

Infamous Crimes

While revising other features of their electoral laws, states extended the disfranchisement of felons and ex-felons. Roughly two dozen states had taken such action before the Civil War; by 1920, all but a handful had made some provision for barring from suffrage men who had been convicted of a criminal offense, usually a felony or "infamous" crime, one that in common law prohibited its perpetrator from testifying under oath in court. (See chapter 3 and table A.15.) In the South, these measures often were more detailed and included lesser offenses, targeting minor violations of the law that could be invoked to disfranchise African Americans.[83]

Elsewhere, the laws lacked socially distinct targets and generally were passed in a matter-of-fact fashion. Constitutional conventions and legislatures sometimes quibbled over the changing definition of felony and over specific lists of crimes that would bring disfranchisement. (Electoral fraud was on everybody's list.) There also was some disagreement—and some variety, from state to state—regarding the duration of the exclusion. In almost all states, felons were disfranchised while they remained in prison; in many, disfranchisement was implicitly or explicitly permanent, although many states made it possible for ex-felons to be restored to their civil rights, usually by the governor. Rarely, however, were objections voiced to the principle of disfranchisement in either legislatures or constitutional conventions. The courts upheld such laws, concluding that the states had both a right to disfranchise ex-felons and a compelling interest in doing so. In 1890, the U.S. Supreme Court validated the exclusion of felons in elections held in federal territories.[84]

The widespread support for such laws is noteworthy because, as recent legal analysts have pointed out, there has never been a particularly persuasive or coherent rationale for disfranchising felons and ex-felons. In their classical and English origins, these laws were primarily punitive in nature, and the punitive thrust clearly was present in the United States for much of the nineteenth century. Yet the efficacy of disfranchisement as a punishment was always dubious, since there was no evidence that it would deter future crimes; nor (except in the case of voting crimes) did disfranchisement appear to be an appropriate or significant form of retribution. For this reason, perhaps, the states in the late nineteenth century drifted toward a different rationale: that disfranchisement of felons was necessary to protect the integrity of elections and—in the words of a much-cited Alabama Supreme Court decision—"preserve the purity of the ballot box." Proponents argued that men who could not be legally relied on to tell the truth (which was formally why they could not testify in court) would corrupt the electoral process. They also expressed the fear that enfranchised ex-felons might band together and vote to repeal the criminal laws. Both arguments were at best conjectural.[85]

Why then were felons and ex-felons disfranchised, so widely and with so little debate? The answer appears to reside in a notion that generally was unspoken but infiltrated all debates about suffrage during this period: this was, simply, that a voter ought to be a moral person. Although state laws rarely made explicit mention of moral standing as a qualification for suffrage and the difficulty of imposing a morality test was manifest, the idea persisted that there were moral boundaries to the polity. Discerning or agreeing on those boundaries admittedly was difficult—as the debates over pauper exclusions and corruption revealed—but men who had been convicted of crimes were easy to distinguish and label.

Full membership in the political community therefore depended on proper behavior and perhaps even proper beliefs: coexisting uneasily with the broad claim that the franchise was a right was the resurgent notion that the state could draw a line between the worthy and the unworthy, that it could determine who was fit to possess the rights of citizenship. Disfranchising felons in effect was a symbolic act of political banishment, an assertion of the state's power to exclude those who violated prevailing norms. It is telling that one of the most important court cases involving these issues dealt with a Utah law that made it a crime (and therefore a cause for disfranchisement) for a man to practice, or even advocate, bigamy. Equally revealing, perhaps, is the fact that the same state legislature that drafted New York's literacy test expressed its disapproval of the political opinions of some citizens by preventing five legally elected Socialists from taking their seats. The speaker of the New York assembly declared that "socialist ballots" would not be recognized until the party had become "thoroughly American."[86]

Native Americans

> Again, there is no overwhelming political necessity, as in the case
> of the negroes, requiring us to make citizens of the Indians. When

we remember that our country is being invaded, year by year, by the undesirable classes driven out of Europe because they are a burden to the government of their birth; that as many as seventy thousand immigrants have landed on our shores in a single month, made up largely of Chinese laborers, Irish paupers, and Russian Jews; that the ranks are being swelled by adventurers of every land—the Communist of France, the Socialist of Germany, the Nihilist of Russia, and the cut-throat murderers of Ireland—that all these persons may become citizens within five years, and most of them voters under State laws as soon as they have declared their intentions to become citizens—we may well hesitate about welcoming the late "untutored savages" into the ranks of citizenship.

—G. M. LAMBERTSON, "INDIAN CITIZENSHIP,"
American Law Review, 1886

Native Americans continued to occupy a special place in American law and society. At the close of the Civil War, the vast majority of Native Americans, although born in the United States, were not citizens, and they could attain citizenship only through treaties, not through the naturalization laws that applied to white foreigners. Unlike blacks and immigrants, they were not needed for their labor, but the lands that they controlled were coveted by settlers, miners, and railroad corporations. Although extolled as noble savages by the humanitarian reformers who controlled Indian policy for much of the late nineteenth century, they were the targets of a war of attrition, as well as a resettlement program, that rapidly destroyed the way of life of some of the largest tribes. They were also few in number, totaling less than 250,000 at their population nadir in 1900.

In 1865, most Native Americans were unable to vote, largely because they lacked citizenship; and for the next sixty years the ability of Indians to become citizens traveled a bumpy and circuitous road. The Fourteenth Amendment set things in motion with its declaration that "all persons born or naturalized in the United States, and subject to the jurisdiction thereof, are citizens of the United States." In response to claims that the amendment effectively transformed Indians into citizens, the Senate Judiciary Committee, in 1870, issued a report rejecting that interpretation. Native Americans who retained relations with their tribes, the committee concluded, were not born under the jurisdiction of the United States and thus were not covered by the amendment. A year later, a federal district court in Oregon agreed, holding that Indian tribes were "independent political communities" not fully subject to the legal jurisdiction of the national government. In 1884, in the landmark case of *Elk v. Wilkins*, the U.S. Supreme Court ended debate on the issue by concluding that the Fourteenth Amendment did not confer citizenship on John Elk, an Indian who was born on tribal lands. The Court further maintained that Elk, who had left his tribe and lived in Omaha, could not attain citizenship simply by assimilating: whether he had "so far advanced" as to "be let out of the state of pupilage" was a decision to be made by the nation whose ward he was. Accordingly, Elk's right to vote—he had brought suit after being unable to cast a ballot in Omaha— was not protected by the Fifteenth Amendment.[87]

Nonetheless, it was the formal policy of the United States to encourage Indian citizenship and Indian assimilation into American society. Although Congress continued to grant citizenship through treaties with individual tribes until 1871, the major thrust of policy became the conferral of citizenship on Indians who were abandoning tribal ways and becoming "civilized." In 1887 Congress passed the General Allotment (or Dawes) Act, which granted citizenship to all Native Americans who "adopted the habits of civilized life," as well as those who accepted private allotments of what had been tribal lands. (One key goal of the act was to free up tribal lands for white settlement.) Thanks in part to the General Allotment Act and in part to a congressional act passed in 1901, more than half of all Indians were citizens by 1905. This number was augmented after World War I, when citizenship was conferred upon Indians who had served in the military and been honorably discharged. Finally, in response to partisan politics in the West, bureaucratic politics in Washington, and the wartime service of Native Americans, Congress in 1924 declared that all Indians born in the United States were citizens.[88]

Meanwhile, states had been taking steps on their own. In Massachusetts in 1869, for example, Republicans and ex-abolitionists who thought it hypocritical to deny Indians the same rights they demanded for southern blacks succeeded in passing legislation declaring all Indians to be "citizens of the Commonwealth . . . entitled to all the rights, privileges and immunities" of citizenship; foreshadowing the Dawes Act, the Indian Enfranchisement Act also provided that all Indian lands would revert to individual ownership and therefore could be sold to non-Indians. By the early twentieth century, as table A.16 indicates, nearly all states with Native American populations had enacted similarly double-edged constitutional or statutory provisions. On the one hand, they—explicitly or implicitly—enfranchised some Native Americans, generally those who had assimilated or "severed their tribal relations." At the same time, states disfranchised Indians who continued to belong to tribes, or were "not taxed" or "not civilized."[89]

The prevailing policy was clear, if difficult to apply: Native Americans could become voters, but only by surrendering or repudiating their own culture, economic organization, and societal norms. Membership in the polity was conditioned on good behavior, on adopting a culture and style of life deemed appropriate by the states that had militarily conquered the Indian tribes. Since good and appropriate behavior was not always forthcoming, many of the states with the largest Native American populations proceeded to devise new rationales for disfranchising Indians after the Citizenship Act of 1924 was passed.

Sovereignty and Self-Rule

An important by-product of the evolution of voting laws, South and North, was the increasingly precise delineation of the powers of federal, state, and municipal governments in determining suffrage law. During Reconstruction, the federal government had asserted its jurisdiction in unprecedented ways with the passage of the Fourteenth and Fifteenth Amendments, as well as the enforcement acts. For several decades thereafter, federal activity to protect the rights enshrined in those amendments persisted, even in the North. Between 1877 and 1893, more than half of all federal appropriations for electoral supervision were expended in New York.[90]

Yet the tilt toward the nationalization of the right to vote proved to be both short-lived and fragmentary. Congress's decisions to adopt a narrow version of the Fifteenth Amendment, to repeal key provisions of the enforcement acts, and not to enact the Lodge Force Bill effectively left the federal government on the sidelines during most contests over the franchise. Washington's role was circumscribed further by Supreme Court decisions that definitively severed the link between citizenship and suffrage and that interpreted the Fifteenth Amendment as prohibiting only the most flagrant and intentional forms of discrimination. Indeed, the court cases spawned by the Fourteenth and Fifteenth Amendments led to a formal articulation of state supremacy that was merely implicit in the nation's Constitution. As the Supreme Court declared in *Pope v. Williams* in 1904, "the privilege to vote in a state is within the jurisdiction of the state itself, to be exercised as the state may direct, and upon such terms as to it may seem proper, provided, of course, no discrimination is made between individuals, in violation of the Federal Constitution." States in effect could do as they wished, as long as they did not disfranchise men solely and overtly because of race. Had the Wilson amendment passed, of course, the story would have been different: many of the restrictions on suffrage adopted by northern and western, as well as southern, states would have been unconstitutional. But those who had opposed the Wilson amendment because it would inflate the power of the national government had won a long-lasting victory: suffrage in 1915 was not much more of a federal concern than it had been in 1800.[91]

The courts also drew increasingly numerous, if sometimes jagged, lines between state constitutional authority and the power of state legislatures. While the states had great freedom to set suffrage qualifications in their constitutions, state legislatures had far less latitude. Suffrage remained a matter of fundamental or constitutional, rather than statute, law: legislatures, as a rule, were permitted to enact laws that concretized or carried out constitutional provisions, but they did not possess the power to alter suffrage qualifications. Practices, though, varied among states; as noted in chapter 4, several southern legislatures enacted disfranchising laws without bothering to amend their constitutions, and some state courts permitted legislatures to take steps that blurred the boundaries between procedural and substantive regulation. A New York court, for example, found in 1920 that "legislative regulations" could be reasonable even if they burdened citizens unequally: "the wit of man cannot devise a method transcending all inequality and discrimination."[92]

In many states, moreover, the courts allowed legislatures to adopt non-standard suffrage qualifications in referenda or in elections for offices that were not explicitly named in state constitutions. In 1893, for example, the Florida Supreme Court concluded in the oft-cited case of *Lamar v. Dillon* that "where the Constitution does not fix the right of suffrage or prescribe the qualifications of voters, it is competent for the legislature . . . to do so." Such reasoning made it possible for voting to be restricted to taxpayers or property owners in state elections dealing with public expenditures; it also opened the doors for women to vote in school board elections.[93]

The same reasoning revived the possibility of municipal franchise qualifications different from those obtaining in state elections. In contrast to their late-eighteenth- and early-nineteenth-century predecessors, however, such qualifications could not be determined by cities and towns alone. As discussed in chapter 2, the legal subservience of municipalities to states was well established in American law by the mid-nineteenth century: Judge John "Dillon's rule"—that state power over municipalities was "supreme and transcendent," that municipalities had no "inherent right of local self-government which is beyond legislative control"—was articulated at length in a landmark treatise published in 1872. Despite several jurisprudential challenges, it remained dominant, in part because conservatives believed that property interests would be better protected by state governments than by cities. Dillon himself supported some taxpaying restrictions on voting and eventually left the bench to become a prominent railroad lawyer. Dillon's rule, however, did permit municipalities and state legislatures to jointly agree on distinctive suffrage qualifications for municipal elections, particularly in states that enacted "home rule" provisions for cities. Although never widespread, distinctive municipal franchise regulations were adopted in Tulsa, Kansas City, Deer Park, Maryland, and Oklahoma City, among other places, and they continued to surface throughout the twentieth century.[94]

The New Electoral Universe

> Though the sovereignty is in the people, as a practical fact it resides in those persons who by the Constitution of the state are permitted to exercise the elective franchise.
>
> —JUDGE THOMAS M. COOLEY, 1868

> I cannot attempt to describe the complicated and varying election laws of the different States.
>
> —JAMES BRYCE, 1888

By the beginning of World War I, the ebullient, democratic political culture of the mid-nineteenth century had given way to a more constrained and segmented political order. Throughout the nation, large slices of the middle and upper classes, as well as portions of the working class, had ceased to believe in universal suffrage—and had acted on their beliefs. In the South, blacks and many poor whites had been evicted wholesale from electoral politics. In the North and West, exclusions were on a smaller scale, but still numerous: depending on the state or city in which he lived, a man could be kept from the polls because he was an alien, a pauper, a lumberman, an anarchist, did not pay taxes or own property, could not read or write, had moved from one state to another in the past year, had recently moved from one neighborhood to another, did not possess his naturalization papers, was unable to register on the third or fourth Tuesday before an election, could not prove that he had canceled a prior registration, been convicted of a felony, or been born in China or on an Indian reservation. Although some women had gained the franchise, and all others would within a few years, the same dense cluster of voting laws applied to them as well. It can be no surprise, in light of this legal history, that turnout at elections dropped during the latter half of this period. Voting was not for everyone.[95]

This sustained, nationwide contraction of suffrage rights had several root causes. Stated most broadly, those who wielded economic and social power in the rapidly changing late nineteenth century found it difficult to control the state (which they increasingly needed) under conditions of full democratization. In the South, the abolition of slavery, coupled with the beginnings of industrialization and the compelling need for a docile, agricultural labor force, created pressures that overwhelmed fledgling democratic institutions. In the North and West, the explosive growth of manufacturing and of labor-intensive extractive industries generated class conflict on a scale that the nation had never known. As Max Weber noted long ago, it is during periods of rapid economic and technological change that class becomes most salient and class issues most prominent. The United States was not the only country whose political institutions were profoundly shaken by the stresses of industrialism.[96]

Yet these economic and class factors would not by themselves, in all likelihood, have produced such a marked and widespread narrowing of the entries to voting booths. Equally critical was the fact that the threatening lower orders consisted largely of men who were racially different or came from different ethnic, cultural, and religious backgrounds. What transpired in the South seems unimaginable in the absence of racial hostility and prejudice. Similarly, the changes in voting laws in the North and the West were made possible, and shaped, by the presence of millions of immigrants and their children, indeed by the very foreignness of Jews and Chinese, of the Irish and Italian Catholics, of Indians and Mexicans. Their ethnic identities, fused with their class position, made these new (or Native) Americans seem both threatening and inferior, necessary and legitimate targets of political discrimination; rolling back the franchise would have been a far more difficult task in a racially and ethnically homogeneous society. It was the convergence of racial and ethnic diversity with class tension that fueled the movement to "reform" suffrage.

One other factor, admittedly more speculative, also may have played a role: the absence of war. In light of the rest of the nation's history, it does not seem coincidental that this prolonged period of franchise contraction occurred during a prolonged period of peace. (The United States did launch an imperial war in 1898, but it was relatively brief, did not require mass recruitment, and was fought largely by eager volunteers.) The wartime conditions that commonly spawned pressures for franchise expansion simply were not present; forces tending in the opposite direction thus could triumph all the more readily. Indeed, from the era of Reconstruction to World War I, the United States never had much of an army nor any need for military mobilization. The political aftermath of the Spanish-American War, moreover, paralleled the antidemocratic drift of domestic politics. In annexed territories overseas, the national government, led by Republicans, deprived men who were racially and ethnically different of political rights, a step easily sanctioned by the claim that Filipinos, Hawaiians, and Cubans were not ready for self-government and that suffrage always had been a matter of expediency. Not even the Constitution, with its very limited protection of voting rights, followed the flag. Southern Democrats applauded these imperial policies, seeing in them Republican recognition of the wisdom of disfranchisement in the South.[97]

The parallels between North and South, of course, ought not be overdrawn. What transpired in the southern states was far more draconian, sweeping, and violent. The disfranchisement was massive rather than segmented, the laws were enforced brutally, and they were always administered with overtly discriminatory intent. In New York and Massachusetts, an illiterate immigrant could gain the franchise by learning to read; for a black man in Alabama, education was beside the point, whatever the law said. That the redemption of the North was far milder than the parallel movement in the South is testimony not only to the significance of race but also to differences in the South's social structure and political organizations. Northern society was too fluid, heterogeneous, and urban to permit the successful imposition of a project as sweeping as the Mississippi plan. At the same time, the existence of an already competitive party system, with elite and middle-class elements supporting each party, meant that efforts at wholesale disfranchisement—as was contemplated in New York in the 1870s—were certain to encounter fierce resistance and likely to meet defeat. Moreover, the ability of the dominant parties to integrate and incorporate many working-class and immigrant voters made mass disfranchisement unnecessary: the Democratic Party in the North (unlike the overwhelmingly black Republican Party in the South) did not threaten the established order.[98]

Both North and South, however, the legal contraction of the franchise made a difference. Millions of people—most of them working class and poor—were deprived of the right to vote in municipal, state, and national elections. Their exclusion from the electorate meant that the outcomes of innumerable political contests were altered, different policies were put into place, different judges appointed, different taxes imposed. Third-party insurgencies were deprived of a potential electoral base, and the relative strength of the two major parties, in at least some cities and states, was reversed. Many of the core institutions of the modern American state—institutions built and solidified between Reconstruction and World War I— were indeed shaped and accepted by a polity that was far from democratic. It was an apt symbol of the era that Congress voted to enfranchise residents of the District of Columbia in 1871 and then disfranchised them a few years later, transforming the city into a municipal corporation governed by an appointed commission.[99]

—SIX—

Women's Suffrage

To get the word "male" in effect out of the Constitution cost the women of the country fifty-two years of pauseless campaign. . . . During that time they were forced to conduct 56 campaigns of referenda to male voters; 480 campaigns to get legislatures to submit suffrage amendments to voters; 47 campaigns to get state constitutional conventions to write woman suffrage into state constitutions; 277 campaigns to get state party conventions to include woman suffrage planks; 30 campaigns to get presidential party conventions to adopt woman suffrage planks in party platforms, and 19 campaigns with 19 successive Congresses.

—CARRIE CHAPMAN CATT
AND NETTIE R. SHULER,
Woman Suffrage and Politics (1926)

MR. HALFHILL: Now, gentlemen, this question of franchise is not, as has been sometimes debated and urged, an inalienable right; it is a conferred right, and it must be conferred under our theory of government and under our organization of society.

MR. FACKLER: If suffrage is a conferred right and not a natural one, who conferred that right on us?

—OHIO CONSTITUTIONAL CONVENTION, 1912

*T*HE HISTORY OF VOTING RIGHTS FOR WOMEN carved its own path through the political landscape. As half the population, women constituted the largest group of adults excluded from the franchise at the nation's birth and for much of the nineteenth century. Their efforts to gain the right to vote persisted for more than seventy years, eventually giving rise to the nation's largest mass movement for suffrage, as well as a singular countermovement of citizens opposed to their own enfranchisement. Women enjoyed (or at least possessed) different, more intimate relationships with the men who could enfranchise them than did other excluded groups, such as African Americans, aliens, or the propertyless. Moreover, the debates sparked by the prospect of enfranchising women had unusual features—with fairly conventional propositions about political rights and capacities contending with deeply felt and publicly voiced fears that female participation in electoral politics would undermine family life and sully women themselves.

Yet distinctive as this history may have been, it always ran alongside and frequently intersected with other currents in the chronicle of suffrage. The broad antebellum impulse toward democratization helped to fuel the movement for women's rights; decades later, the reaction against universal suffrage retarded its progress. Black suffrage and women's suffrage were closely linked issues everywhere in the 1860s and in the South well into the twentieth century; similarly, the voting rights of immigrants and the poor pressed repeatedly against the claims of women in the North and West. To some degree, this interlacing was inherent and structural. Women, after all, were not a socially segregated group; they were black and white, rich and poor, foreign-born and native. But the links between the evolution of suffrage for women and for men also were shaped by more contingent events: by the rhythms of social change, the dynamics of partisan politics, and the accidents of historical timing.

From Seneca Falls to the Fifteenth Amendment

The movement to enfranchise women in the United States had its legendary beginnings at a convention held in July 1848, in the small town of Seneca Falls, New York. The convention was the brainchild of two women, Elizabeth Cady Stanton and Lucretia Mott. Mott, from Philadelphia, was already a well-known public figure, a Quaker minister and ardent abolitionist, revered for her compassionate manner and eloquence as a speaker. Stanton, a generation younger and the daughter of a judge, was married to Henry B. Stanton, a prominent abolitionist who recently had settled in Seneca Falls, not far from Rochester. The two women renewed an earlier acquaintance while Mott was visiting a friend in the nearby town of Waterloo. Their conversations led to a publicly announced call for a "convention" to "discuss the social, civil, and religious rights of woman."[1]

The convention, held in a local church and featuring Mott as a speaker, attracted nearly three hundred people, including many men. Most of those who attended were from Seneca Falls, Waterloo, or Rochester; roughly a quarter were Quakers. After two days of discussion, one hundred of the participants approved and signed a set of resolutions calling for equal rights for women, including "their sacred right to the elective franchise." The convention's Declaration of Sentiments, drafted by Stanton and modeled on the Declaration of Independence, declared "that all men and women are created equal" and protested the denial to women of "this first right of a citizen, the elective franchise, thereby leaving her without representation in the halls of legislation" and "oppressed on all sides." Laws made only by men, the declaration detailed, relegated women to an inferior place in the social, civil, and economic order.[2]

That women throughout the nation lacked the right to vote in 1848 reflected beliefs and values long embedded in the politics and culture of the United States and western Europe. Although women were regarded as intelligent adults, they were viewed as having capacities different from those of men, capacities appropriate to private life and the domestic sphere rather than the public world of politics. More decisively perhaps, women—who were envisaged and treated in law as members of families rather than as autonomous individuals—were excluded from the polity for the same reason that the poor and propertyless were disfranchised in the late eighteenth century: they purportedly lacked the "independence" necessary for participation in electoral politics. Economically dependent on men, as well as legally subservient to them, women, in Blackstonian fashion, could be controlled by men and thus could not be responsible political actors. Concomitantly, women were not believed to need the franchise because, in a gendered version of "virtual representation," their interests were defended by the men in their families, presumably husbands and fathers.[3]

To be sure, not everyone accepted such views, even in the late eighteenth century. Abigail Adams's well-known admonition that her husband "remember the ladies" was only one expression of the belief that the rights of women ought to be enlarged, and some of her contemporaries, unlike Adams, even believed that women could play a public role in political life. Moreover, the experience of New Jersey, where women participated in elections for more than a decade, suggests that the enfranchisement of women was neither unthinkable nor catastrophically disruptive of the political order. Even William Griffith, one of the state's vocal opponents of female suffrage, stressed that the primary "mischief" caused by women voting was that it gave "the towns and populous villages . . . an unfair advantage over the country" because women could get to the polls more easily in the towns.[4]

Nonetheless, women remained outside the polity throughout the first half of the nineteenth century, and efforts to promote their inclusion were rare. The idea of enfranchising women was raised briefly at a few constitutional conventions in the antebellum era; Kentucky in 1838 went so far as to permit propertied widows and unmarried women to vote in school elections. But the issue was not widely debated during this period, and most references to women, in constitutional discussions of suffrage, were designed to demonstrate that voting was a privilege, not a right: since everyone agreed that women should not vote, it clearly could *not* be a right. As Abigail Adams's husband had noted, any claim that voting was a right logically led to the enfranchisement of even women and children.[5]

The timing of the Seneca Falls convention—and the emergence of women's suffrage as a public issue—was far from accidental. The decades preceding Seneca Falls had witnessed the expansion of an urban and quasi-urban middle class in much of the North, a growing concentration of city and townspeople, some of them professionals, who valued and embraced an expansion of civil, economic, and political rights. At the same time, the number of women in the paid labor force increased sharply, leading many women to be exposed as individuals—not simply as family members—to the vicissitudes of the market and the consequences of state policies. These shifts in the social structure fostered diverse efforts to rethink and promote the rights of women in the family, churches, and society at large. In addition, the antislavery movement proved to be a breeding ground—and training ground—for advocates of women's rights: actively abolitionist women were frustrated by being treated as second-class members of the movement, while some male abolitionists were led, by the logic of their own convictions, to embrace gender as well as racial equality.[6]

Of equal importance were the spillover effects of the era's broader democratizing currents. The termination of property and taxpaying restrictions on voting, as well as debates about the enfranchisement of aliens and African Americans, threw open the logical and rhetorical doors to the further expansion of suffrage. If the propertyless (who also had been viewed as dependent) could vote, if noncitizens could vote, if voting were indeed a natural right, then why should women continue to be excluded? The Pandora's box had, in fact, been opened, and it proved difficult to slam shut: ar-

guments that had been mobilized to enfranchise men could readily be applied to women as well. To at least some women, the refusal of political
leaders to acknowledge these parallels underscored the need for a suffrage
movement—and the need for conventions (not just meetings) that would
reestablish fundamental principles of governance much as state constitutional conventions were doing. It was likely not coincidental that the Seneca
Falls gathering occurred in the wake of a New York State Constitutional
Convention that had ridiculed, and given short shrift to, the idea of enfranchising women.[7]

In fact, the meeting at Seneca Falls was only one of numerous conventions called to promote women's rights in the late 1840s and early 1850s; its
special place in historical memory, as Nancy Isenberg has pointed out, stems
partially from Stanton's subsequent role as the preeminent leader and
chronicler of the movement. In the spring of 1850, a similar convention was
held in Salem, Ohio; with men sitting quietly in the balcony, women drew
up and debated resolutions to be forwarded to the forthcoming state constitutional convention. Several months later, the first national Woman's
Rights meeting was convened in Worcester, Massachusetts, initiating a series of annual events to mobilize support for full citizenship for women and
their equal treatment under the law.[8]

Although suffrage had been one demand among many in 1848, it soon became foremost on the agenda of a growing feminist movement that held
meetings, sponsored lectures, and petitioned legislatures throughout the
1850s. "The Right of Suffrage," resolved the second national convention in
1851, "is . . . the corner-stone of this enterprise, since we do not seek to protect woman, but rather to place her in a position to protect herself." This demand, as historian Ellen DuBois has pointed out, was a radical one: it implied
that the interests of women could not be adequately protected as long as men
held a monopoly on political power, that women had to be empowered rather
than protected. Nonetheless, the argument for suffrage generally was couched
in traditional republican language: voting was a right that ought to belong to
all adults, including women; all of the governed had the right to choose their
governors. Familiar as the rhetoric may have been, the movement was slow to
garner support: although significant measures were passed to improve the
legal and economic status of women, no states granted them the franchise in
the 1850s. At the beginning of the Civil War, suffrage advocates, most of
whom were strongly invested in the antislavery cause, temporarily scaled back
their efforts to give the war, and black rights, priority.[9]

As the war ended and Reconstruction began, leaders of the suffrage movement, including Stanton and her indefatigable collaborator, Susan B. Anthony, were optimistic about its prospects. (Anthony, also a Quaker and a former teacher from western Massachusetts and upstate New York, had begun working with Stanton in 1851.) The public embrace of democracy was as broad as it ever had been; the war and the plight of the freedmen had energized the language of universal rights; and the Republican Party, home of the staunchest advocates of civil and political rights, was firmly in power. What the suffragists anticipated was a rising tide of prodemocratic sentiment that would lift women, as well as African Americans, into the polity. We intend, declared Stanton, "to avail ourselves of the strong arm and the blue uniform of the black soldier to walk in by his side." Suffragists also felt that their claim to the franchise had been strengthened by the energetic support women had lent to the war effort: such activities presumably had neutralized the oft-repeated argument that women should not vote because they did not bear arms. As one supporter noted,

> True, the women did not go to the battle-field, with muskets and bayonets in their hands, and fight to put down the rebellion; but they did render services at home during the war equally as valuable as fighting, and highly auxiliary to the success of the Union Army. . . . They did their full share in saving the Republic.[10]

Yet the suffragists were doomed—or at least slated—to be disappointed. Within a few months of the war's end, Republican leaders and male abolitionists began to signal their lack of enthusiasm for coupling women's rights to black rights. "One question at a time," intoned Wendell Phillips. "This hour belongs to the negro." The Fourteenth Amendment, drafted in late 1865 and ratified in 1866, disheartened suffragists and made clear that the Republican Party could not be counted on to promote suffrage for women. While offering strong, if indirect, federal support to black enfranchisement, the amendment undercut the claims of women by adding the word *male* to its pathbreaking guarantee of political rights. Although well aware of the strategic concerns that prompted such language, Stanton, in a prescient warning, declared that "if that word 'male' be inserted, it will take us a century at least to get it out."[11]

Offended by the text of the Fourteenth Amendment and feeling betrayed by their former abolitionist allies, suffragists launched an energetic campaign to fuse the causes of women and blacks in the name of equal rights. Stanton, in a speech delivered in 1867, flatly rejected not only the "principle" that suffrage was a "gift of society" (which she claimed would "take us back to monarchies and despotisms") but the notion that "women and negroes" ought to be enfranchised "as women and negroes, and not as citizens of a republic." Similarly, Henry Ward Beecher, a staunch supporter of women's rights, urged "not that women have the right of suffrage—not that Chinamen or Irishmen have the right of suffrage—and that native born Yankees have the right of suffrage—but that suffrage is the inherent right of mankind." Stanton, Beecher, and their allies campaigned vigorously to achieve universal suffrage through both state constitutional reforms and the federal government.[12]

Meanwhile, the number of Republicans committed to enfranchising the freedmen was growing rapidly; but many of these men, whatever their personal convictions, feared that this goal would be jeopardized by simultaneously pursuing the controversial cause of women's suffrage. Republican leaders, even Radicals, sought to separate the issues, to enfranchise blacks first and women later. The result of this divergence of strategy and principle was a growing, often hostile schism between the two movements: some abolitionists and African Americans actively opposed the drive for woman suffrage, while many feminists denigrated the abilities and qualifications of African Americans. Stanton herself objected to having "the colored man enfranchised before the women . . . I would not trust him with all my rights; degraded, oppressed himself, he would be more despotic with the governing power than even our Saxon rulers are." At a New York Constitutional Convention, one delegate opposed a law allowing "the black men of the South, fresh from the chains of slavery, to go to the ballot-box and vote on all the great questions involving the interests of this nation, while you deny the same right to educated, patriotic women." This schism led Stanton and some of her allies into a brief flirtation with the Democratic Party, which had a more prosuffrage track record than the Republicans on issues other than race; it was played out with particular clarity—and destructive force— in Kansas, where separate referenda were placed before the electorate by the legislature in 1867. While many Republicans campaigned not only for black suffrage but against enfranchising women, some advocates of female suffrage, including Anthony, allied themselves with overtly racist Democrats who opposed black enfranchisement. The upshot was the popular defeat of both African-American and woman suffrage.[13]

During this same period, Stanton, Anthony, and other suffragists also sought to build an alliance with the fledgling postwar labor reform movement, centered around the National Labor Union (NLU). The equal rights vision of many suffrage advocates meshed well with the broad, class-based politics of the NLU, a multifaceted organization founded in 1866 that appeared to have picked up the mantle of reform discarded by the Republicans. But the alliance proved to be short-lived, if not stillborn. Middle-class suffragists such as Stanton, believing as they did in the reconciliation of capital and labor, never fully grasped the sense of class antagonism that informed the NLU's politics and program. At the same time, the trade unions of the NLU, seeking to protect the jobs of their own members, remained antagonistic to the entry of women into their trades. By the early 1870s, a series of small but grating conflicts had undermined the possibility of substantial collaboration.[14]

With the passage and ratification of the Fifteenth Amendment in 1869 and 1870, the causes of black (male) and women's suffrage were decisively severed. Discrimination against African-American men was constitutionally prohibited, bringing the national drive for suffrage expansion to a close and leaving the status of women at best unchanged; indeed, arguably, women were worse off, because the Fifteenth Amendment appeared to implicitly condone political discrimination based on sex. After twenty years, the drive for women's suffrage had failed, and the political crisis of Reconstruction had, in the form of the Fourteenth and Fifteenth Amendments, erected new constitutional obstacles to enfranchisement.

The defeat of this initial mobilization stemmed from constraints of ideology and partisan politics. Although support for female suffrage had grown rapidly and many thousands of men and women had publicly endorsed the cause in petitions and meetings, there was still substantial resistance to the proposition that women could be participants in the public sphere. Despite the movement's pointed arguments and visibility, little had occurred to shatter the traditional consensus that had kept women out of the polity in the first place. The surge in democratic sentiments, so palpable at midcentury and so fervently embraced by some Republicans during Reconstruction, had its limits: the nation's political leaders, almost certainly reflecting the views of a majority of their constituents, declined to promote women's suffrage, just as they had backed away from more inclusive versions of the Fifteenth Amendment. There may well have been, as one delegate to the Illinois Constitutional Convention of 1869–70 declared, "a wonderful revolution taking place in the minds of all the people of the country with reference to the right of suffrage." But that revolution was beginning to stall, even as the delegate was speaking. "Equal rights" was a powerful slogan, but a minority view. As important, the political contingencies that drove Republicans to endorse black suffrage were lacking in the case of women. Women did not seem (to men) to be endangered by their inability to vote, and nowhere did the enfranchisement of women seem likely to vest Republicans or Democrats with any discernible partisan advantage.[15]

Citizenship and Taxes

In the wake of their political defeats in Congress and within the Republican Party, some suffragists turned briefly to a legal strategy for gaining the right to vote. The strategy was suggested by the first section of the Fourteenth Amendment, which declared that "all persons" born or naturalized in the United States were citizens of the nation and the state in which they resided. Women, as "persons," were unquestionably citizens, and the franchise, suffragists maintained, was an intrinsic feature of citizenship: the Constitution, therefore, already guaranteed women the right to vote in federal elections. As was frequently pointed out, various dictionaries, including Webster's, actually defined an American citizen as someone entitled to vote and hold office. Susan B. Anthony gave this equation a broadly political, if ambivalently egalitarian, rationale:

> If we once establish the false principle, that United States citizenship does not carry with it the right to vote in every State in this Union, there is no end to the petty freaks and cunning devices that will be resorted to, to exclude one and another class of citizens from the right of suffrage . . . it will not always be the rich and educated who may combine to cut off the poor and ignorant; but we may live to see the poor, hard-working, uncultivated day laborers, foreign and native born, learning the power of the ballot and their vast majority of numbers, combine and amend State constitutions so as to disfranchise the Vanderbilts and the A. T. Stewarts, the Conklings and Fentons . . . . Establish this precedent, admit the right of the States to deny suffrage, and there is no power to foresee the confusion, discord, and disruption that may await us. There is, and can be, but one safe principle of government—equal rights to all.[16]

This view was activated into legal combat when women in several locales (including Anthony) went to the polls and either voted or, if refused the ballot, filed suit to exercise a right that they claimed they already possessed. The most consequential of these legal actions (because it went to the Supreme Court) proved to be a suit brought by Virginia Minor and her lawyer husband, Francis, in 1872 against a St. Louis registrar who had prevented her from registering to vote. The Minors maintained that the Missouri Constitution and its voter registration law, which restricted the ballot to men, violated the U.S. Constitution in at least two ways: they infringed on Virginia Minor's right of free speech, which was protected by the First Amendment, and they contravened the Fourteenth Amendment's command that states not abridge the "privileges or immunities" of citizens of the United States. Voting, the Minors claimed, was one of those privileges. Although the argument was a coherent one, the justices of the Supreme Court unanimously disagreed. Upholding a lower court decision, they ruled in 1875 that suffrage was not coextensive with citizenship and thus that states possessed the authority to decide which citizens could and could not vote. Bringing an end to debates that had surfaced periodically for decades, the Court formally ratified the severance of national citizenship from suffrage that the late-eighteenth-century authors of the Constitution had devised as a solution to their own political problems. In so doing, and in reiterating the principle that suffrage was a state rather than a federal matter, the Court was bolting the gates on the simplest and shortest road to female suffrage.[17]

The rulings in the women's suffrage cases did not take place in a legal or political vacuum: lurking in the background was the apprehension that the franchise was already too broad. This apprehension fostered resistance to claims that voting was a national right and colored legal arguments assigning the federal government only a narrow role in shaping the franchise. In rebuffing the claims of women in Washington, D.C., for example, a federal judge in 1871 observed that the breadth of the franchise in the cities was producing "political profligacy and violence verging upon anarchy." Categorically rejecting the proposition that there existed a natural or constitutional right to the franchise, the judge noted that "the fact that the practical working of the assumed right would be destructive of civilization is decisive that the right does not exist." In taking this approach, the judges in *Minor v. Happersett* and similar cases were self-consciously laying the legal groundwork for decisions that would limit the ability of the federal government to prevent racial discrimination in the South as well as discrimination against workers and immigrants in the North.[18]

Suffragists took another legal tack as well: they promoted tax rebellions among female property owners in the late 1860s and early 1870s. In scattered locales throughout the country, women refused to pay their taxes as long as they were prevented from voting, insisting that it was unconstitutional to impose the obligations of citizenship on them while they were deprived of political rights. "No taxation without representation" remained a resonant slogan, which activists buttressed with research demonstrating that women in fact paid a sizable portion of the taxes in many municipalities. The depth of feeling about this incongruence between the tax and voter rolls was made clear in the small town of Glastonbury, Connecticut, where two elderly sisters, Abby Hadassah Smith and Julia Evelina Smith, announced in 1869 that they would refuse to pay taxes on their farm until the town permitted them to vote. As historian Linda Kerber has recounted, the Smith sisters—educated, single women with abolitionist backgrounds and some involvement in the suffrage movement—dug in their heels for years, forcing the tax assessor to go to their home and seize their cows to pay off their overdue taxes. Although a series of court battles that dragged on for a decade resulted in a technical victory for the women, they were never enfranchised, and the Connecticut courts—like their counterparts elsewhere—gave little credence to the claim that taxpaying and voting had to go hand in hand.[19]

Although it would take another half century for women to acquire the right to vote, the optimism that suffrage advocates felt in the 1860s was realistically grounded in their own ideological vision and political experience. Supporters of women's suffrage sincerely and deeply believed not only in the rightness of their cause but in the power of their simple egalitarian arguments: women were capable adult citizens and as such ought to be able to choose the lawmakers and laws that governed them. These suffragists, moreover, lived in an era when a righteous cause—the abolition of slavery—had triumphed over ferocious, entrenched opposition. They had witnessed not only the end of slavery but also an extraordinary transformation of popular views and laws regarding black suffrage: within a decade, an idea supported only by those on the fringes of politics had acquired the backing of the Republican Party and then been embedded in the Constitution. Suffragists thus had good reason to believe that profound ideological and political changes could not only happen, but happen quickly, particularly in the overheated climate of sectional conflict and war; and if one accepted the premise that voting was a right, natural or otherwise, it was not a long leap from black to women's suffrage.[20]

What Stanton and Anthony and their allies could not have foreseen, however, was that the mid-nineteenth-century wave of prodemocratic sentiment already had crested. It would not continue to swell, sweeping away all obstacles to an expanded suffrage. An antidemocratic undertow had already begun during the Know-Nothing agitation, and by the late 1860s it was growing stronger. Black suffrage triumphed—albeit temporarily—not because the polity had become convinced of the virtues of equal rights or universal suffrage but due to the unique political exigencies of Reconstruction and the political goals of the Republican Party. Since these singular conditions did not create comparable pressures to enfranchise women, the drive for suffrage fell short, leaving the issue stranded on shore just as the tides of democracy began to recede.

Regrouping

> We do not concur with those who predict that the question of Suffrage for women will speedily demand public action or engross public attention . . .
>
> *New York Times*, 8 March 1869

> The question of woman suffrage is, in my opinion, one of the most important of the political problems of this century.
>
> —Mr. Ewing, Ohio
> Constitutional Convention, 1874

> Our political system is based upon the doctrine that the right of self-government is inherent in the people. . . . Women are a portion of the people, and possess all the inherent rights which belong to humanity. They, therefore, have the right to participate in the government.
>
> —Mr. Sears, Ohio
> Constitutional Convention, 1874

> I deny, Mr. Chairman, that there is one scintilla of truth in the assertion that woman is oppressed. Men shield and protect and de-

> fend her as a being better than themselves. . . . The male, at least
> in all species which form unions of any degree of permanence. . .
> defends and protects the female and her young ones. Thus, if a
> herd of elephants is menaced, the most powerful tuskers take their
> station on the side where danger appears. . . . If bisons are attacked
> by wolves, the bulls form a circle. . . . A gorilla will encounter any
> danger in defense of his mate.
>
> —MR. CAPLES, CALIFORNIA
> CONSTITUTIONAL CONVENTION, 1879

The defeats of the late 1860s left the movement for women's suffrage divided but unbowed. Ironically, perhaps, the political debates of Reconstruction had served to magnify the importance of the right to vote: while pressing the cause of black suffrage, Republican Charles Sumner, for example, had declared that the ballot was "the great guarantee and the only sufficient guarantee" of human rights. Advocates of women's rights increasingly agreed with Sumner, and they remained determined that women soon would acquire this "Columbiad of our political life." For the next two decades, against the backdrop of a changing political climate and an increasingly industrial society, these advocates pursued their goal through diverse means in Washington and in the states.[21]

Once it became clear that women would not be enfranchised on the arm of the black soldier, several different strategies emerged. The first, embraced by the National Woman Suffrage Association (NWSA), founded by Stanton and Anthony in 1869, was to pressure the federal government into enfranchising women throughout the nation; this was to be done through a national organization controlled and shaped by women themselves. The second strategy was to convince state legislatures and constitutional conventions to amend state constitutions to include women in the electorate; this approach was favored by the American Woman Suffrage Association (AWSA), which was founded a few months after the NWSA and headed by Lucy Stone and her husband, Henry Blackwell, both veterans of the abolitionist and antebellum suffragist movements. Stone, raised in a wealthy family in western Massachusetts, was an early graduate of Oberlin College and a popular public speaker; Blackwell, from Ohio, was a dedicated reformer with a lifelong penchant for failed entrepreneurial schemes. The third strategy, more local and decentralized, yet overlapping with that of

AWSA, was to wring "partial" or "limited" suffrage (on issues such as schooling, prohibition, and municipal taxes) from state authorities.[22]

NWSA's approach in key respects was an extension of Radical Reconstruction: despite their break with former abolitionist allies, their distress at the Fifteenth Amendment, and their sometimes disparaging comments about black suffrage, Stanton and Anthony retained a commitment to equal rights and, for a time at least, a desire to build bridges to labor. Government "based on caste and class privilege cannot stand," declared Stanton in 1869, and she was convinced that political rights were the solvent that would dissolve these social boundaries. Accordingly, NWSA's strategy was to pressure the federal government to offer women the same constitutional protections given to freedmen in the Fifteenth Amendment. This view was embodied in a draft constitutional amendment introduced in Congress by Radical Republican George Julian in 1869: it declared that "the right of suffrage in the United States shall be based on citizenship" and that "all citizens . . . shall enjoy this right equally without any distinction or discrimination whatever founded on sex." In the increasingly conservative and pro–states rights political climate of the 1870s, however, this initial version of the Sixteenth Amendment—which tacitly would have nationalized suffrage in ways akin to the Wilson amendment—made little headway.[23]

Anthony consequently drafted a new and narrower version in the late 1870s that was first presented to the Senate by Aaron A. Sargent of California in 1878. Modeled on the Fifteenth Amendment, it stated simply that "the right of citizens of the United States to vote shall not be denied or abridged by the United States or by any state on account of sex." Although NWSA also lobbied for the expansion of women's economic and social rights, securing the passage of this amendment was the focal point of its activities, and the organization's political allies introduced the measure into Congress every year. In 1882, both houses of Congress appointed select committees on women's suffrage, each of which recommended passage of an amendment. Four years later, thanks in part to the energetic support of Republican Henry Blair of New Hampshire, the amendment was finally brought to a vote on the Senate floor, where, to the great disappointment of suffragists seated in the galleries, it was decisively defeated in January 1887 by a margin of thirty-four to sixteen (with twenty-six abstentions), a far cry from the two-thirds positive vote required for passage. In an echo of the regional politics that remained so salient even after the end of Reconstruction, no southern senator voted in favor of the amendment, while twenty-two voted against it. For another half dozen years, Congress continued to grapple with the issue, but after 1893, no congressional committee reported it favorably until late in the Progressive era.[24]

The state-by-state strategy of the AWSA bore little fruit as well. Although the issue was debated in numerous constitutional conventions, and referenda were held in eleven states (eight of them west of the Mississippi) between 1870 and 1910, concrete gains were few. The territory of Wyoming enfranchised women in 1869, a policy affirmed at statehood in 1889; Utah did the same in 1870 and 1896 (interrupted by a brief period when the federal government stripped Utah's women of the suffrage as a curious step in its effort to rid the territory of polygamy); and Idaho and Colorado granted suffrage to women in the mid-1890s. Everywhere else, referenda failed, or the writers of new constitutions chose not to present the proposition to voters for ratification. (See table A.20).[25]

There were, however, a significant number of locales—states, counties, and municipalities—where partial suffrage was adopted, permitting women to vote in municipal elections, on liquor licensing matters, or for local school boards and on issues affecting education. This unique, even anomalous development—enabling women to vote in certain elections but not in others—was made possible by the complex architecture of voting laws. In most states, the suffrage requirements for "nonconstitutional" elections did not have to be identical to those for offices named in state constitutions; they also could be altered by legislation rather than the cumbersome and difficult process of constitutional amendment (see chapter 5).

The most common form of partial enfranchisement involved schools: legislatures, recognizing women's responsibility for childrearing, as well as their education experience, responded to pressure from the suffrage movement by permitting women to vote on matters affecting schooling. Nearly all state legislatures considered adopting laws of this type, and by 1890, more than twenty states had done so. (See table A.17.) Although activists generally viewed school suffrage as a stepping-stone, an entering wedge for broader electoral participation, legislators tended to view the matter differently: as a gesture to placate prosuffrage forces and an assertion that school matters were distinct from "politics."[26]

Placating suffragists, as well as temperance reformers, also was the primary motivation behind laws permitting women to vote on liquor licenses and other matters related to the sale of alcoholic beverages. In many states, such laws were demanded by the large, rapidly growing Woman's Christian

Temperance Union (WCTU), which argued that women had a special interest in voting on such matters because of the impact of alcohol on the family and the links between drunkenness and domestic violence. Similarly, in the 1880s and 1890s, women in a few states were granted the right to vote in municipal elections, or if they were taxpayers, to vote on tax and bond issues. Although sanctioned by the notion that municipal governance was a form of "housekeeping," such laws also were a response to the suffrage movement's ongoing agitation in behalf of the inseparability of taxation and representation. Indeed, there was a conservative twist to this expansion of the franchise, since it appealed to those who believed that voting should be restricted to property owners and taxpayers.[27] (See table A.18.[28])

The limited roster of successes, however, does not do justice to the strength of the movement in the 1870s and 1880s. Local prosuffrage organizations proliferated, referenda were held in numerous states, and after vigorous campaigns, hundreds of thousands of men voted in favor of women's suffrage, a development that would have been unthinkable forty years earlier. Moreover, even in states where the issue was not submitted to a popular vote, suffrage organizations were active, state legislators were obligated to vote on suffrage bills year after year, and support for enfranchisement often cut across party lines. In Massachusetts, for example, both parties were divided on the issue, and Democrat Ben Butler twice ran for governor on prosuffrage planks. At the Illinois Constitutional Convention of 1869–70, delegates voted forty to twenty-one to submit the question to the voters, only to reverse that vote by a narrow margin a month later. A few years later, in Pennsylvania, the issue was the subject of a lively debate at the constitutional convention, and in the 1880s the Indiana House of Representatives voted several times to endorse women's suffrage, only to see its actions blocked by Senate filibusters encouraged by fears that female voters would restrict the sale of intoxicating liquors. In California, the constitutional convention of 1878–79 devoted a tremendous amount of time and energy to the question; after prolonged and passionate debate, suffrage was restricted to men by a margin of only ten votes.[29]

One reason for the growing support was the power of prosuffrage arguments. Impressively diverse, these arguments were voiced not only by suffrage activists but also by political figures, usually but not always Republican, who found themselves in legislatures or constitutional conventions where they had to think through and vote on the issue. The most common argument remained the natural or universal rights view put forward at Seneca Falls and throughout the 1850s. "Woman's right to the ballot seems so clear that it is like some of the mathematical axioms which it is difficult to more clearly define than by stating them," declared an Ohioan in 1874.

> Each individual on entering a state of society surrenders a portion of natural rights, and in return therefore receives, among others, the political right of the elective franchise. A woman is an individual, and when she enters into a state of society and thereby surrenders a portion of her natural rights, she receives in return therefore the right of the elective franchise, equally with man. . . . If the syllogism be correct the right inevitably follows, and where logic leads I cheerfully follow.

"Whatever rights are given to one citizen ought to be given . . . to every other citizen," echoed Eli T. Blackmer, superintendent of the San Diego public schools, at the California Constitutional Convention of 1878. Although voting was not a "natural right," conceded Democrat John Campbell, the youngest member of Pennsylvania's constitutional convention of 1872–73, it was a "political right" that ought not be denied to women. Evoking the traditional language of American republicanism, all Americans were believed to be entitled to self-government—and all Americans included women. An Ohio delegate insisted that "woman . . . have a voice in the enactment of laws to which she is subject. . . . There should be, with us, no subject class. In a genuine, democratic republican government, the governed are also the governors." The governor of Kansas, in 1871, insisted that in a "true republic—a 'government of the people, by the people, for the people,'" there should be no "favored class of 'white male citizen.'"[30]

Emerging alongside these traditional views was another, more essentialist strand of argument: that women possessed particular qualities or virtues that would improve the character of politics and governance. Such views began to be uttered by Stanton and other suffragists in the late 1860s, and they were embraced by many male politicians who seemed more comfortable stressing women's unique virtues rather than their similarity to men. The presence of women, it was argued, would elevate the tone of politics and put an end to "scoundrelism and ruffianism at the polls," particularly in urban areas. Enfranchising women would "tend to impart integrity and honesty to politics, and to control the tricks of those who make politics their trade." In addition, female voters would be less corruptible and more likely to promote policies favoring social justice, peace, and sobriety: "when our mothers, wives, and sisters vote with us, we will have purer legislation, and better execution of the laws, fewer tippling shops, gambling halls, and brothels." According to this line of argument, which became preeminent by the end of the 1870s, women ought to be enfranchised not because they were identical to men but precisely because they were different—and the qualities that made them different would be a boon to American political life.[31]

For some men, at least, this essentialist vision—the notion that women had special qualities and virtues—was both Christian and Jeffersonian, emotional as well as political. In Texas in 1875, for example, a delegate to the constitutional convention introduced the following resolution:

That women, being by the ordinances of nature, the mother of all living human beings . . . and that, as mother, wife, sister and daughter, she has the first care of our lives, is our nurse in childhood, our mentor in youth, our companion, helper and consoler in manhood, our comforting, ministering and sustaining angel in death, even at the birth, trial, death and resurrection of Jesus . . . and that, in this land of republican faith and representative, democratic government, by every recognition of modern, enlightened Christian civilization, she is morally and mentally man's equal; that the same "inalienable rights" that Jefferson has made household words . . . are as much woman's as man's; . . . and inasmuch as woman is of the people, and must be governed by the laws made by the people, and is often a taxpayer, there is no reason, political, human or divine . . . why she should not have the same rights at the ballot-box that man has.[32]

This essentialist argument could have a conservative thrust as well: the virtues of women could be counted on to preserve the traditional social order, to protect property, order, and stability, particularly against the vices of the urban working class.[33]

Other arguments were also mobilized. Prosuffrage convention delegates maintained (probably inaccurately) that the public desired woman suffrage and thus that the conventions should respond to the will of the people. Some of their allies invoked the principle of "no taxation without representation," while others claimed that enfranchisement would provide economic benefits and workplace protection to the growing number of female wage earners. More intellectually minded advocates offered broad historical portraits, pointing to the progressive enlargement of the franchise as a sign of the steady and beneficent erosion of oppression and "aristocracy." John M. Broomall, a former congressman and Republican delegate to the Pennsylvania Constitutional Convention of 1872–73, concluded a lengthy speech by announcing that

> This thing is coming. It is only a question of time. The progress is onward. For thirty years I have been an advocate of universal self-government, and during that time I have marked the progress of it steadily onward. At first, nobody was a man, in the sense of the "governed," unless he was a white man; and indeed some white men were hardly counted. . . . That word "white". . . was washed out with blood.

He continued:

> Four hundred years ago women, according to the popular notion of that day, had no souls. . . . Still later than that, the women were beasts of burden. . . . Still the world moves, and in our time they have been granted equal civil rights with men. The next step is coming, and there are those living who will see it. . . . That step is equality of all human beings both before the law and in the making of the law. Thus it is that the world moves, and the man who is not prepared to keep pace with its motion had better get out of the way.[34]

Still others, both politicians and female suffragists, put forward a more conservative—and ominous—rationale: that it was wrong for the polity to enfranchise ignorant blacks and foreigners while barring educated, native-born white women. One delegate to Ohio's constitutional convention in 1873 lamented the decision "to confer this great privilege upon the ignorant alien—the Chinaman, the Japanese, the Ashantees, and to everything that wears human hair from any part of God's earth, because they are 'male,' and yet withhold it from the American woman who may desire it, for the only reason that she is a female." Similarly, a Californian in 1879 asked whether there was

> any right, or justice, or decency, in a law which gives the elective franchise to the most ignorant, debased, and brutal man in the land, whether born here or abroad, and denies it to Mrs. Stanton, a cultivated and intellectual woman, descended from revolutionary forefathers, and able to go before a committee of the United States Senate and make an argument on constitutional law that would have done credit to any gentleman on this floor or in this nation?

At times in the 1870s and 1880s, this rationale went a giant step beyond fairness and acquired a more overtly politicized, racist edge: female suffrage would benefit society because white native-born women outnumbered— and would outvote—blacks, the Chinese, aliens, or transients. The political dominance of "Americans," therefore, would be insured by the enfranchisement of women.[35]

Faced with this powerful array of arguments, opponents of women's suffrage in the 1870s, 1880s, and 1890s responded with expressions of an altogether different conception of gender roles, with convictions heavily laden with moralism, religion, and fears of social and familial turmoil. In sharp and revealing contrast to other debates about the franchise, opponents of expansion rarely argued that women lacked the intelligence to participate in politics or that their enfranchisement would damage the political order. Instead they insisted that women themselves would be degraded by participating in politics, that their nature made them unsuitable for the rough-and-tumble world of politics. "I believe that women occupy in many respects a higher position than men," observed a Californian in 1879, "and I, for one, do not wish to drag them down from that exalted sphere." Some maintained that the prospect of being dragged down "into the very filth and mire of degradation and human infamy" would mean that only the "worst" women actually would vote, while others (including antisuffrage women) claimed that most women in fact did not want to be enfranchised. Opponents of women's suffrage also invoked repeatedly the notion that voting ought to be linked to military service—which led to the following memorable exchange between two delegates to the California convention of 1879:

> Mr. CAPLES: What is political sovereignty? It is the fruits of the sword. It has always been the fruits of the sword. . . . Where would be that power that you represent at the ballot box today but for that sword that has maintained it from the time of the Revolution down to the present day. . . . The right to vote, the power of sovereignty, does rest right squarely upon the basis of the ability of men to wield the sword.
>
> Mr. McFARLAND: I would like to ask the gentleman if he holds that the right to vote depends upon skill in wielding the sword? If that be so, I know a little actress who can run the gentleman through the ribs in two minutes.

Opponents further insisted that voting was not a natural right and that women did not need to vote because their civil rights already were amply protected. "If there be any one thing settled in the long discussion of this subject it is that suffrage is not a natural right, but is simply a means of government," declared New York delegate (and later senator and secretary of war) Elihu Root in 1894. "The question is therefore a question of expediency."[36]

But the core of the opposition was more emotional: a deeply felt anxiety that enfranchising women would deform natural gender roles and destroy family life. "What is this demand that is being made?" asked the irrepressible Mr. Caples in California in 1879.

> This fungus growth upon the body of modern civilization is no such modest thing as the mere privilege of voting, by any means. . . . The demand is for the abolition of all distinctions between men and women, proceeding upon the hypothesis that men and women are all the same. . . . Gentlemen ought to know what is the great and inevitable tendency of this modern heresy, this lunacy, which of all lunacies is the mischievous and most destructive. It attacks the integrity of the family; it attacks the eternal degrees of God Almighty; it denies and repudiates the obligations of motherhood.

Statements such as Caples's—remarkable as they sound to twentieth-century ears—were not uncommon during this period. A few years earlier, a Pennsylvania politician, W. H. Smith, declared that he opposed the "pernicious heresy" of women's suffrage because "my mother was a woman, and further, because my wife is a woman." If women could vote, "the family . . . would be utterly destroyed." An Ohioan viewed "this attempt to obliterate the line of demarcation . . . between the sexes" as "one phase of the infidelity of our time." That infidelity often was overtly sexualized: admitting women into the public arena would encourage promiscuity, undermine the purity of women, and expose them to the irresistible predations of men. In addition, the sexual charms and seductiveness of women would distort the ways in which men voted: "the young lady would control everything with the young gallants," insisted an Ohio politician. Those who resisted reform further claimed that the enfranchisement of women would create dissension within families, that inescapably there would be arguments between husband and wife that would fracture the family, "the most ancient and uninterrupted social community"; it would produce "horrible strife and derangement of domestic relations." "The whole country—every household," noted the much-agitated Mr. Smith, "would or might be the scene of everlasting quarrels."[37]

Advocates of suffrage devoted considerable energy to rebutting such views. They spurned the notion that "self-government" was "degrading" as "sentimental twaddle" and denied flatly that "only low class women would vote." They countered the idea that "woman" was "outside her sphere when she casts her ballot" by pointing out both that higher education once had been considered outside the sphere of women, and that women themselves ought to determine the boundaries of their sphere. That enfranchising women would destroy the family was dismissed as baseless, as was the charge that voting would somehow erode the special virtues of females. In response to the claim that the franchise ought to be yoked to military service, a California politician asked, "is fighting all there is to be done in this country? . . . Look at the greatest heroes of the wars of the world, and tell me who of them all did as much as Miss Florence Nightingale?" A Pennsylvanian with similar views asked whether clergymen, who did not fight, also should be excluded from the polls. By the mid-1870s, proponents frequently invoked the precedent of Wyoming, where women voted and nothing calamitous had occurred.[38]

Although advocates of suffrage surely got the better of the argument, their rhetorical sallies did not vanquish the opposition. Far from it. Logical arguments could carry the movement only so far, and resistance was firmly lodged in several different quarters. Most fundamentally, perhaps, many women themselves were either opposed, or relatively indifferent, to their own enfranchisement. In the United States, as elsewhere, the demand for suffrage was most resonant among middle-class women, women from families engaged in the professions, trade or commerce, and educated women who lived in cities and developing towns. These were the women whose experiences and desires clashed most directly with traditional norms and who were most likely to seek the independence, autonomy, and equality that enfranchisement represented. Yet such women, although more numerous with each passing year, were far from a majority in 1880. Farm women, living in greater isolation and in more traditional social structures, were less responsive to calls for suffrage as well as more difficult to mobilize into collective action (they were, however, increasingly active in women's clubs, which sometimes led them into more politicized activities). Similarly, urban working-class women, many from immigrant families, did not rush to join a movement that addressed their pressing economic needs only obliquely and sometimes seemed inhospitable to the foreign-born. Upper-class women, meanwhile, often became the leaders of formally organized antisuffrage campaigns and organizations: defending what Susan Marshall (among others) has called their "gendered class position," these women, who already had access to power and could wield influence through their wealth, had little need for the ballot and little interest in democratization.[39]

The political pressure that suffragists could exert thus was limited by their numbers, too limited to overcome the entrenched ideological and psychological resistance of many male voters and politicians. The campaigns for suffrage, moreover, generated organized opposition from some interest groups. The identification of suffrage with temperance and prohibition, for example, sparked an antisuffrage reaction among brewers and liquor retailers. This reaction was shared by some immigrants who felt culturally assaulted by the attack on alcohol, not to mention (although it rarely is mentioned) the rather large number of individuals who simply liked to drink or wanted the freedom to have a drink. Machine politicians also were dubious about women's suffrage—in part for cultural reasons and in part because they always sought to keep the electorate as manageable as possible. Equally skeptical, and sometimes downright hostile, were conservative members of the economic elite who took seriously the proposition that women would promote egalitarian social reforms. Reinforcing these diverse sources of antagonism was the generally declining faith in democracy. "At the bottom of this opposition is a subtle distrust of American institutions, an idea of 'restricted suffrage' which is creeping into our republic through so-called aristocratic channels," observed Harriette R. Shattuck in 1884. To some degree (and to a degree that later would grow) the resistance to enfranchising women was a resistance to enfranchising any new voters at all.[40]

These broad social and political patterns help to explain the particularly slow progress of women's suffrage in the South. There were, of course, active suffragists in the region, both white and black; there also were male politicians, usually Republican, who embraced the cause in constitutional conventions and state legislatures. Still, the movement was slow to gather steam: suffrage organizations were far smaller and less visible than in the North, no referenda were held, and even school-district suffrage remained a rarity. This lag had two critical sources. The first was the South's predominantly rural, agricultural social structure. The social strata most receptive to woman suffrage—urban, professional, educated, middle-class—emerged belatedly and slowly in the South. Most women continued to live in an entirely agricultural world, while elite women from plantation and textile-manufacturing families often joined a vocal antisuffragist countermovement. The second reason that the movement lagged was race. Although suffrage advocates argued that their enfranchisement would solidify white supremacy—because white

women outnumbered black men and women—this claim made little headway with white male Southerners: to them, women's suffrage meant opening
the door to a large new constituency of black voters, something to be avoided
at all costs. As Senator Joseph E. Brown of Georgia put it in 1887, little
could "be said in favor of adding to the voting population all the females of
that race." In addition, the movement for a national suffrage amendment was
repellent to southern Democrats, who perceived such an amendment as yet
another federal threat to states' rights.[41]

If the South was particularly resistant to enfranchising women, the West
was unusually receptive. All of the states that fully enfranchised women in the
nineteenth century were west of the Mississippi, as were most states that held
referenda on the issue. This regional pattern has elicited from historians an
array of plausible, if not altogether convincing, explanations: the egalitarian
influences of frontier life, the desire to encourage settlement, a western revival
of a Puritan urge to purify politics, the opportunities presented by the con-
vening of constitutional conventions at statehood, the egalitarian thrust of
western Populism, and a heightened valuing of women resulting from unusually large male-to-female population ratios. Recent studies, however, have
suggested that these broad western phenomena may have been less significant
than the unusual political circumstances that prevailed in the handful of states
(Wyoming, Colorado, Idaho, and Utah) where suffrage was achieved. In Colorado, for example, the temporary strength of the People's Party appears to
have been crucial to the 1893 success of women's suffrage. In Utah, the enfranchisement of women was certainly—if not simply—linked to the complex politics of gender spawned by the efforts of a Mormon territory, with a
tradition of polygamy, to gain national acceptance and statehood.[42]

Indeed, the history of the right to vote in general suggests that the search
for any single-factor explanation of regional differences is misguided:
groups of nonvoters, as a rule, gained the franchise only when there was a
convergence of several different factors—from a list of possibilities that included grassroots pressure, ideological resonance, wartime mobilization,
economic incentives, class interest, and partisan advantage. Some of these
(e.g., grassroots mobilization and ideological appeal) were present in numerous states, both east and west of the Mississippi—which is why debates
over enfranchising women often were sharply contested and closely fought.
What seems to have tipped the balance in a handful of western states (as
well, perhaps, as in western states that dominated the first twentieth-
century wave of suffrage victories) was a combination of several additional

ingredients. One was a more fluid pattern of party competition, due in part to the strength of the insurgent Farmers' Alliance and shortly later, the People's Party. Another was that western states tended to be dominated by land-owning farm families yet included a highly visible number of working-class transients who labored in mining, railroading, and agriculture. Since the latter group consisted overwhelmingly of single males, the enfranchisement of women offered discernible political benefits to the settler population at the expense of workers in extractive industries (and the companies that sometimes were believed to control their votes).[43]

Finally, most western states between 1850 and the 1890s did not experience the massive growth of an industrial working class that triggered such an antidemocratic reaction in the East and Midwest. The region's swing against democracy was more mild and emotionally focused on the largely male Chinese population. Although the West did share in the nation's ideological retreat from universal suffrage, the relative shallowness of that retreat may have left open a larger political space in which the political rights of women could be considered and embraced.

Doldrums and Democracy

> I think it was Wendell Phillips who said something like this, "if women are like men, then they certainly possess the same brain and that should entitle them to the ballot; if they are not like men, then they certainly need the ballot, for no man can understand what they want." And we ask you upon those lines to give the ballot to women.
>
> —Carrie Chapman Catt to the
> Delaware Constitutional Convention, 1897

> I provide a home for my wife, and I expect her to do her share in maintaining it, and I think that is reasonable enough. If we give women the vote our wives will soon be absorbed in caucuses instead of in housekeeping. They will be drafted on juries too. When I come home at night I expect my wife to be there, and not in a political caucus or locked up in a jury room with eight or ten men.
>
> —Assemblyman Shea of
> Essex, New York, 1910

In October 1893, the *New York Times* declared in an editorial that "the cause of woman suffrage does not seem to have made the least progress in this part of the country in the last quarter of a century, if indeed it has not lost ground." Although the *Times* was hardly an unbiased observer—it would editorialize against woman suffrage well into the twentieth century—its observation was difficult to dispute. Only a tiny portion of the nation's women was fully enfranchised, interest was flagging in many states, and as the *Times* observed, most of the women who were entitled to vote in school board elections did not show up at the polls. The optimistic days when woman suffrage seemed to be a goal within easy reach were over.[44]

Suffrage activists responded to their lack of success—and to the economic and political circumstances that had changed around them—by unifying the two competing suffrage organizations into the National American Woman Suffrage Association (NAWSA) in 1890. Although Stanton and Anthony were the first two presidents of the merged association, power was gradually handed off to a younger generation of leaders, including Anna Howard Shaw, who had risen from a childhood of frontier poverty to gain a medical degree, and Carrie Chapman Catt, a former teacher and journalist from Iowa. Catt, who proved to have exceptional administrative talents, spent years transforming NAWSA from a loosely run association into an efficient organization that carefully tracked its membership and finances, established permanent headquarters in each state, sponsored courses in political science and economics, and coordinated national, state, and local campaigns. By the end of the 1890s, NAWSA had created branches in every state, founded hundreds of local clubs, generated large quantities of literature, and was pressuring politicians everywhere. NAWSA also began to target and raise funds from wealthy, upper-class women, some of whom for the first time were lending their support to the movement.[45]

These organizational changes were accompanied by shifts in ideology—or at least by shifts in the emphases placed on various arguments. Mirroring the broader middle- and upper-class disenchantment with democracy, suffragists placed less weight on equal rights arguments, which implied that everyone, male and female, should possess the right to vote. They stressed instead the more palatable essentialist theme that feminine qualities would be a welcome addition to the polity: that theme, in addition to conforming with traditional notions of gender roles, had the advantage of avoiding the implication that blacks and immigrant workers also should be enfranchised. This essentialist emphasis was reinforced by the increasingly common claim that women had distinct economic and social interests that could only be protected by possession of the right to vote.[46]

As important, white middle-class suffragists placed new weight on the argument that the enfranchisement of women would compensate for and counterbalance the votes of the ignorant and undesirable. This conservative notion, with its unmistakable class and racial edge, had been voiced since the late 1860s, but only in the late 1880s and 1890s did it become commonplace.[47] Catt herself decried the enfranchisement of some Native Americans and spoke disparagingly of immigrants, particularly those from eastern and southern Europe.

> Today there has arisen in America a class of men not intelligent, not patriotic, not moral, nor yet not pedigreed. In causes and conventions, it is they who nominate officials, at the polls through corrupt means, it is they who elect them and by bribery, it is they who secure the passage of many a legislative measure.

The best means of limiting the influence of such voters and of perpetuating "the American Republic" was to enfranchise native-born American women. "The census of 1890 proves that women hold the solution in their hands. . . . Expediency demands it as the policy which alone can lift our nation from disgrace." Olympia Brown, a Universalist minister from Wisconsin, gave more precise numbers in 1889.

> There are in the United States three times as many American-born women as the whole foreign population, men and women together, so that the votes of women will eventually be the only means of overcoming this foreign influence and maintaining our free institutions. There is no possible safety for our free school, our free church or our republican government, unless women are given the suffrage and that right speedily.[48]

In the South, of course, the American Republic was thought to be threatened not by immigrants but by blacks, and some suffragists offered to meet that threat through what Henry Blackwell, as early as 1867, called "the statistical argument." (Blackwell's reiteration of this argument, entitled "A Solution to the Southern Question," was published by NAWSA in 1890.) As Mississippi native Belle Kearney put it at the NAWSA convention of 1903, "Anglo-Saxon women" were "the medium through which to retain the supremacy of the white race over the African." Kearney maintained that the "enfranchisement of women would insure immediate and durable white supremacy, honestly attained." To be sure, the relationship between women's suffrage and black enfranchisement in the South was byzantine. Many white suffragists declined to play the race card, and even some who did were motivated less by a commitment to white supremacy than by the search for a potent line of attack. In addition, the ranks of southern suffragists included a growing number of African-American women. The most strident antagonists of black rights, moreover, belonged to the anti–women's suffrage camp: one of the principal arguments against female enfranchisement from 1890 to 1920 was that it would open an additional door to black voting and possibly to federal intervention in election laws. Nonetheless, the currency of the statistical argument, particularly coupled with NAWSA's own tolerance of segregation, highlighted the distance that the movement had traveled from the equal rights impulses of the 1860s. At the 1903 NAWSA meeting, held in New Orleans, the executive board formally affirmed its recognition of "states' rights," effectively permitting southern chapters to bar blacks from membership.[49]

In both the North and South, the notion that women were the antidote to undesirable voters led many suffragists, including Stanton, to join the conservative chorus calling for literacy tests as a means of shaping the electorate. In a well-known article entitled "Educated Suffrage," Stanton in 1895 proposed doing away with the "ignorant foreign vote" by instituting a test for "intelligent reading and writing." Speaking to a Senate committee in 1898, she declared that "the popular objection to woman suffrage is that it would 'double the ignorant vote.' The patent answer to this is 'abolish the ignorant vote'" (which Stanton, in any case, believed was "solid against woman's emancipation"). At the 1902 convention of NAWSA, she insisted that immigrants "not become a part of our ruling power until they can read and write the English language intelligently and understand the principles of republican government." Although Stanton's longstanding radicalism kept her xenophobia in check (she opposed immigration restriction and pressed hard for free, compulsory education), she and many other suffragists effectively abandoned the principle of universal suffrage in favor of increasingly popular class-based limitations on electoral participation. They were not unopposed in this stance: Stanton's own daughter, Harriot Stanton Blatch, publicly dissented from her mother's view in the 1890s. But advocacy of restrictions on the right to vote had entered the mainstream of feminist thought.[50]

The sources of this ideological shift were several. White, native-born, middle-class women, like their male counterparts, had less faith in democracy and universal suffrage than they had possessed thirty years earlier. Women, as well as men, reacted to the political turmoil in the South, to massive immigration, and to the growth of urban political machines by concluding that the franchise should be restricted—even while arguing that the portals to politics should be opened to them. In addition, as historian Steven Buechler has pointed out, changes in the nation's social structure altered the class location and attitudes of many suffrage advocates: with the growth of a national elite and a foreign-born working class, the midcentury view of a relatively porous boundary separating workers from members of the middle class was becoming untenable. Given such a shift, suffragists who embraced middle-class values found themselves sliding from the "class blind" ideology of equal rights to the more class-conscious embrace of "educated suffrage." This conservative tilt was accentuated by the entry into the suffrage movement of upper-class women who self-consciously sought to defend the existing social order through politics. Finally, many suffragists—whatever their deepest convictions—may have resorted to these restrictionist and even racist claims in order to counter their opponents' arguments and win adherents in an increasingly conservative political climate. As was often true in public debates, each side's utterances were partial reflections of the arguments of their adversaries.[51]

If feminists believed that their conservative posture would speed the passage of new suffrage laws, they were sorely mistaken. Despite the more sophisticated organizing techniques developed by Catt and her colleagues, the 1890s and 1900s witnessed few concrete gains, and the period from 1896 to 1910 came to be known among suffragists as "the doldrums." During this period, only six referenda on suffrage were held, three of them in Oregon: all six were soundly defeated. Although the issue was raised repeatedly in state legislatures and constitutional conventions, there were no new additions to the suffrage column. New York rebuffed its suffragists in 1894, as did California in 1896, and Washington in 1898. In 1895, Massachusetts even underwent the demoralizing spectacle of a mock (or nonbinding) referendum on municipal suffrage that was overwhelmingly defeated and for which only 23,000 women (out of a possible 600,000) turned out to vote. To be sure, some progress was made in achieving partial suffrage for women: school suffrage laws were passed in several states; Michigan, Kansas, and New York permitted property-owning women to cast ballots on financial issues; and the city of Annapolis rewrote its charter to permit female taxpayers to vote. (See tables A.17 and A.18.) Yet even on this limited front, setbacks were common: most legislative proposals for school and municipal suffrage were defeated; California's governor vetoed as unconstitutional an 1899 bill that would have granted municipal and school board suffrage; legislatures debated but uniformly rejected bills to permit women to vote in presidential elections; and the courts in several states, including Michigan and New Jersey, ruled that partial suffrage bills violated state constitutions.[52]

The paucity of victories had multiple sources. As was true before 1890, the social base of the women's movement remained limited, despite the addition of some upper-class recruits. Well into the twentieth century, for example, the nation's women's clubs declined to endorse the cause of suffrage. Similarly, traditional gender ideology remained strong, reinforced by religious world views that were resistant to social change. In Delaware in 1897, for example, delegate Edward G. Bradford insisted that enfranchisement would "strike a blow at the harmony . . . of the home" and at "the Christian civilization of the nineteenth century." His colleague, Wilson T. Cavender, expressed his belief that women possessed a "maternal duty imposed by the law of nature" and "by that duty God has placed an obstacle in the way of their becoming a part and parcel of a Government." In addition, liquor interests as well as businessmen opposed to social reform once again mounted effective campaigns against enfranchisement, particularly after they were alerted by the victories of the mid-1890s that women's suffrage could win.[53]

Undergirding and perhaps outweighing all of these factors, however, was the conservative reluctance to expand the franchise at all, the distrust of democracy that reached its emotional peak precisely during the "doldrums." "Tory anti-suffragism," as historian Sara Graham aptly dubbed such sentiments (to distinguish them from traditional antisuffrage views, grounded in notions of feminine ideals and separate spheres), was gaining strength with each passing year. In 1897, Carrie Chapman Catt, addressing Delaware's constitutional convention, noted that "there is growing in this country a great skepticism concerning man suffrage. If that were not true, our own cause of woman suffrage would grow more rapidly than it is growing." The following year, Mary Jo Adams, an early historian of suffrage, wrote that

the day has passed when the incapacity of women for political duties was maintained; and the opposition today seems not so much against *women* as against any more voters at all. Suffrage is not an "inalienable right" of the citizen, of the tax-payer or of anybody else. It exists for the good of the State and whatever is for its best interests is right. . . . The advocates of the measure claim that government would be better if women had a participation in it. The opponents say that woman suffrage would merely add to the number of votes, already unmanageably large, without vitally affecting results.

Adams's observation was astute. In the South, the statistical argument was simply no match for the frenzied political circus that was disfranchising blacks and poor whites in one state after another. Meanwhile, in the North, the parallel push for suffrage for educated women collided head-on with the powerful middle- and upper-class desire to shrink the electorate. As Abraham Kellogg put it at the New York Constitutional Convention of 1894, "before we double twice over the voting population . . . with its untold possibilities of corruption," the state ought to "bend its efforts towards purifying the Augean stables which we now have to contend with rather than to incur the possibility of new evils which we know not of." By 1901, the aging Susan B. Anthony, a witness to a half century of struggle, concluded that one of the three "great obstacles to the speedy enfranchisement of women" was "the inertia in the growth of democracy which has come as a reaction following the aggressive movements that with possibly ill-advised haste enfranchised the foreigner, the negro, and the Indian."[54]

Whatever its statistical validity, the anti-black, anti-immigrant, and anti–working class argument in favor of women's suffrage was inescapably weakened by its own internal contradictions. Voicing the argument at all meant jeopardizing or forgoing the political support of large groups of actual and potential voters; it also implicitly sanctioned the antifeminist view that voting was not a right and that the franchise could legitimately be restricted by the state. An antidemocratic argument in favor of enlarging the franchise could neither overwhelm nor outflank the simpler and more consistent conservative view that the polity should be as narrowly circumscribed as possible.

A Mass Movement

Even as the doldrums dragged on, organizational and ideological shifts were under way that would soon change the movement's direction and fortunes; the first decade of the twentieth century proved to be less a period of failure than of fruitful stock taking and coalition building. Under the leadership of Catt and Blatch, among others, NAWSA continued to systematize its organization, while adopting tactics pioneered by British suffragists and the political left. Equally important was the formation of new, more militant organizations, such as the Equality League (1907) and later the Congressional Union (1913) and the Woman's Party (1916), led by Alice Paul, a highly educated Quaker social worker. Paul, who had traveled to England to study as a young woman, served an apprenticeship in militance with British suffragists, including participation in a hunger strike that had terminated only when she was fed by force.

Both in and out of NAWSA, the movement became more tightly run, better funded, and more militant in the decade beginning in 1905: suffrage organizations implanted themselves in towns, cities, wards, and precincts throughout the country; they imaginatively generated attention-getting demonstrations of strength; and they pressured political leaders in Washington and the states. In New York, the Woman Suffrage Party adopted Tammany Hall's techniques of precinct-level organizing; in California, the Equal Suffrage Association canvassed door to door and distributed millions of pamphlets. A steady increase in the number of educated urban women helped to swell the ranks of suffragists.[55]

At the same time, the movement became socially and ideologically more diverse, attracting both elite and working-class supporters to complement its middle-class base. The addition of the latter was encouraged by increasingly audible progressive voices, by the movement's growing interest in social reform and receptivity to working-class women. The turning point for NAWSA came at its 1906 convention, at which child labor reformer Florence Kelley sharply attacked the movement's class and ethnic prejudices. "I have rarely heard a ringing suffrage speech which did not refer to the 'ignorant and degraded' men, or the 'ignorant immigrants' as our masters. This is habitually spoken with more or less bitterness. But this is what the workingmen are used to hear applied to themselves by their enemies in times of strike." Urging her fellow suffragists to abandon such language, Kelley called for a renewed commitment to social reform, particularly compulsory education and child labor laws. Her views were seconded at the convention by settlement house pioneer Jane Addams, who grounded a call for enfranchisement in the observation that the governance of modern cities was largely a matter of "housekeeping" that required the particular talents and experiences of women. Notably, Addams also seized the occasion to debunk the notion that women should be excluded from voting because they did not bear arms: although that notion may have had "a certain logic" in medieval cities that were constantly at war, it was irrelevant in a world where the welfare of the city was threatened not by military attack but by social, industrial, and medical problems.[56]

Not all suffragists embraced the progressive views of Kelley and Addams, but many did, and the tactical failure of the tilt toward xenophobia and elitism was apparent to all. As a result, the movement shifted direction once again, became more inclusive (at least of whites), and more openly identified with social reform. After 1906, calls for educated suffrage became less frequent, and in 1909, NAWSA formally reversed its support of education qualifications for voting. Linked to the growing concern with social reform, moreover, was a new stress on the economic roles and needs of women. "It is with woman as a worker that the suffrage has to do," observed Harriot Stanton Blatch, one of the key architects of this ideological turn. Although Blatch wrote extensively about the economic importance of household labor, it was the size and nature of the paid female labor force that buttressed the claim that working women had a particularly compelling need to be enfranchised. By 1900, roughly one fifth of the labor force was female, and many of these women held poorly paid, semiskilled jobs; in 1905, there were 50,000 women in New York's garment industry alone. As activists tried to impress on politicians and on the middle-class public, women were not a transient presence in industry, and they therefore needed to wield political power in order to protect themselves. "No one needs all the powers of the fullest citizenship more urgently than the wage-earning woman," Florence Kelley had declared in 1898.[57]

This new emphasis on working women had both ideological and pragmatic attractions for suffragists. Female workers were, in the words of historian Nancy Cott, admirable "exemplars of independent womanhood"; they also were vulnerable and exploited victims of industrial capitalism whose plight readily tapped the broad impulses of Progressive-era social reform. Moreover, to stress the needs of working women was to treat them tacitly as an interest group, an ideological reconfiguration that (as Cott has pointed out) fused essentialist and egalitarian claims. Finally, some suffragists, such as Blatch, Kelley, Adams, Anna Howard Shaw, and New York settlement house founder Lillian Wald, believed that suffrage would never be achieved until it had gained the electoral support of working-class men—which meant emphasizing class as well as gender issues. The defeat of a 1912 suffrage referendum in Ohio was widely attributed to the lack of labor support.[58]

Meanwhile, working women themselves, as well as their activist leaders, displayed new interest in acquiring the right to vote. This arose in part because of their difficulty unionizing and winning workplace conflicts: although the number of organized women workers was on the rise, progress was slow, and many women were losing faith in the leadership of male trade unionists. More important, female wage earners, in and out of the labor movement, were increasingly convinced that state intervention could ameliorate their working conditions and that such intervention would be forthcoming only if they were enfranchised. Despite their early skepticism about the significance of suffrage, many women workers and their supporters—most notably those who belonged to the Women's Trade Union League (WTUL), a cross-class organization founded in 1902 to promote the unionization of women—came to believe that enfranchisement was the key to the passage of legislation that would improve the wages, hours, health, and workplace safety of women. "Behind suffrage," organizer Leonora O'Reilly declared, "is the demand for equal pay for equal work." Some WTUL activists went a step further, concluding that women's lack of political power was the critical source of their economic exploitation. "The disfranchised worker is always the lowest paid," insisted a WTUL resolution presented to the New York State Federation of Labor in 1914. "Working women must use the ballot in order to abolish the burning and crushing of our bodies for the profit of a very few," lamented a garment worker after a fire at the Triangle shirtwaist factory killed more than one hundred women. Similarly, black women—a disproportionate number of whom held working-class jobs—became increasingly engaged in the struggle for suffrage.[59]

Not surprisingly, the engagement of working-class women was accompanied by the strengthening of trade union and socialist support. The American Federation of Labor had endorsed women's suffrage as early as 1892, but its support was tepid until the WTUL and other suffrage organizations began to appeal to working-class interests. By 1915, even the politically cautious AFL president, Samuel Gompers, formally asked all trade unionists to offer active support to the suffrage movement. "There are two tremendous movements for freedom at the present time," Gompers wrote in an official AFL bulletin, "the labor movement and the woman suffrage movement. . . . Men must join the women in the effort to solve their common problem, or else they will find women used against them as competitors." Similarly, Socialists had long endorsed suffrage in principle and their leader, Eugene V. Debs, had been an unflagging supporter, but it was only in the 'teens that Socialists began to campaign vigorously for the ballot. Although support from labor and Socialists drew fire (albeit a rather self-satisfied fire) from antisuffragists, those movements helped to invigorate the suffrage drive while also serving as a training ground for organizers.[60]

Thanks in part to this convergence of working-class interest in suffrage with the suffragists' interest in the working class, the campaign for women's suffrage became a mass movement for the first time in its history after 1910. Not coincidentally, the movement also began to win some new victories. Washington permitted women to vote in 1910, followed by California in 1911, and Arizona, Kansas, and Oregon the following year; Illinois, in 1913, decided to allow women to vote in presidential elections and for all state and local offices not provided for in its constitution; and the next year, Montana and Nevada adopted full suffrage. In 1912, Congress expressly authorized the territory of Alaska to enfranchise women if its legislature so chose. (See tables A.19 and A.20.)

A large and geographically variable roster of factors contributed to these successes: among them were imaginative organizing techniques, persuasive and charismatic leadership (notably, Jeannette Rankin in Montana), the strength of the Progressive Party and the progressive wing of the Republican Party, increasing support among Democrats, the appeal of social reform endeavors linked to women's suffrage, and the persistence of prohibitionist sentiment (coupled with the persistent prohibitionist campaigns of some suffragists). Yet even in the western states, far from the densely populated immigrant cities of the East and Midwest, the shift in working-class sentiment played a key role. In Washington, suffrage was supported by the state federation of labor, and a straw poll revealed that union members overwhelmingly favored the referendum. In California, where the margin of victory was slight, a sharp rise in the prosuffrage working-class vote proved to be critical. Although women's suffrage was defeated in the San Francisco area (and received its greatest support in rural counties), an energetic working-class suffrage organization, the Wage Earners' Suffrage League, helped to substantially increase the prosuffrage vote in working-class districts: from 25 percent in the unsuccessful referendum of 1896 to more than 40 percent in 1911. The working class, in both San Francisco and Los Angeles, was more favorably disposed to suffrage than were either the middle classes or the urban elite.[61]

Such victories reinvigorated the movement, as did other tangible signs of progress. In 1910, President William H. Taft agreed to address the annual convention of NAWSA, endorsing the cause in remarkably opaque and ambivalent prose.

> In the first place popular representative government we approve and support because on the whole every class, that is, every set of individuals who are similarly situated in the community, who are intelligent enough to know what their own interests are, are better qualified to determine how those interests shall be cared for and preserved than any other class, however altruistic that class may be; but I call your attention to two qualifications in that statement. One is that the class should be intelligent enough to know its own interests. The theory that Hottentots or any other uneducated, altogether unintelligent class is fitted for self-government at once or to take part in government is a theory that I wholly dissent from—but this qualification is not applicable here. The other qualification to which I call your attention is that the class should as a whole care enough to look after its interests, to take part as a whole in the exercise of political power if it is conferred. Now if it does not care enough for this, then it seems to me that the danger is, if the power is conferred, that it may be exercised by that part of the class least desirable as political constituents and be neglected by many of those who are intelligent and patriotic and would be most desirable as members of the electorate.

Taft's reference to Hottentots infuriated many suffragists, but what mattered politically was that he spoke at all. That same year, a petition favoring a federal amendment, signed by more than 400,000 women, was presented to Congress. In 1912, the Progressive Party endorsed women's right to vote, and in March 1913, Woodrow Wilson's inauguration was partially eclipsed by a suffrage parade of 5,000 women in Washington. The following year, a Senate committee reported favorably on a federal amendment, and for the first time in decades a draft amendment was brought to the floor of Congress for a vote. Throughout these years, the issue garnered far more attention in the press than it ever had before, while suffragists ratcheted up the pressure to change both state and federal laws.[62]

Nonetheless, opposition remained strong, particularly in the eastern half of the country. Although the movement was sturdy enough to compel numerous states to hold referenda on women's suffrage, defeats were far more common than victories. In 1912, referenda had negative outcomes in Ohio, Wisconsin, and Michigan (where the result was repeated in 1913); in 1914, the men of North and South Dakota, Nebraska, Missouri, and Ohio (again) voted similarly; the following year, suffrage proposals were defeated by large margins in the industrial states of New York, New Jersey, Pennsylvania, and Massachusetts. In nearly all of these states, political machines (generally Democratic but Republican in Pennsylvania), liquor interests, elite opponents of democratization, and immigrant groups (particularly Germans, but some of the Irish as well) contributed to the defeats. So too did the durability of traditional beliefs that could not be reconciled with the enfranchisement of women.[63]

The strength and persistence of such beliefs ought not be underestimated, however tempting it may be to regard them as mere window dressing for more material, political, or ethnic interests. At the 1912 Ohio Constitutional Convention, for example, the standard array of prosuffrage arguments (including numerous invocations of the needs of female workers and the positive stance of the labor movement) repeatedly was countered by a profoundly different social vision, grounded in religion, culture, and individual life experiences. One delegate, after extensively quoting the Bible, including the phrase from Corinthians that "the head of every woman is the man," insisted that enfranchisement would "blot out three of the most sacred words known in the world's vocabulary of six thousand years, namely, mother, home, and heaven." Another spoke reverentially of his mother, a widow "who took in long rolls of wool to spin for her neighbors" and who never voted. Several lamented that voting was a "burden" that they ought not place on the "shoulders" of women and that only "unwomenly" women would vote; another characterized the agitation for suffrage as "a sex war." One eloquent opponent announced with a telling sense of social and generational resentment,

> I stand here as the apostle of the old man—mere man—tyrannical man. The old fellow who brings home the rent—who eats out of a kettle at noon, and fills it with kindling to carry home in the evening. The old fellow who pays for the food and heat and light, who puts up the insurance premiums, and occasionally wrestles with a chattel mortgage . . . the old fellow who has hewn the wood and drawn the water, who has tunnelled our mountains, who has bridged our rivers, who has built our railroads . . . and who now stands in the presence of it all wearing plain clothes, holding up horny hands, weary in body and mind, quietly receiving the assurance that he is indeed a tyrant.

It was testimony to the growth of prosuffrage sentiment that the Ohio convention voted to hold a referendum on the issue: numerous delegates announced that they personally opposed suffrage but did not want to bear the responsibility of preventing its passage. But the traditional gender ideology that they voiced was sufficiently widespread that the referendum failed in 1912 and again in 1914.[64]

Although no referenda were held in the South during this period, the suffrage movement there also gained strength. A new surge of organizing began in 1910, rooted in an urban and quasi-urban middle class that had grown rapidly in preceding decades: that middle class spawned southern New Women who were educated, had held professional or white-collar service jobs, and were married to (or the children of) professionals and small businessmen. This new generation of white southern suffragists—women such as Gertrude Weil from the railroad juncture town of Goldsboro, North Carolina, or Margaret Caldwell of Nashville, the daughter of a doctor and wife of a car dealer—was motivated by concerns very similar to those of their northern counterparts, and they joined hands with NAWSA and other national organizations, reviving or building chapters throughout the South. By 1913, every southern state had a suffrage organization allied with NAWSA; within a few years, Virginia's organization had 13,000 members and Alabama possessed eighty-one local suffrage clubs. These women were joined (although usually not in the same organizations) by numerous African-American women who believed with good reason that they, more than anyone perhaps, had a compelling need to be enfranchised. Notably, some southern suffragists, like their northern colleagues, made concerted efforts to reach out to the South's emerging labor movement and to link the cause of suffrage to the exploitation of working people. "We have no right," declared Virginia's Lucy Randolph Mason, "to stand idly by and profit by the underpaid and over-driven labor of people bound with the chains of economic bondage."[65]

Despite such efforts, the soil for democratic expansion remained less fertile in the South. Not only was the middle class relatively small and the rural world large and difficult to reach, but antisuffrage forces were strong and well organized. In addition to the liquor interests and political machines, such as those in New Orleans and parts of Texas, suffragists had to contend with active and well-financed antisuffrage organizations, led by upper-class women and men tied both to the world of plantation agriculture and to the new industrial South of textiles and railroads. This elite opposition was grounded in southern variants of traditional gender ideology and in a fierce class-based antagonism to the types of social reform (including labor reform) that many suffragists advocated.[66]

The opposition also had a great deal to do with race. By the latter years of the Progressive era, African Americans had been successfully disfranchised throughout the South, and most whites were intent on keeping it that way. Politicians were loath to tinker at all with electoral laws, and they feared that black women might prove to be more difficult to keep from the polls than black men—because black women were believed to be more literate than men and more aggressive about asserting their rights, and also because women would be unseemly targets of repressive violence. "We are not afraid to maul a black man over the head if he dares to vote, but we can't treat women, even black women, that way," fretted a senator from Mississippi. Although some white suffragists continued to advance the statistical argument that woman suffrage would insure white supremacy, that rhetorical claim made no more headway after 1910 than it had in the 1890s.[67]

Faced with this opposition, in a one-party political system that left little room for dissent, suffragists found it difficult to make much progress. In 1912, after a perfunctory debate, the Virginia legislature voted eighty-eight to twelve against a state amendment; the state senate declined to vote on the issue at all. In Louisiana, both branches of the legislature rejected a bill that would have permitted white women to vote in Democratic primaries, and the electorate then rebuffed a proposal for school suffrage. Although Arkansas's legislature did approve a suffrage referendum (that was not submitted to the people because of a technicality), as did the lower house in Alabama, most state governments declined to promote referenda on the issue and some reacted derisively to suffrage proposals. In 1916, for example, the state senate of Georgia set a hearing on women's suffrage for the day after the legislature adjourned.[68]

Compounding the difficulties faced by southern suffragists was another issue, the growing support nationally for a federal amendment. If women's suffrage itself was unpopular in much of the South, a federal constitutional amendment was anathema. Not implausibly, many Southerners were convinced that a federal amendment would open the doors to Washington's intervention in elections, to enforcement—so glaringly absent—of the Fifteenth Amendment and any subsequent amendment that might appear to guarantee the voting rights of black women. In addition to strengthening antisuffragism, this issue split the southern suffrage movement itself, often along lines coinciding with suffragists' attitudes toward racial equality. While some suffragists welcomed the prospect of a federal strategy (either on principle or because it was more likely to succeed than state efforts), others—most vocally, Kate Gordon of Louisiana—denounced the possibility. Gordon, a champion of women's suffrage as a bulwark against black political power, resigned her leadership position in NAWSA to protest the organization's renewed efforts to promote a federal amendment. In 1913, she founded the Southern States Woman Suffrage Conference to focus on passage of state laws and convincing the national Democratic Party to endorse suffrage on a state-by-state basis. Gordon's new organization—which she thought should replace NAWSA's in the South—proved to be short-lived, but by 1915 it was evident that the two currents in the southern movement coexisted very uneasily with one another.[69]

The Nineteenth Amendment

> To fail to ask for the suffrage amendment at this time would be treason to the fundamental cause for which we, as a nation, have entered the war. President Wilson has declared that "we are at war because of that which is dearest to our hearts—democracy; that those who submit to authority shall have a voice in the Government." If this is the basic reason for entering the war, then for those of us who have striven for this amendment and for our freedom and for democracy to yield today, to withdraw from the battle, would be to desert the men in the trenches and leave them to fight alone across the sea not only for democracy for the world but also for our own country.
>
> —ANNA HOWARD SHAW, HEARING BEFORE
> THE HOUSE COMMITTEE ON WOMAN SUFFRAGE, 1918

In 1914 and 1915, the suffrage movement stood at a crossroads. Although women were fully enfranchised in some states and had partial suffrage in many, the movement for political equality still faced an uphill, obstacle-laden struggle. Victories had been won, but defeats were more numerous, and none of the heavily populated states of the Northeast and Midwest had granted women the right to vote. The social base of the movement was broader than ever, but key segments of the electorate remained antagonistic, most politicians were waffling, and the opposition was better organized.

Not surprisingly, the mixed record of wins and losses—coming after fifty years of effort—spawned a vigorous strategic debate. Some NAWSA ac-

tivists favored a continuation of efforts to alter state constitutions: this strategy had yielded victories, and it had the virtue of deflecting the opposition
of states' rights advocates, particularly (but not exclusively) in the South.
Proponents of a state strategy also were mindful that Congress had defeated
a proposed federal amendment in 1914 and early 1915. On the other hand,
state campaigns required a massive investment of resources, and they
seemed almost unwinnable both in the South and in other states (such as
Minnesota and New Mexico) whose constitutions could be amended only
through elaborate, multilayered electoral procedures. Passage of a federal
amendment, in contrast, would demand only congressional approval (by a
two-thirds vote) followed by votes in the legislatures of three quarters of the
states. It was for these tactical reasons—in addition to the principle that all
of the nation's female citizens should be enfranchised—that Alice Paul and
her friend Lucy Burns (also a veteran of the militant wing of the British
movement) split off from NAWSA to create the Congressional Union,
which would focus single-mindedly on a federal amendment.[70]

In 1915, with the reelection of Carrie Chapman Catt as its president,
NAWSA too began to tilt decisively toward a federal strategy. The text of
the Nineteenth Amendment, still modeled on the Fifteenth, was simple
and straightforward:

> Section 1. The right of citizens of the United States to vote shall not be de-
> nied or abridged by the United States or any State on account of sex.
> Section 2. Congress shall have power, by appropriate legislation, to enforce
> the provisions of this article.

Catt devised a "Winning Plan" of building support in the thirty-six states
most likely to ratify an amendment; under her leadership, NAWSA also
managed to increase its membership from 100,000 to 2 million by 1917.
Meanwhile, the Congressional Union intensified its efforts, and as a cadre
organization, smaller and more focused than the sprawling heterogeneous
NAWSA, became increasingly militant in its tactics. Although not by design, the combination of the Congressional Union's militance and
NAWSA's more moderate yet insistent lobbying was emerging as a potent
strategic force, a political pincers' movement that kept the public spotlight
and political pressure on both parties.[71]

In 1916, the Congressional Union and NAWSA catapulted the issue of
women's suffrage, for the first time, into the mainstream of national party pol-

itics. The partisan lineup on the issue was—as it long had been—complex and fluid. Support for women's suffrage was most common among reform-minded Republicans, but the party itself was not united, either nationally or in most states. Vehement opposition came both from Tory Republicans, who wished to turn the clock back on democratization, and from those who resisted social reform, such as New York's Senator James Wadsworth. Another stalwart Republican opponent was Senator Henry Cabot Lodge, the author of the 1890 "force" bill to guarantee black voting rights in the South. The Democratic Party was also divided: its southern wing and urban machines generally had opposed women's suffrage, and the party's embrace of states' rights mitigated against a federal amendment. Yet there were many prosuffrage Democratic politicians, including Champ Clark of Missouri, who became the powerful Speaker of the House in the 'teens.[72]

Breaking with the suffrage movement's tradition of nonpartisanship, the Congressional Union—and its organizational offspring, the Woman's Party and the National Woman's Party—attempted in 1914 and again in 1916 to mobilize women who were already enfranchised to vote against Democratic candidates. Despite that threat, President Woodrow Wilson declined to endorse women's suffrage, evasively reiterating his view that suffrage was a state issue; the national Democratic Party was similarly unresponsive. (The Republican platform of 1916, in contrast, endorsed the cause, albeit in watered-down language.) When the votes were counted, the suffragists' strategy appeared to have failed: Wilson was reelected, the Democrats won most states where women had voted, and there was no evidence that Democratic congressional candidates had suffered because of their party's stance on the voting rights of women.[73]

Nonetheless, the 1916 elections set in motion two distinctive partisan dynamics that had surfaced periodically in suffrage struggles since the 1840s. The first resulted from the partial enfranchisement of women: some women already could vote in all elections, and many could vote in some elections. As Alice Paul and her allies realized, such circumstances gave women leverage to reward or punish politicians because of their (or their party's) stance on the Nineteenth Amendment. That this leverage was not particularly effective in 1916 did not mean that it would remain inconsequential: Democrats in states such as California, where women did vote, still had good reason to press the national party to endorse women's suffrage. The second dynamic was that of the "endgame," the dynamic of possible or impending victory: once it seemed likely or even possible that women's suffrage eventually would be achieved, either nationally or in an individual state, the potential political cost of a vote against enfranchisement rose dramatically. Such a vote all too easily could earn the enmity of a large group of future constituents. The invariable upshot of such circumstances (and a clear sign that a suffrage contest had entered its endgame) was pressure on political leaders to jump on the bandwagon, or at the very least, to get out of the road.

The operation of these dynamics accelerated in 1917. Beginning in January, the National Woman's Party began the unladylike activity of picketing the White House day after day, carrying signs contrasting Wilson's broadly stated democratic utterances with his position on women's suffrage. As the picket lines grew larger and occasionally more vociferous, the Washington police began arresting the women, which led to trials, jail terms, and hunger strikes for prominent social figures as well as dedicated recent college graduates. The courts eventually dismissed all charges against the picketers, but small-scale acts of disruption and civil disobedience continued in various locales. NAWSA, meanwhile, intensified its less flamboyant efforts on all fronts, raising money, holding public demonstrations, and lobbying state and national political leaders. Indeed, by 1917, the National Woman's Party's dramatic militance was serving to make NAWSA appear increasingly moderate and acceptable to mainstream politicians. State legislators in six midwestern and northeastern states (Michigan, Ohio, North Dakota, Rhode Island, Nebraska, and Indiana) responded to these efforts by adopting the precedent set in Illinois: without constitutional amendments, they altered their laws to permit women to vote in presidential elections. (See table A.19.)[74]

In November 1917, the male voters of New York made an even more striking decision, approving a state constitutional amendment that enfranchised women in all elections. This stunning victory, reversing the outcome of a referendum held only two years earlier, was made possible by a remarkable shift in the working-class and immigrant neighborhoods of New York City. Districts that had opposed suffrage in 1915 voted in favor in 1917, by margins large enough to tilt the balance in the state tally. The efforts of the WTUL and others to build a cross-class coalition finally had paid off. The Democratic machine politicians of New York had proven to be receptive to those efforts and shrewd enough to read the political winds: dropping their longstanding opposition, they remained officially neutral in the referendum, and in the end, actively worked for its passage. After the victory, one suffrage leader declared that "we owe a great debt to Tammany Hall," and many credited Democratic politicians, especially Tammany boss Charlie Murphy, for the victory.[75]

The shift of Tammany to the prosuffrage column was both an emblem of and stimulant to a seismic shift in the politics of suffrage: between 1915 and 1920, machine politicians dramatically reversed course and began to favor the enfranchisement of women. Sensing correctly that suffrage was likely to triumph, that it would not necessarily damage their interests, and that their own constituents supported it, Democratic machine leaders in New York, Boston, Chicago, Cleveland, and other cities joined hands with NAWSA and the National Woman's Party to promote suffrage reform; the Republican organization made a similar about-face in Pittsburgh and Philadelphia. Simultaneously, if more spottily, organized labor—rapidly growing in the wartime economic boom—strengthened its ties to the suffrage movement. In Connecticut, for example, a strong alliance emerged between the National Woman's Party and the International Association of Machinists (IAM), which counted among its members thousands of munitions workers in Bridgeport. In 1919, one activist wrote to Alice Paul that Sam Lavit, the head of the Bridgeport IAM local, had "done more for the National Woman's Party in Connecticut than any other man." In most states, thus, the two primary organizational expressions of working-class power—political machines and the labor movement—climbed on the suffrage bandwagon. At the Massachusetts Constitutional Convention of 1917–1918, the primary argument made in behalf of suffrage expansion was that it would benefit the "working girls and women" who were exploited in the factories and shops of the Bay State.[76]

1917, of course, also was the year that the United States entered World War I. The war, and preparations for it, briefly retarded and then accelerated the progress of suffrage reform. When President Wilson and Congress declared war, NAWSA, in deference to the war effort, decided to suspend its congressional lobbying, although it continued grassroots efforts to build support for a federal amendment. Militant and pacifist (often Quaker) suffragists, however, ignored NAWSA's directives, organizing picket lines and hunger strikes, while excoriating the president for fighting for democracy abroad while undercutting it at home. These militant suffragists were often denounced as unpatriotic (or worse) by an increasingly strident antisuffrage movement that linked the right to vote with feminism, radicalism, socialism, and "German Kultur."[77]

But the most critical impact of the war was the opportunity it gave suffragists to contribute to the mobilization and in so doing, to vanquish the age-old argument that women should not vote because they did not bear arms. NAWSA converted its local chapters into volunteer groups that provided Americanization classes, distributed food, and cooperated with the Red Cross. Missouri's suffragists, thousands of whom, carrying yellow parasols, had lined the streets at the Democratic convention in St. Louis in 1916, feverishly sold bonds and thrift stamps, knitted clothes, and gave gifts to soldiers and sailors. In New York, the Woman Suffrage Party sold more than a million dollars' worth of bonds between the declaration of war and the fall referendum of 1917, the first direct electoral test of the impact of war on the suffrage movement. The leadership of NAWSA also offered its political support—always especially valued during wartime—to the Wilson administration; both Catt and Anna Howard Shaw served on the Women's Committee of the Council on National Defense.[78]

The suffragists' adroit handling of the war crisis, coupled with continuing (if often behind the scenes) political pressure on Congress and the president, was rewarded in January 1918. The president, in an extraordinary address, announced his support of a federal suffrage amendment "as a war measure." The next day, the House of Representatives, reversing its stance of only three years earlier, voted in favor of the Nineteenth Amendment: the victory was won by one vote, with the Democrats splitting almost evenly while more than 80 percent of Republicans voted favorably. Importantly, most of the congressmen who changed their position in those few years came from states that recently had adopted some form of women's suffrage.[79]

The Senate, where antisuffrage southern Democrats constituted a proportionally larger bloc, took an additional year and a half to endorse the amendment. Addressing the Senate in September 1918, Wilson again pressed the links between war and enfranchisement. Women's suffrage, he declared, was "essential to the successful prosecution of the great war of humanity in which are engaged. . . . We have made partners of the women in this war. Shall we admit them only to a partnership of sacrifice and suffering and toll and not to a partnership of privilege and of right? This war could not have been fought . . . if it had not been for the services of women." Notably, Wilson was extending rather than rejecting the traditional notion that suffrage ought to be tied to military service: as was appropriate, perhaps, in the nation's first modern war (which demanded a new level of mass mobilization), the president claimed that women should be enfranchised because of their contributions to the war rather than despite their failure to bear arms.[80]

Suffragists too stressed their wartime role, even threatening to diminish their support if suffrage were not forthcoming. They also campaigned hard in the 1918 elections, helping to generate new Republican majorities in Congress. After months of relentless political pressure and careful targeting of Republican and Democratic holdouts, the Senate—by a large Republican majority and a small Democratic one—finally came on board in the summer of 1919. The combination of broad, multiclass support, war, and the endgame dynamics of party competition had put the amendment over the top.[81] Notably, congressional support for the Nineteenth Amendment was centered among politicians of both parties who had displayed some commitment to issues of social justice and civil rights; its last-ditch opponents were almost entirely Southerners and old-stock, probusiness Republicans such as Henry Cabot Lodge.[82]

The fight was not quite over. NAWSA's leaders recognized that ratification depended on winning virtually every state outside of the South and the border states; they also believed it essential to move quickly, before the aura of wartime faded. Meanwhile, antisuffragists geared up for battle, denouncing the Nineteenth Amendment as a violation of states' rights and a giant step toward socialism and free love. Fortunately for the suffragists, however, the political tides were running in their favor, and NAWSA's finely honed organization was well prepared for the task of navigating the Nineteenth Amendment through state legislatures. The amendment was approved with remarkable speed in much of the Northeast and Midwest; the western states, where women already were enfranchised, did not lag far behind. Texas, Oklahoma, and Connecticut proved to be battlegrounds, but successes in the first two lessened the sting of defeat in the southern New England state.[83]

To no one's surprise, the South remained recalcitrant. In the hope of wooing southern votes, some politicians, such as Jeannette Rankin, as well as activists such as Catt and Paul, tried to reassure Southerners that the amendment did not threaten white supremacy (it meant "the removal of the sex restriction, nothing more, nothing less"); and NAWSA opportunistically distanced itself from black suffragists. But despite their rather unprincipled efforts, the South remained opposed, with the full-throated cry of states' rights giving tortured voice to the region's deep anxieties about race. Nowhere were those anxieties more vividly manifested than in Louisiana and Mississippi, where Kate Gordon and her followers actively and successfully worked to defeat the amendment; in the end, it was approved only by the four border states of Kentucky, Tennessee, Texas, and Arkansas. Nonetheless, women everywhere, including Kate Gordon, were enfranchised. On August 18, 1920, Tennessee, by a margin of one vote, became the thirty-sixth state to vote positively on the amendment; a week later, after ratification had been formally certified, the Nineteenth Amendment was law.[84]

Aftermath

It is a well-known irony in American history that politics did not change very dramatically after women were enfranchised. The electorate nearly doubled in size between 1910 and 1920, but voting patterns and partisan alignments were little affected. The largest movement for voting rights in the nation's history did not spark the revolution that some had feared but instead coincided with the return to "normalcy" in American politics. Warren Harding and Calvin Coolidge were the first presidents elected with a sizable number of women's votes, and conservative Republicans dominated political life throughout the 1920s. Women, moreover, did not rush out to vote in huge numbers: electoral turnout was even lower among women than among men. Political life in the 1920s was not nearly as vibrant or energetic as it had been in the 1890s or the latter years of the Progressive era; despite the identification of women with social reform, reforms were few during the first decade that women could vote.[85]

To be sure, the entry of women into the electorate, as scholars recently have pointed out, did have many subtle and longer-range consequences for political life. New issues, particularly those affecting women and children, were injected into the political arena, even if concrete reforms were slow to materialize. The social welfare programs of the 1930s were colored by the concerns of the female electorate and often promoted by women who had cut their political and organizational teeth in the suffrage movement. To cite the most obvious example, Franklin Roosevelt's appointment of Frances Perkins as secretary of labor (and as the first woman to hold a cabinet position) would not have happened without the Nineteenth Amendment. Women, and the experiences of the suffrage movement, also had an impact on the practice of politics—including interest group formation and techniques of voter education—and on the evolution of political cultures within each of the major parties.[86]

Nonetheless, the aftermath of victory was low-key, if not anticlimactic, a fact not unrelated to the movement's success in the first place. The victories of the suffrage drive were built in part on the ever-widening perception among men that the enfranchisement of women would not significantly transform politics or policy. This perception gained currency thanks to the federal structure of voting laws and the piecemeal way in which women first were enfranchised. As was pointed out again and again in twentieth-century debates, nothing particularly unusual had happened to politics or voting patterns in states that had enfranchised women in the 1880s and 1890s, such as Colorado and Wyoming: by the time that the federal amendment was approved, women already were voting in many state and local elections, as well as in numerous foreign countries, without jarring or revolutionary consequences. The states that enfranchised women early did not even enact prohibition laws! The machine politicians who eventually tilted in favor of suffrage learned from these experiences, concluding correctly that their organizations would not be threatened by the votes of women. Similarly, the suffragists' prediction that the enfranchisement of women would not jeopardize white supremacy in the South proved to be on the mark: although some (but not many) black women were able to register to vote, the Democratic Party remained firmly in power, segregation and black disfranchisement persisted, and the federal government steered clear of voting rights issues for another four decades.[87]

Sex, thus, did not prove to be a significant line of cleavage in the American electorate: some gender gaps in voting did occur in the early years (as well as more recently), but they were not large, and few issues sharply divided men and women. Moreover, despite the coalitions formed during the suffrage struggle, women as a group did not develop lasting alliances with other disadvantaged citizens, such as blacks and immigrants, nor did the foray of the suffrage movement into partisan politics lead to durable party loyalties. Women certainly were empowered by enfranchisement, and their lives consequently (if gradually) may have changed in a host of different ways, but they tended to vote for the same parties and candidates that their husbands, fathers, and brothers supported. Class, race, ethnicity, and religion remained the more salient predictors of a person's voting behavior. The domestic and familial conflict over politics so vividly feared by anti-suffragists never materialized. Nor did possession of the vote automatically give women full and equal citizenship in matters such as jury duty or office holding.[88]

The very absence of dramatic change after 1920 inescapably leaves one wondering what the adamant resistance was all about. Why, given the rather placid outcome, did so many men oppose women's suffrage for so long? Why did it take women seventy years after Seneca Falls to become enfranchised? The historical record points to three overarching factors. The first, simply, was fear of the unknown: no one knew—especially in the nineteenth century—exactly what would happen if women voted, which permitted many different types of anxieties—political, social, and psychological—to be projected onto the specter of woman suffrage. The enfranchisement of women was something new and untested that could reach into the public and private lives of all men.

The second sustained source of resistance was the persistence of deeply ingrained standards of femininity and masculinity that appeared to be threatened by the prospect of women voting. Grounded in culture, social patterns, and the division of labor, these standards led men (and some women as well) to believe that suffrage would genuinely be a pernicious heresy, a violation of divine law, a threat to the family, or a source of promiscuity and debasement. The right to vote was an expression of masculine power, exercised in the male sphere of public life; for women to claim such power was to rob men of a piece of their identities, alter their social roles, and threaten their legal dominance over women. In the end, of course, suffrage did not generate any profound transformation in gender roles or even a powerful feminist movement. But people believed that it would, and they acted on their beliefs.

The third overarching factor was the coincidence of historical timing that brought the issue of women's suffrage to the fore just as faith in broadly distributed political rights was beginning to diminish. By the latter decades of the nineteenth century, the celebratory democratic rhetoric of the 1830s and 1840s had receded into almost-dim memory. To many, voting once again had become a privilege rather than a right, and the size of the electorate a matter of expediency rather than principle. To grant that women had a *right* to vote could only undercut the rationale for laws designed to restrict a male electorate that already seemed too large and unmanageable. This conservative impulse, widely present in the middle and upper classes, substantially narrowed the path down which the women's suffrage movement was obliged to travel and in so doing, significantly retarded its progress.[89]

Overcoming this resistance required an immense movement, shrewdly led by experienced political operatives, energized by the participation of millions. It also took more than that. Success did not come to the suffrage movement until images and norms of gender roles began to shift under the gradual but sturdy pressure of changes in the social structure, until local experiences and evolving beliefs could relax some of the apprehensions about the potential consequences of enfranchisement. Electoral majorities in favor of suffrage were mustered only when divisions between and within the major political parties could be exploited by a single-issue movement; and victory was ushered in at the end by war. Elizabeth Cady Stanton's Civil War vision of entering the polity alongside the blue-uniformed black soldier was never realized. Yet the final and decisive victories of the movement that she founded were achieved while millions of men were in uniform and millions of women were mobilized to abet their military efforts.[90]

PART III

Toward Universal Suffrage— and Beyond

A NEW ERA IN THE HISTORY of the right to vote began after World War I. The passage of the Nineteenth Amendment brought the prolonged struggle for women's suffrage to an end, nearly doubling the size of the nation's electorate. At roughly the same time, there occurred a marked slowdown of legal and political initiatives to shrink the polity. The flurries of activity that had been so visible since the 1850s—the movements and countermovements, the recurrent state constitutional debates, the writing and revising of complex legislation aimed at blacks, immigrants, and workers, among others—subsided in the 1920s. For several decades thereafter, the broad contours of suffrage law remained remarkably stable.

That stability would disintegrate in the 1960s. Pressures that had been mounting since World War II—reinforced by socioeconomic change, an inspired grassroots movement, and the ideological climate of the cold war—fractured the edifice of voting law and precipitated a broad reconstruction of the legal principles governing the franchise. This transformation began with efforts to remedy the nation's most glaring limitation on suffrage, the exclusion of African Americans from political life in the South; but it did not end there. In the course of the 1960s and the early 1970s, the right to vote was effectively nationalized for the first time in the history of the United States, and the ability of individual states to keep men and women from the polls was severely limited by newly democratic rules emanating from Congress and from the federal judiciary. By the early 1970s, the United States, formally at least, had something very close to universal suffrage.

SEVEN

The Quiet Years

The Council of State Governments investigated state suffrage laws, and their results show a poor substitute for the "universal suffrage" guaranteed by the Constitution. Citizens may be disqualified from voting for more than fifty reasons, and every state except Michigan has at least one provision for disqualification. Alabama has twenty-five and South Carolina twenty-eight. On the credit side, Illinois and Pennsylvania have only one each, and Vermont two. The average is about six. Convicted felons are barred in forty states. Lesser crimes that are punished by disfranchisement range from betting on an election to wife beating. Treason, electoral bribery, bigamy, perjury, adultery, malfeasance in office, receiving stolen goods, and miscegenation are all reasons for losing the right to vote in at least one state. Five states bar Indians and Rhode Island specifically bars Narragansett Indians. Insane persons, idiots, illiterates, incompetents, soldiers, sailors, and "immoral persons" are generally disfranchised. Disqualification of paupers, the infamous poll taxes in eight states, and some amazing registration and residence requirements make the list almost complete. Add to this the terrorism which prevents Negroes and unpopular minorities from voting, and the wonder is that anyone is left to go to the polls.

—*The New Republic*, 1940

Stasis and Its Sources

In 1928, William B. Munro, a professor of political science and history at Harvard, published an article in *The Forum* entitled "Intelligence Tests for Voters." Munro, a past president of the American Political Science Association, echoed E. L. Godkin in wistfully concluding that "universal suffrage has come to stay." Munro continued,

> But this does not mean that universal suffrage will always continue to be interpreted as excluding nobody. On the contrary there is every reason to expect that it will gradually be trimmed at the edges, as have so many other principles in the American philosophy of government.

For Munro, redefining universal suffrage—so that it would not be universal—was desirable because "the complexities of government" had increased so rapidly that

> about twenty percent of those who get on the voters' list have no business to be there. Taking the country as a whole, the total number of these interlopers must run into the millions. There are enough of them to swing an election. Can rational men be fairly expected to place unwavering faith in a system of suffrage which commits the destinies of a great nation into such hands as these?

Munro acknowledged that there was not "even a remote possibility" that the United States could eliminate the "interlopers" by reinstituting property qualifications, but he believed that the problem could at least begin to be solved if all states followed the recent example of New York and instituted "intelligence tests" for voters: "by eliminating the least intelligent stratum of the applicants for suffrage, as New York State is now doing," the nation would heighten the competence of the electorate and avoid the "revulsion from the extreme implications of democracy" that seemed to be sweeping Europe.[1]

Munro was not alone in his beliefs. Many Americans in the 1920s and 1930s remained skeptical (at best) of universal suffrage, and the rise of fascism, as well as the threat of socialism, in Europe only deepened their concern. Even before the trauma of the Great Depression cast doubts on the viability of both capitalism and democracy, numerous American intellectuals and political leaders believed that they saw in Europe an updated version of the Blackstonian nightmare: an excess of democracy leading to mobocracy that in turn would degenerate into dictatorship. Munro himself complained that "the world suffered from a democracy complex" in the years just after World War I. A United States Army training manual in the late 1920s warned its readers that democracy gave birth to "demogagism," "anarchy," and "communistic" attitudes toward property.[2]

Those who held such views, like their nineteenth-century predecessors, saw intelligence or literacy tests as a critical check against the power of the mob and the "extreme implications" of democracy. A 1924 article in the *Educational Review* also praised New York's law, insisting that "illiteracy, practically synonymous with ignorance, should have no place in the voting population of America." A few years later, Dr. William J. Hickson, director of the "psychopathic" laboratory of the Municipal Court of Chicago, asserted that limiting the vote to "those of superior intelligence" would help eradicate crime, and in 1931, Professor Harrison R. Hunt of Michigan State College urged the annual meeting of the Eugenics Research Association to support the limitation of suffrage to the nation's "natural aristocrats." "One might almost say," observed the professor, "that it is self-evident that men are created unequal." Throughout the 1920s and early 1930s, the *New York Times* reported with pride the workings of New York's requirement that all new voters either present evidence of their education or pass an intelligence test, in English, designed by the state department of education. Thousands of people failed the test each time that it was given, and thousands more were believed to have foregone the opportunity to vote because they chose not to be tested. New York City's superintendent of schools was convinced that the state's experience with the test was "so satisfactory that other states will rapidly follow our lead."[3]

Other states in fact did not follow New York's lead: Oregon, in 1924, was the last state to institute any kind of literacy test for voting, bringing to a halt a movement that had begun in Connecticut in 1855. Indeed, New York itself, through its supreme court, rebuffed a 1934 effort by the Honest Ballot Association to require literacy of all (not just new) voters, and several states made provisions for assisting illiterate voters at the polls. Yet if the pendulum was no longer swinging toward franchise restriction, neither did it travel very far in the opposite direction. No states that had literacy qualifications for voting repealed them in the decades following World War I; in the 1940s, eighteen states (seven in the South) continued to exclude voters who could not demonstrate their literacy in English. In the South, the administration of these laws was designed primarily to exclude blacks: as Senator Theodore Bilbo observed in 1946, in Mississippi "a man to register must be able to read and explain . . . a Constitution that damn few white men and no niggers at all can explain." As late as 1959, the Supreme Court, in *Lassiter v. Northampton County Board of Electors*, upheld the legitimacy of state laws that made the ability to read and write a qualification for voting.[4]

The nation's experience with literacy tests was emblematic of the broader history of suffrage from 1920 until World War II—and in some respects, until the early 1960s. Despite skirmishes large and small, partisan as well as ideological, there were few major changes in the laws governing the right to vote. In the South, where suffrage had provoked the most bitter and violent conflicts, the dense web of restrictions woven between 1890 and 1910 continued to disfranchise nearly all blacks and many poor whites. The diverse techniques that southern states had adopted to insure white supremacy remained in force, and the federal government—ostensibly respecting the right of states to set their own suffrage laws—colluded in the fiction that the Fifteenth Amendment was still the law of the land.[5]

Indeed, the most significant legal reforms in the South before World War II had a greater impact on whites than on blacks. These were the decisions by three states (North Carolina, Louisiana, and Florida) to repeal their poll taxes. (Georgia, in addition, responded to the exigencies of the Great Depression by eliminating the disqualification of citizens who were delinquent in paying property taxes.) The poll tax, of course, had a class, as well as racial, thrust, and, once white Democratic primaries had been instituted in the one-party region, some critics believed that the poll tax served primarily to keep poor whites out of politics. Consequently, opposition could be mounted that would not be fatally tarred with the brush of race. In North Carolina in 1920, white voters from the west voted overwhelmingly to abolish the poll tax (and to lower the residency requirement), despite some opposition from the eastern Black Belt.[6]

More flamboyantly, Huey Long, in the 1930s, spearheaded a movement to abolish Louisiana's tax: he did so both to enhance his support among poor whites and to undercut the power of conservative sheriffs who bought votes by paying the poll taxes of poor voters. Long dismissed opposition claims that repeal would open elections to blacks, arguing that registration laws and the white primary were sufficient obstacles to black enfranchisement. Persuaded by Long's appeal to class interest, a huge majority of Louisiana's white voters supported repeal. A few years later, in Florida, the poll tax was repealed by a coalition of liberals led by Claude Pepper and by Miami politicians who were fed up with the corruption that the poll tax was facilitating. In each of these states, poll tax repeal was the consequence of political conflicts among whites and had the effect of increasing the number of white voters. Although blacks also registered in significant numbers in Florida's cities, Huey Long's prediction was largely accurate: other racially exclusive laws kept the vast majority of blacks in all three states from voting, whether they paid their poll taxes or not. The legal armor of the white South was only slightly dented.[7]

Similarly, in the North, the patterns of inclusion and exclusion established before World War I endured, with some trimming and stitching around the edges. Immigrants who sought to vote continued to face relatively high barriers to citizenship, including literacy tests, a sharply increased naturalization fee, and limitations on their political views. In the 1920s, Arkansas (as noted in chapter 5) put an end to the nation's faltering experiment with alien voting; moving in the opposite direction, California eliminated its ban on voters of Chinese descent in 1926, and Oregon followed suit a year later. Rhode Island in 1928 liberalized its franchise by eliminating the property qualification for municipal voting, and Pennsylvania eliminated its taxpaying requirement in 1933. By 1940, there were no poll taxes in the North, although property and tax qualifications for voting on bond and assessment issues persisted in numerous states, including Michigan, Utah, Nevada, and Montana. Paupers continued to be excluded in a dozen states; the "insane" and "incompetent" were disfranchised nearly everywhere; and convicted felons faced an array of detailed laws that kept them from voting during and after periods of incarceration.[8]

In fact, most of the legal changes that occurred during this period were relatively technical and dealt with issues of residence and registration. All states retained residency qualifications, typically of one year but ranging from six months (in rural states, mostly in the Midwest) to two years (in a handful of southern states in addition to Rhode Island); nearly all had shorter county and district residency requirements as well. Modifications of the residency laws generally involved their application to unusual or anomalous cases: students, soldiers, inmates of institutions, migrant workers, absentees, and people who owned two homes or had difficulty furnishing proof that they had any domicile at all. In most northern states, the drift of the law was mildly expansive, as state courts tried to protect the right of individuals to vote somewhere; in addition, provisions for absentee voting became more flexible. Still, students who were not demonstrably independent of their parents usually could not establish legal residency where they attended school; neither could soldiers where they were stationed; nor could inhabitants of mental institutions and poorhouses. In quantitative terms, the significance of the laws affecting anomalous cases paled in comparison with the durational requirements themselves: the United States remained a highly mobile society, and residency rules, both state and local, continued to keep large numbers of voters from the polls.[9]

Voter registration laws, already widespread by 1920, became nearly universal by 1940: only Arkansas, whose state constitution prohibited such procedures, lacked some scheme for registering and enrolling voters prior to elections. In numerous states, detailed and complex registration rules remained a procedural obstacle to voting, much as they had been prior to World War I. There were, however, two broad trends in these laws between 1920 and the 1950s. The first, lessening a procedural burden that had generated vociferous complaints and partisan conflict, was the spread of permanent rather than periodic registration systems: voters who did not change their place of residence remained on the registry lists and did not have to repeat the process of registering before each election or every two or four years. (In some states, voters were dropped from the rolls if they did not cast their ballots during a defined period.) The second trend was toward the increasing uniformity of registration rules within states: although initially targeted at large cities, registration laws, usually at the insistence of urban politicians, were made applicable to all prospective voters within a state. In 1934, the Supreme Court for the first time affirmed the constitutionality of registration schemes. Upholding a decision by the Indiana Supreme Court (*Blue v. State ex rel. Brown*), the justices ruled that state registration laws were legitimate as long as they were reasonable and uniform.[10]

On the whole, thus, the years between 1920 and World War II constituted—with a few exceptions—a period of stasis in the legal and political history of the right to vote. To a considerable degree, this stasis reflected a relaxation of elite and middle-class apprehensions about the breadth of the franchise. Although the men and women who had favored restrictions on the right to vote did not suddenly discover a new enthusiasm for universal suffrage, neither did they press for more severe limitations. William B. Munro's call for action struck a much shallower chord than Francis Parkman's had a half century earlier.

That this was so stemmed in part from the success of the laws already in force and from the political stability of the era of "normalcy." In the South, there was little perceived need for action, because the disfranchising laws of earlier decades were working well: only a tiny fraction of the region's blacks voted, and single-party rule was secure. Similarly, in the Northeast and Midwest, the Republican Party retained a strong grip on most states through the 1920s; meanwhile, concerns about the immigrant working class were eased by the sharp drop in immigration that began during World War I and was perpetuated by the restriction acts of 1921 and 1924. (The virtual cessation of Asian immigration lowered the temperature in the West.) Throughout the nation, moreover, those who had feared a broad franchise were reassured by the uneventful passage of women into electoral politics.

Conservatives in all likelihood were also reassured by the ongoing decline in electoral participation that had begun after the election of 1896 and accelerated by the 1920s. In the South, turnout plummeted to roughly 20 percent in presidential elections, and even in the North, it fell to less than 60 percent, a sharp contrast to late-nineteenth-century elections in which more than 80 percent of potential voters cast their ballots. In nonpresidential years, the vote totals were even lower. How much of this drop was due to indifference or the lack of party competition, rather than legal restraints, was—and remains—unclear, but there is no doubt that fewer people were casting their ballots and that turnout was lowest (outside of the South) among women, immigrants and their children, and the poor.[11]

As historians have noted, the decline in turnout produced some peculiar, yet temporary, handwringing among its political beneficiaries. In the 1920s, mainstream northern newspapers, commentators, and politicians (there was very little handwringing in the South) lamented the fall in electoral participation and even debated the merits of making voting compulsory. Scholars began studying nonvoting, and civic organizations sponsored Get Out the Vote campaigns in 1924 and subsequent election years. Even President Calvin Coolidge got into the act. In 1926, in a remarkable speech to the Daughters of the American Revolution, Coolidge pointed out both that turnout had been extremely low in 1924 (when he was elected) and that in 1922 not a single senator had received the votes of a majority of eligible voters. "Citizenship in America," Coolidge declared, "is not a private enterprise but a public function . . . . The shirking of" the "responsibilities of citizenship" constituted "a serious danger" to the nation. Precipitated by the mistaken perception that turnout was falling because respectable middle-class citizens were not bothering to vote, these laments became less frequent once studies revealed that nonvoters were disproportionately poor and working class: the potential voters who had been feared most were not wielding electoral strength in proportion to their numbers. Indeed, after the 1920s, public expressions of concern about declining participation acquired a ritualistic tone, while turnout itself, despite a brief upturn in the 1930s, continued its long-run slide and retained its class skew.[12]

There were other reasons as well for the slowdown in efforts to narrow the breadth of the franchise, reasons tied to structural changes in political life and governmental institutions. One such change was a piecemeal erosion of popular control over government agencies and decisions. Proposals for de-democratizing government, particularly municipal government, had been a staple of "reform" thought in the late nineteenth century: "the elective principle is not the proper one to be generally applied in large centres of population," urged Frank Goodnow, an influential commentator in 1897. One means of translating such ideas into action was a structural reform that became extremely popular during the Progressive era: the replacement of mayors and ward-based aldermen with appointed city managers and commissioners elected at large in nonpartisan contests. Sponsored by businessmen throughout the nation, this structural innovation vitiated the influence of political machines and their working-class constituents, while favoring wealthy probusiness candidates who could mount citywide campaigns. Openly designed on a corporate model, the commission-manager structure removed many policy decisions from direct popular influence. By the 1920s, more than 600 city governments had been restructured in this way, and by the late 1960s, almost half of the nation's cities were governed by city managers and commissioners. State and county governments too witnessed a proliferation of appointed commissions and managers, often with broad powers over domains such as water resources, utilities, policing, and transportation. One key demand of many Progressive reformers was "the short ballot"—a reduction in the number of offices for which one voted—and the short ballot meant fewer officials directly accountable to the populace.[13]

Similarly, it was in the late nineteenth and early twentieth centuries that the federal government began to entrust major policy responsibilities to commissioners and agency heads who were appointed for lengthy terms and (often) could not be removed by elected officials. The prototype of such institutions was the Interstate Commerce Commission, created in 1887 to regulate railroad practices (such as rebates and discriminatory rates) that had become the object of widespread public rage and the focus of bitter political conflict. Several decades later, the hottest political issue of the era, the monopolization of industry, was entrusted to the Federal Trade Commission, while control of the nation's money supply (and interest rates) was vested in the powerful Federal Reserve Board. Created in the name of efficiency and expertise, such agencies served in part to insulate important policy decisions from popular control.

These new institutional arrangements became increasingly important in the twentieth century, taking the nation down a path presciently suggested in 1879 by a worried critic of universal suffrage in *The Atlantic Monthly* (see chapter 5). "The subjects of voting can be much reduced," the unnamed commentator had proposed. Although American political life had countercurrents as well (such as the Progressive-era provisions for initiatives and referenda, direct primaries, and the popular election of senators), there was an unmistakable drift, at all levels of governance, toward a more managerial state and a shrinking spectrum of decisions that could be directly affected by elections.

The power of individual voters was limited further by the organization of political life and competition. Put simply, the choices open to voters narrowed. In the 1920s, single-party dominance was the rule in many states, and even after the electoral realignment of the 1930s put an end to Republican control of the industrial Northeast and Midwest, numerous states remained uncompetitive. Moreover, everywhere voters typically had a choice between only two parties—and two parties that were not all that unlike each other. The rebellious third and fourth and fifth parties that flourished in the late nineteenth century—mostly local but some rising to regional and national strength—gave way to the reification and institutionalization of a two-party system. In some states, such as Ohio and Illinois, dissident or "un-American" parties were banned from the ballot, and in New York in 1920, the legislature refused to seat elected Socialists. More commonly, third-party movements were discouraged by rules prohibiting fusion tickets and limiting the appearance and placement on the ballot of non–major party candidates. Such laws had been pioneered by Republicans as a means of undercutting the Populists in the 1880s and 1890s, but the model long outlived the Populist revolt. In 1947, for example, the Wilson-Pakula Act in New York took direct aim at the coalition-building efforts of left-leaning Congressman Vito Marcantonio by making it nearly impossible for a candidate belonging to one party to even enter the primary of another party. Later in the twentieth century, the two-party system further was incorporated into the state through a system of partial public financing of electoral campaigns that was effectively available only to the major parties.[14]

One revealing variant of this pattern involved the election of state appellate court judges. Between 1846 and 1912, nearly all states opted for an elected judiciary—in part owing to popular pressure to make judges accountable to the people, and in part because political leaders, as well as leaders of the bar, sought to enhance the legitimacy and authority of the courts. This formal democratization, however, was undercut in several stages by the introduction of nonpartisan elections for judges and by the rise of merit screening of potential nominees by bar associations and committees of lawyers in the 1930s and 1940s. Although ostensibly designed to improve the quality and independence of the judiciary, these innovations also served to diminish its popular accountability. Voters were left choosing among candidates about whom they knew little (since party labels had been a critical source of information) and whose views already had been approved by the legal establishment. The upshot was a sharp decline in voting for judges and a virtual guarantee that incumbents would remain on the bench as long as they wished. By 1940, at least two states (California and Missouri) had partially returned to a system of appointing state court judges.[15]

Other techniques for limiting the impact of democratization also were available, such as gerrymandering. Whether gerrymandering was more common in the twentieth century than in the nineteenth is unclear, but certainly it was deployed with frequency to control or influence electoral outcomes. Similarly, malapportionment often served to diminish the political power of the immigrant and ethnic working class. In many states, rural counties and districts were systematically overrepresented (relative to their population) in one or both branches of the state legislature.[16]

Against this changing institutional backdrop, as historians and political scientists have long noted, organized interest groups became increasingly prominent political actors. This trend, begun in the late nineteenth century, became far more pronounced in the twentieth: lobbyists, representing organized interests such as bankers and individual industries, became a permanent presence in Washington and state capitals, while the interest groups themselves became significant constituencies for political leaders. The state served as a broker among organized interests, who played an increasingly active role in shaping government decisions. What this meant, of course, was that those who had the resources and skills to do so acquired a voice—often a loud voice—that spoke to government officials through nonelectoral channels. The locus of policy formation was shifting from the hustings to the hearing room or the headquarters of regulatory commissions and agencies.[17]

This broad assembly of changes in politics and the structure of government gradually took the wind out of the sails of advocates of further suffrage restriction. Franchise restriction had always had risks: it violated the nation's official commitment to democracy and opened the door to partisan reprisals and further exclusions. After 1920, fewer people seemed to think that those risks were worth taking. The perceived threats to the established order that loomed so large in the 1870s and 1890s lost their vivid coloration and seemed increasingly manageable without further shrinking the electorate.

The stasis of voting law between 1920 and World War II also was grounded in an altogether different phenomenon: the absence of significant pressure to expand the franchise. The dynamics of war were not in play; the alignment of political parties favored stability; and importantly, grassroots movements were weak. In the North and West, both the social composition and social location of the disfranchised were such that collective action was highly unlikely. With the exception of Native Americans, Asians, and Hispanics, the disfranchised did not constitute coherent, distinctive, or easily identifiable social groups. Although liberal intellectuals and organs of opinion (such as the *New Republic*, cited earlier) frequently registered their dismay over the scope of legal disfranchisement, mobilizations of the illiterate or the itinerant were improbable.

Equally improbable was collective action on the part of paupers, felons, people who had lost their naturalization papers, or individuals who had difficulty navigating their way through byzantine registration laws. Such legal restrictions had an unmistakable class bias, but they did not disfranchise the working class per se; most of the working class indeed was enfranchised, and the proportion rose as immigration slowed and the children of immigrants came of age. Those who remained outside the polity were numerous, but they were scattered, socially marginal, transient, or (in theory, at least) only temporarily disfranchised. As a result, they were unlikely either to organize or to attract the interest of any major political party. Partisan pressure to expand the franchise was confined to eliminating financial barriers to voting in a few northern states and smoothing out some of the rougher edges of registration requirements.

The South was the potential exception to this pattern—since blacks constituted a very large and identifiable bloc of disfranchised voters—and some African Americans, particularly in the cities, actively pursued changes in the suffrage laws. Eschewing Booker T. Washington's advice to accept Jim Crow and concentrate on self-advancement (and tacitly embracing the position of W.E.B. DuBois that voting rights were essential to black freedom), these men and women attempted to vote and pressed—usually through the courts—for an end to poll taxes, the white primary, and discriminatory literacy tests. But the activists were small in number. Most southern blacks lived in a predominantly rural world where collective action was exceedingly difficult; thanks to sharecropping and the crop-lien system (which kept them in a state of debt peonage), they also were propertyless, economically dependent on those who controlled political life, fearful of reprisals, and often resigned to an all-encompassing and seemingly inescapable system of repression.

The structure of southern politics, moreover, provided few opportunities for prying open the doors to the polls. Although rife with factionalism and ideological conflict, the state Democratic parties did not countenance dissent on race: although alliances between poor whites and blacks always were theoretically possible, no white faction that dared to support black enfranchisement could hope to survive long enough to build a coalition with prospective African-American voters. Nor did national politics afford much of an opening. The Republican Party in the 1920s had no need of the black vote (or the South) to win national elections, while the Democrats had no partisan incentive to rock the boat of black disfranchisement. This tableau began to shift only in the 1930s when, thanks to black migration and the popularity of the New Deal, the African-American vote in the North became larger, more contested, and potentially critical to some electoral outcomes. Yet voting remained a matter of state law, and despite the egalitarian rhetoric of both parties, neither was eager to promote federal seizure of one of the cornerstones of states' rights.[18]

The final years of the 1930s, however, did witness the emergence of a significant, if unsuccessful, political effort to expand suffrage in the South: the movement to abolish the poll tax. Building on actions sponsored by the National Association for the Advancement of Colored People, the movement was galvanized by southern white liberals—most of them intellectuals and activists rather than political leaders—who came together to foster a drive to abolish the tax qualification. They were actively supported by New Dealers (including Eleanor Roosevelt and at times the president himself), who were frustrated by conservative southern opposition to economic and social reform; the cause also was promoted by organized labor, which viewed the poll tax as a key to the low wages of southern workers and therefore a threat to labor's welfare nationally. Members of this broad coalition—an interregional pressure group rather than a grassroots movement—were convinced that the poll tax was not only "un-American" but an impediment to social and economic progress in the South. Eliminating it, they believed, would enfranchise poor whites and blacks, democratize politics in the South, and hasten the downfall of conservatives who controlled key committees in the House and Senate.[19]

After the failure of attempts to promote poll tax reform within southern states (other than the scattered victories mentioned earlier), the loosely co-alescing movement turned its attention to Washington and to Congress. There advocates of repeal faced a significant legal obstacle: the Supreme Court in 1937, in *Breedlove v. Suttles*, had unanimously upheld Georgia's poll tax qualification for state and local elections. The reformers filed a law-suit challenging the poll tax in federal elections alone, but it too was re-buffed by the courts in the early 1940s. Congressional supporters then drafted legislation making it unlawful for a poll tax to be imposed in any na-tional election: they maintained that the tax bred corruption and that it was an "arbitrary . . . qualification by which large numbers of citizens are pro-hibited from voting simply because they are poor." Less euphemistically, a member of the Senate Judiciary Committee cited Senator Carter Glass's speeches at the Virginia Constitutional Convention forty years earlier as ir-refutable evidence that poll taxes were adopted to disfranchise blacks and thus violated the Fourteenth and Fifteenth Amendments.[20]

Conservative southerners fought the bill tooth and nail, couching their opposition in constitutional terms: Congress, they argued, lacked the au-thority to pass legislation altering a state's voting qualifications. Such action only could be carried out by the states themselves or through the unwieldy process of amending the federal Constitution. Thanks in part to the new political climate generated by World War II (to be discussed later in this chapter), the House of Representatives passed the bill, but it then was killed by a southern filibuster in the Senate. This frustrating legislative scenario was repeated several times in subsequent years, until efforts to repeal the poll tax through federal legislation were abandoned. But the battle lines had been drawn and the first shots fired in a resurgent struggle to nationalize suffrage and eliminate discrimination in the South.[21]

Franklin Roosevelt and the Death of Blackstone

The 1930s also witnessed an extraordinary series of events—or nonevents—revolving around the political rights of the very poor. As noted in earlier chapters, paupers in nearly a dozen states were disfranchised in the nine-teenth century, reflecting both disciplinary attitudes toward the poor and the belief that men and women considered dependent ought not vote. Such laws remained on the books, with little controversy, until the crisis of the Great Depression transformed millions of workers into relief recipients who could be legally labeled as paupers.

The drama began in fall 1932, a grim moment when the nation seemed frozen in depression, thousands of people were starving, millions were job-less, and more than a few were beginning to take to the streets in protest. As the bitter election campaign between Franklin Roosevelt and Herbert Hoover was drawing to a close, Mrs. E. F. Wellman, the Republican chair of the Board of Registration in Lewiston, Maine, acquired a list of relief re-cipients from the town's overseers of the poor and proceeded to strike 350 recipients from the rolls of eligible voters. According to Mrs. Wellman, Maine's pauper exclusion clause rendered these men and women ineligible. Her action appeared to be the start of a process that would disfranchise 1,000 voters in Lewiston alone and thousands more in other cities and towns in Maine.

A counterattack came quickly. Enraged at what he regarded as an unjust and partisan act, Herbert E. Holmes, the Corporation Counsel of Lewiston and a Democratic candidate for the state senate, immediately sent a telegram to President Hoover:

> Republican organization here has invoked obsolete pauper law . . . to strike
> from voting lists about one thousand unemployed voters . . . . Believed here
> to constitute first step in nation-wide campaign to disfranchise unemployed
> and prevent them from voting in national election. I urge you to advise local
> officials against this injustice to hapless victims of existing emergency.

Hoover did not respond. Republicans in Maine, however, insisted that pol-itics had nothing to do with the registration board's action: they were sim-ply enforcing the state constitution. One of the state's leading newspapers defended Mrs. Wellman, pointing out that Mr. Holmes "is not the judge of whether a law has become 'obsolete.'"[22]

The uproar in Lewiston was followed by a Republican attempt to dis-franchise an additional 129 relief recipients in Waterville, Maine. It too pro-voked heated commentary in the national press and in other states that had pauper exclusion provisions. The commentary was self-satisfied in Massachusetts, where a prescient state legislature had enacted a law early in the depression specifying that no one would be "deemed" a pauper who "to the best of his ability, has attempted to provide for himself and his dependents . . . and who, through no crime or misdemeanor of his own, has come into grievous need and receives aid or assistance given temporarily." Yet numerous other states had not been so prescient, and, as the New York *World-Telegram* noted, all could invoke the pauper exclusion clauses in their constitutions to disfranchise victims of the depression. This would be, the *World-Telegram* concluded, "the worst irony" that could "befall a man if, in addition to losing his job, he was deliberately robbed of his vote." That worst irony, however, turned out to be rare: relatively few of the unemployed were barred from voting in 1932. Maine, despite the efforts of Mrs. Wellman and her colleagues, voted Democratic for the first time in decades.[23]

The issue did not die; instead it was resuscitated by the New Deal's unprecedented efforts to provide federal aid to the unemployed. In 1934, the banner of disfranchisement was carried by the New York State Economic Council (NYSEC), an association of anti–New Deal businessmen headed by prominent Republicans, including former United States Attorney General (and former chair of President Hoover's law enforcement commission) George W. Wickersham. Claiming to have 50,000 members, the NYSEC was an influential voice urging lower taxes and reduced government expenditures to promote business recovery; it also opposed "compulsory" unemployment insurance, denounced the American Federation of Labor as "un-American," and recommended the passage of laws outlawing general and sympathetic strikes.[24]

Among the council's most celebrated proposals was "the withholding from all persons receiving public unemployment relief the right of suffrage during the period in which such relief is being received." Put forward in the summer of 1934, just as the country was moving politically leftward, this proposition immediately drew national attention—both because millions of jobless workers were receiving relief and because the rationale for the proposal was politically inflammatory. Unlike the registration board of Lewiston, the council claimed that disfranchisement was warranted not because there were laws on the books but because the growth of New Deal programs had created a huge and potentially dangerous bloc of voters. Relief recipients, it was argued, were indebted to those who had created the relief programs and would vote to perpetuate and enlarge those programs. "If the millions now receiving relief should organize . . . and wield the power of organized voters," insisted Merwin K. Hart, the president of the council and a vigorous opponent of unemployment insurance, "they could hamstring any effort to bring about economic recovery." Implicit in the NYSEC's argument was the conviction that the great mass of relief recipients, beholden to the New Deal, would vote for the Democrats in order to keep relief funds and tax dollars flowing in their direction.[25]

Although Wickersham and his colleagues never mentioned William Blackstone or Chancellor Kent, their argument for disfranchisement had deep historical roots. In the millions of citizens on the payroll of the Civil Works Administration (CWA) or receiving relief through the Federal Emergency Relief Administration (FERA), the NYSEC saw the nightmare that Blackstone had characterized and Kent had predicted: an army of "dependents" marching to the polls; a mass of propertyless men ready to seize the property of others (through taxes); men "with no will of their own" who easily could be manipulated by a clever politician or demagogue, such as Franklin Roosevelt or even Huey Long. That New Deal administrators announced $135 million in relief appropriations shortly before the 1934 elections only added fuel to the flames; so too did widespread (if unsubstantiated) reports that aid was being given only to those who promised to vote Democratic. In the harsh, disordered, and to some, frightening social order of the mid–1930s, where the poor were numerous and supported by the state, the dangers of a broad suffrage once again loomed large.[26]

According to a survey conducted by the NYSEC, 35 percent of all candidates for the legislature and Congress in New York supported disfranchisement. National support was sufficiently widespread that a countermovement was launched to promote a Twenty-second Amendment to the United States Constitution to guarantee the citizenship rights of the unemployed. The economic council had overplayed its hand, however—or played it at the wrong historical moment. In the dire conditions of the depression, it was clear to almost all Americans—as had not been clear even a decade earlier—that the unemployed were victims of a crisis in capitalism, that they were jobless "through no fault of their own," and that they sought relief not because they were slothful but because jobs did not exist. For businessmen (whom many blamed for the depression in the first place) to try to deprive unfortunate working people of their political rights seemed unfair, even grotesque. Democratic politicians, labor spokesmen, and letter writers to newspapers heaped scorn on the idea; more than one asked if the

NYSEC also planned to disfranchise businessmen and farmers who received any form of government aid. In October 1934, President Roosevelt himself addressed the issue. Asked for his response to a report that officials in twelve states were taking action to deny the franchise to persons on relief, the president declared that no man who was "out of work and willing to work" possibly could be regarded as a pauper, according to any "honest" conception of the law. Disfranchising the jobless, he insisted, would be "a thoroughly un-American procedure."[27]

In the end, the number of relief recipients actually disfranchised in 1934 was small. In some locales, pauper laws were invoked; in others, such as West Virginia, they were explicitly and publicly ignored; a compromise in Maine led to the laws being applied only to those receiving municipal rather than federal relief. In Kansas, transients (largely agricultural workers) who voted were warned that they would be taken off the "transient relief" rolls. But no new voting restrictions were enacted, and it is likely that far more of the unemployed were disfranchised because of poll taxes and residency requirements than regulations expressly excluding paupers and relief recipients. Turnout, moreover, was unusually high in the 1934 elections, and the liberal wing of the Democratic Party gained unprecedented strength. The heirs of Chancellor Kent were on the run.[28]

Yet wariness of relief recipients persisted. Throughout the New Deal, Republicans attacked the administration for the partisan use of public funds in the distribution of relief and jobs. Roosevelt was accused of being a masterful and manipulative politician using federal tax dollars to build a national political machine; the large relief programs were decried as sources of corruption fostering a permanent, government-supported army of indigents. In fact there was some basis for Republican concern: not only were relief funds sometimes distributed to gain partisan advantage, but by 1938 an organization of 400,000 Works Progress Administration (WPA) workers and other relief recipients pledged that it would organize politically to elect congressmen who supported higher relief wages. The policy conflict that flowed from such charges, however, did not focus on disfranchisement: it centered instead on the size of the relief budget and on efforts to insulate the administration of relief from politics. The most significant law to emerge from this controversy was the Hatch Act, which prevented federal employees from participating in political campaigns.[29]

Nonetheless, the idea of disfranchising the unemployed had one more moment in the sun. In September 1938, a small group of conservative, anti–New

Deal women, calling itself the Women's Rebellion, revived the demand that relief recipients be deprived of their voting rights. The group was led by Mrs. Sarah O. Hulswit of Suffern, New York, who was identified in the press as the wife of the manager of the Rockland Gas Company. Mrs. Hulswit explained that she and her colleagues feared that if millions of relief recipients continued to vote, they would perpetuate themselves "and there would never be an end of the depression." She also attacked the New Deal's "buying and coercion of votes," declaring that "millions are no longer free to vote as they wish," and warning that the "WPA and relief vote is building up a situation similar to that existing in Germany and Russia." Mrs. Hulswit and her fellow members of the Women's Rebellion were not alone in raising the issue. In an article in the *North American Review*, Cal Lewis declared that "the pauper vote should be an important public question" since "such a large part of the voters in many states are not self-supporting." Lewis claimed that in many states, "the pauper vote may hold the balance of political power."[30]

The strategy of the Women's Rebellion was to approach the attorneys general in states with pauper exclusion laws and demand that the laws be enforced. New Jersey and Rhode Island were targeted first. In New Jersey, the case for disfranchising recipients of federal aid was logically compelling: WPA jobs went only to those who had been on relief for two months, relief recipients had to take a pauper's oath, and the state constitution expressly banned paupers from voting. The legal logic notwithstanding, the "rebellious women" achieved little. New Jersey's attorney general stated that only a formal investigative procedure could determine whether or not a person was a pauper; "in my judgment," the attorney general continued, "it is inconceivable" that the category of pauper would apply to "those who, because of the unusual economic conditions, are receiving assistance through the agencies of the federal government." It was notable that the attorney general, like most opponents of franchise restriction, argued not that paupers should be enfranchised, but rather that relief recipients were not paupers. Even more telling, Warren Barbour, the Republican candidate for the United States Senate from New Jersey, announced that the proposed restriction was "unthinkable" and that he personally would "engage eminent counsel to oppose in the courts any attempt at preventing WPA employees or relief clients from voting in the coming election."[31]

The Women's Rebellion fared poorly in other states as well, although New Hampshire placed before its voters a circuitous constitutional amendment to permit the state legislature to define *pauper*. Despite the cries of political corruption and the fears of some conservatives, the idea of disfranchising relief recipients ran counter to the prevailing tides. A survey conducted by *Fortune* in 1939 revealed that only 18 percent of Americans favored such action—a figure high enough to suggest that nineteenth-century fears of the poor were still alive and well, yet low enough to explain why the notion was embraced primarily by men and women who were not running for office. In the eyes of most citizens, the dependent poor were victims; the New Deal remained popular; and the growth of fascism in Europe was strengthening American identification with democracy. Once again President Roosevelt gave voice to the popular mood. When asked his views of the crusade of the Women's Rebellion, Roosevelt breezily responded that the logical outcome of such a crusade would be to limit the franchise to men of "academic distinction." He then recalled that a group of Harvard students had once agitated to restrict suffrage to men with bachelor's degrees, provoking Harvard's president, Charles W. Eliot, to comment that with such a restriction the United States would "remain a republic for just about three years."[32]

The significance of Roosevelt's comments resided as much in their cavalier tone as in their content. The president could be flippant about the issue precisely because he knew that his was the majority view: in the wake of the stock market crash and the collapse of the pro-business ideology of the 1920s, Roosevelt, a Harvard graduate himself, could safely ridicule the notion of government by an educated elite. In addition, Roosevelt was expressing a confidence, characteristic of the New Deal, that a democratic polity could be managed successfully, that government could juggle the competing claims of diverse social and economic interests, and that it could smooth the inherent tensions between industrial capitalism and popular government. While the New York State Economic Council and the Women's Rebellion echoed longstanding conservative apprehensions—perpetuating a line of thought that had run from Blackstone and Kent to Parkman and Munro—Roosevelt was the embodiment of a more optimistic faith.

In early November 1936, on the eve of the presidential elections, Roosevelt, at home in Hyde Park, New York, gave an extemporaneous speech to his fellow residents of Dutchess County. Announcing that he wanted to tell them "a few things" that were "in my heart at the end of this campaign," he reflected on American constitutional history and on the history of the county. "At the time of the first election, after the Constitution was ratified," he observed, very few men—of course there were no women voting in those days—comparatively few men voted. The reason for that was that in the early days of the United States the franchise was limited to property holders. Most of this Dutchess County of ours in the early days of the republic was inhabited by tenant farmers. A tenant farmer could not vote because he was not a freeholder and only freeholders could vote in this and the other counties of the State of New York . . . . Today we have a very different proposition . . . . You do not have to be the owner of real estate in order to vote.

"In the early days of the nation," the president then noted, "the results of an election could not be called the rule of the majority"; but things had changed, and "today you have a different situation and by midnight tomorrow night . . . whatever the result is, it will be definitely, clearly, and conclusively the will of the majority."[33]

Roosevelt was not the first president to celebrate the virtues of democracy or to applaud the end of property requirements for voting. But his self-conscious excursion into history, in the midst of a profound economic crisis that had brought class issues to the forefront of national politics, had an unmistakable symbolic resonance. The president's embrace of a broad suffrage, unbounded by economic qualifications, underscored one of the central messages and thrusts of the New Deal: industrial capitalism and political democracy could coexist. Just as he rebuffed socialist critics who believed that capitalism had failed, he dismissed conservatives who were clamoring for the resurrection of electoral bans on the dependent poor or the "economic unfit." That this resurrection did not occur, that Mrs. Wellman, the NYSEC, and the Women's Rebellion made so little progress—despite the threatening presence of millions of dependent "paupers"—was a measure of the New Deal's success and a sign that the ghosts of Blackstone and Kent finally had been put to rest.[34]

War and Race

The equilibrium in voting laws was decisively disrupted by World War II. Fighting a long and difficult war on both the Atlantic and Pacific fronts compelled the United States to mobilize almost all men of military age, including many who were not enfranchised: roughly one million African Americans as well as thousands of Native Americans and men of Asian descent. Drafting these men into military service inescapably raised the troubling issue of fairness that had surfaced as early as the American Revolution: Could men be obliged to risk their lives to protect a society and government that did not give them a voice in its politics? This question shot to the surface of political life during the war and was kept there, in the war's aftermath, by veterans—cadres of young Americans who, by dint of their military service, felt entitled to the full rights of citizenship and were unabashed about demanding those rights.

The impact of World War II also was shaped by the particular goals of the war and the nature of America's adversaries. The Atlantic Charter was precise in declaring that the war's objectives included the restoration of democracy to all European nations, as well as an end to racial and ethnic discrimination. In the popular mind and in wartime propaganda, the ideology of racial superiority espoused by the Nazis loomed as an evil that had to be vanquished. Yet, as the Nazis and the Japanese frequently pointed out, the presence of systematic discrimination in the United States undercut America's posture as the standard bearer of democracy. World War II was an ideological as well as a military war, and its ideological dimension exposed the undemocratic features of American political life. In doing so, the war recast democratization as a matter of compelling national interest and therefore as an appropriate, indeed imperative, concern of the national government.[35]

Alongside such strategic considerations was a broader shift in beliefs and temperament: World War II spawned a popular embrace of democracy more vigorous than any that had occurred since the most optimistic moments of Reconstruction. In sharp contrast to the 1930s, when many intellectuals and opinion leaders thought that capitalist democracy was on its last legs, the war against Germany and Japan (and then the cold war) led many Americans to renew their identification with democratic values. That identification, coupled with the repugnance of Nazi ideology, significantly strengthened the movement to end racial discrimination at home. Sensitive to this shift in values and to the growing electoral strength of northern blacks, both political parties, and particularly the Republicans, vigorously supported black rights in their national electoral campaigns.[36]

The tensions between the democratic goals of the war and the limits of democracy at home offered black leaders an opportunity that they seized to good effect. In contrast to their stance during World War I (which was to defer racial issues while uniting behind the war effort), African-American political figures invoked the anti-Nazi and antiracialist ideology of the war to press for an end to discrimination at home. "Prove to us," declared one activist, "that you are not hypocrites when you say this is a war for freedom." The well-known March on Washington Movement focused attention on discriminatory practices in the armed services and among defense contractors; the campaign to abolish the poll tax gathered steam, as noted earlier; and the NAACP, whose membership rose from 50,000 to more than 400,000, announced that the war for freedom would be fought on "two fronts," abroad and at home. Declaring that "we shall not abate one iota our struggle for full citizenship rights in the United States," the NAACP renewed its legal assault on lynching, social segregation, and disfranchisement. In making such pronouncements, activists had the support of an increasingly assertive African-American community, particularly among the millions who either joined the army or took advantage of the booming wartime economy to migrate to northern and southern cities to take jobs in industry. "If I've got to die for democracy," observed one black soldier, "I might as well die for some of it right here and now."[37]

Not surprisingly, the first concrete steps prompted by the war involved soldiers. In 1942, with five million men and women already mobilized in the armed forces, Congress—building on Civil War and World War I precedents—took steps to permit these soldiers to vote, creating the machinery for ballots to be distributed overseas and at military bases across the nation. By the 1940s, most states already had laws that permitted absentee soldiers to register and vote, but the Soldier Voting Act of 1942, as well as its successor in 1944, went a step further, standardizing and federalizing that right. These acts also reignited the process of stretching the definition of residence as a voting qualification: during and after the war, new laws and court decisions permitted some soldiers to vote in the towns where they were stationed, exempted inhabitants of soldiers' homes from residency restrictions, and even allowed veterans who were students to vote in municipalities where they attended school.[38]

The significance of the Soldier Voting Acts, however, went beyond matters of residence. When the legislation came before Congress in 1942, liberal legislators seized the occasion to include a provision exempting any soldier from having to pay a poll tax: although many Southerners correctly viewed this provision as an entering wedge in the battle for poll tax repeal (one wrote to his daughter that "all white people in Alabama are buying pistols and other ammunition in preparation for the race war which is coming"), the idea of taxing soldiers in the field was so unpalatable that southern congressmen did little to block its passage. Several states even passed laws temporarily abolishing the poll tax for all soldiers. To be sure, southern state governments, after bitter fights in Congress, retained administrative control over absentee voting and thereby were able to limit the number of black soldiers who actually cast ballots. Nonetheless, the Soldier Voting Act was an important step. The federal government's disapproval of poll taxes had become a matter of law, and the wartime climate of opinion contributed to the repeal of the poll tax in Georgia in 1945 as well as to the postwar passage of state laws exempting veterans from poll taxes.[39]

A far more significant victory for black voting rights came in 1944, with the Supreme Court's stunning decision that the white primary was unconstitutional. By 1920, racially exclusive primary elections in the Democratic Party had become the norm not only in all southern state elections but in nearly every county in the South: since electoral outcomes invariably were determined in primaries, this was an extremely tidy and efficient vehicle for black disfranchisement. The legal journey that led to its demise was a circuitous one, a shuttle between Washington and Texas that stretched back into the 1920s.

The first legal blow against the white primary was struck in 1927, when the United States Supreme Court overturned the primary law in Texas on the grounds that it violated the equal protection clause of the Fourteenth Amendment. The Lone Star State then turned around and adopted a new law that did not mandate but merely sanctioned a Democratic Party rule restricting its primaries to whites. The Court responded in 1932 by declaring that law too to be unconstitutional. Unwilling to surrender, the Democratic Party of Texas, ostensibly acting on its own initiative as a private political association, elected to bar blacks from membership in the party—which meant that they could not participate in primary elections. The Court accepted this practice in *Grovey v. Townsend* in 1935, repeating a line of argument from Reconstruction-era cases that private rather than state actions were not subject to federal oversight. Although the Court's 1927 and 1932 decisions had signaled an incipient willingness of the federal judiciary to intervene in voting rights cases, *Grovey v. Townsend* represented a triumph for the stubborn ingenuity of white supremacists in the South.[40]

In 1944, however, the Supreme Court reversed *Grovey v. Townsend*. In a new case, *Smith v. Allwright*, the Court concluded that the exclusion of nonwhites from membership in the Democratic Party in Texas was indeed unconstitutional. The Court grounded its decision (and its willingness to overturn a judgment made only nine years earlier) in the implications of a

1941 electoral corruption case, *United States v. Classic et al.*, in which it had ruled that the Constitution's implicit guarantee of a right to vote (in article 1, sections 2 and 4) applied to primaries as well as general elections. Consequently, when "the privilege of membership in a party . . . is also the essential qualification for voting in a primary," party rules, sanctioned by law, become "the action of the state," subject to the requirements of the Fifteenth Amendment. The Democratic Party thus was not a "voluntary association," free to adopt regulations that discriminated on the basis of race.[41]

The Court's abrupt about-face (the majority opinion acknowledged that none of the facts had changed since *Grovey*) had multiple sources, some of them—as always—unacknowledged in the legal prose. One key was that the composition of the Court had changed dramatically between 1935 and 1944: only two of the justices who had ruled in *Grovey* were still on the Court at the time of *Smith*, and several of Roosevelt's appointees were experienced, liberal, Democratic politicians, well attuned to the politics of black suffrage. The New Deal justices appointed by Roosevelt, moreover, were far more willing than their predecessors to assert the power and jurisdiction of the federal government: the Court's willingness to extend federal authority over state voting laws was entirely in keeping with its actions in other domains.

Of perhaps equal importance, the justices were not immune to events transpiring in the world around them: much as they were sensitive to the exigencies of the Great Depression in other landmark rulings, they were well aware of the links between the ideological dimensions of World War II and the exclusion of blacks from voting in the South. One shrewd contemporary commentator, Supreme Court reporter Arthur Krock of the *New York Times*, attributed the decision in *Smith v. Allwright* directly to the wartime shift in thinking about racial equality in the United States. In analyzing the case, Krock observed that the "real reason for the" decision was "that the common sacrifices of wartime have turned public opinion and the court against previously sustained devices to exclude minorities from any privilege of citizenship."[42]

The impact of the *Smith* decision was rapid and far-reaching. Indeed, pioneering attorney and then Supreme Court Justice Thurgood Marshall, who argued the case with William H. Hastie, later stated that he regarded it as his most important victory, more important than the famous school desegregation case, *Brown v. Board of Education*. Although many African Americans remained reluctant to test the new legal order, tens of thousands began to line up to register for Democratic primaries throughout the South. Several states truculently attempted to circumvent the Court's decision by repealing all laws governing primary elections (thus ostensibly restoring political parties to the status of voluntary associations or "private clubs") and by continuing to hold racially exclusive elections, but the courts brought an end to those efforts through subsequent rulings.

The white primary, probably the most efficacious method of denying the vote to African Americans, was dead. Enraged by this development, white southern politicians fumed at the federal courts and vowed to resist the intrusion of the federal government into their affairs: they immediately began constructing and reinforcing other techniques for disfranchisement, including extensive racial gerrymandering and physical intimidation. "The best way to stop niggers from voting," pointed out Mississippi's diehard Senator Theodore Bilbo, "is to visit them the night before the election." This pattern of resistance would persist for decades, perpetuating discrimination against black voters, but the wall of exclusion had been seriously breached: between 1940 and 1947, the percentage of southern blacks registered to vote quadrupled from 3 to 12 percent and the numbers continued to rise thereafter.[43]

The war also generated pressures for Washington to ease the restrictions on immigrants from Asia. Under existing law, Asian migrants were few in number and could not become American citizens. This discrimination became a wartime diplomatic issue because China was an ally, India was strategically located, and the Japanese attempted to mobilize support throughout Asia by portraying the United States as an anti-Asiatic nation fighting with Britain to restore Anglo-Saxon imperialism. Madame Chiang Kai-shek herself lobbied American congressmen to endorse repeal of the Chinese exclusion laws, while critics of American immigration policies maintained that successful prosecution of the war would be hindered by racial discrimination against Asians. An Indian scholar, for example, wrote that

> Hitler's justification of Nazi oppression in Europe is supposedly based on the right of the mythically superior Nordic to superimpose his *Kultur* on the other so-called inferior peoples of Europe. If the United States is successfully to combat such dangerous ideas, it can ill afford to practice racial discrimination in its relations with Asiatic countries . . . . America cannot afford to say that she wants the people of India to fight on her side and at the same time maintain that she will not have them among her immigrant groups.

These diplomatic and ideological concerns, coupled with the presence in the armed forces of thousands of men of Chinese, Indian, Korean, Filipino, and even Japanese descent, led Congress to reconsider the ban on Asian immigration and citizenship. Between 1943 and 1946, almost all of those bans were lifted. Within a few years, the courts had taken the further step of nullifying state laws that obstructed the enfranchisement of naturalized citizens from particular (generally Asian) nations.[44]

The energy unleashed by the war carried over into its aftermath. Although the movement to repeal the poll tax fizzled, black organizations continued to pressure the federal government, while the growing number of African-American voters in the North made clear that they would use their political leverage to back candidates and parties that endorsed full citizenship for blacks. Returning black veterans in the South (as well as Mexican-American veterans in Texas and elsewhere) sought to make good on the nation's rhetorical promises. Throughout the region, black veterans lined up—often very publicly—to register to vote in general elections and in Democratic primaries; in Birmingham, a column of ex-soldiers marched through the city's streets to the registrar's office, much as earlier generations of soldiers had done during the Revolutionary War and the War of 1812. The rejections that these veterans often encountered—ranging from closed registration offices to grotesquely rigged literacy tests to violent beatings—attracted widespread national attention. In Georgia, Texas, and South Carolina, blacks who had voted or engaged in civil rights events were killed; in other episodes, overly assertive veterans were murdered. Perhaps more flagrantly than ever before, men who had risked their lives for the nation were being denied their political rights.[45]

These developments, coupled with other outbreaks of racial violence in the South, led President Truman to create a national Committee on Civil Rights in late 1946. Chaired by Charles Wilson, the president of General Electric, the committee, Noah's Ark-like, counted among its members two African Americans, two women, two labor leaders, two businessmen, and two Southerners (Frank P. Graham, the liberal president of the University of North Carolina, and M. E. Tilley of the Women's Society of Christian Services). The extraordinarily honest report issued by the committee, entitled *To Secure These Rights* (a phrase taken from the Declaration of Independence), was a self-conscious milestone in the history of the federal government's stance toward voting and civil rights. Invoking the precedents of the Revolutionary period and Reconstruction, the report proclaimed that the nation stood once again at a critical juncture: although "the right of all qualified citizens to vote" was "considered axiomatic by most Americans," the franchise in fact was "barred to some citizens because of race; to others by institutions or procedures which impede free access to the polls." It singled out for attention the disfranchisement of blacks in the South and Native Americans in several western states, as well as discriminatory naturalization laws that kept men and women from some nations from becoming citizens.[46]

The committee's recommendations for addressing these problems were straightforward: it proposed congressional action to abolish poll taxes as voting prerequisites, to protect the rights of "qualified persons" to participate in federal elections, and to bar discrimination based on race, color, or "any other unreasonable classification" in state and federal elections. The committee also urged New Mexico and Arizona to enfranchise "their Indian citizens," and called for a modification of the naturalization laws "to permit the granting of citizenship without regard to the race, color, or national origin of applicants." To promote enforcement of these laws and others already on the books, the committee also recommended strengthening the civil rights section of the Justice Department.[47]

More important, perhaps, than these specific proposals was the committee's underlying and deliberate message: "the National Government of the United States must take the lead in safeguarding the civil rights of all Americans." Sensitive to the constitutional issues involved and to the political freight of states' rights, the committee nonetheless was calling for federal guarantees of the right to vote, for what amounted to a nationalization of the franchise. The report justified federal action on three grounds: first, that suffrage limitations and discrimination were producing a "moral erosion" of the nation, particularly in the South; second, that discrimination had negative consequences for the economy; and third, that the international interests of the United States were jeopardized by limitations on democracy at home.[48]

This last factor was stressed repeatedly and was grounded not in the threat of Nazism but in the new ideological rivalry of what soon would be labeled the cold war. In the emerging hostile competition with the Soviet Union, racial discrimination in the United States was an Achilles' heel of the American claim to represent truly democratic values. The committee's report cited a letter from Acting Secretary of State Dean Acheson noting that "the existence of discrimination against minority groups in the United States is a handicap in our relations with other countries." The report reprinted a press dispatch indicating that "Communist propagandists in Europe" were successfully scoring points with other nations by publicizing incidents of racial discrimination in the American South; it also pointed out that men and women around the non-European world were acutely sensitive to the ways in which their relatives and countrymen were treated in the United States. Faced with a global propaganda war, the United States could not afford to let states' rights and regional histories poke holes in the fabric of democracy. "Interference with the right of a qualified citizen to vote locally cannot today remain a local problem," the report concluded. "An American diplomat cannot forcefully argue for free elections in foreign lands without meeting the challenge that in many sections of America qualified voters do not have free access to the polls. Can it be doubted that this is a right which the national government must make secure?"[49]

President Truman may well have gotten more than he bargained for from his Committee on Civil Rights. A moderate on racial issues, he had voted for repeal of the poll tax but was hardly a member of the Democratic Party's most liberal wing. In addition, he found himself caught in a political crossfire as he looked ahead to the presidential election of 1948: although reluctant to antagonize the southern wing of his own party, he needed the votes of northern blacks—who were being courted both by the Republicans and by the much more liberal Henry Wallace. Practical politician that he was, Truman responded to this dilemma with compromise, issuing executive orders to desegregate the armed forces and promote fair employment practices by the federal government, while declining to press for the full range of reforms advocated by his Committee on Civil Rights. This stance helped Truman's election effort—despite the defection of both Dixiecrats and Wallace supporters—and it solidified the identification of black voters with the Democratic Party.[50]

But the president's stance also left the campaign for black voting rights without strong leadership in the federal government. For a decade following the publication of the civil rights committee's report, Washington in fact did little to follow up on the call for national suffrage regulations and an end to racial discrimination in voting. Whatever efforts were made in Congress were blocked by powerful southern politicians who, thanks to their seniority, chaired key committees. These same conservative politicians tried, with some success, to turn the dynamics of the cold war against reform, arguing—with a bit of truth and a great deal of hyperbole—that Communists were prominent in the civil rights movement. Without a strong push from

Washington, southern blacks made only modest gains: their attempts to register and vote were consistently met with discriminatory education tests (such as explicating clauses of the Constitution to the satisfaction of a white registrar), legal challenges, procedural obstacles, outright refusal, and sometimes violence. In some urban areas, significant numbers of African Americans did register and vote, and they even succeeded in electing blacks and liberal whites to office. Yet most rural blacks—lacking education and resources, economically and physically intimidated—remained disfranchised. In 1956, in the South as a whole, barely one quarter of all black adults were registered to vote; in 1960, the percentage was only a few points higher.[51]

"Our Oldest National Minority"

The most immediate impact of the president's Committee on Civil Rights—and perhaps of World War II itself—may well have been on Native Americans rather than African Americans. Although all Indians had been granted citizenship in 1924, the states with the largest Native-American populations had continued to balk at granting them suffrage. Several states had challenged the ability of reservation Indians to meet residency requirements, and Colorado in 1936 maintained that Native Americans were not state citizens. These obstacles had been removed gradually through court decisions, but as the Committee on Civil Rights pointed out, Arizona and New Mexico still disfranchised the great majority of their Native-American residents. Within a year of the report's publication—and within a few weeks of one another—both states ceased such practices.[52]

In Arizona, the disfranchisement of Indians was rooted in a clause of the state constitution that provided that "no person under guardianship . . . shall be qualified to vote at any election." In 1928, in the case of *Porter v. Hall*, the Arizona Supreme Court had ruled that this clause was applicable to reservation Indians who lived "under the laws, rules, and regulations of the United States government" and thus were not subject to the jurisdiction of the state of Arizona. For two decades, this decision went unchallenged. In the aftermath of World War II, however, numerous Native-American veterans attempted to register, and two of them, when refused, filed suit in 1948. The resulting court case led to a sharp rejection of *Porter* and the "tortuous" logic that supported it. Justice Levi Udall, speaking for the court, argued that Native Americans were not under guardianship of a type envisioned by the state constitution, that the state government had never intended to apply such a provision to Native Americans, and that no court in any other state had ever upheld the application of the guardianship clause to Native Americans. Udall cited *To Secure These Rights* and concluded that "suffrage is the most basic civil right, since its exercise is the chief means whereby other rights may be safeguarded. To deny the right to vote, where one is legally entitled to do so, is to do violence to the principles of freedom and equality."[53]

Almost simultaneously, federal courts were hearing a New Mexico case that challenged its constitutional denial of the franchise to "Indians not taxed." As late as 1940, five states had enforced such laws, despite a 1938 legal opinion from the Department of the Interior that they violated the Fifteenth Amendment. By 1948, four of these states (Idaho, Maine, Mississippi, and Washington) had dropped their "Indians not taxed" provisions, but New Mexico, with one of the largest Native-American populations, had not done so, insisting that there be "no representation without taxation." Consequently, in 1948, Miguel Trujillo, a Native-American ex-Marine sergeant, filed suit after he was denied the right to vote because he did not pay taxes on his property—although he was subject to all other state taxes. A three-judge federal panel, after pointing out that whites who paid no taxes were not disfranchised, concluded that New Mexico's constitution violated the Fourteenth and Fifteenth Amendments. Notably, the court alluded to the wartime service of Native Americans. "It is perhaps not pertinent to the question here, but we all know that these New Mexico Indians have responded to the needs of the country in time of war. . . . Why should they be deprived of their rights to vote now because they are favored by the federal government in exempting their lands from taxation?"[54]

Attorneys for the National Congress of American Indians labeled the Trujillo decision a "smashing victory for civil rights for our oldest national minority." Yet the long struggle for Indian suffrage was not quite over. In 1956, the attorney general of Utah issued an opinion (reversing one delivered sixteen years earlier) that an 1897 law denying residency to anyone who lived on an "Indian or military reservation" still applied to Native Americans and thus prohibited them from voting. The state's supreme court agreed, arguing that residency was determined not merely by geographic location but by culture and legal status: Indians remained subject to special protection by the federal government, they spoke their own language, and were "not as conversant with nor as interested in government as other citizens." On appeal, the decision in the case, *Allen v. Merrell*, was vacated by the United States Supreme Court and returned to Utah for rehearing. The state's legislature, bowing to the currents of the law and public opinion, rendered the case moot by repealing the original legislation.[55]

Native Americans in some states continued to encounter literacy tests as well as procedural obstacles to voting and registration; in subsequent decades, they also faced occasional legal challenges, usually on the grounds that their exemption from property taxes undermined their eligibility to participate in elections. By the mid–1950s, however, the basic suffrage rights of Native Americans were legally secure. Thereafter, Indians, although few in number, came to constitute an important voting bloc in several western states as well as in many towns and counties. Thanks to the courts, the federal government, and 25,000 World War II veterans, they were full citizens at last.[56]

EIGHT

Breaking Barriers

ℬETWEEN THE LATE 1950S AND EARLY 1970S, the legal underpinnings of the right to vote were transformed more dramatically than they had been at any earlier point in the nation's history. In a cascading series of congressional enactments and court decisions, virtually all formal restrictions on the suffrage rights of adult citizens were swept away, and the federal government assumed full responsibility for protecting and guaranteeing those rights. Almost exactly a century after Congress, led by Henry Wilson, had first debated the imposition of national, universal suffrage, it became the law of the land.

The historical stars were well aligned for such a transformation. In the South, a determined movement of African Americans stared down the threat of violence and reprisals to force the issue of voting rights into the public eye. The expansive dynamics of military mobilization and international competition were kept in motion by the cold war and the distant, but very hot, war in Vietnam. The Supreme Court, fueled by an enlarged conception of citizenship and a willingness to extend the powers of the national government, was actively promoting the rights of the disadvantaged. In addition, public opinion, molded by antitotalitarian conflict with Germany and the Soviet Union, was broadly supportive of democratic principles; the solvent of rapid economic growth took the edge off class antagonism; and for a time at least, both major political parties saw more to gain than to lose from a broadening of the franchise.

For millions of Americans, these legal changes had concrete consequences as simple as they were profound. A poor black woman in Alabama who could not set foot in a polling place in 1958 could pull a voting-machine lever for a black candidate in 1972. A Puerto Rican-born resident of New York who failed the English-language literacy test in 1960 would receive voting information in Spanish in 1980. Eighteen-year-old soldiers who were sent to Vietnam during the Tet Offensive of 1968 could not vote in that year's tumultuous election, but their eighteen-year-old counterparts during the Gulf War could cast ballots wherever they were stationed. These were not small changes.

Race and the Second Reconstruction

> As Americans, we must also realize and accept the fact that the responsibility of worldwide leadership carries with it a concomitant duty of providing the world with examples of freedom and liberty for all in our daily lives. Any intolerance or discrimination or deprivation of our constitutionally guaranteed rights and privileges resound and reverberate throughout the globe . . .
>
> —HOUSE REPORT 291, ACCOMPANYING
> H.R. 6127, THE CIVIL RIGHTS ACT OF 1957

> It seems that neither Thaddeus Stevens nor Charles Sumner ever advocated any such thing as is found in the present proposed legislation, which has the effect of making the United States the parent guardian of minority groups, and the pursuer of all of the other citizens in the United States . . .
>
> Why swap the harmony and unity prevailing over this country today for proposals that will undoubtedly bring chaos, dissension and strife into this land so rich with promise for the future, that promise being predicated upon a glorious past.
>
> —HOUSE MINORITY REPORT
> ON H.R. 6127, 1957

Washington and the South

The South was a cauldron of racial tension in the 1950s. Throughout the region—and particularly in its many small and medium-sized cities— African Americans pressed forward against the boundaries of America's caste system, demanding an end to social segregation and second-class citizenship. Sometimes led by national and regional organizations, such as the NAACP, trade unions, or the newly formed Southern Christian Leadership Conference, and sometimes acting entirely on local initiative, black citizens marched, rallied, boycotted buses, wrote petitions, and filed lawsuits to challenge the Jim Crow laws that had kept them in their place for more than half a century. Encouraged by the Supreme Court's 1954 decision, in *Brown v. Board of Education*, that separate was not equal, the black community focused particular attention on the integration of schools and institutions of higher learning. African Americans also kept the spotlight on the right to vote, which was always at the heart of the civil rights movement. Convinced that the franchise was an important right in itself and the key to securing other civil rights, hundreds of thousands of African Americans, acting alone and in organized registration drives, attempted to enter their names on registry lists and participate in elections. "Once Negroes start voting in large numbers," observed one black newspaper, "the Jim Crow laws will be endangered." "Give us the ballot and we will fill our legislative halls with men of good will," declared the Reverend Martin Luther King, Jr. to a crowd of nearly 30,000 people in front of the Lincoln Memorial in 1957.[1]

The push for civil rights encountered formidable opposition, which evolved into a semiformal policy of "massive resistance" after the *Brown* decision. To be sure, an increasing number of white Southerners were recognizing the inevitability, and even desirability, of integration; many advocates of a modernized New South sought to remove the stigma attached to the region's racial practices, while the mechanization of agriculture diminished the reliance on semicaptive black labor. Nonetheless, resistance to equal rights remained fierce and sometimes violent. Mayors and governors refused to integrate schools and public facilities; legislatures declared that they would not dismantle Jim Crow; sheriffs arrested and beat black protesters and their white allies. Meanwhile, the fortunes of liberal or populist white politicians who displayed any sympathy with blacks, such as Earl Long in Louisiana and Jim Folsom in Alabama, were spiraling into decline.[2]

The widespread resistance to integration only underscored the black community's need for political rights, but throughout the 1950s their efforts to vote were thwarted more often than not. In seven states (Alabama, Georgia, Louisiana, Mississippi, North Carolina, South Carolina, and Virginia), literacy tests kept African Americans from the polls: failure of the test could result simply from misspelling or mispronouncing a word. In 1954, Mississippi instituted a new, even more difficult "understanding test," complete with a grandfather clause exempting those already registered. Black residents of the five remaining poll tax states (Alabama, Arkansas, Mississippi, Texas, and Virginia) faced not only an economic hurdle but also discriminatory administration: poll tax bills were not sent to blacks, and receipts were hard to obtain. In Alabama, prospective registrants had to be accompanied by white citizens who would "vouch" for them. In Louisiana, members of the White Citizens Council purged black registrants from the voting lists for minor paperwork irregularities, and a 1960 law provided for the disfranchisement of a person of "bad character"—which included anyone convicted of refusing to leave a movie theater or participating in a sit-in. Registrars in many towns and cities thwarted black aspirants by not showing up at the office or by simply refusing to register blacks when they did. Those who were adamant about registering could lose their jobs, have loans called due, or face physical harm. More than a few were killed.[3]

It was apparent to nearly all black leaders that the civil rights movement could succeed only with significant backing from the federal government: the black community by itself could not compel city and state authorities to cease discriminating. But Washington, although sympathetic, was hesitant. Liberal Democrats in Congress were eager to take action—at least to implement the recommendations of Truman's Commission on Civil Rights—but their influence was offset by the power of southern Democrats. Republicans were similarly torn: while the desire to court black voters reinforced the party's traditional pro–civil rights principles, many Republicans also hoped to make inroads into the solid South by winning over white southern voters.

President Dwight Eisenhower, meanwhile, was cautious through most of his first term, favoring gradual change, reliance on the judiciary, and a limited role for the federal government. By 1956, however, the worsening situation in the South (including the murder of two Mississippi voting rights workers), coupled with prodding from Attorney General Herbert Brownell, persuaded the president to act. He gave Brownell—who was convinced that new laws were needed—the go ahead to send to Congress a civil rights bill that the Justice Department had been preparing for months. For more than a year, the legislation wended its way through Congress, where it was streamlined and watered down to avoid a southern filibuster. Senate Majority Leader Lyndon B. Johnson, aspiring to the presidency and hoping to serve as a bridge between the two warring wings of his party, played a critical role in shaping the final legislation; another aspirant to the Oval Office, Vice President Richard Nixon, also lent indispensable support.[4]

The Civil Rights Act of 1957—the first civil rights bill passed by Congress in more than eighty years—was a modest piece of legislation, so modest that it was roundly criticized by African-American activists. The bill created a national Civil Rights Commission, elevated the Civil Rights section into a full-fledged division of the Justice Department, and authorized the attorney general to seek injunctions and file civil suits in voting rights cases. The operative heart of the measure was a strengthening of the machinery that the Justice Department and federal judges could utilize to respond to violations of existing voting rights laws, including the Fifteenth Amendment. Well-intentioned as the bill surely was, it had few teeth and little impact: the Justice Department was sluggish in initiating suits, southern federal judges were sometimes unreceptive, and the entire strategy of relying on litigation inescapably meant that progress would be slow. Between 1956 and 1960, only 200,000 additional blacks were registered to vote in the South. The ineffectiveness of the bill led to the passage in 1960 of a second Civil Rights Act, stronger than the first, but conceptually similar and still modest in its reach.[5]

Rhetorically and politically, however, the Civil Rights Act of 1957 did push the voting rights agenda forward, largely through the creation of the Commission on Civil Rights (CCR). The bipartisan commission, instructed to report to Congress and the president within two years, energetically pursued complaints, held hearings, and conducted field investigations. Its report, issued in 1959, contained vivid, detailed confirmation of claims that had been streaming forth from African Americans in the South. (The commission's report also pointed to a growing problem in New York, where natives of Puerto Rico by the scores of thousands were being denied the franchise because of their inability to pass the state's English-language literacy exam.) The critical source of nonvoting by blacks, the CCR reported, was the brazen refusal of southern authorities to permit blacks to register, as well as their willingness to intimidate those who tried. In the end, the CCR concluded,

> legislation presently on the books is inadequate to assure that all our qualified citizens shall enjoy the right to vote. There exists here a striking gap between our principles and our everyday practices. This is a moral gap . . . . It runs counter to our traditional concepts of fair play. It is a partial repudiation of our faith in the democratic system. It undermines the moral suasion of our national stand in international affairs.

The commission's recommendations included the appointment of federal registrars who would be dispatched to the South and empowered to register voters. The three Northerners on the commission, including its chairman, went further, calling for a new constitutional amendment that "would give the right to vote to every citizen who meets his State's age and residence requirement, and who is not legally confined at the time of registration or election." Although the precedent was unmentioned, the proposed amendment bore a strong resemblance to the Wilson amendment of the 1860s.[6]

The Civil Rights Commission thus lent its prestige and authority to calls for further federal action and the de facto, if not de jure, nationalization of the right to vote. Whether such calls would be heeded depended on a complex political calculus. Both parties were engaged in balancing acts, trying to court northern black and southern white voters simultaneously; for the Democrats this also was a tension between the two regional wings of their own party. Election returns of the 1950s made clear, however, that the balance was unstable and could not continue for long. The rapidly growing black electorate had become influential in many northern states, and black voters, although tending to vote Democratic, could be wooed by pro–civil rights candidates from either party. Eisenhower's victories in some southern states, moreover, indicated that single-party dominance in that region was cracking. An additional ingredient in the calculus was the likelihood that black voters would be enfranchised in the South in the foreseeable future and would be unsympathetic to any party that had opposed their enfranchisement. The Civil Rights Acts of 1957 and 1960 were bipartisan compromises constructed to appease competing political interests, but it was apparent that difficult choices loomed on the horizon.[7]

The pace of governmental activity began to quicken in 1960, largely because the political temperature was soaring in the South. A sit-in at a segregated luncheon counter in Greensboro, North Carolina, sparked a wave of civil disobedience by young African Americans who refused to adhere to the strictures of Jim Crow; freedom riders rode buses to try to integrate interstate transportation; in Birmingham and other cities, mass movements challenged segregation and disfranchisement; efforts to register black voters even reached into the Deep South bastions of white supremacy in rural Alabama and Mississippi. In the latter state, in 1963, 80,000 African Americans, echoing a strategy from the Dorr War in 1840s Rhode Island, participated in a mock gubernatorial election.[8]

The growing militance of the black freedom movement only stiffened the opposition. The governors of Alabama and Mississippi refused to desegregate their universities; voting districts were gerrymandered to dilute the influence of blacks who did manage to register; freedom riders were beaten and their buses burned; police arrested protestors by the thousands; bombs were tossed into black churches; and activists were occasionally—as in Mississippi in 1964—murdered in cold blood. In 1961, the CCR (whose life had been extended by the 1960 legislation) reported that "in some 100 counties in eight Southern States," discriminatory laws, arbitrary registration rulings, and threats of "physical violence or economic reprisal" still kept most "Negro citizens . . . from exercising the right to vote."[9]

The commission also concluded that the federal government's reliance on county-by-county litigation was too "time consuming, expensive, and difficult" to bring an end to discriminatory voting practices. "Broader measures are required," the CCR intoned, urging Congress once again to pass legislation "providing that all citizens of the United States shall have a right to vote in Federal or State elections" if they could meet reasonable age and residency requirements and had not been convicted of a felony.[10]

Neither Congress nor President John Kennedy was ready to bite that bullet. Although Kennedy's narrow electoral victory owed a great deal to black voters, he lacked a strong popular mandate, had limited influence with Congress, and did not regard civil rights as a high-priority issue. His approach, accordingly, was nearly as cautious as Eisenhower's: the Justice Department filed lawsuits to enforce the Civil Rights Acts, and the administration supported what had become an uncontroversial constitutional amendment to ban poll taxes in federal elections (only four states still had poll taxes). More innovatively, the Kennedy administration fostered the creation of a Voter Education Project that channeled the energies of civil rights activists into a campaign to promote voter registration. These efforts bore some fruit. Rulings by federal judges stripped away more of the legal camouflage that was sheltering discrimination; the Twenty-fourth Amendment was ratified with relatively little opposition; and black registration in the South rose to more than 40 percent by 1964. Still, the pace of legal progress was outstripped by the acceleration of conflict in the South. Consequently, the administration in 1963 drafted an omnibus civil rights bill designed to give strong federal support to equal rights, although it said little about voting rights per se.[11]

Kennedy did not live to witness the passage of his civil rights bill, but Johnson successfully seized the moment after Kennedy's assassination to urge the bill's passage as a tribute to the late president. As important, Johnson himself was elected to the presidency in 1964 with an enormous popular vote, offering the first southern president in a century the opportunity to complete the Second Reconstruction. Personally sympathetic to the cause of black suffrage, bidding for a place in history, and prodded by the nationally televised spectacle of police beatings and arrests of peaceful, prosuffrage marchers in Selma, Alabama, Johnson went to Congress in March 1965 to urge passage of a national Voting Rights Act. "The outraged conscience of a nation" demanded action, he told a joint session of Congress. "It is wrongly—deadly wrong—to deny any of your fellow Americans the right to vote," he reminded his former colleagues from the South. Then, rhetorically identifying himself with the civil rights movement, he insisted that "it is really all of us, who must overcome the crippling legacy of bigotry and injustice. And we *shall* overcome."[12]

Johnson's words, spoken to a television audience of 70 million and to a somber, hushed Congress that interrupted him forty times with applause, were sincere, principled, and moving. Yet, astute politician that he was, the president also knew that the Democrats' political balancing act was over: with the Civil Rights Act of 1964, the party had decisively tilted away from the white South and toward black voters, and now it was going to need as many black voters as possible to have a chance of winning southern states. Johnson understood that the politics of suffrage reform once again had entered its endgame: black enfranchisement would become a reality, and few politicians in either party wished to antagonize a new bloc of voters by opposing their enfranchisement.

The Voting Rights Acts

The Voting Rights Act of 1965 contained key elements demanded by civil rights activists and the Commission on Civil Rights; it also bore a strong resemblance to the never-passed Lodge Force Bill of the 1890s. Designed as a temporary, quasi-emergency measure, the act possessed an automatic "trigger" that immediately suspended literacy tests and other "devices" (including so-called good character requirements and the need for prospective registrants to have someone vouch for them) in states and counties where fewer than 50 percent of all adults had gone to the polls in 1964; the suspensions would remain in force for five years. In addition, the act authorized the attorney general to send federal examiners into the South to enroll voters and observe registration practices. To prevent the implementation of new discriminatory laws, the act prohibited the governments of all affected areas from changing their electoral procedures without the approval (or "preclearance") of the civil rights division of the Justice Department. States could bring an end to federal supervision only by demonstrating to a federal court in Washington that they had not utilized any discriminatory devices for a period of five years. Finally, the act contained a congressional "finding" that poll taxes in state elections abridged the right to vote, and it instructed the Justice Department to initiate litigation to test their constitutionality.[13]

The Voting Rights Act was passed by an overwhelming majority, as moderate Republicans joined with Democrats to carry out what Johnson called the "tumbling" of "the last of the legal barriers" to voting. Some conservative Republicans and southern Democrats voted negatively, but recognizing the inevitability of the bill's triumph and the political wisdom of supporting it, forty southern congressmen voted favorably. Hailed by one activist as "a milestone" equal in importance to the Emancipation Proclamation, the legislation had an immediate impact, particularly in the Deep South. Within a few months of the bill's passage, the Justice Department dispatched examiners to more than thirty counties in four states; scores of thousands of blacks were registered by the examiners, while many more were enrolled by local registrars who accepted the law's dictates to avoid federal oversight. In Mississippi, black registration went from less than 10 percent in 1964 to almost 60 percent in 1968; in Alabama, the figure rose from 24 percent to 57 percent. In the region as a whole, roughly a million new voters were registered within a few years after the bill became law, bringing African-American registration to a record 62 percent.[14]

The Voting Rights Act of 1965 was indeed a milestone in American political history. A curious milestone, to be sure, since the essence of the act was simply an effort to enforce the Fifteenth Amendment, which had been law for almost a century. But the very fact that it had taken so long for a measure of this type to be adopted was a sign of its importance. Racial barriers to political participation had been a fundamental feature of American life, and resistance to racial equality was deeply ingrained; so too was resistance to federal intervention into the prerogatives of the states. That such resistance was finally overcome in the 1960s was a result of the convergence of a wide array of social and political forces: the changing socioeconomic structure of the South, the migration of blacks to southern cities, the growing electoral strength of African-American migrants in the North, the energies of the civil rights movement, the vanguard role played by black veterans of World War II, and a renewed American commitment to democracy occasioned by international struggles against fascism and communism. As is often the case, more contingent factors played a role as well—including the postassassination election of a skillful southern president, the talents of civil rights leaders such as Martin Luther King, Jr., and technological changes in media coverage that brought the violence and ugliness of a "southern" problem into the homes of citizens throughout the nation.

The Voting Rights Act did not suddenly put an end to racial discrimination in southern politics. To a considerable degree, the locus of conflict shifted from the right to vote to the value of the vote (to be further discussed later in this chapter), but reports from the field made clear, to the Justice Department and the CCR, that racial obstacles to enfranchisement per se also persisted long after 1965. As a result, the act was renewed three times after its initial passage, despite a political climate that grew more conservative with each passing decade. In 1970, despite significant reluctance in the Nixon administration and congressional jockeying to weaken the measure, the bill was renewed for five years, while the ban on literacy tests was extended to all states. In 1975, the act was extended for an additional seven years, and its reach enlarged to cover "language minorities," including Hispanics, Native Americans, Alaskan Natives, and Asian Americans; the "language minority" formulation was, in effect, a means of redefining race to include other groups who had been victims of discrimination. In 1982, despite the Reagan administration's anti–civil rights posture, the act's core provisions were extended for an additional twenty-five years. Throughout this period, the Justice Department, as well as the Civil Rights Commission, worked actively to promote black enfranchisement and reviewed thousands of proposed changes in electoral law.[15]

The debates surrounding these renewals—and they were substantial—were grounded in a new partisan configuration that in part was a consequence of the Voting Rights Act itself. By the late 1960s, all southern states contained a large bloc of black voters whose loyalty to the Democratic Party had been cemented by the events of the Kennedy and Johnson years; since these voters constituted a core Democratic constituency, Democratic politicians, even within the South, generally supported efforts to shore up black political rights. At the same time, conservative white Southerners, joined by some migrants into the region, flocked to the Republican Party, reviving its fortunes in the South and becoming a critical conservative force in the national party.

Efforts to weaken the Voting Rights Act, or even to let it expire, invariably came from these southern Republicans and from national Republican leaders—such as Nixon and Reagan—who wanted and needed their support. The party of Lincoln, as one critic quipped, had donned a "Confederate uniform." That almost all of these Republican efforts failed—despite the conservative drift of the 1970s and 1980s—was a clear sign that the nation had turned a corner, that formal racial barriers to enfranchisement were dead. In 1982, even South Carolina Republican Senator Strom Thurmond, who had led the Dixiecrat exodus from the Democratic Party in 1948, voted in favor of extending the Voting Rights Act, marking the first time in his astonishingly long career that he had supported passage of a civil rights bill.[16]

The Warren Court

The eradication of racial restrictions on the franchise also was promoted by federal courts in general, and by the Supreme Court in particular. As a matter of constitutional law, this was not a particularly difficult or pathbreaking exercise: the Fifteenth Amendment was explicit in rejecting racial bars, and many, but not all, judges believed that the Fourteenth Amendment—which guaranteed the "equal protection of the laws" and prohibited states from abridging "the privileges or immunities of citizens"—was also applicable to discriminatory franchise rules. Indeed, well before the 1960s, the New Deal Supreme Court had begun to shed its predecessors' willful blinders about the realities of southern politics and discard the once-prevalent principle that laws that were not overtly discriminatory in their language did not violate the Fifteenth Amendment. In 1939, the Supreme Court had invalidated an Oklahoma law (adopted after the 1915 nullification of the state's grandfather clause) that imposed a discriminatory registration scheme on blacks; in 1944, it had abolished the white primary; and in 1949, in *Schnell v. Davis*, it had ruled that Alabama's "understanding test" was used arbitrarily to eliminate black voters. In 1960, the Supreme Court also upheld a provision of the 1957 Civil Rights Act authorizing the federal government to take legal action against registrars who were engaging in discriminatory practices.[17]

Yet the Voting Rights Act required the Court to go substantially further, particularly in permitting Congress to authorize what amounted to a federal takeover of state voting law. Not surprisingly, six southern states (South Carolina, Alabama, Georgia, Louisiana, Mississippi, and Virginia) challenged the core provisions of the bill, arguing that they "exceed the powers of Congress and encroach on an area reserved to the States by the Constitution." The Supreme Court emphatically rebuffed that challenge in 1966 in *South Carolina v. Katzenbach*, concluding that the disputed features of the Voting Rights Act "are a valid means for carrying out the commands of the Fifteenth Amendment." The Court's opinion, written by Chief Justice Earl Warren, included a detailed historical account both of "the blight of racial discrimination in voting, which has infected the electoral process . . . for nearly a century" and of the failure of milder forms of federal intervention to "cure the problem of voting discrimination." Given these failures, Warren concluded, the "array of potent weapons" provided by the Voting Rights Act was a reasonable and legitimate exercise of Congress's duty to enforce the Fifteenth Amendment. "Hopefully, millions of non-white Americans will now be able to participate for the first time on an equal basis in the government under which they live."[18]

In related cases, the Warren Court invoked the equal protection clause of the Fourteenth Amendment in defense of the Voting Rights Act. In *Katzenbach v. Morgan*, the Court upheld the provision of the act that prohibited the use of New York's English-language literacy test to disqualify natives of Puerto Rico who were American citizens and had been educated in Spanish-speaking American schools. (New York had hundreds of thousands of Puerto Rican–born residents in the 1960s.) The Court in effect was utilizing the Fourteenth Amendment to extend the antidiscrimination requirements of the Fifteenth to minorities who were not of a different "race"; it also recognized the power of Congress to enact such an extension. Three years later, in 1969, the Court ruled, in *Gaston County, N.C. v. the United States*, that a North Carolina literacy test administered without overt racial bias could be barred under the Voting Rights Act: looking behind the law to its social context, the Court concluded that segregated and inferior school systems made it more difficult for blacks to pass the literacy test. In 1970, in *Oregon v. Mitchell*, the Court ruled that the Fifteenth Amendment gave Congress the power to ban literacy tests or "other devices" that discriminated against blacks in state as well as federal elections.[19]

By the end of the 1960s, thus, two precepts had been clearly and irretrievably etched into federal law. The first was that racial barriers to the exercise of the franchise, whether simple or sophisticated, direct or indirect, were illegal. The second was that Congress, backed by the courts, possessed the authority to take vigorous, even extraordinary, measures to dismantle any such racial barriers. After a century of contorted excursions through constitutional byways, reinforced—if not prompted—by a lack of political will, the simple brevity of the Fifteenth Amendment had returned to center stage. That critical fact was underscored by Chief Justice Warren in the literary flourish with which he concluded his opinion in *South Carolina v. Katzenbach.* "We may finally look forward," he wrote, "to the day when truly 'the right of citizens of the United States to vote shall not be denied or abridged by the United States or by any State on account of race, color, or previous condition of servitude.'"[20]

Universal Suffrage

Racial barriers were not the only ones to fall between the late 1950s and early 1970s. In an extraordinary burst of activity, Congress, the Supreme Court, and state legislatures took a rapid-fire series of steps to expand the franchise along several different axes. Such action was prompted in part by the debates surrounding black voting rights: If it was wrong to deny or obstruct the enfranchisement of African Americans, how could it be legitimate for states to disqualify other citizens, such as the very poor or the mobile? The issue of race effectively reopened the venerable Pandora's box of suffrage rules, and a host of other restrictions came pouring out.

They landed, moreover, in a receptive ideological climate shaped by World War II and the cold war, in which the virtues of democracy were being trumpeted from almost every point on the political spectrum; even if such trumpetings at times were less than sincere, they made it difficult to oppose a broad franchise. The bars to suffrage also landed in an economically thriving nation, basking in the glow of two decades of prosperity, in which both political parties appeared convinced that the elixir of economic growth had permanently diluted the class tensions and distributional politics of the past.

Of equal importance, the Supreme Court, both reflecting and reinforcing the popular mood, broke new doctrinal ground through its embrace of democracy as a core constitutional value, a jurisprudential move that had been developing since the 1940s. The Warren Court came to see itself as the guardian of formal democratic rights, and it fashioned the equal protection clause of the Fourteenth Amendment into a formidable weapon with which to protect the ability of citizens to participate in democratic processes. Since Congress declined to pass a constitutional amendment (proposed in 1963) "to establish a free and universal franchise throughout the United States," that weapon proved to be critical to the nation's culminating effort to adopt universal suffrage.[21]

Wealth Is Not Germane

Economic barriers to voting were among the first to fall: although pecuniary restrictions on the franchise were relatively few in the mid–twentieth century, they did exist, and there was nothing in federal law to prohibit their application (or resuscitation) as long as they were not racially discriminatory. One of these restrictions was eliminated through the Twenty-fourth Amendment (1964), which banned poll taxes in federal elections. Enacted more than a decade after the poll tax had ceased to be a burning civil rights issue, the amendment nonetheless stemmed more from concerns about race than class. Congress (as noted earlier) pushed the issue further in section 10 of the Voting Rights Act by declaring that it viewed poll taxes, in state as well as federal elections, to be an infringement of constitutional rights. The Voting Rights Act based this declaration on the claim that poll taxes not only were racially discriminatory but that they kept "persons of limited means from voting," and that there was no legitimate state interest in requiring "the payment of a poll tax as a precondition to voting." To settle the question, the act directed the attorney general to seek a test of the constitutionality of poll taxes in the federal courts.

The test case sought by Congress came before the Supreme Court in 1966. *Harper et al. v. Virginia Board of Elections et al.* originated in a suit by several Virginia residents who challenged the state poll tax; a district court had dismissed their complaint, citing the Supreme Court's 1937 decision in *Breedlove v. Suttles*.[22] The residents' appeal to the Supreme Court produced a ringing, but not unanimous, declaration that "a State violates the Equal Protection Clause of the Fourteenth Amendment whenever it makes the affluence of the voter or payment of any fee an electoral standard." In his majority opinion, Justice William O. Douglas, perhaps the most liberal member of the Warren Court, reached well beyond the issue of poll taxes to insist that wealth was "not germane to one's ability to participate intelligently in the electoral process," that "wealth or fee paying has . . . no relation to voting qualifications; the right to vote is too precious, too fundamental to be so burdened or conditioned." He justified the applicability of the equal protection clause by claiming that it "is not shackled to the political theory of a particular era. In determining what lines are unconstitutionally discriminatory, we have never been confined to historic notions of equality. . . . Notions of what constitutes equal treatment for purposes of the Equal Protection Clause *do* change."[23]

The two dissenting opinions filed in the case, by Justices Hugo Black and John Harlan (joined by Potter Stewart), took direct aim at the ideological basis of the majority's invocation of the equal protection clause. All of the justices agreed that poll taxes were repugnant, but the dissenters argued that financial qualifications for voting were not necessarily irrational or arbitrary and therefore did not fall under the scope of the equal protection clause: it was not for the courts, they held, but for Congress or the American people (through a constitutional amendment) to adopt a new political theory. "Property and poll-tax qualifications, very simply, are not in accord with current egalitarian notions of how a modern democracy should be organized," Harlan concluded, but it was up to the "legislatures" to "modify the law to reflect such changes in popular attitudes." The dissenters in effect were arguing that democracy should be expanded only through democratic means, while the majority was insisting that universal suffrage was already an established value that the judiciary was obliged to protect.[24]

The dissenters in fact may have had the more cogent and historically grounded legal argument. Since the nation's founding, there had always been plausible—if elitist—rationales for economic qualifications, and as Black pointed out, Douglas never even attempted to show why such qualifications were arbitrary, capricious, or irrelevant. Moreover, even putting aside longstanding debates about the proper role of the judiciary in American governance, there was much to be said for allowing the people, or their elected representatives, to determine the shape of the polity. Nonetheless, the majority opinion reflected another set of historical truths: that there was always conflict about the breadth of the franchise and that those who possessed it could not necessarily be counted on to extend the right to others. Faced with this reality, it made sense for an insulated institution such as the Court to defend what it believed to be a fundamental feature of American politics. Or, stated somewhat differently, if the nation truly embraced the political theory that it celebrated, if—as was so widely proclaimed in American public life—the United States was the embodiment and standard bearer of democratic values, then it was reasonable for the Court to ensure that the nation's laws matched those values.[25]

As a matter of constitutional law, *Harper*'s significance resided in its innovative use of the equal protection clause of the Fourteenth Amendment.

From a broader, more historical standpoint, the case's significance was far greater and less technical: almost two centuries after the nation's founding, economic restrictions on voting had been abolished in all general elections. What once had been believed to be the most essential qualification for the franchise—the possession of property—formally had been judged irrelevant. The United States may have been the first nation to begin dismantling class limitations on the suffrage, but it was among the last to complete the process. That this final step was taken during a period of unprecedented wealth and prosperity, in an era marked by the celebration of the United States as a society in which class boundaries had dissolved (if they ever existed) was surely not a coincidence. Nor, perhaps, was it a coincidence that the author of the *Harper* opinion (like the chief justice himself) had grown up in dire poverty.[26]

The 1960s also witnessed the abolition of another vestigial class limitation on suffrage: the disfranchisement of paupers. Roughly half of the states that once had pauper exclusions had repealed them by 1960, but such laws—though rarely enforced after the 1930s—remained on the books in Delaware, Maine, Massachusetts, New Hampshire, Oklahoma, Rhode Island, South Carolina, Texas, Virginia, and West Virginia. (Missouri, in addition, excluded persons kept in "poorhouses.") As late as 1956, Congress, in drawing up a poll tax amendment (which eventually became the Twenty-fourth Amendment) considered adding a clause to permit states to retain their pauper exclusion provisions. In 1957, the Oklahoma Supreme Court tacitly sanctioned that state's pauper exclusion, while concluding that it did not apply to persons receiving old-age assistance.[27]

Still, by the 1960s such laws appeared to most Americans to be archaic and indefensible. Oklahoma eliminated its requirement in a referendum in 1964, and Maine did the same the following year. The *Harper* decision was the final nail in the coffin: its broad language made clear that pauper exclusion laws no longer could withstand judicial scrutiny. As a result, state legal codes and constitutions were revised to bring the letter of the law into line with the new reading of the federal Constitution. Remarkably, this process revealed that many Americans still believed that the dependent poor ought to remain disfranchised. In 1972, Massachusetts held a referendum on deleting the pauper exclusion clause from its constitution: the referendum passed, but more than 400,000 people (roughly 20 percent of the electorate) voted against it—and Massachusetts, in 1972, was the only state carried by the liberal Democratic presidential candidate, George McGovern. The people of Rhode Island affirmed that state's long history of contrariness by rejecting such an amendment altogether.[28]

The attack on economic qualifications quickly carried over into the last domain in which they endured: municipal or special-purpose elections that restricted the franchise to those who owned property or paid taxes. Once again the Supreme Court, rather than state governments or Congress, led the attack, and once again the equal protection clause of the Fourteenth Amendment was the Court's primary weapon. In *Kramer v. Union Free School District* (1969), the Court considered a challenge to the New York law that permitted residents of some school districts to vote in school elections only if they owned taxable real property in the district or had a child enrolled in the public schools. With Justices Stewart, Harlan, and Black again dissenting, the Court ruled that the law violated the equal protection clause. Writing for the majority and self-consciously establishing a precedent, Chief Justice Warren declared that any "statutes which deny some residents the right to vote" had to come under the "strict scrutiny" of the Court, that the Court's usual deference "to the judgment of legislators does not extend to decisions concerning which resident citizens may participate in the election of legislators and other public officials." This was so "because statutes distributing the franchise constitute the foundation of our representative society."[29]

Strict scrutiny was a concept that would loom large in later suffrage law, and what it meant was that any restriction on the franchise had to be "necessary to promote a compelling state interest." To pass strict scrutiny, exclusionary laws also had to be tailored with great precision, so that "all those excluded" were clearly less interested in or affected by the election's outcome than those who were permitted to vote. In typical judicial fashion, the Court declined to address the first issue—whether in theory there could be a state interest compelling enough to warrant exclusions in school elections—while announcing that New York's law had failed the second test. Many residents excluded by the law had an interest in the quality of the schools and were affected by the school budget and property tax rates.

What the Court had done in effect was to recognize the potential legitimacy of property-based restrictions in special elections, while setting the bar very high—almost impossibly high. Its stance was elaborated in another case decided simultaneously, *Cipriano v. Houma*. In that case, the Court overturned a Louisiana law that permitted property taxpayers alone to vote on the issuance of revenue bonds by a municipal utility: since the bonds were to be paid from the revenues of the utility, and nontaxpayers also used and paid for the utility, the Court ruled that the exclusion of nontaxpayers was illegitimate. The following year, the Court issued a similar yet more far-reaching decision regarding an Arizona statute that restricted the franchise to real property owners in elections approving the issuance of general obligation bonds (that would be paid back through taxes). In *City of Phoenix, Arizona v. Koldziejski,* the Court ruled that non–property owners were just as interested as property owners in public facilities funded through bonds, and they contributed to tax revenues by paying rent. The Arizona statute consequently was struck down. Within two years of the *Phoenix* decision, similar laws in nine other states were either repealed or overturned by the lower courts. One of the more significant, if relatively invisible, late-nineteenth- and twentieth-century strategies for circumventing the absence of general property qualifications had met its end.[30]

In the 1970s and 1980s, however, an increasingly conservative Supreme Court did establish a narrow exception to the ban on property requirements. In a series of cases beginning with *Salyer Land Company v. Tulare Lake Basin Water Storage District* (1973) and continuing through *Ball v. James* (1980), the Court ruled that participation in elections for entities such as water storage districts could be predicated on the ownership of property. The Court found that the powers and purposes of such entities were extremely limited and that the costs of their decisions were borne almost entirely by landowners. (The Court's "one person, one vote" rule, to be further discussed later in this chapter, also was suspended in such circumstances.) Although liberals on the Court dissented vigorously from what appeared to be a resurrection of class-based franchise requirements, the loophole was tiny and remains so to this day. The same was true of the Court's approval of the participation of property-owning nonresidents in some elections.[31]

Literacy Untested

The demise of literacy tests—which had served as a class barrier as well as a means of racial and ethnic screening—followed a different course. In 1959 (as noted in chapter 7), the Supreme Court—including Justice Douglas—sanctioned literacy tests as long as they were not administered in a racially discriminatory fashion; a decade later, in the *Gaston* case, the Court ruled that literacy tests were unacceptable in locales where schools had been segregated. Meanwhile, the Voting Rights Act already had led to the suspension of literacy tests in most southern states in 1965, a suspension that was extended to all states, for five years, in 1970.

The nationalization of the suspension of literacy tests had complex political roots: it was strongly advocated by the Nixon administration on the ostensibly principled grounds that literacy tests were discriminatory and antidemocratic wherever they occurred—and they were in force in a dozen northern states. "Voting rights," declared Attorney General John Mitchell, "is not a regional issue. It is a nationwide concern for every American." Extending the ban to all states, however, also was a means of placating southern opinion: it removed the regional stigma from the legislation and tweaked northern liberals, from states such as New York and California, with the implicit charge that their own houses might be in less than perfect order.[32]

In upholding the nationwide suspension of literacy tests in *Oregon v. Mitchell* (1970), the justices of the Supreme Court (in an array of concurring opinions) declined to repudiate the Court's earlier decision in *Lassiter* or to take a stance against literacy tests per se; instead it effectively nationalized the logic of the *Gaston* ruling. Blacks, as well as Native Americans and other minorities, received unequal and inferior educations in many locales in and out of the South, and this bias in educational opportunities hindered their ability to pass literacy tests. High rates of interstate migration, moreover, meant that literacy tests administered in states such as Arizona and New York could have the effect of disfranchising African Americans trained in segregated southern schools. "In imposing a nationwide ban on literacy tests," wrote Justice Black, "Congress has recognized a national problem for what it is—a serious national dilemma that touches every corner of our land." Although Justice Douglas hinted at other rationales as well (e.g., that thanks to radio and television, literacy was no longer necessary for a voter to become informed), the core of the Court's decision was that a national ban on literacy tests constituted a reasonable means of enforcing the Fifteenth Amendment.[33]

In light of the Court's argument, as well as evidence of ongoing inequalities in education, it is not surprising that in 1975 Congress decided with little debate to make the ban on literacy tests permanent. The conditions that had generated the national proscription of such tests in 1970 had not disappeared, and they seemed unlikely to disappear in the foreseeable future. Whether members of Congress supported a permanent ban because they subscribed to the constitutional argument linking education with literacy tests is unclear; surely there were numerous political leaders who simply believed that literacy was not a legitimate or meaningful qualification for voting. Whatever the rationale, literacy tests disappeared after 1975, and the permanent ban was never challenged in the Supreme Court. By 1975, most states even had provisions permitting the illiterate to receive assistance when voting (except by their employer or union representative), and the Voting Rights Act of 1975 required bilingual ballots and registration materials in areas with significant minority populations.[34]

This assembly of laws and rulings produced a dramatic change in the ground rules for voting in some states. In New York, for example, the presence of an English-language literacy test—once heralded as a model for the entire nation—meant that Italian and Jewish immigrants had been obliged to learn English and become literate in order to vote. After 1975, the Empire State was compelled not only to permit illiterate Hispanic and Asian-American citizens to vote but also to furnish them with ballots in their own language.

Mobile Voters

The nationwide banning of literacy tests was accompanied by the federal government's first effort to remove yet another obstacle to enfranchisement: lengthy durational residency requirements. Although some states had shortened their requirements, one year was still the norm, with shorter periods demanded in individual precincts and counties. The impact of these laws, in a society as peripatetic as the United States, was significant: according to one estimate, they kept 15 million people from voting in the 1964 elections. Congress, encouraged by Attorney General Mitchell, took direct aim at this issue in the 1970 amendments to the Voting Rights Act. With little fanfare or controversy, the 1970 legislation prohibited the states from imposing more than a thirty-day residency requirement in presidential elections; at the same time, it mandated that those who had relocated less than thirty days prior to an election could cast absentee ballots from their previous state of residence.[35]

The sources of this action are obscure, although several plausible hypotheses can be offered. Included as part of the Nixon administration's package of amendments to the 1965 Voting Rights Act, the short residency rule certainly (and perhaps deliberately) buttressed the Republican Party's presentation of itself as an advocate of universal suffrage and national reform. The rule also was a safe, uncontroversial means of responding to a resurgence of public concern about the decline in electoral turnout, a concern that may have increased its valence during the tumultuous 1960s. For Republicans and Democrats alike, moreover, the very process of thinking through the validity of other franchise qualifications easily could have led to the conclusion that lengthy residency requirements simply were unfair and undemocratic. Once the spotlight was focused on the issue of voting rights, all of the holes in the fabric were illumined.

In addition—and certainly more speculatively—the shift in thinking about residency rules may have been tied to a long-run change in the nature of geographic mobility in the United States. In the nineteenth century, when most of the residency rules were drafted, the most mobile Americans were workers, particularly semiskilled and unskilled workers. During the middle decades of the twentieth century, that pattern began to shift: the working class became less mobile, and the middle and upper classes far more mobile. Residency requirements by 1970 thus were screening out not only working-class transients but also the kinds of respectable middle-class voters that the laws originally had been designed to protect.[36]

The thirty-day rule in presidential elections was upheld by the Supreme Court in *Oregon v. Mitchell*. With only Justice Harlan dissenting, the Court found that Congress had the authority to regulate federal elections in this manner, through article 1, section 4 of the Constitution (which gives Congress the right to alter the "times, places and manner of holding" federal elections), article 4, section 2 (the privileges and immunities clause), or through the enforcement clause of the Fourteenth Amendment. Several of the justices also grounded their decisions in a constitutionally derived right of interstate travel, which was impeded by lengthy residency laws.[37]

Two years later, the Court took an additional giant step, prompted in part by a host of inconsistent rulings in the lower courts: it determined that Tennessee's residency requirement for *state* elections (one year in the state and ninety days in the county) violated the equal protection clause. Subjecting the law to the "strict scrutiny" test, the Court reversed a 1965 decision and concluded, in *Dunn v. Blumstein*, that no "compelling state interest" was served by any residency requirement longer than the period necessary for carrying out the process of registration. The "purity of the ballot box" could best be protected through other laws, and durational requirements were too crude a device for "assuring the knowledgeable exercise of the franchise." The Court suggested that a thirty-day residency period was sufficient, although in later cases it granted Arizona and Georgia permission to adopt fifty-day residency rules. Even before the *Dunn* decision, several states, such as Illinois, had been considering dramatic reductions in their residency requirements—in Illinois, this change was advocated both by rural Republicans and by Chicago Democrats who complained that people were disfranchised when they moved across the street—but the Supreme Court's action cut that process short.[38]

Other longstanding features of residency rules went overboard as well. As early as 1965, in *Carrington v. Rash*, the Supreme Court overturned a Texas law (similar to those in many states) that prevented members of the military from establishing residency. The state could not, the Court ruled, use "occupation" as a basis for discrimination; nor could it "fence out" from the franchise any segment of the population because of the way in which it might vote. Servicemen thus were subject to the same residency criteria (physical presence combined with intention) as other citizens. In addition, the rights of students were enhanced, through a long series of state and federal court cases.[39] Students also benefited from a general loosening of the legal definition of residency: in place of the traditional notion that one had to have the intention of remaining in a locale permanently or indefinitely, the intention to remain "for the time at least" began to suffice. By the 1980s, the courts were even ruling that the homeless could establish residency for voting purposes, in parks or wherever else they regularly slept; a state could not deny individuals the right to vote because they had "untraditional" residences or could not afford housing. The thrust of the law clearly had become to include rather than exclude, to incorporate citizens into the polity rather than to screen them out. At the end of the twentieth century, the definition of residency was broader than it ever had been, durational requirements in most states had been cut by 90 percent, and absentee ballots, almost everywhere, had become relatively easy to obtain.[40]

The Age of Reason

The years between 1970 and 1972 also witnessed the culmination of a long, if sporadic, campaign to lower the voting age. Since the nation's founding, a voting age of twenty-one—a carryover from colonial and English precedents—had been a remarkable constant in state laws governing the franchise. Proposals for lowering the age limit had appeared during or after every major war, on the grounds that men who were old enough to fight for their country were old enough to participate in its political decisions. Reasonable as this argument may have sounded, it had little effect on the prevailing consensus that twenty-one was the age of political maturity.[41]

The challenge to that consensus mounted during the mass mobilization of World War II. In 1942, in response to a lowering of the draft age to eighteen, Republican Senator Arthur Vandenberg and Democratic Representative Randolph Jennings sponsored a constitutional amendment to lower the voting age as well. "If young men are to be drafted at eighteen years of age to fight for their Government," declared Vandenberg, "they ought to be entitled to vote at eighteen years of age for the kind of government for which they are best satisfied to fight." Jennings pointed out that one quarter of the army, half the marine corps, and more than a third of the navy consisted of men under age twenty-one. The amendment received strong support from the National Education Association, which argued that the twentieth-century increase in the number of students graduating from high school meant that eighteen-year-olds now were amply prepared for full citizenship. The Vandenberg-Jennings proposal was referred to a committee, where it died a quiet death—to be joined in subsequent years by other, similar proposals. Numerous states also considered lowering the voting age during World War II, but only one, Georgia, did so.[42]

During the 1950s and into the 1960s, youth organizations, the National Education Association, and veterans groups such as the American Legion and the Veterans of Foreign Wars continued to press for state action, but their defeats were many and their successes few (Kentucky, Alaska, and Hawaii). As advocates of women's suffrage had discovered decades earlier, amending state constitutions was a slow and trying process. The youth vote movement, moreover, was inescapably weakened by the fact that its membership was inherently transitory. In Washington, however, support for a reduction in the voting age was growing. Perhaps reflecting his own military background, President Eisenhower in 1952 noted that "if a man is old enough to fight he is old enough to vote," and two years later he formally endorsed the idea of a constitutional amendment to lower the voting age.[43]

Eisenhower was joined by figures as diverse as liberal Democratic Senator Hubert Humphrey, Republican Kenneth Keating, and Oregon's maverick independent, Wayne Morse: both Republicans and Democrats thought they might reap partisan benefits from a lowered voting age. Although advocates of reform invariably pointed to the desirability of harnessing the energies of the young and drawing youth into politics, the primary argument, buttressed by the Korean War and the maintenance of a large cold war peacetime army, remained the link between military service and voting.[44]

One of the few public figures to question that link was Congressman Emanuel Celler, a New York Democrat with a high-ranking position on the critical House Judiciary Committee. "To my mind, the draft age and the voting age are as different as chalk is from cheese," Celler maintained. "The thing called for in a soldier is uncritical obedience, and that is not what you want in a voter."

> To say that he who is old enough to fight is old enough to vote is to draw an utterly fallacious parallel. No such parallel exists. The ability to choose, to separate promise from performance, to evaluate on the basis of fact, are the prerequisites to good voting. Eighteen to twenty-one are mainly formative years where the youth is racing forward to maturity. His attitudes shift from place to place. These are the years of the greatest uncertainties, a fertile ground for the demagogues. Youth attaches itself to promises, rather than to performance. These are rightfully the years of rebellion rather than reflection. We will be doing a grave injustice to democracy if we grant the vote to those under twenty-one.

Although polling data indicated that most Americans favored a reduction in the voting age (support rose dramatically between 1939 and 1952), Celler's views were shared widely enough to thwart any federal action; opposition also came from those who believed that the voting age was a state rather than federal matter. Congressional proponents of a lower voting age, moreover, simply did not regard it as a high-priority item.[45]

All this changed during the war in Vietnam. The unpopularity of the war spawned a widespread draft resistance movement, massive protests of college students, and an alarming radicalization of the young. In the political climate of the mid– and late 1960s, the issue of eighteen-, nineteen-, and twenty-year-olds voting acquired an unprecedented urgency; indeed, their lack of enfranchisement served, rhetorically at least, to underscore the absence of democratic support for the war and to legitimize resistance to the draft. As a result, numerous states began to reconsider the voting age, and support for a federal constitutional amendment became increasingly widespread, both among Republicans, including conservative Senator Barry Goldwater and President Nixon, and among liberal antiwar Democrats who believed that they would attract a majority of the youth vote. Meanwhile, formal lobbying and pressure group organizations appeared, including Let Us Vote (LUV) and the Youth Franchise Coalition, an umbrella group backed by a unique coalition of youth groups, liberal Democratic activists, the NAACP, church organizations, the National Student Association, the United Auto Workers, and some Republicans. The *New York Times* endorsed an age reduction on the grounds that "young people . . . are far better prepared educationally for the voting privilege than the bulk of the nation's voters have been through much of its history."[46]

The denouement of the drama was a tribute to the arcane workings of Congress and the intricacies of federalism. In the spring of 1970, with little advance notice, Senators Edward Kennedy, Warren Magnuson, and Majority Leader Mike Mansfield added a proposal for reducing the voting age, in all elections, to the amendments being prepared to the Voting Rights Act. Contrary to widely held views, Kennedy and Mansfield, backed by some constitutional scholars, maintained that Congress alone could change the voting age, that a constitutional amendment was not required. After a heated but brief debate, the Senate approved the measure by a wide, bipartisan margin and included it in its extension of the Voting Rights Act.[47]

This created a quandary for the House, particularly for Congressman Celler, now the chair of the Judiciary Committee. Most members of the House were convinced that the legislation was unconstitutional, many were reluctant to enfranchise student protestors, and Celler had vowed to kill the bill. If the House did not accept the entire Senate package, however, the Voting Rights Act extension would either go back to the Senate, where it could be filibustered to death, or to a conference committee, where numerous provisions of the carefully wrought act might be challenged and revised. Unwilling to jeopardize the extension of the Voting Rights Act, Celler and his colleagues reluctantly caved in and supported the age reduction as part of the package. Although he too thought the age reduction clause unconstitutional, President Nixon signed the bill, while urging its speedy testing in the courts.[48]

The issue came to the Supreme Court in *Oregon v. Mitchell.* Citing the equal protection clause, as well as the enforcement clause of the Fourteenth Amendment, four of the justices concluded that Congress did in fact have the right to lower the voting age in all elections. "It is a reasoned judgment," concluded Justice Douglas, "that those who have such a large 'stake' in modern elections as 18-year-olds, whether in times of war or peace, should have political equality." Four others reached the opposite conclusion, ruling that the age of enfranchisement was up to the states, for both federal and state elections. The balance was tipped by Justice Black, who rejected the equal protection argument but concluded that the Constitution, in article 1, section 4, gave Congress the right to set the voting age in—and only in—federal elections. The upshot of this complex verdict was a voting age of eighteen in federal elections coexisting with an age limit of twenty-one in almost all states.[49]

The prospect of a two-tiered age limit was an administrative and logistical nightmare for state election officials. Voters under age twenty-one would have to be registered and tracked separately; cities and towns would have to either purchase additional voting machines (and set them up in age-segregated booths) or utilize special machines constructed to permit selective blocking of particular electoral contests. The projected costs ran into the millions of dollars, and some states were not sure that the changes could be carried out before the 1972 elections. Compounding the problem was the fact that many states could not possibly alter their own constitutions to adopt a lower state voting age by 1972: doing so often required votes in successive legislatures followed by popular referenda.[50]

Faced with this crisis, Congress moved expeditiously to rectify the mess that it had helped to create. A month after the *Oregon* decision, now-Senator Jennings Randolph introduced a proposal for a constitutional amendment that barred the United States or any state from denying or abridging the right to vote of any citizen aged eighteen or over on account of age. In March 1971, the Senate, with no dissenting votes, approved the amendment. Within a few weeks, the House had done the same, with negative votes cast by only nineteen members, mostly conservative Republicans or southern Democrats. State legislatures then rushed to ratify the amendment. By the end of June, thirty-eight states had done so, and the Twenty-sixth Amendment was law. The ratification process was by far the most rapid in the history of the republic. At a White House ceremony certifying the ratification, President Nixon announced that he believed in "young Americans" who would "infuse into this country some idealism, some courage, some stamina, some high moral strength."[51]

A National Franchise

By 1975, the nation had witnessed a legal revolution, a revolution far broader in scope than the phrase "the second Reconstruction" might suggest. What occurred in the course of a decade was not only the reenfranchisement of African Americans but the abolition of nearly all remaining limits on the right to vote. Poll taxes, literacy tests, understanding clauses, pauper exclusions, and good character provisions had been swept away. Property and tax requirements for voting in special elections had been all but eliminated; durational residency qualifications had been drastically cut and the definition of residency broadened; the voting age had been lowered to eighteen, and language barriers had been dropped. The total number of new voters added to the electorate cannot be counted with precision, but the figure was surely in excess of twenty million.[52]

This revolution also constituted a nationalization of the right to vote. The Voting Rights Acts, coupled with a succession of Supreme Court decisions, effectively brought to a close the era of state control over suffrage. That long era had begun, in the late eighteenth century, when the founding fathers, for pragmatic political reasons, had chosen not to tinker with the laws already in place in the ex-colonies; and state supremacy had remained largely intact, despite the limits imposed by the Fourteenth, Fifteenth, and Nineteenth Amendments. Only in the 1960s and 1970s did the process of nationalization become broad-gauged and sweeping.

The impulse, and perhaps the will, to nationalize and expand the right to vote stemmed from a unique historical conjuncture, a confluence of forces pressing in the same direction. The international ideological competition of the cold war; the dynamics of military mobilization, accentuated by the war in Vietnam; the presence of a militant grassroots movement, primarily among blacks and later among students; the broad acceptance of formal democratic values that was a legacy of World War II: all of these forces contributed to the impulse to formally democratize the American polity. Once set in motion by the civil rights movement, moreover, the process of suffrage reform played out its own internal, if ultimately revolutionary, logic. The political leaders of the 1960s found themselves thinking through the issue of voting rights in a manner unparalleled since Reconstruction. Wittingly or not, they retraced the path traveled by Henry Wilson and his colleagues, journeying from a focus on black enfranchisement to an embrace of universal suffrage.

But in the 1960s and 1970s, in contrast to the 1860s and 1870s, this intellectual path was traversed at a time when class tensions were easing rather than accelerating, when they were at a historic low rather than a historic high. The New Deal's politically successful management of economic crisis, followed by extraordinary postwar prosperity and the bipartisan embrace of a politics of growth (rather than distribution) had put to rest many of the late-nineteenth- and early twentieth-century apprehensions about universal suffrage. In addition, the national government already had asserted its supremacy over the states in numerous legal and political domains.[53]

Furthermore, by the 1960s it was abundantly clear to both Congress and the courts that universal suffrage would not be achieved by the decentralized actions of the fifty states, each with its own historical legacy, its own political conflicts, its own minorities, and special issues. If the polity was going to be democratized, it would require action by the national government, in the name of the nation's publicly professed values. Notably—and reflecting historical precedents and the step-by-step dynamics of the intellectual and political process under way—the nationalization of suffrage was achieved not by the passage of a single national law but through a series of actions that compelled the states to adjust their laws to match the nation's democratic self-image and convictions. The piecemeal quality of this indirect approach was reflected in congressional passage of two constitutional amendments and three voting rights acts, as well as earlier civil rights acts.

The Supreme Court's views ran remarkably parallel to those of Congress; the two institutions in fact reinforced and prodded one another. Indeed, difficult as it is to discern the precise mechanisms through which political beliefs are mediated into constitutional interpretation, there can be little doubt that the Court's discovery of the applicability of the equal protection clause to voting rights represented the Court's own embrace of the internal logic of suffrage reform. If discriminating against blacks was wrong—and it was clearly proscribed by the Fifteenth Amendment—so too was discriminating against the very poor, the propertyless, the mobile, and the Spanish speaking. The Court's use of the equal protection clause was, in effect, a means of extending the ban on racial bars stated explicitly in the Fifteenth Amendment to other forms of discriminatory disfranchisement not expressly mentioned in the Constitution. The combination of the Court's rulings and congressional action meant that, despite the absence of a national suffrage law, state voting requirements in 1975 were far more uniform and substantially more democratic than those that existed a decade earlier.

The symbolic capstone of this legal revolution was provided, once again, by a change in the governmental structure of the nation's capital. Since 1874, after a brief experiment with democratic rule, the District of Columbia had been governed by a federally appointed commission. During the following century, and particularly after World War II, residents of Washington, many of them African American, periodically had demanded home rule for the city and representation in Congress. Their efforts invariably had been blocked—by, among others, Mississippi Senator Theodore Bilbo, who chaired the Senate Committee on the District, and later, South Carolina Representative John McMillan, the chair of the House Committee on the District of Columbia. By the late 1960s, however, what one Washington resident called "the absurdity that the capital of the leading nation of the free world is itself not free" had become too glaring to overlook, particularly given the city's African-American majority. In 1967, President Johnson, an advocate of home rule, succeeded in pushing through Congress a compromise reorganization plan that created an elected city council. Three years later, the district was permitted to elect a nonvoting representative to Congress. In 1973, after McMillan had been succeeded by an African-American chair of the key House committee, Congress passed the District of Columbia Self-Government and Governmental Reorganization Act, which gave the city an elected mayor as well as a city council. That act finally brought self-government to the "800,000 Americans—more people than in ten states of the Union" who had been "second-class citizens." Democracy had even come to Washington.[54]

The Value of the Vote

> And history has seen a continuing expansion of the scope of the right of suffrage in this country. The right to vote freely for the candidate of one's choice is of the essence of a democratic society, and any restrictions on that right strike at the heart of representative government. And the right of suffrage can be denied by a debasement or dilution of the weight of a citizen's vote just as effectively as by wholly prohibiting the free exercise of the franchise.
>
> —CHIEF JUSTICE EARL WARREN,
> MAJORITY OPINION, *Reynolds v. Sims* (1964)

The achievement of an essentially unrestricted national franchise did not bring an end to controversies over voting. Indeed, the legal transformation wrought in the 1960s segued—logically and then chronologically—into a prolonged series of conflicts over a related yet distinct issue: the value of each individual's vote. This critical, if perhaps ill-fated, development occurred for two reasons. First, the process of thinking about and redefining the breadth of the franchise led lawmakers, judges, and civilians almost inescapably to examine the electoral structures—such as the size of legislative districts—in which votes were cast. Second, conservatives, particularly in the South, repeatedly attempted to reduce the impact of an enlarged franchise by altering these structures, by changing the rules of the political game. The conflict over democratization thus endured, although the legal terrain shifted—from the right to vote itself to apportionment, districting, and the structure of representation.

Into the Thicket: One Person, One Vote

The stage was set for these conflicts by a series of Supreme Court rulings in the early 1960s, before passage of the Voting Rights Act. In *Baker v. Carr*, decided in 1962, the Court determined that the apportionment of state legislative seats in Tennessee could be challenged in federal courts under the equal protection clause of the Fourteenth Amendment. The ruling was a narrow, technical one (focused on whether inequalities of apportionment were a "justiciable" constitutional issue), but its implications were so potentially far-reaching that it provoked a lengthy and powerful dissent from Justice Felix Frankfurter, joined by Justice Harlan. Pointing to a historical record demonstrating that most state legislatures (as well as the federal government) had long been built on districts with unequal populations, Frankfurter insisted that the issue belonged to a "class of political controversy which, by the nature of its subject, is unfit for federal judicial action." Harlan maintained that he could "find nothing in the Equal Protection Clause or elsewhere in the Federal Constitution which expressly or impliedly supports the view that state legislatures must be so structured as to reflect with approximate equality the voice of every voter." Such a proposition "strikes deep into the heart of our federal system." The majority disagreed, and in so doing, plunged into what Frankfurter had called the "political thicket" of apportionment issues, a terrain that the courts had never before entered.[55]

A year later, in *Gray v. Sanders*, the Court built on *Baker v. Carr* and struck down Georgia's "county unit" primary system that weighted "rural votes more heavily than urban votes and weighted some small rural counties heavier than other larger rural counties." According to the Court, this violated not only the equal protection clause but the very notion of equality undergirding American democracy. In another of his ringing phrases, Justice Douglas—undeterred by the historical record that Frankfurter had laid out in great detail—maintained that "the conception of political equality from the Declaration of Independence, to Lincoln's Gettysburg Address, to the Fifteenth, Seventeenth, and Nineteenth Amendments can mean only one thing—one person, one vote." In 1964, the Court again took aim at Georgia, because the populations of its congressional districts were not even roughly similar: this, the Court ruled, ran afoul of article 1, section 2 of the Constitution (which provided that representatives should be chosen "by the people"). "To say that a vote is worth more in one district than in another would . . . run counter to our fundamental ideas of democratic government."[56]

Later that same year, in *Reynolds v. Sims*, the Court further extended the power of the federal government over state electoral arrangements by striking down Alabama's districting system for its state legislature because it permitted counties with only 25 percent of the state's population to elect a majority of the representatives to both legislative branches. (Only Justice Harlan dissented; Frankfurter had retired.) Citing the equal protection clause once again, Chief Justice Warren, for the Court, declared that "legislators represent people, not trees or acres" and that the "right to vote" of those living in underrepresented areas "is simply not the same right to vote as that of those living in a favored part of the State." Confronting an obvious counterargument head-on, Warren insisted that unequal state apportionment schemes could not be analogized to the United States Senate or the electoral college: those arose "from unique historical circumstances," including the "compromise and concession indispensable to the establishment of our federal republic." The states that formed the union once had been "sovereign entities," which was not true of counties, cities, or other "political subdivisions." It was legitimate therefore for each state to have two senators, regardless of its population, but it was not legitimate for state legislatures to mirror that structure.[57]

In key respects, the arguments and the history leading to the Court's embrace of one person, one vote closely paralleled its repudiation of economic qualifications for voting in *Harper v. Virginia*. Justices Frankfurter and Harlan surely were correct that neither the founding fathers nor the authors of the Fourteenth Amendment believed that an arithmetic equality of votes had to underlie all schemes of representation. The justices also were on solid ground in claiming that it was not irrational for states to factor in other considerations (such as geography or balancing rural versus urban interests) in devising systems of representation, and that these were essentially political matters or questions of political philosophy that belonged more appropriately in the hands of elected legislators than the judiciary. Yet Douglas and Warren too had a point. Democracy indeed could be undone or circumvented through districting mechanisms as well as through disfranchisement, and the historical record strongly suggested that those who wielded disproportionate power in state governments were unlikely to surrender that power voluntarily. It was unrealistic to expect that an undemocratic distribution of power could be reformed democratically. Consequently, if the judiciary did not act, if it failed to establish a yardstick for assessing the democratic content of electoral structures, the door would be open to a wide range of abuses.

The upshot of this assembly of cases was a broadening of the legally operative definition of the right to vote. By 1965, the Constitution was interpreted to mean that individuals not only had the right to register, cast their ballots, and have their ballots counted, but also that they had the right to have their votes count as much as the votes of other citizens. Votes could not be weighted more heavily in some locales than in others; nor could voting districts be significantly unequal in population. The federal government, moreover, had assumed responsibility for judging the legality and legitimacy of federal, state, and local electoral arrangements—and it would have to make those judgments and apply the one person, one vote standard each time that the nation's population was counted.

Preclearance and the Totality of Circumstances

By the late 1950s, the city of Tuskegee, Alabama, contained a sizable number of African Americans who had succeeded in becoming registered voters. Indeed, black registrants were sufficiently numerous that they posed a threat to white political control of the city. To meet this threat, the state legislature completely redrew the city's boundaries, creating a bizarre twenty-eight-sided municipality with an almost entirely white population: blacks found themselves consigned to the surrounding counties, where they lacked the numbers to wield much influence. The legislature's step was not unprecedented: racial districting had been a common form of political warfare throughout the South, particularly in the years before the wholesale disfranchisement of the black population. What happened in Tuskegee was unusually flagrant, however, and the city's black citizens, emboldened by the civil rights movement, mobilized collectively to protest the new city boundaries. In response to these protests, and acting under the Civil Rights Act of 1957, the Justice Department promoted a lawsuit by local black citizens. For the first time in the twentieth century, the Supreme Court in 1960 heard a case involving racial gerrymandering (*Gomillion v. Lightfoot*), and led by Justice Frankfurter, the Court ruled that the legislature's action was a clear violation of the Fifteenth Amendment.[58]

The events in Tuskegee (and similar developments elsewhere) served notice to civil rights activists and Justice Department lawyers that many white Southerners were not prepared to share political power with blacks. If the federal government insisted on black enfranchisement, conservative Southerners would attempt to vitiate its consequences by altering the structures of representation. Deannexation, as had occurred in Tuskegee, was one way of doing so; annexation (of white populations) was another. Racial gerrymandering could take the form of cracking (i.e., dividing minority voters into several districts) or stacking (i.e., loading voters into a single district). In the numerous cities with white majorities but sizable black populations, whites could maintain a monopoly on political power by having all city council members elected "at large" rather than from single-member districts. A similar result could be achieved by insisting on majority runoffs rather than plurality victories. Given the long history of racial discrimination and the recent history of massive resistance to civil rights, it would have been surprising if southern whites in the 1960s had not turned to such mechanisms to remain in power.

No doubt it was with this in mind, as historian J. Morgan Kousser has argued, that the Voting Rights Act insisted on the federal "preclearance" of any new "voting qualification or prerequisite to voting or standard, practice, or procedure with respect to voting" in all locales that had a history of discrimination. As Attorney General Nicholas Katzenbach testified to Congress during hearings on the Voting Rights Act, "there are an awful lot of things that could be started for purposes of evading the Fifteenth Amendment if there is the desire to do so." The preclearance procedure—requiring targeted states and counties to get federal approval for any new or changed electoral procedures—was a mechanism designed to prevent recalcitrant white Southerners from undermining the effectiveness of black enfranchisement.[59]

The scope of the preclearance provision (section 5) was unclear during the first years after passage of the Voting Rights Act, and the mechanism was little used. This changed dramatically in 1969, as a result of a cluster of lawsuits that came before the Supreme Court. Originating in Mississippi and Virginia, these cases involved an array of different alterations in electoral structures: a shift from district to at-large voting for county supervisors, the appointment rather than election of superintendents of education, new rules governing the ability of independent candidates to secure a place on the ballot, and modifications in the procedures for write-in ballots. Bringing the cases together under one decision (*Allen v. State Board of Elections*), the Court ruled that all of these changes were subject to the pre-clearance provision of the Voting Rights Act. Rejecting the claim that section 5 applied only to laws governing the registration of voters, the Court concluded that the Voting Rights Act "was aimed at the subtle, as well as the obvious" and thus that all modifications of electoral laws were to be screened by the Justice Department for their potentially discriminatory effects. Two years later, the Court affirmed this broad interpretation, finding that the preclearance provision applied also to municipal annexations and the relocation of polling places.[60]

The Court's actions meant that any state or county covered by the trigger mechanism of the Voting Rights Act (i.e., those with histories of discrimination) had to clear all changes in its electoral rules with the Justice Department. This requirement generated heavy traffic in the wake of the 1970 Census, as states redistricted to meet the one person, one vote requirement of *Reynolds v. Sims* and tried to seize the opportunity to create racially biased structures and procedures. Despite the initial hesitance of the Nixon administration, the Justice Department enforced the Voting Rights Act with some vigor; it consequently found itself screening thousands of changes in electoral law, more than two hundred of which were rejected. In subsequent years, in response to the ingenuity of southern conservatives, the federal courts enlarged the reach of the preclearance provision, as did Congress with its 1975 extension of the Voting Rights Act to cover language minorities.[61]

In addition, the courts wrestled with constitutional challenges to potentially discriminatory schemes that were not subject to the preclearance clause: those adopted before 1965 (and thus were not changes in the law per se) and those in states and counties not under direct federal supervision. In 1971, in an Indiana case, the Court made clear that multimember districts (i.e., those in which more than one representative was elected by a particular geographic unit) were not necessarily unconstitutional, but were suspect—because they created an opportunity for elections to be structurally stacked against black voters. In 1973, the Court went a step further, unanimously striking down multimember districts in two Texas counties because they diluted the votes of African Americans and Mexican Americans. Its decision was based on a close inspection of the "totality of circumstances" enveloping the districting system, including the state's lengthy history of racial discrimination. Implicit in the ruling was the notion that blacks and Hispanics would have greater political representation if districts were smaller and each elected only one official. The totality of circumstances standard was refined and given specificity by a circuit court in *Zimmer v. McKeithen* (1973), and the Zimmer test was widely applied for the remainder of the 1970s. In practice, the test rendered at-large and multimember district elections suspect throughout the South.[62]

The totality of circumstances standard emerged from the Court's dawning recognition of the complexity of the problem that it faced: How in effect was a court to tell whether a districting system—or any other electoral arrangement—discriminated against blacks or other minorities? The easy cases were those where discriminatory *intent* could be established, but by the 1970s, southern lawmakers—having learned the lesson of *Gomillion*—were sufficiently sophisticated to make intent difficult to prove. New laws invariably were accompanied by racially neutral justifications, such as administrative efficiency. Alternatively, a finding of discrimination could be based on the *effects* of new electoral arrangements, but this too had hazards: the fact that an electoral structure left minorities unrepresented, for example, did not prove unlawful discrimination. Interest groups that could not muster a majority always were unrepresented as a result of elections; that was how the system worked. The totality of circumstances standard—which embraced both intentions and effects—was a strategy for coping with this dilemma, but it did not necessarily provide clear answers. The standard implied that courts ought to consider the effects of electoral arrangements, but how were the effects of an annexation or districting system to be gauged? What was it that had to be measured, and to what should such measures be compared? What was the yardstick that told whether the effects of at-large voting or deannexation were illegally discriminatory?[63]

The most obvious answer to such questions would have been the adoption of some form of proportional representation for racial minorities: the percentage of minority elected officials ought to be roughly comparable to the minority percentage of the population. If African Americans constituted one third of the inhabitants of a city or state, they should have one third of the representatives, and a legitimate electoral structure would make that happen. Without such a standard, the voices of a long-oppressed minority would continue to be muffled. Yet this obvious answer was not easy to accept. A system of racially based proportional representation was repugnant to the traditional American emphasis on individual rather than group rights; it violated the integrationist norm of race blindness; and it conveyed the balkanizing implication that blacks could only be represented adequately by other blacks. In addition, racially based proportional representation privileged the collective political rights of some groups over others. If blacks and Hispanics were entitled to a certain percentage of a city's representatives, what about Asians, Jews, Catholics, or union members?[64]

The Supreme Court struggled, with much internal debate, to find some middle ground on which to stand, a way to be sensitive to the history of racial discrimination without imposing proportional representation or opening a new Pandora's box of claims for representation by nonracially defined social or political groups.[65] The result was something of a muddle, shaped in part by the growing conservatism of the post–Warren Court. In 1973, the Court allowed Petersburg, Virginia, to annex white neighborhoods from an adjacent county (which would give the city a white rather than black majority); at the same time, however, it advised the city to switch to district rather than at-large elections to give blacks greater representation. Two years later, the Court permitted nearby Richmond to annex a white neighborhood and adopt a new districting system, because the overall plan "fairly" recognized "the minority's political potential" and offered African Americans representation "reasonably equivalent to their political strength in the enlarged community." The next year, a majority of the Court veered in a different direction, sanctioning a New Orleans proposal that would increase black representation on the city council from what it had been, but not to a level proportional to the black population of the city. The Court did not consider the plan to be in violation of the Voting Rights Act because there was no "retrogression" in the "effective exercise of the electoral franchise" by blacks. Liberal dissenters on the Court objected loudly, stressing that the absence of "retrogression" was a woefully inadequate standard and that there had to be "legislative representation roughly proportional to the Negro population."[66]

In 1977, in *United Jewish Organizations of Williamsburgh, Inc. v. Carey*, the Court dealt head-on, if clumsily, with the balkanizing issue: it rejected the Fourteenth and Fifteenth Amendment claims of a group of 30,000 Hasidic

Jews in Brooklyn who found themselves split up between two districts because of an apportionment plan that sought to produce "nonwhite majorities" in those districts. The Jewish community claimed that the plan greatly diminished its chance of electing one of its own members to office. The Court ruled, however, that for the purposes of districting Hasidic Jews were simply "white" (whatever their own view of their cultural identity), that whites on the whole were adequately represented, and that it was permissible for race to be used as a factor in drawing district boundaries.[67]

This less-than-coherent attempt to find middle ground came to an abrupt halt in 1980, when the Supreme Court jettisoned the Zimmer criteria and the totality of circumstances standard in *City of Mobile, Alabama v. Bolden*. Mobile had been governed since 1911 by a three-person commission, chosen in at-large elections. Although Mobile's population was 35 percent black, no African American ever had been elected to the commission. Applying the totality of circumstances approach, a federal district court (sustained by the appeals court) found sufficient evidence of dubious voting practices and historical discrimination to rule that black voting strength had been diluted in violation of the Fourteenth and Fifteenth Amendments and the Voting Rights Act. A very fragmented Supreme Court (issuing six separate opinions) overturned the verdict, concluding that there was insufficient evidence of discriminatory intent and that only actions undertaken with "racially discriminatory motivation" were unconstitutional or illegal under the Voting Rights Act. The Court ruled that the absence of black commissioners was not by itself evidence of discrimination, that there was no Fourteenth Amendment right to proportional representation, and that at-large voting always disadvantaged minorities of different types. Four of the justices further maintained that the Fifteenth Amendment applied only to the actual exercise of the franchise, not to vote dilution or districting.[68]

Mobile v. Bolden simplified the law while making it far more difficult for claims of vote dilution to be sustained. Proving an overt discriminatory intent, rather than deducing intent from the consequences of a law, was extremely difficult: in the immediate aftermath of the decision, numerous suits were dismissed or withdrawn, judgments reversed, and challenges to at-large voting systems turned down in the lower courts because of lack of evidence of deliberate discrimination. Civil rights advocates were enraged by what appeared to be the Court's reversal of precedent and its becoming—in the words of Justice Marshall's vehement dissent—"an accessory to the perpetuation of racial discrimination."[69]

Thanks to the happenstance of timing, the reign of *Bolden* was brief. In 1982, when the Voting Rights Act was being renewed by Congress, liberal Democrats, joined by moderate Republicans, rewrote the law to put greater emphasis on effects than on intent. Recognizing the near impossibility of proving deliberate and purposeful discrimination, section 2 of the amended law, as drafted by Senator Robert Dole, prohibited any voting standard or procedure that "results in a denial or abridgement of the right of any citizen ... to vote on account of race or color." This replaced the original language, which implied that a state law violated the Voting Rights Act only if discriminatory intent could be established. The amended act underscored this shift by declaring that a standard or procedure was illegal if

> based on the totality of circumstances, it is shown that the political processes leading to nomination or election in the State or political subdivision are not equally open to participation by members of a class of citizens protected by subsection (a) in that its members have less opportunity than other members of the electorate to participate in the political process and to elect representatives of their choice. The extent to which members of a protected class have been elected to office in the State or political subdivision is one circumstance which may be considered.

In a disclaimer important to conservatives and some smaller minority groups, the bill also contained an explicit rejection of proportional representation: "Provided, That nothing in this section establishes a right to have members of a protected class elected in numbers equal to their proportion in the population."

The totality of circumstances standard had been restored. Two days after President Reagan signed the Voting Rights Act extension, the Supreme Court signaled the change in direction by easing the requirements for establishing proof of intent in Fourteenth Amendment cases, ruling that circumstantial evidence could be sufficient to establish discrimination.[70]

Defining Dilution

Restoring the totality of circumstances approach also meant restoring its attendant problems and confusions. As a result, the lower courts were uncertain about how to proceed and inconsistent in their rulings. In 1986, the Supreme Court attempted to clarify matters in a North Carolina redistricting case,

Thornburg v. Gingles. In yet another fragmented decision, the Court articulated a set of conditions that had to be met to establish that a multimember or at-large districting plan illegally diluted the votes of an African-American minority. First, the minority had to be "sufficiently large and geographically compact to constitute a majority of a single district." Second, it had to be "politically cohesive." Third, there had to be evidence, over time, that whites voted as a bloc in such a way as to "usually" defeat black candidates. Other factors (such as those from the Zimmer test) could certainly be weighed to help determine whether a plan was illegally discriminatory, but the presence of racially polarized voting—measured through standard statistical methods—was the heart of what became known as the Gingles test. If whites tended strongly to vote for white candidates and blacks for black candidates, then a legitimate districting system ought to produce both white and black representatives.[71]

The *Gingles* decision was hailed as a victory for civil rights advocates, largely because it confirmed the Court's retreat from the imposition of an "intent" standard. But *Gingles* did not end either the confusion or juridical zigzagging. For one thing, its guidelines were not readily applicable to all types of vote dilution cases, particularly those where multimember districts were not at stake. In addition, many of the key terms of the Gingles test were subject to interpretation, including *geographic compactness, cohesive, usually,* and even *majority.* (Could blacks and Hispanics, for example, be combined to form the majority of a new single-member district?) It also was unclear to the lower courts whether the three prongs of the Gingles standard had replaced the totality of circumstances approach or whether they should serve instead as an efficient way to do a first screening of potential claims. Nonetheless, the decision facilitated the adjudication of many cases, and it encouraged both the lower courts and the Justice Department to promote single-member and "minority opportunity" districts in the numerous locales where the Gingles criteria were met. Indeed, the Court's ruling served as a mandate, for state lawmakers as well as Justice Department officials engaged in the preclearance process, to create "majority-minority" voting districts in cities and states that contained sizable minority populations and had a record of racially polarized voting.[72]

It was precisely that mandate that led to the next sharp turn in the road. In redrawing the boundaries of congressional districts after the 1990 Census, legislators in North Carolina devised a plan that would create two predominantly black districts: this was done after an earlier plan with only one minority district was rejected by the Justice Department as insufficiently sensitive to the rights of black citizens. The shape of the second majority-minority district, the Twelfth, was "dramatically irregular," snaking 160 miles along an interstate highway between Charlotte and Durham: an African-American state representative quipped that if "you drove down the interstate with both car doors open, you'd kill most of the people in the district." That the boundaries of the Twelfth District were drawn with close attention to its racial composition was undisguised.

This new districting plan was challenged in a lawsuit filed by five white residents who claimed that their Fourteenth Amendment rights to equal protection had been violated by this pro–African American racial gerrymander. Those who brought the suit did not and could not claim that the votes of whites had been diluted: even if there were two black representatives to Congress, the white population still would be overrepresented in comparison to its proportion of the population. The plaintiffs charged instead that creating districts on the basis of race was per se unconstitutional and "violated their constitutional right to participate in a 'color-blind' electoral process." Two of the three judges on an appeals court panel (both of whom had initially heard *Gingles* as well) rebuffed this claim and dismissed some of its more arcane arguments.[73]

The Supreme Court, however, reversed that decision by a narrow five to four vote in *Shaw v. Reno* (1993). Writing for the majority, Justice Sandra Day O'Connor (joined by Justices Rehnquist, Scalia, Kennedy, and Thomas) ruled that districting plans based on race were subject to "strict scrutiny" and that the North Carolina proposal was "so irrational on its face" that it could only be understood as an attempt to "segregate voters" racially. By ignoring traditional districting criteria (compactness, most importantly) and drawing boundaries based "solely" on race, North Carolina legislators were engaging in a form of "racial classification" that posed "a risk of lasting harm to our society." According to O'Connor, racial classification itself was a wrong: racially defined voting districts, such as North Carolina's Twelfth, would exacerbate patterns of bloc voting, reinforce racial stereotyping by suggesting that "members of the same racial group" voted alike, and lead elected officials to believe that their "primary obligation" was to represent only members of their own racial group rather than the entire district. At the heart of O'Connor's opinion was the insistence on the constitutional and moral primacy of color-blindness. "Racial gerrymandering, even for remedial purposes, may balkanize us into competing racial factions; it threatens to carry us further from the goal of a political system in which race no longer matters—a goal that the Fourteenth and Fifteenth Amendments embody, and to which the Nation continues to aspire." Minority opportunity districts thus were illegal if they departed significantly from traditional conceptions of compactness.[74]

The dissents to O'Connor's opinion were sharp. In the last opinion that he wrote before retiring, Justice Byron White maintained that the appropriate question was not whether there were racial classifications but whether such classifications discriminated "against anyone by denying equal access to the political process"; in this case, he asserted, they clearly did not. White also insisted that the geography of a district was irrelevant to the constitutional issues. Justice David Souter pointed out that the Voting Rights Act required legislators to classify voters according to race in locales with a history of bloc voting; and since the Court was not challenging the Voting Rights Act, it seemed contradictory to deem racial classification to be illegal. Several of the dissenters, as well as many civil rights lawyers, voiced the hope that the holdings in *Shaw* would be confined to unusual cases, instances in which minority opportunity districts were as geographically bizarre as they were in North Carolina.[75]

Such hopes were disappointed. Shortly after *Shaw* was decided, a challenge was mounted to Georgia's districts, particularly its elongated majority-minority Eleventh District. This challenge was sustained by the Supreme Court in *Miller v. Johnson*, which broadened and developed the reasoning in *Shaw*. Although acknowledging that race commonly and legitimately would be a consideration in districting decisions, the Court ruled that it could not be the predominant factor and could not submerge traditional districting principles; a majority-minority district could withstand close scrutiny only if "convincing evidence" were presented that such remedial action was necessary for compliance with the Voting Rights Act. The majority opinion, written by Justice Kennedy, criticized the Justice Department for pressuring states to maximize black representation and hinted that the Voting Rights Act itself might violate the Fourteenth Amendment.[76]

Meanwhile, in another Georgia case, *Holder v. Hall*, the Court declined to offer support to black plaintiffs seeking to increase their voice in government. The case originated in Bleckley County, Georgia, a county that was 20 percent black. Bleckley had been governed since 1912 by a one-person commission, and the elected commissioner always had been white. In the mid–1980s, the Georgia legislature authorized the county to adopt a six-person commission, five of whom would be elected by single-member districts, but the electorate voted not to adopt the plan. Six African-American voters sued, seeking to compel the courts to institute a multimember commission so that blacks could be represented in the county government. In a fragmented set of opinions, the Court refused to do so. Justice Kennedy argued that the size of a county's government was not a "standard, practice, or procedure" under the Voting Rights Act; both he and Justice O'Connor further believed that the courts could not take action in the absence of a benchmark indicating how large a government body should be or what degree of minority representation would be appropriate. The logic was peculiar, but clearly stated. "Where there is no objective and workable standard for choosing a reasonable benchmark by which to evaluate a challenged voting practice, it follows that the voting practice cannot be challenged as dilutive."[77]

Far more controversial was the concurrence written by Justice Clarence Thomas (joined by Justice Antonin Scalia): it amounted to a wholesale assault on recent trends in voting rights law by the Court's one African-American justice. Calling for "a systematic reassessment," Thomas maintained that the legal definition of the "right to vote" ought to be narrowed back to its pre–1969, pre-*Allen* parameters: he argued that the Voting Rights Act guaranteed individuals the right to cast their votes and have them "fairly counted" but not the right to be protected against vote dilution. "By construing the Act to cover potentially dilutive electoral mechanisms, we have immersed the federal courts in a hopeless project of weighing questions of political theory—questions judges must confront to establish a benchmark concept of an 'undiluted' vote." Thomas rejected the notion that proportionality was an apt benchmark and dismissed the totality of circumstances standard as "an empty incantation . . . that serves to hide the drive for proportionality that animates our decisions." Even more "pernicious," Thomas maintained, was the prevailing assumption "that members of racial and ethnic groups must all think alike on important matters of public policy." Although much criticized, Thomas's opinion certainly made clear his own objective: undoing the 1982 amendments to the Voting Rights Act and terminating the Court's attempts to superintend the racial composition of electoral districts.[78]

These three cases—*Shaw, Miller,* and *Holder*—were critical steps in what was becoming a disorderly retreat from the effort to prevent the dilution of minority votes and promote the election of minority officials. In a handful of additional cases decided between 1994 and 1998, an always divided and sometimes splintered Supreme Court promoted color-blind districting while refusing to outlaw majority-minority districts per se. The Court ruled that states had no obligation to maximize the number of such districts as long as minorities were reasonably represented, yet it refused to endorse demographic proportionality as a benchmark of reasonableness. The Court continued to insist, as it had in *Miller*, that race could not be the predominant factor in districting, but it offered no clear definition of *predominance* and declined to reveal how minority opportunity districts could be created without conscious effort. The Court was divided about the importance of compactness or bizarre shapes in drawing district boundaries, and it seemed bewildered by the challenge of disentangling racial motives from the more traditional (and acceptable) partisan motives that had long played a role in districting decisions. On more than one occasion, opinions suggested that a collision was brewing between the Voting Rights Act and the Fourteenth Amendment: the former seemed to mandate race-conscious remedies, while the latter was interpreted as a constitutional requirement to be color-blind.

Not surprisingly, uncertainty reigned among the lower courts and in the civil rights division of the Justice Department. In 1996, the confusion and bitterness surrounding the issue prompted the generally temperate Justice Souter to call for the Court's "withdrawal from the presently untenable state of the law." An apt symbol of the state of affairs was the enduring uncertainty of the boundaries of North Carolina's congressional districts: districting schemes designed to satisfy the cross pressures of the law shuttled from the legislature to the Justice Department to the district court to the Supreme Court and then back again. *Shaw v. Reno* (which became known as Shaw I) was followed by *Shaw v. Hunt* (Shaw II) in 1996; in November 1999, a third legal incarnation was about to be heard by a panel of federal judges.[79]

Politics and Theory

The conflicts over districting and dilution issues—conflicts that have split the Supreme Court, generated sharp polemics among legal scholars, and helped to kill President Clinton's nomination of Lani Guinier as Assistant Attorney General for Civil Rights in 1993—have had multiple sources. Most superficially, these conflicts have been partisan. African Americans as well as Latinos have tended to vote overwhelmingly Democratic, and enhancing their voting power consequently serves the interests of the Democratic Party and disadvantages Republicans. (The partisan advantages of particular schemes are, however, not always obvious: creating a predominantly black district, for example, could help the Democrats to win in that district while hurting its chances elsewhere.) State legislators always have drawn district boundaries and devised other electoral mechanisms with one eye on their partisan impact, and it is no accident that the political parties and allied foundations have played a role in voting rights litigation. Conservative Republican Senator Jesse Helms, for example, filed an amicus brief in *Shaw v. Reno*. Partisan interests no doubt also shaped the thinking of formal, ostensibly neutral participants in the battle, including district court judges and Justice Department lawyers. Even the august members of the Supreme Court do not seem to be immune to ideological considerations that serve partisan interests: the Court often has divided largely on partisan lines—and broad swings in its position have coincided with its changing political composition.[80]

The legal knots and partisan alignments have also mirrored broader currents in popular attitudes toward race. The egalitarian impulses so celebrated in the 1960s have been blunted in recent decades, and large segments of white society have come to oppose programs that have privileged racial minorities in order to remedy and rectify past injustices. Affirmative action policies, in hiring and education, have been strenuously attacked by Republican politicians and often been vitiated by elected officials or successfully challenged in the courts. That the implementation of the Voting Rights Act has drawn similar fire is altogether congruent with this conservative drift: the act, particularly as amended and as interpreted by the Warren Court, constituted an affirmative action program in the arena of electoral participation. Particularly for Republicans, consistently supported by a majority of white voters in the South, opposition to the aggressive enforcement of the Voting Rights Act has been a popular as well as self-interested stance.

The Supreme Court's difficulties with vote dilution have deeper roots as well, roots both theoretical and historical. Justice Thomas was correct to point out that vote dilution cases had drawn the Court into questions of "political theory" and that there was no generally accepted theory of representation undergirding American politics. Historically, structures of representation in the United States had been grounded in the relatively unarticulated (and untested) presumption that both individual and communal interests ought to be, and could be, served through geographically based voting units. The right to vote and to representation inhered in the individual, but the communities to which they belonged also had some collective interests and therefore deserved to have some voice in governance—which was why counties were represented in many legislatures and all states had United States senators. In the course of the nineteenth and twentieth centuries, however, the identification of individuals with their once-homogeneous geographic communities declined, while their sense of belonging to other types of communities—religious, racial, ethnic, occupational—became more salient. Concomitantly, the laws governing elections, like most areas of law, increasingly stressed the primacy and protection of individual rights. This trend culminated in the one person, one vote doctrine that emerged from the Supreme Court in the 1960s: voting was judged to be a purely individual right that took precedence over any communal or collective interests. The equal weighting of individual votes could not be undermined by the representation of "trees, land," particular economic interests, or any other feature of a geographic community.[81]

This purely individualistic conception of the right to vote was a coherent one, and given many features of the nation's history, it was natural that the Court embraced it. But the conception of voting as a purely individual right could produce a truly egalitarian politics only if one presumed that there were no structural biases in the ways in which individual votes were aggregated. Yet this was not the case in the United States in 1965 or 1970: a host of electoral rules led to the aggregation of individual votes in such a way as to make it extremely difficult for members of long-oppressed minority groups to elect candidates whom they preferred. This lack of representation of minority communities and their community interests became recognized as the problem of vote dilution: what was diluted, after all, was not the individual's vote but the community's influence. The Supreme Court's early decisions in dilution cases, beginning with *Allen* in 1969, constituted a recognition of this fact, as well as a largely tacit effort to reincorporate communal interests into the structures of representative government.

Doing so, however, raised two inevitable and critical questions. First, which communities were to be represented? The Court dodged most of the hornets in that nest by invoking the language of the Fifteenth Amendment and the Voting Rights Act: only racial and some "minority language" communities; not Hasids, who were assigned to the white community. The answer was clear, if intellectually unsatisfying.

The second question was more difficult: If representation were to be based even in part on communal interests, how much representation were communities entitled to? This seemingly abstract question had to be answered for judges to decide cases; otherwise, they could not know whether communities already had sufficient representation. As Justice Thomas and others noted, however, there were no guidelines in the Constitution or elsewhere in American law that addressed the issue. The most obvious approach would have been to decide that representation should be proportional to the demographic size of the minority community, but both Congress and the Court resisted such a decision—in part because there were no agreed-on norms that would have justified it, and in part because it would have meant explicitly jettisoning the more accepted individualistic theory of representation. As a result, the Court was unmoored and drifted uneasily for more than two decades between the Scylla of pure individualism and the Charybdis of demographic proportionality. Without a normative theory of representation, the issues before the Court were insoluble. Either some benchmark—some standard of adequate community representation—had to be adopted, or, as an increasing number of judges seemed to be thinking, the effort to prevent vote dilution would have to be abandoned.[82]

This impasse has led a number of scholars—most visibly, Harvard law professor and former friend of Bill Clinton, Lani Guinier—to propose a more far-reaching transformation of American electoral procedures: the replacement of winner-take-all elections in single-member districts with a broad-based system of proportional representation. Under proportional representation schemes (and there are many), the losers in elections are not left completely unrepresented; as long as they reach a certain threshold of votes, parties or slates of candidates still win seats in city councils, county commissions, and legislatures. Minorities therefore can be represented without contorting the boundaries of political units. Such arrangements, moreover, can circumvent the ideological hazards of essentialism (e.g., presuming that all blacks have identical interests) and of privileging particular communities. All minority groupings—not simply racial ones—would have a chance at representation, and the groupings (or communities) themselves could be fluid over time, depending on the ways in which individuals defined their own interests. Proportional representation would encourage the emergence of multiple parties, and individuals could vote for a black candidate in one election, a class-based candidate in the next, and a Hasid in the third.[83]

Whether the legal and political struggles over the "value of the vote" will generate such a radical shift in electoral rules is beyond the reckoning of this historian; nor can any reliable predictions be made about the future leanings of the Supreme Court or the viability of the Voting Rights Act. What is clear is that, despite its increasing unpopularity, the federal government's attack on vote dilution succeeded in altering electoral rules in many jurisdictions throughout the nation: at-large elections are far less common than they were in 1965, as are other potentially discriminatory mechanisms. Also evident is that the achievement of virtually universal suffrage opened the doors both to knotty new problems and new forms of contestation over the distribution of political power. The issues that have bedeviled Congress and the courts for several decades could not have come into the spotlight—or even come into focus—until the barriers to enfranchisement came down. Only when people had the vote could they become concerned with the value or effectiveness of their vote. The conflicts over representation and vote dilution thus represent the fruits—if often bitter—of an achievement that has taken centuries.

Two Uneasy Pieces

Felons and Ex-Felons

The impulse to expand the franchise in the 1960s and early 1970s was strong enough to reach even the most unpopular and least powerful group of disfranchised citizens: men and women who had been convicted of crimes. In 1974, all but a handful of states continued to impose the penalty of disfranchisement on felons or those convicted of "infamous" or specified crimes. In roughly half the states, this disability was permanent, although in many it could be lifted, at least in theory, through a pardon or an appeal to designated state officials. Elsewhere, the deprivation of political rights was for a fixed period or coincided with a criminal's period of incarceration (or probation); in some states, it stretched through parole, and in many, absentee ballot rules effectively barred even detainees awaiting trial. The precise list of crimes that triggered disfranchisement varied considerably from state to state. Major crimes were on the list almost everywhere, but lesser offenses—including vagrancy, breaking a water pipe, participating in a common-law marriage, and stealing edible meat—could do the trick in particular states.[84]

The heightened interest in suffrage, sparked initially by the civil rights movement, led many lawmakers as well as prisoners' rights advocates to question the validity and utility of such laws. Permanent disfranchisement in particular seemed to be a draconian response to a single offense, and the fact that convicted felons were disproportionately nonwhite sharpened sensitivity to the issue. Once closely examined, moreover, the lack of a compelling rationale for criminal disfranchisement was difficult to miss. As a penal measure, disfranchisement did not seem to serve any of the four conventional purposes of punishment: there was no evidence that it deterred crimes; it was an ill-fitting form of retribution; it did not limit the capacity of criminals to commit further crimes; and it certainly did not further the cause of rehabilitation. Indeed, many critics argued that it did just the opposite, preventing ex-felons from resuming a full and normal position in society.[85]

Equally shaky were the arguments—inherited from the late nineteenth century—that felon disfranchisement was necessary to safeguard the political system. The vision of felons and ex-felons banding together to elect officials who would soften the criminal code seemed divorced from reality. Nor was there evidence to support the claim that a man or woman who once had broken the law would be particularly likely to engage in electoral corruption or permanently lacked the moral competence to make political judgments. The purity of the ballot box did not appear to be threatened by the prospect of felons or ex-felons participating in elections.[86]

The weakness of the old rationales, coupled with a new emphasis on the ideal of rehabilitation, prompted numerous states to reconfigure their laws. The primary thrust of these reforms was the elimination of lifetime disfranchisement: more than fifteen states took this step between the late 1960s and 1998. In addition, some states narrowed the range of crimes that resulted in disfranchisement, while others tried to iron out inconsistencies—for example, different treatment for convicted felons who were or were not incarcerated. These changes were significant but did not go very far; the idea of lessening the burdens imposed on criminals was hardly popular, and amending state constitutions could be an arduous procedure. In both Rhode Island and Idaho, the electorate rejected proposals to restore the franchise to felons or ex-felons.[87]

Meanwhile, the transformation of voting rights law opened the door to challenges to criminal disfranchisement in both state and federal courts. (There were remarkably few court cases dealing with this issue prior to the 1960s.)[88] The first wave of challenges was based on the equal protection clause of the Fourteenth Amendment. In 1966, in California, two conscientious objectors who had served prison terms during World War II sued to be reinstated as voters: they had been permanently disfranchised under a California law that barred all those convicted of infamous crimes, a category interpreted to mean all felonies. The California Supreme Court, in *Otsuka v. Hite*, found that their refusal to enter the armed forces had been based on religious grounds and therefore could not reasonably be construed as a crime so "infamous" that it branded the perpetrators as "morally corrupt and dishonest men." The Court concluded that the phrase *infamous crimes* in the California Constitution ought to be interpreted to disfranchise only those who could "reasonably be deemed to constitute a threat to the integrity of the elective process." Although the Court implicitly recognized the state's right to bar some criminals, the blanket disfranchisement of all convicted felons was not permissible under the Fourteenth Amendment.[89]

A year later, a federal appeals court reached the opposite conclusion in a challenge to New York's law by a man who had been convicted under the Smith Act for conspiring to overthrow the government. In a frequently cited opinion, Judge Henry Friendly concluded not only that the plaintiff's crime was potentially linked to the integrity of the electoral process but also that there was nothing unreasonable or unconstitutional about criminal disfranchisement statutes. Invoking Lockean principles, Friendly declared that "a man who breaks the laws he has authorized his agent to make for his own governance could fairly have been thought to have abandoned the right to participate in further administering the compact. . . . It can scarcely be deemed unreasonable," he continued, "for a state to decide that perpetrators of serious crimes shall not take part in electing the legislators who make the laws . . . the prosecutors who must try them . . . or the judges who are to consider their cases." This "is especially so" given the "heavy incidence of recidivism and the prevalence of organized crime." The equal protection clause, according to Friendly, did not require New York to permit "convicted mafiosi to vote for district attorneys or judges."[90]

Mafiosi aside, equal protection challenges gained new teeth as a result of the Supreme Court's assertion in *Dunn v. Blumstein* that any statute limiting the exercise of the franchise (a "fundamental right") ought to be subject to the "strict scrutiny" of the courts. This meant that proponents of such laws had to demonstrate that they served a compelling state interest and were both necessary and narrowly tailored to satisfy that interest. In 1972, accordingly, a ninth circuit appeals court sustained the claim of a paroled felon who had been denied the right to vote by the state of Washington. Invoking strict scrutiny, the court observed,

> courts have been hard pressed to define the state interest served by laws disenfranchising persons convicted of crimes. . . . Search for modern reasons to

sustain the old governmental disenfranchisement prerogative has usually ended with a general pronouncement that a state has an interest in preventing persons who have been convicted of serious crimes from participation in the electoral process or a quasi-metaphysical invocation that the interest is preservation of the "purity of the ballot box."

The court concluded that the state had not established the necessity of such laws, and it quoted Justice Douglas's opinion in *Harper* (doing him one better in terms of rhetoric) as grounds for application of the Fourteenth Amendment.

> Earlier in our constitutional history, laws disenfranchising persons convicted of crime may have been immune from attack. But constitutional concepts of equal protection are not immutably frozen like insects trapped in Devonian amber. "Notions of what constitutes equal treatment for purposes of the Equal Protection Clause do change."[91]

A year later, the California Supreme Court reached a similar conclusion, after hearing another equal protection challenge to the state's lifetime disfranchisement of persons convicted of infamous crimes. (California's constitution had been modified in 1972, giving the legislature more leeway to determine the scope of the exclusion; perhaps aptly, in a state combating smog and so reliant on automobiles, operating a motor vehicle with a faulty muffler could put one at risk of disfranchisement.) The case was initiated as a class action by three ex-felons who had served their prison terms but were still unable to vote. The court, building on federal decisions, concluded that any deprivation of this critical right should come under strict scrutiny; although it conceded a compelling state interest in preventing electoral corruption, the disfranchisement statute was too blunt and ineffective an instrument for furthering that goal. The statute caught in its web far too many individuals who posed no threat whatsoever to the integrity of the electoral system; besides, the state had available to it more precise and efficacious methods of protecting the sanctity of the ballot box. Going beyond its earlier decision in *Otsuka*, the Court found that the criminal disfranchisement clause of the California Constitution violated the equal protection provisions of the federal Constitution.[92]

The decision was appealed to the U.S. Supreme Court, where it was overturned. The ruling, in *Richardson v. Ramirez*, was based on section 2 of the

Fourteenth Amendment, which specified that representation in Congress would be reduced for any state that denied the franchise to adult male citizens "except for participation in rebellion, or other crime." The Court (with Justices Brennan, Douglas, and Marshall dissenting) construed this clause—the interpretation of which was heatedly debated—as a constitutional license for states to disfranchise convicted criminals. Acknowledging that "the legislative history bearing on the meaning of the relevant language . . . is scant indeed," Justice Rehnquist, speaking for the majority, concluded that the authors of the Fourteenth Amendment must have intended to permit the states to disfranchise convicted criminals. Since the exclusion of felons had an "affirmative sanction" from the Constitution, it differed from "other state limitations on the franchise which have been held invalid under the Equal Protection Clause." California's law therefore was not subject to strict scrutiny and was not unconstitutional. The Court did acknowledge that a "more modern view" of the issue, stressing the rehabilitation of ex-felons, might well lead to different laws, but it regarded that as an issue to be addressed in a "legislative forum."[93]

Soon thereafter, the state of California in fact did modify its criminal disfranchisement provisions, limiting the disability to the terms of a person's sentence.[94] Still, the Court's ruling in *Ramirez* effectively closed the door on equal protection challenges to the disfranchisement of criminals.[95] In 1985, in *Hunter v. Underwood*, however, the Court carved out an exception after examining the remarkably detailed criminal disfranchisement provisions that had been in force in Alabama since 1901: these provisions disfranchised (among many others) all persons convicted of any crime involving moral turpitude, a characterization that included numerous nonfelony offenses such as vagrancy. Based both on the nature of the specified laws and on the overt statements of those who had passed them, the Court concluded that Alabama's criminal exclusion did violate the equal protection clause because it was designed to discriminate against blacks. States had the right to disfranchise criminals but not with a racially discriminatory intent.[96] (See table A.15.)

The reach of *Hunter* was limited, since few states—and none outside the South—had legal codes and track records that demonstrated intent as clearly as did Alabama's. In the 1990s, a district court even upheld Mississippi's ban on felon voting because its law, although originally adopted with discriminatory intent, later had been amended and reenacted: this "removed" the "discriminatory taint" from the disfranchisement provision. (One of the more remarkable changes in Mississippi's law was the 1968 addition of murder and rape to the list of crimes that resulted in disfranchisement: these had not originally been believed to be "black" crimes.) Nonetheless, the ruling in *Hunter* pointed toward a new avenue of approach to the issue: the claim that criminal disfranchisement statutes were illegal because they discriminated against blacks and Hispanics. This argument was first put forward in *Wesley v. Collins* in 1986, but it was rebuffed: in a sketchy decision, the courts ruled that when Tennessee's disfranchisement law was "viewed in the context of the 'totality of circumstances,' it is apparent that the challenged legislation does not violate the Voting Rights Act."[97]

Despite this setback, the approach continued to gain adherents among both civil rights and prisoners' rights activists, many of whom believed the *Wesley* decision to be flawed. By the 1990s, something close to a full-blown legal strategy was being proposed, grounded in two well-documented empirical findings. The first was that a hugely disproportionate number of prison inmates and convicted felons were black or Hispanic. In the early 1990s, for example, 63 percent of all prisoners in Illinois were black (compared to 15 percent of the population); in New York, where parolees could not vote, 49 percent were black and 31 percent Hispanic. Roughly 80 percent of New York's prison inmates also belonged to minorities. The second key finding was that minorities were treated in a discriminatory fashion by the criminal justice system: blacks and Hispanics were targeted by the police and arrested far more often than were whites. Minorities also were far more likely to be sentenced to prison, and for longer terms, than were whites convicted of committing the same crimes. These racial disparities were particularly visible in drug-related cases, which had come to constitute a sizable proportion of all felony convictions. Discrimination in the justice system thus made minorities more vulnerable to disfranchisement. The argument was deepened, sociologically if not legally, by the claim that racial discrimination kept many minorities in disadvantaged socioeconomic circumstances, which made them more likely to commit crimes. Opposition to criminal disfranchisement also was buttressed politically by the argument that electoral turnout levels among the poor already had fallen to a perilous low and that the state should seek to reverse rather than aggravate the trend.[98]

This strategy made a small amount of headway in the mid-1990s, with several lower courts suggesting that the Voting Rights Act could "apply to felon disenfranchisement laws."[99] Whether it will yield any victories in the future remains uncertain, particularly in light of the confusion surrounding the Voting Rights Act itself. But there is no doubt that the scale of the problem is significant. Although, by the late 1990s, only ten states continued to impose lifetime disfranchisement on convicted felons, every state except Maine, Massachusetts, Utah, and Vermont possesses a criminal disfranchisement law of one type or another; most continue to exclude not only those in prison but also men and women on probation and parole. Given the enormous increase in the size of the prison population, linked in part to an explosion of arrests for drug-related offenses, these laws are estimated to keep roughly 4 million people from voting. Their impact on minority populations is extraordinary, especially in those states that have retained permanent disfranchisement. Nationwide, 14 percent of black males are barred from voting because they are in prison or have been convicted of felonies. In Alabama and Florida, nearly one out of every three black men is disfranchised, and in Iowa, Mississippi, New Mexico, Virginia, Washington and Wyoming, the ratio is only slightly lower.[100]

At the beginning of the twenty-first century, convicted felons constitute the largest single group of American citizens who are barred by law from participating in elections. Although their participation rates in elections would likely be low, their numbers are certainly sufficient to affect the outcomes of elections in numerous states. That this group remains disfranchised despite the transformation of voting laws in the 1960s and 1970s reflects not only its racial composition but also its utter lack of political leverage. Indeed, convicted felons—mostly minority males, many of them young—probably possess negative political leverage: it would be costly to any politician to embrace their cause. Their ongoing exclusion from the polity also is a stark sign of the limits of the legal revolution that has occurred. Although race, class, mobility, literacy, and the ability to speak English have ceased to be formal impediments to voting, good behavior is still required. However weak or unsubstantiated the rationales for felon disfranchisement may be, states have retained, and exercise, the power to banish the unlawful and the unruly from politics. By the late twentieth century, voting had become a right belonging to all American citizens, but it has remained a right that can be lost or taken away as a means—largely symbolic—of promoting social discipline.

Immigrants and Aliens Redux

After playing a large, even leading role in the drama of voting rights in the nineteenth and early twentieth centuries, immigrants quickly receded from view. The key to the shift lay in the numbers: immigration levels plummeted during World War I, remained very low until the late 1940s, and rose only gradually between 1950 and 1965. Those who did come for the most part were easily absorbed into American society and into the political institutions created in earlier decades. The potentially most troublesome group (from the vantage point of natives) was the hundreds of thousands of men and women from Mexico who served as a reserve army of labor for American agriculture in the Southwest and West. The political threat posed by Mexicans, however, was greatly diminished by their low rate of naturalization—the result both of their desire to retain Mexican citizenship and of the federal government's *bracero* program, which admitted scores of thousands of Mexican laborers each year on expressly temporary visas.[101]

By the time that immigration rates began to rise significantly, during the final quarter of the twentieth century, the transformation of suffrage law already was well under way, and new legal principles protected immigrants against forms of discrimination that had been widespread in 1880 and 1910. Literacy tests could not be imposed; mastery of English was not essential (after 1975); geographic mobility was not penalized; and special requirements, such as waiting periods or the presentation of naturalization documents, fell by the wayside, at least in part because of the looming umbrella of the equal protection clause. Immigrant citizens could not be treated differently than other citizens, which meant that they had to be gradually incorporated into the polity.[102]

Yet not all foreign-born residents of the United States were citizens: indeed, the percentage who were naturalized dropped from nearly 80 percent in 1950 to 40 percent in 1990. By 1996, there were 10.5 million legally resident aliens in the nation, most of whom had come from either Asia or Latin America. In addition, the number of illegal aliens was estimated to be in the vicinity of 5 million throughout the 1980s and 1990s. Whether legal or illegal, these noncitizens all lacked political rights. Felons may have been the largest single group of disfranchised citizens, but aliens by far were the largest group of adults barred from participation in American politics.[103]

The laws governing the voting rights (or lack thereof) of these men and women were unusually clear-cut. After the nation's experiment with declarant alien voting had come to a close in the 1920s, all states required voters to be citizens. The federal government did not insist on but allowed that qualification: citizenship was considered to be a reasonable qualification for voting, one that did not violate any tenets of the Constitution. Although several attempts were made to include aliens under the broad canopy of the equal protection clause, these made little headway in the courts.[104]

The resurgence of immigration, however, reignited interest in alien voting, particularly in local elections. The argument for stretching the boundaries of the franchise was straightforward: in many communities, thousands of noncitizens paid taxes, owned homes, held jobs, and had children in public schools. They contributed to the public purse, were affected by public policies, and sometimes were subject to military service: consequently, they ought to have a voice in government. Stated somewhat differently, they were de facto if not de jure citizens; they behaved as citizens, even if they lacked official status. Between the late 1970s and 1990s, this view was buttressed by a growing awareness of global population movements among professionals as well as manual workers and by the growth of regional economic structures and organizations, particularly in Europe, that diminished the salience of national boundaries. Indeed, in Europe, the notion that people should vote where they lived and worked was the subject of high-level policy discussions, accompanied by significant experiments in transnational voting. Sweden, Denmark, Norway, and Finland all granted suffrage in local elections to immigrants who had met fairly minimal residency requirements.[105]

This assembly of concerns prompted a number of locales to offer at least limited suffrage to noncitizen residents. Beginning in 1968, New York authorized aliens whose children were in public schools to vote in community school board elections; Chicago subsequently did the same; and parents in Los Angeles and San Francisco sought similar rights in the 1990s. In 1992, moreover, the small, Washington-area city of Takoma Park joined a number of its Maryland neighbors by amending its charter to enfranchise noncitizens in all local elections: the decision was prompted by a 1990 redistricting, which revealed that wards that were equal in population had very unequal numbers of eligible voters—because some neighborhoods were filled with alien residents. The city, which had a reputation as a bastion of progressive politics, then voted to permit noncitizens to participate in elections. Its action sparked a controversy in the Maryland legislature, but Takoma Park and other communities with similar regulations successfully defended their home rule right to expand the franchise.[106]

Takoma Park has not been widely emulated, and there is little reason to believe that it will be. Although the size of the immigrant population is large, particularly in some states, the conditions that fostered the nineteenth-century alien suffrage laws—the desire to attract settlers, most critically—no longer obtain. Meanwhile, arguments about equity, fairness, and the nature of citizenship easily are overwhelmed by the fears spawned by the new waves of non-European immigration. Nativism once again has reared its head, and public policy debates—in California, for example—center more on contracting than expanding the rights of immigrants. State legislatures, thus, are highly unlikely to seriously entertain proposals for alien voting, and the courts already have made their position clear. "Voting and citizenship are so inextricably bound in this country that it's hard to imagine one without the other," editorialized the *San Francisco Examiner* in 1996. That was not always true, but it may be now.[107]

Getting the Electorate to the Polls

> The Congress finds that—
>
> 1) the right of citizens of the United States to vote is a fundamental right;
>
> 2) it is the duty of the Federal, State and local governments to promote the exercise of that right; and
>
> 3) discriminatory and unfair registration laws and procedures can have a direct and damaging effect on voter participation in elections for Federal office and disproportionately harm voter participation by various groups, including racial minorities.
>
> —THE NATIONAL VOTER
> REGISTRATION ACT OF 1993

In 1988, two prominent scholar-activists, Frances Fox Piven and Richard A. Cloward, published an influential book entitled *Why Americans Don't Vote*. Their subject, as the title suggests, was the extraordinarily low electoral turnout among Americans, particularly poor and young Americans. Although the authors presented a complex historical and structural analysis of this phenomenon, they wrote with a particular target in mind: the registration laws that in almost all states governed the procedures through which eligible adults could become voters. To Piven and Cloward, these laws loomed as the critical source of nonparticipation (and thus powerlessness) of the nation's poorest and least well-educated citizens: they did not constrict the right to vote per se, but they constituted a major class-biased obstacle to the exercise of that right. Many other scholars—if less single-minded in their analyses—agreed that the registration laws were an impediment to a fully participatory democracy.[108]

Registration laws (described in chapter 5) emerged in the nineteenth century as a means of keeping track of voters and preventing fraud; they also served—and often were intended to serve—as a means of keeping African-American, working-class, immigrant, and poor voters from the polls. First placed on the books between the 1850s and World War I, registration laws frequently were revised by state legislatures in the course of the twentieth century. In some states, procedures were simplified and made easier; elsewhere they remained complex and difficult to navigate. As always, the devil was in the details: the laws specified when and where people could register, how often they had to register, whether or not the names of nonvoters were periodically "purged," the procedures to be followed if a voter moved from one precinct to another, the hours that registry offices were open, and the documentation that had to be presented to registrars. In 1974, the federal courts, while affirming the legitimacy of reasonable and uniform registration procedures, made clear that such details mattered: the courts struck down a Texas law permitting registration only during a four-month period, long before elections, because it imposed too onerous a burden on prospective voters and thus impeded their right to vote.[109]

The concern that registration procedures were depressing turnout—and therefore ran counter to the new spirit of voting laws in general—led many states in the 1970s and 1980s to streamline their registration procedures. Some permitted registration by mail; others allowed voters to register at a wide range of public offices; a few even allowed voters to register on election day. But the effects of some of these reforms (such as registration by mail) often were slight, and numerous states resisted such actions altogether. As a result, the federal government began to consider the imposition of national voter registration standards. As early as 1962, a presidential commission, reflecting concerns about low levels of turnout, recommended significant reforms in state registration laws.[110]

The first major proposals for national legislation came in the 1970s. Between 1972 and 1976, Congress considered several bills that would have required the states to permit postcard or mail-in registration: these were defeated by a coalition of Republicans and southern Democrats. In 1977 President Jimmy Carter offered the National Uniform Registration Act, which mandated election-day registration. To Carter's stated surprise, his bill encountered fierce opposition in Congress: almost all Republicans opposed it (on the grounds that it would facilitate corruption), as did many conservative Democrats, and a few liberals as well. Carter attributed the opposition to the reluctance of incumbents to expand their own electorates, which could make reelection more problematic. Yet as Carter surely knew, there were partisan factors as well. Easing registration requirements was widely perceived as a step that would help Democrats and hurt Republicans: most of the new enrollees were expected to be poor, members of minority groups, or young, and all of these groups tended to vote Democratic.[111]

Despite their defeats in Congress, proponents of registration reform, spurred on by the election of Ronald Reagan, renewed their efforts in the 1980s. One proposal was to coordinate all registration through the Postal Service, but opposition to the idea was too widespread (including among postal workers) for it to get very far. Another was "agency registration," permitting prospective voters to enroll at a variety of public facilities, such as libraries, welfare offices, and motor vehicle bureaus: the latter seemed particularly promising, since 85 percent of adult Americans had drivers' licenses that periodically had to be renewed and already served as identification papers. This idea had been adopted by Michigan in 1977 and subsequently was embraced by other states, thanks in part to the energetic lobbying of a broad coalition of progressive and good government groups, including the League of Women Voters and Project SERVE, which Piven and Cloward themselves had helped to found. In addition to state legislation, bills calling for agency and motor vehicle bureau registration, as well as registration by mail and election-day registration, were introduced in Congress in the late 1980s.[112]

The rationale put forward for these proposals was straightforward and ostensibly nonpartisan. Low voter turnout was deemed to be a defect of American politics, and making registration easier, it was argued, would go a long way toward solving the problem: more than 80 percent of Americans who were registered did in fact participate in elections. Proponents maintained that the United States was almost unique in placing the burden of registration on the individual (rather than the state); they also pointed out that countries and states with less burdensome registration procedures tended to have higher turnout. Turnout in Michigan, for example, had increased by more than 10 percent after passage of its "motor voter" bill. Facilitating registration thus would improve the health and vitality of the polity.[113]

Proponents of reform also had a partisan, or political, agenda. Progressives such as Piven and Cloward wanted to enhance the voting strength of disadvantaged groups whose interests were being ignored or worse by Reagan Republicanism. Not surprisingly, thus, most Republicans opposed the reforms, although they too defended their position in nonpartisan terms. Republicans argued that registration by mail and same-day registration would increase fraud and that agency registration would be unduly expensive. Some also insisted that any federal law would be an unconstitutional intrusion into an arena traditionally regulated by the states. Senator Mitch McConnell, a Kentucky Republican who led the fight against national legislation, even denied that a "turnout problem" existed. "Low voter turnout is a sign of a content democracy," he proclaimed.[114]

Federal registration bills came to the floor of Congress between 1988 and 1991: their usual fate was to be filibustered to death by Republicans who opposed the legislation but did not want to vote directly against it. In the spring of 1992, however, some key Republican defections, coupled with a looming election, led to the passage of a compromise motor voter bill. As he had threatened to do, President George Bush vetoed the legislation, arguing that it "imposes an unnecessary and costly federal regime on the states" and was "an open invitation to fraud and corruption." The president also maintained that the bill was "constitutionally suspect."[115]

Less than a year later, George Bush was a private citizen, and his successor, Bill Clinton, signed the National Voter Registration Act of 1993 into law. The bill was passed by large majorities in the House and Senate after several key compromises ended weeks of acrimonious partisan wrangling. In its final form, the bill required the states to provide three procedures for registration (in addition to any the state already possessed) in federal elections: the simultaneous application for a driver's license and voter registration; registration by mail; and registration at designated public agencies, including those offering public assistance and services to the disabled. The law did not apply to state and local elections, but it would obviously affect them—since, as had been true with federal age regulations, maintaining a separate registration system for nonfederal elections would be difficult and expensive.[116]

The Motor Voter bill, as it was called, took effect on January 1, 1995. Its impact on registration levels was rapid. Millions of voters availed themselves of the opportunity to register or reregister at motor vehicle bureaus or through the mail. In less than two years, there was a net addition of 9 million registrants (slightly less than 20 percent of the unregistered) to the electorate. Fulfilling Democratic hopes and Republican fears, the new registrants were disproportionately young, black, high-school educated, and Democratic, although in the South the law also seemed to stimulate registration in Republican strongholds. But this surge in registration did not quickly translate into higher turnout at elections. In 1996, half of all potential voters stayed home: turnout was lower than it had been in any presidential election since 1924. The 1998 congressional elections were no better at sparking the interest of voters. Significant as the registration issue surely was, something else was ailing the body politic.[117]

The persistence of dismal turnout, however, ought not obscure the significance of the National Voter Registration Act; nor should its nickname, the Motor Voter bill, be allowed to trivialize the legislation's meaning. The registration measure was the final act of the drama that had begun in the 1960s: it completed a lurching yet immensely important forty-year process of nationalizing the voting laws and removing obstacles to the ballot box. As such, the Motor Voter bill was also a critical step in dismantling the multiple impediments to voting that had been erected between the 1850s and World War I. By the end of the twentieth century, what had been a long historical swing toward contraction of the franchise had been decisively reversed.

Conclusion:
The Project of Democracy

$\mathscr{T}$HIS IS A STORY WITH A PARTIALLY HAPPY ENDING. At the opening of the twenty-first century (and the new millennium), nearly all adult citizens of the United States are legally entitled to vote. What once was a long list of restrictions on the franchise has been whittled down to a small set of constraints. Economic, gender-based, and racial qualifications have been abolished; literacy tests are gone, if not forgotten; residency requirements have been reduced to a matter of weeks; the age of political maturity has been lowered; and the burden of registration has been rendered less onerous. The proportion of the adult population enfranchised is far greater than it was at the nation's founding or at the end of the nineteenth century. That there exists a right to vote rather than the privilege of voting is clearly established in law as well as in popular convictions.

Yet getting here has taken a very long time. The elementary act of voting—of participating in the shaping of our laws and the selection of our lawmakers—was, for many decades, reserved to white English-speaking literate males, a majority of whom belonged to the respectable classes. As late as 1950, basic political rights were denied to most African Americans in the South, as well as significant pockets of voters elsewhere, including the illiterate in New York, Native Americans in Utah, many Hispanics in Texas and California, and the recently mobile everywhere.

That it took so long for universal suffrage to be achieved reflects elements of our history that fit uneasily into the official portrait of the United States as the standard bearer of democracy and representative government. One such element—known to scholarly specialists but widely ignored in popular culture—is that the right to vote has never been formally enshrined in our nation's constitutional order. At the country's birth, there were few believers in universal suffrage, even for males: the Bill of Rights guaranteed Americans freedom of speech and the right to bear arms, but it did not guarantee the right to participate in elections. Not until 1868, with the passage of the Fourteenth Amendment, did the phrase "the right to vote" appear in the federal Constitution, and to this day the nation's fundamental law contains no affirmative embrace of universal suffrage. State constitutions did make voting an affirmative right, but not for all residents; and the guarantees afforded by state constitutions were highly variable and subject to revision.

In addition, large and influential sectors of the population have frequently opposed democratization and the extension of political rights to all Americans. They did so both to defend their own interests and because their beliefs and prejudices led them to view others as something less than responsible or worthy citizens. Most men did not want to enfranchise women until the twentieth century; most whites did not want to enfranchise blacks or other racial minorities in their own states; the native-born often were resistant to granting suffrage to immigrants; the wealthy at times sought to deny political citizenship to the poor; established community residents preferred to fence out new arrivals. There is nothing peculiarly American or particularly surprising about these patterns; those who possess political power commonly are reluctant to share it, and they have easily developed or embraced ideas that justify and legitimize that reluctance.

It took powerful forces, as well as decades of conflict and change, to overcome resistance to a broad franchise. Two of the largest social movements in American history were devoted to achieving suffrage for women and for blacks; smaller, less celebrated campaigns of agitation were mounted by militiamen in the early nineteenth century, by workers in Rhode Island, by Asians, Native Americans, and young people in the twentieth century. The eventual success of these movements was made possible by the dynamics of party competition, by economic changes that spawned new patterns of labor force participation (e.g., among women), and by surges of urbanization that lessened the isolation and heightened the visibility of some excluded groups (e.g., blacks and Native Americans). The expansion of suffrage also depended heavily on ideological shifts, on the spread of democratic values in the first half of the nineteenth century, and on a renewed commitment to them in the mid-twentieth. The expansion depended too on war: the most prominent peaks in the history of the franchise in the United States were the Revolutionary War, the Civil War, World Wars I and II, and the first decades of the cold war. Each of these conflicts contributed significantly to the broadening of the right to vote.

Powerful as the forces promoting democratization may have been, their progress was not inexorable and the outcome was far from certain. From the perspective of the late twentieth century, it is all too easy to invest the triumph of universal suffrage with an aura of inevitability; but the contested history suggests otherwise. Contingencies of timing and politics dot the chronological landscape: had New York and Massachusetts waited until 1830 or 1840 before removing property qualifications, much of the Northeast might have ended up embroiled in a large version of the Dorr War; had Radical Republicans not successfully pressed for the Fourteenth and Fifteenth Amendments (the latter passed during the final days of a session of Congress), the twentieth-century struggle for civil rights might have been far more arduous; were it not for the war in Vietnam, the voting age still might be twenty-one. The interaction of underlying processes with critical events that had independent causes shaped the contours of suffrage history—and there was little that was predestined about the timing or consequences of those interactions.

The lack of inevitability—despite de Tocqueville's "invariable rule of social behavior"—also is suggested by the reversals of direction that characterize the history. Not only was there a prolonged period when the franchise on the whole was tightened rather than expanded, but there were numerous occasions on which particular groups lost political rights that they once had possessed: women in New Jersey in the early nineteenth century; blacks in the mid-Atlantic states before 1860 and in the South after 1890; naturalized Irish immigrants during the Know-Nothing period; aliens in the late nineteenth and early twentieth centuries; men and women who were on public relief in Maine in the 1930s; and countless citizens who suddenly found themselves confronted with extended residency requirements or newly complex registration rules. To be sure, all of these restraints on the franchise were eventually removed, but a path so long and winding suggests contingency and conflict rather than a clear and sure destination.

The evolution of suffrage in the United States is a story with many parallels in the histories of other nations; indeed, nearly all of the key ingredients in this contested history appeared elsewhere as well. Property and tax qualifications were commonplace in nineteenth-century Europe; in some nations, such as Hungary, class-based restrictions were so finely tuned that members of specific occupations were prohibited from voting. Poor relief recipients were disfranchised in England and Japan; literacy tests were deployed to disfranchise peasants in Italy; racial barriers were erected in several Canadian provinces; and both Australia and New Zealand for many decades refused to fully enfranchise their aboriginal populations. Lengthy residency requirements aimed primarily at mobile workers were common, and detailed registration rules (in England, after 1885, e.g.) kept countless individuals from the polls. Similarly, almost all European nations have been resistant to enfranchising the foreign-born, although such resistance was (and is) most often expressed in the erection of high barriers to citizenship. Not surprisingly, conflicts over districting and apportionment (e.g., Britain's "rotten boroughs") also have been widespread.[1]

The dynamics of change too have been transnational. Across the world, grassroots movements (often tied to labor unions) pressed for inclusion in the polity; party competition cracked numerous exclusionary walls; and broad-gauged ideological shifts made suffrage restriction less and less defensible. Both Bismarck and Disraeli in the late 1860s—much like the Republicans who acted at almost exactly the same time—expanded the franchise to strengthen the state and their own political factions. Moreover, war served as a stimulus to democratization in many nations. The enfranchisement of soldiers, for example, was an issue in Britain in World War I; and the dynamics of wartime mobilization contributed to expansion of the suffrage in Belgium, parts of Canada, and Italy (where the Libyan campaign, in 1912, led to the enfranchisement of soldiers and veterans who did not meet the normal age requirement). The cause of women's suffrage, of course, was promoted by both world wars. In a rather different pattern, military defeat—and thus the imposition of new political regimes—resulted in the broadening of the franchise in Germany and Austria. Class tensions slowed the progress of woman suffrage in England (among other places), and they also produced reversals in the progress of democratization in France, Germany, and Italy. Although France was the first nation to adopt a broad franchise, the right to vote contracted several times after brief spells of expansion. In Germany, Austria, and Italy, universal suffrage was adopted during the second decade of the twentieth century but became meaningless with the suspension of political rights under fascism.[2]

Even these brief international comparisons make clear that the basic forces shaping the history of suffrage in the United States were not unique: they were—and are—grounded in the realities of class and ethnic conflict in the industrial capitalist world of the nineteenth and twentieth centuries. The American experience, to be sure, had several distinctive features: the early abolition of property requirements; the presence of slaves and afterward a large, repressed, and regionally concentrated racial minority; the scale of immigration and the facility with which immigrants could become citizens. Each of these features had a significant impact on the details and rhythms of the history of suffrage in the United States, particularly on the backsliding that marked the late nineteenth and early twentieth centuries. Yet these distinctive features also interacted with broader currents—economic, social, and political—that were common to the western world. Conflicts over the breadth of the right to vote have been nearly universal in the political life of modern nations for the past two centuries.

All of which brings us back to the fact that the ending to the story is only partially happy. Although the formal right to vote is now nearly universal, few observers would characterize the United States as a vibrant democracy, as a nation where the equality of political rights offers release to a host of engaged and diverse political voices. The most telling symptom of the malady is the low level of popular participation in American elections: in recent years, only half of all eligible adults have voted in presidential elections, and fewer than 40 percent generally cast their ballots in other contests. Electoral turnout has declined significantly over the last century, and it is markedly lower in the United States than in most other nations.[3]

In theory, of course, nonvoting could be a sign of contentment, of a satisfied electorate. But portraits of the nonvoting population make this rosy interpretation difficult to sustain: turnout is lowest among the poor, minorities, and the less well-educated. In a pattern distinctively American, turnout correlates positively with social class: those with more education and higher incomes are far more likely to vote than are their less advantaged fellow citizens. The people who are least likely to be content and complacent (and most likely to need government help) are those who are least likely to vote.[4]

As debates among political scientists have made clear, there are numerous factors that contribute to this low and class-skewed turnout. Yet it is not a coincidence that nonvoters come disproportionately from the same social groups that in earlier decades were the targets of restrictions on the franchise itself. Despite the Motor Voter bill, there remain procedural obstacles to registration that have a heavy impact on the poor and uneducated. Perhaps more important, the political institutions and culture that evolved during the era of restricted suffrage spawned a political system that offers few attractive choices to the nation's least well-off citizens. The two major political parties operate within a narrow, ideological spectrum; the programmatic differences between candidates often are difficult to discern; the core social and economic policies of both parties are shaped largely by the desire to foster economic growth and therefore to satisfy the business and financial communities. Ideas and proposals that might appeal to the poor and are commonplace in other nations—such as national health insurance or laws enhancing job security—have been beyond the pale of modern American political discourse.[5]

The range of choices offered to the public has been kept narrow, in part through the increasing institutionalization of the two-party system: rules governing ballot access limit the ability of dissident parties to mount national campaigns; public funding goes only to parties that already are established; and the persistence of winner-take-all elections makes it exceedingly difficult for new parties to gradually acquire influence, visibility, and strength. (Notably, the only third party to have made any headway in recent years—the Reform Party—has no distinctive ideology or program and was underwritten by an iconoclastic billionaire.) Meanwhile, the two major parties have displayed little interest in altering the political equation (and rocking the boat) by reaching out to nonvoters: most tellingly, perhaps, the Democratic Party—the more likely beneficiary of an increase in turnout—has focused less on mobilizing the disaffected than on winning the suburban swing vote and remaining in the good graces of Wall Street. This political strategy led even a member of President Clinton's cabinet, Robert B. Reich, the former secretary of labor, to conclude that "the great mass of non-voters . . . didn't vote in 1996 because they saw nothing in it for them."[6]

Low levels of electoral turnout are not the only problem. As political scientist Sidney Verba and his colleagues have pointed out in an important study of civic voluntarism, voting is one of several forms of political participation open to Americans and vital to the health of democracy. Other avenues of participation, however, such as volunteering time or contributing money, are even more class correlated: people with more money, more education, and middle-class skills are far more likely than working-class citizens to engage in all forms of political activism. As a result, the voices of the more privileged are

heard more loudly in the halls of governance, and the ideal of democracy—
that all voices be heard equally—is consistently undermined.[7]

Indeed, the raw and growing power of money in politics serves as a coun-
terweight to the democratic thrust of the twentieth-century broadening of
suffrage. Critical governmental decisions are made by regulatory commissions and agencies that are beyond the direct reach of electoral politics but
accessible to well-funded lobbyists and organized interest groups. Congressional committees and state legislatures hear not only the distant and diffuse
voices of the electorate but the nearby and insistent voices of those who roam
the corridors of power. Even institutions ostensibly insulated from public influence, such as the all-important Federal Reserve Board, have constituencies to which they listen, and these constituencies are comprised largely of
the wealthy and the well-positioned. Former secretary Reich is not the only
commentator to regard Federal Reserve Board Chairman Alan Greenspan as
"the most powerful man in the world," and those who get to express their
views to Greenspan are not a random cross-section of the population.[8]

In addition, the direct role of money in elections is enormous. Campaigns, waged largely on television, have become extraordinarily expensive,
and candidates who cannot raise large war chests are doomed to failure. The
need to raise such sums has made candidates and parties altogether dependent on the wealthy and on organized influence groups, who in turn exert a
grossly disproportionate influence on the political parties and the positions
they espouse. Blue-collar workers and welfare recipients do not sleep in the
Lincoln bedroom or air their views with high-ranking officials at $1,000 a
plate dinners; they rarely get to testify before congressional committees either. Indeed, if current trends continue, the actual casting of ballots may be
in danger of becoming a pro forma ritual designed to ratify the selection of
candidates who have already won the fund-raising contests.

The current state of American politics makes clear that universal suffrage
is a necessary but not sufficient condition for a fully democratic political
order. No political system can claim to be democratic without universal suffrage, but a broad franchise alone cannot guarantee to each citizen an equal
voice in politics and governance. The arrangements and institutions that sur-
round the conduct of elections—such as districting, apportionment, the
structure of representation, the financing of campaigns, and the organization
of activist groups—all can promote or vitiate the equality of political rights.
These institutions and rules often are contested, just as the right to vote was
contested for a century and three quarters. The current debate over campaign

financing and the use of soft money can be viewed as the latest battle in the two-centuries-old war over the democratization of politics in the United States; at the moment, antidemocratic forces are winning that battle, and in so doing, are undercutting the achievement of universal suffrage.[9]

Yet the sweep of history suggests that democracy should not be imagined or understood as a static condition or a fixed set of rules and institutions; it may be more valuable—and accurate—to think instead of democracy as a project.[10] One critical lesson of the history of suffrage in the United States and elsewhere is that modern societies always have contained individuals and social groups who oppose equal and universal political rights. In capitalist societies (and at present, we have none other) there always have been private interests and centers of power that are or believe themselves to be threatened by democratic control of the state. In socially diverse nations, ethnic, racial, and religious antagonisms often have sparked the impulse to suppress or restrict the rights of minorities. Even individual issues have sometimes loomed so important that factions have sought to deny political voice to their adversaries. On the other hand, there always have been individuals and groups pressing in the opposite direction, for greater democratization and equality. As a result, the very structures and rules of electoral politics periodically become touchstones and lightning rods of conflict.

This lesson drawn from the history of suffrage should lead us to expect recurrent skirmishing once universal suffrage has been achieved. The effects of a restricted suffrage can be replicated, or at least approximated, by cleverly unequal districting or by complex registration requirements. Even if one person, one vote principles are applied to districting, regulations governing the access of parties to the ballot can influence the outcome of elections; so too can the design of electoral systems (majority versus plurality victors or "winner take all" versus proportional representation, e.g.) or the structure of campaign financing. As American political parties discovered long ago, changing the rules is one way to win.[11]

It would, alas, be utopian to expect that such conflicts will ever subside: that any tamperproof set of rules or institutions can be devised; that competing interests will not seek to alter electoral regulations; or that changing conditions will not recurrently create the need for new arrangements. History offers no examples of political institutions that can permanently guarantee genuine political equality. Democracy therefore must remain a project, a goal, something to be endlessly nurtured and reinforced, an ideal that cannot be fully realized but always can be pursued.

This notion of democracy as a project, as well as the contested history of democracy, ought to inform American—and other—efforts to promote democratic regimes in nations with different political traditions and troubled recent pasts. The business of exporting democracy has been booming since the end of the cold war, and American experts and consultants have been dispatched throughout the globe to offer advice regarding the erection of new political institutions. Thus far, the track record of such efforts has been mixed: blueprints drawn up in Washington do not necessarily fit foreign landscapes, and the creation of formally democratic electoral procedures does not guarantee a redistribution of power and influence. Military leaders, party bosses, and business moguls have been endlessly inventive in devising methods of circumventing or overriding procedural democracy. Our own history suggests that this ought not be a surprise. Growing a democracy takes time, and it is often easier to pay lip service to popular government than to live with its decisions. This is not to say that the United States ought to be tolerant of abuses or cast a blind eye to oligarchies masquerading in constitutional garb. But if Americans are to be involved at all in such international efforts, and if our goal truly is to promote democracy—and not simply capitalism—we must recognize the real scope of the endeavor and be prepared to provide long-term support to those individuals and forces who will be struggling for popular government for some time to come.[12]

At home too, there is, and always will be, much to be done. The ideal of democracy—that all individuals are not only born equal but remain equally worthy—surely is an admirable one. The principle that no person's interests and needs are more important than those of anyone else—and thus that all individuals should have an equal chance of influencing government policy—seems well worth fighting for.[13] The project of democracy has never been unanimously embraced in the United States, but it has animated and shaped a great deal of our history. For more than two centuries, men and women who were committed to that project have pressed it forward, despite ceaseless and sometimes forceful opposition. The history of the right to vote is a record of the slow and fitful progress of the project, progress that was hard won and often subject to reverses. The gains so far achieved need to be protected, while the vision of a more democratic society can continue to inspire our hopes and our actions.

State Suffrage Laws, 1775–1920

A Note on the Tables and Sources

The tables presented in this appendix represent an effort to assemble, as completely as possible, a factual skeleton of the evolution of suffrage in the United States. That no similar compilation exists anywhere in print is a remarkable fact—and the rationale for publishing these tables here.

Three limits to this collection should be noted. First is that the tables deal largely with the years prior to 1920. This chronological limit was set because state laws changed relatively little after that date, federal law became paramount by the 1960s, and legal materials for the post–1920 period are more readily accessible in reference volumes. Second, this assembly does not include detailed presentations of all of the disfranchising laws passed in the South between 1890 and 1920: this is so because such presentations previously have been published in the work of other historians (cited in chapter 4). Finally, this collection omits data regarding registration laws. This decision was made for reasons of feasibility: state voter registration laws for the last century generally have been complex, lengthy, and subject to frequent changes. A preliminary attempt to produce such a tabular presentation yielded an incomplete document more than fifty pages long.

The sources listed at the end of these tables are those in which constitutional provisions, statutes, and court cases mentioned in the tables were found. The list does not include the hundreds, perhaps thousands, of vol-

umes (particularly of statutes) that were examined to confirm other sources
or to find that no relevant laws were listed.

The procedures that yielded these tables were as follows. The first sources
to be examined were the texts of all of the state constitutions that were ever
in force between the American Revolution and the mid–twentieth century.
These were supplemented by readings of all of the state constitutional conventions for which transcripts of the proceedings exist. Systematic studies
of the statutes and case law then were conducted for a set of critical states:
Massachusetts, New York, Pennsylvania, California, Colorado, Florida,
Ohio, Texas, Illinois, Oregon, and Indiana. Less systematic but sometimes
extensive research was undertaken for all other states. These efforts were
complemented through the use of multistate compilations of the laws that
were periodically put together either by scholars or (more commonly) by
state officials and constitutional conventions preparing to revise their own
laws.

In addition, a substantial secondary literature was consulted. One of the
more chastening features of this research effort, however, was the discovery
that much of the secondary literature was unreliable in details: inconsistencies and contradictions among secondary sources (and between secondary
and primary sources) abounded. All problematic items in the secondary literature thus were treated simply as leads back into the state constitutions,
codes, session laws, and court cases. Items are included in the tables only
when they could be verified.

I am reasonably confident that these tables are comprehensive with respect to constitutional provisions: that is, they include all constitutional requirements (on the subjects examined) that were in force at any point
during the period. Comprehensiveness with respect to statutes (as well as
case law), however, is more difficult to achieve. In most states, some (usually minor) dimensions of suffrage law could be shaped by statutory provisions, court decisions, and even municipal regulations; some of these
changes may well have escaped my notice, particularly for those states
where the annual session laws were not exhaustively examined. Local residency requirements, for example, might have shifted back and forth without leaving an imprint on periodic codifications of a state's laws; the same
was true of laws permitting women to vote for school boards. It is, thus,
possible that there are (presumably minor) errors of omission in some of the
tables: this caution would apply primarily to tables A.10, A.11, A.13, A.15,
and A.17 to A.19.

Finally, it should be noted that, in all of the tables, the dates accompanying particular legal provisions are the earliest dates on which I have found such provisions. Unless otherwise indicated, these laws remained in force for the duration of the period covered by each table.

TABLE A.1 Suffrage Requirements: 1776–1790

State	Property or Taxpaying Requirement	Residency	Gender[1]	Race
Connecticut: 1715 (S)[2]	Freehold estate worth 40 shillings per year or 40 pounds personal estate.	—	—	—
Delaware: 1776 (C) and 1734 (S)	"Freeholder . . . and has 50 acres of land or more well seated, and 12 acres or more thereof cleared," or "is otherwise worth 40 pounds money of this government clear estate."	2 years in state.	—	—
Georgia: 1777 (C)	"Possessed in his own right of 10 pounds value, and liable to pay tax in this State, or being of any mechanic trade."	6 months in state.	Male	White
Georgia: 1789 (C)	Paid all taxes for year preceding the election.	6 months in county.	—	—
Maryland: 1776 (C)	Freehold of 50 acres or property above value of 30 pounds.	No requirement if 50-acre freeholder; otherwise, 1 year in county.	Freemen	—
Massachusetts:1780 (C)	Freehold estate with annual income of 3 pounds, or any estate worth 60 pounds to vote for Senate; property must be owned in same town as residence to vote for House.	No requirement to vote for Senate; 1 year in town to vote for House.	Male	—
New Hampshire: 1784 (C)	Poll tax.	No requirement.	Male	—
New Jersey: 1776 (C)	Worth 50 pounds proclamation money, clear estate in the same.	1 year in county.	—	—
New York: 1777 (C)[3]	For Assembly: "Freeholder, possessing a freehold of the value of 20 pounds, . . . or have rented a tenement therein of the yearly value of 40 shillings, and been rated and actually paid taxes to this State." Exceptions for "every person who now is a freeman of the city of Albany, or who was made a freeman of the city of New York on or before" 14 October 1775. For Senate: Owners of freeholds valued at "one hundred pounds, over and above all debts charged thereon."	6 months in county.	Male	—

State: Year (Type)	Property / Tax Requirement	Residency	Gender	Race
North Carolina: 1776 (C)	Freehold of 50 acres of land owned for 6 months prior to election to vote for Senate; must have paid public taxes to vote for House of Commons.	1 year in county.	Freemen	—
Pennsylvania: 1776 (C)	Paid public taxes in year prior to election (or the sons of freeholders).	1 year in state.	Freemen	—
Pennsylvania: 1790 (C)	Paid state or county tax within 2 years of election, assessed at least 6 months before the election. Exempt if under age 22 and the son of a qualified voter.	2 years in state.	Freemen	—
Rhode Island: 1762 (S)	Freehold worth 40 pounds or 40 shillings per year, or the eldest son of a freeholder.	—	—	—
South Carolina[4]: 1778 (C)	Freehold of 50 acres of land owned for 6 months prior to election, or paid a tax the preceding year, or was taxable the present year, at least 6 months previous to said election, in a sum equal to tax on 50 acres of land.	1 year in state.	Male	White
South Carolina: 1790 (C)	"Freehold of 50 acres of land or a town lot, of which he hath been legally seized and possessed at least six months before such election, or not having such a freehold or town lot, hath been a resident in the election district in which he offers to give his vote 6 months before the said election, and hath paid a tax the preceding year of 3 shillings sterling."	2 years in state.	Male	White
Vermont: 1786 (C)[5,6]	No requirement.	1 year in state.	Freemen	—
Virginia: 1776 (C) and 1762 (S)	"Freehold . . . in at least 50 acres of land, if no settlement be made upon it, or 25 acres, with a plantation and house thereon, at least 12 feet square," or town lot with house "at least 12 feet square."	Must own property 1 year prior to the election, unless received by inheritance, marriage, or marriage settlement.	Male	White

[1] Noted below if gender was expressly mentioned. Only in New Jersey were women permitted to vote.
[2] (S) = statute, (C) = constitution.
[3] Also required all Quakers to pledge allegiance to the state.
[4] Also required that a voter must "acknowledge the being of a God, and believe in a future state of rewards and punishments."
[5] Came into effect with statehood in 1791.
[6] The 1776 constitution also required individuals to be "of a quiet and peaceable behaviour."

TABLE A.2 Property and Taxpaying Requirements for Suffrage: 1790–1855

State	Date of Statehood[1]	Property Requirement	Taxpaying Requirement
Alabama	1819	1819 (C)[2]: None.	1819 (C): None.
Arkansas	1836	1836 (C): None.	1836 (C): None.
California	1850	1849 (C)[3]: None.	1849 (C): None.
Connecticut		1715 (C): Freehold estate worth 40 shillings per year or 40 pounds personal estate.	1715 (S): None.
		1796 (S): Freehold worth $7 a year or possession of personal property worth $134.	1796 (S): None.
		1817 (S): Freehold requirement dropped.	1817 (S): Paid taxes or served in militia.
		1818 (C): Freehold reinstated with taxpaying and militia alternatives.	1818 (C): Taxpaying and militia alternatives to freehold requirement.
		1845 (C): Freehold requirement dropped.	1845 (C): Taxpaying requirement dropped.
Delaware		1734 (S): "Freeholder . . . and has 50 acres of land or more well seated, and 12 acres or more thereof cleared" or "is otherwise worth 40 pounds money of this government of cleared estate."	1734 (S): None.
		1792 (C): None.	1792 (C): "Paid a State or county tax . . . assessed at least six months before the election." Exempt if under age 22 and the son of a qualified voter.
		1831 (C): None.	1831 (C): Paid county tax within 2 years, assessed at least 6 months before the election. Exempt if under age 22.
Florida	1845	1838 (C)[4]: None.	1838 (C): None.
		1845 (C): None.	1845 (C): None.
Georgia		1789 (C): None.	1789 (C): Paid all taxes for year preceding the election.
		1798 (C): None.	1798 (C): Paid all taxes for year preceding the election.
Illinois	1818	1818 (C): None.	1818 (C): None.
		1848 (C): None.	1848 (C): None.

State	Date	Property requirement	Taxpaying requirement
Indiana	1816	1816 (C): None. 1851 (C): None.	1816 (C): None. 1851 (C): None.
Iowa	1846	1846 (C): None.	1846 (C): None.
Kentucky	1792	1792 (C): None. 1799 (C): None. 1850 (C): None.	1792 (C): None. 1799 (C): None. 1850 (C): None.
Louisiana	1812	1812 (C): Exempt from taxpaying requirement if "purchased lands from the United States."	1812 (C): Paid state tax in last 6 months or purchased land from the United States. 1845 (C): None. 1852 (C): None.
Maine	1820	1819 (C)[5]: None.	1819 (C): None in general elections. 1821–33 (S): Paid poll or local tax to vote in town elections.
Maryland		1776 (C): Freehold of 50 acres or property above value of 30 pounds. 1801 (S): Freehold requirement dropped. 1810 (C): None. 1851 (C): None.	1776 (C): None. 1801 (S): None. 1810 (C): None. 1851 (C): None.
Massachusetts		1780 (C): Freehold estate with annual income of 3 pounds, or any estate worth 60 pounds to vote for Senate; property must be owned in same town as residence to vote for House. 1821 (C): Property requirement dropped.	1780 (C): None.
Michigan	1837	1835 (C)[6]: None. 1850 (C): None.	1821 (C): Paid any state or county tax assessed within 2 years, unless exempted from taxation. 1835 (C): None. 1850 (C): None.
Mississippi	1817	1817 (C): None.	1817 (C): Paid state or county tax or enrolled in local militia, unless exempt from military service.
Missouri	1821	1832 (C): None. 1820 (C)[7]: None.	1832 (C): Militia/taxpaying requirement dropped. 1820 (C): None.
New Hampshire		1784 (C): None. 1792 (C): None.	1784 (C): Poll tax. 1792 (C): "Persons excused from paying taxes at their own request" excluded.

(continues)

State	Date of Statehood[1]	Property Requirement	Taxpaying Requirement
New Jersey		1847 (S): None.	1847 (S): Those previously excused from paying taxes can vote after having paid all taxes assessed for a year prior to the election.
		1776 (C): Worth 50 pounds proclamation money, clear estate in the same.	1776 (C): None.
		1807 (S): Worth 50 pounds; any person who paid a state or county tax, or had his name enrolled upon a tax duplicate for the last state or county tax deemed to be worth 50 pounds.	1807 (S): Worth 50 pounds; any person who paid a state or county tax, or had his name enrolled upon a tax duplicate for the last state or county tax, deemed to be worth 50 pounds.
		1844 (C): Property requirement dropped.	1844 (C): Tax requirement dropped.
New York		1777 (C): For Asembly: "freeholder, possessing a freehold of the value of 20 pounds... or have rented a tenement therein of the yearly value of 40 shillings, and been rated and actually paid taxes in this State." Exceptions for "every person who is now a freeman of the city of Albany, or who was made a freeman of the city of New York on or before" 14 October 1775. For Senate: owners of freeholds valued at "one hundred pounds, over and above all debts charged thereon."	1777 (C): See property requirements for 1777.
		1804 (S): Those who rent a tenement worth $25 a year or meet 1777 property requirements.	—
		1821 (C): Property requirement dropped for whites. If a "man of color," must have been for 1 year "seized and possessed of a freehold estate of the value of $250 over and above all debts and incumbrances charged thereon."	1821 (C): If white, "shall have, within the year next preceding the election," paid a state or county tax on real or personal property; or shall by law be exempted from taxation; or "shall have performed within that year military duty in the militia" or as a fireman; or, if meeting special residency requirements, shall have labored on public highways.

State		
North Carolina	1826 (C): None for whites; same requirement as 1821 for "men of color."	1826 (C): If "man of color," 1821 property and tax requirements still in effect.
	1846 (C): None for whites; same requirement as 1821 for "men of color."	1846 (C): If "man of color," 1821 property and tax requirements still in effect.
	1776 (C): Freehold of 50 acres of land to vote for Senate; none for House of Commons.	1776 (C): Must have paid taxes to vote for House of Commons.
	1835 (C): To vote for Senate, freehold of 50 acres for 6 months prior to election; to vote for House of Commons and governor, none.	1835 (C): Must have paid taxes to vote for House of Commons and governor.
	1854 (C)[8]: None.	1854 (C): Must have paid public taxes.
Ohio 1803	1802 (C)[9]: None.	1802 (C): Must have paid or been charged with state or county tax; not applicable to white males above age 21, who are "compelled to labor on the roads" and have resided 1 year in the state.
		1851 (C): Tax requirement dropped.
Pennsylvania	1851 (C): None.	
	1790 (C): None.	1790 (C): Paid state or county tax within 2 years, assessed at least 6 months before the election; exempt if under age 22 and son of a qualified voter.
	1838 (C): None.	1838 (C): Paid state or county tax within 2 years, assessed at least 12 days before the election; exempt if under age 22.
		1762 (S): None.
Rhode Island	1762 (S): Freehold worth 40 pounds or 40 shillings per year, or the eldest son of a freeholder.	
	1842 (C): Ownership of real estate worth $134 or renting an estate for $7 per annum. Native-born male citizen, resident in the state for two years and in the city or county for one year, may vote if he pays a tax of $1 or performs military duty for at least one day in year preceding election. No one shall be allowed to vote for the Providence city council or to vote on any proposal to impose a tax or authorize expenditures, in any city or town, unless he has paid a tax on real estate worth $134 in year preceding election.	1842 (C): See property requirements. Also a registry tax of $1, or "such sum as with his other taxes shall amount to one dollar." Those performing military duty and mariners at sea for the year exempt.

(continues)

TABLE A.2   (continued)

State	Date of Statehood[1]	Property Requirement	Taxpaying Requirement
South Carolina		1790 (C): Freehold of 50 acres or a town lot, owned 6 months prior to election; taxpaying alternative.	1790 (C): If resident for 6 months, must have paid tax year preceding election of 3 shillings sterling.
		1810 (C): Freehold of 50 acres or a town lot, owned for 6 months prior to election; or residence in the election district for 6 months.	1810 (C): Tax requirement dropped.
Tennessee	1796	1796 (C): Freehold in the county wherein he may vote, or inhabitant of any one county in the state 6 months.	1796 (C): None.
		1834 (C): Freehold requirement dropped.	1834 (C): None.
Texas	1845	1845 (C): None.	1845 (C): None.
Vermont	1791	1786 (C)[10]: None.	1786 (C): None.
		1793 (C): None.	1793 (C): None.
		1828 (C): None.	1828 (C): None.
Virginia		1762 (S): "Freehold . . . in at least 50 acres of land, if no settlement be made upon it, or 25 acres, with a plantation and house thereon, at least 12 feet square," or town lot with house "at least 12 feet square."	1762 (S): None.
		1804 (S): Must own land for 6 months prior to election.	1804 (S): None.
		1830 (C): Must meet the qualifications of previous Constitution and laws or be "possessed, or whose tenant for years, at will, or at sufferance is possessed, of an estate or freehold in land of the value of twenty-five dollars, and so assessed to be if any assessment thereof be required by law" or "possessed as tenant in common, joint tenant, or partner of an interest in or share of land, and having an estate of freehold therein, such interest or share being of the value of twenty-five dollars, and so assessed to be if any assessment thereof be required by law" or persons "entitled to a reversion or vested remainder in fee, expectant on an estate for life or lives, in land of the value of fifty dollars, and so assessed to be if any assessment thereof be required by law . . . each and every such citizen, unless his title shall have come to him by descent, devise, marriage or marriage settlement, having been so possessed or	1830 (C): See 1830 property requirements.

entitled for six months" or "shall own and be himself in actual occupation of a leasehold estate, with the evidence of title recorded two months before he shall offer to vote, of a term originally not less than five years, of the annual value or rent of twenty dollars" or persons "who for twelve months next preceding has been a housekeeper and head of a family within the county, city, town, borough, or election district where he may offer to vote, and shall have been assessed. . . within the preceding year, and actually paid the same" and "in the case of two or more tenants in common, joint tenants, or partners in possession, reversion, or remainder, having interest in land, the value whereof shall be insufficient to entitle them all to vote, they shall together have as many votes as the value of the land shall entitle them to; and the legislature shall by law provide the mode in which their vote or votes shall in such case be given."

1850 (C): Property requirement dropped.
1848 (C): None.

1850 (C): Tax requirement dropped.
1848 (C): None.

Wisconsin	1848	

[1]If not one of the original 13 states.
[2](C) = constitution, (S) = statute.
[3]Came into effect with statehood in 1850.
[4]Came into effect with statehood in 1845.
[5]Came into effect with statehood in 1820.
[6]Came into effect with statehood in 1837.
[7]Came into effect with statehood in 1821.
[8]Amendment proposed by the General Assembly of 1854 and submitted to the people in 1856; ratified on 6 August 1856.
[9]Came into effect with statehood in 1803.
[10]Came into effect with statehood in 1791.

TABLE A.3   Chronology of Property Requirements for Suffrage: 1790–1855

Year	Number of States in Union	Number of States with Property Requirements	States with Property Requirements	Year Requirement Adopted	Year Requirement Terminated
1790	13	10	Connecticut	1715	1817
			Delaware	1734	1792
			Rhode Island	1762; 1842 with exemptions for native-born citizens.	—
			Virginia	1762	1850
			Maryland	1776	1801 in elections for state officials, 1810 for all elections.
			New Jersey	1776; 1807 with taxpaying alternative.	1844
			North Carolina	1776; requirement for Senate, none for House.	1854
			New York	1777; exceptions for freemen of Albany in 1777 or freemen of New York in 1775 in Assembly elections	1821 for whites only.
			Massachusetts	1780	1821
			South Carolina	1790 with taxpaying alternative; 1810 with residency alternative.	—
1800	16	10	Tennessee	1796 with residency alternative.	1834
1810	17	9			
1820	23	9	Connecticut	1818 with taxpaying and militia alternatives.	1845
1830	24	8			
1840	26	7			
1850	31	4			
1855	31	3[1]			

[1]In 1855, the three states with property requirements were Rhode Island, New York, and South Carolina; however, Rhode Island exempted native-born citizens, New York's requirement only applied to African Americans, and South Carolina offered a residency alternative.

TABLE A.4 Race and Citizenship Requirements for Suffrage: 1790–1855

State and Year of Statehood[1]	Date of Requirement	Race	Citizenship	Native Americans
Alabama (1819)	1819 (C)[2]	White	U.S. citizen	—
Arkansas (1836)	1836 (C)	White	U.S. citizen, citizen of the state for 6 months	—
California (1850)	1849 (C)[3]	White	U.S. citizen or Mexican citizen who became a U.S. citizen under the Queretaro Treaty of 1848	The legislature may by a two-thirds vote admit "to the right of suffrage, Indians, or the descendants of Indians, in such special cases as such a proportion of the legislative body may deem just and proper."
Connecticut	1715 (S)	No requirement	—	—
	1818 (C)	White	U.S. citizen	—
	1845 (C)	White	U.S. citizen	—
Delaware	1734 (S)	No requirement	—	—
	1792 (C)	White	No requirement	—
	1831 (C)	White	Citizen	—
Florida (1845)	1838 (C)[4]	White	U.S. citizen	—
Georgia	1789 (C)	No requirement[5]	Citizen of state	—
	1798 (C)	No requirement[5]	Citizen of state	—
Illinois (1818)	1818 (C)	White	No requirement	—
	1848 (C)	White	Citizen, or inhabitant of state on 1 April 1848	—
Indiana (1816)	1816 (C)	White	U.S. citizen	—
	1851 (C)	"No negro or mulatto"	U.S. citizen or alien declarant with 1 year of U.S. residence	—
Iowa (1846)	1846 (C)	White	U.S. citizen	—

(continues)

TABLE A.4 (continued)

State and Year of Statehood[1]	Date of Requirement	Race	Citizenship	Native Americans
Kentucky (1792)	1792 (C)	No requirement	Citizen	—
	1799 (C)	"Negroes, mulattoes, and Indians excepted"	Citizen	"Indians" specifically excluded
Louisiana (1812)	1850 (C)	White	Citizen	—
	1812 (C)	White	U.S. citizen	—
	1845 (C)	White	U.S. citizen for 2 years	—
	1852 (C)	White	U.S. citizen	—
Maine (1820)	1819 (C)[6]	No requirement	U.S. citizen	"Indians not taxed" excluded
Maryland	1776 (C)	No requirement	No requirement	—
	1801 (S)	White		—
	1810 (C)	White	Citizen of state	—
	1851 (C)	White	U.S. citizen	—
Massachusetts	1780 (C)	No requirement	No requirement	—
	1807[7]	—	—	Inhabitants of incorporated plantations not entitled to vote for governor or lieutenant governor; this effectively excluded many Indians
Michigan (1837)	1821 (C)	No requirement	Citizen	—
	1835 (C)[8]	White	Citizen or inhabitant of state at time of signing of 1835 constitution	"Every civilized male inhabitant of Indian descent, a native of the United States and not a member of any tribe, shall be an elector and entitled to vote"
	1850 (C)	White	U.S. citizen or inhabitant residing in state on 24 June 1835 or inhabitant who had declared his intention to become a citizen.	
Mississippi (1817)	1817 (C)	White	U.S. citizen	—
	1832 (C)	White	U.S. citizen	—

State	Year			
Missouri (1821)	1820 (C)[9]	White	U.S. citizen	—
New Hampshire	1792 (C)	No requirement	No requirement	—
	1813 (S)	No requirement	Citizen	—
New Jersey	1776 (C)	No requirement	No requirement	—
	1807 (S)	White	Citizen	—
	1844 (C)	White	U.S. citizen	—
New York	1777 (C)	No requirement	No requirement	—
	1804 (S)	—	Citizen	—
	1821 (C)	White or "man of color" meeting property and tax requirements	Citizen; if a "man of color," citizen of state for 3 years	—
	1826 (C)	Same as 1821	Same as 1821	—
	1846 (C)	Same as 1821	Citizen for 10 days; if "man of color," citizen for 3 years	—
North Carolina	1776 (C)	No requirement	No requirement	—
	1835 (C)	White[10]	No requirement	—
Ohio (1803)	1802 (C)[11]	White	No requirement	—
	1809 (S)	—	U.S. citizen	—
	1851 (C)	White	U.S. citizen	—
Pennsylvania	1790 (C)	No requirement	Citizen	—
	1838 (C)	White	U.S. citizen	—
Rhode Island	1762 (S)	No requirement	—	—
	1842 (C)	No requirement	U.S. citizen	Members of the Narragansett tribe excluded
South Carolina	1790 (C)	White	Citizen of state	—
	1810 (C)	White	Citizen of state	—

(continues)

TABLE A.4 *(continued)*

State and Year of Statehood[1]	Date of Requirement	Race	Citizenship	Native Americans
Tennessee (1796)	1796 (C)	No requirement	No requirement	—
	1834 (C)	White; "*Provided,* That no person shall be disqualified from voting in any election on account of color, who is now, by the laws of this State, a competent witness in a court of justice against a white man."	U.S. citizen and citizen of the county "wherein he may offer his vote" for 6 months	—
Texas (1845)	1845 (C)	"Indians not taxed, Africans, and descendants of Africans" excluded	U.S. citizen or person "who is at the time of the adoption of this Constitution by the Congress of the United States a citizen of the Republic of Texas" or no requirement if a resident of Texas for 6 months before the acceptance of the 1845 constitution by Congress	"Indians not taxed" excluded
Vermont (1791)	1786 (C)[12]	No requirement	No requirement	—
	1793 (C)	No requirement	No requirement	—
	1828 (C)	No requirement	U.S. citizen or freeman before the 1828 amendment[13]	—
Virginia	1762 (S)	White	—	—
	1830 (C)	White	"Citizen of the commonwealth"	—
	1850 (C)	White	"Citizen of the commonwealth"	—

| Wisconsin (1848) | 1848 (C) | White | U.S. citizen or alien declarant (see also Native Americans) | "Persons of Indian blood who have once been declared by law of Congress to be citizens of the United States, any subsequent law of Congress notwithstanding," or "civilized persons of Indian descent, not members of any tribe" could vote |

[1]If not one of the original 13 states.

[2](C) = constitution, (S) = statute.

[3]Came into effect with statehood in 1850.

[4]Came into effect with statehood in 1845.

[5]Georgia's 1777 constitution explicitly limited the franchise to whites, but the constitutions of 1789 and 1798 did not. All secondary sources agree that blacks could not vote, but a very extensive research effort has not turned up a clear legal basis for that exclusion—although there are indications that only whites could become state citizens.

[6]Came into effect with statehood in 1820.

[7]*In Re Opinion of the Justices* (1807), 3 Mass 568.

[8]Came into effect with statehood in 1837.

[9]Came into effect with statehood in 1821.

[10]"No free Negro, free mulatto, or free person of mixed blood, descended from negro ancestors to the fourth generation inclusive (though one ancestor of each generation may have been a white person), shall vote for members of the Senate or House of Commons."

[11]Came into effect with statehood in 1803.

[12]Came into effect with statehood in 1791.

[13]Noncitizens remaind able to vote in local elections until 1864.

TABLE A.5 Chronology of Race Exclusions: 1790–1855

Year	Number of States in Union	Number of States with Race Exclusions	States with Race Exclusions	Year Requirement Adopted
1790	13	3	Virginia	1762
			Georgia	1777[1]
			South Carolina	1790
1800	16	5	Delaware	1792
			Kentucky	1799
1810	17	8	Maryland	1801 by statute, 1810 by constitutional amendment
			Ohio	1803
1820	23	14	New Jersey	1807 by statute, 1844 by constitution
			Louisiana	1812
			Indiana	1816
			Mississippi	1817
			Connecticut	1818
			Illinois	1818
			Alabama	1819
1830	24	15	Missouri	1821
1840	26	20	New York	1821: Different requirements for whites and for men "of color"[2]
			Tennessee	1834: White, but "no person shall be disqualified from voting in any election on account of color, who is now . . . a competent witness in a court of justice against a white man"
			North Carolina	1835
			Arkansas	1836
			Michigan	1837
			Pennsylvania	1838
1850	31	25	Florida	1845
			Texas	1845
			Iowa	1846
			Wisconsin	1848
			California	1850
1855	31	25		

[1]See table A.4.
[2]New York is not counted as a state with a race exclusion, although the stiff property requirement for "men of color" was obviously discriminatory.

TABLE A.6 Pauper Exclusions: 1790–1920

State	All Paupers	Inmates of Institutions	Inmates Barred from Residence in Locale of Institution
Arizona	—	—	1910 (C)[1,2]
Arkansas	1873 (C) 1874 (C): No exclusion	—	—
California	—	—	1849 (C)[3]
Colorado	—	—	1879 (C)
Connecticut	—	—	1902 (S)[4]
Delaware	1831 (C)	—	—
Idaho	—	—	1889 (C)[5]
Illinois	—	—	1877 (S)[6]
Kansas	—	—	1859 (C)[7]
Louisiana	1845 (C)[8]	1898 (C): Inmates of any charitable institution, except the Soldier's Home.	—
Maine	1819 (C)[9]	—	—
Massachusetts	1821 (C)[10] 1881 (S): Civil War veterans exempted.	—	—
Michigan	—	—	1908 (C)[11]
Minnesota	—	—	1857 (C)[12]
Missouri	—	1875 (C)	1875 (C)
Montana	—	—	1889 (C)
Nevada	—	—	1864 (C)
New Hampshire	1792 (C) 1847 (S): Exclusion may be reversed if cost of public assistance is reimbursed. 1881 (S): Honorably discharged veterans of the Civil War exempted.	—	—

(continues)

TABLE A.6 (continued)

State	All Paupers	Inmates of Institutions	Inmates Barred from Residence in Locale of Institution
New Hampshire (continued)	1901 (S): Persons receiving aid within 90 days of the election.	—	—
New Jersey	1844 (C)	—	—
New York	—	—	1894 (C)
Oklahoma	—	1907 (C): Any person kept in a poorhouse at public expense, except federal, Confederate, and Spanish-American ex-soldiers or sailors.[13]	—
Oregon	—	—	1857 (C)[14]
Pennsylvania	—	—	1873 (C)[15]
Rhode Island	1842 (C)	—	—
South Carolina	1810 (C)	—	—
	1895 (C): Paupers supported at public expense.	1868 (C)	—
Texas	1876 (C): Paupers supported by any county.	—	—
Virginia	1830 (C)[16]	—	—
	1902 (C)	—	—
Washington	—	—	1902 (C)
West Virginia	1861 (C)	—	1889 (C)

[1](C) = constitution, (S) = statute.
[2]Came into effect with statehood in 1912.
[3]Came into effect with statehood in 1850.
[4]"If any person shall be supported in any town as a pauper by the payment to such town of any weekly or other regular sum of money from any other town, his legal residence for the purposes of registration shall be the town to which he is chargeable."

[5]Came into effect with statehood in 1890.

[6]Inmates cannot gain residence by moving to an institution, but are considered residents of the locale that they lived in prior to institutionalization; honorably discharged soldiers and sailors excepted.

[7]Came into effect with statehood in 1861.

[8]Repealed by 1868 constitution.

[9]Came into effect with statehood in 1820.

[10]In 1811, paupers were excluded from town and district elections (Mass. *Gen. Laws*, 1811, Chap. 9).

[11]Inmates cannot gain residence while kept at any asylum at public expense; honorably discharged soldiers, seamen and marines excepted.

[12]Came into effect with statehood in 1858.

[13]Oklahoma Territory had excluded paupers in 1890.

[14]Came into effect with statehood in 1859.

[15]Bar affirmed by Pennsylvania Supreme Court in 1877 despite fact that inmates were generally not permitted to return to their homes to vote (see Steinfeld, 1989: 335).

[16]Repealed by 1870 constitution.

TABLE A.7 Suffrage Exclusions for Criminal Offenses: 1790–1857

State[1]	Date of Requirement	Constitutional Exclusion[2]	Constitutional Authorization of State Legislatures to Exclude Felons[3]
Alabama	1819 (C)[4]	—	"Laws shall be made to exclude from . . . suffrage . . . those who shall hereafter be convicted of bribery, perjury, forgery, or other high crimes and misdemeanors."
California	1849 (C)[5]	Persons convicted of any infamous crime.	"Laws shall be made to exclude from . . . the right of suffrage those who shall hereafter be convicted of bribery, perjury, forgery, or other high crime."
Connecticut	1818 (C)	Those convicted of bribery, forgery, perjury, dueling, fraudulent bankruptcy, theft, or other offense for which an infamous punishment is inflicted.	—
Delaware	1831 (C)	Those convicted of a felony.	"The legislature may impose the forfeiture of the right of suffrage as a punishment for crime."
Florida	1838 (C)[6]	—	"Laws shall be made by the General Assembly to exclude from . . . suffrage those who shall have been, or may thereafter be, convicted of bribery, perjury, forgery, or other high crime or misdemeanor." Also, "the General Assembly shall have power to exclude from . . . the right of suffrage, all persons convicted of bribery, perjury, or other infamous crimes."
Illinois	1818 (C)	—	"The General Assembly shall have full power to exclude from the privilege of electing or being elected any person convicted of bribery, perjury, or any other infamous crime."
Indiana	1816 (C)	—	"The General Assembly shall have full power to exclude from electing, or being elected, any person convicted of any infamous crime."
	1851 (C)	—	"The General Assembly shall have power to deprive of the right of suffrage, and to render ineligible any person convicted of an infamous crime."
Iowa	1846 (C)	Those convicted of any infamous crime.	—

State	Year		
Kentucky	1792 (C)	—	"Laws shall be made to exclude from . . . suffrage those who thereafter be convicted of bribery, perjury, forgery, or other high crimes and misdemeanors."
	1850 (C)	—	"Laws shall be made to exclude from . . . suffrage those convicted of bribery, perjury, forgery, or other crimes or high misdemeanors."
Louisiana	1812 (C)	Persons engaged in a duel with deadly weapons against a citizen of Louisiana.	"Laws shall be made to exclude from . . . suffrage those who shall thereafter be convicted of bribery, perjury, forgery, or other high crimes or misdemeanors."
	1845 (C)	Persons "under interdiction" or "under conviction of any crime punishable with hard labor."	—
Maryland	1851 (C)	Persons "convicted of larceny or other infamous crime" unless pardoned by the executive; persons convicted of bribery at elections "forever disqualified from voting."	—
Minnesota	1857 (C)[7]	Those convicted of treason or felony until restored to civil rights.	—
Mississippi	1817 (C)	—	"Laws shall be made to exclude from . . . suffrage, those who shall thereafter be convicted of bribery, perjury, forgery, or other high crimes or misdemeanors."
Missouri	1820 (C)[8]	Persons convicted of electoral bribery, for ten years.	"The General Assembly shall have power to exclude . . . from the right of suffrage, all persons convicted of bribery, perjury, or other infamous crime."
New Jersey	1844 (C)	Those convicted of felonies unless pardoned or restored by law to the right of suffrage.	"The legislature may pass laws to deprive persons of the right of suffrage who shall be convicted of bribery."
New York	1821 (C)	—	"Laws may be passed excluding from the right of suffrage persons . . . convicted of infamous crimes."
	1846 (C)	—	"Laws may be passed excluding from the right of suffrage all persons who have been or may be convicted of bribery, larceny, or of any other infamous crime" and for wagering on elections.

(continues)

TABLE A.7 Suffrage Exclusions for Criminal Offenses: 1790–1857

State[1]	Date of Requirement	Constitutional Exclusion[2]	Constitutional Authorization of State Legislatures to Exclude Felons[3]
Ohio	1802 (C)[9]	—	"The legislature shall have full power to exclude from the privilege of voting . . . any person convicted of bribery, perjury, or otherwise infamous crime."
	1851 (C)	—	"The General Assembly shall have the power to exclude from the privilege of voting . . . any person convicted of bribery, perjury, or other infamous crime."
Oregon	1857 (C)[10]	Those convicted of crimes punishable by imprisonment.	—
Rhode Island	1842 (C)	Those convicted of bribery or of any crime deemed infamous at common law, until expressly restored to the right of suffrage by act of General Assembly.	—
Tennessee	1834 (C)	—	"Laws may be passed excluding from the right of suffrage persons who may be convicted of infamous crimes."
Texas	1845 (C)	—	"Laws shall be made to exclude . . . from the right of suffrage those who shall hereafter be convicted of bribery, perjury, forgery, or other high crimes."
Vermont	1793 (C)	"Any elector who shall receive any gift or reward for his vote, in meat, drink, moneys, or otherwise, shall forfeit his right to elect at that time, and suffer such other penalty as the law shall direct."	State supreme court empowered until 1830s to disenfranchise those guilty of bribery, corruption, or other crimes.

Virginia	1830 (C)	Those convicted of an infamous offense.	—
	1850 (C)	Those convicted of electoral bribery or an infamous offense.	—
Wisconsin	1848 (C)	Persons "convicted of treason or felony.... unless restored to civil rights." Also a permanent disqualification for direct or indirect involvement in dueling.	"Laws may be passed excluding from the right of suffrage all persons ... convicted of bribery, or larceny, or any infamous crime," and betting on elections.

[1]States not listed had no provisions for the exclusion of felons.
[2]In 1837, Arkansas passed a law excluding felons without any apparent prior constitutional authorization.
[3]Presumably, all state legislatures that were instructed (rather than simply enabled) to pass restrictive laws did so. Among states where legislatures were permitted but not required to pass legislation, laws were passed in Delaware, Indiana, Louisiana, Missouri, New York, Illinois, Ohio, and Tennessee.
[4](C) = constitution.
[5]Came into effect with statehood in 1850
[6]Came into effect with statehood in 1845.
[7]Came into effect with statehood in 1858.
[8]Came into effect with statehood in 1821.
[9]Came into effect with statehood in 1803.
[10]Came into effect with statehood in 1859.

TABLE A.8   Labor Force Changes in Selected States: 1820–1850

State	Ratio of Persons Engaged in Agriculture to Persons Engaged in Commerce and Manufactures			Number Employed in Manufactures	
	1820	1840	1850	1820	1850
Maine	4.6	4.1	2.0	7,643	28,078
New Hampshire	5.4	4.0	1.7	8,699	27,092
Massachusetts	1.4	0.9	0.4	33,464	165,938
Rhode Island	1.7	0.7	0.4	6,091	20,881
Connecticut	2.4	1.8	0.8	17,541	47,770
Vermont	5.5	5.0	2.8	8,484	8,445
New York	3.6	2.3	1.0	60,038	199,349
New Jersey	2.3	1.9	0.7	15,941	37,311
Pennsylvania	2.1	1.7	0.8	60,215	146,766
Delaware	4.0	3.5	1.4	2,821	3,888
Maryland	3.4	2.8	0.6	18,640	30,124
Ohio	5.4	3.6	1.9	18,956	51,489
Indiana	16.8	6.3	3.6	3,229	14,342
Illinois	10.0	6.7	3.9	1,007	12,065
Missouri	5.8	6.8	2.2	1,952	16,850
Michigan	2.5	7.4	2.9	196	9,290

Sources: U.S. Census 1820, *Aggregate Amount of Each Description of Persons in the United States* (Washington, 1821), 1; U.S. Census 1850, *Occupations of the Male Inhabitants*, vol. 1 (Washington, 1853), lxvii–xxx; U.S. Census 1850, *Compendium of the Seventh Census* (Washington, 1854), 125–29.

TABLE A.9 Summary of Suffrage Requirements in Force: 1855

State	Race	Residence[1]	Citizenship	Property	Taxpaying	Military Service Personnel Cannot Acquire Residence or Vote	Criminal Exclusion in Place or Authorized by State Constitution	Other Exclusions
Alabama: 1819 constitution	White	1 year in state, 3 months in county, city, or town	U.S. citizen	—	—	Yes*	Yes	—
Arkansas: 1836 constitution	White	6 months in state	U.S. citizen; state citizen for 6 months	—	—	Yes*	Yes	—
California: 1849 constitution	White	6 months in state, 30 days in county or district	U.S. citizen	—	—	Yes	Yes	Idiots, insane persons
Connecticut[2]: 1818 constitution, 1845 and 1855 amendments	White	1 year in state, 6 months in town	U.S. citizen	—	—	—	Yes	Literacy
Delaware: 1831 amendment	White	1 year in state, 1 month in county	Citizen	—	Paid county tax within 2 years, assessed 6 months prior to election, exempt if under age 22	Yes	Yes	Paupers, idiots, insane persons
Florida: 1838 constitution, 1847 amendment	White	1 year in state, 6 months in county	U.S. citizen	—	—	—	Yes	—
Georgia: 1798 constitution	White (see table A.4)	6 months in county	State citizen	—	Paid all taxes for year prior to election	—	—	—

(continues)

TABLE A.9 (continued)

State	Race	Residence[1]	Citizenship	Property	Taxpaying	Military Service Personnel Cannot Acquire Residence or Vote	Criminal Exclusion in Place or Authorized by State Constitution	Other Exclusions
Illinois: 1848 constitution	White	1 year in state[3]	Citizen[4]	—	—	—	Yes	—
Indiana: 1851 constitution	White	6 months in state, 60 days in township, 30 days in precinct or ward	U.S. citizen or alien declarant with 1 year of U.S. residence	—	—	Yes*	Yes	—
Iowa: 1846 constitution	White	6 months in state, 20 days in county	U.S. citizen	—	—	Yes	Yes	Idiots, insane persons
Kentucky: 1850 constitution	White	2 years in state or 1 year in county, town, or city; 60 days in precinct	Citizen	—	—	—	Yes	—
Louisiana: 1852 constitution	White	12 months in state, 6 months in parish	U.S. citizen	—	—	Yes*	Yes	Paupers
Maine: 1819 constitution	"Indians not taxed" excluded	3 months in state	U.S. citizen	—	—	Yes	—	Paupers, persons under guardianship
Maryland: 1851 constitution	White	1 year in state, 6 months in county or Baltimore	U.S. citizen	—	—	—	Yes	Any person "under guardianship as a lunatic, or . . . non compos mentis"
Massachusetts: 1780 constitution, 1821 amendment	Indians living on incorporated plantations cannot vote for governor or lieutenant governor	1 year in state, 6 months in town or district	Citizen	—	Paid any state or county tax assessed within 2 years, unless legally exempted	—	—	Paupers, persons under guardianship

Michigan: 1850 constitution	White or "civilized male" Indian, "not a member of any tribe"	For citizens, 6 months in state, 20 days in township, for alien declarant, 2 years in state, 6 months in county	U.S. citizen, or inhabitant of state on 24 June 1835 or 1 January 1850, or alien declarant	—	—	Yes	—	—
Mississippi: 1832 constitution	White	1 year in state, 4 months in county, city, or town	U.S. citizen	—	—	—	Yes	—
Missouri: 1820 constitution	White	1 year in state, 3 months in county or district	U.S. citizen	—	—	Yes*	Yes	—
New Hampshire: 1792 constitution, 1847 statute	—	6 months in state, 3 months in town	Citizen	—	Poll tax[5]	—	—	Paupers
New Jersey: 1844 constitution	White	1 year in state, 5 months in county	U.S. citizen	—	—	Yes	Yes	Paupers, idiots, insane persons
New York: 1846 constitution	Separate requirement for "men of color"	1 year in state, 4 months in county, 30 days in district	Citizen for 10 days; if "man of color," state citizen for 3 years	For "men of color," only†	If "man of color," must have paid tax on estate[6]	Yes	Yes	—
North Carolina: 1776 constitution, 1835 and 1854 amendments	White	—	—	—	Must have paid "public taxes"	—	—	—
Ohio: 1851 constitution	White	1 year in state, resident of county, township, or ward "as may be presented by law"	U.S. citizen	—	—	Servicemen stationed in state cannot acquire residence	Yes	Idiots, insane persons

(continues)

TABLE A.9 *(continued)*

State	Race	Residence[1]	Citizenship	Property	Taxpaying	Military Service Personnel Cannot Acquire Residence or Vote	Criminal Exclusion in Place or Authorized by State Constitution	Other Exclusions
Pennsylvania: 1838 constitution	White	1 year in state, 10 days in election district	U.S. citizen	—	Paid state or county tax within 2 years, assessed at least ten days prior to elections; exempt if under age 22	—	—	—
Rhode Island: 1842 constitution	—	1 year in state, 6 months in town or city (property req.); 2 years in state and 6 months in city or county (tax req.)	U.S. citizen	Nonnative citizens must own real estate worth $134 or rent such an estate for $7 per annum	Native-born male citizens must pay tax of $1 or perform military duty for one day in year preceding election	Yes	Yes	Paupers, lunatics, persons non compos mentis, persons under guardianship
South Carolina: 1790 constitution, 1810 amendment	White	2 years in state, 6 months in district if not meeting freehold requirement	State citizen	Freehold of 50 acres of land or a town lot owned for 6 months; or resident of district for 6 months	—	Yes[7]	—	Paupers
Tennessee: 1834 constitution	White[8]	6 months in county	U.S. citizen	—	—	—	Yes	—
Texas: 1845 constitution	"Indians nottaxed, Africans and descendants of Africans" excluded	1 year in state, 6 months in county, district, city, or town	U.S. citizen[9]	—	—	Yes*	Yes	—

Vermont: 1793 constitution, 1828 amendment	—	1 year in state	U.S. citizen or freeman before 1828 (except local elections)	—	Yes	Required to be of "quiet and peaceable behavior"
Virginia: 1850 constitution	White	2 years in state, 12 months in county, city, or town	Citizen of commonwealth	Yes[10]	Yes	Paupers, persons "of unsound mind"
Wisconsin: 1848 constitution	White, or "persons of Indian blood" who are U.S. citizens or "civilized" and "not members of any tribe"	1 year in state	U.S. citizen or alien declarant or native American as specified	—	Yes	Persons under guardianship, non compos mentis, or insane

*All military personnel excluded from voting, without mention of residence.

[1]In most states, residence could not be gained or lost by the following: employment in the service of the United States or the state, navigation of the state's waterways or the high seas, attendance at a college or seminary of learning, residence at an almshouse or asylum at public expense, or confinement in prison.

[2]Voters also had to "sustain a good moral character."

[3]Or resident on 1 April 1848.

[4]Unless an inhabitant of the state on 1 April 1848.

[5]Those excused from paying taxes at their own request were excluded, but they could regain the franchise after having paid all taxes assessed for the year prior to election.

[6]"Men of color" were exempt from direct taxation by the state unless they owned an estate of the value of $250.

†See table A.2 for details.

[7]"Non-commissioned officers and private soldiers of the army of the United States" excluded.

[8]Tennessee stipulated that voters must be white, but added that "no person shall be disqualified from voting in any election on account of color, who is now by the laws of this State, a competent witness in a court of justice against a white man."

[9]Or person who is at the time of statehood a citizen of the Republic of Texas, or resident of Texas for six months "immediately preceding the acceptance of this Constitution by the Congress of the United States."

[10]"Non-commissioned officers and private soldiers of the army of the United States" excluded; servicemen stationed in the state cannot acquire residence.

TABLE A.10 States with Taxpaying Requirements for Suffrage: 1870–1921

State	Date of Requirement	Taxpaying Requirement[1]
Alabama	1901 (C)[2]	Poll tax of $1.50 for those age 21 to 45; legislature authorized to increase maximum age "to not more than 60 years." After 1 January 1903, if using property alternative to literacy requirement, paid all taxes on that property.
Arizona	1910 (C)[3]	"Questions upon bond issues or special assessments shall be submitted to the vote of real property tax payers."
Arkansas	1893 (C)	Poll tax. Must present receipt or other evidence that tax has been paid.
Delaware	1897 (C)	1831 tax requirement repealed.
Florida	1885 (C)	"The legislature shall have power to make the payment of the capitation tax a prerequisite for voting, and all such taxes received shall go into the school fund."
Georgia	1889 (S)	Poll tax of $1.
	1866 (S)	Poll tax of $1.
	1868 (C)	Paid taxes required for year preceding election.
	1907 (S)	Paid all taxes since the 1877 constitution at least 6 months prior to election.
Kansas	1905 (S)	Only taxpayers vote for drainage district officers.
Kentucky	1892 (S)	Municipality can require poll tax in municipal election.
Louisiana	1898 (C)	If younger than 60, paid poll tax of $1 per annum for two years. If using property alternative to literacy requirement, paid all taxes on that property.
Maryland	1921 (C)	Repealed.
	—	Legislature enacted numerous laws permitting various communities to restrict municipal franchise to taxpayers.
	1908 (S)	Taxpaying requirement for local elections in Annapolis unless other criteria met.[4]
Massachusetts	1881 (C)	Exemption from poll tax for Civil War veterans who were paupers.
	1891 (C)	1821 tax requirement repealed.
Mississippi	1890 (C)	Paid all taxes for 2 preceding years by February 1 of the election year. Exemption for ministers with 6 months residence in district. Also $2 poll tax, except for persons who are "deaf and dumb or blind, or who are maimed by loss of hand or foot; said tax to be a lien only upon taxable property."
Montana	1889 (C)	"Upon all questions submitted to the vote of the taxpayers of the State, or any political division thereof, women who are taxpayers and possessed of the qualifications for the right of suffrage required by men by this Constitution equally, with men, have the right to vote."
Nevada	1864 (C)	Annual poll tax "and the legislature may, in its discretion, make such payment a condition to the right of voting." Payment of poll tax not required for those in army or navy.
	1865 (S)	Every male inhabitant between ages 21 and 60 must pay poll tax of $4 unless exempted by law.

State	Type/Year	Requirement
New Hampshire	1902 (C)	Excludes persons excused from paying taxes at their own request.
	1913 (S)	Poll tax of $2 for every male inhabitant between age 21 and 70 except paupers, insane persons or others exempt by law.
New York	1910 (S)	To vote for School district officers must own property in the district liable to taxation for school purposes, or be the parent or guardian of a child of school age.
North Carolina	1876 (C)	Poll tax.
Oklahoma	1907 (S)	Taxpayers only may vote to authorize incurring of debts by city or town.
Pennsylvania	1873 (C)	Paid state or county tax at least 1 month before the election.
	1913 (S)	Paid taxes on or before the last day of registration.
Rhode Island	1888 (C)	Property requirement repealed for state elections, but registry tax of $1 or other tax must be paid. To vote in city elections or on any proposition to impose a tax, paid tax on property worth at least $134.
	1896 (C)	"No person shall at any time be allowed to vote in the election of the city council of any city, or upon any proposition to impose a tax or for the expenditure of money in any town or city, unless he shall within the year next preceding have paid a tax assessed upon his property therein valued at least $134."
South Carolina	1895 (C)	Poll tax; if registering for the first time after 1 January 1898, paid all property taxes collectible during previous year. Proof of payment required. In addition, property/taxpaying alternative to literacy test: paid all taxes collectible during previous year on property assessed at $300 or more.
Tennessee	1870 (C)	Poll tax; proof of payment required.
Texas	1876 (C)	Paid property tax to vote in municipal elections to "determine expenditure of money or assumption of debt."
	1883 (C)	Poll tax of $1.
	1902 (S)	Paid poll tax and produced receipt by February 1 of election year.
	1910 (S)	Exemptions from poll tax for those over 60, Indians not taxed, insane persons, blind persons, deaf and dumb persons, persons who have lost a hand, persons who have lost a foot, persons permanently disabled.
Utah	1896 (C, S)	Counties, cities, and school districts may incur debt only if approved by a majority of property taxpayers.
Vermont	1915 (S)	For town meetings, paid taxes due February 15 before the meeting unless exempt from taxes.
Virginia	1876 (C)	Paid the capitation tax required by law for year preceding election.
	1902 (C)	If using property alternative to literacy requirement between 1902 and 1903, paid "state taxes aggregating at least one dollar" on the property. If registered after 1 January 1904, paid poll taxes for the 3 years preceding registration at least 6 months prior to the election. Exemption for Civil War veterans.

[1] For taxpaying requirements prior to 1870 see table A.2. After 1870, those requirements remained in force in Delaware, Massachusetts, New Hampshire, Pennsylvania, and Rhode Island.

[2] (C) = constitution, (S) = statute.

[3] Came into effect with statehood in 1912.

[4] Declared unconstitutional in 1915 because of grandfather clause.

TABLE A.11   States with Property Requirements for Suffrage: 1870–1920

State	Date of Requirement	Property Requirement[1]
Alabama	1875 (C)[2]	Constitutional ban on education or property qualifications for suffrage.
	1901 (C)	Exempt from literacy requirement if owning 40 acres of land or real estate assessed at $300.
Arizona	1910 (C)[3]	"Questions upon bond issue or special assessments shall be submitted to the vote of real property tax payers."
Georgia	1907 (S)	Owners of at least 40 acres of land assessed for taxation at $500 exempt from literacy requirement.
Idaho	1889 (C)[4]	Constitutional ban on property qualifications for voting except in school elections, elections creating indebtedness, or irrigation district elections.
Louisiana	1898 (C)	Owners of property worth $300 on which all taxes paid exempt from literacy requirement.
	1921 (C)	No requirement.
Maryland	—	Legislature enacts laws for diverse cities and towns permitting restrictions of municipal suffrage to owners of real estate.[5]
Michigan	1908 (C)	Must own taxable property in district or territory to vote on any question "which involves the direct expenditure of public money or the issue of bond."
Nebraska	1881 (S)	Can vote for school board only if parent of school-age child or owns real property or assessed for personal property.
New York	1910 (S)	To vote for school district officers must own property in district liable to taxation for school purposes, or be the parent or guardian of a child of school age.
Oregon	1898 (S)	To vote in school election must have property with a value of at least $100 or children of school age.
Rhode Island	1888 (C)	Property requirement for state elections repealed. To vote in city council elections anywhere, "or upon any proposition to impose a tax, or for the expenditure of money in any town or city," paid a tax assessed upon property worth at least $134.
	1896 (S)	Property owners exempt from registration requirement.
South Carolina	1895 (C)	If registered after 1 January 1898, property/taxpaying alternative to literacy test: paid all taxes collectible during previous year on property assessed at $300 or more.
Texas	1876 (C)	See table A.10.
Utah	1895 (C)[6]	"Except in elections levying a special tax or creating indebtedness, no property qualification shall be required for any person to vote or hold office."
Virginia	1902 (C)	In 1902 and 1903 a property alternative to literacy requirement. General Assembly may prescribe property qualification not exceeding $250 for county, city, or town elections.

[1]For property requirements prior to 1870 see table A.2. Rhode Island's 1842 property requirement remained in force until 1888.
[2](C) = constitution, (S) = statute.
[3]Came into effect with statehood in 1912.
[4]Came into effect with statehood in 1890.
[5]This practice was upheld by the Maryland Court of Appeals in *Hanna v. Young*, 84 Md. 179 (1896).
[6]Came into effect with statehood in 1896.

TABLE A.12 States with Special Provisions Affecting Aliens and Immigrants: 1870–1926

State	Declarant Aliens Permitted to Vote	Termination of Declarant Alien Voting	Naturalized Citizens Required to Present Naturalization Papers	Waiting Periods and Other Restrictions
Alabama	1867 (C)[1]	1901 (C)	—	—
Arkansas	1868 (C)	1926 (C)	—	—
California	—	—	1872 (S)	1879 (C): Naturalization 90 days prior to election.
Colorado	1876 (C)	1902 (C)	1891 (S): If challenged.	1876 (C): Declarant 4 months prior to election.
Connecticut	—	—	1902 (S)	—
Florida	1868 (C)	1895 (S)	1868 (C)	—
Georgia	1868 (C)	1877 (C)	—	—
Indiana	1851 (C)	1921 (C)	—	—
Kansas	1859 (C)[2]	1917 (C)	—	—
Louisiana	1879 (C)	1898 (C)	—	—
Massachusetts	—	—	1855 (S)	1885 (S): Must be naturalized more than 30 days before registration. 1887: 1885 law declared unconstitutional[3]
Michigan	1850 (C)	1894 (C)[4]	—	1850 (C): Declarant 6 months prior to election.
Minnesota	—	—	—	1857 (C)[5]: U.S. citizen for 3 months.
Missouri	1870 (C)	1924 (C)	1883 (S)	1870 (C): Declarant "not less than one year nor more than five years before he offers to vote."
Montana	1889 (C): For 5 years after the adoption of this constitution.	1894 (C)	1909 (S)	—

(continues)

State	Declarant Aliens Permitted to Vote	Termination of Declarant Alien Voting	Naturalized Citizens Required to Present Naturalization Papers	Waiting Periods and Other Restrictions
Nebraska	1867 (C) 1875 (C)	1918 (C) —	— —	1875 (C): Declarant at least 30 days prior to election.
Nevada	—	—	1913 (S)	1846 (C): Citizen for 10 days.
New York	—	—	1866 (S)	1874 (C): Citizen for 20 days. 1894 (C): Citizen for 90 days.
North Dakota	1889 (C)	1913 (C)	—	1889 (C): Declarant at least 1 year and not more than 6 years prior to election.
Ohio	—	—	1857 (S)	—
Oregon	1857 (C)[6]	1914 (C)	—	1857 (C)[7]: Declarant 1 year preceding election.
Pennsylvania	—	—	1915 (S)	1873 (C): U.S. citizen for 1 month.
Rhode Island	—	—	1912 (S)	—
South Dakota	1889 (C)	1918 (C)	—	1896 (C): Declarant not less than 6 months prior to election.
Texas	1869 (C) 1876 (C)	1918 (S): Repealed for primaries. 1921 (S): Repealed for all elections.	—	1918 (S): No interpreters at polls. No assistance from election judges unless citizen for 21 years. 1895 (C)[8]: U.S. citizen for 90 days. 1912 (S): Naturalized citizens must be able to read and speak English language, unless incapacitated.
Utah	—	—	—	
Washington	—	—	—	

West Virginia	—	1908 (C)[9]	1908 (S)
Wisconsin	1848 (C)	1895 (C)	—
Wyoming	1889 (C)[10]: Provides for expiration of alien voting in 1895.		—

[1] (C) = constitution, (S) = statute.
[2] Came into effect with statehood in 1861.
[3] *Kinern v. Wells* (1887) 11 Ne. 916.
[4] Inhabitants residing in Michigan either on 24 June 1835 on 1 January 1850, and those of foreign birth who declared their intention to become U.S. citizens 2 years and 6 months prior to 8 November 1894 remain entitled to vote.
[5] Came into effect with statehood in 1858.
[6] Came into effect with statehood in 1859.
[7] Came into effect with statehood in 1859.
[8] Came into effect with statehood in 1896.
[9] To be eligible to vote, citizens must have declared before 1 December 1908 their intention to become citizens. The right to vote under this provision expired on 1 December 1912.
[10] Came into effect with statehood in 1890.

TABLE A.13 Literacy Requirements for Suffrage: 1870–1924

State[1]	Literacy Requirements	Exemptions	Assistance to Illiterates
Alabama	1875 (C)[2]: "No education qualification for suffrage . . . shall be made by law." 1901 (C): After 1 January 1903, must be able to "read or write any article of the Constitution of the United States in the English language."	— 1901 (C): Those unable to read or write due to physical disability; owners of 40 acres of property or real estate assessed for taxation at $300.	— —
Arizona	1912 (S): Must be able to "read the Constitution of the United States in the English language in such manner as to show he is neither prompted nor reciting from memory, and to write his name."	—	—
Arkansas	—	—	1891 (S): Election judges may assist illiterates.
California	1911 (C): Excludes those "who shall not be able to read the Constitution in the English language and write his or her name."	1911 (C): Those with physical disabilities, those currently enfranchised, and those over age 59 at time amendment takes effect.	—
Colorado	1876 (C): "The General Assembly may prescribe, by law, an educational qualification for electors, but no such law shall take effect prior to" 1890.	-	1891 (S): Assistance provided for any voter who declares under oath that he cannot read or write. Interpreters provided for those who cannot speak or understand the English language.
Connecticut	1855 (C): Must be able to read any article of the Constitution or any section of the state statutes. 1902 (S): Must "read at least three lines of the Constitution or of the statutes of this State, other than the title or enacting clause, in such manner as to show that he is not prompted nor reciting from memory."	1855 (C): Those who could vote before 1855. 1902 (S): No one will be held ineligible by reason of blindness or defective sight.	— —

State			
Delaware	1897 (C): Must be able to read Constitution and write name if becoming eligible to vote after 1 January 1900.	—	1897 (C): Those who cannot read or write due to physical disability.
Florida	1868 (C): Constitution authorizes education qualifications, but none passed by legislature. 1885 (C): No requirement.	—	1877 (S)
Georgia	1907 (S): Must be able to read in English any paragraph of state or U.S. Constitution and write the same in English.	1907 (S): All veterans of all wars and their descendants; "all persons who are of good character, and understand the duties and obligations of citizenship under a republican form of government"; those who are prevented from reading and writing due to physical disability but can understand and give a reasonable interpretation of state or U.S. Constitution; owners of at least 40 acres of land assessed for taxation at the value of $500.	—
Illinois	—	—	—
Kentucky	—	—	1891 (S): Any voter who declares under oath that he cannot read the English language shall be assisted in marking his ballot. 1890 (C): The legislature shall "provide that persons illiterate, blind, or in any way disabled, may have their ballots marked as herein required."
Louisiana	1898 (C): Must demonstrate ability to read or write in English or mother tongue.	1898 (C): Owners of property; those who could vote on or before 1 January 1867, and their sons and grandsons; foreign-born males naturalized prior to 1 January 1898, if registered prior to 1 September 1898 and if resident in state for five years preceding registration.	—

(continues)

State[1]	Literacy Requirements	Exemptions	Assistance to Illiterates
Louisiana (continued)	1921 (C): Must demonstrate ability to read and write in English or mother tongue.	1921 (C): Those physically disabled; also those "of good character and reputation, attached to the principles of the Constitution of the United States and of the State of Louisiana, and . . . able to understand and give a reasonable interpretation of any section of either Constitution when read to him by the registrar, and he must be well disposed to the good order and happiness of the State of Louisiana and of the United States and must understand the duties and obligations of citizenship under a republican form of government."	If disabled.
Maine	1893 (C): Must be able to read the Constitution in English and write his name.	1893 (C): Those prevented from reading or writing by physical infirmities; those 60 years or older at time of amendment.	—
Massachusetts	1857 (C): Must be able to read the Constitution in English and write his name.	1857 (C): Those with physical disabilities; also, "any person who now has the right to vote," and those "who shall be sixty years of age or upwards at the time this Amendment shall take effect."	—
	1892 (S): Must be able to read state constitution in English and write his name.	1892 (S): "Those who cannot read or write because of physical disability or . . . those who had the right to vote on May 1, 1857."	—
Mississippi	1868 (C): "No educational qualification shall ever be required for any person to become an elector."	—	—

	1890 (C): "On or after the first day of January, AD, 1892, every elector shall . . . be able to read any section of the Constitution of this State; or he shall be able to understand the same when read to him, or give a reasonable interpretation thereof."		—
Missouri	1865 (C): After 1 January 1876, must be able to read and write.	1865 (C): Those who were qualified electors before 1 January 1876, and those prevented from reading and writing by physical disability.	—
New Hampshire	1875 (C): No requirement. 1902 (C): Must be able to read the constitution in English and to write.	1902 (C): Those currently enfranchised; those age 60 or more on 1 January 1903, and those with physical disabilities that prevent them from meeting requirement.	— —
New Mexico	1910 (C): "The right of any citizen of the State to vote . . . shall never be restricted, abridged, or impaired on account of . . . inability to speak, read, or write the English or Spanish languages, except as may otherwise be provided by this Constitution."		—
New York	1921 (C): After 1 January 1922, no person shall become entitled to vote by attaining majority, by naturalization, or otherwise, unless such person is also able to read and write in English.	1921 (C): Those with physical infirmities preventing them from reading or writing; those who were electors before 1 January 1922.	1896 (S): Any voter who has made an oath of illiteracy shall be assisted in filling his ballot. —

(continues)

State[1]	Literacy Requirements	Exemptions	Assistance to Illiterates
North Carolina	1876 (C): Must be able to read and write any section of the constitution in English.	1876 (C): Those who were qualified voters on 1 January 1867, and lineal descendants of such persons.	—
North Dakota	1899 (C): "The legislature shall by law establish an educational test as a qualification." Legislature declined to do so.	—	1891 (S)
Ohio	—	—	1891 (S): Assistance may be given to voters for any reason.
		—	1896 (S): Assistance may be given only for reasons of physical infirmity.
Oklahoma	1907 (C): Must be able to read and write any section of the state constitution.	1907 (C): Those who were qualified voters on 1 January 1866, and lineal descendants of such persons.[4]	—
Oregon	1924 (C, S): Must be able to read the constitution in English and write name.	—	—
South Carolina	1895 (C): Until 1 January 1898, must be able to read any section of the state constitution submitted by the registration officer, or understand and explain it when read by registration officer. After 1 January 1898, must be able to read and write any section of this constitution submitted to him by registration officer.	1985 (C): Those who have paid all taxes collectible during previous year on property assessed at $300 or more.	—

State[1]	Literacy/understanding requirement	Exemptions	
Virginia	1902 (C): In 1902 and 1903, must be able to read any section of state constitution "and to give a reasonable explanation of the same; or, if unable to read such section, able to understand and give a reasonable explanation thereof when read to him by the officers." After 1904, must apply for registration in own handwriting.	1902 (C): Property owners; wartime veterans and their descendants.	—
Washington	1896 (C): Must be able to read and speak English. 1912 (S): "If naturalized, must furnish satisfactory evidence that he is capable of reading and speaking the English language so as to comprehend the meaning of ordinary English prose."	1912 (C): Those qualified to vote at time act takes effect; also those incapacitated through physical infirmity, if they present evidence of literacy in English prior to incapacity.	—
Wyoming	1889 (C)[5]: Must be able to read state constitution	1889 (C): Those prevented from reading by physical disability.	—

[1] States not listed had no provisions for literacy requirements.
[2] (C) = constitution, (S) = statute.
[3] Came into effect with statehood in 1912.
[4] Declared unconstitutional in 1915 in *Guinn v. Oklahoma* 238 U.S. 347 (1915); this case also invalidated all similar "grandfather clauses" that had the obvious intent of racial discrimination.
[5] Came into effect with statehood in 1890.

TABLE A.14 Residency Requirements for Suffrage: 1870–1923

State	Length of Residence Required	No Residency Gained by			No Loss of Residence for Soldiers or Others Traveling on Public Business	Other
		Military Personnel Stationed in Towns and Cities	Students	Residence in Almshouse or Other Institutions		
Alabama	1867 (C)[1]: 6 months in state, 6 months in county.	1867 (C)	—	—	—	—
	1875 (C): 1 year in state, 3 months in country, 30 days in precinct, district, or ward.	*				1875 (C): General Assembly may change residency length in any town with more than 5,000 inhabitants.
	1901 (C): 2 years in state, 1 year in county, 3 months in precinct or ward.[2]	*				1901 (C): Residency requirement, until 20 December 1902, not applicable to veterans, their descendants, and "all persons who are of good haracter and cwho understand he duties and tobligations of citizenship under a republican form of government." After 1 January 1903, not applied to those who meet literacy requirements or are owners of land worth $300.
Arizona	1910 (C)[3]: 1 year in state.	1910 (C)	1910 (C)	1910 (C)	1910 (C)	—
Arkansas	1868 (C): 6 months in state.	1868 (C)	—	—	—	—
	1873 (C): 6 months in state, 10 days in county.	*				—
	1874 (C): 12 months in state, 6 months in county, 1 month in precinct or ward.	*				—
California	1849 (C)[4]: 6 months in state, 30 days in county or district.[5]	1849 (C)	1849 (C)	1849 (C)	1849 (C)	—

1879 (C): 1 year in state, 90 days in county, 30 days in election district.	*	*	*	*	—
1894 (C): 1 year in state, 30 days in election precinct.	*	*	*	*	—
Colorado	1876 (C)	1876 (C)	1876 (C)	1876 (C)	—
1876 (C): 6 months in state; and 1877 (S): 30 days in county.					
1881 (S): 6 months in state, 90 days in county, 30 days in city or town, 10 days in ward or precinct.	*	*	*	*	—
1903 (S): 1 year in state, 90 days in county, 30 days in city or town, 10 days in ward or precinct.	*	*	*	*	—
Connecticut	—	—	—	—	—
1845 (C): 1 year in state, 6 months in town.					
Delaware	1831 (C)	—	—	—	—
1831 (C): 1 year in state, 1 month in county.					
1897 (C): 1 year in state, 3 months in county, 30 days in election district.	*	—	—	—	—
Florida	1868 (C)	—	—	—	—
1868 (C): 1 year in state, 6 months in county.					
Georgia	1868 (C)	—	—	—	—
1868 (C): 6 months in state, 30 days in county.					
1877 (C): 1 year in state, 6 months in county.	*	—	—	—	—
Idaho	1889 (C)	1889 (C)	1889 (C)	1889 (C)	—
1889 (C): 6 months in state, 30 days in county.					
1891 (S): For county seat elections, 6 months in county and 90 days in precinct.	*	*	*	*	—

(continues)

State	Length of Residence Required	No Residency Gained by			No Loss of Residence for Soldiers or Others Traveling on Public Business	Other
		Military Personnel Stationed in Towns and Cities	Students	Residence in Almshouse or Other Institutions		
Illinois	1870 (C): 1 year in state, 90 days in county, 30 days in election district.	1870 (C)	—	—	—	—
	*					
Indiana	1851 (C): 6 months in state, 60 days in township, 30 days in ward or precinct; for declarants, 1 year in U.S.	1851 (C)	—	1877 (S)	—	—
					1851 (C)	—
Iowa	1857 (C): 6 months in state, 60 days in county.	1857 (C)	—	—	—	—
Kansas	1859 (C)7: 6 months in state, 30 days in township or ward.	1859 (C)	1859 (C)	1859 (C)	1859 (C)	—
Kentucky	1850 (C): 2 years in state or 1 year in county, town, or city, 60 days in precinct.	—	—	—	1850 (C)	—
	1891 (C): 1 year in state, 6 months in county, 60 days in precinct.	1891 (C)	—	—	1891 (C): No provision	—
Louisiana	1868 (C): 1 year in state, 10 days in parish	—	—	—	—	—
	1879 (C): 1 year in state, 6 months in parish, 30 days in ward or precinct.	1879 (C)	1879 (C)	—	1879 (C)	—
	1898 (C): 2 years in state, 1 year in parish, 6 months in precinct.[8]	*	*		*	—

State	Residence Requirement				
Maine	1921 (C): 2 years in state, 1 year in parish, 4 months in municipality, 3 months in precinct.[9]	*	—	*	—
Maryland	1819 (C)[10]: 3 months in state.	1819 (C)	—	1864 (S)	—
	1867 (C): 1 year in state, 6 months in legislative district of Baltimore city or of the county.	—	—	—	—
Massachusetts	1821 (C): 1 year in state, 6 months in town or district.[11]	—	—	—	—
Michigan	1850 (C): 6 months in state, 20 days in township or ward; for declarants, 2 years and 6 months in state prior to 8 November 1894.	—	—	—	—
Minnesota	1908 (C): 6 months in state, 30 days in city or township.[12]	1908 (C)	1908 (C)	1908 (C)	1908 (C)
	1857 (C): 6 months in state, 30 days in election district.	1857 (C)	—	—	—
	1874 (S): 3 months in ward.	*	—	—	1893 (S): No residence for voting purposes can be gained by any "person employed temporarily" cutting timber "or in the construction or repair of any railroad, canal, municipal or other work of public nature."
Mississippi	1868 (C): 6 months in state, . 1 month in county	—	—	—	—

(continues)

TABLE A.14 *(continued)*

State	Length of Residence Required	No Residency Gained by			No Loss of Residence for Soldiers or Others Traveling on Public Business	Other
		Military Personnel Stationed in Towns and Cities	Students	Residence in Almshouse or Other Institutions		
Mississippi *(continued)*	1890 (C): 2 years in state, 1 year in election district or incorporated city or town.	—	—	—	—	
Missouri	1870 (C): 1 year in state, 60 days in county, city, or town. *	1875 (C) *	1875 (C) *	1875 (C) *	1875 (C) *	—
	1883 (S): 1 year in state, 60 days in city, 20 days in precinct.					
	1917 (S): 1 year in state, 60 days in county.					No military personnel permitted to vote.
Montana	1889 (C): 6 months in state, and (S) 30 days in county.	1889 (C)	1889 (C)	1889 (C)	1889 (C)	—
	1893 (S): 1 year in state, 30 days in county. *	*	*	*	*	—
Nebraska	1866 (S): 6 months in state, 20 days in county, 10 days in precinct.	—	—	—	—	—
	1869 (S): 40 days in county. *	1875 (C)	—	—	—	—
Nevada	1864 (C): 6 months in state, 30 days in district or county.[13]	1864 (C)	1864 (C)	1864 (C)	1864 (C)	—
New Hampshire	1860 (S): 6 months within town.[14]	—	—	—	—	—
New Jersey	1844 (C): 1 year in state, 5 months in county.	1844 (S)	—	—	1844 (C)	—

State	Requirement					
New Mexico	1910 (C)[15]: 12 months in state, 90 days in county, 30 days in precinct.	1910 (C)	1910 (C)	—	1910 (C)	—
New York	1846 (C): 1 year in state, 4 months in county, 30 days in district; for "man of color," 3 years in state.	—	—	—	—	—
	1874 (S): 1 year in state, 4 months in county, 30 days in election district.	—	—	—	1874 (S)	—
North Carolina	1868 (C): 12 months in state, 30 days in county.	—	—	—	—	—
	1876 (C): 2 years in state, 6 months in county, 4 months in precinct, ward, or other election district.	—	—	—	—	—
North Dakota	1889 (C): 1 year in state, 6 months in county, 90 days in precinct.	1889 (C)	—	—	1889 (C)	—
	1923 (S): 1 year in state, 90 days in county, 30 days in precinct.	—	—	—	—	—
Ohio	1851 (C): 1 year in state; local requirements "as may be provided by law."	1851 (C)	—	—	—	—
	1857 (S): 1 year in state, 30 days in county, 20 days in township, village, or ward of city or village.	—	1914 (S)	—	—	—

(continues)

TABLE A.14 *(continued)*

State	Length of Residence Required	No Residency Gained by			No Loss of Residence for Soldiers or Others Traveling on Public Business	Other
		Military Personnel Stationed in Towns and Cities	Students	Residence in Almshouse or Other Institutions		
Oklahoma	1907 (C): 1 year in state, 6 months in county, 30 days in precinct.	1907 (C)	—	—	—	—
Oregon	1857 (C)[16]: 6 months in state.[17]	1857 (C)	1857 (C)	1857 (C)	1857 (C)	—
Pennsylvania	1838 (C): 1 year in state, 10 days in election district.[18]	—	—	—	—	—
	1873 (C): 1 year in state, 2 months in election district; 6 months in state for previously qualified elector or native-born state citizen, returning after absence.	1873 (C)	1873 (C)	1873 (C)	1873 (C)	—
Rhode Island	1842 (C): 1 year in state, 6 months in town or city if owning real estate worth $134 or "which shall rent for seven dollars per annum"; or 2 years in state, 6 months in town or city if taxpayer registered at least 7 days before voting. *	—	—	—	—	—
	1888 (C): 2 years in state, 6 months in town and city.	—	—	—	1864 (C)	—

	1896 (S): For election of general officers and members of General Assembly, 1 year in state, 6 months in town or city; for election of civil officers and on all questions in town or district meetings, 2 years in state, 6 months local.	—	—	—	—
South Carolina	1868 (C): 1 year in state, 60 days in county.	1868 (C)	—	—	—
	1895 (C): 2 years in state, 1 year in county, 4 months in polling precinct; 6 months in state for ministers and public school teachers.	1895 (C)	1895 (C)	1895 (C)	—
South Dakota	1889 (C): 1 year in U.S., 6 months in state, 30 days in county, 10 days in election precinct.	1889 (C)	—	1889 (C)	—
Tennessee	1870 (C): 12 months in state, 6 months in county.	—	—	—	—
Texas	1869 (C): 1 year in state, 60 days in county.	—	—	—	No soldier, seaman, or marine may vote.
	1876 (C): 1 year in state, 6 months in county.	—	—	—	—
Utah	1895 (C)[19]: 1 year in state or territory, 4 months in county, 60 days in precinct.	—	—	—	—
Vermont	1793 (C): 1 year in state.	—	—	—	—
	1913 (S): 3 months in town to vote for General Assembly or justices.	—	—	—	—

(continues)

TABLE A.14 (continued)

State	Length of Residence Required	No Residency Gained by				
		Military Personnel Stationed in Towns and Cities	Students	Residence in Almshouse or Other Institutions	No Loss of Residence for Soldiers or Others Traveling on Public Business	Other
Virginia	1870 (C): 12 months in state, 3 months in county, city, or town.	1870 (C)	—	—	—	—
	1902 (C): 2 years in state, 1 year in county, city, or town, 30 days in precinct.[20]	*	1902 (C)	1902 (C)	1902 (C)	—
Washington	1889 (C): 1 year in state, 90 days in county, 30 days in city, town, ward, or precinct.	1889 (C)	1889 (C)	—	1889 (C)	—
West Virginia	1863 (C): 1 year in state, 30 days in county.	—	—	—	—	—
	1872 (C): 1 year in state, 60 days in county.	1872 (C)	—	—	—	—
Wisconsin	1848 (C): 1 year in state.	—	—	—	—	—
	1882 (C): 1 year in state, maximum of 30 days in district.	—	—	—	—	—
	1898 (S): 1 year in state, 10 days in election district.					
Wyoming	1889 (C)[21]: 1 year in state or territory, 60 days in county.	1889 (C)	—	—	—	—
	1911 (S): 1 year in state, 60 days in county, 10 days in district.[22]	*	—	—	1911 (S)	—

*Preceding provision still in place.

[1](C) = constitution, (S) = statute.

[2]Those who moved within the state within 3 months of an election allowed to vote in the precinct from which they moved.

[3]Came into effect with statehood in 1912.

[4]Came into effect with statehood in 1850.

[5]1874 statute: Those who moved within the state within 30 days of an election allowed to vote in precinct from which they moved.

[6]Came into effect with statehood in 1890.

[7]Came into effect with statehood in 1861.

[8]Can vote in previous election district within 6 months of moving.

[9]Can vote in previous election district within 3 months of moving.

[10]Came into effect with statehood in 1820.

[11]1892 statute: For 6 months after moving within the state, residents retain the right to vote in the district from which they moved.

[12]Can vote in previous election district for 30 days after moving within the state.

[13]1915 statute: Can vote in previous election district for 30 days after moving within the state.

[14]Can vote in previous election district for 6 months after moving within the state.

[15]Came into effect with statehood in 1912.

[16]Came into effect with statehood in 1859.

[17]In 1897 and again in 1916, 30-day requirements were added for counties, towns, and precincts—only to be dropped a few years later.

[18]"But a citizen of the United States, who had previously been a qualified voter of this state and removed therefrom and returned, and who shall have resided in the election district and paid taxes as aforesaid, shall be entitled to vote after residing in the state six months."

[19]Came into effect with statehood in 1896.

[20]Can vote in previous election district for 30 days after moving within the state.

[21]Came into effect with statehood in 1890.

[22]Can vote in previous election district for 10 days after moving within the state.

TABLE A.15   Disenfranchisement of Felons and Others Convicted of Crimes: 1870–1920

State	Persons Excluded	Duration of Exclusion[1]
Alabama	1867 (C)[2]: Those convicted of treason, embezzlement of public funds, malfeasance in office, crime punishable by imprisonment in penitentiary, or bribery.	—
	1901 (C): Those convicted of treason, murder, arson, embezzlement, malfeasance in office, larceny, receiving stolen property, obtaining property or money under false pretenses, perjury, suborNation of perjury, robbery, assault with intent to rob, burglary, forgery, bribery, assault and battery on the wife, bigamy, living in adultery, sodomy, incest, rape, miscegenation, crime against nature or crime involving moral turpitude; also any person convicted as a vagrant or tramp, or of election fraud.	—
Arizona	1910 (C)[3]: Those convicted of a felony.	Until restored to civil rights.
Arkansas	1868 (C): Those convicted of treason, embezzlement of public funds, malfeasance in office, crimes punishable by law with imprisonment in penitentiary, or bribery.	—
	1873 (C): Persons convicted in any court in any state of a crime punishable by law with death or confinement in penitentiary.	Until pardoned or sentence commuted.
	1874 (C): Those convicted of a felony.	—
	1893 (C): Those presons "as may for the commission of some felony be deprived of the right to vote by law passed by the General Assembly."	—
California	1894 (S): Those convicted of a felony.	—
	1849 (C)[4]: Those convicted of any infamous crime. Also, "laws shall be made to exclude from . . . the right of suffrage, persons convicted of bribery, perjury, forgery, malfeasance in office or other high crimes."	—
	1879 (C): Those convicted of infamous crime or convicted of embezzlement or misappropriation of public money. In addition, "laws shall be made to exclude from . . . the right of suffrage, persons convicted of bribery, perjury, forgery, malfeasance in office or other high crimes."	—

State		
Colorado	1894 (C): Those convicted of any infamous crime or those hereafter convicted of the embezzlement or misappropriation of public money.	—
	1876 (C): Those confined in public prison.	While in prison.
Connecticut	1818 (C): Those convicted of bribery, forgery, perjury, dueling, fraudulent bankruptcy, theft, or any offense for which an infamous punishment is inflicted.	—
	1902 (S): Those convicted three times, as minors, of offenses punishable by imprisonment, or fine and imprisonment; those convicted of a crime (as specified under 1818 constitution) within a year prior to reaching their majority.	—
Delaware	1831 (C): Those convicted of a felony.	—
	1852, 1874 (S): Election bribery.	—
	1897 (C): Those convicted of a felony or election bribery.	—
Florida	1868 (C): Those convicted of a felony or wagering on election results. In addition, the legislature "shall enact the necessary laws to exclude from . . . the right of suffrage, all persons convicted of bribery, perjury, larceny, or of infamous crime."	Until restored to civil rights.
	1868 (S): Those convicted of a felony, bribery, perjury, larceny, or other infamous crime; those convicted of betting on an election.	For election betting, 2 years from date of conviction.
Georgia	1868 (C): "Those convicted of treason, embezzlement of public funds, malfeasance in office, crime punishable by law with imprisonment in the penitentiary, or bribery."	—
	1877 (C): Those convicted of treason against the state, of embezzlement of public funds, malfeasance in office, bribery, or larceny, or of any crime involving moral turpitude punishable by the laws of this state with imprisonment in penitentiary.	Until pardoned.
Idaho	1889 (C)[5]: Those "convicted of treason, a felony, embezzlement of the public funds . . . or other infamous crime, or who, at the time of such election, is confined in prison on conviction of a criminal offense." Also those convicted of buying or selling votes.	Until restored to the rights of citizenship.

(continues)

TABLE A.15 *(continued)*

State	Persons Excluded	Duration of Exclusion[1]
Illinois	1870 (C): "The General Assembly shall pass laws excluding from the right of suffrage persons convicted of infamous crimes."	—
	1872 (S): Persons convicted of any crime, punishable by confinement in penitentiary.	Until restored to the right to vote by pardon.
Indiana	1851 (C): "The General Assembly shall have power to deprive of the right of suffrage, and to render ineligible any person convicted of an infamous crime."	—
	1852 (S): Those convicted of infamous crimes.	
	1881 (S): Those in prison for any felony or misdemeanor.	While in prison.
Iowa	1857 (C): Those convicted of any infamous crime.	—
Kansas	1859 (C)[6]: Those convicted of a felony, dishonorably discharged from the service of the United States, guilty of defrauding the United States government or any state, guilty of giving or receiving a bribe, and any person who has voluntarily borne arms against the United States government.	Until restored to civil rights.
Kentucky	1850 (C): Laws shall be made to exclude persons sentenced to prison for larceny, robbery, forgery, counterfeiting, perjury, or "any such like crime."	—
	1851 (S): Persons sentenced as earlier specified.	—[7]
	1890 (C): Those convicted of treason, a felony, or bribery in an election, or of such high misdemeanor as the General Assembly may declare; also "persons, who, at the time of the election, are in confinement . . . for some penal offense." "High misdemeanors" added by legislature (1892).	Until restored to civil rights by executive pardon.
Louisiana	1870 (C): Those indicted or convicted of treason, perjury, forgery, bribery, or other crime punishable by imprisonment.	—
	1879 (C): Those convicted of treason, embezzlement of public funds, malfeasance in office, larceny, bribery, illegal voting, or other crime punishable by hard labor or imprisonment.	—

State		
	1898 (C): Those convicted of any crime punishable by imprisonment, those actually confined in prison, and all indicted persons.	Until pardoned with express restoration of franchise.
	1921 (C): Those convicted of any crime punishable by imprisonment, those involved in election bribery, those confined in prison, and all indicted persons.	—
Maine	1819 (C)[8]: No exclusion.	—
Maryland	1867 (C): Those convicted of larceny or other infamous crime, and those involved in election bribery.	Until pardoned by governor.
Massachusetts	1821 (C): No exclusion.	—
Michigan	1850 (C): No exclusion.	—
	1908 (C): No exclusion.	—
Minnesota	1857 (C)[9]: Those convicted of treason or a felony.	Until restored to civil rights.
Mississippi	1868 (C): Those convicted of bribery, perjury, or other infamous crime. In addition, "the legislature shall pass laws to exclude from office and from suffrage those who shall hereafter be convicted of bribery, perjury, forgery, or other high crimes or misdemeanors."	—
	1876 (S): Those convicted of bribery, perjury, forgery, or other infamous crimes.	—
	1880 (S): Grand larceny and all felonies added to 1876 list.	Until pardoned.
	1890 (C): Those convicted of "bribery, burglary, theft, arson, obtaining money or goods under false pretenses, perjury, forgery, embezzlement, or bigamy."	—
Missouri	1870 (C): Those convicted of bribery, perjury, or other infamous crimes; those convicted of betting on election results.	—
	1875 (C): "The General Assembly may enact laws excluding from the right of voting all persons convicted of a felony or other infamous crime."	—
	1879 (S): Those convicted of bribery, perjury, other infamous crime, or any misdemeanor linked to voting (e.g., betting).	—
	1899 (S): In addition to 1879 list: arson, burglary, robbery or larceny, and those confined in any prison.	Until pardoned; minimum of 1 year after conviction.

(continues)

TABLE A.15 (continued)

State	Persons Excluded	Duration of Exclusion[1]
Missouri (continued)	1917 (S): Those convicted of any felony or infamous crime, any misdemeanor connected with voting, those confined in any public prison.	Until pardoned; permanent for second conviction.
Montana	1889 (C): No exclusion.	—
	1909 (S): Those convicted of a felony.	Until pardoned.
Nebraska	1867 (C): No exclusion.	—
	1875 (C): Those convicted of treason or a felony.	—
Nevada	1864 (C): Those convicted of treason or a felony.	Until restored to civil rights.
New Hampshire	1792 (C): No exclusion.	—
	1912 (C): Those convicted of treason, bribery, or election law offenses.	—
New Jersey	1844 (C): Those convicted of felonies.	Until pardoned or restored by law to right of suffrage.
	1866 (S): Election bribery.	Ten years.[10]
New Mexico	1910 (C)[11]: Those convicted of felonious or infamous crimes.	Until restored to political rights.
New York	1846 (C): "Laws may be passed excluding . . . all persons who have been or may be convicted of bribery, of larceny, or of any infamous crime" and persons involved in betting on elections.	—
	1847 (S): Those convicted of bribery or any infamous crime or who bet on the results of any election.	Until pardoned and restored to all rights of a citizen.
	1894 (C): "The legislature shall enact laws excluding from the right of suffrage all persons convicted of bribery or any infamous crime."	—
North Carolina	1868 (C): No exclusion.	—
	1876 (C): Those convicted of or who have confessed to a crime punishable by imprisonment.	Until restored to citizenship in the manner prescribed by law.
North Dakota	1889 (C): Those convicted of treason or a felony.	—
Ohio	1835 (S): Those convicted of any crime punishable by 1 year in prison.	—
	1841 (S): Those imprisoned in penitentiary and those convicted of bribery and election offenses.	Until pardoned by governor.
	1877 (S): Those convicted of a felony.	1881 (S): Franchise restored to those leaving prison who did not violate any rules while incarcerated.

State		
	1898 (S): Those convicted of a felony or imprisoned in penitentiary of any state.	Until pardoned or sentence is reversed or annulled.
Oklahoma	1907 (C): Those convicted of a felony and any person in a public prison.	Until citizenship restored.
Oregon	1857 (C)[12]: Those convicted of crimes punishable by imprisonment.	—
Pennsylvania	1838 (C): No exclusion.	—
Rhode Island	1873 (C): Those convicted of willful violation of election laws.	Four years from date of conviction.
	1842 (C): Those convicted of bribery or any crime deemed infamous by common law.	Until restored to right of suffrage by act of General Assembly.
South Carolina	1868 (C): Those confined in any public prison. But "no person shall be disfranchised" for any crime committed while a slave. In addition, "the General Assembly shall never pass any law that will deprive any of the citizens of this State of the right of suffrage except for treason, murder, robbery, or dueling."	—
	1895 (C): Those convicted of burglary, arson, obtaining goods or money under false pretenses, perjury, forgery, robbery, bribery, adultery, bigamy, wife beating, housebreaking, receiving stolen goods, breach of trust with fraudulent intent, fornication, sodomy, incest, assault with intent to ravish, miscegenation, larceny, or crimes against election laws.	Until pardoned by governor.
South Dakota	1889 (C): Those convicted of treason or a felony.	Until restored to civil rights.
Tennessee	1841 (S): Those convicted of bribery, larceny, or any other offense declared infamous.	Until restored to citizenship.
	1870 (C): "Laws may be passed excluding from the right of suffrage persons . . . convicted of infamous crimes."	—
	1871 (S): Those convicted of bribery, offering to bribe, larceny, or any other felony.	—
Texas	1869 (C): Those convicted of a felony or confined in prison.	While confined in prison.
Utah	1876 (C): Those convicted of a felony.	Until rights restored by governor.
	1895 (C)[13]: Those convicted of treason.	Until restored to civil rights.

(continues)

TABLE A.15 *(continued)*

State	Persons Excluded	Duration of Exclusion[1]
Vermont	1793 (C): Those convicted of involvement in electoral bribery.	The elector shall forfeit his right for that election.
	1884 (S): Those convicted of a felony.	Until rights restored.
Virginia	1870 (C): Those convicted of bribery in an election, embezzlement of public funds, treason, or a felony.	—
	1902 (C): "Persons who, prior to the adoption of this Constitution, were disqualified from voting, by conviction of crime, either within or without this State; persons convicted after the adoption of this Constitution, either within or without this State, of treason, or of any felony, bribery, petit larceny, obtaining money or property under false pretenses, embezzlement, forgery, or perjury."	Until disabilities have been removed.
Washington	1889 (C): Those convicterd of infamous crimes.	—
West Virginia	1863 (C): Those convicted of bribery in an election, treason, or a felony.	—
Wisconsin	1848 (C): Those convicted of treason, felony, or involvement in a duel.[14]	Until restored to civil rights.
	1849 (S): Those convicted of bribery.	—
Wyoming	1889 (C)[15]: Those convicted of infamous crimes.	Until restored to civil rights.

[1]Disfranchisement for specific criminal convictions were permanent unless otherwise specified.

[2](C) = constitution, (S) = statute.

[3]Came into effect with statehood in 1912.

[4]Came into effect with statehood in 1850.

[5]Came into effect with statehood in 1890.

[6]Came into effect with statehood in 1861.

[7]Between 1851 and 1873, forfeiture of suffrage was for 10 years.

[8]Came into effect with statehood in 1820.

[9]Came into effect with statehood in 1858.

[10]In 1871, the term of disfranchisement became indeterminate, presumably permanent; beginning in 1906, it was five years for a first offense and permanent thereafter.

[11]Came into effect with statehood in 1912.

[12]Came into effect with statehood in 1859.

[13]Came into effect with statehood in 1896.

[14]Dueling provision repealed in 1883.

[15]Came into effect with statehood in 1890.

TABLE A.16 Native–American Voting Rights: 1870–1920

State[1]	Date	Provision
California	1849 (C)[2, 3]	The legislature may, "by a two-thirds concurrent vote," admit "to the right of suffrage, Indians, or the descendants of Indians, in such special cases as . . . the legislative body may deem just and proper."
Idaho	1889 (C)[4]	Excludes "Indians not taxed, who have not severed their tribal relations and adopted the habits of civilization."
Maine	1819 (C)[5]	Excludes Indians not taxed.
Massachusetts	1869 (S)	"Indians and people of color, heretofore known and called Indians . . . are citizens of the Commonwealth . . . entitled to all the rights, privileges, and immunities" of citizenship.
	1892 (S)	"Indians residing within this commonwealth shall, as citizens thereof, have all the rights, privileges and immunities, and be subject to all the duties and liabilities, to which all other citizens of the Commonwealth are entitled and subject."
Michigan	1850 (C)	Includes "civilized male inhabitants of Indian descent, native of the United States and not a member of any tribe."
	1908 (C)	Includes "every inhabitant of Indian descent, a native of the United States."
Minnesota	1857 (C)[6]	Includes "persons of mixed white and Indian blood who have adopted the customs and habits of civilization; persons of Indian blood residing in the State, who have adopted the language, customs and habits of civilization, after an examination before any district court of the State, in such manner as may be provided by law."
	1917[7]	Denied the right to vote to all "tribal Indians." To vote, Indians had to sever relationships with tribes.
Mississippi	1868 (C)	Excludes Indians not taxed.
	1890 (C)	Excludes Indians not taxed.
Montana	1897 (S)	Excludes from residency "any person living on an Indian or military reservation, unless that person previously had acquired a residence in a county of Montana and is in the employ of the government while living on a reservation."[8]
New Mexico	1910 (C)[9]	Excludes Indians not taxed.
North Dakota	1889 (C)	Includes "civilized persons of Indian descent who shall have severed their tribal relations two years next preceding such election."
	1896 (S)	"No Indian or person of Indian descent who has not received a final patent conveying the title in free of lands allotted to him within the boundaries of this State, pursuant to an act of the Congress of the United States, approved February 8, 1887 . . . shall be deemed a qualified elector . . . or be entitled to the rights and privileges of an elector unless he was born within the limits of the United States, and has voluntarily taken up his residence within this State separate and apart from any tribe of Indians therein, and adopted the habits of civilized life, and is in no manner subject to the authority of any Indian chief or council or Indian agent of the United States."

(continues)

TABLE A.16 (continued)

State[1]	Date	Provision
North Dakota (continued)	1913 (C)	Includes "civilized persons of Indian descent who shall have severed their tribal relations two years next preceding such election."
Oklahoma	1907 (C)	Includes "persons of Indian descent, native of the United States."
Rhode Island	1842 (C)	Excludes members of the Narragansett tribe.
Texas	1869 (C)	Excludes Indians not taxed.
Washington	1889 (C)	Excludes Indians not taxed.
	1896 (C)	"Indians not taxed shall never be allowed the elective franchise."
Wisconsin	1848 (C)	Includes "persons of Indian blood who have once been declared by laws of Congress to be citizens of the United States," or "civilized persons of Indian descent, not members of any tribe."
	1882 (C)	Includes "persons of Indian blood who have once been declared by law of Congress to be citizens of the United States, any subsequent law of Congress to the contrary notwithstanding; [and] civilized persons of Indian descent not members of any tribe."
	1893 (S)	Includes "any civilized person being a descendant of the Chippewas of Lake Superior, or any other Indian tribe, and residing within this State, and not upon any Indian reservation, who shall make and subscribe to an oath . . . that he is not a member of any Indian tribe, and has no claim upon the United States for aid and assistance from any appropriation made by Congress for the benefit of Indians, and that he thereby relinquishes all tribal relations, and right to claim or receive any aid from the United States."

[1] States not listed had no provisions specifically concerning Native Americans.
[2] (C) = constitution, (S) = statute.
[3] Came into effect with statehood in 1850.
[4] Came into effect with statehood in 1890.
[5] Came into effect with statehood in 1820.
[6] Came into effect with statehood in 1858.
[7] Opsahl v. Johnson, 163 N.W. 988 (Minn. 1917).
[8] Because there was a residency requirement of one year in Montana, this statute effectively disfranchised those living on Indian reservations.
[9] Came into effect with statehood in 1912.

TABLE A.17 States and Territories Permitting Women to Vote in Elections Dealing with Schools Prior to the Nineteenth Amendment

State[1]	Date Enacted[2]
Kentucky	1838 (S)[3]: Widows and unmarried women who owned property subject to taxation for school purposes.
Michigan	1855 (S): Taxpayers.
Kansas	1861 (S)[4]
Colorado	1876 (C)
Minnesota	1878 (C)
Mississippi	1878 (S): "Patrons" of schools.
New Hampshire	1878 (S)
Massachusetts	1879 (S)
Mississippi	1880 (S): Heads of families.
New York	1880 (S)
Vermont	1880 (S)
Oregon	1882 (S)
Territory of Dakota	1883 (S)
Nebraska	1883 (S)
Wisconsin	1886 (S)
Territory of Arizona	1887 (S)
New Jersey	1887 (S)[5]
Idaho	1889 (C)
Montana	1889 (C)
North Dakota	1889 (C)
Territory of Oklahoma	1890 (S)
Washington	1890 (S)
Illinois	1891 (S)
Connecticut	1893 (S)
Kentucky	1893 (S): Widows and unmarried women who are taxpayers or have school-age children.
Ohio	1894 (S)
Iowa	1895 (S): Taxpayers.
Delaware	1898 (S): Taxpayers.
New Mexico	1910 (C)
Kentucky	1912 (S): Literate women.

[1]Does not include states with full suffrage for women.
[2]In some instances (e.g., in New Jersey, as indicated in n. 5), these laws were later modified or declared unconstitutional by state courts or legislatures. This table does not indicate all such modifications.
[3](C) = constitution, (S) = statute.
[4]Although article 2, section 23 of the 1859 constitution was believed by some to enfranchise women in school elections, the Kansas Supreme Court decided otherwise in *Wheeler v. Brady*, 15 Kan. 26 (1875).
[5]Restricted by *Landis v. Ashworth*, 31 A. 1017 (New Jersey, 1895) and *State v. Board of Education of Cranbury Township*, 31 A. 1033 (New Jersey, 1895) to voting only on school appropriations, and not for officers.

TABLE A.18   States Permitting Women to Vote in Municipal Elections or on Tax and Bond Issues Prior to the Nineteenth Amendment

State[1]	Date Enacted
Kansas	1887 (S)[2]: Municipal.
Montana	1889 (C): Tax issues.
Michigan	1893 (S): Literate women in school, village, and city elections.[3]
Iowa	1894 (S): Municipal elections on any proposition to issue bonds or increase taxes.
Louisiana	1898 (C): Tax issues.
New York	1906 (S): Property owners on tax issues and in town meetings.
Michigan	1909 (S): Financial expenditures and bond issues; limited to owners of property assessed for taxes.
New York	1910 (S): Property owners on bond issues.
Illinois	1913 (S): Offices established by statute and for all officers of cities, villages, and towns, except police magistrates.
Florida	1915 (S): Municipal: for offices and on issues determined by city or town.
Indiana	1917 (S): County and municipal officers not provided for in the constitution, and for delegates to the Constitutional Convention.[4]
North Dakota	1917 (S): County surveyors, county constables, and all officers of cities, villages, and towns (except police magistrates and city justices of the peace) and upon all questions or propositions submitted to a vote of the electors of such municipalities or other political subdivisions.
Nebraska	1917 (S): Municipal officers.
Vermont	1917 (S): Municipal officers; must be a taxpayer.

[1]Does not include states with full suffrage for women.

[2](C) = constitution, (S) = statute.

[3]Declared unconstitutional in *Coffin v. Board of Election Commissioners of Detroit*, 56 N.W. 567 (Mich. 1893).

[4]Statute declared unconstitutional by Indiana Supreme Court in *Board of Election Commissioners of Indianapolis v. Knight*, 117 N.E. 565 (Ind. 1917).

TABLE A.19 States Permitting Women to Vote in Presidential Elections Prior to the Nineteenth Amendment

State[1]	Date Enacted
Illinois	1913 (S)
Arkansas	1917 (S): Primary elections.
Indiana	1917 (S)[2]
Michigan	1917 (S)
Nebraska	1917 (S)
North Dakota	1917 (S)
Rhode Island	1917 (S)
Ohio	1917 (S)[3]
Texas	1918 (S): Primary elections and nominating comventions.[4]
Indiana	1919 (S)
Iowa	1919 (S)
Maine	1919 (S)
Minnesota	1919 (S)
Missouri	1919 (S)
Ohio	1919 (S)
Tennessee	1919 (S)
Wisconsin	1919 (S)

[1]Does not include states with full suffrage for women.

[2]Statute declared unconstitutional: see table A.18.

[3]Law was suspended from operation by the filing of a referendum petition and subsequently was defeated by voters on 6 November 1917.

[4]Women exempt from poll tax required of men in 1918 election, but were required to pay the poll tax beginning 1 January 1919.

TABLE A.20   States and Territories Fully Enfranchising Women Prior to the Nineteenth Amendment

State	Date Enacted
Territory of Wyoming	1869
Territory of Utah	1870[1]
Territory of Washington	1883[2]
Territory of Montana	1887
Wyoming	1889[3]
Colorado	1893
Utah	1895[4]
Idaho	1896
Arizona	1910[5]
Washington	1910
California	1911
Kansas	1912
Oregon	1912
Territory of Alaska	1913
Montana	1914
Nevada	1914
New York	1917
Michigan	1918
Oklahoma	1918
South Dakota	1918

[1]Annulled by Congress in 1887.
[2]Declared unconstitutional by Supreme Court of the Territory in 1887.
[3]Came into effect with statehood in 1890.
[4]Came into effect with statehood in 1896.
[5]Came into effect with statehood in 1912.

APPENDIX SOURCES

MULTISTATE SOURCES, TABLES A.1–A.16

Adams, Willi Paul, *The First American Constitutions: Republican Ideology and the Making of the State Constitutions in the Revolutionary Era*, Rita and Robert Kimber, trans. (Chapel Hill, NC, 1980).

Aylsworth, Leon, "The Passing of Alien Suffrage," *American Political Science Review* 25 (February 1931): 114–16.

Evans, Taliesin, *American Citizenship and the Right of Suffrage in the United States* (Oakland, Calif., 1892).

Green, Fletcher M., *Constitutional Development in the South Atlantic States, 1776–1860: A Study in the Evolution of Democracy* (Chapel Hill, NC, 1930).457

Jones, Samuel, *A Treatise on the Right of Suffrage* (Boston, 1842).

Kousser, J. Morgan, *The Shaping of Southern Politics: Suffrage Restriction and the Establishment of the One-Party South, 1880–1910* (New Haven, CT, 1974).

Kruman, Marc S., "The Second American Party System and the Transformation of Revolutionary Republicanism," *Journal of the Early Republic* 12, 4 (1992): 509–37.

Lowell, Kendrick, and Harold Salisbury, eds., *General Constitutional and Statutory Provisions Relative to Suffrage Published by the Legislative Reference Bureau of the Rhode Island State Library* (Providence, 1912).

McCool, Daniel, "Indian Voting," in Vine Deloria, Jr., ed., *American Indian Policy in the Twentieth Century* (Norman, OK, 1985), 105-33.

McGovney, Dudley O., *The American Suffrage Medley: The Need for a National Uniform Suffrage* (Chicago, 1949).

Native and Alien. The Naturalization Laws of the United States: Containing Also the Alien Laws of the State of New York (Rochester, NY, 1855).

Porter, Kirk H., *A History of Suffrage in the United States* (Chicago, 1918).

Raskin, Jamin B., "Legal Aliens, Local Citizens: The Historical Constitutional and Theoretical Meanings of Alien Suffrage," *University of Pennsylvania Law Review* 141 (April 1993): 1391–1470.

"Restoring the Ex-Offenders Right to Vote: Background and Developments" (note), *American Criminal Law Review* 11 (1973): 721-70.

Rosberg, Gerald M., "Aliens and Equal Protection: Why Not the Right to Vote?" *Michigan Law Review* 75 (April-May 1977): 1092-1136.

Steinfeld, Robert J., "Property and Suffrage in the Early American Republic," *Stanford Law Review* 41, 2 (January 1989): 335–76.

Swindler, William, ed., *Sources and Documents of United States Constitutions*, 11 Vols. (Dobbs Ferry, NY, 1973–1988).

Thorpe, Francis, ed., *Federal and State Constitutions*, 7 Vols. (Washington, 1909).

Williamson, Chilton, *American Suffrage: From Property to Democracy, 1760–1860* (Princeton, 1960).

STATE SOURCES, TABLES A.I–A.I6

Alabama

McMillan, Malcolm C., *Constitutional Development in Alabama, 1798–1901: A Study in Politics, the Negro, and Sectionalism* (Chapel Hill, NC, 1955).

Ormond, John J., Arthur P. Bagby, George Goldthwaite, eds., *The Code of Alabama* (Montgomery, AL, 1852).

Arkansas

Chism, Ben B., ed., *A Digest of the Election Laws of the State of Arkansas* (Little Rock, AR, 1891).

Digest of the Statutes of Arkansas (1894).

Gould, Josiah, ed., *A Digest of the Statutes of Arkansas* (Little Rock, AR, 1858).

Journal of the Proceedings of the Convention Met to Form a Constitution and a System of State Government for the People of Arkansas (Little Rock, AR, 1838).

California

Bowman, J. F., ed., *Election Laws of the State of California* (San Francisco, 1872).

General Election Laws of California, Compiled by the Legislative Counsel Bureau and Issued by the Secretary of State (Sacramento, 1918).

Waite, E. G., ed., *The Election Laws Governing Primary, City, County, State, and Presidential Elections* (Sacramento, 1892).

Colorado

Act of February 18, 1881, 1881 Colorado Laws 113, 114.

Act of March 26, 1891, ch. 28, 1891 Colorado Laws 160.

Colorado, *General Laws*, ch. 926 and 928 (1877).

Laws Passed at the Fourteenth Session of the General Assembly of the State of Colorado, Convened at Denver, the Seventh Day of January, 1903 (Denver, 1903).

Laws Passed at the Third Session of the General Assembly of the State of Colorado, Convened at Denver, on the Fifth Day of January, 1881 (Denver, 1881).

McClees, Nelson O., ed., *Colorado Election Law, 1891–1893* (1893).

Connecticut

The General Statutes of the State of Connecticut (New Haven, 1866).

Journal of the Proceedings of the Convention of Delegates, Convened at Hartford, August 26, 1818, for the Purpose of Forming a Constitution of Civil Government for the People of the State of Connecticut (Hartford, 1902).

State of Connecticut Election Laws (1906).

Delaware

Delaware Session Laws 1891, chap. 38.

Laws of Delaware (Milford, 1898).

Laws of the State of Delaware (New Castle, 1797).

Manual of the Registration and Election Laws of the State of Delaware for the City of Wilmington (Dover, 1892).

Revised Statutes of Delaware, 1852 (Dover, 1852).

Revised Statutes of the State of Delaware (Wilmington, 1874).

Revised Statutes of the State of Delaware (Wilmington, 1893).

Florida

Act of February 27, 1877, ch. 3021, 1877 Fla. Laws 69.

The Acts and Resolutions Adopted by the Legislature of Florida at its First Session (1868) (Tallahassee, 1868).

"The Committee on the Rights of Suffrage and Qualification of Officers," *Territorial Florida Journalism*, reproduced from the *Floridian*, 15 December 1838.

Georgia

Act of February 7, 1785, Ga., *General Laws* (1785).

Bryan v. Walton, 14 Ga. 185 (1853).

Clark, R. H., T. R. R. Cobb, and D. Irwin, eds., *Code of the State of Georgia* (Atlanta, 1861).

Idaho

Pinkham, A. J., ed., *General Election Laws of the State of Idaho, Passed at the First Session of the Legislature and Approved February 25th, 1891* (Boise City, 1891).

Illinois

Act Regulating Elections, sec. 8, 1821 Illinois Laws 74, 77.

Act Regulating Elections, sec. 21, 1822 Illinois Laws 53, 61 (1823).

Act Relative to Criminal Jurisprudence, Illinois Rev. Code, sec. 162 (1827).

Cole, Arthur, ed., *The Constitutional Debates of 1847* (Springfield, 1919).

Election Laws of the State of Illinois, Including the Act of 1865, Known as the "Registry" Law: The Act of 1872, Known as the "General Election" Law: The Act of 1891, Known as the "Australian Ballot" Law, with Forms and Instructions to Aid Election Officers in Carrying the Same into Effect (Springfield, 1892).

Gray, William S., John L. Dryer, and Rodney H. Brandon, eds., *Proceedings of the Constitutional Convention of the State of Illinois, Convened January 6, 1920*, 5 Vols. (Springfield, 1922).

Hurd, Harvey, ed., *Revised Statutes of the State of Illinois, 1874, Comprising the Revised Acts of 1871–2 and 1873–4, Together with All Other General Statutes of the State, in Force on the First Day of July, 1874* (Springfield, 1874).

Hurd, Harvey, ed., *Revised Statues of the State of Illinois 1908, Containing All the General Statutes of the State in Force January 1, 1909* (Chicago, 1909).

Journal of the Constitutional Convention of the State of Illinois, January 7, 1862 (Springfield, 1862).

Journal of the Convention Assembled at Springfield, June 7, 1847 for the Purpose of Altering, Amending, or Revising the Constitution of the State of Illinois (Springfield, 1847).

"Journal of the Illinois Constitutional Convention, 1818," *Journal of the Illinois State Historical Society* 6 (October 1913): 273.

Purple, N. H., ed., *A Compilation of the Statutes of the State of Illinois, of a General Nature, in Force January 1, 1856, Collated with Reference to Decisions of the Supreme Court of Said State, and to Prior Laws Relating to the Same Subject Matter* (Chicago, 1856).

Starr, Merritt, and Russell H. Curtis, eds., *Annotated Statutes of the State of Illinois in Force January 1, 1885*, vol. 1 (Chicago, 1885).

Woods, Harry, ed., *Illinois Election Laws 1913* (Springfield, 1913).

Indiana

Dunn, J. P., ed., *General Laws*, ch. 47 (1879).

Indiana, *Revised Manual of the Election Law of Indiana* (Indianapolis, 1891).

Laws of the State of Indiana Passed at the Special Session, 1881 (Indianapolis, 1881).

The Revised Statutes of Indiana, collated and annotated by James S. Frazer, John H. Stotsenburg, and David Turpie (Chicago, 1881).

The Revised Statutes of the State of Indiana (Indianapolis, 1843).

The Revised Statutes of the State of Indiana, vol. 1 (Indianapolis, 1852).
The Statutes of the State of Indiana: Containing the Revised Statutes of 1852 (Indianapolis, 1870).

Kansas

Act of February 22, 1905, ch. 215, 1905 Kan. Laws 306, 312, 314.
State ex rel. Gilson v. Monahan, 72 Kan. 492 (1905).

Kentucky

Act of June 30, 1892, ch. 65, art. 1, sec. 5, 1892 Ky. Acts 106, 107.
Acts of the General Assembly of the Commonwealth of Kentucky (Frankfort, 1852).
Bullitt, Joshua F., and John Feland, *The General Statutes of Kentucky, with notes of decisions concerning the Constitution and other laws thereof* (Louisville, 1887).
Bullock, Edward I., and William Johnson, eds., *The General Statutes of the Commonwealth of Kentucky* (Frankfort, 1873).
Kentucky, *General Laws*, ch. 1439–40, 1478–80 (1894).
Revised Statutes of Kentucky (Frankfort, 1852).
Stanton, Richard H., *The Revised Statutes of Kentucky* (Cincinatti, 1860).

Maine

Act of February 6, 1833, ch. 49, sec. 1, 1833 Me. Laws 51–52.
Act of March 19, 1821, ch. 114, sec. 1, 1834 Me. Laws 549–56.
Act of March 25, 1864, ch. 278, 1864 Me. Laws 209.
The Debates and Journal of the Constitutional Convention of the State of Maine, 1819–1820 (Augusta, 1894).

Maryland

Act of April 8, 1908, ch. 545, sec. 4, 1908 Md. Laws 347–48.
Pole, J. R., "Suffrage and Representation in Maryland from 1776 to 1810: A Statistical Note and Some Reflections," *Voters, Parties, and Elections: Quantitative Essays in the History of American Popular Voting Behavior*, ed. Joel H. Silbey and Samuel T. McSeveney (Lexington, Mass., 1972), 61–71.
Registration and Election Laws of Maryland. Including All Amendments Thereto and Including the Acts of the Extra Session of the General Assembly of 1917; Also Containing the Primary Election Law, the Senatorial Primary Law, and the Corrupt Practices Law (Annapolis, 1917).

Massachusetts

A Compilation of the Laws in Force Relating to Elections: Containing the Act of 1874, Chapter 376, in Which Were Incorporated the Provisions of the Several Acts Relating to Elections Passed Since the General Statutes; and the Other Acts Relating to Elections Passed in 1874, 1875 and 1876; Together with the Provisions of the General Statutes Relating to Elections Which Remain in Force (Boston, 1876).
Laws Relating to Elections (Boston, 1893).
Massachusetts, *General Laws*, ch. 376, sec. 12 (1874).
Plane, Ann Marie, and Gregory Button, "The Massachusetts Indian Enfranchisement Act: Ethnic Contest in Historical Context, 1849–1869," *Ethnohistory* 40, 4 (1993):, 587–618.
Pole, Jack R., "Suffrage and Representation in Massachusetts: A Statistical Note," *William and Mary Quarterly* 14 (October 1957), 560-92.
Report of the Commissioners of the Revision of the Statutes in Five Numbers (Boston, 1858).

Michigan

Cooley, Thomas, ed., *The Compiled Laws of the State of Michigan*, vol. 1 (Lansing, 1857).
Dorr, Harold, ed., *The Michigan Constitutional Conventions of 1835–1836: Debates and Proceedings* (Ann Arbor, 1940).

Journal of the Proceedings of the Convention to Form a Constitution for the State of Michigan, 1835 (Detroit, 1835).

Public Acts of the Legislature of the State of Michigan Passed at the Regular Session of 1895 (Lansing, 1895).

Minnesota

General Election Law of Minnesota, Chapter 4, General Laws, 1893 (St. Paul, 1893).

Mississippi

Laws of the State of Mississippi (Jackson, 1876).

Laws of the State of Mississippi (Jackson, 1880).

McCardle, William H., and Robert Lowry, *A History of Mississippi, From the Discovery of the Great River by Hernando de Soto, Including the Earliest Settlement Made by the French, Under Iberville, to the Death of Jefferson Davis* (Jackson, 1891).

Thompson, R. H., "Suffrage in Mississippi," *Publications of the Mississippi Historical Society*, vol. 1, ed. Franklin L. Riley (Oxford, 1898), 25–49.

Missouri

Hardin, Charles H., ed., *The Revised Statutes of the State of Missouri*, vol. 1 (Oxford, 1856).

Journal of the Missouri State Convention, June 12, 1820 (St. Louis, 1820).

Laws of Missouri (Jefferson City, 1899).

Laws of Missouri Passed at the 49th General Assembly (Jefferson City, 1917).

Laws of Missouri Passed at the Session of the 32nd General Assembly (Jefferson City, 1883).

Missouri, *Revised Statutes*, sec. 5492 (1879).

Sullivan, John, ed., *Election Laws of the State of Missouri and the Federal Naturalization Laws, 1920* (Jefferson City, 1920).

Montana

Montana, *Compiled Statutes* (1888).

Montana, *Gen. Laws*, ch. 7 (1893).

Montana, *Revised Code* (1915).

Yoder, A. N., ed., *Election Laws of the State of Montana with Annotations* (Helena, 1910).

Nebraska

Act of April 1, 1899, ch. 59, sec. 1, 1899 Neb. Laws 286.

Act of February 15, 1869, 1869 Neb. Laws 95, 103.

Act of February 28, 1883, ch. 72, sec. 2, 1883 Neb. Laws 288–90.

Act of March 1, 1881, ch. 78, 1881 Neb. Laws 331, 338–39.

Act of March 29, 1889, ch. 78, sec. 3, 1889 Neb. Laws 539, 542–44.

Nebraska, *Revised Statutes*, ch. 17, sec. 33 (1866).

Nebraska, *General Statutes*, ch. 20, sec. 29 (1873).

Nebraska, *Compiled Statutes*, ch. 26, sec. 3 (1881).

Laws, Joint Resolutions, and Memorials Passed by the Legislative Assembly of the State of Nebraska, 1879 (Lincoln, 1879).

Nevada

Brodigan, George, ed., *Election Laws of 1916, Pamphlet* (Carson City, 1915).

New Hampshire

Chase, William, and Arthur Chase, eds., *The Public Statutes of the State of New Hampshire and General Laws in Force January 1, 1901* (Concord, 1900).

Laws of the State of New Hampshire (Exeter, 1815), 250.

Lyon, G. Parker, ed., *The Compiled Statutes of the State of New Hampshire* (Concord, 1854).

New Hampshire, *Gen. Laws*, ch. 2341, sec 1 (1860).

New Hampshire Primary and Election Laws (Manchester, 1925).

The Public Laws of the State of New Hampshire, to Which is Prefixed the Constitution of New Hampshire, with a General Index (Manchester, 1925).

New Jersey

Act Relative to Bribery, ch. 399, 1871 N.J. Laws 70–71.

Constitution of the State of New Jersey, 1844 (Trenton, 1844).

Elmer, Lucius Q. C., ed., *A Digest of the Laws of New Jersey*, 2d ed. (Philadelphia, 1855).

Pole, J. R., "The Suffrage in New Jersey, 1790–1807," *Proceedings of the New Jersey Historical Society*, vol. 71 (Edison, 1953), 39-61.

Proceedings of the New Jersey State Constitutional Convention of 1844 (Trenton, 1942).

Supplement to Act for the Punishment of Crimes, ch. 206, 1906 N.J. Laws 384–86.

Supplement to Act to Regulate Elections, ch. 291, 1866 N.J. Laws 705.

New York

Birdseye, Clarence, Robert Cumming, and Frank Gilbert, eds., *Annotated Consolidated Laws of the State of New York as Amended to January 1, 1910 Containing Also the Federal and State Constitutions with Notes of Board of Statutory Consolidation, Tables of Laws and Index*, vol. 2 (New York, 1909).

Comparative View of the State Constitutions: Manual of the New York State Constitutional Convention 1846 (Albany, 1849).

The Constitution of the State of New York, November 3, 1846 (Albany, 1849).

Donnan, George, ed., *The Complete Election Code of the State of New York; Containing the Ballot Reform Law, Rural Registration Act, and Other Election Laws as Are in Force in 1890, with Notes, Explanations, Forms, and Instructions* (Albany, 1890).

Duer, John, et al., eds., *The Revised Statutes of the State of New York* (Albany, 1846).

Edmonds, John, ed., *Statutes at Large of the State of New York Containing the General Statutes Passed in the Years 1863, 1864, 1865, and 1866, With a Reference to All the Decisions Upon Them*, vol. 6. (New York, 1868).

Edwards, Isaac, ed., *Supplement to the Fifth Edition of the Revised Statutes of the State of New York, Containing the Amendments and General Statutes Passed Since the Fifth Revision* (Albany, 1863).

Gunn, L. Ray, *The Decline of Authority: Public Economic Policy and Political Development in New York, 1800–1860* (Ithaca, 1988), 171.

Journal of the Convention of the State of New York, 1846 (Albany, 1846).

Laws of the State of New York, Passed at the 95th Session of the Legislature, vol. 2. (Albany, 1872).

May, Mitchell, ed., *State of New York. The Election Law Being Chapter 17 of the Consolidated Laws Containing Amendments of 1914 Together With Notes and Instructions and Political Calendar* (Albany, 1914).

New York State Constitutional Convention, 1846, Documents (Albany, 1849).

North Carolina

Sanders, John L., ed., *Amendments to the Constitution of North Carolina 1776–1970* (Chapel Hill, 1970).

North Dakota

Act of March 7, 1891, ch. 66, N.D. Laws 171, 180.

Con. Res., 5th Leg. (N.D. 1897).

Hall, Thomas, ed., *Election Laws of the State of North Dakota* (Devils Lake, 1914).

Power v. Williams, 53 N.D. 54 (1925).

Supplement to the 1913 Compiled Laws of North Dakota 1913–1925 (Rochester, 1916).

Ohio

Act of March 7, 1835, section 41, 1834 Ohio Laws 33, 41.

Act of March 20, 1841, section 25, 1840 Ohio Laws 13, 19.

Act of March 31, 1881, 1881 Ohio Laws 89–91.

Acts of a General Nature and Local Laws and Joint Resolutions Passed by the 52nd General Assembly of the State of Ohio (Columbus, 1857).

Bates, Clement, ed., *The Annotated Revised Statutes of the State of Ohio, Including All Laws of a General Nature in Force January 1, 1900,* 2d ed. (Cincinnati, 1899).

Curwen, Maskell, ed., *The Public Statutes at Large of the State of Ohio: From the Close of Chase's Statutes, February 1833 to the Present Time,* vol. 1 (Cincinnati, 1853).

Daugherty, M. A., John Brasee, and George Okey, eds., *The Revised Statutes and Other Acts of a General Nature of the State of Ohio in Force January 1, 1880,* 2d ed. (Columbus, 1882).

Graves, Chas, ed., *The Election Laws of the State of Ohio and the United States of America. Applicable to the Conduct of Elections and the Duties of Officers in Connection Therewith* (Columbus, 1914).

Kinney, Charles, ed., *The Election Laws of the State of Ohio and of the United States of America So Far as They Relate to the Conduct of Elections and the Duties of Officers in Connection Therewith* (Columbus, 1898).

Ohio, *Revised Statutes,* ch. 40, sec. 71 (1860).

Patterson, Isaac F., ed., *The Constitutions of Ohio* (Cleveland, 1912).

Report of the Debates and Proceedings of the Convention for the Revision of the Constitution of the State of Ohio, 1850–1851, 2 vols. (Columbus, 1851).

Smith, Rufus, and Alfred Benedict, eds., *The Verified Revised Statutes of the State of Ohio Including All Laws of a General Nature in Force January 1st, 1890,* 4th ed. (Cincinnati, 1891).

Swan, Joseph R., ed., *Statutes of the State of Ohio, of a General Nature, in Force August, 1854* (Cincinnati, 1854).

Thompson, Carmi, E. M. Fullington, and U. G. Denman, *The General Code of the State of Ohio* (Cincinnati, 1910).

Throckmorton, Archibald, et al., *The General Code of the State of Ohio, Revised to 1921* (Cleveland, 1921).

Winkle, Kenneth J., *The Politics of Community: Migration and Politics in Antebellum Ohio* (Cambridge, 1988), 174–75.

Oregon

General and Special Laws, 20th Assembly (Salem, 1898).

Olcott, Ben, ed., *General Laws and Joint Resolutions and Memorials Enacted and Adopted by the 28th Regular Session of the Legislative Assembly* (Salem, 1915).

Pennsylvania

Digest of the Election Laws of Pennsylvania, and an Index to the Same, Corrected to January 1, 1916, as Compiled for Smull's Legislative Hand Book (Harrisburg, 1916).

Dunlop, James, ed., *The General Laws of Pennsylvania, From the Year 1700 to April, 1849,* 2d ed. (Philadelphia, 1849).

Rhode Island

Election Laws of the State of Rhode Island (Providence, 1912).

Tennessee

McClure, Wallace, *State Constitution-Making With Especial Reference to Tennessee* (Nashville, 1916).

Shannon, R. T., ed., *Annotated Code of Tennessee* (Nashville, 1896).

Thompson, Seymour, and Thomas M. Steger, eds., *Statutes of Tennessee* (St. Louis, 1871).

Texas

Citizens Advisory Committee on Revision of the Constitution of the State of Texas, *Interim Report to the Fifty-sixth Legislature and the People of Texas* (n.p., 1959).
Lightfoot, Jewel, ed., *The Terrell Election Law with Annotations from the Decisions of the Courts and Opinions of the Attorney General's Department* (Austin, 1910).
Moffett, Jonas W., ed., *Constitution of the State of Texas* (Austin, 1922).
1928 Complete Texas Statutes (Kansas City, 1928).
Sayles' Annotated Civil Statutes of the State of Texas (St. Louis, 1898).

Utah

Act of April 5, 1896, ch. 130, 1896 Utah Laws 467, 480–81, 497.
Act of February 27, 1897, ch. 12, 1897 Utah Laws 25–27.
Utah, *Compiled Laws Annotated* (Salt Lake City, 1917).

Vermont

Vermont, *Compiled Laws*, ch. 85 (1824).
Martin v. Fullam, 90 Vt. 163 (1916).

Virginia

Pole, Jack R., "Representation and Authority in Virginia from the Revolution to Reform," *Journal of Southern History* 24, 1 (1958): 16-50.
The Statutes at Large: Being a Collection of All the Laws of Virginia, From the First Session of the Legislature, in the Year 1619, vol. 7 (Richmond, 1820).

Washington

Howell, I. M., ed., *State of Washington. General Election Laws Including Laws for Commission Form of Government* (Olympia, 1912).

West Virginia

The Election Laws of West Virginia Including "Registration Act" of 1908 and "Corrupt Practices Act of 1908" (Charleston, 1910).

Wisconsin

Act of August 21, 1848, 1848 Wis. Laws 191–92.
Cunningham, T. J., ed., *The Registry and Election Laws of the State of Wisconsin with Forms and Instructions for the Use of County, City, Village and Town Officers* (Madison, 1894).
Sanborn, Arthur, and John Berryman, eds., *Wisconsin Statutes of 1898* (Chicago, 1898).
Wisconsin, *Revised Statutes*, ch. 6, sec. 2 (1849).
Wisconsin, *General Laws*, ch. 39, sec. 1 (1883).

Wyoming

Houx, Frank, ed., *Election Laws of the State of Wyoming* (Sheridan, 1911).
Primary Registration and Election Laws of the State of Wyoming In Force From and After January 21, 1891 (Cheyenne, 1891).

MULTISTATE SOURCES, TABLES A.17–A.20:
SUFFRAGE RIGHTS FOR WOMEN

Evans, Taliesin, *American Citizenship and the Right of Suffrage in the United States* (California, 1892).

Flexner, Eleanor, *Century of Struggle: The Woman's Rights Movement in the United States* (Cambridge, Mass., 1959).

Kendrick, Lowell, and Harold P. Salisbury, eds., *General Constitutional and Statutory Provisions Relative to Suffrage Published by the Legislative Reference Bureau of the Rhode Island State Library* (Providence, 1912).

Maule, Frances, ed., *"The Blue Book," Woman Suffrage, History, Arguments, and Results* (New York, 1917).

Stapler, Martha, ed., *The Woman Suffrage Yearbook 1917* (New York, 1917).

Swindler, William, ed., *Sources and Documents of United States Constitutions,* vols. 1–11 (Dobbs Ferry, 1973–1988).

Thorpe, Francis, ed., *Federal and State Constitutions,* 7 vols. (Washington, DC, 1909).

STATE SOURCES, TABLES A.17–A.20

California

The Statutes of California and Amendments to the Constitution Passed at the Extra Session of the 39th Legislature, 1911 (San Francisco, 1912).

Colorado

McClees, Nelon O., ed., *Colorado Election Law 1891–1893* (n.p., 1893).

Connecticut

General Statutes of Connecticut, Revision of 1901 (Hartford, 1902).
State of Connecticut Election Laws (1906).

Florida

Act of June 4, 1915, ch. 6940, sec. 1, 1915 Florida Laws 312.
Act of May 12, 1915, ch. 7154, sec. 35, 1915 Florida Laws 529.
Special Acts Adopted by the Legislature of Florida, vol. 2. (Tallahassee, 1915).

Idaho

Pinkham, A. J., ed., *General Election Laws of the State of Idaho, Passed at the First Session of the Legislature and Approved February 25th, 1891* (Boise City, 1891).

Illinois

Laws of the State of Illinois (Springfield, 1891).

Indiana

Roach, William, ed., *Laws of the State of Indiana, Passed at the Seventy-first Regular Session of the General Assembly* (Indianapolis, 1919).

Kansas

Kansas, *General Statutes,* ch. 92, art. 3, sec. 20 (1868).
State of Kansas, Session Laws of 1887 (Topeka, 1887).
State of Kansas Session Laws, 1909 (Topeka, 1909).

Kentucky

Acts of the General Assembly of the Commonwealth of Kentucky (Frankfurt, 1912).
Acts of the General Assembly of the Commonwealth of Kentucky (Frankfurt, 1920).
Kentucky Statutes (Louisville, 1894).

Massachusetts

Laws Relating to Elections (Boston, 1893).

Michigan

Acts of the Legislature of the State of Michigan (Lansing, 1855).
Compiled Laws of the State of Michigan, 1915 (Lansing, 1915).
Michigan Reports, vol. 97 (Chicago, 1894), 188–97.
Public Acts of the Legislature of the State of Michigan (Lansing, 1875).
Public Acts of the Legislature of the State of Michigan, 1917 (Lansing, 1917).

Mississippi

Laws of the State of Mississippi (Jackson, 1878).
The Revised Code of the Statute Laws of the State of Mississippi (Jackson, 1880).

Nebraska

Laws, Resolutions and Memorials Passed by the Legislature of the State of Nebraska (Lincoln, 1917).

Nevada

Brodigan, George, ed., *Election Laws of 1916, Pamphlet* (Carson City, 1915).

New York

Laws of the State of New York, Passed at the 133rd Session of the Legislature, vol. 1 (Albany, 1910).

North Dakota

The Australian Ballot Act and Other Acts Constituting the Election Laws of North Dakota (Bismarck, 1891).
Supplement to the 1913 Compiled Laws of North Dakota 1913–1925 (Rochester, 1916).

Ohio

Bates, Clement, ed., *The Annotated Revised Statutes of the State of Ohio, Including All Laws of a General Nature in Force January 1, 1900*, 2d ed. (Cincinnati, 1899).
Daugherty, M. A., John Brasee, and George Okey, eds., *The Revised Statutes and Other Acts of a General Nature of the State of Ohio in Force January 1, 1880*, 2d ed. (Columbus, 1882).
Kinney, Charles, ed., *The Election Laws of the State of Ohio and of the United States of America So Far as They Relate to the Conduct of Elections and the Duties of Officers in Connection Therewith* (Columbus, 1898).
Smith, Rufus, and Alfred Benedict, eds., *The Verified Revised Statutes of the State of Ohio Including All Laws of a General Nature in Force January 1st, 1890*, 4th ed. (Cincinnati, 1891).
Thompson, Carmi, E. M. Fullington, and U. G. Denman, *The General Code of the State of Ohio* (Cincinnati, 1910).
Throckmorton, Archibald, et al., eds., *The General Code of the State of Ohio, Revised to 1921* (Cleveland, 1921).

Oregon

General Laws of Oregon, 12th Regular Session (Salem, 1882).

Rhode Island

Election Laws of the State of Rhode Island (Providence, 1912).

Texas

Howard, George, ed., *General and Special Laws of the State of Texas Passed by the 4th Called Session of the 35th Legislature* (Austin, 1918).

Vermont

The Public Statutes of Vermont 1906 (Concord, 1907).

Washington

Howell, I. M., *State of Washington. General Election Laws Including Laws for Commission Form of Government* (Olympia, 1912).

Wisconsin

Cunningham, T. J., ed., *The Registry and Election Laws of the State of Wisconsin with Forms and Instructions for the Use of County, City, Village and Town Officers* (Madison, 1894).

Wyoming

Primary Registration and Election Laws of the State of Wyoming In Force From and After January 21, 1891 (Cheyenne, 1891).

NOTES

INTRODUCTION

1. Richard M. Scammon and Alice V. McGillivray, eds., *America Votes*, vol. 20 (Washington, 1992): 9; Raymond E. Wolfinger and Steven J. Rosenstone, *Who Votes* (New Haven, 1980), 1; *New York Times*, 13 November 1988; Walter Dean Burnham, "The Turnout Problem," in A. James Reichley, ed., *Elections American Style* (Washington, DC, 1987), 97–133. Other, more recent statistics are cited in the conclusion.

2. Herbert Croly, *The Promise of American Life* (1909; reprint, New York, 1964), 2, 6; Special Message to the Congress: The American Promise, 15 March 1965, *Public Papers of the Presidents of the United States: Lyndon B. Johnson, 1965*, vol. 1 (Washington, 1965), 281–87. Cf. Robert Wiebe, *Self Rule: A Cultural History of American Democracy* (Chicago, 1994), 1, 8.

3. Congressional Quarterly, *Guide to U.S. Elections*, 2d. ed. (Washington, 1985), 324.

4. Among many discussions of the turnout problem, see the numerous and influential writings of Walter Dean Burnham (including "The Turnout Problem"), as well as Frances F. Piven and Richard A. Cloward, *Why Americans Don't Vote* (New York, 1988).

5. See, e.g., J. Morgan Kousser, *The Shaping of Southern Politics: Suffrage Restriction and the Establishment of the One-Party South, 1880–1910* (New Haven, 1974); Steven Lawson, *Black Ballots: Voting Rights in the South, 1944–1969* (New York, 1976); William Gillette, *The Right to Vote: Politics and the Passage of the Fifteenth Amendment* (Baltimore, 1965). Numerous works on this subject are cited herein, chaps. 4, 7, and 8.

6. See, e.g., chap. 6.

7. Chilton Williamson, *American Suffrage: From Property to Democracy, 1760–1860* (Princeton, 1960); Marchette G. Chute, *The First Liberty: A History of the Right to Vote in America, 1619–1850* (New York, 1969).

8. Dudley O. McGovney, *The American Suffrage Medley: The Need for a National Uniform Suffrage* (Chicago, 1949); Kirk H. Porter, *A History of Suffrage in the United States* (Chicago, 1918). One other useful, if dated, synthetic study is Albert J. McCulloch, *Suffrage and Its Problems* (Baltimore, 1929). J. Morgan Kousser has written a brief overview of the history of suffrage in Jack P. Greene, ed., *The Encyclopedia of American Political History*, vol. 3 (New York, 1984), 1236–58. At a state level, see also Richard P. McCormick, *The History of Voting in New Jersey: A Study of the Development of Election Machinery, 1664–1911* (New Brunswick, NJ, 1953). Peter H. Argersinger's work on Gilded Age elections and election laws is much needed and important but limited in chronological scope; see, e.g., "'A Place on the Ballot': Fusion Politics and Antifusion Laws," *American Historical Review* 85 (1980): 287–306; "The Value of the Vote: Political Representation in the Gilded Age," *Journal of American History* 76 (June 1989): 59–90.

9. Herbert Butterfield, *The Whig Interpretation of History* (New York, 1951). The term *progressive* is used here not to allude to Progressive historians, such as Charles Beard, but rather to capture the conviction that history represents progress.

10. Alexis de Tocqueville, *Democracy in America*, J. P. Mayer and Max Lerner, eds., George Lawrence, trans. (New York, 1966), 52–53.

11. Cf. Robert J. Steinfeld, "Property and Suffrage in the Early American Republic," *Stanford Law Review* 41 (January 1989): 335–37; Frank W. Blackmar, "History of Suffrage in Legislation in the United States," *The Chautauquan* 22 (October 1895): 34.

12. William B. Munro, *The Government of American Cities*, 4th ed. (New York, 1928), 147–48. This quote appeared also in the 1926 edition of Munro's book (but not in the 1912 or 1916 editions).

13. Mary Jo Adams, *The History of Suffrage in Michigan*, Publications of the Michigan Political Science Association, vol. 3, no. 1 (Ann Arbor, March 1898), 37.

14. James Schouler, "Evolution of the American Voter," *American Historical Review* 2 (July 1897): 665–74; Francis N. Thorpe, "A Century's Struggle for the Franchise in America," *Harper's Magazine* 94 (January 1897), 215.

15. Porter, *Suffrage*, vii, 4. The sense of conflict and contingency endured, among some analysts, into the 1920s and even later. See, e.g., Arthur W. Bromage, "Literacy and the Electorate: Expansion and Contraction of the Franchise," *American Political Science Review* 24 (1930): 946; Harold F. Gosnell, *Democracy: The Threshold of Freedom* (New York, 1948).

16. E. E. Schattschneider, *The Semisovereign People: A Realist's View of Democracy in America* (Hinsdale, 1960), 100–101; Sidney Verba, Norman Nie, and Jaeon Kim, *Participation and Political Equality: A Seven-Nation Comparison* (New York, 1978), 5; Williamson, *American Suffrage*. For other examples of this view see V. O. Key, Jr., *Politics, Parties, and Pressure Groups*, 5th ed. (New York, 1964), 597; William H. Flanigan and Nancy H. Zingale, *Political Behavior of the American Electorate*, 4th ed. (Boston, 1979), 10–13; Jay A. Sigler, *American Rights Policies* (Homewood, IL, 1975), 111. Kousser (*Shaping*, 3) observes that political scientists interested in voting laws have tended to focus on extensions of the suffrage while ignoring contractions, while Steinfeld ("Property and Suffrage," 336*n*) notes that constitutional law casebooks tend to contain implicit Whig histories of the suffrage. There are some exceptions, scholars who acknowledge that the road to a broader suffrage in the United States has been slow and uneven. See, e.g., Judith Shklar, *American Citizenship—The Question for Inclusion* (Cambridge, 1991), 13–14; William H. Riker, *Democracy in the United States* (New York, 1965), 50; Flanigan and Zingale (cited earlier on the other side of the issue), *Political Behavior*, 10.

17. Munro, *Government*, 134. The surprising lack of interest in the subject is noted also by Peter Argersinger, "Regulating Democracy: Election Laws and Dakota Politics, 1889–1902," *Midwest Review* 5 (Spring 1983): 1; see also James A. Morone, *The Democratic Wish: Popular Participation and the Limits of American Government* (New York, 1990), 20.

18. The point that scholars from both the political right and left have tended to ignore this issue also is made in Göran Therborn, "The Rule of Capital and the Rise of Democracy," *New Left Review* 103 (May-June 1977): 3–41.

19. See, e.g., Stein Rokkan, with Angus Campbell, Per Trosvik, and Henry Valen, *Citizens, Elections, Parties: Approaches to the Comparative Study of the Processes of Development* (New York, 1970); T. H. Marshall, *Class, Citizenship, and Social Development* (New York, 1964); Seymour Martin Lipset, "Some Social Requisites of Democracy: Economic Development and Political Legitimacy," in Charles F. Cnudde and Deane E. Neubauer, eds., *Empirical Democratic Theory* (Chicago, 1969); Reinhard Bendix, *Nation-Building and Citizenship: Studies of Our Changing Social Order* (Berkeley, 1977). See also Therborn, "Rule of Capital."

20. On this theme see Shklar, *American Citizenship*, esp. 28–29.

21. Frederick Jackson Turner, "Contributions of the West to American Democracy," *Atlantic Monthly* 91 (January 1903), 83–96; Schattschneider, *Semisovereign People*, 100–101; Gosnell, *Democracy*, 20–23, 31; Flanigan and Zingale, *Political Behavior*, 9; Robert C. Brooks, *Political Parties and Electoral Problems* (New York, 1923), 361–62; Ronald P. Formisano, *The Transformation of Political Culture: Massachusetts Parties, 1790s–1840s* (New York, 1983), 4.

22. A rare discussion of the role of war in the evolution of suffrage (albeit with different conclusions) is Manfred Berg, "Soldiers and Citizens: War and Voting Rights in American History," in David K. Adams and Cornelis A. Van Minnen, eds., *Reflections on American Exceptionalism* (Staffordshire, England, 1994), 188–225; the subject also is alluded to in Marc W. Kruman, "Legislatures and Political Rights," in Joel H. Silbey, ed., *Encyclopedia of the American Legislative System*, vol. 3 (New York, 1994), 1235–51.

23. See chap. 5 for details regarding this incident.

24. Notions of American exceptionalism commonly are grounded in the claim that there is a uniquely weak relationship between class and politics in the United States.

25. For comparative and international perspectives on the history of suffrage see Charles Seymour and Donald P. Frary, *How the World Votes: The Story of Democratic Development in Elections* (Springfield, MA, 1918); Gosnell, *Democracy*; Rokkan, *Citizens*; Therborn, "Rule of Capital"; see also chap. 8 and the conclusion.

26. Schattschneider, *Semisovereign People*, 105; Raymond E. Wolfinger and Steven J. Rosenstone, *Who Votes?* (New Haven, 1980), 13–25; Burnham, "Turnout Problem," 126; see also the conclusion. Some of these subjects will be analyzed in detail in a forthcoming volume, tentatively entitled *The Free Gift of the Ballot*, focusing on the history of working-class electoral participation.

PART ONE

1. Adams quoted in Charles Francis Adams, *The Works of John Adams, Second President of the United States*, vol. 9 (Boston, 1856), 377–78; Davis quoted in Arthur Charles Cole, ed., *The Constitutional Debates of 1847* (Springfield, IL, 1919), 564. On the word *democracy* see, e.g., Roy N. Lokken, "The Concept of Democracy in Colonial Political Thought," *William and Mary Quarterly* 16 (October 1984): 571–73.

CHAPTER ONE

1. Franklin quote from *The Casket, or Flowers of Literature, Wit and Sentiment*, vol. 4 (Philadelphia, 1828), 181; this story is cited also in P. M. Zall, ed., *Ben Franklin Laughing: Anecdotes from Original Sources by and About Benjamin Franklin* (Berkeley, 1980), 149–50. Jack N. Rakove, *The Beginnings of National Politics: An Interpretive History of the Continental Congress* (New York, 1979), 361–99; idem, *Original Meanings: Politics and Ideas in the Making of the Constitution* (New York, 1996), 23–36.

2. Rakove, *Original Meanings*, 46, 58–59, 83; Wilbourn E. Benton, ed., *1787: Drafting the United States Constitution*, vol. 1 (College Station, TX, 1986), 19–32; William G. Carr, *The Oldest Delegate: Franklin in the Constitutional Convention* (Newark, 1990), 169–71.

3. Kirk H. Porter, *A History of Suffrage in the United States* (Chicago, 1918), 12–13; Robert J. Dinkin, *Voting in Provincial America* (Westport, 1977), 36; see also Robert J. Steinfeld, "Property and Suffrage in the Early American Republic," *Stanford Law Review* 41 (January 1989): 339–40; Chilton Williamson, *American Suffrage: From Property to Democracy 1760–1860* (Princeton, 1960), 12–19; Jack P. Greene, *Imperatives, Behaviors, and Identities: Essays in Early American Cultural History* (Charlottesville, 1992), 246–48. Among the best monographic studies are those of Jack R. Pole, e.g., *Political Representation in England and the Origins of the American Republic* (London, 1966); "Suffrage Reform and the American Revolution in New Jersey," *Proceedings of the New Jersey Historical Society* 74 (July 1956): 181; "Suffrage and Representation in Maryland from 1776 to 1810: A Statistical Note and Some Reflections," *Voters, Parties, and Elections: Quantitative Essays in the History of American Popular Voting Behavior*, ed. Joel H. Silbey and Samuel T. McSeveney (Lexington, 1972); see also Gary B. Nash, *The Urban Crucible: Social Change, Political Consciousness, and the Origins of the American Revolution* (Cambridge, MA, 1979).

4. Steinfeld, "Property," 340; Charles Seymour and Donald P. Frary, *How the World Votes: The Story of Democratic Development in Elections*, vol. 1 (Springfield, 1918), 210–11; Williamson, *American Suffrage*, 3–12; Greene, *Imperatives*, 248–57; Ireton quoted in Dinkin, *Voting*, 36–46, 251; Edmund S. Morgan, *Inventing the People* (New York, 1988), 68–69; Jack R. Pole, *The Pursuit of Equality in American History* (Berkeley, 1978), 44–45; Nash, *Urban Crucible*, 367–68; Robert J. Dinkin, "The Suffrage," *Encyclopedia of the North American Colonies*, vol. 1, ed. Jacob E. Cooke (New York, 1993), 369–70.

5. Dinkin, *Voting*, 34–35; Williamson, *American Suffrage*, 15; Richard P. McCormick, *The History of Voting in New Jersey: A Study of the Development of Election Machinery, 1664–1911* (New Brunswick, NJ, 1953), 62.

6. Williamson, *American Suffrage*, 15; Dinkin, *Voting*, 34.

7. Dinkin, *Voting*, 33; Marc W. Kruman, *Between Authority and Liberty: State Constitution Making in Revolutionary America* (Chapel Hill, NC, 1997), 104.

8. Greene, *Imperatives*, 249–50.

9. Ibid., 249; Dinkin, *Voting*, 31–32; there appears to be some scholarly disagreement regarding the number of colonies that excluded Jews. Richard Boeckel, *Voting and Nonvoting in Elections* (Washington, D.C., 1928), 521; Jack R. Pole, "Representation and Authority in Virginia from Revolution to Reform," *Journal of Southern History* 24 (February 1958): 18; Williamson, *American Suffrage*, 15–16.

10. Native Americans apparently voted in parts of New England; free blacks voted in North Carolina; and aliens voted in Pennsylvania and South Carolina. Dinkin, *Voting*, 32; James H. Kettner, *The Development of American Citizenship, 1608–1870* (Chapel Hill, NC, 1978), 122; Jamin B. Raskin, "Legal Aliens, Local Citizens: The Historical, Constitutional, and Theoretical Meanings of Alien Suffrage," *University of Pennsylvania Law Review* 141 (April 1993): 1399–1401.

11. Dinkin, *Voting*, 30; Greene, *Imperatives*, 249.

12. Julian A. C. Chandler, "The History of Suffrage in Virginia," Johns Hopkins University Studies in Historical and Political Science Series, ed. Herbert B. Adams, no. 19 (Baltimore, 1901), 15; Pole, "Representation and Authority," 17; Pole, *Political Representation*, 141; Donald S. Lutz, *The Origins of American Constitutionalism* (Baton Rouge, 1988), 75–76.

13. Chandler, "Suffrage in Virginia," 14, 19; Williamson, *American Suffrage*, 16–17, 18, 36–37; Pole, *Political Representation*, 48, 88–89, 142; Nash, *Urban Crucible*, 31–32; Pole, "Suffrage Reform," 561–62; Jon C. Teaford, *The Municipal Revolution in America: Origins of Modern Urban Government, 1650–1825* (Chicago, 1975), 30–32; Williamson notes that in some places municipalities gave their residents a broader franchise for voting in provincial as well as local elections (pp. 16–17). Indeed, as Pole suggests, qualifications for all elections may well have varied among communities within individual colonies (*Political Representation*, 142). Robert E. Brown, *Middle-Class Democracy and the Revolution in Massachusetts, 1691–1780* (Ithaca, 1955), 79–80, 99.

14. Dinkin, *Voting*, 31; Chandler, "Suffrage in Virginia," 10–11, 23; B. Katherine Brown, "The Controversy over the Franchise in Puritan Massachusetts, 1954–1974," *William and Mary Quarterly* 33 (April 1976): 213, 231, 233; Pole, *Political Representation*, 37, 138–39, 142–43; Teaford, *Municipal Revolution*, 30–32. Whether there was much public agitation against suffrage restrictions has been little investigated by historians, some of whom regard the absence of evidence of conflict as a sign of acquiescence on the part of the excluded. Dinkin, *Voting*, 37; Pole, *Political Representation*, 33; Chandler, "Suffrage in Virginia," 23.

15. Chandler, "Suffrage in Virginia," 10; Dinkin, *Voting*, 37; Pole, *Political Representation*, 88–89, 137–39, 143–45; Nash, *Urban Crucible*, 30; Merrill Jensen, *The Articles of Confederation* (Madison, 1966), 8–9; Steinfeld, "Property," 339; Brown, "Controversy," 216–22.

16. Pole, "Representation and Authority," 17–18; Dinkin, *Voting*, 31, 33; Chandler, "Suffrage in Virginia," 12–13.

17. Brown, "Controversy," 232; Chandler, "Suffrage in Virginia," 11.

18. For an excellent and judicious summary of the evidence see Dinkin, *Voting*, 40–49; see also Williamson, *American Suffrage*, 20–39. On the debate among historians see also Brown, "Controversy," 216–22; Brown, *Middle-Class Democracy*, 19–20, 25–30, 37, 43–45, 60, 195; Carl Becker, *The United States: An Experiment in Democracy* (New York, 1920), 35–36; Pole, *Political Representation*, 141–47. Most of the available statistics and estimates are for the mid-eighteenth century.

19. Brown, "Controversy," 223–41; Jack R. Pole, *Paths to the American Past* (New York, 1979), 233–34; idem, "Suffrage Reform," 561; Williamson, *American Suffrage*, 38–39; Dinkin, *Voting*, 46–49; Nash, *Urban Crucible*, 29; Eric Foner, *Tom Paine and Revolutionary America* (New York, 1976), 56–57.

20. Dinkin, *Voting*, 40–48; Nash, *Urban Crucible*, 63, 363, 451; Jensen, *Articles*, 17.

21. Dinkin, *Voting*, 40–49; Nash, *Urban Crucible*, 63, 266, 351. As Dinkin, among others, has pointed out, the available evidence varies in quality from place to place.

22. Epigraph from *Maryland Gazette*, 15 August 1776, cited in Kruman, *Between Authority and Liberty*, 95.

23. On interpretations of the revolution see Carl L. Becker, "The History of Political Parties in the Province of New York, 1760–1776," *Bulletin of the University of Wisconsin*, no. 286, History Series, vol. 2, no. 1 (Madison, WI, 1907), 5; Becker, *United States*, 34–35; Gordon S. Wood, *The Radicalism of the American Revolution* (New York, 1992), 232; Brown, *Middle-Class Democracy*, v–vi; Pole, *Paths*, 228–29.

24. Greene, *Imperatives*, 260–61; Mark D. Hall, *The Political and Legal Philosophy of James Wilson, 1742–1798* (Columbia, MO, 1997), 108–9; *The Oxford English Dictionary*, 2d ed., vol. 6 (1989), 144; for the best overview of these arguments see Willi Paul Adams, *The First American Constitutions: Republican Ideology and the Making of the State Constitutions in the Revolutionary Era* (Chapel Hill, NC, 1980), 207–27. By the seventeenth century, *suffrage* was being used to refer to collective opinions or the expression of collective opinions, but it was only in the late eighteenth and nineteenth centuries that the term began to be commonly used to refer to the right to vote.

25. Pole, *Paths*, 245.

26. Oscar Handlin and Mary Flug Handlin, *The Popular Sources of Political Authority: Documents on the Massachusetts Constitution of 1780* (Cambridge, MA, 1966), 437; J. Allen Smith, *The Growth and Decadence of Constitutional Government* (New York, 1930), 29.

27. Michael Levin, *The Spectre of Democracy: The Rise of Modern Democracy as Seen by Its Critics* (New York, 1992), 45; Gordon S. Wood, *The Creation of the American Republic: 1776–1787* (Chapel Hill, NC, 1969), 178–79.

28. Sir William Blackstone, *Commentaries on the Laws of England*, facsimile of the first edition of 1765–1769, vol. 1 (Chicago and London, 1765), 165; Williamson, *American Suffrage*, 10–12, 62; John Phillip Reid, *The Concept of Representation in the Age of the American Revolution* (Chicago, 1989), 39–40.

29. Chilton Williamson, "American Suffrage and Sir William Blackstone," *Political Science Quarterly* 68 (1953): 552–54; Foner, *Tom Paine*, 122–23; John Adams, *Thoughts on Government* (Philadelphia, 1776), 209–11.

30. Adams, *First American Constitutions*, 209–10; Greene, *Imperatives*, 254, 257, 259, 260–61; Williamson, *American Suffrage*, 10–11; Pole, *Pursuit of Equality*, 42–43; Elisha P. Douglass, *Rebels and Democrats: The Struggle for Equal Political Rights and Majority Rule During the American Revolution* (Chapel Hill, NC, 1955), 28; Levin, *Spectre of Democracy*, 85–86; Wood, *Radicalism*, 56, 178–79; Williamson, "American Suffrage," 554.

31. Greene, *Imperatives*, 260–61; Wood, *Radicalism*, 178–79; Williamson, "American Suffrage," 556.

32. On Paine's views see Foner, *Tom Paine*, 142–44.

33. Charles Francis Adams, *The Works of John Adams, Second President of the United States*, vol. 10 (Boston, 1856), 268; see also J. Morgan Kousser, *The Shaping of Southern Politics, Suffrage, and the Establishment of the One-Party South* (New Haven, 1974), 1261; Pole, *Pursuit of Equality*, 45–46.

34. Max Farrand, ed., *The Records of the Federal Convention of 1787*, vol. 2 (New Haven, 1966), 203–4; Drew R. McCoy, *The Elusive Republic: Political Economy in Jeffersonian America* (Chapel Hill, NC, 1980), 128–32; Pole, *Paths of Equality*, 245–46; Levin, *Spectre of Democracy*, 87; Adams, *Works*, vol. 10, 267–68.

35. W. J. Shepard, "Suffrage," *Encyclopedia of the Social Sciences*, ed. Edwin R. A. Seligman (New York, 1934), 448; Harold F. Gosnell, *Democracy: The Threshold of Freedom* (New York, 1948), 16; Adams, *First American Constitutions*, 215.

36. Handlin and Handlin, *Popular Sources*, 487, 562; for additional examples of the use of the language of rights see ibid., 34–36, 266–67, 550, 562, 580–81.

37. Ibid., 248–49, 277, 302; Adams, *First American Constitutions*, 184–85.

38. Adams, *Works*, vol. 9, 375–78; for a later iteration in 1817 see vol. 10, 267–68.

39. Handlin and Handlin, *Popular Sources*, 36.

40. Marc Kruman also has used the phrase *Pandora's box* in reference to the Adams quotation. Kruman, *Between Authority and Liberty*, 89.

41. Ibid., 92–95.

42. Handlin and Handlin, *Popular Sources*, 231; see also Douglass, *Rebels and Democrats*, 293–94.

43. Handlin and Handlin, *Popular Sources*, 385.

44. Ibid., 483; Adams, *First American Constitutions*, 127.

45. Wood, *Radicalism*, 96–97, 258–59; Handlin and Handlin, *Popular Sources*, 341; for a full discussion of theories of representation see Reid, *Concept of Representation*, 43–62.

46. Handlin and Handlin, *Popular Sources*, 584.

47. Ibid., 254.

48. Douglass, *Rebels and Democrats*, 256; quote from Elector cited in Steven Rosswurm, *Arms, Country, and Class: The Philadelphia Militia and "Lower Sort" During the American Revolution, 1775–1783*

(New Brunswick, NJ, 1987), 89–90. See also Williamson, *American Suffrage*, 79–82; Kruman, *Between Authority and Liberty*, 98–99.

49. Farrand, *Records*, vol. 2, 204–8; Benton, *1787*, vol. 1, 235; Lawrence D. Cress, *Citizens in Arms: The Army and the Militia in American Society to the War of 1812* (Chapel Hill, NC, 1982), 59.

50. In several of the colonies, there were movements to liberalize the franchise even prior to independence.

51. Douglass, *Rebels and Democrats*, 251–56; Rosswurm, *Arms, Country, Class*, 55–69.

52. Pole, *Political Representation*, 260, 268, 271–75; Nash, *Urban Crucible*, 378–80; Foner, *Tom Paine*, 63–64, 126–32; Douglass, *Rebels and Democrats*, 251–52, 255–56, 268–69; Rosswurm, *Arms, Country, Class*, 12, 55–69, 71, 77, 86–93, 97, 99–105, 252–53; Williamson, *American Suffrage*, 92–96; Wood, *Creation*, 169; Robert L. Brunhouse, *The Counter-Revolution in Pennsylvania, 1776–1790* (New York, 1971), 227.

53. Kruman, *Between Authority and Liberty*, 91, 99–100; Douglass, *Rebels and Democrats*, 51–52, 54; Pole, "Suffrage and Representation in Maryland," 62–63; Charles G. Steffen, *The Mechanics of Baltimore: Workers and Politics in the Age of Revolution, 1763–1812* (Urbana, 1984), 61–64, 92–93; Adams, *First American Constitutions*, 206; Williamson, "American Suffrage," 108–10.

54. Adams, *First American Constitutions*, 205; J. R. Pole, "The Suffrage in New Jersey, 1790–1807," *Proceedings of the New Jersey Historical Society* 71 (January 1953): 39–41, 57–59, 69, 113–14, 186–87, 192–93.

55. Fletcher M. Green, *Constitutional Development in the South Atlantic States, 1776–1860: A Study in the Evolution of Democracy* (Chapel Hill, NC, 1930), 87; Williamson, *American Suffrage*, 104–5.

56. Williamson, "American Suffrage," 105–6; Douglass, *Rebels and Democrats*, 331; Jere R. Daniell, *Experiment in Republicanism: New Hampshire Politics and the American Revolution, 1741–1794* (Cambridge, 1970), 108, 167–79.

57. Williamson, *American Suffrage*, 107–8; Adams, *First American Constitutions*, 205; Linda G. DePauw, *The Eleventh Pillar: New York State and the Federal Constitution* (Ithaca, NY, 1966), 141–47; Becker, "Parties in New York," 141, 166, 252; Nash, *Urban Crucible*, 362–63; L. Ray Gunn, *The Decline of Authority: Public Economic Policy and Political Development in New York, 1800–1860* (Ithaca, NY, 1988), 66–67; Peter J. Galie, *Ordered Liberty: A Constitutional History of New York* (New York, 1996), 40, 45.

58. Williamson, *American Suffrage*, 110; Douglass, *Rebels and Democrats*, 116–30; Green, *Constitutional Development*, 86.

59. Michael A. Bellesiles, *Revolutionary Outlaws: Ethan Allen and the Struggle for Independence on the Early American Frontier* (Charlottesville, 1993), 47, 136–41, 161–63, 258, 260; Williamson, "American Suffrage," 97–99.

60. Pole, "Representation and Authority," 16, 17, 25, 28; Douglass, *Rebels and Democrats*, 294; Chandler, "Suffrage in Virginia," 16, 17; Adams, *First American Constitutions*, 203–4; Williamson, "American Suffrage," 85, 111–15.

61. Regarding Massachusetts see: Handlin and Handlin, *Popular Sources*, esp. 19–50, 113, 163, 182, 192–93, 202–28, 286–94, 309–27, 402, 410–11, 437–59, 476–99, 510–86 passim, 616, 644, 685–95, 702–45, 767, 771–97, 805–43ff., 860–70, 894–95, 907–8; Nash, *Urban Crucible*, 359, 380–81; Robert J. Taylor, *Western Massachusetts in the Revolution* (Providence, RI, 1954), 89; Brown, *Middle-Class Democracy*, 394; Pole, *Political Representation*, 73, 178–86, 205–14; Douglass, *Rebels and Democrats*, 177–83; Samuel E. Morison, "Struggle over the Adoption of the Constitution of Massachusetts, 1780," *Proceedings of the Massachusetts Historical Society*, vol. 50 (Boston, May 1917), 389, 390, 391; idem, *A History of the Constitution of Massachusetts* (Boston, 1917), 18–31; Adams, *First American Constitutions*, 90–91, 184–85, 200–203; Williamson, "American Suffrage," 100–102.

62. Handlin and Handlin, *Popular Sources*, 312; Stephen E. Patterson, *Political Parties in Revolutionary Massachusetts* (Madison, WI, 1973), 171–96.

63. Handlin and Handlin, *Popular Sources*, 437; Pole, *Political Representation*, 73, 344, 510; Douglass, *Rebels and Democrats*, 199–200.

64. Patterson, *Political Parties*, 234–47, 251–54; Pole, "Suffrage Reform," 565, 570; Brown, *Middle-Class Democracy*, 384–85, 390–91; Taylor, *Western*, 99–100; Douglass, *Rebels and Democrats*, 204–5.

65. In some states, conflicts continued after the drafting of the first constitutions. See Williamson, *American Suffrage*, 131–36.

66. J. Morgan Kousser, "Suffrage," *The Encyclopedia of American Political History*, vol. 3, ed. Jack P. Greene (New York, 1984), 1238; Greene, *Imperatives*, 262; Pole, "Representation and Authority," 27.

67. Kousser, "Suffrage," 1238.

68. See Porter, *History of Suffrage*, 14–17.

69. Chandler, "Suffrage in Virginia," 17; Pole, "Suffrage Reform," 293–94; Pole, *Political Representation*, 55; idem, "Representation and Authority," 18, 27.

70. Teaford, *Municipal Revolution*, 66–67; Williamson, *American Suffrage*, 103, 123–24; *Perpetual Statutes of 1788 for Massachusetts*, 21–22, 25–27; Pole, "Suffrage Reform," 562–64.

71. Teaford, *Municipal Revolution*, 66–67.

72. Ibid., 71–75, 82–89.

73. Jonathan Elliot, *Debates on the Adoption of the Federal Constitution, in the convention held at Philadelphia, in 1787; with a diary of the debates of the Congress of the Confederacy; as reported by James Madison, a member, and deputy from Virginia*, vol. 5 (Philadelphia, 1859), 335; Farrand, *Records*, vol. 2, 139–40, 151, 153, 163–65; Rakove, *Original Meanings*, 83, 224–25.

74. Elliot, *Debates*, vol. 5, 386.

75. Ibid., 387; variations in the accounts of these debates can be found in Farrand, *Records*, vol. 2, 201–11.

76. Elliot, *Debates*, vol. 5, 385–89; Benton, *1787*, vol. 1, 233–35; Carr, *Oldest Delegate*, 109.

77. Pole, *Political Representation*, 71–76, 358–61; McCoy, *Elusive Republic*, 128–32; Farrand, *Records*, vol. 1, 132, 422, 465–66; ibid., vol. 2, 225; ibid., vol. 3, 146–47, 450–55; Benton, *1787*, vol. 1, 234–37, 1535.

78. Benton, *1787*, vol. 1, 19–20; Raskin, "Legal Aliens," 1402; Robert M. Taylor, ed., *The Northwest Ordinance 1787: A Bicentennial Handbook* (Indianapolis, IN, 1987), 49. The District of Columbia also was directly governed by the federal government, but between 1790 and 1802 everyone in Washington, D.C., was disfranchised. Frank W. Blackmar, "History of Suffrage in Legislation in the United States," *The Chautauquan* (October 1895): 32. For a different interpretation see Rakove, *Original Meanings*, 225.

79. James Madison, *Federalist*, no. 52; Elliot, *Debates*, 385; Thornton Anderson, *Creating the Constitution: The Convention of 1787 and the First Congress* (University Park, 1993), 94–97.

80. See Richard Greene, "Congressional Power Over the Elective Franchise: The Unconstitutional Phases of Oregon v. Mitchell," *Boston University Law Review* 52 (1972): 516–28; Rogers Smith, *Civic Ideals: Conflicting Visions of Citizenship in U.S. History* (New Haven, 1997), 115.

81. For estimates regarding the number of persons eligible to vote see Adams, *First American Constitutions*, 198–207; Greene, *Imperatives*, 259–60; Becker, "Parties in New York," 10–11; Williamson, "American Suffrage," 111–12; DePauw, *Eleventh Pillar*, 141–59. Regarding socioeconomic changes and growing inequality see Handlin and Handlin, *Popular Sources*, 35; Nash, *Urban Crucible*, 324–27, 379–83; Billy G. Smith, ed., *Life in Early Philadelphia: Documents from the Revolutionary and Early National Periods* (University Park, PA, 1995), 9–11; Jeffrey G. Williamson and Peter H. Lindert, *American Inequality: A Macroeconomic History* (New York, 1980), 44–46, 295–303; Jackson T. Main, *The Social Structure of Revolutionary America* (Princeton, 1965), 33–47, 277, 287.

82. See Williamson, *American Suffrage*, 115–16; William B. Munro, "Intelligence Tests for Voters," *Forum* 80 (December 1928): 824–25; Kruman, *Between Authority and Liberty*, 107–8; Boeckel, *Voting*, 521; Wood, *Radicalism*, 6–7, 232, 234; Rosswurm, *Arms, Country, Class*, 253; John Shy, *A People Numerous and Armed: Reflections on the Military Struggle for American Independence*, rev. ed. (Ann Arbor, 1990), 240–62.

CHAPTER TWO

1. Sanford quote from *A Report of the Debates and Proceedings of the Convention of the State of New York; Held at the Capitol in the City of Albany, on the 28th Day of August, 1821* (New York, 1821), 97; Harlow W. Sheidley, *Sectional Nationalism: Massachusetts Conservative Leaders and the Transformation of America, 1815–1836* (Boston, 1998), 35–36; Robert P. Sutton, *Revolution to Secession: Constitution Making in the Old Dominion* (Charlottesville, 1989), 73–74.

2. Townshend quote from *Report of the Debates and Proceedings of the Convention for the Revision of the Constitution of the State of Ohio, 1850–51*, vol. 2 (Columbus, OH, 1851), 550. The tendency of the courts

in general was to protect suffrage, as a constitutional right, from interference by the legislature. In principle, legislatures were permitted to implement and regulate the suffrage but not to change its breadth. See, e.g., Charles Theodore Russell, *The Disfranchisement of Paupers: Examination of the Law of Massachusetts* (Boston, 1878).

3. Eldon C. Evans, *A History of the Australian Ballot System in the United States* (Chicago, 1917), 1–10; L. E. Fredman, *The Australian Ballot: The Story of an American Reform* (Lansing, 1968), 21–23.

4. See, e.g., Massachusetts, *General Laws* (1791), chap. 26; (1793), chap. 40; (1809), chap. 25; (1855), chap. 416; John Duer et al., *The Revised Statutes of the State of New York, As Altered by Subsequent Enactments*, vol. 1 (Albany, 1846), pt. 1, chap. 6, Titles I and IV, 129–37; *Statutes of the State of New York, of a Public and General Character, Passed From 1829 to 1851*, vol. 1, Samuel Blatchford, comp. (Auburn, NY, 1852), Elections, General Elections, Title 1, 435–43; *Supplement to the Fifth Edition of the Revised Statues of the State of New York*, arr. Isaac Edwards (Albany, 1863), 42; *Spragins v. Houghton*, 3 Ill. (2 Scam.) 377 (1840). The emergence of such laws also is reflected in reports on disputed elections; see, e.g., Luther S. Cushing, *Reports of Controverted Elections to the House of Representatives of the Commonwealth of Massachusetts, From 1780 to 1852* (Boston, 1853). For a discussion of the legal history of residence definitions see Kenneth J. Winkle, *The Politics of Community: Migration and Politics in Antebellum Ohio* (Cambridge, UK, 1988), 48–87.

5. Fletcher M. Green, *Constitutional Development in the South Atlantic States, 1776–1860: A Study in the Evolution of Democracy* (Chapel Hill, NC, 1930), 270.

6. Louisiana and Tennessee did make property ownership a means—though not the exclusive means—of qualifying for the franchise. Florida, in its 1838 constitution, notably declared that "no property qualification for eligibility to office, or for the right of suffrage, shall ever be required in this state." *Comparative View of the State Constitutions, Manual for the New York State Constitutional Convention, 1846* (Albany, 1849), 172.

7. Robert M. Taylor, *The Northwest Ordinance 1787: A Bicentennial Handbook* (Indianapolis, 1987), 47–49, 118; Franklin B. Hough, ed., *American Constitutions: Comprising the Constitution of Each State in the Union, and of the United States*, vol. 1 (Albany, 1872), 333; Charles Kettleborough, *Constitution Making in Indiana: A Source Book of Constitutional Documents with Historical Introduction and Critical Notes*, vol. 1 (Indianapolis, 1916), xcii–xciii, 3, 48.

8. Kirk H. Porter, *A History of Suffrage in the United States* (Chicago, 1918), 132–33; Arthur C. Cole, ed., *The Constitutional Debates of 1847* (Springfield, IL, 1919), 536–37; Kettleborough, *Constitution Making in Indiana*, vol. 1, 56, 58; R. H. Thompson, "Suffrage in Mississippi," *Publications of the Mississippi Historical Society*, vol. 1, ed. Franklin L. Riley (Oxford, 1898), 30; Dudley O. McGovney, *The American Suffrage Medley: The Need for a National Uniform Suffrage* (Chicago, 1949), 137; Malcolm C. McMillan, *Constitutional Development in Alabama, 1798–1801: A Study in Politics, the Negro and Sectionalism* (Chapel Hill, NC, 1955), 11–14.

9. Notably, however, Illinois insisted that electors be white, which was not the case in Ohio or Indiana. Richard Peters, ed., *The Public Statutes at Large of the United States of America from the Organization of Government in 1780 to March 3, 1845* (Boston, 1848), vol. 2, 173–75, vol. 3, 289–91, 428–31, vol. 5, 49–50; "An Act in Relation to the Formation of a State Government in Wisconsin," in W. T. Madison, ed., *Laws of the Territory of Wisconsin* (Simeon Mills, WI, 1846), 5–12; George Minot, ed., *The Public Statutes at Large of the United States of America from December 1, 1845 to March 3, 1851* (Boston, 1857), 56–58; "An Act to Enable the People of Michigan to form a Constitution and State Government," *Acts Passed at the Extra and Second Session of the Sixth Legislative Council of the Territory of Michigan* (Detroit, 1835), 72–77.

10. Porter, *History of Suffrage*, 133–34.

11. Mass., *Gen. Laws* (1811), chap. 9.

12. Thompson, "Suffrage in Mississippi," 33; Chilton Williamson, "American Suffrage and Sir William Blackstone," *Political Science Quarterly* 68 (1953): 125.

13. Edmund J. James, *The Charters of the City of Chicago. Part 1, The Early Charters, 1833–1837* (Chicago, 1898), 39; Williamson, "American Suffrage," 162.

14. Julian A. C. Chandler, "The History of Suffrage in Virginia," Johns Hopkins University Studies in Historical and Political Science Series, ed. Herbert B. Adams, no. 19 (Baltimore, 1901), 20;

Williamson, "American Suffrage," 190, 220–23; J. R. Pole, *Political Representation in England and the Origins of the American Republic* (New York, 1966), 293–94; *The Constitution of the State of New York, Nov. 3, 1846* (Albany, 1849), 1069–79; *Charter of the City of Milwaukee*, Published by Order of the Common Council (Milwaukee, 1849), 6.

15. James Fenimore Cooper, *The American Democrat* (1838; reprint, New York, 1956), 139–43.

16. Gerald E. Frug, *Local Government Law* (St. Paul, 1988), 56–61.

17. Jon C. Teaford, *The Municipal Revolution in America: Origins of Modern Urban Government, 1650–1825* (Chicago, 1975), 79–90; John F. Dillon, *Commentaries on the Law of Municipal Corporations*, vol. 1 (Boston, 1911), 26–27, 37–39, 635–36; Hendrik Hartog, *Public Property and Private Power: The Corporation of the City of New York in American Law, 1730–1870* (Chapel Hill, NC, 1983), 4, 237; Gerald E. Frug, "The City as a Legal Concept," *Harvard Law Review* 93 (1980): 1101–8.

18. Teaford, *Municipal Revolution*, 82–89; Frank W. Blackmar, "History of Suffrage in Legislation in the United States," *The Chautauquan* 22 (October 1895): 28–34; Mass., *Gen. Laws* (1822), chap. 110, sec. 1–8, 23–24; Chandler, "Suffrage in Virginia," 20, 52; John V. Mering, *The Whig Party in Missouri* (Columbia, MO, 1967), 72–75; Hartog, *Public Property*, 135–39; Pole, *Political Representation*, 293–94.

19. Mary Jo Adams, *The History of Suffrage in Michigan*, Publications of the Michigan Political Science Association, vol. 3, no. 1 (Ann Arbor, March 1898), 42–43, 50–53.

20. Green, *Constitutional Development*, 249; Adams, *Suffrage in Michigan*, 37–38; Kettleborough, *Constitution Making in Indiana*, vol. 1, ccxxvi, 106, 304–5; Roy H. Akagi, "The Pennsylvania Constitution of 1838," *Pennsylvania Magazine of History and Biography* 48 (1924): 328.

21. Winkle, *Politics of Community*, 49–65, 83–87, 172–75.

22. Gerald M. Rosberg, "Aliens and Equal Protection: Why Not the Right to Vote?" *Michigan Law Review* 75 (April-May 1977): 1096–97; James H. Kettner, *The Development of American Citizenship, 1608–1870* (Chapel Hill, NC, 1978), 28; H. Sidney Everett, "Immigration and Naturalization," *Atlantic Monthly* 75 (March 1895): 349–50; *Reports of the U.S. Immigration Commission*. Vol. 39, *Immigration Legislation*, Senate Document no. 758 (Washington, DC, 1911), 6.

23. Jamin B. Raskin, "Legal Aliens, Local Citizens: The Historical, Constitutional and Theoretical Meanings of Alien Suffrage," *University of Pennsylvania Law Review* 141 (April 1993): 1402.

24. Gerald L. Neuman, "'We Are the People': Alien Suffrage in German and American Perspective," *Michigan Journal of International Law*, 13 (Winter 1992): 291–96; Raskin, "Legal Aliens," 1400–1403.

25. *The Naturalization Laws of the United States*, comp. by "member of the bar," *containing also the Alien Laws of the State of New York* (Rochester, 1855) 9-11; *Immigration Commission*, vol. 39, 6; Everett, "Immigration and Naturalization," 349–50; John P. Gavit, *Americans by Choice* (1922; reprint, Montclair, NJ, 1971), 66–77; Taliesin Evans, *American Citizenship and the Right of Suffrage in the United States* (Oakland, CA, 1892), 14–15.

26. Among the key court cases see *Johnston v. England* (1817), *Ohio Unreported Judicial Decisions Prior to 1823*, ed. Ervin H. Pollack (Indianapolis, 1952), 149–59; or the more widely cited *Spragins v. Houghton*, 3 Ill. (2 Scam.) 377 (1840); and Rosberg, "Aliens and Equal Protection," 1095–96.

27. Raskin, "Legal Aliens," 1403–4; Richard P. McCormick, *The History of Voting in New Jersey: A Study of the Development of Election Machinery, 1664–1911* (New Brunswick, NJ, 1953), 110; Rosberg, "Aliens and Equal Protection," 1097–99.

28. Raskin, "Legal Aliens," 1403–5.

29. For the debate in Wisconsin regarding alien suffrage see Milo M. Quaife, ed., *The Convention of 1846*, Publications of the State Historical Society of Wisconsin, Collections, vol. 27, Constitutional Series, vol. 2 (Madison, 1919), 207–78; *Journal of the Convention to form a constitution for the State of Wisconsin, with a sketch of the debates, begun and held at Madison, on the fifteenth day of December, eighteen hundred and forty-seven* (Madison, 1848), 146–91.

30. Calculated from data in *Naturalization Laws*, 87.

31. For an examination of the politics leading to Michigan's law see Ronald P. Formisano, *The Birth of Mass Political Parties, Michigan, 1827–1861* (Princeton, 1971), 81–101; see also *The Michigan Constitutional Conventions of 1835–36 Debates and Proceedings*, ed. Harold M. Dorr (Ann Arbor, 1940), 177–257, 511; regarding Indiana, see Kettleborough, *Constitution Making in Indiana*, vol. 1, xcvi–xcix, civ–cix; and *Report of the Debates and Proceedings of the Convention for the Revision of the Constitution of*

the State of Indiana (Indianapolis, 1850), 1292–1305; for listings of chronology see articles by Raskin, Rosberg, and Neuman.

32. For a partial chronicle of the states that adopted alien suffrage see Neuman, "Alien Suffrage," 297–300; see also Raskin, "Legal Aliens," 1391–1470; and Rosberg, "Aliens and Equal Protection," 1095–99. As Rosberg points out, there is some uncertainty about the number of states that did ever have alien suffrage provisions in part because such provisions may have appeared in statutes rather than constitutional clauses; tables A.4 and A.12 list all of the states in which I found such provisions. See also Albert J. McCulloch, *Suffrage and Its Problems* (Baltimore, 1929), 140–41. For debates regarding alien suffrage see *Debates Indiana 1850*, vol. 2 (Indianapolis, 1850), 1292–1305; *Report of the Debates and Proceedings of the Convention for the Revision of the Constitution of the State of Kentucky, 1849* (Frankfort, 1849), 445–617.

33. Quaife, *Convention of 1846*, 235–38.

34. *Spragins v. Houghton*, 3 Ill. (2 Scam.) 377, 408 (1840); see also Neuman, "Alien Suffrage," 300–310.

35. Frederick J. Turner, "Contributions of the West to American Democracy," *Atlantic Monthy* 91(January 1903): 83–96; idem, *The Frontier in American History* (New York, 1920), 192. Donald Frary and Charles Seymour also advance an argument supporting the notion of the frontier as a democratizing influence, but this is disputed by Avery Craven and Walter Johnson. Donald Frary and Charles Seymour, *How the World Votes: The Story of Democratic Development in Elections*, vol. 1 (Springfield, IL, 1918), 228–33; Avery Craven and Walter Johnson, *The United States: Experiment in Democracy* (Boston, 1947), 288. See also Edward Pessen, *Jacksonian America: Society, Personality, and Politics* (Homewood, IL, 1969), 128–29, 157–58.

36. Green, *Constitutional Development*, 159–62; J. R. Pole, "Representation and Authority in Virginia from the Revolution to Reform," *Journal of Southern History* 24 (February 1958): 35; Pole, *Political Representation*, 314–17ff.

37. Roger W. Shugg, *Origins of Class Struggle in Louisiana: A Social History of White Farmers and Labourers During Slavery and After, 1840–1875* (Baton Rouge, 1939), 120–28; Perry H. Howard, *Political Tendencies in Louisiana* (Baton Rouge, 1957), 24–25; Green, *Constitutional Development*, viii, 190–95, 300; Chandler, "Suffrage in Virginia," 21–38.

38. Chilton Williamson, *American Suffrage: From Property to Democracy, 1760–1860* (Princeton, 1960), 228–29.

39. Merrill D. Peterson, ed., *Democracy, Liberty, and Property—The State Constitutional Conventions of the 1820s* (Indianapolis, 1966), 135; Frary and Seymour, *World Votes*, vol. 1, 233.

40. Williamson, *American Suffrage*, 210–12.

41. Charles G. Steffen, *The Mechanics of Baltimore: Workers and Politics in the Age of Revolution, 1763–1812* (Urbana, IL, 1984), 121; Edmund S. Morgan, *Inventing the People* (New York, 1988), 185–86; Pole, *Political Representation*, 318; Sean Wilentz, *Chants Democratic: New York City and the Rise of the American Working Class, 1788–1850* (New York, 1984), 175; John Spencer Bassett, "Suffrage in the State of North Carolina, 1776–1861," *American Historical Association: Annual Report of the American Historical Association for 1895* (Washington, DC, 1896), 281; *Michigan Conventions 1835–36*, 74; Green, *Constitutional Development*, 266; Pole, *Political Representation*, 307; Kathleen N. Conzen, *Immigrant Milwaukee, 1836–1860: Accommodation and Community in a Frontier City* (Cambridge, MA, 1976), 195.

42. Pole, *Political Representation*, 307–9; idem, "Representation in Virginia," 33–34.

43. Peterson, *Democracy*, 377–87; see also Pole, *Political Representation*, 320–21.

44. Chandler, "Suffrage in Virginia," 32–44.

45. Sutton, *Revolution to Secession*, 60–66.

46. Ibid., 72–103; William G. Shade, *Democratizing the Old Dominion: Virginia and the Second Party System, 1824–1861* (Charlottesville, 1996), 59–77.

47. Donald R. Hickey, *The War of 1812: A Forgotten Conflict* (Urbana, IL, 1989), 110–13, 221–23.

48. *Debates and Proceedings in the State Convention Held at Newport, September 12th, 1842, For the Adoption of a Constitution of the State of Rhode Island* (Providence, 1859), 36, 45–47, 53–60; Quaife, *Convention of 1846*, 223–35; *Constitution New York 1846*, 1015–16; Green, *Constitutional Development*, 190–95, 269; Cole, *Constitutional Debates 1847*, 516, 532, 535, 543–44, 561, 574–75, 577–78, 603, 605–6; *Constitution of the State of New York 1821* (Albany, 1849), 77–78; Samuel Jones, *A Treatise on the Right of Suffrage* (Boston, 1842), 150; *New York Debates 1821*, 118, 121, 141, 144, 179; *American Mercury*, 9 June 1818.

49. Williamson, *American Suffrage*, 188; *Massachusetts Convention of Delegates, Journal of Debates and Proceedings in the Convention of Delegates, 1821* (Boston, 1853), 253; Lindley S. Butler, ed., *The Papers of David S. Reid*, vol. 1. (1993–97), 253; Shade, *Democratizing the Old Dominion*, 58.

50. Peterson, *Democracy*, 280, 408–9; Rogers M. Smith, *Civic Ideals: Conflicting Visions of Citizenship in U.S. History* (New Haven, 1997), 173; Sutton, *Revolution to Secession*, 88–89, 96; Alison G. Freehling, *Drift Toward Dissolution: The Virginia Slavery Debate of 1831–32* (Baton Rouge, 1982), 72. See also *Proceedings of the Maryland State Convention, to Frame a New Constitution. Commenced at Annapolis, November 1, 1850* (Annapolis, 1850), 136.

51. Cole, *Constitutional Debates 1847*, 517–18, 525, 553, 570–608; *Journal of the convention assembled at Springfield, June 7, 1847, in pursuance of an act of the general assembly of the State of Illinois, entitled "An act to provide for the call of a convention," approved, February 20, 1847, for the purpose of altering, amending, or revising the constitution of the State of Illinois* (Springfield, IL, 1847), 47–48, 76–77, 180, 196–205; *Journal of the Convention for the Formation of a Constitution for the State of Iowa, Begun and Held at Iowa City, First Monday of May Eighteen Hundred and Forty-Six* (Iowa City, 1846), 52–53.

52. John Ashworth, *"Agrarians" and "Aristocrats": Party Political Ideology in the United States, 1837–1846* (London, 1983), 1, 8–36, 53–57, 61, 114–15, 153, 161, 225; regarding race see ibid., 221–23; Marc W. Kruman, "The Second American Party System and the Transformation of Revolutionary Republicanism," *Journal of the Early Republic* 12 (1992): 525–30; Lee Benson, *The Concept of Jacksonian Democracy: New York as a Test Case* (Princeton, 1961), 10–11; Ronald P. Formisano, *The Transformation of Political Culture: Massachusetts Parties, 1790s–1840s* (New York, 1983), 268–78; Joel H. Silbey, *The American Political Nation, 1838–1893* (Stanford, 1991), 8–10, 30–31; James A. Morone, *The Democratic Wish: Popular Participation and the Limits of American Government* (New York, 1990), 86–87; John L. Brooke, *The Heart of the Commonwealth* (New York, 1989), 247–48; Rush Welter, *The Mind of America, 1820–1860* (New York, 1975), 179–235.

53. John H. Aldrich, *Why Parties? The Origin and Transformation of Political Parties in America* (Chicago, 1995), 97–115; Porter, *History of Suffrage*, 124–25; Neuman, "'We Are the People,'" 292–310; Shade, *Democratizing the Old Dominion*, 108–9; Laura J. Scalia, *America's Jefferson Experiment: Remaking State Constitutions, 1820–1850* (DeKalb, IL, 1999), 7–8; Fredman, *Australian Ballot*, ix, 21–23; Evans, *History of the Australian Ballot*, 1–16.

54. For accounts of the partisan dynamics contributing to suffrage reform in different states see Frary and Seymour, *World Votes*, vol. 1, 233; Benson, *Concept of Jacksonian Democracy*, 7–11; Formisano, *Birth of Mass Political Parties*, 81–101; Howard, *Political Tendencies*, 51–53; William H. Adams, *The Whig Party of Louisiana* (Lafayette, LA, 1973), 41–49; Shugg, *Origins of Class Struggle*, 126–31.

55. Frary and Seymour, *World Votes*, vol. 1, 233; Benson, *Concept of Jacksonian Democracy*, 10–11; Craig Hanyan, *De Witt Clinton and the Rise of the People's Men* (Montreal, 1996), 233–34.

56. Mering, *Whig Party*, 71–75.

57. Bassett, "Suffrage," 282; see also ibid., 281–84; Green, *Constitutional Development*, 266–70; Kruman, "Second American Party System," 531; Thomas E. Jeffrey, "Beyond 'Free Suffrage': North Carolina Parties and the Convention Movement of the 1850s," *North Carolina Historical Review* 62 (1985): 393–94, 415; idem, "'Free Suffrage' Revisited: Party Politics and Constitutional Reform in Antebellum North Carolina," *North Carolina Historical Review* 59 (1982): 24–30, 35–38; *Papers of David Reid*, vol. 1, (Raleigh, NC, 1933), xxxv–xxxix, 231, 249; ibid., vol. 2, 84.

58. Jack R. Pole, "Suffrage Reform and the American Revolution in New Jersey," *Proceedings of the New Jersey Historical Society* 74 (July 1956): 581; Kettleborough, *Constitution Making in Indiana*, vol. 1, xcvii; *Journal of the Convention to Form a Constitution for the State of Wisconsin 1848*, 168, 175–78; Henry R. Mueller, *The Whig Party in Pennsylvania: Studies in History, Economics, and Public Law* (New York, 1922), 36–37; Williamson, *American Suffrage*, 184–85; Stephen E. Maizlish, *The Triumph of Sectionalism: The Transformation of Ohio Politics, 1844–1856* (Kent, OH, 1983), 176–78; Floyd B. Streeter, *Political Parties in Michigan, 1837–1860* (Lansing, 1918), 27–29, 165; Cole, *Constitutional Debates of 1847*, 551, 567; for debates about alien voting see ibid., 524–608.

59. Jarvis M. Morris, *A Neglected Period of Connecticut's History, 1818–1850* (New Haven, 1933), 291–317; Philip C. Davis, *The Persistence of Partisan Alignment: Issues, Leaders, and Voters in New Jersey, 1840–1860* (Ann Arbor, 1978), 106–12.

60. Ashworth, *"Agrarians" and "Aristocrats,"* 153–54; Kruman, "Second American Party System," 531–32; idem, "Legislatures and Political Rights," in Joel H. Silbey, ed., *Encyclopedia of the American Legislative System*, vol. 3 (New York, 1994), 1240.

61. Sheidley, *Sectional Nationalism*, 39–59.

62. Jeffrey, "'Free Suffrage' Revisited," 25–45; idem, "Beyond 'Free Suffrage,'" 415; idem, *State Parties and National Politics: North Carolina, 1815–1861* (Athens, GA, 1989), 206–15.

63. Sutton, *Revolution to Secession*, 122–41; Shade, *Democratizing the Old Dominion*, 264–83; Peter J. Galie, *Ordered Liberty: A Constitutional History of New York* (New York, 1996), 75–91.

64. Chandler, "Suffrage in Virginia," 26; George Ticknor Curtis, *Letters of Phocion* (n.p., n.d., *Daily Advertiser and Courier*, Boston, 1853), 117; Ashworth, *"Agrarians" and "Aristocrats,"* 10.

65. *Massachusetts Debates 1821*, 256; *Debates New York 1821*, 97; Peterson, *Democracy*, 199–200.

66. *Massachusetts Debates 1821*, 252; William Griffith, *Eumenes, being a collection of papers, written for the purpose of exhibiting some of the more prominent errors and omissions of the constitution of New Jersey* (Trenton, 1799), 46; Peterson, *Democracy*, 381–82, 402–3; see also one of the first American treatises on the subject, Isaac Hillard, *The Rights of Suffrage* (Danbury, CT, 1804).

67. James Cheetham, *A Dissertation Concerning Political Equality, and the Corporation of New York* (New York, 1800), vi, 25.

68. *Massachusetts Debates 1821*, 250; for similar arguments see also ibid., 247, as well as Curtis, *Phocion*, 118–19.

69. *Journal of the Convention of the State of New York, Begun and Held at the Capitol in the City of Albany, On the First Day of June, 1846* (Albany, 1846), 1016; *Niles' Register*, 21 October 1820, 115; *Debates Ohio 1850–1851*, vol. 2, 635.

70. *Debates New York 1821*, 97.

71. For examples of arguments regarding the military and militia service see *Niles' Register*, 21 October 1820, 115; *Debates New York 1821*, 118, 121, 141, 179; *Journal New York 1846*, 1015–16; Williamson, *American Suffrage*, 188, 227; *Convention 1847 Illinois*, 513, 532; Quaife, *Convention of 1846*, 249–50.

72. Williamson, *American Suffrage*, 202; *Debates New York 1821*, 130; Benson, *Concept of Jacksonian Democracy*, 7–10.

73. Peterson, *Democracy*, 202–5; Williamson, *American Suffrage*, 192, 202.

74. *Massachusetts Debates 1821*, 253.

75. Peterson, *Democracy*, 197–98, 404.

76. Williamson, *American Suffrage*, 231–32; Peterson, *Democracy*, 407–10.

77. *Massachusetts Debates 1821*, 247; Jones, *Treatise*, 84.

78. *Massachusetts Debates 1821*, 251; for an example of the Blackstonian argument see the report on the Connecticut Legislature in the *American Mercury*, 9 June 1818.

79. Gordon S. Wood, *The Radicalism of the American Revolution* (New York, 1992), 269–70; *Debates New York 1821*, 193; Peterson, *Democracy*, 391–93.

80. *Massachusetts Convention 1821*, 251–52; *American Mercury*, 9 June 1818.

81. *Debates New York 1821*, 115–16; part of what is quoted is from a slightly different version of Kent's speech, reprinted in Peterson, *Democracy*, 193–97. Kent, like many of his Blackstonian ancestors, actually voiced both arguments (that workers would be controlled by their employers and that they would rise up independently against the interests of property), however contradictory they may have been. Yet his emphasis, unlike Quincy's, was on the fear of the urban poor seizing the property of the rich in their own interest.

82. *Debates New York 1821*, 115–16, 128, 137, 143.

83. Cole, *Constitutional Debates of 1847*, 534–35, 594–95; Green, *Constitutional Development*, 190–95; Peterson, *Democracy*, 196–97.

84. Shugg, *Origins of Class Struggle*, 126.

85. Jones, *Treatise*, 180.

86. Williamson, *American Suffrage*, 263–72; Rosalind L. Branning, *Pennsylvania Constitutional Development* (Pittsburgh, 1960), 25. Even that most democratic state, Vermont, imposed property qualifications for voting in local elections throughout the first half of the nineteenth century.

87. Williamson, *American Suffrage*, 204–7, 255–72.

88. Ibid., 255–56, 263–72; Marguerite G. Bartlett, *The Chief Phases of Pennsylvania Politics in the Jacksonian Period* (Allentown, PA, 1919), 128; Pessen, *Jacksonian America*, 128–29; Marchette G. Chute, *The First Liberty: A History of the Right to Vote in America, 1619–1850* (New York, 1969), 313.

89. Richard P. McCormick, "Suffrage Classes and Party Alignments: A Study in Voter Behavior," *Mississippi Valley Historical Review* 46 (December 1959): 397–410; Williamson, *American Suffrage*, 241.

90. Alexis de Tocqueville, *Democracy in America* (London, 1835), 53; Brooke, *Heart of the Commonwealth*, 325–26; William E. Gienapp, "'Politics Seem to Enter into Everything': Political Culture in the North, 1840–1860," *Essays on American Antebellum Politics, 1840–1860*, ed. Stephen Maizlish and John Kushma (College Station, TX, 1982), 15–22, 62–65; Walter Dean Burnham, "Those High Nineteenth-Century American Voting Turnouts: Fact or Fiction?" *Journal of Interdisciplinary History* 16 (Spring 1986): 613–44 ; Williamson, *American Suffrage*, 195; Harry Watson, *Liberty and Power: The Politics of Jacksonian America* (New York, 1990), 232; McCormick, "Suffrage Classes," 405–10; idem, "New Perspectives on Jacksonian Politics," *American Historical Review* 65 (January 1960): 291–98; Ronald P. Formisano, "Boston, 1800–1840: From Deferential-Participant to Party Politics," *Boston 1700–1980: The Evolution of Urban Politics*, ed. Ronald P. Formisano and Constance K. Burns (Westport, 1984), 34–35; Walter Dean Burnham, "The Turnout Problem," *Elections American Style*, ed. A. James Reichley (Washington, 1987), 113–15.

CHAPTER THREE

1. Kelso quoted in *Report of the Debates and Proceedings of the Convention for the Revision of the Constitution of the State of Indiana* (Indianapolis, 1850), 172; Judith A. Klinghoffer and Lois Elkin, "'The Petticoat Electors': Women's Suffrage in New Jersey," *Journal of the Early Republic* 12 (Summer 1992): 161–93; Marion T. Wright, "Negro Suffrage in New Jersey, 1776–1875," *Journal of Negro History* 33 (April 1948): 176; Irwin N. Gertzog, "Female Suffrage in New Jersey, 1790–1807," *Women and Politics* 10 (1990): 52–57; Richard P. McCormick, *The History of Voting in New Jersey: A Study of the Development of Election Machinery, 1664–1911* (New Brunswick, NJ, 1953), 93–100; Rowland Berthoff, "Conventional Mentality: Free Blacks, Women, and Business Corporations as Unequal Persons, 1820–1870," *Journal of American History* 76 (December 1989): 768; Edward R. Turner, "Women's Suffrage in New Jersey: 1790–1807," *Smith College Studies in History* 1 (October 1915–July 1916): 67–85; Marc W. Kruman, *Between Authority and Liberty: State Constitution Making in Revolutionary America* (Chapel Hill, NC, 1997), 103–6.

2. James M. Burns, *The Vineyards of Liberty* (New York, 1982), 392–93; Marchette Gaylord Chute, *The First Liberty: A History of the Right to Vote in America, 1619–1850* (New York, 1969), 313; Charles H. Wesley, "Negro Suffrage in the Period of Constitution-Making, 1787–1865," *Journal of Negro History* 32 (April 1947): 152–56; *The Seventh Census of the U.S.: 1850*, vol. 4 (Washington, DC, 1850), 83; Rogers Smith, *Civic Ideals: Conflicting Visions of Citizenship in United States History* (New Haven, 1997), 263–68. As indicated in the notes to tables A.4 and A.5, Georgia did not constitutionally bar blacks, and the legal history is obscure, but it seems certain that free blacks did not vote.

3. Merrill D. Peterson, ed., *Democracy, Liberty, and Property—The State Constitutional Conventions of the 1820s* (Indianapolis, 1966), 215; *Journal of the Convention of the State of New York, Begun and Held at the Capitol in the City of Albany, On the First Day of June, 1846* (Albany, 1846), 1027.

4. *Eighth U.S. Census, Population of the United States in 1860* (Washington, DC, 1864), ix; Lee Benson, *The Concept of Jacksonian Democracy: New York as a Test Case* (Princeton, 1961), 303–20; Phyllis F. Field, *The Politics of Race in New York: The Struggle for Black Suffrage in the Civil War Era* (Ithaca, NY, 1982), 28–77; Charles M. Snyder, *The Jacksonian Heritage, Pennsylvania Politics, 1833–48* (Harrisburg, PA, 1958), 105; Chilton Williamson, *American Suffrage: From Property to Democracy, 1760–1860* (Princeton, 1960), 189–90; Jarvis M. Morris, *A Neglected Period of Connecticut's History, 1818–1850* (New Haven, 1933), 318–31; Wright, "Negro Suffrage," 174–75; Leon F. Litwack, *North of Slavery: The Negro in the Free States, 1790–1860* (Chicago, 1961), 79–90.

5. Milo M. Quaife, ed., *The Convention of 1846*, Publications of the State Historical Society of Wisconsin, Collections, vol. 27, Constitutional Series, vol. 2 (Madison, 1919), 214–16, 223–35, 278; *Pro-*

ceedings and Debates of the Convention of the Commonwealth of Pennsylvania to Propose Amendments to the Constitution, Commenced at Harrisburg, May 2, 1837, vol. 9 (Harrisburg, 1838), 321; Report of the Debates and Proceedings of the Convention for the Revision of the Constitution of the State of Indiana (Indianapolis, 1850), 233, 247, 251; The Constitution of the State of New York, Nov. 3, 1846 (Albany, 1849), 1034; Daniel J. Ryan, History of Ohio: The Rise and Progress of an American State (New York, 1912), 115; Report of the Debates and Proceedings of the Convention for the Revision of the Constitution of the State of Ohio, 1850–1851, vol. 2 (Columbus, OH, 1851), 635–38; Leonard P. Curry, The Free Black in Urban America, 1800–1850 (Chicago, 1981), 216–19, 329n.

6. Curry, Free Black, 216–24.

7. Peterson, Democracy, 225; Journal New York 1846, 1029. See also Debates Indiana 1850, 245.

8. Quaife, Convention of 1846, 241–48.

9. Journal New York 1846, 1016; Debates Ohio 1850–1851, vol. 2, 549–51; Roy H. Akagi, "The Pennsylvania Constitution of 1838," Pennsylvania Magazine of History and Biography 47 (1924): 318–19, 354; Proceedings of Pennsylvania, 1838, 232. Efforts to define white frequently ended up in court cases; see, e.g., two Ohio cases decided in 1842, Jeffries v. Ankeny, 11 Ohio 372 (1842) and Thacker v. Hawk, 11 Ohio 376 (1842). For an example of a petition from blacks see Wright, "Negro Suffrage," 185–86.

10. Journal New York 1846, 1035; Debates Indiana 1850, 232; see also ibid., 228, 253–54, 277–80; Rufus B. Smith and Alfred B. Benedict, eds., The Verified Revised Statutes of the State of Ohio, including All Laws of a General Nature in Force January 1st, 1890, vol. 1 (Cincinnati, 1891), 236, 458–59; Curry, Free Black, 224.

11. David Montejano, Anglos and Mexicans in the Making of Texas, 1836–1986 (Austin, TX, 1987), 38–39; F. Ross Brown, Report of the Debates in the Convention of California on the Formation of the State Constitution, in September and October, 1849 (Washington, D.C., 1850), 67; see also ibid., 61–75, 305–9; Harold M. Dorr, ed., The Michigan Constitutional Conventions of 1835–36, Debates and Proceedings (Ann Arbor, 1940), 246.

12. Jeannette Wolfley, "Jim Crow, Indian Style: The Disenfranchisement of Native Americans," American Indian Law Review 16 (1991): 167–202; R. Alton Lee, "Indian Citizenship and the Fourteenth Amendment," South Dakota History 4 (Spring 1974): 199–206; Felix Cohen, Handbook on Federal Indian Law (Charlottesville, 1982), 157–58.

13. Wolfley, "Jim Crow," 171–72; Mary Jo Adams, The History of Suffrage in Michigan (Ann Arbor, 1898), 21–25; Acts of the General Assembly of the State of Georgia (Milledgeville, GA, 1840), 32; see also table A.4.

14. Robert J. Steinfeld, "Property and Suffrage in the Early American Republic," Stanford Law Review 41 (January 1989): 335–72.

15. William M. Gouge, Debates of the Delaware Convention, for Revising the Constitution of the State, or Adopting a New One; Held at Dover, November, 1831 (Wilmington, 1831), 15; Steinfeld, "Property and Suffrage," 358; Proceedings of the New Jersey State Constitutional Convention of 1844 (Trenton, 1942), 88.

16. Proceedings New Jersey 1844, 87–91, 430–33; Quaife, Convention of 1846, 208–9; J. R. Pole, "The Suffrage in New Jersey, 1790–1807," Proceedings of the New Jersey Historical Society 71 (January 1953): 3–8. On David Naar see Ruth M. Patt, The Sephardim of New Jersey (New Brunswick, NJ, 1992).

17. Steinfeld, "Property and Suffrage," 335–72; Charles Theodore Russell, The Disfranchisement of Paupers: Examination of the Law of Massachusetts (Boston, 1878), 21–25; Octavius Pickering, Reports of Cases Argued and Determined in the Supreme Judicial Court of Massachusetts, vol. 14 (Boston, 1849), 341–44; cf. David Montgomery, Citizen Worker: The Experience of Workers in the United States with Democracy and the Free Market During the Nineteenth Century (New York, 1993), 22.

18. Howard Itzkowitz and Lauren Oldak, "Restoring the Ex-Offender's Right to Vote: Background and Developments," The American Criminal Law Review 11 (1973): 695, 721–27.

19. Ibid., 727; Journal of the Convention assembled at Springfield, June 7, 1847, in pursuance of an act of the general assembly of the State of Illinois, entitled "an act to provide for the call of a convention," approved February 20, 1847, for the purpose of altering, amending, or revising the constitution of the State of Illinois (Springfield, 1847), 47; Journal of the Proceedings of the Convention of Delegates, Convened at Hartford, August 26, 1818, for the purpose of forming a Constitution of Civil Government of the People of the State of Connecticut (Hartford, 1901), 47; Debates Indiana 1850, 65, 913; Proceedings New Jersey 1844, 1, 4, 95–99, 433; Journal of the Illinois Constitutional Convention, 1818, in Journal of the Illinois State Historical Society

6 (October 1913): 373; Charles Kettleborough, *Constitution Making in Indiana: A Source Book of Constitutional Documents with Historical Introduction and Critical Notes*, vol. 1 (Indianapolis, 1916), 58, 108, 224–25, 249, 306; Dorr, *Michigan 1835–36 Debates*, 170–73; *Journal of the Convention to form a constitution for the state of Wisconsin, with a sketch of the debates, begun and held at Madison, on the fifteenth day of December, eighteen hundred and forty-seven* (Madison, 1848), 144, 514–15, 639; *Comparative View of the State Constitutions, Manual for the New York State Constitutional Convention, 1846* (Albany, 1849), 184, 240–60; *The Debates and Journal of the Constitutional Convention of the State of Maine 1819–1820* (Augusta, 1894), 123–25; *Journal New York 1846*, 2; *Journal of the Proceedings of the Convention met to form a Constitution and a system of state Government for the People of Arkansas: At the Session of the Said Convention held at Little Rock, in the Territory of Arkansas which commenced on the fourth day of January, and ended on the thirtieth day of January, one thousand eight hundred and thirty-six* (Little Rock, 1836), 23; *Journal in the Committee of the whole, of the convention of the people of the state of Delaware, assembled at Dover, by their delegates, December 7 and 8, 1852, and afterwards, by adjournment from March 10 to April 30, 1853* (Wilmington, 1853), 77; *Constitution of the State of Indiana: Adopted in Convention at Corydon, on the 29th of June, A.D. 1816* (Washington, D.C., 1816), 22; Joseph R. Swan, ed., *Statutes of the State of Ohio in Force August, 1854* (Cincinnati, 1854), art. 4, sec. 1–5, xxiii; John Duer et al., *The Revised Statutes of the State of New York* (Albany, 1846), 129; George F. Taylor, "Suffrage in Early Kentucky," *Register of the Kentucky Historical Society* 61 (January 1963): 31. For an interesting debate about such provisions see J. Ross Browne, ed., *Report of the Convention of California* (1849), entered, according to act of Congress by J. Ross Browne, in District Court of the District of Columbia, 1850, 253–54.

20. It also should be noted that many states during this period attempted to clarify the meaning of residence, and in so doing explicitly excluded as residents soldiers and seamen who were temporarily stationed in their state, as well as college students. See, e.g., Quaife, *Convention of 1846*, 743; *Convention Wisconsin* (1847), 207–8, 268–69; *Proceedings New Jersey 1844*, 92–101, 429; *Comparative View 1846*, 184; *Constitution New York 1846*, 8; and the Massachusetts case, *Williams v. Whiting*, 11 Mass. 424 (1814).

21. Samuel R. Jones, *A Treatise on the Right of Suffrage* (Boston, 1842), 127, 169; *Journal of the Convention of the State of Mississippi: Held in the Town of Jackson* (Jackson, 1832), 45–63; *Debates Indiana 1850*, 1295–1307; *Debates Ohio 1850–51*, vol. 2, 9–10; *Journal New York 1846*, 111; *Convention Wisconsin* (1847), 129; Quaife, *Convention of 1846*, 208; *Massachusetts Convention of Delegates, Journal of Debates and Proceedings in the Convention of Delegates, 1821* (Boston, 1853), 249–50, 554–55; Isaac Sharpless, *Two Centuries of Pennsylvania History* (Philadelphia, 1900), 311; Henry R. Mueller, *The Whig Party in Pennsylvania* (New York, 1922), 36–37; James F. Cooper, *The American Democrat* (1838; reprint, New York, 1956), 140–44.

22. Sharpless, *Pennsylvania History*, 311; Kenneth J. Winkle, *The Politics of Community: Migration and Politics in Antebellum Ohio* (Cambridge, 1988), 60–85; Roger W. Shugg, *Origins of Class Struggle in Louisiana: A Social History of White Farmers and Labourers During Slavery and After, 1840–1875* (Baton Rouge, 1939), 128–31.

23. Winkle, *Politics of Community*, 60–85; J. Allen Smith, *The Growth and Decadence of Constitutional Government* (New York, 1930), 37–38; Fletcher M. Green, *Constitutional Development in the South Atlantic States, 1776–1860: A Study in the Evolution of Democracy* (Chapel Hill, NC, 1930), 280–85; Shugg, *Origins of Class Struggle*, 128–31; Perry H. Howard, *Political Tendencies in Louisiana* (Baton Rouge, 1957), 51–53; *Comparative View 1846*, 143–44, 184; see also Peter Way, *Common Labour: Workers and the Digging of North American Canals 1780–1860* (Cambridge, Eng., 1993), 180–81.

24. Joseph P. Harris, *The Registration of Voters in the United States* (Washington, D.C., 1929), 67–70; *A Report of the Debates and Proceedings of the Convention of the State of New York; Held at the Capitol in the City of Albany, on the 28th Day of August, 1821* (New York, 1821), 148.

25. Harris, *Registration of Voters*, 69–70; Massachusetts, *Acts and Laws, 1801*, chap. 38; *Journal New York 1846*, 148, 176–77; *Capen v. Foster*, 29 Mass. 485 (1832).

26. Joel H. Silbey, *The Partisan Imperative* (New York, 1985), 141–53; Williamson, *American Suffrage*, 273–77; *Constitution New York 1846*, 65; *Proceedings of the Maryland State Convention, to Frame a New Constitution. Commenced at Annapolis, November 1, 1850* (Annapolis, 1850), 82; *Proceedings of the New Jersey State Constitutional Convention of 1844* (Trenton, 1942), 86–92; Kettleborough, *Constitution Making in Indiana*, vol. 1, ciii, cvii, cx–cxiii, 396–465; *Convention Wisconsin* (1847), 144.

27. Jones, *Treatise*, 132; *Proceedings New Jersey 1844*, 100–103; see also ibid., 96, 434; Kettleborough, *Constitution Making in Indiana*, vol. 1, cxv–cxvii; *Journal New York 1846*, 2, 91.

28. *Arguments Proving the Inconsistency and Impolicy of Granting to Foreigners the Right of Voting* by A Disciple of the Washington School (1810; reprint, Philadelphia, 1844); *Speeches of Hon. Garrett Davis delivered in the Convention to Revise the Constitution of Kentucky, December 1849* (Frankfort, 1855); *Proceedings New Jersey 1844*, 76–87; *Proceedings Maryland 1850*, 94; *Journal New York 1846*, 129; John Duer, Benjamin Butler, and John Spencer, *The Revised Statutes of the State of New York*, vol. 1 (Albany, 1846), 138–39; *Debates Indiana 1850*, 1304; Kirk H. Porter, *A History of Suffrage in the United States* (Chicago, 1918), 115–18.

29. For an articulate example of these reservations to broadening the franchise see Jones, *Treatise*, 20–21.

30. For examples of such views (and many more could be cited) see Selig Perlman, *A Theory of the Labor Movement* (New York, 1928); John R. Commons and Helen L. Sumner, *History of Labour in the United States*, vol. 1 (New York, 1926); Amy Bridges, "Becoming American: The Working Classes in the United States Before the Civil War," *Working-Class Formation: Nineteenth-Century Patterns in Western Europe and the United States*, ed. Ira Katznelson and Aristide R. Zolberg (Princeton, 1986), 37–38; Alan Dawley, *Class and Community: The Industrial Revolution in Lynn* (Cambridge, MA, 1976).

31. Montgomery, *Citizen Worker*, 24–50. An important quantitative question arises here: What percentage of American workers (or male workers) was enfranchised during this period? Remarkably, this question (which, as noted in the preface, launched the present study) has never been systematically investigated.

32. Marvin Meyers, *The Jacksonian Persuasion: Politics and Belief* (Stanford, 1957), 247n.6, 248–49; Montgomery, *Citizen Worker*, 3–5, 17–18; *Proceedings New York 1821*, 140–46.

33. I disagree with Montgomery's conclusion (*Citizen Worker*, 22) that the "wage contract" took its place alongside property ownership as a "badge of participation in the polity." Although true perhaps for skilled workers, the wage contract did not similarly empower the unskilled and semiskilled.

34. *Proceedings and Debates of the Virginia State Convention of 1829–30* (Richmond, 1830), 158.

35. Marvin E. Gettleman, *The Dorr Rebellion–A Study in American Radicalism, 1833–1849* (New York, 1973), 6–7; Williamson, *American Suffrage*, 243–45; George M. Dennison, *The Dorr War: Republicanism on Trial, 1831–1861* (Lexington, 1976), 14, 28.

36. Seth Luther, *An Address on the Right of Free Suffrage* (Providence, 1833), 14–16, 23; Gettleman, *Dorr Rebellion*, 8–9.

37. Gettleman, *Dorr Rebellion*, 21–28; Dennison, *Dorr War*, 13–19.

38. Dennison, *Dorr War*, 37, 43–45; Gettleman, *Dorr Rebellion*, 25–35.

39. Gettleman, *Dorr Rebellion*, 25–35, 42–47; Montgomery, *Citizen Worker*, 19–21.

40. Gettleman, *Dorr Rebellion*, 64–83.

41. Ibid., 64–90; Dennison, *Dorr War*, 33, 53.

42. Gettleman, *Dorr Rebellion*, 101–3.

43. John Ashworth, *"Agrarians" and "Aristocrats": Party Political Ideology in the United States, 1837–1846* (London, 1983), 225–29.

44. Gettleman, *Dorr Rebellion*, 89–144, 160–73; Dennison, *Dorr War*, 96.

45. Williamson, *American Suffrage*, 259.

46. "Note, Political Rights as Political Questions: The Paradox of *Luther v. Borden*," *Harvard Law Review* 100 (1987): 1127–45; Gettleman, *Dorr Rebellion*, 177, 199.

PART TWO

1. *Anderson v. Baker*, 23 Md. 531 (1865), cited in Frederick C. Brightly, *A Collection of Leading Cases on the Law of Elections in the United States* (Philadelphia, 1871), 38. Cf. Joel H. Silbey et al., eds., *History of American Electoral Behavior* (Princeton, 1978), 141–42.

2. See Herbert G. Gutman, *Work, Culture, and Society in Industrializing America* (New York, 1976), 234–59; Lawrence M. Lipin, *Producers, Proletarians, and Politicians: Workers and Party Politics in Evansville and New Albany, Indiana, 1850–87* (Urbana, 1994), 45–180, 212–46; David Montgomery, *Citizen Worker: The Experience of Workers in the United States with Democracy and the Free Market During the Nineteenth Century* (New York, 1993), 115–57.

3. "Limited Sovereignty in the United States," *Atlantic Monthly* 43 (February 1879): 185–92.

CHAPTER FOUR

1. Ira Berlin, Barbara J. Fields, Steven F. Miller, Joseph P. Reidy, and Leslie S. Rowland, *Free at Last: A Documentary History of Slavery, Freedom, and the Civil War* (New York, 1992), 497–500.

2. Ibid., 500–505.

3. Ibid.

4. William E. Gienapp, *The Origins of the Republican Party 1852–1856* (New York, 1987), 93; Stephen Erie, *Rainbow's End: Irish-Americans and the Dilemmas of Urban Machine Politics, 1840–1985* (Berkeley, 1988), 26; George H. Haynes, "The Causes of Know-Nothing Success in Massachusetts," *American Historical Review* 3 (1897–98): 70–71.

5. Dirk Hoerder, ed., *Labor Migration in the Atlantic Economies: The European and North American Working Classes During the Period of Industrialization* (Westport, CT, 1985), 3–31; for the eighteenth century cf. Bernard Bailyn, *The Peopling of British North America* (New York, 1986), and idem, *Voyagers to the West: A Passage in the Peopling of America on the Eve of the Revolution* (New York, 1986). In the twentieth century, the settler–worker distinction also seems germane, although it changes shape: highly educated migrants, such as physicians and engineers, have many of the characteristics of "settlers," while unskilled "workers" still abound. This distinction generally overlaps with—but is not identical to—flows of migration from different countries; in many instances, moreover, settlers intend to remain in the United States permanently, while workers do not.

6. *Report of the Debates and Proceedings of the Convention for the Revision of the Constitution of the State of Indiana, 1850* (Indianapolis, 1850), 1295, 1300, 1302, 1312; Jamin B. Raskin, "Legal Aliens, Local Citizens: The Historical, Constitutional and Theoretical Meanings of Alien Suffrage," *University of Pennsylvania Law Review* 141 (1993): 1406–9; Gerald M. Rosberg, "Aliens and Equal Protection: Why Not the Right to Vote?" *Michigan Law Review* 75 (1977): 1098; Gerald L. Neuman, "'We Are the People': Alien Suffrage in German and American Perspective," *Michigan Journal of International Law* 13 (Winter 1992): 298.

7. Michael F. Funchion, "The Political and Nationalist Dimensions," *The Irish in Chicago*, ed. Lawrence J. McCaffrey et al. (Urbana, IL, 1987), 62; cf. Kirk H. Porter, *A History of Suffrage in the United States* (Chicago, 1918), 122.

8. Robert Ernst, *Immigrant Life in New York City, 1825–1863* (New York, 1949), 162; Eric Foner, *Free Soil, Free Labor, Free Men: The Ideology of the Republican Party Before the Civil War* (New York, 1970), 230–31; Tyler Anbinder, *Nativism and Slavery: The Northern Know Nothings and the Politics of the 1850s* (New York, 1992), 122; John W. Le Barnes, *The Amendment to the Constitution Argument of John W. Le Barnes, Esquire, upon the Unconstitutionality, Injustice and Impolicy of the Proposed "Two Years Amendment"* (Boston, 1859), 10; Rudolph Vecoli, *The People of New Jersey* (Princeton, 1965), 138–39; Erie, *Rainbow's End*, 27; William E. Gienapp, "'Politics Seem to Enter into Everything': Political Culture in the North, 1840–1860," *Essays on American Antebellum Politics, 1840–1860*, ed. William E. Gienapp et al. (College Station, TX, 1982), 22–28.

9. Charles Kettleborough, *Constitution Making in Indiana: A Source Book of Constitutional Documents with Historical Introduction and Critical Notes*, vol. 1 (Indianapolis, 1916), civ–cv, and ibid., vol. 2 (Indianapolis, 1916), 11–16, 40; *Debates Indiana 1850*, 1295ff.; *Journal of the Convention of the State of New York, Begun and Held at the Capitol in the City of Albany, On the First Day of June, 1846* (Albany, 1846), 1036; Porter, *History of Suffrage*, 116–18; Arthur W. Bromage, "Literacy and the Electorate: Expansion and Contraction of the Franchise," *American Political Science Review* 24 (1930): 951; Roger W. Shugg, *Origins of Class Struggle in Louisiana: A Social History of White Farmers and Labourers During Slavery and After, 1840–1875* (Baton Rouge, 1939), 128–29; Vecoli, *New Jersey*, 138–41.

10. On the South see W. Darrell Overdyke, *The Know-Nothing Party in the South* (Baton Rouge, 1950); Leon C. Soulé, *The Know Nothing Party in New Orleans: A Reappraisal* (Baton Rouge, 1961); Jean H. Baker, *Ambivalent Americans: The Know-Nothing Party in Maryland* (Baltimore, 1977).

11. Anbinder, *Nativism and Slavery*, 103; Gienapp, *Origins of the Republican Party*, 92–96; Stephen E. Maizlish, "The Meaning of Nativism and the Crisis of the Union: The Know-Nothing Movement in the Antebellum North," *Essays on American Antebellum Politics, 1840–1860*, ed. William E. Gienapp et al. (College Station, TX, 1982), 168, 181; Richard P. McCormick, *The History of Voting in New Jersey: A Study of the Development of Election Machinery, 1664–1911* (New Brunswick, NJ, 1953), 142–43. In Louisiana,

notably, the Know-Nothings dropped their religious plank and religious exclusion. Soulé, *Know Nothing Party*, 66.

12. Gienapp, *Origins of the Republican Party*, 96; Anbinder, *Nativism and Slavery*, 106, 121–22.

13. Gienapp, *Origins of the Republican Party*, 92; Maizlish, "Nativism," 166–67; Haynes, "Causes," 67–82; Benjamin Tuska, *Know-Nothingism in Baltimore 1854–1860* (New York, n.d.), 6, 15–16, 20; Harry J. Carman and Reinhard H. Luthin, "Some Aspects of the Know-Nothing Movement Reconsidered," *South Atlantic Quarterly* 39 (April 1940): 218; Anbinder, *Nativism and Slavery*, 32–43, 128; John L. Brooke, *The Heart of the Commonwealth* (New York, 1989), 385–86; Formisano, *Parties*, 339; Baker, *Ambivalent Americans*, 141–45; Michael F. Holt, *The Rise and Fall of the American Whig Party: Jacksonian Politics and the Onset of the Civil War* (New York, 1999), 845–46. An economic slowdown in 1854 may have intensified the antagonism of native-born workers; overall, the proportion of farmers voting for the Know-Nothings was low in comparison to city and town dwellers.

14. Haynes, "Causes," 71; Vecoli, *New Jersey*, 138–41; Anbinder, *Nativism and Slavery*, 255–56; Stephen E. Maizlish, *The Triumph of Sectionalism: The Transformation of Ohio Politics, 1844–1856* (Kent, OH, 1983), 176–78; Gienapp, *Origins of the Republican Party*, 427–28; Joel H. Silbey, *The Partisan Imperative: The Dynamics of American Politics Before the Civil War* (New York, 1985), 141–42.

15. Haynes, "Causes," 72–73; Anbinder, *Nativism and Slavery*, 137–38, 256–57; Silbey, *Partisan Imperative*, 141–56; Tuska, *Know-Nothingism in Baltimore*, 15–16; Gienapp, *Origins of the Republican Party*, 428; A. C. Bernheim, "The Ballot in New York," *Political Science Quarterly* 4 (1889): 131–34; Fred Siegel, "Artisans and Immigrants in the Politics of Late Antebellum Georgia," *Civil War History* 27 (1981): 221–30. For similar issues in Ohio see Anbinder, *Nativism and Slavery*, 258–59; and Maizlish, "Nativism," 190–98, 221–30; see also *Journal of the Constitutional Convention of the State of Oregon held at Salem, Commencing August 17, 1857, together with the Constitution adopted by the people, November 9, 1857* (Salem, 1882), 321, 361–62.

16. Anbinder, *Nativism and Slavery*, 137–41, 254; John R. Mulkern, *The Know-Nothing Party in Massachusetts* (Boston, 1990), 156–58, 211, 219; Le Barnes, *Amendment*, 8–14; Porter, *History of Suffrage*, 118; Dale Baum, "Know-Nothingism and the Republican Majority in Massachusetts: The Political Realignment of the 1850s," *Journal of American History* 64 (March 1978): 974–76; Donald B. Cole, *Immigrant City: Lawrence, Massachusetts, 1845–1921* (Chapel Hill, NC, 1963), 34–38; Bromage, "Literacy and the Electorate," 950–51.

17. Anbinder, *Nativism and Slavery*, 141–42, 248–53, 267; Le Barnes, *Amendment*, 14; Baum, "Know-Nothingism," 975; idem, *The Civil War Party System: The Case of Massachusetts, 1848–1876* (Chapel Hill, NC, 1984), 44–48; Gienapp, *Origins of the Republican Party*, 423, 427, 428, 444–46; Edward L. Pierce, *Letter of Edward L. Pierce, Esq. of Chicago* (Boston, 1857), 16. Some historians of Know-Nothingism, including Mulkern, Haynes, Holt, and Formisano, see the movement as a response to modernization and rapid social change as well as immigration; these interpretations tend to emphasize the quasi-populist content of the movement.

18. Henry Ward Beecher, "Universal Suffrage: An Argument," delivered at Plymouth Church, Brooklyn, 12 February 1865, (Boston, 1865), 10; Marion T. Wright, "Negro Suffrage in New Jersey, 1776–1875," *Journal of Negro History* 33 (April 1948): 198, 211–15; Manfred Berg, "Soldiers and Citizens: War and Voting Rights in American History," *Reflections on American Exceptionalism*, ed. David K. Adams and Cornelis A. Van Minnen (Staffordshire, England, 1994), 194–200.

19. Eric Foner, *Reconstruction: America's Unfinished Revolution, 1863–1877* (New York, 1988), 27, 60, 62–66, 75, 110–14; Leon Litwack, *Been in the Storm So Long: The Aftermath of Slavery* (New York, 1979), 522–36; William Gillette, *The Right to Vote: Politics and the Passage of the Fifteenth Amendment* (Baltimore, 1965), 21–22; Xi Wang, *The Trial of Democracy: Black Suffrage and Northern Republicans, 1869–1910* (Athens, GA, 1997), 11–18; Barbara J. Fields, *Slavery and Freedom on the Middle Ground: Maryland During the Nineteenth Century* (New Haven, 1985), 133.

20. Beecher, "Universal Suffrage," 5–11; see also J. K. H. Willcox, "Suffrage a Right Not a Privilege," speech delivered to the Universal Franchise Association, 19 July 1867 (Washington, D.C., 1867).

21. Robert R. Dykstra and Harlan Hahn, "Northern Voters and Negro Suffrage: The Case of Iowa," *Voters, Parties, and Elections*, ed. Joel H. Silbey and Samuel T. McSeveney (Lexington, MA, 1972), 156–57, 203–5, 215; Wright, "Negro Suffrage," 176, 198, 202–17; Gillette, *Right to Vote*, 25–27; Foner, *Reconstruction*, 223.

22. Foner, *Reconstruction*, 60, 186–87.

23. Ibid., 131, 252, 258; Gillette, *Right to Vote*, 22–24; William L. Scruggs, "Citizenship and Suffrage," *North American Review* 177 (December 1903): 840.

24. Foner, *Reconstruction*, 241–42, 255; Gillette, *Right to Vote*, 22–25.

25. Foner, *Reconstruction*, 277, 314; Gillette, *Right to Vote*, 28–29; Dan T. Carter, *When the War Was Over: The Failure of Self-Reconstruction in the South, 1865–1867* (Baton Rouge, 1985), 248–50.

26. Wang, *Trial of Democracy*, 29–35; Foner, *Reconstruction*, 272, 314; Gillette, *Right to Vote*, 28–32.

27. Wang, *Trial of Democracy*, 35–40; Foner, *Reconstruction*, 272–79; Gillette, *Right to Vote*, 31.

28. Foner, *Reconstruction*, 280–84, 330, 342, 425ff.; James M. McPherson, *Ordeal by Fire: The Civil War and Reconstruction* (New York, 1982), 542–45; petition cited in Michael Les Benedict, *The Fruits of Victory: Alternatives in Restoring the Union 1865–1877* (Philadelphia, 1975), 118.

29. Foner, *Reconstruction*, 215, 291, 314–15, 470–71; Gillette, *Right to Vote*, 32–33, 38–39; McPherson, *Ordeal by Fire*, 65, 529–42; Felice A. Bonadio, "Ohio: A 'Perfect Contempt of All Unity,'" *Radical Republicans in the North: State Politics During Reconstruction*, ed. James C. Mohr (Baltimore, 1976), 85–92; see also the rest of the volume.

30. Gillette, *Right to Vote*, 32–34, 48–49; John M. Mathews, *Legislative and Judicial History of the Fifteenth Amendment* (Baltimore, 1909), 20–21; McPherson, *Ordeal by Fire*, 545; Michael Les Benedict, *A Compromise of Principle: Congressional Republicans and Reconstruction, 1863–1869* (New York, 1974), 325–31.

31. Gillette, *Right to Vote*, 42–54; F. Rives, J. Rives, and George A. Bailey, eds., *The Congressional Globe*, 40th Cong., 3d sess. (Washington, D.C., 1869), 643, 744.

32. Gillette, *Right to Vote*, 56–57; *Congressional Globe*, 1009, 1014, 1035.

33. *Congressional Globe*, 672, 709, 1009, 1010, 1035–39, 1626–28, 1641, Appendix, 153–54; Mathews, *Fifteenth Amendment*, 22–33; Gillette, *Right to Vote*, 57. On Wilson's links with the Know-Nothings see Richard H. Abbott, *Cobbler in Congress: The Life of Henry Wilson, 1812–1875* (Lexington, KY, 1972), 58–78; Ernest McKay, *Henry Wilson, Practical Radical: A Portrait of a Politician* (Port Washington, NY, 1971), 88–93.

34. *Congressional Globe*, 1036–37, 1628, 1641, 1869.

35. Ibid., 1010, Appendix, 165–69.

36. Ibid., 1030, 1035, 1038; McPherson, *Ordeal by Fire*, 545–46; Mathews, *Fifteenth Amendment*, 30–34; Gillette, *Right to Vote*, 58–74.

37. *Congressional Globe*, 705–6, Appendix, 285; *New York Times*, 15 February 1869; Gillette, *Right to Vote*, 56–57; Benedict, *Compromise of Principle*, 321–35.

38. *Congressional Globe*, 1029–30, 1040, 1044, 1425–28, 1440, 1466, 1625, 1627–28; Gillette, *Right to Vote*, 64–76, 88–90; see also Earl M. Maltz, *Civil Rights, The Constitution, and Congress, 1863–1869* (Lawrence, KS, 1990), 142–56.

39. *Congressional Globe*, 1291, 1307, 1625–41; Gillette, *Right to Vote*, 64–65, 70–90; Benedict, *Compromise of Principle*, 331–35.

40. *New York Times*, 8 March 1869; Foner, *Reconstruction*, 446.

41. Gillette, *Right to Vote*, 147–54; Foner, *Reconstruction*, 446.

42. Gillette, *Right to Vote*, 148–57; Foner, *Reconstruction*, 446–47.

43. Gillette, *Right to Vote*, 79–139; Wang, *Trial of Democracy*, 49–51.

44. Phillips and Douglass cited in Wang, *Trial of Democracy*, 50–53; *New York Times*, 8 March 1869; Garfield cited in Foner, *Reconstruction*, 449.

45. Foner, *Reconstruction*, 272–78, 323–24; Julian A. C. Chandler, *The History of Suffrage in Virginia* (Baltimore, 1901), 56–64.

46. *Journal of the Constitutional Convention of the State of Illinois* (Springfield, 1862), 191, 1021; *General Laws, and Joint Resolutions, Memorials and Private Acts, Passed at the Third Session of the Legislative Assembly of the Territory of Colorado* (Denver, 1864), 77–78; Albert G. Burr, "Address to the People of Illinois" speech delivered March 1862 (Springfield, 1862), 53; George McCrary, *A Treatise on the American Law of Elections* (Chicago, 1880), 46; *Journal of the Constitutional Convention of New York, 1872–73*, 22, 167–69, 176, 197–98, 338–39, 457; *Debates and Proceedings of the Pennsylvania Constitutional Convention, 1872–73*, vol. 2, 29–32; *Official Report of the Proceedings and Debates of the Third Constitutional Convention of Ohio, 1873*, vol. 2 (Cleveland, 1874), 1937–38; Marc W. Kruman, "Legislatures and Political Rights," *Encyclopedia of the American Legislative System*, vol. 3, ed. Joel H. Silbey (New York, 1994),

1241. Pennsylvania also attempted to disfranchise deserters permanently, but the law was declared unconstitutional in a state court because it constituted a legislative narrowing of a constitutional right.

47. Neuman, "'We Are the People,'" 298; Rosberg, "Aliens and Equal Protection," 1096, 1099; Raskin, "Legal Aliens," 1408–15; Kruman, "Legislatures," 1245–53.

48. Gordon quoted in *Report of the Proceedings and Debates of the Constitutional Convention, State of Virginia, held in the city of Richmond, June 12, 1901 to June 24, 1901*, comp. James H. Lindsay (Richmond, 1906), 3061–62. William Gillette, *Retreat from Reconstruction, 1869–1879* (Baton Rouge, 1979), 37–41; Foner, *Reconstruction*, 422–23.

49. McPherson, *Ordeal by Fire*, 564–66; Foner, *Reconstruction*, 424–35, 559–60.

50. Gillette, *Retreat from Reconstruction*, 37; McPherson, *Ordeal by Fire*, 566–67; Foner, *Reconstruction*, 454–57, 558, 586; Wang, *Trial of Democracy*, 57–92, 118–19.

51. Foner, *Reconstruction*, 423–24, 428–29, 587–96.

52. Wang, *Trial of Democracy*, 120–21, 161, 300; Bernard Grofman et al., *Minority Representation and the Quest for Voting Equality* (New York, 1992), 6–7.

53. Foner, *Reconstruction*, 588–93; J. Morgan Kousser, "Suffrage," *The Encyclopedia of American Political History*, vol. 3, ed. Jack P. Greene (New York, 1984), 1245–47; idem, *The Shaping of Southern Politics: Suffrage Restriction and the Establishment of the One-Party South, 1880–1910* (New Haven, CT, 1974), 11–44; Walter L. Fleming, ed., *Documentary History of Reconstruction*, vol. 2 (New York, 1966), 434–35.

54. Wang, *Trial of Democracy*, 216–32.

55. *Congressional Record*, 51st Cong., 1st sess., vol. 21, pt. 7 (1890), 6537–67, 2d sess., vol. 22, pt. 1 (1890), 21–26; Joseph A. Fry, *John Tyler Morgan and the Search for Southern Autonomy* (Knoxville, TN, 1992), 54–55; Wang, *Trial of Democracy*, 209–11.

56. *Congressional Record*, 51st Cong., 1st sess., vol. 21, pt. 7 (1890), 6543; George F. Hoar, *Autobiography of Seventy Years*, vol. 2 (New York, 1903), 150–65; John A. Garraty, *Henry Cabot Lodge: A Biography* (New York, 1953), 116–25.

57. *Congressional Record*, 51st Cong., 1st sess., vol. 21, pt. 7 (1890), 6548–54, 6672–75, 2d sess., vol. 22, pt. 1 (1890), 75–80; Wang, *Trial of Democracy*, 239–46; Rayford W. Logan, *The Negro in American Life and Thoughts: The Nadir, 1877–1901* (New York, 1903), 62–66.

58. George R. Brown, ed., *Reminiscences of Senator William M. Stewart of Nevada* (New York, 1908), 297–307; Wang, *Trial of Democracy*, 228–52; Franklin L. Burdette, *Filibustering in the Senate* (Princeton, NJ, 1940), 51–57; Russell R. Elliot, *Servant of Power: A Political Biography of Senator William M. Stewart* (Reno, NV, 1983), 127–31; Dorothy G. Fowler, *John Coit Spooner: Defender of Presidents* (New York, 1961), 132–58; Stanley P. Hirshson, *Farewell to the Bloody Shirt: Northern Republicans and the Southern Negro, 1877–1893* (Bloomington, IN, 1962), 143–65; Homer Socolofsky, *The Presidency of Benjamin Harrison* (Lawrence, KS, 1987), 60–65; Richard Bensel, *Sectionalism and American Political Development: 1880–1980* (Madison, WI, 1984), 76–78.

59. Wang, *Trial of Democracy*, 255–59.

60. Since the story of black (and some poor white) disfranchisement is well known and well documented, here it is summarized. For a complete and persuasive account see Kousser, *Shaping of Southern Politics*.

61. Kousser, *Shaping of Southern Politics*, 139–45.

62. *Virginia Proceedings, 1901*, 3067; Robert C. Brooks, *Political Parties and Electoral Problems* (New York, 1923), 364–65; Kousser, *Shaping of Southern Politics*, 5, 63–65; McPherson, *Ordeal by Fire*, 618–19; C. Vann Woodward, *Origins of the New South* (Baton Rouge, 1951), 321–49. As Kousser explains (p. 50), multiple voting-box arrangements required voters to put ballots for each office (or group of offices) into a separate voting box. Those placed in the wrong box would not be counted, and the order of the boxes could be changed repeatedly to outwit illiterate voters. Regarding failed efforts at disfranchisement in Maryland (with the exception of some local property requirements) see Margaret L. Callcott, *The Negro in Maryland Politics, 1870–1912* (Baltimore, 1969). For Texas see David Montejano, *Anglos and Mexicans in the Making of Texas, 1836–1986* (Austin, 1987), 140–45.

63. *Virginia Proceedings, 1901*, 3076–77; Kousser, *Shaping*, 47–50, 59, 83–86.

64. *Virginia Proceedings, 1901*, 3046–47, 3056, 3058–59, 3060–61; see also ibid., 3062–76. Texas citation from Kousser, *Shaping of Southern Politics*, 58, 112, 200–201.

65. *Virginia Proceedings, 1901*, 3062, 3069, 3074; Kousser, *Shaping of Southern Politics*, 68–71, 129, 168–71, 191, 246–49; Matthew J. Schott, "Progressives Against Democracy: Electoral Reform in Louisiana, 1894–1921," *Louisiana History* 20 (Summer 1979): 247–60.

66. See Kousser, *Shaping of Southern Politics*, 238–50; cf. Jerrold G. Rusk and John J. Stucker, "The Effect of the Southern System of Election Laws on Voting Participation," *The History of American Electoral Behavior*, ed. Joel H. Silbey et al. (Princeton, NJ, 1978), 220ff.; James B. Drake, "Making Voting Compulsory," *Machinists' Monthly Journal* 19 (August 1907): 759–60; on North Carolina see Glenda E. Gilmore, *Gender and Jim Crow: Women and the Politics of White Supremacy in North Carolina, 1896–1920* (Chapel Hill, NC, 1996), 119–25, 256*n*.

67. Kousser, *Shaping of Southern Politics*, 43–44, 60–62, 236–37; Bensel, *Sectionalism*, 81; Bruce A. Campbell, *The American Electorate: Attitudes and Action* (New York, 1979), 24; Rusk and Stucker, "Effect of the Southern System," 200, 247–48; Wang, *Trial of Democracy*, 260–61.

68. John F. Reynolds, *Testing Democracy: Electoral Behavior and Progressive Reform in New Jersey, 1880–1920* (Chapel Hill, NC, 1988), 122–23; Arthur Holcombe, *State Government in the United States* (New York, 1926), 85–86; *Williams v. Mississippi*, 170 U.S. 213 (1898); Loren P. Beth, *The Development of the American Constitution, 1877–1917* (New York, 1971), 110–11; Kousser, *Shaping of Southern Politics*, 57, 250–57; Wang, *Trial of Democracy*, 253–66; Rogers Smith, *Civic Ideals: Conflicting Visions of Citizenship in United States History* (New Haven, CT, 1997), 383–85, 428–29, 451–53.

69. *Guinn v. United States*, 238 U.S. 347 (1915); *Myers v. Anderson*, 238 U.S. 368 (1915); for a labor protest against the southern laws see *United Mine Workers' Journal* (14 August 1913): 7.

CHAPTER FIVE

1. *Washington Post*, 20 February 1899, cited in the *Coast Seamen's Journal*, 8 March 1899, 7; see also exchange of letters between E. B. Smith and E. L. C. Morse, *The Nation*, 9 July 1903 and 30 July 1903. The term *sans-culottes* is from the French Revolution: it referred loosely to urban-dwelling men of the people, who supported the Jacobin republic.

2. Eric Foner, *Reconstruction: America's Unfinished Revolution, 1863–1877* (New York, 1988), 497–98.

3. Herbert G. Gutman, *Power and Culture: Essays on the American Working Class* (New York, 1987), 380–94.

4. Francis Parkman, "The Failure of Universal Suffrage," *North American Review* 263 (July-August 1878): 7.

5. Parkman, for example, made one brief reference to "priests" but otherwise did not mention Catholicism.

6. Charles Francis Adams, Jr., "The Protection of the Ballot in National Elections," *Journal of Social Science* 1 (June 1869): 108–9; Alexander Winchell, "The Experiment of Universal Suffrage," *North American Review* 136 (February 1883): 129; William L. Scruggs, "Citizenship and Suffrage," *North American Review* 177 (December 1903): 844–45; Frank J. Scott, *The Evolution of Suffrage* (New York, 1912), 7; Melvin G. Holli, *Reform in Detroit: Hazen S. Pingree and Urban Politics* (New York, 1969), 172; David Montejano, *Anglos and Mexicans in the Making of Texas, 1836–1986* (Austin, 1987), 130–31. For a broader expression of racial antagonism (against non–Anglo-Saxons of all types) see Josiah Strong, *Our Country: Its Possible Future and Its Present Crisis* (New York, 1886). Cf. James Bryce, *The American Commonwealth*, vol. 2 (New York, 1941), 103.

7. Howard B. Grose, *Aliens or Americans?* (Cincinnati, 1906), 214–16; see also ibid., 248–49, 255; Winchell, "Experiment," 126–27, 131; John R. Commons, *Races and Immigrants in America* (New York, 1907), 220–21.

8. "The Crime Against the Suffrage in Washington," *The Nation* 26 (27 June 1878): 415; Parkman, "Failure of Universal Suffrage," 4, 8; Richmond Mayo Smith, *Emigration and Immigration: A Study in Social Science* (New York, 1890), 83–90.

9. Edward L. Godkin, "The Democratic View of Democracy," *North American Review* 101 (July 1865): 109–10, 113–14; *Anderson v. Baker*, 23 Md. 531 (1865), cited in Frederick C. Brightly, *A Collec-*

tion of Leading Cases on the Law of Elections in the United States (Philadelphia, 1871), 33–34; Parkman, "Failure of Universal Suffrage," 10, 20.

10. *The Outlook* 68 (27 July 1901): 711–12; Scruggs, "Citizenship and Suffrage," 839–40.

11. John Martin Luther Babcock, "The Right of the Ballot: A reply to Francis Parkman and Others Who Have Asserted 'The Failure of Universal Suffrage,'" reprinted from the *Boston Herald*, 15 March 1879 (Boston, 1879), 4–13.

12. "Sincere Demagogy," *Atlantic Monthly* 44 (October 1879): 489–90; "Universal Suffrage," *The Nation* 3 (8 November 1861): 371–72; George W. Julian, "Suffrage a Birthright," *International Review* 6 (1879): 16–17. For other examples see Francis N. Thorpe, "A Century's Struggle for the Franchise in America," *Harper's Magazine* 94 (January 1897): 207–15; Commons, *Races and Immigrants*, 184; Maurice Maeterlink, "Universal Suffrage," *The Bookman* 19 (March-August 1904): 133–35; E. B. Smith, "Debasement of Suffrage," *The Nation* 77 (9 July 1903): 28–29. Cf. McGerr, *Decline of Popular Politics*, 45–52.

13. Among the commentators noting a decline in faith in a broad suffrage (in addition to those expressly cited earlier) were James Schouler, "Evolution of the American Voter," *American Historical Review* 2 (July 1897): 669; Commons, *Races and Immigrants*, 3–4; Edward L. C. Morse, "The Debasement of Suffrage," *The Nation* 76 (25 June 1903): 515; idem, "The Suffrage Again," *The Nation* 77 (30 July 1903): 93; Edward L. Godkin, *Problems of Modern Democracy: Political and Economic Essays*, ed. Morton Keller (Cambridge, MA, 1966), 123; "Topics of the Time: A Recent Election and Universal Suffrage," *Century Magazine* 67 (January 1904): 474–75; cf. J. Morgan Kousser, *The Shaping of Southern Politics: Suffrage Restriction and the Establishment of the One-Party South, 1880–1910* (New Haven, CT, 1974), 251–52; Foner, *Reconstruction*, 492–93; Michael McGerr, *The Decline of Popular Politics: The American North, 1865–1928* (New York, 1986), 43–5; McGerr attributes the *Nation* article in the chapter epigraph to Jonathan B. Harrison. The two quotations are from Charles Seymour and Donald P. Frary, *How the World Votes: The Story of Democratic Development in Elections*, vol. 2 (Springfield, IL, 1918), 321–22; William B. Munro, "Intelligence Tests for Voters," *The Forum* 80 (December 1928): 828–30.

14. Godkin, *Problems of Modern Democracy*, 146–47, 201–2.

15. "Limited Sovereignty in the United States," *Atlantic Monthly* 43 (February 1879): 190–93.

16. Holli, *Reform in Detroit*, 172–74; Winchell, "Experiment," 125, 133–34; Scruggs, "Citizenship and Suffrage," 845–46; Parkman, "Failure of Universal Suffrage," 5, 12–13, 20.

17. The history of electoral laws presented here is based on the following sources: all extant transcripts of the debates and proceedings of constitutional conventions held in all states during this period; all state constitutions and amendments in force at any time between 1870 and 1920; a systematic examination of the statutes and case law in roughly a dozen states; a less systematic canvass of statutes and case law in other states; and secondary sources. All quotations and laws cited are indicated in notes, but broader generalizations are based on these other sources as well; see also tables and sources in the appendix.

18. Peter Argersinger has very ably analyzed many of the technical laws that influenced political outcomes during the Gilded Age; see "'A Place on the Ballot': Fusion Politics and Antifusion Laws," *American Historical Review* 85 (April 1980): 287–306; idem, "The Value of the Vote: Political Representation in the Gilded Age," *Journal of American History* 76 (June 1989): 59–90; idem, "New Perspectives on Election Fraud in the Gilded Age," *Political Science Quarterly* 100 (Winter 1985–86): 669–87; idem, "Regulating Democracy: Election Laws and Dakota Politics, 1889–1902," *Midwest Review* 5 (Spring 1983): 1–19. See also John Buenker, "The Politics of Resistance: The Rural-Based Yankee Republican Machines of Connecticut and Rhode Island," *New England Quarterly* 47 (June 1974): 212–37; Terrence J. McDonald, *The Parameters of Urban Fiscal Policy: Socioeconomic Changes and Political Culture in San Francisco, 1860–1906* (Berkeley, 1986), 160; Donald B. Cole, *Immigrant City: Lawrence, Massachusetts, 1845–1921* (Chapel Hill, NC, 1963), 42–49. For examples of contemporary opinion about the inequalities inherent in district voting see Simeon Stetson, *The People's Power or How to Wield the Ballot* (San Francisco, 1883); and "Legal Disfranchisement," *Atlantic Monthly* 69 (April 1892): 542–46.

19. The subject of compulsory voting still awaits its historian. See J. Allen Smith, *The Growth and Decadence of Constitutional Government* (New York, 1930), 54; Alfred R. Conkling, *City Government in the United States* (New York, 1895), 200; Albert B. Hart, "The Exercise of the Suffrage," *Political Science Quarterly* 7 (June 1892): 307–29; Frederick Holls, "Compulsory Voting," *Annals of the American Acad-*

emy of Political and Social Science 1 (1890–91): 586–614; *Debates in the Massachusetts Constitutional Convention, 1917–1918*, vol. 3 (Boston, 1920): chap. 8.

20. The two best monographs dealing with the politics of suffrage history (those of McCormick and Reynolds, cited herein) are both about New Jersey.

21. Geoffrey Blodgett, *The Gentle Reformers: Massachusetts Democrats in the Cleveland Era* (Cambridge, MA, 1966), 117–18; Dale Baum, *The Civil War Party System: The Case of Massachusetts, 1848–1876* (Chapel Hill, NC, 1984), 11–13; Nathan Matthews, *Municipal Charters* (Cambridge, MA, 1914), 20. Massachusetts courts also had ruled that men who had been exempted from taxation due to poverty for two successive years before they were seventy (at which time they were exempted from taxation due to age) were not entitled to vote. George W. McCrary, *A Treatise on the American Law of Elections* (Chicago, 1880), 64–65. Regarding Delaware see *Debates and Proceedings of the Constitutional Convention of the State of Delaware, Commencing December 1, 1896* (Milford, 1958), vol. 1, 334–40, 770–76; ibid., vol. 2, 1141–70; ibid., vol. 5, 3495–501. Dudley O. McGovney, *The American Suffrage Medley: The Need for a National Uniform Suffrage* (Chicago, 1949), 116. Delaware for a time imposed a registration fee in place of a poll tax.

22. Evelyn Sterne, "All Americans: The Politics of Citizenship in Providence, 1840 to 1940," (Ph.D. diss., Duke University, 1998), chap. 1; Buenker, "Politics of Resistance," 222–36; Samuel T. McSeveney, *The Politics of Depression: Political Behavior in the Northeast, 1893–1896* (New York, 1972), 13–14.

23. *Debates and Proceedings of the Pennsylvania Constitutional Convention, 1872–73*, vol. 1 (Harrisburg, 1873), 626–34, 639–46, 649–57, 707, 711; A. D. Harlan, *Pennsylvania Constitutional Convention 1872 and 1873: Its Members and Officers and the Result of Their Labors* (Philadelphia, 1873); Rosalind L. Branning, *Pennsylvania Constitutional Development* (Pittsburgh, 1960), 93–94, 135; Edward McPherson, *A Hand-Book of Politics For 1890* (Washington, 1890), 57; Clinton R. Woodruff, "Election Methods and Reforms in Philadelphia," *Annals of the American Academy of Political and Social Science* 17 (March 1901): 192–95.

24. *Debates and Proceedings of the Constitutional Convention of the State of Illinois, 1869*, vol. 1 (Springfield, 1870), 736; Isidor Loeb and Floyd Shoemaker, eds., *Debates of the Missouri Constitutional Convention of 1875*, vol. 12 (Columbia, 1944), 343–65; Charles Kettleborough, *Constitution Making in Indiana*, vol. 2 (Indianapolis, 1916), 365, 370, 387, 394; Charles T. Russell, *Manhood Suffrage Under Constitutional Guaranty: An Argument in Favor of Rescinding the Provision in the State Constitution Establishing the Payment of a State or County Tax as a Qualification of Voters* (Boston, 1879), 11; *Debates and Proceedings of the Constitutional Convention of the State of California, 1878*, vol. 1 (Sacramento, 1880), 86; *Debates in the Texas Constitutional Convention of 1875* (Austin, 1930), 167–89.

25. "The Rights of Taxpayers," *Harper's Weekly* 21 (7 April 1877): 263; "Municipal Politics," *Harper's Weekly* 21 (28 April 1877): 323; "Voting in Cities," *Harper's Weekly* 21 (29 September 1877): 758–59; "The City Amendments," *Harper's Weekly* 21 (10 November 1877): 879; "Distrust of the People," *Harper's Weekly* 22 (9 May 1878): 187; "The Constitutional Amendment on City Government," *The Nation* 26 (14 February 1878): 108–9; McGerr, *Decline of Popular Politics*, 49. For an argument in favor of a taxpaying requirement for municipalities while retaining "universal suffrage" for state elections see Cuthbert Mills, "Universal Suffrage in New York," *The International Review* 8 (1880): 199–211.

26. McGovney, *American Suffrage Medley*, 113; *Journal of the Constitutional Convention of the State of Texas, 1875* (Galveston, 1875), 53, 139, 176, 315; Leon Fink, *Workingmen's Democracy: The Knights of Labor and American Politics* (Urbana, IL, 1983), 72; Act of 22 February 1905, chap. 215, Kan. *Laws* (1905), 306, 312, 314. Maryland gave municipalities the right to limit the franchise to taxpayers through public local laws. See, e.g., Md. *Pub. Loc. Laws*, art. 12, sec. 74 (1888). These municipal laws, which generally had to be passed both by town councils and by the state legislatures, were difficult to track, and the listing here is not comprehensive.

27. *Spitzer v. Village of Fulton*, 64 N.E. 957, 958 (N.Y. 1902); *Myers v. Anderson*, 238 U.S. 368, 380 (1915); *State ex rel. Gilson v. Monahan*, 72 Kan. 492 (1905). See also *Hanna v. Young*, 84 Md. 179 (1896).

28. For an example of a constitutional debate on this issue see *Debates Pennsylvania 1872–73*, vol. 1, 706–10. The precise number of pauper exclusions in effect is unclear. Table A.6 lists all those that I have been able to detect. Robert Steinfeld believes that there were more, but he does not offer a comprehensive list; see Steinfeld, "Property and Suffrage," *Stanford Law Review* 41 (January 1989): 372–73.

29. *Massachusetts Report 124, Cases Argued and Determined in the Supreme Judicial Court of Massachusetts, January-June, 1878* (Boston, 1879), 596–98.

30. Steinfeld, "Property and Suffrage," 372–73; Charles T. Russell, Jr., *The Disfranchisement of Paupers* (Boston, 1878), 3–5, 19–31; regarding the legal definition of *pauper* and an attempt to change the outcome of an election because a man who was allegedly a pauper had been permitted to vote see Edward P. Loring and Charles T. Russell, Jr., *Reports of Contested Elections in the Senate and House of Representatives of the Commonwealth of Massachusetts* (Boston, 1886), 139–42. On unemployment and tramps see Alexander Keyssar, *Out of Work: The First Century of Unemployment in Massachusetts* (New York, 1986), 130–42.

31. *The Morning Mercury* (New Bedford), 1 February 1898; unidentified newspaper article in the Ashley Scrapbooks, vol. 9, New Bedford Public Library; *Machinists' Monthly Journal* (April 1898): 192–93.

32. Burns quoted in *Official Report of the Proceedings and Debates of the Third Constitutional Convention of Ohio, 1873* (Cleveland, 1874), 1903–4. Many workers, of course, also came to favor immigration restriction but did so because they feared economic competition, not because they decried the influence of immigrants on political life.

33. *Debates Ohio 1873*, 1800, 1802, 1903–4.

34. *Debates Missouri 1875*, vol. 5, 16; *Journal of the Texas Constitutional Convention, 1875*, 40–41, 92–93; Taliesin Evans, *American Citizenship and the Right of Suffrage in the United States* (Oakland, CA, 1892), 59; *Debates California 1878*, vol. 1, 146; Albert J. McCullough, *Suffrage and Its Problems* (Baltimore, 1929), 53; Holli, *Reform in Detroit*, 67. Cf. Joseph H. Brewer et al., *Proceedings and Debates of the Constitutional Convention of the State of Michigan, 1907*, vol. 2 (Lansing, 1907), 1068–78, 1270–84. As late as 1917, proposals for alien suffrage were introduced at the Massachusetts constitutional convention but were rejected. Raymond L. Bridgeman, *The Massachusetts Constitutional Convention of 1917* (Boston, 1923), 229; Commonwealth of Massachusetts, *The Journal of the Constitutional Convention of the Commonwealth of Massachusetts, 1917* (Boston, 1917), 61, 76, 99, 630.

35. "Show Your Papers," *New York Herald*, 17 October 1888; *Debates Pennsylvania 1872-73*, vol. 1, 89–93, 133, 529, 693–711; McSeveney, *Politics of Depression*, 67; Conkling, *City Government*, 196; William E. Chandler, "Methods of Restricting Immigration," *The Forum* 13 (March 1892): 141–42.

36. *Kineen v. Wells*, 11 NE 916, 922 (Mass. 1887); Massachusetts, *Statutes* (1885), chap. 345; McCrary, *Treatise*, 64–65; William Steele, ed., *Revised Record of the Constitutional Convention of the State of New York, May 8, 1894–September 19, 1894*, vol. 4 (Albany, 1900), 460–78.

37. See Frederick Van Dyne, *A Treatise on the Law of Naturalization of the United States* (Washington, D.C., 1907), 12–13, 40–61, 409–40.

38. M. K. Reely, *Selected Articles on Immigration* (New York, 1917), 62–64; McCullough, *Suffrage and Its Problems*, 149, 151; John B. Moore, "Needed Reform in Naturalization," *The Forum* 13 (June 1892): 476; John P. Gavit, *Americans by Choice* (Montclair, NJ, 1971), 93, 98, 107–8, 124–26; Chandler, "Methods," 133; H. Sidney Everett, "Immigration and Naturalization," *Atlantic Monthly* 75 (March 1895): 348, 351; Don D. Lescohier, "Working Conditions," *The History of Labor in the United States*, vol. 3, ed. Don D. Lescohier, Elizabeth Brandeis, Selig Perlman, and Philip Taft (New York, 1935), 17–23. For examples of judges refusing to naturalize men because of their political beliefs see *The Miners' Magazine* 8 (4 October 1906): 7; ibid., 10 (13 May 1909): 4; ibid., 10 (8 July 1909): 8; ibid., 12 (23 May 1912): 10; ibid., 12 (26 September 1912): 8.

39. Prescott F. Hall, *Immigration and Its Effects Upon the United States* (New York, 1907), 262–80; George M. Stephenson, *A History of American Immigration, 1820–1924* (New York, 1926), 156–69; Smith, *Emigration and Immigration*, 161–67; Lescohier, "Working Conditions," 23–29; Grose, *Aliens*, 95–96; *Proceedings of the New York Convention of the Amalgamated Clothing Workers of America, 1914* (New York, 1914), 92–93; A. T. Lane, "American Trade Unions, Mass Immigration, and the Literacy Test: 1900–1917," *Labor History* 25 (Winter 1984): 18–24; John J. Bukowczyk, "The Transformation of Working-Class Ethnicity: Corporate Control, Americanization, and the Polish Immigrant Middle-Class in Bayonne, New Jersey, 1915–1925," *Labor History* 25 (Winter 1984): 75; Gerd Korman, *Industrialization, Immigrants, and Americanizers: The View from Milwaukee, 1866–1921* (Madison, WI, 1967), 148–55; House Committee on Immigration and Naturalization, "Proposed Changes in Naturalization Laws," Part 6: *Hearings*, 66th Cong., 1st sess., October 1919, 5–27; John W. Briggs, *An Italian Passage: Immigrants to Three American Cities,*

1890–1930 (New Haven, CT, 1978), 134; Gavit, *Americans by Choice*, 255–68; State Committee on Citizenship and Naturalization, State of Illinois, *Citizenship and Naturalization Activities in the United States* (Springfield, 1937), passim.

40. Carl B. Swisher, *Motivation and Political Technique in the California Constitutional Convention, 1878–79* (Claremont, 1930), 11–16, 88–92; Alexander Saxton, *The Indispensable Enemy: Labor and the Anti-Chinese Movement in California* (Berkeley, CA, 1971), 113–38; *Fifteenth Census of the U.S. 1930, Population*, vol. 2 (Washington, D.C., 1933), 402; Chandler, "Methods," 135; Lescohier, "Working Conditions," 18, 32; *Congressional Record*, House, 44th Cong., 2d sess., vol. 5, pt. 1 (28 February 1877), 2004–5; there is evidence that some courts did naturalize a small number of Chinese immigrants.

41. Saxton, *Indispensable Enemy*, 115–34; Gwendolyn Mink, *Old Labor and New Immigrants in American Political Development: Union, Party, and State, 1875–1920* (Ithaca, NY, 1986), 85–86.

42. *Constitution of the State of California, Annotated*, vol. 1, ed. Paul Mason (San Francisco, 1953), 263–66; *Debates California 1878*, vol. 3, 1018–19, 1522; Swisher, *Motivation*, 88–92. Bans on Chinese voting were in the Oregon Constitution of 1857 and the Idaho Constitution of 1889.

43. Herbert J. Bass, "The Politics of Ballot Reform in New York State, 1888–1890," *New York History* 42 (July 1961): 254–62; Charles C. Binney, "The Merits and Defects of the Pennsylvania Ballot Law of 1891," *Annals of the American Academy of Political and Social Science* 2 (July 1891–June 1892): 751–71; John F. Reynolds, *Testing Democracy: Electoral Behavior and Progressive Reform in New Jersey, 1880–1920* (Chapel Hill, NC, 1988), 59; Richard H. Dana, *The Australian Ballot System of Massachusetts*, The City Club of New York (1891), 3–4; and idem, "The Australian System of Voting," *Annals of the American Academy of Political and Social Science* 2 (May 1892): 733–50; Joseph B. Bishop, "The Secret Ballot in 33 States," *The Forum* 12 (1891–92): 587–98; L. E. Fredman, "The Introduction of the Australian Ballot in the United States," *Australian Journal of Politics and History* 13 (August 1967): 204–20; Eldon C. Evans, *A History of the Australian Ballot System in the United States* (Chicago, 1917), 1–31, 40–44; Knights of Labor, Proceedings of the Fifteenth Regular Session of the General Assembly (Toledo, OH, 10 November 1891), 6; *Coast Seamen's Journal* 2 (16 January 1889): 1–2; and ibid., 3 (12 February 1890): 1; *Debates California 1878*, vol. 1, 1368; Argersinger, "A Place on the Ballot," 290–92, 291n; Baum, *Civil War Party System*, 15.

44. Bass, "Politics of Ballot Reform," 254–60; Kousser, *Shaping of Southern Politics*, 52; Phillip Allen, "Ballot Laws and Their Workings," *Political Science Quarterly* 21 (March 1906): 39; Baum, *Civil War Party System*, 16–20; "Successful Ballot Laws," *The Nation* 49 (17 October 1889): 304; A. C. Bernheim, "The Ballot in New York," *Political Science Quarterly* 4 (1889): 151–52; *Debates California 1878*, 1368; *Debates Pennsylvania 1872–73*, vol. 1, 133, 146, 506–7; and ibid., vol. 2, 50–95; Merritt Starr and Russell H. Curtis, eds., *Annotated Statutes of Illinois in Force January 1, 1896*, vol. 2 (Chicago, 1896), chap. 46, sec. 188; *Wickam v. Coyner*, 20 Ohio C.D. 765, 1900 WL 3118, (Ohio Cir 1900).

45. Godkin, "Democratic View," 119; *Revised Record of the Constitutional Convention of the State of New York: April Fifth to September Tenth, 1915*, vol. 3 (Albany, 1916), 2931–43, 2999–3004; Joseph H. Brewer, Charles H. Bender, and Charles H. McCurren, eds., *Proceedings and Debates of the Constitutional Convention of the State of Michigan Convened in the City of Lansing, Tuesday, October 22, 1907*, vol. 2 (Lansing, 1907), 1235.

46. *Debates Missouri 1875*, vol. 4, 158–67; *Proceedings and Debates of the Constitutional Convention of the State of New York, 1867–1868*, vol. 5 (Albany, 1868), 3564; *Revised Record New York 1915*, vol. 3, 3015–28; *Debates Michigan 1907*, vol. 2, 1236; *New York Times*, 25 August 1915.

47. Arthur W. Bromage, "Literacy and the Electorate: Expansion and Contraction of the Franchise," *American Political Science Review* 24 (November 1930): 955–56; *Proceedings of the Constitutional Convention of the State of Illinois, 1920*, vol. 1 (n.p., 1922), 996–99; *Debates Missouri 1875*, vol. 4, 168; *Debates, Michigan, 1907*, vol. 2, 1234–36; *Revised Record New York, 1915*, vol. 3, 2999–3055, 3151–68.

48. *Debates Delaware 1896*, vol. 2, 1046–50; Bromage, "Literacy," 956–59; George H. Haynes, "Educational Qualifications for the Suffrage in the United States," *Political Science Quarterly* 13 (September 1898): 496–98; *New York Times*, 25 August 1915; Massachusetts, *Gen. Laws*, chap. 404, sec. 20 (1889); *Journal and Debates of the Constitutional Convention of the State of Wyoming, 1889* (Cheyenne, 1893), 388–93.

49. Roger Daniels and Eric F. Petersen, "California's Grandfather Clause: The 'Literacy in English' Amendment of 1894," *Southern California Quarterly* 50 (March 1968): 52–54.

50. Bromage, "Literacy," 955–59; *New York Times*, 17 October and 23 October 1921; ibid., 7 November, 9 November, 10 November, 11 November, 12 November, and 21 November 1921; ibid., 2 December and 16 December 1921; *Revised Record, New York, 1915*, vol. 3, 3002; *Journal of the Constitutional Convention of New York*, Convened Wednesday, 4 December 1872 (Albany, 1873), 270–71, 283.

51. Louis Windmuller, "The Qualification of Voters," *Harper's Weekly* 44 (13 October 1900): 975; Bromage, "Literacy," 948–49, 960–62; Commons, *Races and Immigrants*, 194–95; Finla G. Crawford, "Operation of the Literacy Test for Voters in New York," *American Political Science Review* 25 (May 1931): 342–45. For examples of court decisions see *Ferayorni v. Walter*, 202 N.Y.S. 91 (N.Y. Sup. 1923); *Stone v. Smith*, 34 NE 521 (Mass. 1893); and *Guinn v. United States*, 238 U.S. 347 (1915).

52. Johnson quoted in *Arguments of Charles T. Russell, Jr., Counsel for the Respondents and Arthur T. Johnson and Gen. Edgar R. Champlin, Counsel for the Petitioners Before the Committee on Elections on the Part of the House* (Boston, 1891), 21. Stephan Thernstrom, *The Other Bostonians* (Cambridge, MA, 1973), 16–20, 39–42, 220–30; for statistics indicating even higher rates of mobility in San Francisco (and their impact on voting) see McDonald, *Parameters*, 119–20.

53. *Sharp v. McIntire*, 46 P. 115, 116 (Colo. 1896). See also *Kellogg v. Hickman*, 21 P. 325 (Colo. 1889); *Jain v. Bossen*, 62 P. 194 (Colo. 1900); *People v. Turpin*, 112 P. 539 (Colo. 1910); *Sturgeon v. Korte*, 34 Ohio St. 525 (Ohio 1878); *Esker v. McCoy*, 5 Ohio Dec. Reprint 573 (Ohio Com. Pl. 1878); McCrary, *Treatise*, 35–44.

54. *Pope v. Williams*, 193 U.S. 621, 633 (1904).

55. *Debates Illinois 1869*, vol. 2, 1272–74, 1282; Newton Bateman and Paul Selby, eds., *Biographical and Memorial Edition of the Historical Encyclopedia of Illinois*, vol. 1 (Chicago, 1915), 368, 394.

56. *Debates California 1878*, 1016–19, 1362–63; *Debates Pennsylvania 1872–73*, vol. 1, 534–35; see also ibid., 89, 539–40, 628–29; *Journal of New York, 1872–73*, 22, 31–32, 95–96, 281, 291–92.

57. *Debates Pennsylvania 1872–73*, vol. 1, 152–65; *Debates Ohio 1873*, vol. 2, 1860–61, 1938–46; *Dale v. Irwin*, 78 Ill. 170 (Ill. 1875); *Welsh v. Shumway*, 83 N.E. 549 (Ill. 1907); *Wickham v. Coyner*, 20 Ohio C.D. 765 (Ohio Cir 1900); *Parsons v. People* 70 P. 689 (Colo. 1902); McCrary, *Treatise*, 41–44; *In re Goodman*, 40 N.E. 769 (N.Y. 1895); *Matter of Barry*, 58 N.E. 12 (N.Y. 1900).

58. Not surprisingly, perhaps, courts interpreted laws dealing with the voting rights of soldiers with considerable latitude. In 1917, for example, a New York court ruled that men who had left their families and lived on their own for a period and then joined the army could claim their families' homes as their voting residence. The court concluded that "every reasonable facility should be provided for the casting and canvassing of their votes without the strict application of all the formalities provided by the election law." See *People ex rel. Brush v. Schum*, 168 N.Y.S. 391 (N.Y. Sup. 1917).

59. *Debates in the Massachusetts Constitutional Convention, 1917–1918*, vol. 3 (Boston, 1920), 11–12; see also ibid., 4–10, 13–19; Commonwealth of Massachusetts, *Bulletins for the Constitutional Convention, 1917–1918*, vol. 2, Bulletin 23 (Boston, 1919), 209–25; B. Bradwell Helmer, ed., *Revised Statutes of the State of Illinois 1917, containing all the general statutes of the state in force January 1, 1918* (Chicago, 1918), chap. 46, 1396–1400; *Revised Record New York, 1915*, vol. 2 (Albany, 1916), 1587–1605, 1788–98, 1801–22; ibid., vol. 4, 3621–32, 3671, 3680; *Laws Passed at the Twentieth Session of the General Assembly of the State of Colorado* (Denver, 1915), chap. 76, secs. 1–4, 221–24; P. Orman Ray, "Absent Voters," *American Political Science Review* 8 (August 1914): 442–45; "Recent Primary and Election Laws," *American Political Science Review* 13 (May 1919): 264–74. For an indication of labor support for absentee voting see *Coast Seamen's Journal* 29 (15 November 1916): 6; *Seamen's Journal*, 32 (16 July 1919): 2; ibid., 32 (17 August 1919): 9.

60. This issue will be addressed at length in a forthcoming volume. The very rough estimate offered here is based on statistical data for various cities collected in Thernstrom, *Other Bostonians*, 16–20, 39–42, 220–30; these indicate that in general, only 50 to 60 percent of the residents of American cities still lived in the same city a decade later, and that total population turnover was on the order of 300 percent per decade. The full extent of mobility (including within cities or counties) would be substantially higher. How much of this mobility was interstate rather than intrastate is unclear (and surely varied), but presumably 60 to 80 percent of this recorded movement was intrastate. Thernstrom himself concluded that for the years between 1837 and 1921, roughly one quarter of the population living in Boston had not been living there a year earlier: since the figure was higher for lower-status occupations, mobility "must have disfranchised a sizable fraction of the working-class population." Stephan Thernstrom,

"Socialism and Social Mobility," *Failure of a Dream? Essays in the History of American Socialism*, rev. ed., ed. John H. M. Laslett and Seymour M. Lipset (Berkeley, CA, 1984), 415. As indicated in chapter 8, a careful study conducted in the 1960s suggests that residency laws disfranchised 15 to 20 percent of the electorate, but it is hazardous to project such numbers into the more distant past.

61. Regarding the history of registration see Joseph P. Harris, *Registration of Voters in the United States* (Washington, D.C., 1929), esp. 4–6, 65–92. Regarding Massachusetts see *Acts and Laws of Massachusetts* (1801), chap. 38. For examples of objections to registration laws see *Debates California 1878*, 1019; *Debates of the Maryland Constitutional Convention of 1867 (as reprinted from articles reported in the Baltimore Sun)* (Baltimore, 1930), 232–37; Texas Constitutional Convention, *Debates in the Texas Constitutional Convention of 1875* (Austin, 1930), 191–93.

62. Richard P. McCormick, *The History of Voting in New Jersey: A Study of the Development of Election Machinery, 1664–1911* (New Brunswick, NJ, 1953), 148–65; regarding sunset laws and changing poll hours see also Massachusetts, *Statutes* (1869), chap. 62; (1879), chap. 2; (1881), chap. 7; (1884), chap. 299; (1905), chap. 111; Charles E. M. and H. F. Gosnell, *Non-Voting: Causes and Methods of Control* (Chicago, 1924), 233. Several states, including Massachusetts and Illinois, did pass laws requiring employers to give workers time off to vote, but whether employers adhered to these laws is unclear.

63. Reynolds, *Testing Democracy*, 49, 60 69, 121–25, 145–52; McCormick, *History of Voting in New Jersey*, 166; Honorable E. Gurd Grubb, "A Campaign for Ballot Reform," *North American Review* 155 (December 1892): 684–93.

64. Frederick C. Jaher, *The Urban Establishment: Upper Strata in Boston, New York, Charleston, Chicago, and Los Angeles* (Urbana, IL, 1982), 501–5; Kenneth Finegold, *Experts and Politicians: Reform Challenges to Machine Politics in New York, Cleveland, and Chicago* (Princeton, NJ, 1995), 124; Bruce Grant, *Fight for a City: The Story of the Union League Club of Chicago and Its Times, 1880–1955* (Chicago, 1955), 68–79.

65. "An Act Regulating the holding of elections, and declaring the result thereof in cities, villages, and incorporated towns in this State," approved 19 June 1885, in Merritt Starr and Russell H. Curtis, eds., *Annotated Statutes of the State of Illinois, Supplement Embracing Session Laws of 1885 and 1887* (Chicago, 1887), 244–76; Walter C. Jones and Keen H. Addington, eds., *Annotated Statutes of the State of Illinois in Force January 1, 1913*, vol. 3 (Chicago, 1913), 2687–88.

66. Grant, *Fight for a City*, 79.

67. "An Act to regulate Elections, passed March 23, 1850," *General Laws of the State of California, 1850–1864, Inclusive*, vol. 1, ed. Theodore H. Hittell (San Francisco, 1865), 335; Philip J. Ethington, *The Public City: The Political Construction of Urban Life in San Francisco, 1850–1900* (New York, 1994), 219–28.

68. "An Act to provide for the registration of the citizens of this State, and for the enrollment in the several election districts of all the legal voters thereof, and for the prevention and punishment of frauds affecting the elective franchise," *The Statutes of California, Passed at the Sixteenth Session of the Legislature, 1865–66* (Sacramento, 1866), chap. 265, 288–301; Ethington, *Public City*, 220–28.

69. Ethington, *Public City*, 227–28; *The Political Code of the State of California* (Sacramento, 1872), 169–78.

70. William Issell and Robert W. Cherny, *San Francisco, 1865–1932: Politics, Power and Urban Development* (Berkeley, CA, 1986), 127; H. Brett Melendy and Benjamin F. Gilbert, *The Governors of California: Peter H. Burnett to Edmund G. Brown* (Georgetown, CA, 1965), 229; *The Journal of the Assembly during the Twenty-second Session of the Legislature of the State of California, 1877–78* (Sacramento, 1878), 192, 465, 616, 871; "An Act to regulate the registration of voters, and to secure the purity of elections in the city and county of San Francisco," F. P. Deering, *The Codes and Statutes of California, As Amended and in Force at the close of the Twenty-Sixth Session of the Legislature, 1885*, vol. 1 (San Francisco, 1886), 225–28.

71. James M. Kerr, ed., *The Codes of California, As Amended and in Force at the Close of the Thirty-Sixth Session of the Legislature, 1905*, vol. 1 (San Francisco, 1908), sec. 1097, 239, sec. 1094, 233–39; James H. Deering, *The Political Code of the State of California, Adopted March 12, 1872, with Amendments Up to and Including those of the Forty-first Session of the Legislature, 1915* (San Francisco, 1916), sec. 1094, 1097, 1098, subdivision 2a, 1104, 237–45.

72. Harris, *Registration*, 5, 16–17, 255; *New York Times*, 13 October 1908. For examples of New York's frequently changing and detailed registration laws see John W. Edmonds, ed., *Statutes at Large of the State*

of New York: Containing the General Statutes Passed in the Years 1863, 1864, 1865, and 1866 (Albany, 1868), 88th sess. (1865), chap. 740 at 584–91, 89th sess. (1866), chap. 812 at 848–52; A. G. Conant, ed., *Statutes at Large, 1875–1880* (Albany, 1882), 103d sess. (1880), chap. 142 at 928, 103d sess. (1880), chaps. 465, 508 at 1026, 1038; J. C. Thomson, ed., *Statutes at Large 1881–88* (Albany, 1890), 104th sess. (1881), chap. 18 at 4, 109th sess. (1886), chap. 649 at 1007; Clarence F. Birdseye, ed., *The Revised Statutes, Codes and General Laws of the State of New York*, vol. 1 (New York, 1896), 991–98, 1009–12, 1023. See also Howard A. Scarrow, *Parties, Elections, and Representation in the State of New York* (New York, 1983), 81–83. For examples of registration laws in Massachusetts see Massachusetts, *Gen. Laws* (1874), chap. 376; (1877), chaps. 206–8. The conclusions and observations offered here are based not only on the sources cited but on a systematic examination of the registration laws in twenty-two states. By the mid-1920s, nearly all states had registration systems.

73. Holli, *Reform in Detroit*, 191–93; McSeveney, *Politics of Depression*, 67–69; the Pennsylvania registration law (Public Law 49) was passed 17 February 1906, and was followed by Public Law 395 (1907). Bureau for Research in Municipal Government, *Report of the Commission to Revise and Codify the Election Laws of Pennsylvania* (n.p., 1911), Appendix G. On New York see Alexander C. Flick, ed., *History of the State of New York*, vol. 7 (New York, 1935), 203, 206–8, 220; Richard L. McCormick, *From Realignment to Reform: Political Change in New York State 1893–1910* (Ithaca, NY, 1981), 48–54, 106–9, 114–18, 125–27, 243–63; Scarrow, *Parties*, 82–83. For the complex and contested evolution of registration laws in Pennsylvania see Harris, *Registration*, 63–68, 78–81, 363; Philip S. Klein and Ari Hoogenboom, *A History of Pennsylvania* (University Park, 1980), 357–61, 419; Paul B. Beers, *Pennsylvania Politics Today and Yesterday: The Tolerable Accommodation* (University Park, 1980), 28–29, 63; Woodruff, "Election Methods," 181–204; "The Ills of Pennsylvania," *Atlantic Monthly* 88 (1901): 558–66; Bonnie R. Fox, "The Philadelphia Progressives: A Test of the Hofstadter-Hays Theses," *Pennsylvania History* 34 (October 1967): 372–94; *Digest of the Election Laws of Pennsylvania (As Compiled for Smull's Legislative Handbook)* (Harrisburg, 1916).

74. Steven P. Erie, *Rainbow's End: Irish-Americans and the Dilemmas of Urban Machine Politics, 1840–1985* (Berkeley, CA, 1988), 93–97, 249–50; Richard M. Abrams, *Conservatism in a Progressive Era: Massachusetts Politics, 1900–1912* (Cambridge, MA, 1964), 50–51; for an example of the machine adapting to new registration rules see *New York Times*, 4 October 1908.

75. *Daggett v. Hudson*, 3 N.E. 538 (Ohio 1885); *The People ex rel. Smith v. District Court of the Third Judicial District*, 78 P. 679 (Colo. 1904); *People ex rel. Grinnell v. Hoffman*, 8 N.E. 788 (Ill. 1886); *People ex rel. Frost v. Wilson*, 62 N.Y. 186 (N.Y. 1875); *Kineen v. Wells*, 11 N.E. 916 (Mass. 1887); Harris, *Registration*, 305–13. Primary elections—to provide for the direct and ostensibly more democratic selection of candidates—were becoming common throughout the nation during this period. Although it could be claimed that primary elections were purely party affairs and thus that the parties themselves could regulate the right to vote in primaries, both the courts and legislatures increasingly insisted that suffrage rules in primaries be identical to those in general elections. In states where party competition existed, of course, restrictive primary election rules could damage a party's chance to win general elections—which is why primaries did not become a means of restricting the franchise in the North. For an example of laws on primaries see *General Laws, and Joint Resolutions, Memorials and Private Acts, Passed at the Fourth Session of the Legislative Assembly of the Territory of Colorado* (Denver, 1865), 187–88; and *Laws Passed at the Extraordinary Session of the Seventeenth General Assembly of the State of Colorado* (Denver, 1910), chap. 4, sec. 11, 24. For court cases on primary elections see *People v. Board of Election Commissioners of Chicago*, 77 N.E. 321 (Ill. 1906); *People ex rel. Phillips v. Strassheim*, 88 N.E. 821 (Ill. 1909); *Schostag v. Cator*, 91 P. 502 (Cal.1907). See also chapter 7.

76. Harris, *Registration*, 21, 106, 263–64, 302–3, 334–49; Kousser, *Shaping of Southern Politics*, 47–48; Paul Kleppner, *Who Voted: The Dynamics of Electoral Turnout, 1870–1980* (New York, 1982), 60–62; McDonald, *Parameters*, 120; Reynolds, *Testing Democracy*, 145–55. For quite some time, political scientists (including Walter Dean Burnham, Philip Converse, Steven Rosenstone, Raymond Wolfinger, Paul Kleppner, Richard Carlson, Frances Fox Piven, and Richard Cloward) have engaged in a productive scholarly debate regarding the importance of registration in reducing turnout, both historically and in recent years. One summary of this debate is presented in Frances F. Piven and Richard Cloward, *Why Americans Don't Vote* (New York, 1988), 89–109. My own attempt to assess the quantitative issues will appear in a subsequent volume.

77. Registration Commission of Pittsburgh, Minute Books, vol. 1, Report dated 28 February 1907, Archives of Industrial Society, University of Pittsburgh; Reynolds, *Testing Democracy*, 158.

78. For an example of the traditional historical perspective see Abrams, *Conservatism*, 53. For interpretations closer to those presented herein see Samuel P. Hays, "The Politics of Reform in Municipal Government in the Progressive Era," *Pacific Northwest Quarterly* 55 (October 1964): 157–69; and Reynolds, *Testing Democracy*, 122.

79. An excellent examination of the literature on fraud is presented in Argersinger, "New Perspectives on Election Fraud," 669–87; see also Paul Kleppner, *Continuity and Change in Electoral Politics, 1893–1928* (New York, 1987), 168–71; Jaher, *Urban Establishment*, 504–5.

80. Argersinger, "New Perspectives on Election Fraud," 669–86; Genevieve B. Gist, "Progressive Reform in a Rural Community: The Adams County Vote-Fraud Case," *Mississippi Valley Historical Review* 48 (June 1961): 60–78; "Bribery as a Local Custom," *Outlook* 97 (14 January 1911): 42–44.

81. *Neelley v. Farr*, 158 P. 458 (Colo. 1916).

82. Kleppner, *Continuity and Change*, 169–70.

83. "The Disenfranchisement of Ex-Felons: A Cruelly Excessive Punishment," *Southwestern University Law Review* 7 (1975): 124–25; Andrew L. Shapiro, "Challenging Criminal Disenfranchisement Under the Voting Rights Act: A New Strategy," *Yale Law Journal* 103 (October 1993): 537–42.

84. Discussions of the disfranchisement of those convicted of electoral fraud can be found in the constitutional conventions (cited earlier) in Maryland, 1867; New York, 1872 and 1894; Pennsylvania, 1872–73; Texas, 1875; Delaware, 1896; Massachusetts, 1917; Illinois, 1920. Discussions of the disfranchisement (and pardoning) of felons can be found in *Debates Maryland 1867*, 230–31; *Debates Pennsylvania 1872–73*, vol. 1, 133; *Debates Missouri 1875*, vol. 4, 141–51; *Debates Texas 1875*, 259–62; *Debates Ohio 1873*, vol. 2, 1952–57. See also "The Equal Protection Clause as a Limitation on the States' Power to Disfranchise Those Convicted of a Crime," *Rutgers Law Review* 21 (1967): 298–300; *Davis v. Beason*, 133 U.S. 333 (1890).

85. "Equal Protection Clause," 300–301, 310–13; *Washington v. State*, 75 Ala. 582, 51 Am. Rep. 479 (Ala. 1884); "The Need for Reform of Ex-Felon Disfranchisement Laws," *Yale Law Journal* 83 (1974): 584–87; "Restoring the Ex-Offender's Right to Vote: Background and Developments," *American Criminal Law Review* 11 (1973): 721–31; "The Disenfranchisement of Ex-Felons: Citizenship, Criminality, and the Purity of the Ballot Box," *Harvard Law Review* 102 (1989): 1302–17; Shapiro, "Challenging Criminal Disenfranchisement," 560–63.

86. "Ex-Felon Disenfranchisement Laws," 581, 586–88; *Davis v. Beason*, 133 U.S. 333 (1890); "Disenfranchisement of Ex-Felons," 1304–15; Gavit, *Americans by Choice*, 401; *New York Times*, 2 April 1920.

87. Jeanette Wolfley, "Jim Crow, Indian Style: The Disenfranchisement of Native Americans," *American Indian Law Review* 16 (1991): 167–75; Rogers M. Smith, *Civic Ideals: Conflicting Visions of Citizenship in U.S. History* (New Haven, CT, 1997), 390–96; N. D. Houghton, "The Legal Status of Indian Suffrage in the United States," *California Law Review* 19 (1931): 510–12.

88. Wolfley, "Jim Crow," 175–81; John H. Allen, "Denial of Voting Rights to Reservation Indians," *Utah Law Review* 5 (Fall 1956): 251–52; Gary C. Stein, "The Indian Citizenship Act of 1924," *New Mexico Historical Review* 47 (July 1972): 257–70; Felix Cohen, *Handbook of Federal Indian Law* (Charlottesville, VA, 1982), 639–52. The Dawes Act was invoked by a California court in 1917 to justify its refusal to abide by the *Elk v. Wilkins* decision. *Anderson v. Mathews*, 163 P. 902, 904 (Cal. 1917).

89. Ann Marie Plane and Gregory Button, "The Massachusetts Indian Enfranchisement Act: Ethnic Contest in Historical Context, 1849–1869," *Ethnohistory* 40 (Fall 1993): 587–618.

90. Richard F. Bensel, *Sectionalism and American Political Development: 1880–1980* (Madison, WI, 1984), 78, 83.

91. *Pope v. Williams*, 193 U.S. 621, 632 (1904).

92. *Burr v. Voorhis*, 128 N.E. 220 (N.Y. 1920); *Sanner v. Patton*, 40 N.E. 290 (Ill. 1895); *McCafferty v. Guyer*, 59 Penn. 109 (1868), cited in Brightly, *Collection of Leading Cases*, 44–50.

93. *Lamar v. Dillon*, 14 So. 383, 387 (Fla. 1893). Regarding women, see chap. 6.

94. Howard L. McBain, *The Law and the Practice of Municipal Home Rule* (New York, 1916), 11–16, 101–6, 145, 182–86, 581–83; Gerald E. Frug, "The City as a Legal Concept," *Harvard Law Review* 93

(1980): 1062–63, 1109–17; Austin F. MacDonald, *American City Government and Administration*, 3d ed. (New York, 1941), 63–69, 76–87, 253; Jon C. Teaford, *The Unheralded Triumph: City Government in America, 1870–1900* (Baltimore, 1984), 105–22. The supremacy of the state over municipalities was asserted forcefully in *Hunter v. City of Pittsburgh*, 207 U.S. 161 (1907). In general, it was not considered permissible for legislatures unilaterally to impose distinctive suffrage qualifications on individual cities, although they could choose to impose procedural regulations on "classes" of cities, grouped by population. The Kansas City law—which amounted to a tax-induced requirement to vote—later was declared unconstitutional. One rationale for a distinctive municipal suffrage was that cities were corporate rather than political units; see Andrew White, "The Government of American Cities," *The Forum* 10 (December 1890): 357–72.

95. Thomas M. Cooley, *A Treatise on the Constitutional Limitations which rest upon the legislative power of the states of the American union* (Boston, 1883), 758, cited in *State ex. rel. Lamar v. Dillon*, 14 So. at 387; Bryce, *American Commonwealth*, vol. 2, 146. The notion that a new political "universe" appeared early in the twentieth century originated with Walter Dean Burnham, the foremost student of electoral turnout in the United States. See, among Burnham's many works, "The Appearance and Disappearance of the American Voter," *Electoral Participation: A Comparative Analysis*, ed. Richard Rose (Beverly Hills, CA, 1980), 35–73; idem, "The Changing Shape of the American Political Universe," *American Political Science Review* 59 (March 1965): 7–28; idem, *Critical Elections and the Mainsprings of American Politics* (New York, 1970). Cf. Richard L. McCormick, *The Party Period and Public Policy: American Politics from the Age of Jackson to the Progressive Era* (New York, 1986), 274–79. Cf. also Marie-France Toinet, "La participation politique des ouvriers amèricains à la fin du dix-neuvieme siècle," *In the Shadow of the Statue of Liberty: Immigrant Workers and Citizens in the American Republican, 1880–1920*, ed. Marianne Debouzy (Saint Denis, 1988).

96. H. Gerth and C. Wright Mills, eds., *From Max Weber: Essays in Sociology* (New York, 1946), 194.

97. J. B. McMaster, "Annexation and Universal Suffrage," *The Forum* 26 (December 1898): 393–402; C. Vann Woodward, *The Origins of the New South* (Baton Rouge, 1959), 324–26.

98. On the parallels between North and South cf. Kousser, *Shaping of Southern Politics*, 45–46.

99. Evans, *American Citizenship*, 142–43; "The Crime Against the Suffrage in Washington," *The Nation* 25 (27 June 1878): 414–15.

CHAPTER SIX

1. Eleanor Flexner, *Century of Struggle: The Woman's Rights Movement in the United States*, rev. ed. (Cambridge, MA, 1975), 71–77.

2. Ellen C. DuBois, "Beyond the Compact of the Fathers: Equal Rights, Woman Suffrage, and the United States Constitution, 1820–1876," *Journal of American History* 74 (1987): 841; Mary Jo Buhle and Paul Buhle, eds., *Concise History of Woman Suffrage: Selections from the Classic Work of Stanton, Anthony, Gage, and Harper* (Urbana, IL, 1978), 96; Judith Wellman, "The Seneca Falls Women's Rights Convention: A Study of Social Networks," *Journal of Women's History* 3 (Spring 1991): 9–37; Nancy Isenberg, *Sex and Citizenship in Antebellum America* (Chapel Hill, NC, 1998), 1–5, 29–32.

3. Mary Beth Norton, *Liberty's Daughters: The Revolutionary Experience of American Women, 1750–1800* (Ithaca, NY, 1980), 177–93; Ellen C. DuBois, *Feminism and Suffrage: The Emergence of an Independent Women's Movement in America* (Ithaca, NY, 1978), 44–45; DuBois, "Beyond the Compact," 839; Mildred Adams, *The Right to Be People* (Philadelphia, 1967), 5–7.

4. Norton, *Liberty's Daughters*, 188–93; William Griffith, *Eumenes* (Trenton, NJ, 1799), 33–34; George Ticknor Curtis, *Letters of Phocion* (n.p., n.d., *Daily Advertiser and Courier*, Boston, 1853), 118–19. See chap. 3.

5. Marion T. Wright, "Negro Suffrage in New Jersey, 1776–1875," *Journal of Negro History* 33 (April 1948): 172–75; Harold F. Gosnell, *Democracy, the Threshold of Freedom* (New York, 1948), 51; Arthur C. Cole, ed., *The Constitutional Debates of 1847* (Springfield, IL, 1919), 546; Massachusetts Convention of Delegates, *Journal of Debates and Proceedings in the Convention of Delegates* (Boston, 1821), 250; *Proceedings of the New Jersey State Constitutional Convention of 1844* (Trenton, 1942), 438; Milo M. Quaife, ed., *The Convention of 1846*, Publications of the State Historical Society of Wisconsin, Collections, vol. 27,

Constitutional Series, vol. 2 (Madison, WI, 1919), 214–16, 271; *Report of the Debates and Proceedings of the Convention for the Revision of the Constitution of the State of Indiana, 1850* (Indianapolis, 1850), 517–19; Commonwealth of Massachusetts, *Woman Suffrage in the United States*, Bulletins for the Constitutional Convention, 1917–1918, vol. 2, no. 33 (Boston, 1919), 442.

6. Richard J. Evans, *The Feminists* (London, 1977), 31, 45, 47–48, 56–57; DuBois, "Beyond the Compact," 837–40; idem, *Feminism and Suffrage*, 22, 31–32, 39–40; Flexner, *Century of Struggle*, 64–65, 78; Suzanne M. Marilley, *Woman Suffrage and the Origins of Liberal Feminism in the United States, 1820–1920* (Cambridge, MA, 1996), 16–17, 43; Rosalyn Terborg-Penn, *African American Women in the Struggle for the Vote, 1850–1920* (Bloomington, IN, 1998), 14–17; Wellman, "Seneca Falls," 9–32; David Morgan, *Suffragists and Democrats: The Politics of Woman Suffrage in America* (East Lansing, 1972), 13–14; Aileen S. Kraditor, *Up from the Pedestal: Writing in the History of American Feminism* (Chicago, 1968), 14–15. For a compelling analysis of the diverse fronts on which this rethinking was taking place see Isenberg, *Sex and Citizenship*.

7. James Allen Smith, *The Growth and Decadence of Constitutional Government* (New York, 1930), 41–43; Wellman, "Seneca Falls," 19–21; Isenberg, *Sex and Citizenship*, 15–17.

8. Isenberg, *Sex and Citizenship*, 1–6, 15–21, 32–36.

9. DuBois, *Feminism and Suffrage*, 41–46; idem, "Beyond the Compact," 839, 841; Flexner, *Century of Struggle*, 82–83; Isenberg, *Sex and Citizenship*, 17–18, 37; Morgan, *Suffragists and Democrats*, 15; Carol C. Madsen, ed., *Battle for the Ballot: Essays on Woman Suffrage in Utah, 1870–1896* (Logan, UT, 1997), 2–3; Israel Kugler, *From Ladies to Women: The Organized Struggle for Woman's Rights in the Reconstruction Era* (New York, 1987), 37; Terborg-Penn, *African American Women*, 14–17. In Kansas in 1859, for example, a constitutional convention agreed to hear a petition, signed by 252 residents, asking for equal suffrage for women, but it did not act on the petition. *Kansas Constitutional Convention: A reprint of the Proceedings and Debates of the Convention July 1859* (Topeka, 1920), 58–59, 72–76, 86–87, 99.

10. Elisabeth Griffith, *In Her Own Right: The Life of Elizabeth Cady Stanton* (New York, 1984), 110; Dale Baum, "Woman Suffrage and the 'Chinese Question': The Limits of Radical Republicanism in Massachusetts, 1865–1876," *New England Quarterly* 56 (March 1983): 65; *Official Report of the Proceedings and Debates of the Third Constitutional Convention of Ohio, 1873*, vol. 2 (Cleveland, 1874), 1802, 1978; Manfred Berg, "Soldiers and Citizens: War and Voting Rights in American History," *Reflections on American Exceptionalism*, ed. David K. Adams and Cornelis A. Van Minnen (Staffordshire, England, 1994), 197.

11. DuBois, *Feminism and Suffrage*, 59–61; Griffith, *In Her Own Right*, 123.

12. *Proceedings of the First Anniversary of the American Equal Rights Association* (New York, 1867), 7–8, 57.

13. DuBois, *Feminism and Suffrage*, 59–65, 67, 70, 72, 75, 77–78, 79, 80, 87, 95–99, 105–8; Steven M. Buechler, *The Transformation of the Woman Suffrage Movement: The Case of Illinois, 1850–1920* (New Brunswick, NJ, 1986), 5–7; Flexner, *Century of Struggle*, 145–49; Ellen C. DuBois, ed., *Elizabeth Cady Stanton, Susan B. Anthony: Correspondence, Writings, Speeches* (New York, 1981), 88–92; Kraditor, *Up from the Pedestal*, 255; Elizabeth C. Stanton et al., *The History of Woman Suffrage*, vol. 2 (1881; reprint, Salem, NH, 1985), 214, 307–8 (hereafter *HWS*); Griffith, *In Her Own Right*, 119, 123, 134; Baum, "Woman Suffrage," 64; DuBois, "Beyond the Compact," 845–46.

14. DuBois, *Feminism and Suffrage*, 112–60; Buhle and Buhle, *Concise History of Woman Suffrage*, 20–22; DuBois, *Stanton*, 99, 142–43; Buechler, *Transformation*, 40–41, 90.

15. *HWS*, vol. 3, 275; ibid., vol. 2, 788. Dale Baum points out that some Massachusetts Republicans believed that they would benefit from women's suffrage in the short run because a significant proportion of pro-Democratic immigrant women could not meet the literacy or citizenship requirements to vote; Baum, "Woman Suffrage," 68–69. *Debates and Proceedings of the Constitutional Convention of the State of Illinois 1869*, vol. 2 (Springfield, 1870), 1289; for examples of the ideological debates of the period see also ibid., 157, 451, 479, 736, 856, 1277, 1280, 1289, 1291, 1477, 1502.

16. *HWS*, vol. 2, 641–42; *Ohio Constitutional Convention 1873*, vol. 2, 1872; *The Congressional Globe*, 40th Cong., 3d sess., vol. 1 (29 January 1869), 710; *Debates Illinois 1869*, vol. 1, 212.

17. *Minor v. Happersett*, 88 U.S. 162, 163 (1874).

18. Anne F. Scott and Andrew M. Scott, *One Half the People: The Fight for Woman Suffrage* (Philadelphia, 1975), 81–95; DuBois, "Beyond the Compact," 852–60; Martha G. Stapler, *Woman Suffrage Year*

Book 1917 (New York, 1917), 29; Griffith, *In Her Own Right*, 155–56; Kraditor, *Up from the Pedestal*, 241, 250; *New York Times*, 10 February 1875; Flexner, *Century of Struggle*, 168; Carrie S. Burnham, *Suffrage—The Citizen's Birthright* (Philadelphia, 1873), 3–5, 10–11. For a retrospective analysis of these decisions see Francis Minor, *The Law of Federal Suffrage* (n.p., 1889). Notably, Congress in 1871 also declined to enfranchise women in Washington, D.C.

19. Linda K. Kerber, *No Constitutional Right to Be Ladies: Women and the Obligations of Citizenship* (New York, 1998), 81–112.

20. Cf. DuBois, "Beyond the Compact," 845.

21. Quotes in epigraphs from *New York Times*, 8 March 1869; *Ohio Constitutional Convention 1873*, vol. 2, 1802, 1978; *Debates and Proceedings of the Constitutional Convention of the State of California, 1878*, vol. 1 (Sacramento, 1880), 1004–7, 1365. Ann D. Gordon, "Woman Suffrage (Not Universal Suffrage) by Federal Amendment," *Votes for Women! The Woman Suffrage Movement in Tennessee, the South, and the Nation*, ed. Marjorie Spruill Wheeler (Knoxville, 1995), 5; DuBois, "Beyond the Compact," 845.

22. DuBois, *Feminism and Suffrage*, 19, 189–90; Gordon, "Woman Suffrage," 5–22.

23. Gordon, "Woman Suffrage," 3–24; Buhle and Buhle, *Concise History of Woman Suffrage*, 16–22.

24. Flexner, *Century of Struggle*, 176–78, 228; *New York Times*, 26 January 1887; *HWS*, vol. 4, 111.

25. Gordon, "Woman Suffrage," 13–14; Charles Kettleborough, *Constitution Making in Indiana: A Source Book of Constitutional Documents with Historical Introduction and Critical Notes*, vol. 1 (Indianapolis, 1916), cxxiii–cxxiv; Kugler, *From Ladies to Women*, 121, 131, 136, 143–47; Flexner, *Century of Struggle*, 178, 228.

26. Gordon, "Woman Suffrage," 13–14; the detailed story of school suffrage in Michigan, including the attainment of municipal suffrage for women followed by a court decision ruling the law unconstitutional, is recounted in Mary Jo Adams, "The History of Suffrage in Michigan," *Publications of the Michigan Political Science Association* 3 (March 1898): 33–35; Commonwealth of Massachusetts, *Woman Suffrage*, vol. 2, 442–43. For the text of a law see *All the Laws of the State of Illinois Passed by the Thirty-Seventh General Assembly* (Chicago, 1891), 102; and Massachusetts, *Gen. Laws* (1881), chap. 6, sec. 3. For examples of court cases dealing with school suffrage laws see *People ex rel. Ahrens v. English*, 29 N.E. 678 (Ill. 1892); *People ex rel. Tilden v. Welsh*, 70 Ill. App. 641 (Ill. App. 2 Dist. 1896); *In re Inspectors of Election*, 25 N.Y. S. 1063 (Sup. Ct. Suffolk County 1893); *People ex rel Dillon v. Moir*, 115 N.Y.S. 1029 (Sup. Ct. Onandaga County 1908); *Gould v. Village of Seneca Falls*, 118 N.Y.S. 648 (Sup. Ct. Seneca County 1909); *Village of Waverly v. Waverly Waterworks*, 125 N.Y.S. 339 (Sup. Ct. Tioga County 1910); *State ex rel. Taylor v. French*, 117 N.E. 173 (Ohio 1917).

27. Kerber, *No Constitutional Right*, 109, 117–18; Charles A. Beard, *American City Government: A Survey of Newer Tendencies* (New York, 1912), 85; Howard McBain, *The Law and the Practice of Municipal Home Rule* (New York, 1916), 581–83; Adams, *Right to Be People*, 71; *Report of the Committee of the Senate Upon the Relations Between Capital and Labor*, vol. 3 (Washington, DC, 1885), 635–67.

28. The data presented in tables A.17 and A.18 are not altogether comprehensive. No history of any form of partial suffrage has yet been written; the existing secondary compilations of laws are inconsistent, and legal histories in many states are difficult to pin down, because court decisions, legislatures, and city councils frequently changed the laws.

29. Kettleborough, *Constitution Making in Indiana*, vol. 1, cxxiii; Janet Cornelius, *Constitution Making in Illinois 1818–1970* (Urbana, IL, 1972), 70–71; *Debates Illinois 1869*, vol. 1, 129, 156, 212, 451, 472, 487, 510, 532, 560, 613, 679; ibid., vol. 2, 1077, 1277, 1392, 1397–99, 1477, 1502, 1528, 1551, 1725–30, 1840–44; *Debates and Proceedings of the Pennsylvania Constitutional Convention, 1872–73*, vol. 1 (Harrisburg, 1873), 133, 184, 192, 348, 471, 503, 525–65, 589, 601–26, 658, 693; ibid., vol. 2, 69, 148–50, 165; Barbara Allen Babcock, "Clara Shortridge Foltz: Constitution-Maker," *Indiana Law Journal* 66 (1991): 852, 880–90. See also *Debates of the Missouri Constitutional Convention of 1875*, vol. 4 (Columbia, MO, 1944), 122–35; Flexner, *Century of Struggle*, 167; James J. Kenneally, "Woman Suffrage and the Massachusetts 'Referendum' of 1895," *The Historian* 30 (August 1968): 619; for the complex sequence of debates in Texas see A. Elizabeth Taylor, ed., *Citizens at Last: The Woman Suffrage Movement in Texas* (Austin, 1987). For a substantial (but by its own acknowledgment, not comprehensive) listing of the bills introduced into state legislatures see Stapler, *Year Book 1917*.

30. *Ohio Constitutional Convention 1873*, vol. 2, 1817–20, 1969, 1979; *California Constitutional Convention 1878*, vol. 1, 832–34, 1004, 1009; *Debates Pennsylvania 1872–73*, vol. 1, 557–59, 571–78; A. D.

Harlan, *Pennsylvania Constitutional Convention 1872 and 1873: Its Members and the Result of Their Labors* (Philadelphia, 1873), 42; *HWS*, vol. 3, 697.

31. *Ohio Constitutional Convention 1873*, vol. 2, 1828, 1843, 1874–75; see also ibid., 1010, 1819, 1821, 1870; ibid., vol. 2, 1, 1969; *California Constitutional Convention 1878*, vol. 1, 1005, 1366; Harlan, *Pennsylvania Constitutional Convention 1872 and 1873*, vol. 1, 550–63; *HWS*, vol. 2, 562; ibid., vol. 3, 105; DuBois, "Beyond the Compact," 848–52; Buhle and Buhle, *Concise History of Woman Suffrage*, 253.

32. *Journal of the Constitutional Convention of the State of Texas, 1875* (Galveston, 1875), 191–92.

33. DuBois, "Beyond the Compact," 861; Griffith, *In Her Own Right*, 205.

34. *Debates Pennsylvania 1872–73*, vol. 1, 553; Harlan, *Pennsylvania Constitutional Convention 1872 and 1873*, 40; *Ohio Constitutional Convention 1873*, vol. 2, 1862, 1866–75; *California Constitutional Convention 1878*, vol. 1, 832, 1004–14, 1366, 1370.

35. *Ohio Constitutional Convention 1873*, vol. 2, 1802, 1841; *California Constitutional Convention 1878*, vol. 1, 833, 1004–5, 1007, 1010, 1365; *Debates Pennsylvania 1872–73*, vol. 1, 608–10; *HWS*, vol. 3, 52–53, 209; DuBois, "Beyond the Compact," 849–50; Buhle and Buhle, *Concise History of Woman Suffrage*, 319, 337.

36. Charles Francis Adams, "The Protection of the Ballot in National Elections," *Journal of Social Science* 1 (June 1869): 106; *Ohio Constitutional Convention 1873*, vol. 2, 1802, 1830–38, 1960–61, 1967–68, 1978; *California Constitutional Convention 1878*, vol. 1, 1004–7, 1012, 1365; *HWS*, vol. 3, 202, 214–15; cf. *New York Times*, 26 February 1909.

37. *California Constitutional Convention 1878*, vol. 1, 1367; see also ibid., 1012; *Debates Pennsylvania 1872–73*, 540–44; *Ohio Constitutional Convention 1873*, vol. 2, 1831, 1833, 1838, 1863, 1962–65; *Debates and Proceedings of the Constitutional Convention of the State of Delaware Commencing December 1, 1896*, vol. 1 (Milford, 1958), 1006.

38. *Ohio Constitutional Convention 1873*, vol. 2, 1825, 1949; see also ibid., 1824–26, 1841, 1868; *California Constitutional Convention 1878*, vol. 1, 1004–5, 1011–15; *Debates Pennsylvania 1872–73*, vol. 1, 542, 550–52, 557–63, 566–69.

39. Susan E. Marshall, *Splintered Sisterhood: Gender and Class in the Campaign Against Woman Suffrage* (Madison, WI, 1997), 4–12, 19–23, 55–56, 91, 139, 180, 220–21; Kraditor, *Up from the Pedestal*, 15; Buechler, *Transformation*, 115–17, 141, 143; Evans, *Feminists*, 23–29, 44, 90–91.

40. Flexner, *Century of Struggle*, 311–12; Marshall, *Splintered Sisterhood*, 55–56, 91, 180, 221; *HWS*, vol. 4, 21.

41. Elna C. Green, *Southern Strategies: Southern Women and the Woman Suffrage Question* (Chapel Hill, NC, 1997), xiii–xv, 6–8, 10–14, 23–32, 52, 80–98; *HWS*, vol. 4, 98.

42. Gosnell, *Democracy*, 52; Flexner, *Century of Struggle*, 166, 181; Evans, *Feminists*, 27; Beverly Beeton, *Women Vote in the West: The Woman Suffrage Movement 1869–96* (New York, 1986), 1–7, 15–19, 31–48, 111–13, 127–30; Madsen, *Battle for the Ballot*, vii–ix, 6–25; Richard White, *"It's Your Misfortune and None of My Own": A New History of the American West* (Norman, OK, 1991), 353–87; Alan P. Grimes, *The Puritan Ethic and Woman Suffrage* (New York, 1967); *HWS*, vol. 4, 509–18; Marilley, *Woman Suffrage*, 124–58; Jean B. White, "Woman's Place Is in the Constitution: The Struggle for Equal Rights in Utah in 1895," *History of Women in the United States: Historical Articles on Women's Lives and Activities*, vol. 19, part 1, ed. Nancy Cott (Munich, 1992), 69–94 (hereafter cited as *HWUS*).

43. Buechler, *Transformation*, 8; *HWS*, vol. 4, 509–18, 994–98. That political battles over suffrage often were closely fought in the East during this period is made clear by the listing of legislative actions in Stapler, *Year Book 1917*, 27–42: in Michigan, for example, both houses of the legislature approved a women's suffrage amendment as early as 1870, but it was vetoed by the governor (p. 33); in Rhode Island, a suffrage amendment was passed by both houses in 1885, but failed through a technicality; and in 1897, a constitution that included women's suffrage was drafted but rejected on other grounds.

44. Epigraphs from *Debates Delaware 1896*, vol. 1, 436; *HWS*, vol. 5, 270; *New York Times*, 28 April 1910. *New York Times*, 7 October 1893. For an example of a later editorial against suffrage see *New York Times*, 6 December 1908.

45. Sara H. Graham, *Woman Suffrage and the New Democracy* (New Haven, CT, 1996), 6–7, 37–52; Buhle and Buhle, *Concise History of Woman Suffrage*, 32–33.

46. Philip N. Cohen, "Nationalism and Suffrage: Gender Struggle in Nation-Building America," *Signs* 21 (Spring 1996): 712–16; Ellen C. DuBois, "Working Women, Class Relations and Suffrage

Militance: Harriot Stanton Blatch and the New York Woman Suffrage Movement, 1894–1909," *Journal of American History* 74 (June 1987): 37.

47. For early examples see *HWS*, vol. 2, 779–80; ibid., vol. 3, 293–94, 804.

48. Marilley, *Woman Suffrage*, 164–67; *HWS*, vol. 4, 148; Kraditor, *Up from the Pedestal*, 257–61.

49. Green, *Southern Strategies*, 8–18, 85–97; Marilley, *Woman Suffrage*, 167–78; Gordon, "Woman Suffrage," 15–16; on the role of African-American women see Terborg-Penn, *African American Women*; Graham, *Woman Suffrage*, 22–23; Eileen L. McDonagh, "The Significance of the Nineteenth Amendment: A New Look at Civil Rights, Social Welfare and Woman Suffrage Alignments in the Progressive Era," *Women, Politics, and the Constitution*, ed. Naomi Lynn (New York, 1990), 64; Kraditor, *Up from the Pedestal*, 253, 263.

50. Buechler, *Transformation*, 43, 99, 117; *HWS*, vol. 4, 317; ibid., vol. 5, 32, 329–30; Griffith, *In Her Own Right*, 129, 155, 205–6; *New York Times*, 6 February 1898; McDonagh, "Significance of the Nineteenth Amendment," 63–64; Kraditor, *Up from the Pedestal*, 260; DuBois, "Working Women," 34–58.

51. DuBois, "Working Women," 37–40; Griffith, *In Her Own Right*, 194; Buechler, *Transformation*, 121, 137–42; Marilley, *Woman Suffrage*, 9–10, 13–14, 159–86.

52. Flexner, *Century of Struggle*, 230, 256, 271; Commonwealth of Massachusetts, *Woman Suffrage*, vol. 2, 457–58; Sharon H. Strom, "Leadership and Tactics in the American Woman Suffrage Movement: A New Perspective from Massachusetts," *Journal of American History* 62 (September 1975): 299–300; James J. Kenneally, "Woman Suffrage and the Massachusetts 'Referendum' of 1895," *HWUS*, vol. 19, pt. 1, 52–68. On municipal suffrage between 1890 and 1920 see Arthur Holcombe, *State Government in the United States* (New York, 1926), 89; Maureen A. Flanagan, *Charter Reform in Chicago* (Carbondale, IL, 1987), 83–86; *People ex rel. Ahrens v. English*, 29 N.E. 678 (Ill. 1892); *People ex rel. Tilden v. Welsh*, 70 Ill. App. 641 (Ill. App. 2 Dist. 1896); *Scown v. Czarnecki*, 106 N.E. 276 (Ill. 1914); *People ex rel. Jurgensen v. Czarnecki*, 107 N.E. 184 (Ill. 1914); *Franklin v. Westfall*, 112 N.E. 974 (Ill. 1916); *State ex rel. Taylor v. French*, 117 N.E. 173 (Ohio, 1917). For a listing of legislative proposals on full and partial suffrage, their disposition by state legislatures, as well as gubernatorial vetoes and court actions see Stapler, *Year Book 1917*, 27–42.

53. *Debates Delaware 1896*, vol. 1, 1002, 1025; for other examples of constitutional debates see Joseph H. Brewer, Charles H. Bender, and Charles H. McCurren, eds., *Proceedings and Debates of the Constitutional Convention of the State of Michigan, Convened in the City of Lansing, Tuesday, October 22, 1907*, vol. 2 (Lansing, 1907), 966, 1021, 1068–79; for more positive views see ibid., vol. 1, 418–21; Ronald Schaffer, "The Problem of Consciousness in the Woman Suffrage Movement: A California Perspective," *HWUS*, vol. 19, pt. 2, 368; regarding the Pope and suffrage see *New York Times*, 22 April and 23 April 1909.

54. DuBois, "Working Women," 39; *HWS*, vol. 5, 6; *Debates Delaware 1896*, 427; Kraditor, *Up from the Pedestal*, 198; Kenneally, "Woman Suffrage," 63–64; Graham, *Woman Suffrage*, 11–21; Adams, "Suffrage in Michigan," 48; William H. Steele, *Revised Record of the Constitutional Convention of the State of New York, May 8, 1894–September 29, 1894*, vol. 2 (Albany, 1900), 433–36.

55. Nancy F. Cott, *The Grounding of Modern Feminism* (New Haven, CT, 1987), 26–29, 32–33, 53; DuBois, "Working Women," 47–48; Graham, *Woman Suffrage*, 33–37; Strom, "Leadership," 399.

56. Marilley, *Woman Suffrage*, 192–94.

57. DuBois, "Working Women," 34–36, 44–45; *New York Times*, 11 January 1909; *HWS*, vol. 4, 311–13; Marilley, *Woman Suffrage*, 195, 200–201, 205, 208–9; Flexner, *Century of Struggle*, 197, 225–26, 255; Susan Englander, *Class Coalition and Class Conflict in the California Woman Suffrage Movement, 1907–1912* (San Francisco, 1992), 119; Buhle and Buhle, *Concise History of Woman Suffrage*, 367–68; cf. DuBois, *Stanton*, 98–99, 142; *HWS*, vol. 4, 71.

58. Cott, *Grounding of Modern Feminism*, 24, 29–31, 33, 55; Nancy S. Dye, *As Equals and Sisters: Feminism, the Labor Movement, and the Women's Trade Union League of New York* (Columbia, 1980), 8, 18, 125–27; for examples of arguments regarding social reform and women as workers see E. S. Nichols, ed., *Proceedings and Debates of the Constitutional Convention of the State of Ohio, 1912*, vol. 1 (Columbus, 1912), 603, 614, 618, 620.

59. Cott, *Grounding of Modern Feminism*, 22–24, 30–31; Dye, *As Equals and Sisters*, 3–4, 13, 122–25, 132–35, 139–40; Flexner, *Century of Struggle*, 248; DuBois, "Working Women," 46–48; Buechler, *Trans-*

formation, 157–58; Buhle and Buhle, *Concise History of Woman Suffrage*, 374–79; Paula Giddings, *When and Where I Enter: The Impact of Black Women on Race and Sex in America* (New York, 1984), 129.

60. Strom, "Leadership," 303; Mari Jo Buhle, *Women and American Socialism, 1870–1920* (Urbana, IL, 1981), 205, 216–35; Kraditor, *Up from the Pedestal*, 19; *New York Times*, 5 July 1908; ibid., 1 March 1909, 15 September 1915; see also ibid., 2 February, 10 February, 11 February, 21 February, and 25 February 1909; and ibid., 28 February and 24 April 1910; Juliet S. Poyntz, "Revolution and Suffrage," *Justice* 1 (29 March 1919): 6. Regarding Socialists and the Industrial Workers of the World and their ambivalent relation to the movement see Meredith Tax, *The Rising of the Women: Feminist Solidarity and Class Conflict, 1880–1917* (New York, 1980), 179–83; DuBois, "Working Women," 57; Dye, *As Equals and Sisters*, 135.

61. Englander, *Class Coalition*, 2, 6–7, 95–97, 110, 115, 119, 122, 128, 131, 136–41; Buhle, *Women and American Socialism*, 230; Wilda M. Smith, "A Half Century of Struggle: Gaining Woman Suffrage in Kansas," *HWUS*, vol. 19, pt. 1, 135–41; T. A. Larson, "The Woman Suffrage Movement in Washington," *HWUS*, vol. 19, pt. 1, 319–49; Ronald Schaffer, "The Montana Woman Suffrage Campaign, 1911–14," *HWUS*, vol. 19, pt. 1, 352–66; Ronald Schaffer, "California Perspective," 368–90; Marilley, *Woman Suffrage*, 206–7, 210; Graham, *Woman Suffrage*, 27; Stapler, *Year Book 1917*, 28.

62. *New York Times*, 9 January, 16 January, 30 January 1910; ibid., 14 April 1910, 7 February 1915; *HWS*, vol. 5, 270; J. Stanley Lemons, *The Woman Citizen: Social Feminism in the 1920s* (Urbana, IL, 1973), 3.

63. Joseph F. Mahoney, "Woman Suffrage and the Urban Masses," *HWUS*, vol. 19, pt. 2, 417–29; John D. Buenker, "The Urban Political Machine and Woman Suffrage: A Study in Political Adaptability," *HWUS*, vol. 19, pt. 2, 437–41, 449–51; Ronald Schaffer, "The New York City Woman Suffrage Party, 1909–1919," *HWUS*, vol. 19, pt. 2, 460–66; Doris Daniels, "Building a Winning Coalition: The Suffrage Fight in New York State," *HWUS*, vol. 19, pt. 2, 489–90; Eileen L. McDonagh and H. Douglas Price, "Woman Suffrage in the Progressive Era: Patterns of Opposition and Support in Referenda Voting, 1910–1918," *HWUS*, vol. 19, pt. 2, 576–78; Patricia O'Keefe Easton, "Woman Suffrage in South Dakota: The Final Decade, 1911–1920," *HWUS*, vol. 19, pt. 2, 617–34; Louise L. Stevenson, "Women Anti-Suffragists in the 1915 Massachusetts Campaign," *HWUS*, vol. 19, pt. 2, 647–48; Thomas G. Ryan, "Male Opponents and Supporters of Woman Suffrage: Iowa in 1916," *HWUS*, vol. 19, pt. 2, 655–63; Marilyn Grant, "The 1912 Suffrage Referendum: An Exercise in Political Action," *HWUS*, vol. 19, pt. 1, 291–315; Graham, *Woman Suffrage*, 70–73; Paul B. Beers, *Pennsylvania Politics Today and Yesterday: The Tolerable Accommodation* (University Park, 1980), 65–66; *New York Times*, 4 September and 5 September 1912; Flexner, *Century of Struggle*, 269, 280, 306–7, 310–13; Dye, *As Equals and Sisters*, 136; Buechler, *Transformation*, 15. Manuela Thurner points out that many antisuffrage women argued (and likely believed) that women would be more effective advocates of social and political causes without the vote; it seems unlikely, however, that this line of thinking greatly influenced the votes of men who voted against enfranchisement. See Manuela Thurner, "'Better Citizens Without the Ballot': American Antisuffrage Women and Their Rationale During the Progressive Era," *Journal of Women's History* 5 (Spring 1993): 33–60.

64. E. S. Nichols, ed., *Proceedings and Debates of the Constitutional Convention of the State of Ohio, 1913*, vol. 2 (Columbus, 1913), 600–39, 1853–57; quotations from ibid., 604–7, 629, 632–35; cf. Stevenson, "Women Anti-Suffragists," 638–51; and Graham, *Woman Suffrage*, 11–21. On the outcome in Ohio see C. L. Martzloff, "Ohio: Changes in the Constitution," *American Political Science Review* 6 (November 1912): 573–76; Robert E. Cushman, "Voting Organic Laws," *Political Science Quarterly* 28 (June 1913): 207–29; Frank G. Bates, "Constitutional Amendments and Referred Acts, November Election, 1914," *American Political Science Review* 9 (February 1915): 101–7. The examples in Ohio of delegates stating that they opposed suffrage but supported a referendum suggests that the string of referendum defeats between 1912 and 1915 may in fact have been a sign of the movement's growing strength.

65. Green, *Southern Strategies*, xii–xiv, 8, 12–26, 42–44, 157–64; regarding black antisuffragism see ibid., 98–100; on black women and suffrage in general see Ann D. Gordon, ed., *African-American Women and the Vote, 1837–1965* (Amherst, 1997).

66. Green, *Southern Strategies*, 33–55, 80–98; Morgan, *Suffragists and Democrats*, 96.

67. Green, *Southern Strategies*, xiv, 31–32, 36–55, 80–98; Giddings, *When and Where I Enter*, 122–25; Morgan, *Suffragists and Democrats*, 96.

68. Green, *Southern Strategies*, 164; Kenneth R. Johnson, "Kate Gordon and the Woman-Suffrage Movement in the South," *HWUS*, vol. 19, pt. 1, 226–52; B. H. Gilley, "Kate Gordon and Louisiana Woman Suffrage," *HWUS*, vol. 19, pt. 1, 254–71; Stapler, *Year Book 1917*, 27, 29.

69. Green, *Southern Strategies*, 27–29, 39, 167–75; Johnson, "Kate Gordon," 226–51; Morgan, *Suffragists and Democrats*, 141, 146.

70. Epigraph quote cited in *HWS*, vol. 5, 579. Steven M. Buechler, *Women's Movements in the United States: Woman Suffrage, Equal Rights, and Beyond* (New Brunswick, NJ, 1990), 56; Flexner, *Century of Struggle*, 271, 278; Johnson, "Kate Gordon," 227.

71. Buechler, *Women's Movements*, 57–59; Graham, *Woman Suffrage*, 81–98, 150–51.

72. Paul Kleppner, *Continuity and Change in Electoral Politics, 1893–1928* (New York, 1987), 174–75; Buhle and Buhle, *Concise History of Woman Suffrage*, 28–29; Michael L. Goldberg, "Non-partisan and All-partisan: Rethinking Woman Suffrage and Party Politics in Gilded Age Kansas," *Western Historical Quarterly* 25 (Spring 1994): 21–44; Kenneally, "Woman Suffrage," 618–19; *Debates Delaware 1896*, vol. 1, 1041.

73. Graham, *Woman Suffrage*, 84–85; Lemons, *Woman Citizen*, 12.

74. Buechler, *Transformation*, 18; Buechler, *Women's Movements*, 58–61; Flexner, *Century of Struggle*, 292–97.

75. Robert F. Wesser, *A Response to Progressivism: The Democratic Party and New York Politics, 1902–1918* (New York, 1986), 202–3; Dye, *As Equals and Sisters*, 138; Daniels, "Building a Winning Coalition," 472–94; Elinor Lerner examines the remarkable breadth of the Jewish prosuffrage vote in "Jewish Involvement in the New York City Woman Suffrage Movement," *HWUS*, vol. 19, pt. 2, 495–514; as Eileen McDonagh and Douglas Price have pointed out, however, the shift in New York's vote cannot be attributed entirely to Tammany's altered position: in the boroughs outside of Manhattan, where Tammany had less influence, the vote also became more positive between 1915 and 1917. Such data suggest that the immigrant vote itself was changing and that Tammany and other machines were responding to the changing views of their constituents. McDonagh and Price, "Woman Suffrage in the Progressive Era," 575*n*.

76. Carole Nichols, "Votes and More for Women: Suffrage and After in Connecticut," *HWUS*, vol. 18, pt. 2, 428–34; Marilley, *Woman Suffrage*, 199; Buenker, "Urban Political Machine," 441–52; *Debates in the Massachusetts Constitutional Convention, 1917–1918*, vol. 3 (Boston, 1920), 84–86; Cott, *Grounding of Modern Feminism*, 64–65; Marc Karson, *American Labor Unions and Politics* (Carbondale, IL, 1958), 57–58; *American Federationist* 26 (May 1919): 391–92. Mahoney, in "Woman Suffrage and the Urban Masses," 428–36, argues that even in New Jersey in 1915, when the machines staunchly opposed a suffrage amendment, immigrants in working-class wards were no more likely than natives to vote against the enfranchisement of women, suggesting that the "urban masses" were a bit ahead of the political machines in embracing the cause.

77. Graham, *Woman Suffrage*, 99–110; Lemons, *Woman Citizen*, 4–5, 10–12; Cott, *Grounding of Modern Feminism*, 61; Morgan, *Suffragists and Democrats*, 117. Historians are not in agreement about the overall impact of the war, as the sources cited here and elsewhere make clear.

78. Graham, *Woman Suffrage*, 99–127; Walter B. Stevens, *Centennial History of Missouri* (St. Louis, 1921), 508–9; Cohen, "Nationalism and Suffrage," 721–23; Schaffer, "New York City," 467.

79. Flexner, *Century of Struggle*, 303; J. Morgan Kousser, "Suffrage," *The Encyclopedia of American Political History*, vol. 3, ed. Jack P. Greene (New York, 1984), 1246–47.

80. Flexner, *Century of Struggle*, 321–22.

81. The potential political cost of opposition was heightened further by the 1919 decisions of an additional eight states to permit women to vote in presidential elections.

82. Kousser, "Suffrage," 1246–47; Eileen L. McDonagh, "The Significance of the Nineteenth Amendment: A New Look at Civil Rights, Social Welfare, and Woman Suffrage Alignments in the Progressive Era," *Women and Politics* 10 (June 1990): 59–94; idem, "Issues and Constituencies in the Progressive Era: House Roll Call Voting on the Nineteenth Amendment, 1913–1919," *Journal of Politics* 51 (February 1989): 119–36; Cohen, "Nationalism and Suffrage," 721–23; James P. Louis, "Sue Shelton White and the Woman Suffrage Movement in Tennessee, 1913–20," *HWUS*, vol. 19, pt. 2, 405–9; Buenker, "Urban Political Machine," 450; Marilley, *Woman Suffrage*, 216; Morgan, *Suffragists and Democrats*, 122–23, 129–32; for an account of a state branch of NAWSA pressuring Republicans see Nichols, "Votes and More for Women," 436–41.

83. Gordon, "Woman Suffrage," 19; Graham, *Woman Suffrage*, 128–46; Cohen, "Nationalism and Suffrage," 723–24.

84. Johnson, "Kate Gordon," 253; Louis, "Sue Shelton White," 411; Giddings, *When and Where*, 159–70; for an examination of the complexities of the response to the Nineteenth Amendment in North Carolina see Glenda E. Gilmore, *Gender and Jim Crow: Women and the Politics of White Supremacy in North Carolina, 1896–1920* (Chapel Hill, NC, 1996), 220–24. Green, *Southern Strategies*, 179–83, argues that success was possible in those four border states for a convergence of reasons: a relatively high rate of industrialization and urbanization, a relatively small black population, and the durability of political dissent and competition.

85. Glenn Firebaugh and Kevin Chen, "Vote Turnout of Nineteenth Amendment Women: The Enduring Effect of Disenfranchisement," *American Journal of Sociology* 100 (January 1995): 972–96; Maureen A. Flanagan, "The Predicament of New Rights: Suffrage and Women's Political Power from a Local Perspective," *Social Politics* 2 (Fall 1995): 305–30; Cott, *Grounding of Modern Feminism*, 102, 319; McDonagh, "Significance of the Nineteenth Amendment," 59–94; *New York Times*, 22 October 1925; ibid., 21 October 1928; Gosnell, *Democracy*, 56ff.

86. The most thorough exploration of this issue is in Kristi Andersen, *After Suffrage: Women in Partisan and Electoral Politics Before the New Deal* (Chicago, 1996); see also idem, "Women and Citizenship in the 1920s," *Women, Politics, and Change*, ed. Louise Tilly and Patricia Gurin (New York, 1990), 177–98. An important case study is presented in Catherine E. Rymph, "Forward and Right: Shaping Republican Women's Activism, 1920–1967" (Ph.D. diss., University of Iowa, 1998).

87. Gilmore, *Gender and Jim Crow*, 217–24; Green, *Southern Strategies*, 175–76; *New York Times*, 20 September 1920.

88. Lemons, *Woman Citizen*, 63; Cott, *Grounding of Modern Feminism*, 63.

89. This matter of timing—the emergence of women's suffrage during the period of contraction—may help to explain why the United States was not among the first nations to grant women the right to vote.

90. Women were enfranchised during World War I in numerous European countries as well. The impact of the war on suffrage victories has been the subject of some controversy. See, e.g., for a comparative perspective, Evans, *Feminists*, 225–26; Charles Seymour and Donald P. Frary, *How the World Votes*, vol. 2 (Springfield, CA, 1918), 170–71; Gosnell, *Democracy*, 24–25.

CHAPTER SEVEN

1. William B. Munro, "Intelligence Tests for Voters," *The Forum* 80 (December 1928): 823–30.

2. Edward A. Purcell, Jr., *The Crisis of Democratic Theory: Scientific Naturalism and the Problem of Value* (Lexington, 1973), 117–28; Munro, "Intelligence Tests," 825.

3. John R. Voorhis, "An Educational Test for the Ballot," *Educational Review* (January 1924): 1–4; Arthur W. Bromage, "Literacy and the Electorate: Expansion and Contraction of the Franchise," *American Political Science Review* 24 (1930): 948, 956; *New York Times*, 21 November 1923, 4 January 1925, 26 January 1928, 28 March and 7 June 1931. See also *New York Times*, 30 May, 21 September, 3 October, and 22 February 1923, 23 October 1924, 24 September and 27 September 1925, 1 October 1926, 1 October and 26 November 1927, 26 July and 20 September 1928, 17 October and 31 October 1930, 25 October 1931, 25 December 1932, 13 January 1935. For dissenting opinions on the desirability of a stringent literacy test, from Max J. Kohler and Governor Al Smith, see *New York Times*, 18 March 1923, and 23 October 1921.

4. State of Oregon, *Election Laws 1930* (Salem, 1929), 9; *Lassiter v. Northampton County Board of Electors*, 360 U.S. 45, 50–54 (1959); Dudley O. McGovney, *The American Suffrage Medley: The Need for a National Uniform Suffrage* (Chicago, 1949), 59–79; *New York Times*, 6 September and 11 September 1934; Harold W. Stanley, *Voter Mobilization and the Politics of Race: The South and Universal Suffrage, 1952–1984* (New York, 1987), 89. Regarding assistance to illiterate voters see, e.g.: Edgar C. Nelson, *Election Laws of the State of Missouri and Federal Naturalization Laws Revised for 1947–48* (Jefferson City, n.d.), 69; *Simmonds v. Eyrich et al.*, 95 N.E. 2d 595 (Ohio Com. Pl. 1950); *State ex rel. Melvin v. Sweeney*, 94 N.E. 2d 785 (Ohio 1950); *The People ex rel. Dreenan v. Williams*, 131 N.E. 270 (Ill. 1921).

5. Dewey W. Grantham, *The Life and Death of the Solid South: A Political History* (Lexington, 1988), 78–79.

6. Frederic D. Ogden, *The Poll Tax in the South* (Birmingham, 1958), 2–29, 175, 178–85; George B. Tindall, *The Emergence of the New South* (Baton Rouge, 1967), 555, 639–41; Harvard Sitkoff, *A New Deal for Blacks: The Emergence of Civil Rights as a National Issue*, vol. 1, *The Depression Decade* (New York, 1978), 99; McGovney, *Suffrage Medley*, 120–21, 154.

7. Ogden, *Poll Tax*, 178–85; T. Harry Williams, *Huey Long* (New York, 1970), 755–56, 774–75; Tindall, *Emergence*, 640–41.

8. Council of State Governments, *Voting in the United States* (Chicago, 1940), 1–27; Oregon, *Election Laws 1930* (Salem, 1929), 10. In a constitutional amendment, California replaced the phrase "no native of China" with the less racial and later less consequential "no alien ineligible to citizenship." Paul Mason, comp., *Constitution of the State of California, Annotated 1933* (Sacramento, 1933), 310–11; Oregon, in 1927, repealed section 6 of its constitution, which had stated that "no negro, Chinaman, or mulatto shall have the right of suffrage." Hal E. Hoss, comp., *State of Oregon, General Laws Enacted by the 35th Regular Session of the Legislative Assembly 1929 and Constitutional Amendments Adopted June 28, 1927* (Salem, 1929), 5. That it was constitutionally legitimate for states to bar aliens from the polls was affirmed in 1952 by the Supreme Court in *Hariasades v. Shaughnessy*, 342 U.S. 580 (1952). Political restrictions were spelled out in chapter 305 of the Naturalization Law of the United States. Richard Boeckel, *Voting and Non-Voting in Elections* (Washington, 1928), 526–30. For examples of lingering financial requirements see Office of the Secretary of State, *New Hampshire Primary and Election Laws 1929* (Concord, 1929), 1–2, and Rhode Island, *Public Laws* (1929), chap. 1356; for a court case dealing with a property issue (whether ownership of a car could qualify one as a taxpayer) see *City of Montrose v. Niles*, 238 P. 2d 875 (Colo. 1951). General statements regarding the laws of this period are based on various sources indicated in the notes herein and on a reading of the statutes and case law of: New York, Illinois, Ohio, Indiana, Connecticut, Oregon, California, Texas, Colorado, Missouri, Pennsylvania, Mississippi, and North Carolina.

9. *Voting in the United States*, 1–4, 7–27; by 1940, all states except Kentucky, Maryland, Mississippi, New Jersey, and Pennsylvania had some general provision for absentee voting. In New Jersey and Maryland, absentee voting was permitted only for those in military service. The details of the absentee voting laws varied substantially from state to state. For a complete listing see Office of War Information, *State Absentee Voting and Registration Laws* (Washington, DC, 1942). For examples of court cases dealing with residency issues see *Miller v. Trinner*, 224 A.D. 411 (App. Div. 1928); *In re Geis*, 293 N.Y.S. 577 (N.Y. Sup. Ct. 1936); *Watermeyer v. Mitchell*, 9 N.E. 2d 783 (N.Y. 1937); *Application of Davy*, 281 A.D. 137 (App. Div. 1952); *Application of People ex rel. Singer*, 137 N.Y.S. 2d 61 (N.Y. Sup. Ct. 1954); *Application of Neal*, 180 N.Y.S. 2d 332 (N.Y. Sup. Ct. 1957); *Application of Hoffman*, 65 N.Y.S. 2d 107 (N.Y. Sup. Ct. 1946); *Kay v. Strobeck*, 254 P. 150 (Colo. 1927); *Ander v. Pifer*, 146 N.E. 171 (Ill. 1924); *Bullman v. Cooper*, 200 N.E. 173 (Ill. 1936); *Tuthill v. Rendelman*, 56 N.E. 2d 375 (Ill. 1944). For examples of laws affecting students, inmates, and absentees see Archibald H. Throckmorton et al., eds., *The General Code of the State of Ohio: Revised to 1921, Containing All Laws of a General Nature in Force January 1, 1921* (Cleveland, 1921), 1254–55, and William E. Baldwin et al., *Throckmorton's Annotated Code of Ohio, 1930* (Cleveland, 1931), 1432, 1459–60, 1938. Regarding residence law in New York see Benjamin Gassman, *Election Law: Decisions and Procedure*, vol. 2, 2d ed. (Albany, 1962), 634–72.

10. *Blue v. State ex rel. Brown*, 188 N.E. 583 (Ind. 1934); *Voting in the United States*, 1–2; *New York Times*, 9 November 1925, 13 October 1928; news clip dated 20 January 1933, in Pittsburgh elections file, Archives of Industrial Society, University of Pittsburgh; *Laws Passed at the Thirty-second Session of the General Assembly of the State of Colorado, January 3, 1939–April 24, 1939* (Denver, 1939), 332; State of New Jersey, *An Act to Regulate Elections, Approved April 18, 1930* (Trenton, 1932), 170–71; State of New York, *The Election Law* (Albany, 1936); *Illinois Revised Statutes, 1949*, vol. 1, State Bar Association ed. (Chicago, 1949), chap. 46, secs. 4–1 and 5–1 at 1630 and 1639. For an example of a court case in which the court reinstated voters disqualified because of changes in registration procedures see *Schutz v. Merrill*, 273 P. 863 (Cal. Dist. Ct. App. 1928).

11. Michael McGerr, *The Decline of Popular Politics: The American North, 1865–1928* (New York, 1986), 186–88, 207. The term *turnout* often is used with an imprecision—or with two slightly different meanings—that can create havoc with attempts at analysis. Turnout statistics ostensibly and commonly

refer simply to the percentage of eligible voters who voted in a particular election; but to use this term with reference to the South in 1920, for example, is to imply that African Americans were actually "eligible" to vote—which may have been true in theory but was not true in practice. The word itself has an implication of volition, of individual choice about whether or not to vote, which is apt in some circumstances but clearly not in others.

12. *New York Times*, 20 April 1926; see also 9 February and 17 February 1924, 4 February 1926, 3 January, 12 May, and 10 July, 1927, 24 September and 28 September 1931, and 10 November 1935; McGerr, *Decline of Popular Politics*, 187–89.

13. Frank Goodnow, *Municipal Problems* (New York, 1897), 180; Andrew White, "The Government of American Cities," *The Forum* 10 (December 1890): 357–72; Michael Kazin, *Barons of Labor: The San Francisco Building Trades and Union Power in the Progressive Era* (Urbana, 1989), 41–42; Matthew J. Schott, "Progressives Against Democracy: Electoral Reform in Louisiana, 1894–1921," *Louisiana History* 20 (Summer 1979): 257–59; James Weinstein, "Organized Business and the City Commission and Manager Movements," *Journal of Southern History* 28 (May 1962): 166–82; Samuel P. Hays, "The Politics of Reform in Municipal Government in the Progressive Era," *Pacific Northwest Quarterly* 55 (October 1964): 157–69; Martin J. Schiesl, *The Politics of Efficiency: Municipal Administration and Reform in America, 1800–1920* (Berkeley, 1977), 3–5, 69, 134–48, 172–98; Thomas R. Pegram, *Partisans and Progressives: Private Interest and Public Policy in Illinois, 1870–1922* (Urbana, IL, 1992), 96, 104, 191, 199, 215–20; Arthur A. Ekirch, Jr., *Progressivism in America* (New York, 1974), 103; Sarah M. Henry, *Progressivism and Democracy: Electoral Reform in the United States 1888–1919* (Ph.D. diss., Columbia University, NY), 32–52; *New York Times*, 9 February 1924; Melvin G. Holli, *Reform in Detroit: Hazen S. Pingree and Urban Politics* (New York, 1969), 175–79; Kenneth Fox, *Better City Government: Innovation in American Urban Politics 1850–1937* (Philadelphia, 1977), 116–37.

14. William H. Page, ed., *Page's Ohio General Code Annotated: Replacement Volume 4* (Cincinnati, 1945), 52–53; *Illinois Revised Statutes, 1949*, vol. 1, State Bar Association ed. (Chicago, 1949), chap. 46, art. 7, sec. 2; Martin Shefter, "Political Incorporation and the Extrusion of the Left: Party Politics and Social Forces in New York City," *Studies in American Political Development: An Annual*, vol. 1 (New Haven, CT, 1986), 74; Peter H. Argersinger, *Structure, Process, and Party: Essays in American Political History* (Armonk, 1992), 150–71; Eugene J. McCarthy and John C. Armor, "Election Laws: A Case of Deadly Reform," *North Dakota Law Review* 57 (1981): 331–36; *New York Times*, 2 April 1920.

15. Kermit L. Hall, "Progressive Reform and the Decline of Democratic Accountability: The Popular Election of State Supreme Court Judges, 1850–1920," *American Bar Foundation Research Journal*, no. 2 (Spring 1984): 345–69; James Willard Hurst, *The Growth of American Law: The Law Makers* (Boston, 1950), 122–46. Hurst argues that political machines played a large role in selecting judges through the early decades of the twentieth century; cf. a discussion of the merits of an appointed judiciary in William S. Gray, John L. Dryer, and Rodney H. Brandon, *Proceedings of the Constitutional Convention of the State of Illinois, convened January 6, 1920* (Springfield, 1922), 1001, 3824–25.

16. Argersinger, *Structure*, 69–102, 172–90; David Montejano, *Anglos and Mexicans in the Making of Texas, 1836–1986* (Austin, 1987), 292; J. Allen Smith, *The Growth and Decadence of Constitutional Government* (New York, 1930), 61.

17. Richard L. McCormick, *The Party Period and Public Policy: American Politics from the Age of Jackson to the Progressive Era* (New York, 1986), 226.

18. Sitkoff, *New Deal*, 26–27, 30–31, 92–95, 98–99, 102–9; Steven F. Lawson, *Black Ballots: Voting Rights in the South, 1944–1969* (New York, 1976), 57; Tindall, *New South*, 556–59; *New York Times*, 15 July 1929.

19. Lawson, *Black Ballots*, 55–70; Sitkoff, *New Deal*, 64, 125–37. For examples of and reasons for labor's strenuous opposition to the poll tax see *American Federationist* 45 (January 1938): 61–63; American Federation of Labor, *Fifty-ninth Annual Convention* (1939), 456–58; *The Shipyard Worker* 5 (6 June 1941): 5; *Machinists' Monthly Journal* (May 1940): 380–81; *CIO News* 4 (30 June 1941): 6; *Textile Labor* 1 (1 April 1940): 1; *Enginemen's Magazine* 110 (June 1941): 363–64; *UE News* 2 (4 May 1940): 5; ibid., 2 (14 December 1940): 6; see also the papers of the ILGWU, Cornell University, box 26, folder 10.

20. U.S. Senate, 77th Cong., 2d sess., *Report 1662* (27 October 1942), 1–20.

21. Lawson, *Black Ballots*, 57–85; Sitkoff, *New Deal*, 131–37. Each time that the bill came forward, a dozen or more non-Southerners—both Democrats and Republicans—voted with southern senators to

block cloture. A proposed constitutional amendment to eliminate the poll tax in Arkansas was defeated by a margin of more than two to one in a popular election in 1938. McGovney, *Suffrage Medley*, 138; regarding the unusual history of Tennessee's efforts at poll tax reform see ibid., 135–36. The only state to abolish the poll tax in the 1940s was Georgia, which did so during the brief reign of a liberal governor in 1945.

22. *The New Republic*, 12 October 1932, 226; *The Survey* 68 (15 October 1932): 498–99; *The Literary Digest* (17 September 1932): 6.

23. *Literary Digest* (17 September 1932): 6; *Baltimore Sun*, 13 and 14 September 1932; F. W. Grinnell, "The Need of Common Sense in Constitutional Interpretation: The Meaning of the Word 'Pauper' in the Third Amendment," *Massachusetts Law Quarterly* 17 (August 1932); Massachusetts, *Statutes* (1932), chap. 206; Commonwealth of Massachusetts, *General Laws*, Tercentenary ed. (Boston, 1934), chap. 51, 67. The idea of disfranchising the poorest of the unemployed also was being considered by the Conservative government of England at almost the exact same time. *The Garment Worker* 32 (28 October 1932): 4.

24. *New York Times*, 3 February, 6 July, and 17 October 1932; 15 June 1933, 24 March, 6 August, 24 November, and 28 December 1934.

25. *New York Times*, 24 March, 6 August, 14 October, 17 October, 24 November, and 28 December 1934, 8 March 1935.

26. *New York Times*, 8 and 31 October 1934.

27. *New York Times*, 8 August, 10 August, 16 August, 18 October, 21 October, and 4 November 1934, 26 May 1935; *American Federationist* 41 (September 1934): 927–28; Michael B. Scheler, "The Unemployed—Pariahs or Freemen," *American Teacher* 19 (May-June 1935): 17–19.

28. *New York Times*, 21 October 1934; Ernest J. Hopkins, "No Job, No Vote," *The New Republic*, 12 October 1932, 225–26.

29. *New York Times*, 13 September, 6 and 7 October 1934, 10 November, 12 November, 19 November, 23 December, 26 December, 29 December, and 31 December 1935, 1 May, 3 July and 8 July, 5 August, and 26 October 1938, 5 January and 12 January, and 6 July 1939, 18 February and 24 February, 22 April, and 6 October 1940.

30. *New York Times*, 6 September and 11 September 1938; Cal Lewis, "The Pauper Vote," *North American Review* 246 (September 1938): 89.

31. *New York Times*, 6 September, 11 September, and 13 September 1938.

32. *New York Times*, 10 September 1938; *Fortune*, March 1939, 66, 132–33; Purcell, *Crisis of Democratic Theory*, 128–38. That the issue did not altogether die in 1938 is made clear in the *New York Times*, 12 September and 13 September 1939, in coverage of a prodisfranchisement speech by Major General James G. Harbord.

33. *New York Times*, 3 November 1936.

34. Lewis, "The Pauper Vote," 89.

35. Sitkoff, *New Deal*, 299–313; Ward E. Y. Elliott, *The Rise of Guardian Democracy: The Supreme Court's Rulings on Voting Rights Disputes, 1845–1969* (Cambridge, MA, 1974), 76–77.

36. Sitkoff, *New Deal*, 299–313; Purcell, *Crisis of Democratic Theory*, 128–38.

37. Steven F. Lawson, *Running for Freedom: Civil Rights and Black Politics in America Since 1941* (Philadelphia, 1991), 1–20; Tindall, *New South*, 638–43, 712–13, 716; Sitkoff, *New Deal*, 307–25; Lawson, *Black Ballots*, 65–77.

38. Tindall, *New South*, 746; Lawson, *Black Ballots*, 66; W. Brooke Graves, *American State Government*, 4th ed. (Boston, 1953), 115; Robert F. Williams, *The New Jersey State Constitution: A Reference Guide* (New York, 1990), 52–53; *Application of Seld*, 51 N.Y.S. 2d 1, 2 (App. Div. 1944); *Robbins v. Chamberlain*, 75 N.E. 2d 617 (N.Y. 1947); *Kashman v. Board of Elections of Onandaga County*, 282 N.Y.S. 2d 394, 397 (N.Y. Sup. Ct. 1967); Nelson, *Election Laws of the State of Missouri*, 27. Texas eliminated its constitutional bar on soldiers and sailors voting in elections in 1954.

39. Lawson, *Black Ballots*, 65–80; idem, *Running for Freedom*, 17; Elliott, *Guardian Democracy*, 77–78; John Egerton, *Speak Now Against the Day: The Generation Before the Civil Rights Movement in the South* (Chapel Hill, NC, 1995), 218; Ogden, *Poll Tax*, 185–200. In Tennessee, legislation abolishing the poll tax was passed in 1943 but was struck down by the state's courts, only to be revived in the early 1950s. According to Ogden, the poll tax efforts in Tennessee, Georgia, and South Carolina (where the tax was repealed in 1951) were all linked to partisan conflicts among whites—and inspired little opposition.

40. Grantham, *Life and Death of the Solid South*, 27–28; Stanley, *Voter Mobilization*, 88; Lawson, *Running for Freedom*, 14–15; Sitkoff, *New Deal*, 228–29; *Nixon v. Herndon*, 273 U.S. 536 (1927); *Nixon v. Condon*, 186 U.S. 73 (1932); *Grovey v. Townsend*, 295 U.S. 45 (1935). The Texas Supreme Court had permitted primaries to be exclusive because they were "nongovernmental" elections and therefore not subject to federal and state constitutional provisions. Tindall, *New South*, 558.

41. *United States v. Classic et al.*, 313 U.S. 299, 318–319 (1941); *Smith v. Allwright*, 321 U.S. 649, 664 (1944). For a full chronicle of the events leading up to the case (and its aftermath) see Darlene C. Hine, *Black Victory: The Rise and Fall of the White Primary in Texas* (Millwood, NY, 1979).

42. *New York Times*, 4 April 1944; Sitkoff, *New Deal*, 229–37; Elliott, *Guardian Democracy*, 78–80.

43. Stanley, *Voter Mobilization*, 86–89; Tindall, *New South*, 746–48; Egerton, *Speak Now Against the Day*, 380–82, 408–9, 488–89; Elliott, *Guardian Democracy*, 80–81.

44. Ronald Takaki, *Strangers from a Different Shore: A History of Asian Americans* (New York, 1990), 362–78, 407, 413; *Regan v. King*, 49 F. Supp. 222, 223 (1949).

45. Lawson, *Running for Freedom*, 20–35; Numan V. Bartley, *The New South 1845–1980* (Baton Rouge, 1995), 76; Montejano, *Anglos and Mexicans*, 260, 279; cf. Manfred Berg, "Soldiers and Citizens: War and Voting Rights in American History," *Reflections on American Exceptionalism*, ed. David K. Adams and Cornelis A. Van Minnen (Staffordshire, England, 1994), 208–11.

46. *To Secure These Rights: The Report of the President's Committee on Civil Rights* (Washington, DC, 1947), 6–8, 35–40, 139; Bartley, *New South*, 77.

47. *To Secure These Rights*, 151, 160–63.

48. Ibid., 99, 139–48. McGovney's *Suffrage Medley* is, in effect, a tract urging the nationalization of suffrage law.

49. *To Secure These Rights*, 100–101, 146–48.

50. Lawson, *Running for Freedom*, 33–39.

51. Ibid., 39–50; Bartley, *New South*, 171–76. The red-baiting of civil rights initiatives also had occurred in Congress in the 1940s, when a poll tax repeal bill was introduced by left-leaning New York Congressman Vito Marcantonio.

52. Daniel McCool, "Indian Voting," *American Indian Policy in the Twentieth Century*, ed. Vine Deloria, Jr. (Norman, OK, 1985), 107–8; Felix S. Cohen, *Handbook of Federal Indian Law with Reference Tables and an Index* (Washington, 1942), 158; *To Secure These Rights*, 161; Jeanette Wolfley, "Jim Crow, Indian Style: The Disenfranchisement of Native Americans," *American Indian Law Review* 16 (1991): 181–85.

53. *Porter v. Hall*, 271 P. 411, 412 (Ariz. 1928); *Harrison v. Laveen*, 196 P. 2d 456, 461 (Ariz. 1948); N. D. Houghton, "The Legal Status of Indian Suffrage in the United States," *California Law Review* 19 (July 1931): 507, 516–19; Wolfley, "Jim Crow," 186–88; McCool, "Indian Voting," 108–11; Henry Christman, "Southwestern Indians Win the Vote," *American Indian* 4 (1948): 6–10; Cohen, *Federal Indian Law*, 158.

54. Wolfley, "Jim Crow," 184–86; McCool, "Indian Voting," 111–12; *New York Times*, 2 November 1952; Christman, "Southwestern Indians," 6–10.

55. Vine Deloria, Jr. and Clifford M. Lytle, *American Indians, American Justice* (Austin, TX, 1983), 224–25; McCool, "Indian Voting," 108; John H. Allen, "Denial of Voting Rights to Reservation Indians," *Utah Law Review* 5 (Fall 1956): 247–56; Christman, "Southwestern Indians," 10; Helen L. Peterson, "American Indian Political Participation," *Annals of the American Academy* (May 1957): 116–26; *Allen v. Merrell*, 305 P. 2d 490 (Utah 1956); Murlene J. Worth, "Constitutional Law: Restriction of Indian Suffrage by Residence Qualification," *Oklahoma Law Review* 11 (1958): 67–69; Wolfley, "Jim Crow," 188–89.

56. McCool, "Indian Voting," 113–30; Wolfley, "Jim Crow," 186–95; Peterson, "American Indian Political Participation," 121–26.

CHAPTER EIGHT

1. Epigraph quotes from *House Report 291*, 85th Cong., 1st sess., 1 April 1957, 1969, 1977, 1987, 2004. Steven F. Lawson, *Black Ballots: Voting Rights in the South, 1944–1969* (New York, 1976), 125–39,

176; idem, *Running for Freedom: Civil Rights and Black Politics in America Since 1941* (Philadelphia, 1991), 42–43, 47–50, 70.

2. Numan V. Bartley, *The New South, 1945–1980* (Baton Rouge, 1995), 160–222.

3. *Voting: 1961 Commission on Civil Rights Report 1* (Washington, DC, 1961), 31, 69; Lawson, *Black Ballots*, 88, 130–37, 162, 211, 227; idem, *Running for Freedom*, 48–49.

4. Lawson, *Black Ballots*, 139–202; idem, *Running for Freedom*, 56–58; Robert F. Burk, *The Eisenhower Administration and Black Civil Rights* (Knoxville, 1984), 204–50.

5. Lawson, *Black Ballots*, 203–13, 222–49; idem, *Running for Freedom*, 63.

6. *Report of the United States Commission on Civil Rights 1959* (Washington, 1959), 19–145; Lawson, *Black Ballots*, 213–21.

7. Lawson, *Black Ballots*, 150–51, 156–58, 161–63, 165, 221–22; Lawson, *Running for Freedom*, 52–55, 78–79; Bartley, *New South*, 102–3, 232.

8. Lawson, *Running for Freedom*, 79–81, 86–99.

9. *Commission on Civil Rights 1961*, 5; Lawson, *Black Ballots*, 250, 278, 285–86.

10. *Commission on Civil Rights 1961*, 136, 139.

11. Lawson, *Running for Freedom*, 80–86, 94; idem, *Black Ballots*, 256–74, 283, 290, 294, 296–98.

12. Lawson, *Running for Freedom*, 103–17; Lawson, *Black Ballots*, 298–300, 306–12; David J. Garrow, *Protest at Selma: Martin Luther King, Jr., and the Voting Rights Act of 1965* (New Haven, CT, 1978), 106–7; Jack Valenti, "Looking Back," *Washington Post*, 5 August 1990.

13. Lawson, *Running for Freedom*, 114–16; idem, *Black Ballots*, 295–96, 313–23.

14. Lawson, *Black Ballots*, 318–22, 329–39, 341; idem, *Running for Freedom*, 115–16; idem, *In Pursuit of Power: Southern Blacks and Electoral Politics, 1965–1982* (New York, 1985), 15, 19–42; Garrow, *Protest at Selma*, 106–7; Dewey W. Grantham, *The Life and Death of the Solid South: A Political History* (Lexington, 1988), 164–65.

15. Lawson, *In Pursuit of Power*, 127–57, 191–253, 259, 282–303; U.S. Commission on Civil Rights, *State of Civil Rights 1957–1983: The Final Report of the U.S. Commission on Civil Rights* (Washington, DC, 1983), 1–17; Steven F. Lawson, "Preserving the Second Reconstruction: Enforcement of the Voting Rights Act, 1965–1975," *Southern Studies: An Interdisciplinary Journal of the South* 22 (Spring 1983): 55–75; idem, *Running for Freedom*, 185–88, 208–10; Abigail M. Thernstrom, *Whose Votes Count?: Affirmative Action and Minority Voting Rights* (Cambridge, MA, 1987), 51–65; Jeanette Wolfley, "Jim Crow, Indian Style: The Disenfranchisement of Native Americans," *American Indian Law Review* 16 (1991): 190–200; for an impassioned chronicle of ongoing racial discrimination between 1965 and 1972 see Washington Research Project, *The Shameful Blight: The Survival of Racial Discrimination in the South* (Washington, DC, 1972).

16. Lawson, *In Pursuit of Power*, 243, 253, 291–92; idem, *Running for Freedom*, 136–37.

17. *Lane v. Wilson*, 307 U.S. 268 (1939); *Schnell v. Davis*, 336 U.S. 933 (1949); *United States v. Raines*, 362 U.S. 17, 22 (1960); a decision similar to the *Schnell* ruling also came in 1965 in *Louisiana v. United States*, 380 U.S. 145 (1965); regarding the white primary see chap. 7.

18. *South Carolina v. Katzenbach*, 383 U.S. 301, 308, 337 (1966).

19. *Katzenbach v. Morgan*, 384 U.S. 641, 671 (1966); *Gaston County, N.C. v. United States*, 395 U.S. 285, 296 (1969); *Oregon v. Mitchell*, 400 U.S. 112, 118 (1970).

20. Post–1970 cases dealing with the right to vote per se followed the same lines as those discussed here. See, e.g., *Mississippi State Chapter, Operation Push v. Allain*, 674 F. Supp. 1245 (N.D. Miss. 1987).

21. Morton J. Horwitz, *The Warren Court and the Pursuit of Justice* (New York, 1998), xii, 13–14, 74–98; U.S. House, *Hearings Before Subcommittee No. 5* of the Committee on the Judiciary, 88th Cong., 1st sess., ser. no. 4, pt. 1, 1963, 905–6; John H. Ely, *Democracy and Distrust: A Theory of Judicial Review* (Cambridge, MA, 1980), 74. Proposals for resolutions "to establish a free and universal franchise throughout the United States" were introduced by Representatives John D. Dingell and Joseph G. Minish in 1963. They never came to a vote and do not appear to have been seriously considered. *Congressional Record*, 88th Cong., 1st sess., 1963, 109, pt. 1: 57, and pt. 2: 1672.

22. *Breedlove v. Suttles*, 302 U.S. 277 (1937). The Supreme Court, in 1951, also upheld the Virginia state poll tax (over the dissent of Justice Douglas) in *Butler v. Thompson*, 341 U.S. 937 (1951).

23. *Harper et al. v. Virginia Board of Elections et al.*, 383 U.S. 663, 669 (1966).

24. Ibid.

25. For a helpful exegesis of modes of constitutional interpretation see Ely, *Democracy and Distrust*, 73–134; on democratic theory during the period and its link to law see Morton J. Horwitz, *The Transformation of American Law, 1870–1960* (New York, 1992), 254–58.

26. Frank I. Michelman, "Conceptions of Democracy in American Constitutional Argument: Voting Rights," *Florida Law Review* 41 (Summer 1989): 458; Horwitz, *Warren Court*, 6; Ely, *Democracy and Distrust*, 120. As Ely points out (237*n*), the enfranchisement of women never would have required a constitutional amendment had the 1960s interpretation of the equal protection clause been in vogue.

27. *Hines v. Winters*, 320 P. 2d 1114, 1116 (Okla. 1957); U.S. Senate, *Hearings Before a Subcommittee of the Committee on the Judiciary*, 84th Cong., 2d sess., on S. J. Res. 29, 11 and 13 April 1956, 1–9; the original Virginia suit that resulted in the *Harper* decision also challenged Virginia's pauper exclusion law, but that challenge disappeared because the district court ruled that the plaintiffs had been denied the franchise because of their failure to pay poll taxes rather than their being paupers.

28. The Commonwealth of Massachusetts, *Legislative Research Council Report Relative to Voting by Paupers, Senate Document No. 1103* (8 February 1967), 7–26; John F. X. Davoren, Secretary of the Commonwealth, *Election Statistics of the Commonwealth of Massachusetts 1970–72* (Boston, 1972), 499–504; *Boston Globe*, 7 November 1972; *Providence Journal*, 8 November 1972. The pauper exclusion clause in Massachusetts also resulted in a challenge to the state's jury selection system, since jurors were drawn from voting lists. See "The Exclusion of Paupers from Voter Lists and Thereby from Eligibility for Jury Duty," *Suffolk University Law Review* 7 (1973): 369–75.

29. *Kramer v. Union Free School District*, 395 U.S. 623, 627 (1969); Michelman, "Conceptions of Democracy," 462–64.

30. *Cipriano v. Houma*, 395 U.S. 701, 706 (1969); *City of Phoenix, Arizona v. Koldziejski*, 399 U.S. 204, 212 (1970); *Hill v. Stone*, 421 U.S. 289 (1975); *Hayward v. Clay*, 573 F. 2d 187 (4th Cir 1978); *Police Jury of Parish of Vermillion v. Herbert*, 404 U.S. 807 (1971); *Light v. MacKenzie*, 356 N.Y.S. 2d 991 (N.Y. Sup. Ct. 1974); Alan Reitman and Robert B. Davidson, *The Election Process: Voting Laws and Procedures* (Dobbs Ferry, NY, 1972), 26–27; Michelman, "Conceptions of Democracy," 464–65.

31. *Salyer Land Company v. Tulare Lake Basin Water Storage District*, 410 U.S. 719 (1973); *Ball v. James*, 451 U.S. 355 (1981); *State v. Frontier Acres Community Development District Pasco County*, 472 So. 2d 455 (Fla. 1985); *Associated Enterprises, Inc. v. Toltec Watershed Improvement District*, 410 U.S. 743 (1973); *Snead v. City of Albuquerque*, 663 F. Supp. 1084 (D.N.M. 1987). As Michelman points out ("Conceptions of Democracy," 465–72), the Court's attempt to distinguish between different types of government entities and their functions (in comparing the *Ball* decision to *Cipriano*, e.g.) was something less than a model of clarity; cf. *Southern California Rapid Transit District v. Bolen*, 822 P. 2d 875 (Cal. 1992).

32. *Lassiter v. Northampton County Board of Elections*, 360 U.S. 45 (1959); cf. *Castro v. State of California*, 466 P. 2d 244, (Cal. 1970); Lawson, *In Pursuit of Power*, 132–51; Thernstrom, *Whose Votes Count?* 34–35.

33. *Oregon v. Mitchell*, 400 U.S. 112, 133 (1970). For an analysis of the Court's view of literacy requirements, against the backdrop of *Harper* and the Court's general use of the equal protection clause, see Michelman, "Conceptions of Democracy," 480–85.

34. Voting Rights Act Amendments of 1975, *U.S. Statutes at Large* 89 (1975): 400; Reitman and Davidson, *Election Process*, 22–23. New York's literacy test was the subject of considerable legal dispute prior to the national ban. See *U.S. v. County Board of Elections of Monroe County*, 248 F. Supp. 316 (W.D. N.Y. 1965); *Cardona v. Power*, 384 U.S. 672 (1966); *Katzenbach v. Morgan*, 384 U.S. 641 (1966); *Torres v. Sachs*, 381 F. Supp. 309 (S.D. N.Y. 1974). Some states, such as Massachusetts, removed their literacy requirements after the 1970 Voting Rights Act. Massachusetts, *Gen. Laws*, (1971), chap. 382, sec. 8. California did so in 1974. For examples of assistance laws see Massachusetts, *Gen. Laws* (1972), chap. 42, sec. 1; *Laws Passed at the First Regular Session of the Fiftieth General Assembly of the State of Colorado, 1975*, vol. 1, comp. and arr. James C. Wilson, Jr. (Denver, 1975), 177; and *Laws Passed at the First Regular Session of the Fifty-third General Asembly of the State of Colorado, 1981*, vol. 1, arr. and prep. Douglas G. Brown (Denver, 1981), 313. For Illinois see *Puerto Rican Organization for Political Action v. Kusper*, 490 F. 2d 575 (Ill. App. 7th Cir 1973). The 1982 amendments to the Voting Rights Act also included a clause establishing the right of a voter in need of assistance, due to blindness, disability, or illiteracy, to receive such assistance from a person of his or her choice, other than an employer or union official.

35. "Durational Residency Requirements for Voting," *Harvard Law Review* 86 (1972): *n.*107.

36. Stephan Thernstrom, *The Other Bostonians: Poverty and Progress in the American Metropolis, 1880–1970* (Cambridge, MA, 1973), 40–44, 230; Peverill Squire, Raymond E. Wolfinger, and David P. Glass, "Residential Mobility and Voter Turnout," *American Political Science Review* 81 (March 1987): 45–50.

37. *Oregon v. Mitchell*, 400 U.S. 112 (1970).

38. *Dunn v. Blumstein*, 405 U.S. 330, 358 (1972); *Marston v. Lewis*, 410 U.S. 679, 93 S. Ct. 1211 (1973); *Burns v. Fortson*, 410 U.S. 686 (1973); *Hinnant v. Sebesta*, 363 F. Supp. 398 (M.D. Fla. 1973); *Jackson v. Bowen*, 420 F. Supp. 315 (S.D. Ind. 1976). Regarding state action see *Keane v. Mihaly*, 11 Cal. App. 3d 1037 (Cal. App. 4th 1970); *Young v. Gnoss*, 7 Cal. 3d 18 (Cal. 1972); the 1972 revisions of the California Constitution as indicated in *Constitution of the State of California, Annotated* (San Francisco, 1981); *Atkin v. Onondaga County Board of Elections*, 285 N.E. 2d 687 (N.Y. 1972); Colorado's "Act Concerning the Eligibility of New Residents of this State to Vote for Presidential and Vice-Presidential Electors," passed 23 April 1969, as well as "An Act Concerning Elections," passed 17 April 1971, *Laws Passed at the First Regular Session of the Forty-eighth General Assembly of the State of Colorado, 1971*, comp. James C. Wilson, Jr. (Denver, 1971), 548–64; Alan S. Gratch and Virginia H. Ubik, *Ballots for Change: New Suffrage and Amending Articles for Illinois* (Urbana, IL, 1973), 61–71.

39. The rash of legal activity regarding student voting was prompted in good part by the lowering of the voting age (to be discussed).

40. *Carrington v. Rash*, 380 U.S. 89, 96 (1965). Regarding students see *Palla v. Suffolk County Board of Elections*, 286 N.E. 2d 247 (N.Y. 1972); *Auerbach v. Rettaliata*, 765 F. 2d 350 (2d Cir 1985); *Wray v. Monroe County Board of Elections*, 595 F. Supp. 1028 (W.D. N.Y. 1984); *Ramey v. Rockefeller*, 348 F. Supp. 780 (E.D. N.Y. 1972); *Williams v. Salerno*, 792 F. 2d 323 (2d Cir 1986); *Levy v. Scranton*, 780 F. Supp. 897 (N.D. N.Y. 1991); *Walters v. Reed*, 752 P. 2d 443 (Cal. 1988); *Whatley v. Clark*, 482 F. 2d 1230 (5th Cir 1973); *Hershkoff v. Board of Registrars of Voters of Worcester*, 321 N.E. 2d 656 (1974); *Sloane v. Smith*, 351 F. Supp. 1299 (M.D. Pa. 1972); *Lloyd v. Babb*, 196 N.C. 416, 251 S.E. 2d 843 (1979); *Ballas v. Symm*, 494 F. 2d 1167 (5th Cir 1974); *Bright v. Baesler*, 336 F. Supp. 527 (E.D. Ky. 1971); *Dyer v. Huff*, 382 F. Supp. 1313 (D.S.C. 1973). Regarding the homeless see *Collier v. Menzel*, 176 Cal. App. 3d 24 (Cal. App. 2d 1985); *Pitts v. Black*, 608 F. Supp. 696 (S.D. N.Y. 1984); *Fischer v. Stout*, 741 P. 2d 217 (Alaska 1987). Regarding absentee ballots see, e.g., *Laws Passed at the Second Regular Session of the Forty-eighth General Assembly of the State of Colorado 1972*, comp. James C. Wilson, Jr. (Denver, 1972), 305–9; *Laws Passed at the First Regular Session of the Fifty-fourth General Assembly of the State of Colorado, 1983*, arr. Douglas G. Brown (Denver, 1983), 368. The federal government also passed an Overseas Citizens Voting Rights Act in 1975.

41. Wendell W. Cultice, *Youth's Battle for the Ballot: A History of Voting Age in America* (New York, 1992), 2–18.

42. Ibid., 19–30.

43. Ibid., 30–61.

44. Ibid., 30–65, 80–92.

45. Ibid., 40–50.

46. Ibid., 93–112; Ward E. Y. Elliott, *The Rise of Guardian Democracy: the Supreme Court's Rulings on Voting Rights Disputes, 1845–1969* (Cambridge, MA, 1974), 140–41; cf. Manfred Berg, "Soldiers and Citizens," *Reflections on American Exceptionalism*, ed. David K. Adams and Cornelis A. Van Minnen (Staffordshire, England, 1994), 211–14.

47. The negative votes came almost entirely from conservative Republicans and southern Democrats.

48. Cultice, *Youth's Battle*, 116–40; Elliott, *Guardian Democracy*, 141–45.

49. *Oregon v. Mitchell*, 400 U.S. 112, 144 (1970); by 1970, a handful of states had lowered their voting ages to nineteen or twenty. For an analysis of this decision see Richard S. Greene, "Congressional Power over the Elective Franchise: The Unconstitutional Phases of *Oregon v. Mitchell*," *Boston University Law Review* 52 (1972): 509–69.

50. Cultice, *Youth's Battle*, 173–81. Some states, such as Colorado, did manage to lower their voting ages to eighteen in 1971 and 1972.

51. Ibid., 181–215. The reach of the amendment was clarified by the courts in *Gaunt v. Brown*, which determined that states did have the right to deny the franchise (based on age) to any voter who had not reached the age of eighteen by election day. *Gaunt v. Brown*, 341 F. Supp. 1187, *aff'd* 409 U.S. 809 (1972).

52. This is probably a conservative estimate. The age reduction made more than 11 million young men and women eligible; changes in residency law may well have enfranchised an additional 10 million; the number of blacks and Hispanics who could vote was probably in the vicinity of 5 to 6 million; and there were 1 million illiterate citizens in 1970. See Cultice, *Youth's Battle*, 174.

53. On the politics of growth see Alan Wolfe, *America's Impasse: The Rise and Fall of the Politics of Growth* (Boston, 1981).

54. Joan T. Thornell, *Governance of the Nation's Capital: A Summary History of the Forms and Powers of Local Government for the District of Columbia, 1790 to 1973*, U.S. House, Committee on the District of Columbia, 101 Cong., 2d sess. (1990), 1–3, 11–39, 43–53; Steven F. Lawson, "Civil Rights," *Exploring the Johnson Years*, ed. Robert A. Divine (Austin, 1981), 114–15; Lawson, *Black Ballots*, 100.

55. *Baker v. Carr*, 369 U.S. 186, 300, 318, 327 (1962); Ely, *Democracy and Distrust*, 120. Frankfurter first used the phrase in an earlier case, *Colegrove v. Green*, 328 U.S. 549, 556 (1946).

56. *Gray v. Sanders*, 372 U.S. 368, 377 (1963); *Wesberry v. Sanders*, 376 U.S. 1, 8 (1964).

57. *Reynolds v. Sims*, 377 U.S. 533, 563, 573 (1964). Once again, Justice Harlan dissented, citing the inapplicability of the Fourteenth Amendment. Cf. *Avery v. Midland County, Texas*, 390 U.S. 474 (1968), in which the Court held that there could not be "substantial variation from equal population" in districting for local governments. In *Karcher v. Daggett*, 462 U.S. 725 (1983), the Court tightened the permissible latitude allowed in congressional districting.

58. *Gomillion v. Lightfoot*, 364 U.S. 339, 342 (1960); Elliott, *Guardian Democracy*, 82–84; J. Morgan Kousser, *Colorblind Injustice: Minority Voting Rights and the Undoing of the Second Reconstruction* (Chapel Hill, NC, 1999), 53–54, 371; Lawson, *Running for Freedom*, 61–62.

59. Kousser, *Colorblind Injustice*, 60; for a discussion of the breadth of malapportionment and vote dilution see the U.S. Civil Rights Commission, *Voting*, 113–35.

60. *Allen v. State Board of Elections*, 393 U.S. 544, 565 (1969); *Perkins v. Matthews*, 400 U.S. 379, 388 (1971); Lawson, *In Pursuit of Power*, 133, 159–61; Kousser, *Colorblind Injustice*, 59–63; Richard L. Engstrom, "Racial Discrimination in the Electoral Process: The Voting Rights Act and the Vote Dilution Issue," *Party Politics in the South*, ed. Robert P. Steed, Laurence W. Moreland, and Tod A. Baker (New York, 1980), 197–202.

61. Lawson, *In Pursuit of Power*, 133–42, 163–74, 203–12, 217–21; *Georgia v. United States*, 411 U.S. 526 (1973); Engstrom, "Racial Discrimination," 200–203.

62. *Whitcomb v. Chavis*, 403 U.S. 124 (1971); *White v. Regester*, 412 U.S. 755, 769 (1973); *Zimmer v. McKeithen*, 485 F. 2d 1297 (5th Cir 1973); Bernard Grofman, Lisa Handley, and Richard G. Niemi, *Minority Representation and the Quest for Voting Equality* (New York, 1992), 32–34. A divided Court, in the early 1970s, backed away slightly from its insistence on numerical equality in districting, permitting greater variance in the size of districts. *Gaffney v. Cummings*, 412 U.S. 735 (1973); *Mahan v. Howell*, 410 U.S. 315 (1973).

63. Engstrom, "Racial Discrimination," 202–4; Grofman, Handley, and Niemi, *Minority Representation*, 25–27.

64. The Court's awareness of the potentially balkanizing effects was expressed, by Justice White, in his criticism of the district court's holdings in *Whitcomb v. Chavis*. That holding "is expressive of the more general proposition that any group with distinctive interests must be represented in legislative halls if it is numerous enough to command at least one seat and represents a majority living in an area sufficiently compact to constitute a single-member district. This approach would make it difficult to reject claims of Democrats, Republicans, or members of any political organization in Marion County who live in what would be safe districts in a single-member district system but who in one year or another, or year after year, are submerged in a one-sided multi-member district vote. There are also union oriented workers, the university community, religious or ethnic groups occupying identifiable areas of our heterogeneous cities and urban areas." (1875–76)

65. See ibid.

66. Lawson, *In Pursuit of Power*, 216–21; Engstrom, "Racial Discrimination," 205–9; *City of Petersburg, Virginia v. United States*, 354 F. Supp 1021 (D.C. 1972), affirmed 410 U.S. 962 (1973); *City of Richmond v. United States*, 422 U.S. 358 (1975); *Beer v. United States*, 425 U.S. 130 (1976).

67. *United Jewish Organizations of Williamsburgh, Inc. v. Carey*, 430 U.S. 144 (1977); Lynett Henderson, "Lost in the Woods: The Supreme Court, Race, and the Quest for Justice in Congressional Reapportionment," *Denver University Law Review* 73 (1995): 213–14.

68. *City of Mobile, Alabama v. Bolden*, 446 U.S. 55, 62 (1980); Grofman, Handley, and Niemi, *Minority Representation*, 34–38.

69. Grofman, Handley, and Niemi, *Minority Representation*, 37; Lawson, *In Pursuit of Power*, 279–80; Chandler Davidson, "Minority Vote Dilution: An Overview," *Minority Vote Dilution*, ed. Chandler Davidson (Washington, 1984), 2–3.

70. Grofman, Handley, and Niemi, *Minority Representation*, 41; Davidson, "Minority Vote Dilution," 18; Armand Derfner, "Vote Dilution and the Voting Rights Act Amendments of 1982," *Minority Vote Dilution*, ed. Chandler Davidson (Washington, 1984), 145–65. The new wording applied only to claims brought under the Voting Rights Act itself, rather than constitutional claims under the Fourteenth and Fifteenth Amendments.

71. *Thornburg v. Gingles*, 478 U.S. 30, 83 (1986); Grofman, Handley, and Niemi, *Minority Representation*, 48–54.

72. Grofman, Handley, and Niemi, *Minority Representation*, 54–81. For examples of lower courts wrestling with the issues see *Nash v. Blunt*, 797 F. Supp. 1488 (W.D. Mo. 1992), and *Garza v. County of Los Angeles*, 918 F. 2d 763 (9th Cir 1991).

73. Henderson, "Lost in the Woods," 21–22, *n*.137; Andrea Bierstein, "Millennium Approaches: The Future of the Voting Rights Act After Shaw, Degrandy, and Holder," *Hastings Law Journal* 46 (1995): 1508–10; Kousser, *Colorblind Injustice*, 243–76, 377–83.

74. *Shaw v. Reno*, 509 U.S. 630, 657 (1993); Kousser, *Colorblind Injustice*, 383–93; Henderson, "Lost in the Woods," 21–23.

75. *Shaw v. Reno*, 509 U.S. 630, 659–87 (1993).

76. *Miller v. Johnson*, 515 U.S. 900, 923 (1995); Henderson, "Lost in the Woods," 25–38.

77. *Holder v. Hall*, 512 U.S. 874, 880 (1994); Bierstein, "Millennium Approaches," 1512–25. The findings in this case were partially prefigured by the Court's decision in *Presley v. Etowah County Commission*, 502 U.S. 491 (1992), an Alabama case in which, after blacks obtained the right to vote for county commissioners, the powers of those commissioners was sharply restricted: the Court ruled that this did not violate the preclearance provisions of the Voting Rights Act. *New York Times*, 28 January 1992; *Washington Post*, 2 February 1992.

78. For criticisms of Thomas see works by Kousser, Henderson, and Bierstein cited herein.

79. *Johnson v. De Grandy*, 512 U.S. 997 (1994); *Shaw v. Hunt*, 517 U.S. 899 (1996); *Bush v. Vera*, 517 U.S. 952 (1996); *African-American Voting Rights Legal Defense Fund v. State of Missouri*, 994 F. Supp. 1105 (E.D. Mo. 1997); Bierstein, "Millennium Approaches," 1522–25; Donovan L. Wickline, "Note: Walking a Tightrope: Redrawing Congressional District Lines After Shaw v. Reno and Its Progeny," *Fordham Urban Law Journal* 25 (Spring 1998): 641; Judith Reed, "Sense and Nonsense: Standing in the Racial Districting Cases as a Window on the Supreme Court's View of the Right to Vote," *Michigan Journal of Race and Law* 4 (Spring 1999): 389–457; Samuel Issacharoff, Pamela S. Karlan, and Richard H. Pildes, *The Law of Democracy: Legal Structure of the Political Process* (New York, 1998), 590–603; Kousser, *Colorblind Injustice*, 396–455. Justice Ginsburg, in her dissent in *Holder*, agreed with the majority opinion that there was a tension built into the 1982 amendments to the Voting Rights Act because the goal of allowing vote dilution claims to be pressed conflicted with the denial of a "right to proportional representation for minority voters." For examples of recent lower court decisions see *Cleveland County Association for Government by the People v. Cleveland County Board of Commissioners*, 142 F. 3d 468 (D.C. Cir 1998); *Burton v. City of Belle Glade*, 178 F. 3d 1175 (11th Cir 1999); *Chen v. Houston*, 9 F. Supp. 2d 745 (S.D. Tex. 1998); *Quilter v. Voinovich*, 981 F. Supp. 1032 (N.D. Ohio 1997). The author, it should be noted, may live in North Carolina's Twelfth District—depending on the outcome of the latest court case.

80. For an analysis of partisan interests see Kousser, *Colorblind Injustice*, esp. 366–450. Among the most sharply argued of the pieces written by scholars are Kousser, *Colorblind Injustice*, and Thernstrom, *Whose Votes Count?*

81. I owe a debt here to the analysis put forward by Andrea Bierstein in "Millennium Approaches," cited herein.

82. Cf. Reed, "Sense and Nonsense," 418–55, and Grofman, Handley, and Niemi, *Minority Representation*, 53–81.

83. Steven J. Mulroy, "The Way Out: A Legal Standard for Imposing Alternative Electoral Systems as Voting Rights Remedies," *Harvard Civil Rights-Civil Liberties Law Review* 33 (Summer 1998): 333–71; Bierstein, "Millennium Approaches," 1525–30; Lani Guinier, *The Tyranny of the Majority: Fundamental Fairness in Representative Democracy* (New York, 1994); Henderson, "Lost in the Woods," 41–45. Even Justice Thomas, in his opinion in *Holder*, suggested some potential sympathy for a system of proportional representation, or at least an openness to considering "other voting mechanisms . . . that can produce proportional results without requiring division of the electorate into racially segregated districts." Cutting in the opposite direction, in 1997, the Court upheld a Minnesota ban on multiparty candidacies; in her concurring opinion, Justice O'Connor expressed the view that states were free to adopt policies that would advantage the two major parties, reflecting a belief that "political stability is best served through a healthy two-party system." *Timmons v. Twin Cities Area New Party*, 520 U.S. 351, 367 (1997). Preserving a two-party system, of course, would be antithetical to the goals of proportional representation. Mulroy notes that a few lower courts already have begun to consider alternatives to winner-take-all elections. Mulroy, "The Way Out."

84. The articles cited here offer slightly different figures regarding the number of states with provisions of different types. Each contains an inventory of the state laws, the most complete of which is in Howard Itzkowitz and Lauren Oldak, "Note: Restoring the Ex-offender's Right to Vote: Background and Developments," *American Criminal Law Review* 11 (1973): 721–70; "Note: The Need for Reform of Ex-Felon Disfranchisement Laws," *Yale Law Journal* 83 (1974): 582–84; *Vanderbilt Law Review* 23 (1970): 975–87; "Note: The Equal Protection Clause as a Limitation of the States' Power to Disfranchise Those Convicted of a Crime," *Rutgers Law Review* 21 (1967): 298–300; Gary L. Reback, "Note: Disenfranchisement of Ex-Felons: A Reassessment," *Stanford Law Review* 25 (1973): 845–64; Douglas R. Tims, "The Disenfranchisement of Ex-felons: A Cruelly Excessive Punishment," *Southwestern University Law Review* 7 (1975): 124–60; Civil Rights Commission, *Voting, 1961*, 69.

85. Itzkowitz and Oldak, "Restoring," 731–39; Reback, "Disenfranchisement," 858–61; Tims, "Disenfranchisement," 154–60. Tims and others have argued that these laws are subject to attack under the Eighth Amendment of the Constitution, prohibiting cruel and unusual punishment, but these claims have never made much headway in court.

86. "Equal Protection Clause," 309–15; "Need for Reform," 585–88; "Note: The Disenfranchisement of Ex-felons: Citizenship, Criminality, and 'The Purity of the Ballot Box,'" *Harvard Law Review* 102 (1989): 1301–9.

87. Itzkowitz and Oldak, "Restoring," 755–57; Tims, "Disenfranchisement," 126*n*.14. For an excellent example of state deliberations on the issue see *Ohio Constitutional Revision Commission Proceedings Research*, vol. 5 (Columbus, 1977), 2358–66, 2513–35. In Ohio, as elsewhere, such consideration was accompanied by revision of the exclusion of "idiots" and the "insane" and the introduction of the more benign-sounding concept of "mental competence." Regarding the voting rights of the mentally disabled see "Note: Mental Disability and the Right to Vote," *Yale Law Journal* 88 (1979): 1644; Joel E. Smith, "Voting Rights of Persons Mentally Incapacitated," *American Law Reports* 80 (1977): 1116.

88. "Equal Protection Clause," 299–300.

89. *Otsuka v. Hite*, 64 Cal. 2d 596, 598 (Cal. 1966); B. E. Witkin, *Summary of California Law*, vol. 5, 8th ed. (San Francisco, 1974), 3360–62; "Equal Protection Clause," 301–2.

90. *Green v. Board of Elections*, 380 F. 2d 445, 451 (2d Cir 1967). *Green* also ruled that disfranchisement was not cruel or unusual punishment. Florida's law was upheld by a district court in *Beacham v. Braterman*, 300 F. Supp. 182 (S.D. Fla. 1969). New York's courts, in 1972, also ruled that it was permissible for a state statute to prevent incarcerated prisoners awaiting trial from registering to vote and thus from obtaining absentee ballots; there was, however, a dissent that argued that this was discriminatory because those "confined to our prisons awaiting trial are, for the most part, the politically disconnected and the financially disabled." *O'Brien v. Skinner*, 338 N.Y.S. 2d 890 (N.Y. 1972). Regarding *Green* and other cases of this period see Itzkowitz and Oldak, "Restoring," 744–50.

91. *Dillenburg v. Kramer*, 469 F. 2d 1222, 1226 (9th Cir 1972); Itzkowitz and Oldak, "Restoring," 753–54; Reback, "Disenfranchisement," 848–57; Tims, "Disenfranchisement," 133–34.

92. Tims, "Disenfranchisement," 134–36; *Statutes of California and Digests of Measures, 1972*, vol. 2, comp. George H. Murphy (n.p., n.d.), 3382.

93. *Richardson v. Ramirez*, 418 U.S. 24, 43 (1974); Tims, "Disenfranchisement," 138–41.

94. The California Constitution was amended on 5 November 1974 to disqualify electors only "while . . . imprisoned or on parole for the conviction of a felony." *Statutes of California and Digests of Measures, 1974*, vol. 2, comp. George H. Murphy (n.p. n.d.), 3736.

95. In 1983, the federal courts also ruled that states can distinguish among convicted felons as long as the distinction is reasonably related to a legitimate state interest. *Owens v. Barnes*, 711 F. 2d 25 (3d Cir 1983).

96. Between 1967 and 1975, fourteen states dropped their laws enfranchising ex-felons. Tims, "Disenfranchisement," 140–41; *Hunter v. Underwood*, 471 U.S. 222 (1985).

97. *Wesley v. Collins*, 791 F. 2d 1255, 1261 (6th Cir 1986).

98. Andrew L. Shapiro, "Note: Challenging Criminal Disenfranchisement Under the Voting Rights Act: A New Strategy," *Yale Law Journal* 103 (October 1993): 537–66; Andrew L. Shapiro, "Giving Cons and Ex-Cons the Vote," *The Nation* (20 December 1993): 767–68; Alice E. Harvey, "Comment: Ex-Felon Disenfranchisement and Its Influence on the Black Vote: The Need for a Second Look," *University of Pennsylvania Law Review* 142 (January 1994): 1145–89.

99. *Baker v. Pataki*, 85 F. 3d 919, 940 *n*.10 (2d Cir 1996); *Farrakhan v. Locke*, 987 F. Supp. 1304 (E.D. Wash. 1997).

100. *New York Times*, 23 October 1998; *New York Times*, 30 January 1997; Shapiro, "Challenging Criminal Disenfranchisement," 538–39, 564, 566 *n*.146; Shapiro, "Cons," 767–68. Two additional states provided for lifetime disfranchisement after a second felony conviction. A Massachusetts court, in 1983, ruled that incarcerated prisoners had to be provided with the opportunity to register and to vote as absentees. *Cepulonis v. Secy. of Commonwealth*, 452 N.E. 2d 1137 (Mass. 1983).

101. Reed Ueda, *Postwar Immigrant America: A Social History* (Boston, 1994), 33–34, 60; Raymond E. Wolfinger and Steven J. Rosenstone, *Who Votes?* (New Haven, 1980), 92–93.

102. *Van Berkel v. Power*, 254 N.Y.S. 2d 74 (N.Y. Sup. Ct. 1964); this was reversed by an appeals court, but New York's ninety-day waiting period clearly violated *Dunn*, which was decided several years later. Massachusetts dropped its law requiring immigrants to present naturalization papers in 1971.

103. Ueda, *Postwar Immigrant America*, 46–48, 125–28; Jamin B. Raskin, "Time to Give Aliens the Vote (Again)," *The Nation* (5 April 1993): 452; Census Bureau report issued on the Internet on 9 March 1999; Immigration and Naturalization Service Internet report issued on 20 November 1996. One consequence of the termination of the *bracero* program in 1964 was an increase in the flow of Hispanics through illegal channels of migration. Given the size of the alien population, it is hardly surprising that in 1996, the Democrats took steps to try to accelerate the processing of citizenship applications, which led to Republican charges of a "get out the vote conspiracy." *New York Times*, 13 September 1996.

104. Jamin B. Raskin, "Legal Aliens, Local Citizens: The Historical, Constitutional and Theoretical Meanings of Alien Suffrage," *University of Pennsylvania Law Review* 141 (April 1993): 1428, 1431–33; Gerald M. Rosberg, "Aliens and Equal Protection: Why Not the Right to Vote?" *Michigan Law Review* 75 (1977): 1100–101, 1106–10; *Padilla v. Allison*, 38 Cal. App. 3d 784 (Cal. App. 5 1974). Several courts, including the Supreme Courts of Alaska and Colorado, have ruled that the exclusion of aliens did not violate the equal protection clause. A Colorado court concluded flatly that "aliens are not a part of the political community."

105. Raskin, "Legal Aliens," 1395, 1442–45; idem, "Time," 452; Gerald L. Neuman, "We Are the People: Alien Suffrage in German and American Perspective," *Michigan Journal of International Law* 13 (Winter 1992): 259–335; Thomas Hammar, "Dual Citizenship and Political Integration," *International Migration Review* 19 (Fall 1985): 438–47; Yann Moulier-Boutang, "Resistance to the Political Representation of Alien Populations: The European Paradox," *International Migration Review* 19 (Fall 1985): 485–92.

106. Raskin, "Legal Aliens," 1396, 1455, 1457, 1460–69; *Washington Post*, 30 January 1992.

107. *San Francisco Examiner*, 9 February 1996. According to Associated Press files (21 and 26 October 1998), the town of Amherst, Massachusetts, also attempted to grant the vote to noncitizens. In 1997, the residents of Garrett Park, Maryland, voted 142 to 140 not to enfranchise aliens. *Washington Post*, 19 June 1997.

108. Frances Fox Piven and Richard A. Cloward, *Why Americans Don't Vote* (New York, 1988), 17–21; Steven J. Rosenstone and Raymond E. Wolfinger, "The Effect of Registration Laws on Voter Turnout," *American Political Science Review* 72 (1978): 22–45.

109. Rosenstone and Wolfinger, "Effect of Registration Laws," 23–32; *Beare v. Briscoe,* 498 F. 2d 244 (5th Cir 1974); see also *Mississippi State Chapter, Operation Push v. Mabus,* 932 F. 2d 400 (1991); and Deborah S. James, "Note: Voter Registration: A Restriction on the Fundamental Right to Vote," *Yale Law Journal* 96 (June 1987): 1615–40.

110. Piven and Cloward, *Americans,* 178–80. For a revealing example of state deliberations see *Ohio Constitutional Revision Commission Proceedings Research, 1970–1977,* Research Study no. 24 (Columbus, 1977), 2332–51.

111. Piven and Cloward, *Americans,* 181–208, 215; Rosenstone and Wolfinger, "Effect of Registration Laws," 29–33; Wolfinger and Rosenstone, *Who Votes?,* 66; *Congressional Quarterly Almanac* 33 (1977): 779. Prodded by Senator Edward Kennedy, hearings were held on voter registration reform as early as 1971; *Ohio Research,* Study no. 24, 2333–34, 2339–43.

112. Piven and Cloward, *Americans,* 181ff., 209–10, 216–47; regarding the bills introduced in Congress see U.S. House Committee on House Administration, Subcommitee on Elections, *Voter Registration: Hearings on H.R. 3023 and H.R. 3950,* 100th Cong., 2d sess., 19 April, 10 May, and 27 May 1988, and 101st Cong., 1st sess., 21 March 1989.

113. Piven and Cloward, *Americans,* 15–20; House, Subcommittee on Elections, *Hearings,* 10 May 1988, 189.

114. House Committee on House Administration, *Report 101–243 to Accompany H.R. 2190: The National Voter Registration Act of 1989,* 101st Cong., 1st sess., 18 September 1989; Senate Committee on Rules and Administration, *Equal Access to Voting Act of 1989, Hearing on S. 675,* 101 Cong., 1st sess., 10 May 1989; *New York Times,* 13 May 1992. Democrats countered the Republican constitutional argument by pointing out that article 1, section 4 of the Constitution gave Congress the right to regulate "the times, places and manner of holding" federal elections.

115. *Washington Post,* 21 May 1992; Elizabeth Palmer, "Motor Voter Drive Succeeds but Promised Veto Awaits," *Congressional Quarterly Weekly Report* (20 June 1992): 1795; Richard Sammon, "Motor Voter Bill Stalls in Senate," *Congressional Quarterly Weekly Report* (20 July, 1991): 1981; the text of the veto message was printed in *Congressional Quarterly Weekly Report* (4 July 1992).

116. *New York Times,* 18 March 1993; *Congressional Quarterly Almanac* 49 (1993): 199–201.

117. *New York Times,* 21 May, 3 September 1995, 16 and 19 October 1996, 7 February 1996, 7 November 1996, 30 June 1998, 4 and 5 November 1998; *Durham N.C. Herald-Sun,* 27 March 1995. The law was challenged in the courts by several states, including California and New York, but the challenges ultimately were rebuffed by the Supreme Court.

CONCLUSION

1. Göran Therborn, "The Rule of Capital and the Rise of Democracy," *New Left Review* 103 (May-June 1977): 12–19; Martin Pugh, *Electoral Reform in Peace and War, 1906–1918* (London, 1978), 5, 50–51; Neal Blewett, "The Franchise in the United Kingdom, 1885–1918," *Past and Present* 32 (December 1965): 27–56; Charles Seymour and Donald P. Frary, *How the World Votes,* vol. 1 (Springfield, 1918), 13–14, 144, 149, 150, 174–75, 192, 195; and ibid., vol. 2, 69, 85–86, 88–89; Herbert Tingsten, *Political Behavior: Studies in Election Statistics* (Stockholm, 1937), 10–21; Ko-Chih R. Tung, "Voting Rights for Alien Residents—Who Wants It?" *International Migration Review* 19 (Fall 1985): 451–54; Gail G. Campbell, "The Most Restrictive Franchise in British North America? A Case Study," *Canadian Historical Review* 71 (June 1990): 159–88. Cf. Eduardo Posado-Carbo, *Elections Before Democracy: The History of Elections in Europe and Latin America* (London, 1996); and Hilda Sabato, "Citizenship, Political Participation and the Formation of the Public Sphere in Buenos Aires 1850s–1880s," *Past and Present* 136 (August 1992): 139–63.

2. Therborn, "Rule of Capital," 12–19, 21–24; Pugh, *Electoral Reform,* 17, 29, 33, 44, 50–51, 136–37, 144–45, 153–54; Seymour and Frary, *How the World Votes,* vol. 1, 312–13, vol. 2, 91; Stein Rokkan,

Angus Campbell, Per Trosvik, and Henry Valen, *Citizens, Elections, Parties: Approaches to the Comparative Study of the Processes of Development* (New York, 1970), 31, 86–87; Raymond Huard, *Le Suffrage Universel en France, 1848–1946* (Paris, 1991), 9–14, 19–34, 72, 117, 138, 148–49, 355–56, 403–5, 409; Pierre Rosanvallon, *Le Sacre du Citoyen: Histoire du Suffrage Universel en France* (Paris, 1992), 11–12, 445–61; Gaetano Salvemini, *The Origins of Fascism in Italy* (New York, 1973), 60–62, 232–34; Elizabeth Wiskeman, *Europe of the Dictators, 1919–1945* (New York, 1966), 10, 15, 19, 37.

3. Raymond E. Wolfinger and Steven J. Rosenstone, *Who Votes?* (New Haven, 1980), 1; *New York Times*, 13 November 1988, 7 November and 10 November 1996; Frances F. Piven and Richard A. Cloward, *Why Americans Don't Vote* (New York, 1988), 4–19.

4. Rokkan et al., *Citizens*, 38–39; Wolfinger and Rosenstone, *Who Votes?*, 13, 17, 18, 22, 24–34, 90; *New York Times*, 10 November 1994, 11 June 1995, and 11 August 1996; see also the many election-year reports of the Committee for the Study of the American Electorate and the sources cited in the following note.

5. For a sample of the debates regarding the sources of low turnout see various works by Walter Dean Burnham, including *Critical Elections and the Mainsprings of American Politics* (New York, 1970), and "The Appearance and Disappearance of the American Voter," *The Disappearance of the American Voter* (Washington, 1979); Piven and Cloward, *Why Americans Don't Vote*, 17–25; Ruy Teixeira, *The Disappearing American Voter* (Washington, DC, 1992).

6. *New York Times*, 18 October 1990, and 7 October 1996; Robert B. Reich, *Locked in the Cabinet* (New York, 1997), 330. Reich's memoir is dotted with anecdotal material regarding the political strategies of the Clinton administration and the subordination of social policy to the preferences of Wall Street.

7. Sidney Verba, Kay L. Schlozman, and Henry E. Brady, *Voice and Equality: Civic Voluntarism in American Politics* (Cambridge, MA, 1995), 1–13, 23–24, 511–33.

8. Reich, *Locked*, 286; for a more ample attack see William Greider, *Secrets of the Temple* (New York, 1987).

9. Regarding definitions of democracy see Therborn, "Rule of Capital," 4; Rokkan et al., *Citizens*, 26–27.

10. The well-known and quite static notions put forward by Joseph Schumpeter and Robert Dahl are placed in historical context in Morton J. Horwitz, *The Transformation of American Law, 1870–1960* (New York, 1992), 255–58.

11. Cf. E. E. Schattschneider, *The Semisovereign People: A Realist's View of Democracy in America* (Hinsdale, IL, 1960), 104–5.

12. Regarding our efforts overseas see the *New York Times*, 25 October 1999.

13. Cf. Verba, Schlozman, and Brady, *Voice and Equality*, 10.

INDEX

Absentee voting, 440(n9), 450(n100)
    after Civil War to World War I, 150–51
    at end of twentieth century, 277
    implementation in Civil War, 104, 150
    Overseas Voting Rights Act, 446(n40)
Acheson, Dean, 251
Adams, Abigail, 174
Adams, Charles Francis, Jr., 119, 122, 141
Adams, Henry, 102, 104
Adams, John, 1, 2, 11, 29
    and drafting of Massachusetts constitution,
       19
    and Massachusetts constitutional convention
       of 1820, 27
    and "right" to vote, 13, 98, 175
Adams, Mary Jo, xviii, 201–2
Addams, Jane, 203–4
Address on the Right of Free Suffrage (Luther),
    71–72
Affirmative action, 299
African Americans
    activism in 1920–1960 period, 236
    asking for vote after Civil War, 88
    and boundaries of Tuskegee (Ala.), 287–88
    disfranchisement in South after
       Reconstruction, 105–16, 170, 422–23(n65)
    and end of white primaries, 247–49
    Fourteenth Amendment, effect of passage on,
       90–91
    military service in Civil War, 81–82, 88, 89
    race-based apportionment, 287–302
    and Rhode Island suffrage rebellion, 72–73
    and right to vote before 1850, 6, 12, 20,
       54–59, 318, 406(n11), 415(n2)
    and slaves as American peasantry, 70
    and the South in 1950s and 1960s, 252–53,
       257–63
    and Tait's petition to Nashville meeting,
       81–82
    violence against during Reconstruction and
       after in South, 105–6
    and the vote in Civil War and
       Reconstruction, 87–104

    and vote dilution and districting issues,
       284–302
    voting power of in the North, 236
    voting rights of, 1960–1999, 257–68, 274,
       306–8
    and World War II, 244–53
    See also Race
Age. *See* Voting age
Alabama, 31, 92, 113, 163, 209, 210, 246,
    258–59, 263, 264, 266, 286–88, 292, 306,
    308
Algerine laws of Rhode Island, 73–74
Aliens
    enfranchisement of declarant, 32–33, 104–5,
       136–38
    and Equal Protection Clause, 310, 450(n104)
    in 1990s, 309–11, 451(n107)
    rejection of suffrage for in late nineteenth and
       early twentieth centuries, 138, 426(n34)
    and right to vote in colonial era, 406(n11)
    and suffrage, 337–41, 359–61
    suffrage as means of attracting, 38
    and voting 1790–1850, 32–33, 412(n32)
Allen, Ethan, 12, 18
Allen v. Merrell, 254
Allen v. State Board of Elections, 289, 300
American exceptionalism, 67–68
American Federation of Labor (AFL), 205, 2239
American Legion, 278
American Woman Suffrage Association
    (AWSA), 184
    strategy to amend state constitutions to
       include women, 184–85, 186
Annapolis (Md.), 201
Anderson v. Baker, 77
Anthony, Susan B., 177–78, 180–1, 184–85, 197,
    202
Appeal of Forty Thousand Citizens, 57
Appellate court judges, rules regarding election
    of, 234
Apportionment, 128, 234, 285–87
    See also Federal government: vote dilution and
       districting